D0216690

THE PAPERS OF

WOODROW WILSON

VOLUME 55

FEBRUARY 8-MARCH 16, 1919

SPONSORED BY THE WOODROW WILSON
FOUNDATION
AND PRINCETON UNIVERSITY

THE PAPERS OF

WOODROW WILSON

ARTHUR S. LINK, *EDITOR*

DAVID W. HIRST, *SENIOR ASSOCIATE EDITOR*

JOHN E. LITTLE, *ASSOCIATE EDITOR*

FREDRICK AANDAHL, *ASSOCIATE EDITOR*

MANFRED F. BOEMEKE, *ASSOCIATE EDITOR*

DENISE THOMPSON, *ASSISTANT EDITOR*

PHYLLIS MARCHAND AND MARGARET D. LINK,
EDITORIAL ASSISTANTS

Volume 55
February 8-March 16, 1919

PRINCETON, NEW JERSEY
PRINCETON UNIVERSITY PRESS
1986

Copyright © 1986 by Princeton University Press

All Rights Reserved

L.C. card 66-10880

I.S.B.N. 0-691-04737-5

Note to scholars: Princeton University Press sub-
scribes to the Resolution on Permissions of the Association of American University Presses, defining what
we regard as "fair use" of copyrighted works. This Resolution, intended to encourage scholarly use of university press publications and to avoid unnecessary applications for permission, is obtainable from the Press
or from the A.A.U.P. central office. Note, however, that
the scholarly apparatus, transcripts of shorthand, and
the texts of Wilson documents as they appear in this
volume are copyrighted, and the usual rules about the
use of copyrighted materials apply.

Printed in the United States of America
by Princeton University Press
Princeton, New Jersey

E
660
.W717
v. 55

EDITORIAL ADVISORY COMMITTEE

KATHARINE E. BRAND, *EMERITUS*

HENRY STEELE COMMAGER, *EMERITUS*

JOHN MILTON COOPER, JR.

WILLIAM H. HARBAUGH

AUGUST HECKSCHER

RICHARD W. LEOPOLD

ARTHUR M. SCHLESINGER, JR.

BETTY MILLER UNTERBERGER

Standing Order $48.18

87-11400 and 87-12300

9-30-86 Princeton Univ. Press

INTRODUCTION

THIS volume, which covers the period from February 8 through March 16, 1919, opens as the statesmen in Paris are giving first detailed consideration to the military and naval terms of the treaty of peace with Germany. There is much wrangling over the disposition of the German High Seas Fleet but general agreement that Germany should be effectively disarmed, both on land and sea. There is also heated discussion in the Council of Ten in response to Winston Churchill's appeal for a "Grand Crusade" against Bolshevik Russia. Wilson, as he has always done, stands firm against any proposals for military intervention in that country. As the documents also reveal, Wilson grows increasingly frustrated and impatient on account of long-winded and discursive discussions and the failure of his colleagues to confront the controversial issues before them—and all this while eastern and central Europe seem on the verge of starvation and anarchy.

Wilson, in one of the most eloquent speeches of his life, presents a draft of the Covenant of the League of Nations to the Third Plenary Session on February 14 and then leaves for the United States to attend to urgent domestic business upon the expiration of the Sixty-fifth Congress. Upon his arrival in Boston on February 24, he delivers an address on the progress of the peace conference. He then rushes to Washington and spends the next eight days preoccupied with a variety of concerns. In a speech to the members of the Democratic National Committee on February 28, he calls for a great national nonpartisan campaign in behalf of the League of Nations, but pillories and ridicules the opponents of the League. He also gives a dinner at the White House on February 26 for members of the foreign affairs committees of the House and Senate and explains the various articles of the Covenant. On March 3, Senator Lodge responds with his "round robin," signed by enough senators and senators-elect to defeat ratification of any peace treaty, which warned that they could not accept the Covenant "in its present form." Mortified and angered, Wilson hits back in a speech in the Metropolitan Opera House on March 4 by saying that the Covenant would be an integral part of the treaty with Germany, and that senators would have to approve it if they wanted a restoration of peace. Following this address, Wilson meets a group of Irish-American leaders who are beginning to mount a campaign for aggressive American support in Paris of Irish independence. The meeting, which is not harmonious, bodes ill for the fate of the Covenant of the League of Nations.

Wilson lands at Brest on March 13 only to learn from Colonel House that the latter had tentatively approved—in contradiction to Wilson's explicit instructions—among other things, French demands for the establishment of a Rhenish Republic and the separation of the Covenant from the peace treaty with Germany. As this volume ends, Wilson is hard at work to repair House's damage and to get the peace conference back on his, *Wilson's*, track.

"VERBATIM ET LITERATIM"

In earlier volumes of this series, we have said the following: "All documents are reproduced *verbatim et literatim*, with typographical and spelling errors corrected in square brackets only when necessary for clarity and ease of reading." The following essay explains our textual methods and review procedures.

We have never printed and do not intend to print critical, or corrected, versions of documents. We print them exactly as they are, with a few exceptions which we always note. We never use the word *sic* except to denote the repetition of words in a document; in fact, we think that a succession of *sics* defaces a page.

We usually repair words in square brackets when letters are missing. As we have said, we also repair words in square brackets for clarity and ease of reading. Our general rule is to do this when we, ourselves, cannot read the word without having to stop to puzzle out its meaning. Jumbled words and names misspelled beyond recognition of course have to be repaired. We correct the misspellings of names in documents in the footnotes identifying those persons.

However, when an old man writes to Wilson saying that he is glad to hear that Wilson is "comming" to Newark, or a semiliterate farmer from Texas writes phonetically, we see no reason to correct spellings in square brackets when the words are perfectly understandable. We do not correct Wilson's misspellings unless they are unreadable, except to supply in square brackets letters missing in words. For example, he consistently spelled "belligerent" as "belligerant." Nothing would be gained by correcting "belligerant" in square brackets.

We think that it is very important for several reasons to follow the rule of *verbatim et literatim*. Most important, a document has its own integrity and power, particularly when it is not written in perfect literary form. There is something very moving in seeing a Texas dirt farmer struggling to express his feelings in words, or a semiliterate former slave doing the same thing. Second, in Wilson's case it is essential to reproduce his errors in letters which he typed himself, since he usually typed badly when he was in an agitated state. Third, since style is the essence of the person, we would never correct grammar or make tenses consistent, as one correspondent has urged us to do. Fourth, we think that it is very important that we print exact transcripts of Charles L. Swem's copies of Wilson's letters. Swem made many mistakes (we correct them in footnotes from a reading of his shorthand books), and Wilson let them pass. We thus have to assume that Wilson did not read his letters before signing them, and this, we think, is a significant fact.

We think that our series would be worthless if we produced unreliable texts, and we go to considerable effort to make certain that the texts are authentic.

Our typists are highly skilled and proofread their transcripts carefully as soon as they have typed them. The Editor sight proofreads documents once he has assembled a volume and is setting its annotation. The Editors who write the notes read through documents several times and are careful to check any anomalies. Then, once the manuscript volume has been completed and all notes checked, the Editor and Senior Associate Editor orally proofread the documents against the copy. They read every comma, dash, and character. They note every absence of punctuation. They study every nearly illegible word in written documents.

Once this process of "establishing the text" is completed, the manuscript volume goes to our editor at Princeton University Press, who checks the volume carefully and sends it to the printing plant. The galley proofs are read against copy in the proofroom at the Press. And we must say that the proofreaders there are extraordinarily skilled. Some years ago, before we found a way to ease their burden, they queried every misspelled word, inconsistencies in punctuation and capitalization, absence of punctuation, or other such anomalies. Now we write "O.K." above such words or spaces on the copy.

We read the galley proof at least four times. Our copyeditor gives them a sight reading against the manuscript copy to look for remaining typographical errors and to make sure that no line has been dropped. The Editor and Senior Associate Editor, and an Associate Editor sight read them against documents and copy. We then get the page proofs, which have been corrected at the Press. We check all the changes three times. In addition, we get *revised* pages and check them twice.

This is not the end. The Editor, Senior Associate Editor, and an Associate Editor give a final reading to headings, description-location lines, and notes. Finally, our indexer of course reads the pages word by word. Before we return the pages to the Press, she comes in with a list of queries, all of which are answered by reference to the documents.

Our rule in the Wilson Papers is that our tolerance of error is zero. No system and no person can be perfect. There may be errors in our volumes. However, we believe that we have done everything humanly possible to avoid error; the chance is remote that what looks at first glance like a typographical error is indeed an error.

The Editors here take note with much sorrow of the death, on March 18, 1986, of Mathilde (Mme. Paul) Mantoux. She evinced a lively interest in *The Papers of Woodrow Wilson* since the Editor met her in 1962, and she graciously approved our use of extensive translated portions of her husband's *Les Délibérations du Conseil des Quatre*, large portions of which we will begin to print in the next volume. We remember her as a lady who embodied the virtues of her great country.

For their continued review and helpful criticisms, we thank John Milton Cooper, Jr., William H. Harbaugh, Richard W. Leopold, and Betty Miller Unterberger, all members of our Editorial Advisory Committee. We owe a special debt of gratitude to Thomas H. Wright, Esq., and Richard C. Woodbridge, Esq., for help at a critical time. Finally, our thanks to Alice A. Calaprice, our editor at Princeton University Press.

THE EDITORS

Princeton, New Jersey
April 16, 1986

CONTENTS

Introduction, vii
Illustrations, xix
Abbreviations and Symbols, xxi

The Papers, February 8-March 16, 1919
The Paris Peace Conference

Minutes of the Meetings of the Council of Ten
    February 12, 1919, 3 p.m., 104
    February 13, 1919, 3 p.m., 140

Minutes of the Meetings of the Supreme War Council
    February 8, 1919, 3 p.m., 9
    February 10, 1919, 3 p.m., 51
    February 12, 1919, 11 a.m., 95
    February 12, 1919, 5 p.m., 104
    February 14, 1919, 6:30 p.m., 178

Minutes of the Meetings of the League of Nations Commission
    February 8, 1919, 10:30 a.m., 4
    February 10, 1919, 10:30 a.m., 41
    February 11, 1919, 10:30 a.m., 70
    February 13, 1919, 10:30 a.m., 120
    February 13, 1919, 3:30 p.m., 137

Wilson addresses and statements
    Address to the Third Plenary Session of the Peace Conference, February 14,
        1919, 164
    A statement upon leaving France, February 15, 1919, 197

Wilson correspondence
    From Wilson to
        Albert, King of the Belgians, 220
        The American Commissioners, 208
        Newton Diehl Baker, 27, 341
        Bernard Mannes Baruch, 186
        Howard Sweetser Bliss, 81
        Georges Clemenceau, 279
        Josephus Daniels, 343
        Prince Faisal, 183
        Millicent Garrett Fawcett, 183
        Arthur Hugh Frazier, 185
        Carter Glass, 208
        Herbert Clark Hoover, 186(2)
        Edward Mandell House, 178, 202, 229, 230, 299, 326, 392(2), 472
        Morris Jastrow, Jr., 484
        George Lansbury, 187
        Robert Lansing, 209, 231
        Boghos Nubar, 80
        Vittorio Emanuele Orlando, 300
        Raymond Poincaré, 149
        Frank Lyon Polk, 300

Joseph Patrick Tumulty, 532
Wilhelmina, 219
To Wilson from
    Albert, King of the Belgians, 63
    The American Commissioners, 232
    Newton Diehl Baker, 81, 335
    James Levi Barton and Others, 485
    William Shepherd Benson, 27, 515, 522
    Howard Sweetser Bliss, 86, 472
    Tasker Howard Bliss, 28, 511
    Sir Robert Borden, 501
    William Christian Bullitt, 540
    Georges Clemenceau, 335
    George Creel, 363
    Josephus Daniels, 424(2)
    Norman Hezekiah Davis, 113
    Henry Pomeroy Davison, 526
    Prince Faisal, 86
    Ferdinand Foch, 502
    Alfred George Gardiner, 115
    Harry Augustus Garfield, 397, 398
    Pietro Cardinal Gasparri, 493
    James Watson Gerard, 446
    Charles Homer Haskins, 83
    Herbert Clark Hoover, 86, 117
    Edward Mandell House, 178, 201, 203, 212, 213, 223, 233(2), 245, 256,
        283, 304, 305(2), 349(2), 367, 423, 458
    Morris Jastrow, Jr., 438
    Eugene Francis Kinkead, 468
    George Lansbury, 87, 525
    Robert Lansing, 202, 209
    Robert Lansing and Others, 210
    Li Shengto, Wang Yitang, and the Chinese Parliament, 424
    Breckinridge Long, 436
    Julian William Mack and Others, 368, 381
    Porter James McCumber, 491
    David Hunter Miller, 148
    Vittorio Emanuele Orlando, 301
    Thomas Nelson Page, 83
    Nikola Pašić and Others, 87
    Sir Horace Plunkett, 453
    Frank Lyon Polk, 301, 452
    Eleuthérios Vénisélos, 500
    Stephen Samuel Wise, 368

Interviews
    A press conference with American newspaper representatives, 161

Collateral correspondence
    Newton Diehl Baker to Robert Russa Moton, 404
    Tasker Howard Bliss to Newton Diehl Baker and Peyton Conway March,
        404
    Tasker Howard Bliss to Arthur James Balfour, 214
    Gilbert Fairchild Close to Herbert Clark Hoover, 151

David Rowland Francis to Robert Lansing and Others, 234
Carter Glass to Norman Hezekiah Davis, 115
Cary Travers Grayson to Joseph Patrick Tumulty, 495
Robert Lansing to Frank Lyon Polk, 293
William Emmanuel Rappard to Hans Sulzer, 151
Charles Prestwich Scott to Edward Mandell House, 545
Charles Seymour to His Family, 34

Memoranda, reports, aide-mémoire, and position papers
A memorandum by Ray Stannard Baker on American public opinion on the
  League of Nations and the peace conference, 449
Memoranda by William Shepherd Benson on the naval peace terms, 432,
  523, 539
A memorandum by Tasker Howard Bliss suggesting the dispatch of an inter-
  Allied mission to Syria, 4
A memorandum by Tasker Howard Bliss on the opposition of the United
  States to a military campaign in Russia, 214
A memorandum by Tasker Howard Bliss on the military peace terms, 511
A memorandum by Ferdinand Foch on the Rhineland question, 502
A memorandum by the Japanese government on racial equality, 436
A memorandum by Sidney Edward Mezes on the Rhineland question, 475
A memorandum by David Hunter Miller about amendments to the Covenant
  of the League of Nations, 68
A draft of the naval peace terms, 425
A declaration of principles concerning reparation, 29
A memorandum by the United States Naval Advisory Staff on the disposition
  of German and Austrian war vessels, 515
A memorandum by Henry White about the financial needs of Belgium, 200

Diaries
Ray Stannard Baker, 463, 489, 531
Edith Benham, 40, 66
Lord Robert Cecil, 80, 539
Josephus Daniels, 266, 367
Cary Travers Grayson, 3, 36, 41, 94, 120, 159, 197, 201, 202, 205, 207, 217,
  221, 224, 228, 235, 254, 267, 294, 308, 339, 367, 387, 409(2), 442, 448,
  456, 460, 471(2), 473, 479, 486, 496, 529, 538
Edward Mandell House, 88, 155, 193, 499, 538
Florence Haskell Corliss Lamont, 120
Vance Criswell McCormick, 387
David Hunter Miller, 67, 118, 154, 192

General Diplomatic and Military Affairs

Wilson correspondence
From Wilson to
  Newton Diehl Baker, 391
  Robert Lansing, 185
  John Joseph Pershing, 149
  Frank Lyon Polk, 393(2)
To Wilson from
  Newton Diehl Baker, 399
  A memorandum by Tasker Howard Bliss on the reinforcement of Amer-
    ican troops in North Russia, 190

Henry Prather Fletcher, 352
David Rowland Francis, 349
Robert Lansing, 93
John Joseph Pershing, 64
Frank Lyon Polk, 330, 350, 351, 357
Henry White, 187

Collateral correspondence
Tasker Howard Bliss to Newton Diehl Baker, 188
Tasker Howard Bliss to Newton Diehl Baker and Peyton Conway March, 150
Gilbert Fairchild Close to John Joseph Pershing, 151
William Sidney Graves to the Department of State, 493
William Sidney Graves to Peter Charles Harris, 399
Robert Lansing and Vance Criswell McCormick to Frank Lyon Polk, 38
Newton Alexander McCully to William Sowden Sims, 39
Frank Lyon Polk to Robert Lansing and Vance Criswell McCormick, 493
William Sowden Sims to William Shepherd Benson, 39

Domestic Affairs

Wilson addresses and statements
Address in Boston, February 24, 1919, 238
Remarks to members of the Democratic National Committee, February 28, 1919, 309
A statement about Wilson's alleged intention not to seek a third term, March 1, 1919, 340
Address to a conference of governors and mayors, March 3, 1919, 389
Two statements upon the adjournment of the Sixty-fifth Congress, March 4, 1919, 408
Address at the Metropolitan Opera House, March 4, 1919, 413

Wilson correspondence
From Wilson to
William Brockman Bankhead, 302
Edward William Bok, 303
Robert Somers Brookings, 329
Albert Sidney Burleson, 327
Theodore Elijah Burton, 255
Bainbridge Colby, 302
Cleveland Hoadley Dodge, 303
Alvan Tufts Fuller, 343
Charles Mills Galloway, 330
Carter Glass, 256, 279, 342
Thomas Watt Gregory, 276
Walker Downer Hines, 277
David Franklin Houston, 483
Edward Nash Hurley, 341, 394
Thomas Erby Kilby, 327
Robert Lansing, 149, 547
Samuel McCune Lindsay, 157
Breckinridge Long, 279
Samuel Walker McCall, 328
The Members of the House Foreign Affairs Committee, 184

H. Arthur Morgan, 157
Henry Morgenthau, 329
Frank Morrison, 280
Lee Slater Overman, 37
Alexander Mitchell Palmer, 482
James Harry Preston, 232
William Cox Redfield, 156, 343
Edgar Rickard, 393
John Nevin Sayre, 395
Anna Howard Shaw, 281, 299
Joseph Swagar Sherley, 256, 277
William Harrison Short, 186, 208
William Howard Taft, 187, 281, 328
George Carroll Todd, 394
Joseph Patrick Tumulty, 37, 184, 185, 218, 219, 222(2), 225, 226, 231,
    254, 278, 340, 341, 458
Oscar Wilder Underwood, 231
Thomas James Walsh, 280
To Wilson from
  The Atlantic Congress of the League to Enforce Peace, 37
  Bernard Mannes Baruch, 90
  Edward William Bok, 253
  Thomas Lincoln Chadbourne, Jr., 403
  Josephus Daniels, 36, 263, 457
  Felix Cordova Davila, 158, 264
  Jacob McGavock Dickinson, 339
  Cleveland Hoadley Dodge, 265
  Arthur Briggs Farquhar, 439
  Edward Albert Filene, 199, 447
  Charles Mills Galloway, 460
  Charles Mills Galloway and Others, 290
  Harry Augustus Garfield, 362
  John Palmer Gavit, 255
  James Watson Gerard and Others, 65
  Carter Glass, 89, 332, 333, 358, 396, 537
  Carter Glass and William Cox Redfield, 306
  Thomas Watt Gregory, 345, 346
  Norman Hapgood, 292, 439
  Walker Downer Hines, 227, 246, 251, 257, 536
  A memorandum by Walker Downer Hines on railroad legislation, 247
  Gilbert Monell Hitchcock, 437
  Herbert Clark Hoover, 116, 251
  Edward Mandell House, 221, 257
  David Franklin Houston, 395
  Merlin Hull, 158
  Edward Nash Hurley, 532
  Thomas Erby Kilby, 328
  Franklin Knight Lane, 284
  A memorandum by Franklin Knight Lane on the Smith-Bankhead Amer-
    icanization bill, 284
  Robert Lansing, 92
  Asbury Francis Lever, 478
  Dudley Field Malone, 337

William Gibbs McAdoo, 258
Samuel Walker McCall, 292
Vance Criswell McCormick, 206
Royal Meeker, 91
Henry Morgenthau, 288
Frank Morrison, 364
Frank Morrison and Samuel Gompers, 262
Alexander Mitchell Palmer, 339
Frank Lyon Polk, 407
William Cox Redfield, 336
Edgar Rickard, 307, 362
John Nevin Sayre, 365
Charles Michael Schwab, 117
William Harrison Short, 37, 198
Alfred Emanuel Smith, 216
Ellison DuRant Smith, 38
William Howard Taft, 357
William Howard Taft and Abbott Lawrence Lowell, 65
Joseph Patrick Tumulty, 36, 94, 197, 205, 206, 214, 223, 226, 289, 344,
    347, 348(2), 368, 448, 493, 500, 540(2)
Thomas James Walsh, 262
William Bauchop Wilson, 291(2), 447, 478

Collateral correspondence
  Theodore Elijah Burton to Joseph Patrick Tumulty, 278
  Gilbert Fairchild Close to Dudley Field Malone, 407
  Gilbert Fairchild Close to Frank Lyon Polk, 406
  Gilbert Fairchild Close to Charles Michael Schwab, 188
  Albert De Silver to Joseph Patrick Tumulty, 224
  Thomas Watt Gregory to Joseph Patrick Tumulty, 344
  Robert Lansing to Frank Lyon Polk, 547
  William Gibbs McAdoo to Walker Downer Hines, 260
  Timothy O'Brien to Joseph Patrick Tumulty, 407
  Frank Lyon Polk to Robert Lansing, 92
  George Carroll Todd to Thomas Watt Gregory, 478
  Joseph Patrick Tumulty to Cary Travers Grayson, 218, 529
  Joseph Patrick Tumulty to John Sharp Williams, 198

News reports
  A White House dinner with senators and congressmen, 268
  A visit to the Capitol, 295
  An alleged statement on the Irish question, 324
  Endorsement of the creation of a Jewish homeland in Palestine, 386
  A meeting with American-Irish leaders, 421

Personal Affairs

Wilson correspondence
  From Wilson to
    Anita Eugénie McCormick Blaine, 484
    Clinton Tyler Brainard, 484
    Ellen Duane Davis, 304
    Sir Ludovic James Grant, 89
    Allen Schoolcraft Hulbert, 303

Eleanor Randolph Wilson McAdoo, 395
William Gibbs McAdoo and Eleanor Randolph Wilson McAdoo, 283
Thomas L. Snow, 282
Joseph Patrick Tumulty, 392
Frederic Yates, 282
To Wilson from
Anita Eugénie McCormick Blaine, 440
Lord Curzon, 116
Ellen Duane Davis, 265
Eleanor Randolph Wilson McAdoo and William Gibbs McAdoo, 204
Hardwicke Drummond Rawnsley, 387
Francis Bowes Sayre, 234
Jessie Woodrow Wilson Sayre, 216
Howard Duryee Wheeler, 456
Collateral correspondence
Gilbert Fairchild Close to Joseph Patrick Tumulty, 448

Index, 549

ILLUSTRATIONS

Following page 266

Wilson Presents the Covenant of the League of Nations to the Third Plenary Session of the Peace Conference, February 14, 1919. Painting by George Sheridan Knowles
Princeton University Art Museum

Ray Stannard Baker aboard the U.S.S. George Washington
National Archives

David Hunter Miller and Major James Brown Scott
National Archives

Irwin Hood (Ike) Hoover
National Archives

William Christian Bullitt
National Archives

From left to right: Charles C. Wagner, Gilbert Fairchild Close, and Charles Lee Swem
National Archives

On the Bridge as the U.S.S. George Washington *arrives in Boston Harbor*
National Archives

In Mechanic's Hall, Boston, on February 24, 1919
National Archives

ABBREVIATIONS

ACNP	American Commission to Negotiate Peace
ALI	autograph letter initialed
ALS	autograph letter signed
CC	carbon copy
CCL	carbon copy of letter
CCLI	carbon copy of letter initialed
CCLS	carbon copy of letter signed
CCS	carbon copy signed
EMH	Edward Mandell House
FLP	Frank Lyon Polk
FR	*Papers Relating to the Foreign Relations of the United States*
FR 1919, Russia	*Papers Relating to the Foreign Relations of the United States, 1919, Russia*
HCH	Herbert Clark Hoover
Hw, hw	handwriting, handwritten
HwLS	handwritten letter signed
JD	Josephus Daniels
JPT	Joseph Patrick Tumulty
MS, MSS	manuscript, manuscripts
NDB	Newton Diehl Baker
PPC	*Papers Relating to the Foreign Relations of the United States, The Paris Peace Conference, 1919*
RG	record group
RL	Robert Lansing
T	typed
TC	typed copy
TCL	typed copy of letter
TL	typed letter
TLI	typed letter initialed
TLS	typed letter signed
TS	typed signed
TWG	Thomas Watt Gregory
WCR	William Cox Redfield
WGM	William Gibbs McAdoo
WJB	William Jennings Bryan
WW	Woodrow Wilson
WWhw	Woodrow Wilson handwriting, handwritten
WWT	Woodrow Wilson typed
WWTLS	Woodrow Wilson typed letter signed

ABBREVIATIONS FOR COLLECTIONS AND REPOSITORIES

Following the National Union Catalog of the Library of Congress

ATT	Tuskegee Institute
CSt-H	Hoover Institution on War, Revolution and Peace
CtY	Yale University
DLC	Library of Congress

DNA   National Archives
LSE   London School of Economics
MH-BA   Harvard University Graduate School of Business
                        Administration
NjP   Princeton University
PRO   Public Record Office
RSB Coll., DLC   Ray Stannard Baker Collection of Wilsoniana, Library
                        of Congress
SDR   State Department Records
T   Tennessee State Library
WC, NjP   Woodrow Wilson Collection, Princeton University
WDR   War Department Records
WHi   State Historical Society of Wisconsin
WP, DLC   Woodrow Wilson Papers, Library of Congress

SYMBOLS

[February 21, 1919]   publication date of published writing; also date of doc-
                        ument when date is not part of text
[*March 4, 1919*]   composition date when publication date differs
[[February 15, 1919]]   delivery date of speech if publication date differs
**** ***   text deleted by author of document

THE PAPERS OF

WOODROW WILSON

VOLUME 55

FEBRUARY 8-MARCH 16, 1919

THE PAPERS OF
WOODROW WILSON

From the Diary of Dr. Grayson[1]

Saturday, February 8, 1919.

In the morning [afternoon], the President attended a conference of the Supreme War Council. A controversy between Clemenceau and Marshal Foch—a real fight developed over whether German prisoners shall be returned to Germany to work—those with dependent families—also to help put machinery in working order and help pay debt of war indemnities. Foch got up and left the room stiffly; his aide gathered up the papers and followed. No disturbance or notice taken by other Peace Commissioners. Clemenceau went on with the business of the Peace Commission as if nothing had occurred out of the ordinary—not even looking at Foch or in his direction as he left the room.

WW disappointed in Clemenceau—unreliable—tricky—not trustworthy or truthful. Colonel House made a big mistake in his estimate of him to the President—failed to size him up correctly. He was a bit sarcastic to the President.

WW replied sharply to Sir Admiral Wemyss of the British Navy over German ships.

Immediately after luncheon, the President and I posed for a picture at the front door of the Murat Palace. He then attended the afternoon session of the War Council. In the evening, after dinner, the President received three delegations, one from Greece, which bestowed upon him a degree from the University of Athens. In his speech of acceptance, the President said he felt young among the Greeks and praised, in the highest terms, the Greek Premier, Venizelos. A delegation from the University of Cracow, Poland, presented him with a degree, but did not give him a diploma, as they had no parchment. They said they would send it to him as soon as they could get some parchment. The President commented on the work which Mr. Dmowski was doing at the Peace Conference. The third delegation was a Polish War Relief Committee which thanked him for what the United States had done for Poland.

T MS (in the possession of James Gordon Grayson and Cary T. Grayson, Jr.).

[1] About this diary, see n. 1 to the extract from it printed at Dec. 3, 1918, Vol. 53.

A Memorandum by Tasker Howard Bliss

[Paris] February 8th, 1919.

The Military Representatives on the Supreme War Council have decided on the grounds of military convenience that the French shall garrison Syria pending the appointment of a mandatory or other settlement by the League of Nations. Emir Feisal says that if the French send a garrison to Syria and especially if they occupy Damascus, it will constitute a breach of the agreement between his people and the Allies and he will raise the Arab standard and make war on the French. Our experts believe the feeling among the Arab tribes is so strong that this could not be avoided. The French are apparently determined to press the matter in spite of its dangers. The question will be raised at this afternoon's meeting at the Quai D'Orsay. A solution might be found if the President would suggest that the Conference should adopt the proposal made by Emir Feisal yesterday; namely, that the Associated Powers should send a commission to Syria to establish the facts and ascertain the wishes of the people, and that in the meantime no further troops should be sent. If this is done it is probable that an agreement can be reached on the Syrian question which will satisfy the French claims and those of the Arab tribes.

CC MS (WP, DLC).

Minutes of a Meeting of the Commission on the League of Nations

SIXTH MEETING, 8TH FEBRUARY, 1919, AT 10:30 A.M.
President WILSON *in the Chair.*
ARTICLE 16.

Lord Robert Cecil proposed to add the words "as hereinafter provided,"[1] but at the request of President Wilson he withdrew this amendment, and the article was adopted without modification.

ARTICLE 17.

General Smuts presented an amendment (Annex 1).

Mr. Orlando feared that the new draft proposed by the British Delegation might infringe on the sphere of the Conference by defining too closely the territories to which the principle under discussion should be applied. The list of these territories was, more-

---

[1] The members were in the process of amending the so-called Hurst-Miller draft of the Covenant embodied in the minutes of the Commission on the League of Nations printed at Feb. 3, 1919, Vol. 54.

over, necessarily incomplete. The American draft, on the contrary, while fixing the scope of the activities of the League of Nations in regard to the administration of territories, did not prejudice the application of the principle in particular cases, and this appeared to him preferable.

President Wilson replied to this objection that General Smuts' text was based upon a decision of the Conference of the five powers.

Mr. Bourgeois associated himself with President Wilson's remarks, but agreed with Mr. Orlando that it would be preferable to lay down principles without entering into too great detail. He emphasised the moral aspect of the functions which would be discharged by the League of Nations, which should neither be a Super-State nor an additional State created among other States. He added that since the League of Nations was not yet constituted, it appeared to him essential to solve political difficulties in the first instance before determining the part which the League should play. It appeared, therefore, that two successive steps were necessary: (1) the regulation of the problem by international conventions, as, for instance, by a revision of the Act of Berlin,[2] and (2) by handing over to the League of Nations the territories over which it was to exercise its tutelage. Mr. Bourgeois therefore presented an amendment to Article 17 (Annex 2).

Lord Robert Cecil and President Wilson defended the British draft.

President Wilson admitted, however, that in order to meet the objections which had been raised at the beginning of the discussion, the list of territories contained in the first paragraph of the first article of the British amendment might be struck out or preceded by the words "such as" in order to emphasise the fact that this list was not exhaustive.

The Conference agreed to strike out the list.

President Wilson proposed a new paragraph (Annex 3) with the object of extending the scope of the article to certain territories which had been part of the Russian Empire.

Mr. Batalha Reis and *Mr. Hymans* reserved their opinion for the present. They both specially pointed out the consequences which might follow in the future from too broad a wording.

Mr. Larnaude pointed out that it would be preferable not to place in the same category backward countries like certain African colonies and countries which have a very ancient and very complete civilization, but which have been oppressed by foreign domination.

Mr. Vesnitch proposed an amendment intended to facilitate the

[2] See n. 2 to the minutes of the Council of Ten printed at Jan. 28, 1919, 11 a.m., Vol. 54.

complete emancipation of these peoples and their admission into the League of Nations.

Lord Robert Cecil asked Mr. Vesnitch not to insist on his proposal, for reasons of expediency.

Mr. Diamandy supported Mr. Hymans' and Mr. Batalha Reis' observations.

Mr. Veniselos enlarged upon the necessity of leaving no doubt as to the future of the unredeemed Greek territories.

After an exchange of views with Baron Makino, it was agreed to strike out the word "if" in the English text of the last paragraph of sub-article (*b*).

President Wilson summed up the discussion. The matter was then referred to the Drafting Committee, which it was arranged should meet on the following day, at 2:30 at the Hotel Majestic and receive the observations of all members of the Commission interested in the question.

ARTICLE 18.

Lord Robert Cecil read an amendment providing for the creation of a permanent Conference and Labour Office (Annex 4). After a brief discussion the amendment was adopted, subject to the modification of the second part of the amendment as follows:

"And to that end agree to establish as part of the organisation of the League a permanent Labour Commission."

President Wilson suggested the addition of the words "for men, women, and children," after the words "fair and humane conditions of labour." This addition was adopted.

ARTICLE 19.

Lord Robert Cecil proposed to amend the wording of the draft (Annex 5). *President Wilson* explained that the motive of this article was the desire to prevent religious persecutions or wars in the future. *Mr. Hymans* feared that the word "intolerance" might be taken advantage of, and that it might be used to justify appeals to the League of Nations to give judgment on complaints by political parties against governments. *Mr. Batalha Reis* pointed out that whenever a State religion is disestablished its adherents consider themselves as persecuted. *Mr. Orlando* stated that great care would have to be exercised in the wording of such an article, in order to avoid conflict with the constitution of certain States. *Mr. Bourgeois* called attention to the fact that the cases foreseen in the Article under discussion had already been provided for in Article 9, in which internal troubles which threatened peace were mentioned.

After some remarks by *Mr. Batalha Reis* and *Mr. Veniselos* who made the point that the measures contemplated in Article 9 should, of course, be decided unanimously, the question was referred to the Drafting Committee.

The text of Articles 16 and 18 as adopted by the Commission, is contained in Annexes 6 and 7 respectively.

(The Commission adjourned at 1:15. The next Meeting was fixed for Monday, February 10, at 10:30 A.M., in order to discuss the work of the Drafting Committee.)

Annex 1 to Minutes of Sixth Meeting.
ARTICLE 17.

Substitute the following text:

(*a.*) To the colonies, formerly part of the German Empire, and to those territories formerly belonging to Turkey, which incude Armenia, Kurdestan, Syria, Mesopotamia, Palestine, and Arabia, which are inhabited by peoples not able to stand by themselves under the strenuous conditions of the modern world, there should be applied the principle that the well-being and development of such peoples form a sacred trust of civilisation, and that securities for the performance of this trust should be embodied in the constitution of the League.

The best method of giving practical effect to this principle is that the tutelage of such peoples should be entrusted to advanced nations, who, by reason of their resources, their experience, or their geographical position, can best undertake this responsibility, and that this tutelage should be exercised by them as mandatories on behalf of the League.

The character of the mandate must differ according to the stage of the development of the people, the geographical situation of the territory, its economic conditions, and other similar circumstances.

(*b.*) Certain communities, formerly belonging to the Turkish Empire, have reached a stage of development where their existence as independent nations can be provisionally recognised, subject to the rendering of administrative advice and assistance by a mandatory Power, until such time as they are able to stand alone. The wishes of these communities must be a principal consideration in the selection of the mandatory Power.

Other peoples, especially those of Central Africa, are at such a stage that the mandatory must be responsible for the administration of the territory, subject to conditions which will guarantee freedom of conscience or religion, subject only to the maintenance of public order and morals, the prohibition of abuses, such as the slave trade, the arms traffic, and the liquor traffic, and the prevention of the establishment of fortifications or military and naval bases, and of military training of the natives for other than police purposes and the defense of territory, and will also secure equal opportunities for the trade and commerce of other members of the League.

There are territories, such as South-West Africa and certain of the islands in the South Pacific, which, owing to the sparseness of their population, or their small size, or their remoteness from the centres of civilisation, or their geographical contiguity to the mandatory State, and other circumstances, can be best administered under the laws of the mandatory State as if integral portions thereof, subject to the safeguards above mentioned in the interests of the indigenous population.

(c). In every case of mandate, the mandatory State shall render to the League an annual report in reference to the territory committed to its charge.

The degree of authority, control, or administration to be exercised by the mandatory State shall, if not previously agreed upon by the High Contracting Parties, in each case be explicitly defined by the Executive Council in a special Act or Charter.

The High Contracting Parties further agree to establish at the Seat of the League a Mandatory Commission to receive and examine the annual reports of the Mandatory Powers, and to assist the League in ensuring the observance of the terms of all Mandates.

Annex 2 to Minutes of Sixth Meeting.

Substitute the following text:

In conformity with the decisions of the Conference of the Allies the League of Nations regards itself as invested with the moral tutelage of those populations referred to in the Treaty of Peace which have not yet reached the stage of complete development.

The character of this tutelage must differ according to the stage of the development of the peoples, the geographical situation of the territory, its economic conditions, and other similar circumstances.

The conditions and the limits of such tutelage shall be determined by international conventions. The Council of the League of Nations shall indicate the need of new conventions if it deems them necessary to ensure the well-being and development of the populations concerned.

Annex 3 to Minutes of Sixth Meeting.

The provisions of this article can also be applied in respect of other peoples and territories, which are not otherwise disposed of in the Treaty of Peace, of which this Covenant forms a part, or are not definitely constituted as autonomous States.

Annex 4 to Minutes of Sixth Meeting.
ARTICLE 18.

Substitute the following text:

The High Contracting Parties will endeavour to secure and maintain fair and humane conditions of labour, both in their own countries and in all countries to which their commercial and industrial relations extend; and to that end agree to establish as part of the organisation of the League a permanent Conference and Labour office, in accordance with the provisions of the Convention annexed hereto, and to adopt and be bound by all other provisions contained therein.

Annex 5 to Minutes of Sixth Meeting.
ARTICLE 19.

Substitute the following text:

Recognising religious persecution and intolerance as fertile sources of war, the High Contracting Parties agree that political unrest arising therefrom is a matter of concern to the League, and authorise the Executive Council, wherever it is of opinion that the peace of the world is threatened by the illiberal action of the Government of any State towards the adherents of any particular creed, religion, or belief, to make such representations or take such other steps as will put an end to the evil in question.

Annex 6 to Minutes of Sixth Meeting
ARTICLE 16.

The High Contracting Parties entrust to the League the general supervision of the trade in arms and ammunition with the countries in which the control of this traffic is necessary in the common interest.

Annex 7 to Minutes of Sixth Meeting.
ARTICLE 18.

The High Contracting Parties will endeavour to secure and maintain fair and humane conditions of labour for men, women, and children, both in their own countries and in all countries to which their commercial and industrial relations extend; and to that end agree to establish as part of the organisation of the League a permanent Commission of Labour.

Printed copy (WP, DLC).

Hankey's Notes of a Meeting of the Supreme War Council[1]

Quai d'Orsay, February 8, 1919, 3 P.M.

BC-26, SWC-4

M. CLEMENCEAU, in opening the Meeting, said that before continuing the discussion of the previous day which had remained incomplete, he proposed to settle two small matters:

[1] The complete text of these minutes is printed in *PPC*, III, 926-44.

One—relating to the demand of the German National Assembly at Weimar for greater postal facilities in the occupied regions;

The other—relating to a demand of the Germans for the repatriation of their prisoners.

(This was agreed to.)

1. M. CLEMENCEAU read the request made on behalf of the German National Assembly at Weimar and Marshal Foch's suggested reply, (see Appendix "A").

PRESIDENT WILSON asked whether the formula "All liberties compatible with a state of war" offered the Weimar Assembly any considerable facilities as compared with the present conditions.

MARSHAL FOCH stated that the German demand was for full liberty, and the reply offered a conditional freedom.

PRESIDENT WILSON said that he did not wish to grant the Germans any freedom which it was not safe to give them, but it was clearly desirable to assist the Germans in the formation of some authority with which the Allies could deal. It was therefore important to assist the Weimar Assembly. It was clearly undesirable that their letters should take as long as three weeks and their telegrams as long as seven days for delivery.

MR. BALFOUR said that, in his opinion, Marshal Foch's answer was the right one. It might, however, be possible, without touching any question of principle, to ask the administration to hasten the process.

M. CLEMENCEAU said that the delays alleged were probably exaggerated.

MARSHAL FOCH concurred.

PRESIDENT WILSON then proposed that the Council express the hope to Marshal Foch that communications should be hastened as far as possible.

(It was therefore decided to ask Marshal Foch to expedite the delivery of letters and telegrams as far as possible.)

2. M. CLEMENCEAU read the correspondence which had taken place between Herr Erzberger and Marshal Foch on this subject, (see Appendix "B").

PRESIDENT WILSON asked whether he was to understand that Marshal Foch was in favour of the repatriation of German prisoners.

MARSHAL FOCH said that the demand had been presented to him in a manner which suggested that certain categories of prisoners deserved favourable consideration. For instance, the wounded, the unfit, and fathers of large families. He had undertaken to forward to his Government and to support the demand made in regard to certain categories of prisoners.

M. CLEMENCEAU, referring to the demand made by Herr Erz-

berger, pointed out that his request concerned all German prisoners, and, in a subsidiary manner, asked that special treatment
should be accorded to the severely wounded, the sick, those who
had been long in captivity, fathers of large families and all civilians.
He asked Marshal Foch whether he had supported the entire demand, or only a portion of it.

MARSHAL FOCH replied that, in his letter, he had referred only to
certain special categories. The Allies would, themselves, determine
which of these categories deserved consideration.

M. CLEMENCEAU said that it would not be possible for the Governments to give an answer to this request without hearing the
competent Ministers. For instance, in the case of France, the Minister answerable for the restoration of the devast[at]ed districts. The
question had an economic side to it. He, therefore, proposed that
an answer should be sent to Herr Erzberger through Marshal Foch
that the Governments were examining the question and would give
him a reply as soon as possible. As to the fathers of large families,
he, personally, would resist this demand very strongly.

M. SONNINO suggested that the Powers might yield at once concerning certain classes, such as the wounded, the sick, the old and
civilian prisoners, whose retention had no economic value. There
was no doubt in these cases and good will could be shown without
any risk.

MARSHAL FOCH said that he had done no more than transmit a
request and his support in respect to certain classes which might
be considered to deserve special consideration.

(Marshal Foch and General Weygand then withdrew.)

MR. BALFOUR said that he agreed that the competent authorities
should be consulted before a decision was reached on this subject.
He would like to point out that Great Britain, after France, possessed
the greatest number of German prisoners and he would suggest
that the British authorities should also be consulted. The British
Minister dealing with German prisoners might be put in touch with
the French Minister mentioned by M. Clemenceau, and a joint
report might be obtained from them.

(It was therefore decided that no reply should be given to Herr
Erzberger's request for the repatriation of German prisoners until
a joint report had been received from the Competent French and
British Authorities.)

3. M. TARDIEU read and explained the solution proposed by the
Committee on this subject (See Appendix "C"). The committee had
aimed at the simplification of the proposals made on the previous
day. It had not thought it right to lay down the number of Divisions
Germany was to be authorised to keep. The Committee had left

this matter for the decision of the Council. The first request was that the German Government should furnish the full figures of machine guns, field guns, heavy guns, aeroplane motors and sea-planes. An allotment of each would be made for the Divisions the Germans were to keep up. All the surplus would be yielded to the Allies according to Article 2 of the Report. As, however, the enumeration by the Germans might be a lengthy operation, it was proposed under Article 3 that they should yield at once certain quantities of the equipment mentioned.

PRESIDENT WILSON said that his first impression on looking at the document was that the third point was the only one which gave a determinate proposal. He had expected that the result of the Committee's deliberations would be the formulation of a definite demand from Germany in the form of Article 3. Article 2, however, introduced an indeterminate demand. We left it to the Germans to calculate the surplus over and above the equipment of the Divisions we allowed them to maintain. If we did not trust their calculations we should have to verify them. It might be extremely awkward and difficult to achieve this. This was the very sort of difficulty which he wished to avoid. He had hoped that we should be able to make a final demand once and for all in fixed numbers. After that he would like to make a fresh statement to the Germans, not by way of inducement or bargain, but in order to indicate to them our whole temper and the plan we proposed to follow, to the effect that after the surrender of the arms and equipment required of them we should relax the blockade, not only in respect of food but also in respect of raw materials. This we could not do unless assured that the latter would not be used for the disturbance of the peace. We must be certain that in the period elapsing between the renewal of the Armistice and the preliminaries of Peace—a period which he hoped would not exceed six months—the Germans would be unable to set up a stock of big guns and ammunition. He thought it was both wise and fair that Germany should know what we intended to do after imposing these new terms upon them. Much of the irritation caused by the imposition of these terms would, he thought, be removed by proceeding in this manner. He quite saw the necessity of stating the number of divisions Germany should maintain for the preservation of internal order, but he felt that the uncertainty introduced into the demands by Article 2 should be eliminated.

MR. LANSING said that he would like to make an explanation concerning Articles 2 and 3. He had only just seen the English version of the Resolution. The Committee had discussed both an immediate minimum and a final minimum, that is to say, a minimum for immediate delivery and a minimum for ultimate delivery. He had understood that only the former would be specified.

LORD MILNER said that he did not at all disagree with the additional proposal made by the President of the United States. He thought, however, that any such proposal was outside the scope of the Committee's reference. The Committee was appointed to simplify the demands to be made on Germany. It seemed to him that it had suceeded in doing so. It was now apparently considered that the Committee's proposal was itself complicated. To his mind it appeared simple. We began by fixing the strength of the German army. We then allotted to it a fixed number of machine guns, field guns, heavy guns and aeroplanes. We then said to the Germans: "Surrender everything you have of these categories over and above this allotment." This constituted not an indefinite but a definite demand. As, however, its execution would take time, we demanded the immediate cession of certain fixed quantities.

M. TARDIEU said that he agreed with Lord Milner. Article 2 was not really indefinite, because our object was to ensure that no arms or material remained in Germany which would enable her rapidly to equip more forces than we allowed her to maintain.

PRESIDENT WILSON quoted from a report furnished on the previous day,[2] giving an estimate of all the equipment now in Germany over and above the requirements of 30 divisions. He pointed out that the figures were not round figures, but had the appearance of exact statistics. These figures were:

Heavy guns	1,500
Field guns	6,425
Machine guns	41,675

Now the demand for immediate delivery made in Article 2 of the Committee's report was for:

Heavy guns	1,000
Field guns	4,000
Machine guns	20,000

We therefore left the Germans, even after this demand, an excess of:

21,675	Machine Guns
2,425	Field Guns
and 500	Heavy Guns,

over the requirements of the divisions we permitted them to equip. He had understood that the intention had been to demand the surrender of sufficient arms to render the Allies safe. If the figures could be trusted, we were leaving the Germans enough to equip in a short time 60 divisions, rather than 30. If we really knew what quantities they possessed, we could make an exact demand.

M. LOUCHEUR said that if definite quantities were to be demanded,

[2] Annex III to the minutes of the Council of Ten printed at Feb. 7, 1919, 3:30 p.m., Vol. 54.

a great deal more should be required than the Committee had put down. The figures given on the previous day represented what was in possession of the German Armies. The figures took no account of what was in the arsenals and in the factories. If these were added, the figures should be doubled. Since November 1st the Germans had completed the construction of armaments then in process of fabrication. France had done likewise. If definite figures were therefore to be fixed, they must be far bigger than those given.

PRESIDENT WILSON said he wished to recall that when the Armistice Terms were sent to America, the people regarded them as the terms rather of a surrender than of an armistice. Now M. Loucheur would demand of the Germans, in addition, the cession of 82,000 machine guns, 12,000 field guns and 3,000 heavy guns, as in his opinion the numbers given on the previous day should be doubled. If this request were sent to America, people would say that the original figures of the Armistice must have shown astonishing ignorance of the situation in Germany, if the demand then made was so insufficient that an almost equivalent demand must be made now, three months later.

It was very important that the Allies should make a good impression on the world. These continual aggravations of the armistice put the Allies to a moral disadvantage. As far as the interests of safety were concerned, he would be content for himself to leave the Germans in possession of what they had. The Germans were beaten, and they knew it. Their spirit was broken, and they would not renew the struggle.

M. TARDIEU said that Article 2 saved us from the appearance of making extravagant demands. It affirmed the principle that no more armaments should exist in Germany than were required for the maintenance of 30 divisions. If the numbers of those previously existing were suppressed, we should be forced to raise the figures.

M. LOUCHEUR said that in the last three months, according to the normal rate of production, the Germans were in a position to have completed 50 field guns per day, 15 heavy guns, and 200 heavy machine guns, without counting lighter machine guns. It was therefore not surprising if their stock had been greatly increased since November 11th. France was in the same position.

M. CLEMENCEAU said that at the time of the Armistice the experts had worked on hypothetical figures. The same was the case at the present time. He thought the finding of the Committee was a reasonable one, and secured the safety of the Allies.

LORD MILNER added that the proposal had a sort of finality about it. We should not be saying month by month to the Germans, "Give us more and yet more than we previously demanded." The proposal did contain a settlement of the question, at least until the preliminaries of peace had been settled. The demands, moreover, were simplified in that they were confined to certain categories of equipment.

PRESIDENT WILSON said that the demand was not susceptible of successful administration. He had made this point on the previous day, and had been supported in this by so competent a military authority as Marshal Foch. He said that he had a strong distaste for the practice of making reiterated demands. He thought it was fair, however, for the victor to demand information from the vanquished concerning military equipment in his possession. This demand could be made through Marshal Foch before the renewal of the Armistice. Definite figures would then be at hand and the vagueness he complained of would be eliminated. M. Loucheur assumed that German factories had continued turning out armaments at the same rate as before the Armistice. Possibly M. Loucheur had certain knowledge on this subject. If he had not, it appeared very unlikely that this process should have gone on. It was quite likely that little more armament existed in Germany than that with the Armies. The figures for this equipment had been given. He would therefore suggest that Marshal Foch should obtain statistics from the Germans.

LORD MILNER said that this was the demand formulated in Article I of the Report.

PRESIDENT WILSON said that it was suggested as one of the terms of the Armistice. He proposed to make the demand immediately as a preliminary to the renewal of the Armistice.

M. CLEMENCEAU said that the refusal of the Germans to cease hostilities with the Poles afforded the Allies a good pretext for making this demand.

PRESIDENT WILSON agreed.

M. CLEMENCEAU then asked President Wilson to draft a text combining his own views with the suggestion just made concerning Poland.

Should it be impossible to obtain the German reply before February 17th, the next renewal of the Armistice might be for a shorter period than one month.

(The following draft was then read by President Wilson, and adopted:

"It is agreed that an immediate demand shall be made of the Germans that they supply us with all the information now in their hands as to the number of machine guns, of field guns, of heavy guns, of aeroplane motors and of naval aircraft now in their Depots and factories. That they be informed that their refusal to desist from hostilities in Poland, notwithstanding the fact that the Polish authorities have agreed to desist from the use of force against the Germans in Poland, makes this demand for information immediately imperative with a view to determining the terms which shall be exacted when the time comes for the renewal of the armistice.")

4. (*See Appendix "D."*)

ADMIRAL WEMYSS said that the naval questions to be solved were simpler than military questions. The Admirals knew exactly what the conditions were, exactly what they wanted, and what they could get. Delay, however, would render the situation more difficult. The condition of the German Fleet was not as chaotic as it had been at the time of the Armistice. The Allied Admirals had come to the conclusion that they could now fix what should be the state of the German Fleet in time of peace. They could obtain its reduction to that extent at the present time. The Associated Navies had no power of inflicting any damage on Germany to enforce the carrying out of the terms of the Armistice. When the Germans failed to carry out any of the terms, the Navies had to request their colleagues on land to put pressure on them. All this could be stopped by telling the Germans immediately that our requests were not provisional but final. It was possible to lay down at once how many ships Germany should keep; what should be the fate of her naval fortifications, arsenals, etc. How the Allies should dispose of the surrendered ships was a question which concerned the Allies alone and not Germany, and he did not propose to enter into this question at all. The continuance of the blockade was a matter which affected the Navies very materially. It deprived the Fleets of their freedom of action and hampered demobilisation. If final terms could be fixed at once, the Navies would no longer be tied down to their present employment as instruments of the blockade. The spirit of unrest in the world did not leave the Naval Services untouched. A very calming influence on sea-faring folk as a whole would be effected by the settlement of naval peace terms at the next renewal of the Armistice.

M. LEYGUES said that he had no objection to raise as long as the question of the distribution of German ships was left out of account.

ADMIRAL DE BON[3] said that he wished to support Admiral Wemyss. He would specially emphasise the fact that the blockade was depended on to make Germany amenable. It would soon be impossible to carry out this blockade by reason of the demobilisation of the Naval Forces. The most practical way of solving the present difficulties of the Associated Navies was to lay down at once the

---

[3] That is, Vice Adm. Ferdinand Jean Jacques de Bon.

general principles which should form the preliminaries of peace. He would suggest that other Departments of the Governments concerned should do likewise. This would ease the general unrest in the world.

MR. BALFOUR said that on reading the proposals made by the Admirals, he noticed that a number of subjects were introduced, such as the question of Heligoland, the Kiel Canal, the German Colonies, and other territorial questions. These were very important matters concerning which the Council had not been consulted and though he sympathised very much with the trouble experienced by the Associated Navies in continuing the blockade he felt that such subjects could not be introduced into the naval terms of an Armistice.

PRESIDENT WILSON agreed with Mr. Balfour that it was not possible to anticipate the conditions of peace in the renewal of an Armistice. The present Assembly was not concluding peace terms. He would give most careful and friendly study to the document but he thought it quite impossible that many of its provisions should form any part of the Armistice.

Admiral Wemyss explained what was the naval bearing of all the questions entered into. The question was then adjourned.

(It was decided that:

The Blockade of Germany should be discussed on the following Monday.)

5. PRESIDENT WILSON read the following draft:

"(1) Under present conditions many questions not primarily of military character which are arising daily and which are bound to become of increasing importance as time passes should be dealt with on behalf of the United States and the Allies by civilian representatives of these Governments experienced in such questions as finance, food, blockade control, shipping and raw materials.

(2) To accomplish this there shall be constituted at Paris a Supreme Economic Council to deal with such matters for the period of the Armistice. The council shall absorb or replace such other existing interallied bodies and their powers as it may determine from time to time. The Economic Council shall consist of not more than five representatives of each interested Government.

(3) There shall be added to the present International Permanent Armistice Commission two civilian representatives of each associated Government, who shall consult with the Allied High Command, but who may report direct to the Supreme Economic Council."

This Resolution was adopted.

M. CLEMENCEAU said that he understood that he was authorised by the Council to send to Marshal Foch, for communication to the Germans, the proposal relating to the disarmament adopted in paragraph 3.

This was agreed to.

The Meeting then adjourned.

APPENDIX "A"

No. A.A.I.-763 (1) GERMAN DEMAND ON THE SUBJECT OF THE AS-SEMBLY AT WEIMAR.

The Representative of the German Government to the President of the Inter-Allied Commission of the Armistice.

As the National Assembly is to meet on February 6th in Weimar, it is of an urgent necessity that the members of the National Assembly should be free, without any obstacle whatever, in their personal and postal intercourse with their constituents.

At the present time, the forwarding of letters takes as much as three weeks, and telegrams require sometimes 7 days.

In the name of the German Government, I request that the necessary steps should be taken in order that the deputies of the occupied territories may be assured that they will be able to have unrestricted telegraphic and postal intercourse from Weimar with their constituents.

SPA, *February 3rd, 1919.*

(2) SUGGESTED REPLY BY MARSHAL FOCH

Marshal Foch to General Nudant, Spa.

Reply to request No. A.A.I.-763 of the German Commission of Armistice forwarded on February 3rd, number 3.186.

As has been already stated by the High Command of the Allies all liberties *compatible with the state of war* will be granted to allow as far as possible the relations between the German National Assembly and the occupied territories.

But there cannot be any question of the Allies allowing a free and unrestricted exchange of correspondence, and consequently of their giving the assurance asked for on that point by the German Government.

APPENDIX "B" TO IC-136
(TRANSLATION)
I.

To: Marshal Foch.

Sir, By your letter of January 16th you expressed, in a way which deserves our gratitude, the intention of using your credit with the Allied Governments in favour of the repatriation of German prisoners of war, special consideration being given to the most deserving categories.

This promise has awakened in the whole German nation eager and joyful hopes with regard to the return of our brave men.

The German National Assembly which is to meet in a few days at Weimar and of which I have the honour to be a member, will first of all consider the question of the fate of German prisoners of war. The deep emotion produced in the whole nation by the feeling of uncertainty which has hitherto prevailed on their account, will be powerfully and unanimously echoed in the Constituent Assembly of the German people.

The representatives of the nation are sure to ask the Government—and such an inquiry will be fully justified—what they have done to secure the immediate return of our sons. The Government should be in a position to supply the nation with precise and unequivocal information.

I therefore beg you, Sir, kindly to let me know in a few days the result of the intervention to which you had allowed us to look forward. I cannot believe that the Allied Governments have refused to listen favourably to the Marshal to whom they have confidently entrusted the Supreme Command of all their military forces and who conducts the Armistice negotations in their joint names.

Pray accept, Sir, the assurances of my most distinguished and highest consideration. (Signed) ERZBERGER
Secretary of State

Berlin. February 3rd, 1919.[4]

II

Marshal Foch
To: H. E. Herr Erzberger, Secretary of State, President of the German Armistice Commission, Trèves.

Mr. Secretary, I quite understand the concern which Germany has as regards the repatriation of prisoners of war now in the hands of the Allied Governments. It is my intention to forward to these Governments your request asking in particular for the early repatriation of the most deserving cases, and to support it.

As regards relations between the occupied regions and those regions not occupied, I am disposed to allow intercourse so far as is compatible with the security of the Armies, with a view to avoiding any unemployment and consequent disturbances.

(Signed) FOCH

---

[4] There is a TC of this letter in WP, DLC.

Appendix "C"
[Translation]⁵
(Proposal by Committee on the Reduction of
German Armaments)

1. The German Government will report on its own responsibility, within a period of two weeks, the quantities of war material of the following categories, remaining on February 17, 1919, in possession of its combat troops, and in its depots, arsenals, and factories:

> machine guns,
> field guns,
> heavy guns,
> aeroplane engines,
> machines for naval aviation.

2. All material of these various categories in excess of the equipment necessary for * * * will be delivered to the Allies before March 17.

3. Without waiting to fulfill the preceding clauses, the German Government will deliver to the Allies, before March 1, the following minimum numbers of the materials mentioned:

> machine guns   20,000
> field guns   4,000
> heavy guns   1,000
> aeroplane engines   5,000
> machines for naval aviation   250

4. The said quantities will be furnished out of German material, beginning with the most modern types, and, as regards heavy guns, in the following order:

> mobile short guns
> long-range short guns
> mobile long guns
> long-range long guns

5. After the carrying out of the provisions outlined under 1. and 2., all material concealed and brought to light, which is in excess of the figures furnished by the German Government, will be rightfully seized and destroyed.

APPENDIX "D"
NAVAL PEACE TERMS.
JOINT NOTE FROM THE ADMIRALS OF THE ALLIED AND
ASSOCIATED POWERS.
(Translation from the French Text.)

After having received authority from their Governments, the Admirals representing the Admiralties of America, France, Great Brit-

⁵ As printed in *PPC*, III, 937-38. The text in the T MS is in French.

ain, Italy, and Japan held a meeting to study the Peace conditions which it is considered advisable to impose on the enemy at the Peace Conference.

The existing situation was first examined into and may be summed up as follows:

Germany has not yet fulfilled the clauses of the Armistice concerning the handing-over of submarines and merchant ships.

According to authentic information the spirit of anarchy which existed in the Fleet is tending to disappear, and the enemy is re-establishing and re-organising himself.

During this time demobilisation is weakening the Allies' powers of action on land as well as on sea. The continuation of the blockade is weighing exceedingly heavily on all the nations, and it is desirable to set them free from it as soon as possible.

Moreover, the present situation leaves the world in great uncertainty, the effects of which are considerable in every branch of human life. This cannot continue much longer without causing the gravest difficulties.

As regards Austria-Hungary, the difficulties are no less great.

In making the conclusion of Peace dependent on the programme which the Conference has arranged, we have exposed ourselves to an indefinite prolongation of the state of Armistice, in which for nearly three months we have lived in a state of continual discomfort.

For these reasons the Admirals consider that they should ask their Governments that the Peace Conference may examine and decide as soon as possible the definite naval and military conditions to be inserted in the Peace Preliminaries which should be imposed on the enemy Powers. They accordingly submit their proposals on the subject of those conditions.

The other Ministerial Departments might, no doubt, do the same.

If this is so, on the date when the Armistice with Germany is to be prolonged or, in any case, within as short a period as possible, all the enemy Governments might be informed of the conditions to be imposed upon them as preliminaries of peace, those conditions replacing those of the Armistice.

Signed by	*For*
Admiral Benson.	America.
Vice-Admiral de Bon.	France.
Admiral Wemyss.	Great Britain.
Admiral di Revel.[6]	Italy.
Vice-Admiral Takeshita[7]	Japan.

PARIS, 7 February, 1919.

[6] That is, Adm. Paolo Thaon di Revel.
[7] Vice Adm. Isamu Takeshita, Assistant Chief of the Naval General Staff.

NAVAL CLAUSES FOR INSERTION IN THE PRELIMINARY
PEACE TERMS WITH GERMANY.

I. SUBMARINES.

(a) All German submarines, without exception, submarine salvage vessels and docks for submarines (including the Kiel tubular dock) are surrendered to the Allies and the United States of America. Those which can proceed under their own power or be towed shall be taken into Allied ports within a maximum period of fifteen days, to be there sunk or broken-up.

(b) The German submarines which cannot be delivered thus, as well as those which are in course of construction, shall be completely broken-up by the Germans, under the supervision of the Allied Commissioners.

The destruction of these submarines shall be completed within a maximum period of three months after the signature of the preliminaries of Peace.

(c) The materials arising from these submarines may be used, but solely for industrial and commercial purposes. It is forbidden to make use of these materials for works having a warlike object.

Additional clause containing an agreement between the Allies and not for insertion in the Terms with Germany:

(d) All the German submarines, submarine salvage-vessels and docks for submarines, which are surrendered to the Allies, shall be sunk or broken-up under the supervision of the Allies or the United States of America.

The materials arising from the above vessels may be used, but solely for industrial and commercial purposes. It is forbidden to make use of these materials for works having a warlike object.

A maximum period of three months is allowed for the removal of the material and the destruction of the submarines. In the particular case of Japan this period shall not, in any case, be less than 180 days after arrival in Japan.

II. SURFACE VESSELS.

All the German surface warships now interned in Allied or neutral ports, in conformity with the terms of the Armistice, cease to belong to Germany; they are definitely surrendered to the Allies and the United States of America.

The ships shall be sunk or broken-up in the shortest possible time.

III.

The German warships named below shall be delivered to the Allies and the United States of America, at ports to be designated by them, within a period of one month for the purpose of being sunk or broken-up. These vessels should be in condition to proceed under their own power to the places decided on by the Allies; the guns and torpedo material must remain intact.

With these reservations the German Government may remove from these ships, before their surrender, such material as has a commercial value.

These vessels are:

Battleships.

Oldenburg	Posen
Thüringen	Westfalen
Ostfriesland	Rheinland
Helgoland	Nassau

Light Cruisers.

Pillau	Strassburg
Graudenz	Augsburg
Regensburg	Kolberg
Stralsund	Stuttgart

Forty-two modern destroyers

Fifty modern torpedo boats

IV. CONSTRUCTION OF WARSHIPS.

Germany shall stop the construction of all warships now on the slips. These vessels shall be broken up under the supervision of the Allies and the United States of America. The materials arising from the breaking-up of these vessels may be used by Germany on condition that they are used for commercial purposes and on no account for warlike purposes.

Until the signature of the definite Treaty of Peace Germany shall not undertake any new construction of warships, submarines included.

V. HELIGOLAND.

The fortifications, military establishments, and harbours of Heligoland shall be destroyed under the supervision of the Allies, by German labour and at the expense of Germany, within a period to be determined by the Commissioners of the Allied Powers.

The final disposal of the island of Heligoland remains to be decided by the Peace Conference.

VI. ROUTES OF ACCESS INTO THE BALTIC.

In order to secure to free access into the Baltic to all nations, Germany shall not erect any fortifications in the area comprised between the latitudes 55°27′ N. and 54°00′ N. and longitudes 9°00′ and 16°00′ E. of the meridian of Greenwich, nor instal any guns commanding the maritime routes between the North Sea and the Baltic.

The fortifications now existing shall be demolished and the guns removed under the supervision of the Allies.

V.II. KIEL CANAL.

The Kiel Canal shall be open at all times to all war or commercial vessels of every nation. No nation shall benefit by specifically favourable treatment, and no class of vessel shall be excluded from the Canal.

VIII. GERMAN COLONIES.

The German Colonies shall not be returned to Germany.

IX. SUBMARINE CABLES.

The German Cables enumerated below shall not be returned to their previous owners.

The final allocation of these cables will be determined by the decisions of the Prize Courts of the Allies concerned.

> Emden-Vigo.
> Emden-Brest.
> Emden-Teneriffe.
> Emden-Azores (two cables)
> Azores-New York (two cables)
> Teneriffe-Monrovia.
> Monrovia-Pernambuco.
> Monrovia-Lome.
> Lome-Duala.
> Constantinople-Constanza.
> Chifu-Tsingtau-Shang[h]ai.
> Yap-Shang[h]ai.
> Yap-Guam.
> Yap-Menado (Celebes)

X.

German auxiliary cruisers, whether in German or Austrian ports, or interned in neutral ports, and Fleet auxiliaries which could be rapidly turned to commercial purposes or which are converted merchant vessels, shall be treated as are other merchant vessels.

The vessels affected by this clause are enumerated in the attached list. (Appendix I.).[8]

XI.

All Allied or neutral merchant vessels which have been captured, brought into port and condemned by the German Prize Court, shall

---

[8] This and the following appendices not printed in the typed minutes or in *PPC*.

be included in the number of the German merchant vessels which will be surrendered under the heading of Reparation.

XII.

Having in view:

(1) The reiterated and flagrant violations of the Laws of Nations committed at sea by the Germans;

(2) The extensive damage of all sorts caused to the merchant navies of the world by the systematic destruction of merchant vessels carrying passengers and cargoes;

(3) The impossibility, in the greater number of cases, of exactly determining the circumstances to which the losses of vessels are due, the reparation required from Germany (for merchant vessels sunk) will be fixed according to the total number of vessels destroyed by the Germans, whatever the means used for their destruction.

XIII. MINESWEEPING.

Germany shall sweep up all mines in the areas which have been assigned to her in the agreement already entered into between the Allies and the United States of America.

In accordance with this agreement, Germany shall be responsible for sweeping in the following areas:

(1) That portion of the North Sea which lies to the eastward of longitude 4°00′ E. from Greenwich—

(a) between the parallels of latitude 53°00′ N. and 59°00′ N.

(b) to the northward of latitude 60°30′ N.

(2) The Baltic Sea, excluding Russian waters. In regard to these waters further details will be given as soon as the Russian question is determined.

XIV. AIRCRAFT.

The Admirals support the proposals made by the Inter-Allied Committee which has dealt with this subject.

XV. WIRELESS TELEGRAPHY.

(1) The German high-power W/T stations at
Nauen,
Hannover, and
Berlin

shall not be used for the naval, military or political purposes of Germany, or of any State which has been allied to Germany in the war, without the assent of the Allied Powers and the United States of America, which will not be given until they are satisfied that the naval and military stipulations of the Treaty of Peace have been fully carried out. During the intervening period these stations may be used for commercial purposes, but only under the supervision of the Allies and the United States of America, who will decide the wave lengths to be used.

(2) Germany shall not build any more high-power W/T stations in her own territory or that of Austria-Hungary, Bulgaria, or Turkey, until the naval and military stipulations of the Treaty of Peace have been fully carried out.

(3) In the event of Germany violating the provisions of the Treaty of Peace or disregarding the decisions of the International Radio-Telegraphic Conference, the Allies and the United States of America shall be at liberty to withhold the services of their W/T stations from German stations.

(4) Germany shall have only one vote at the next International Radio-Telegraphic Conference, irrespective of the number of independent or semi-independent States into which Germany may be divided.

NAVAL CLAUSES FOR INSERTION IN THE PRELIMINARY PEACE TERMS WITH AUSTRIA-HUNGARY.

I. SUBMARINES AND SURFACE WARSHIPS.

All Austro-Hungarian warships, including submarines and the Danube flotillas, shall be broken-up or sunk as soon as possible by the Allies and the United States of America.

A list is given in Appendix [blank].

II. WARSHIPS UNDER CONSTRUCTION.

The construction of all Austro-Hungarian warships (including submarines) actually on the slips shall cease. These vessels shall be broken-up under the supervision of the Allies and the United States of America; and no new warship construction shall be undertaken by Austria-Hungary before the final Peace is signed.

The material arising from the breaking-up of these vessels may be utilised, but only for commercial purposes.

III. MERCHANT CRUISERS AND FLEET AUXILIARIES.

Austro-Hungarian merchant cruisers and Fleet auxiliaries which can be readily adapted for commercial purposes (or which have been converted from merchant vessels) shall be dealt with as merchant vessels.

The vessels affected are given in Appendix [blank].

T MS (SDR, RG 256, 180.03101/33, DNA).

From William Shepherd Benson

Paris, February 8, 1919.

Memorandum for The President of the United States:

With regard to the proposal of the British this afternoon for a consideration by the Conference of the naval terms for a further extension of the Armistice, I wish to invite your attention to the fact that in all cases so far when it has become necessary to discuss terms of the Armistice the Naval Advisers to the Commissioners have met in formal conference and after reaching an agreement among themselves have submitted their recommendations to the Supreme War Council.

While there have been several suggestions of a possible necessity for extending the terms of the Armistice with Germany, the deliberations of the Naval Advisers since the last extension of the Armistice have been devoted to the question of that body's recommendations regarding Naval terms to be submitted for a preliminary peace. At no time during those deliberations has the question of extension been taken under consideration.

While I have agreed to certain terms contained in the paper drawn up by the Naval Advisers as covering the requirements for preliminary terms of peace, I do not consider that these same terms should be made to comply with the extension of the Armistice. On the contrary I am certainly of the opinion that should it become necessary to extend the Armistice no change whatever should be made in the existing Naval terms of the Armistice.

I beg therefore to suggest that if the Supreme War Council decides that a further extension of the Armistice is advisable, the Naval Advisers be directed to follow the usual procedure and submit the results of their deliberations for approval by the Supreme Body.

Very respectfully,   [W. S. Benson]

CC MS (W. S. Benson Papers, DLC).

To Newton Diehl Baker

Paris. February 8, 1919

For Secretary of War from the President. Very secret and very urgent.

"The question has arisen here whether it is possible to use any of our troops now on this side of the water to garrison portions of the Turkish Empire, such as Constantinople and Armenia and Mesopotamia pending the final determinations of the peace and the designation of mandatories for such regions by the League of Nations. British troops are now occupying these areas and the result is that Great Britain is obliged to maintain much the largest and most burdensome military establishment of the whole group of Associated Powers. It seems to me only fair that we should consider the possibility of sharing the burden of occupations of which nobody but the whole group of nations is to get the benefit. I would very much like your advice; first, as to the legality of sending American troops to those areas, presumably with the assent of Turkey, because we have never been at war with her; second, as to the wisdom of such a step from the point of view of the probable attitude and temper of the people at home and the soldiers themselves; and third, as to the wisdom of such a course from the point of view of public policy. The interest of America in Robert College of Constantinople and in the pitiful fortunes of the Armenians is of such long standing and is so great and genuine that I am assuming that the occupation of Constantinople and Armenia would not strike the people as unreasonable or undesirable in view of the fact that it is clearly true that they would be more welcome and serviceable in those two places than any other troops would be and would be needed in smaller force. The latter statement is also true of the Syrian and Arabian countries, though I suppose our public opinion would not be prepared in any degree for occupation there."

T telegram (SDR, RG 59, 763.72/12770, DNA).

From Tasker Howard Bliss

My dear Mr. President: Paris, February 8th, 1919.

Late on Wednesday afternoon, February 5th, General Sir Henry Wilson, the British Chief of Staff, said to me that you had agreed to have American troops take part in an Allied reinforcement of some thousand men to go to Murmansk, provided I approved. I questioned him as to what the composition of this force was to be (how many British? how many Americans? how many French and Italians?) but could learn nothing definite from him.

I told him that I wished he would give me a written statement of exactly what was wanted and what was proposed to be done. The day following his conversation with me Sir Henry Wilson left for London and has not returned. I am told by a British officer that at the time of his departure he sent me a letter giving me the information I had asked for. This letter has not been received, but I was informed today that a copy was coming over in a British aeroplane that comes daily from London to Paris. It may have so come but it has not come to me. Of course I can give no advice on such a matter without knowing something more definite about it. If, as I hope, I receive the letter tomorrow, I shall at once communicate my views.

Meanwhile, General Pershing informs me that he has also received a communication on this subject. It may be that he will communicate his views to you, in which case I have no doubt they will be the same as mine. I doubt the political or the military wisdom of sending any more troops to North Russia except for the purpose of enabling the force that we now have there to concentrate at Murmansk and Archangel at the earliest moment that it can do so with safety.   Yours respectfully,   Tasker H Bliss

CCL (T. H. Bliss Papers, DLC).

A Declaration[1]

February 8, 1919.

PRINCIPLES OF REPARATION.
(Presented by the Delegation of the United States of America.)

I.

Reparation to be made for all damage directly caused by acts of the enemy clearly in violation of international law as recognized at the time of the commission of the acts.

II.*

Belgium and the occupied areas of France, Roumania, Serbia and Montenegro to be physically restored to a condition as near as possible to that which would have existed had war not occurred; such restoration to be accomplished when practicable by a return of actual property abstracted, otherwise compensation to be made in money or goods.

* Amended at meeting of 14 February (p. 33).[2]

[1] Vance C. McCormick presented this declaration to Wilson on the evening of February 8, and Wilson approved it. The Diary of Vance C. McCormick, printed copy (V. C. McCormick Papers, CtY), Feb. 8, 1919.

[2] The revised version of Section II, submitted at the meeting of the Commission on Reparation of Damage on February 14, reads as follows: "Belgium and the occupied areas of France, Italy, Roumania, Serbia, Greece and Montenegro to be physically restored to a condition as near as possible to that which would have existed had war not occurred: such restoration to be accomplished when practicable by a return of actual property abstracted, otherwise compensation to be made in money or goods. Reservation made provisionally in respect of Poland and Czecho-Slovakia because of the special international situation of these countries." Philip Mason Burnett, *Reparation at the Paris Peace Conference: From the Standpoint of the American Delegation* (2 vols., New York, 1940), II, 318.

III.

Compensation to be made for all physical damage to property of a civilian (i.e., non-military) character, wherever located, provided such damage has been caused directly by German military operations.

IV.

Compensation to be made for all damage directly caused by injuries to civilians directly due to German military operations; this to include death, personal injury, enforced labor, and loss of opportunity to labor or to secure a just reward for labor.

(NOTE: These four principles do not purport to be mutually exclusive in their application.)

APPENDIX I.

The text of that portion of President Wilson's address of Jan. 8, 1918 which relates to restoration, and the text of the Allied qualification thereof.

(It is the view of the American Delegates of the Commission on Reparation that no reparation can be exacted unless (1) it is clearly due in accordance with accepted principles of international law, or (2) it is stipulated in the understanding embodied in the texts given below.)

PRESIDENT WILSON'S POINTS REGARDING RESTORATION OF INVADED TERRITORIES.

VII. Belgium, the whole world will agree, must be evacuated and restored, without any attempt to limit the sovereignty which she enjoys in common with all other free nations. No other single act will serve as this will serve to restore confidence among the nations in the laws which they have themselves set and determined for the government of their relations with one another. Without this healing act the whole structure and validity of international law is forever impaired.

VIII. All French territory should be freed and the invaded portions restored, and the wrong done to France by Prussia in 1871 in the matter of Alsace-Lorraine, which has unsettled the peace of the world for nearly fifty years, should be righted, in order that peace may once more be made secure in the interest of all.

XI. Roumania, Serbia, and Montenegro should be evacuated; occupied territories restored; Serbia accorded free and secure access to the sea; and the relations of the several Balkan states to one another determined by friendly counsel along historically established lines of allegiance and nationality; and international guarantees of the political and economic independence and territorial integrity of the several Balkan states should be entered into.

QUALIFICATION OF THESE CLAUSES BY THE ALLIED GOVERNMENTS,
CONVEYED TO GERMANY IN THE NOTE OF THE SECRETARY
OF STATE OF THE UNITED STATES OF NOVEMBER 5, 1918.

Further, in the conditions of peace laid down in his address to Congress of January 8, 1918, the President declared that invaded territories must be restored as well as evacuated and freed; the Allied Governments feel that no doubt ought to be allowed to exist as to what this provision implies. By it they understand that compensation will be made by Germany for all damage done to the civilian population of the Allies and their property by the aggression of Germany by land, by sea and from the air.

APPENDIX II.
COMMENT ON THE PRINCIPLES OF REPARATION AS PROPOSED BY THE AMERICAN DELEGATES.

I.

Reparation to be made for all damage directly caused by acts of the enemy clearly in violation of international law as recognized at the time of the commission of the acts.

The reparation specified for in the Fourteen Points is not designed to be comprehensive and in derogation of reparation due in accordance with accepted principles of international law. Rather the Fourteen Points proceed from the basis of existing international law and specify the further and special acts of justice necessary for a proper settlement of the war.

We accordingly accept as a first principle that reparation is due for all damage directly consequent upon acts of the enemy clearly in violation of international law as recognized at the time of the commission of the acts in question.

In determining the practical application of this principle we have, to guide us, a large body of international precedent and considerable contractual law, such as the Hague Conventions. The details of the reparation which will be required in pursuance of this principle need not be gone into comprehensively at this time, but such reparation will include the following:

(1) The citizens of the associated countries to be restored to the enjoyment of their property which was in enemy countries at the outbreak of the war. Where restoration in kind cannot be made, pecuniary restitution to be made.

(2) Reparation to be made to Belgium for all losses of whatever character directly attributable to the war. This consequence flows from the fact that the war of Germany against Belgium, unlike that against the other Allies, was violative of inter-

national law, Germany having undertaken by treaty not to make war against Belgium.

(3) Reparation for damage caused by miscellaneous illegal acts, such as:

Deportation of civilians;

Sinking merchant vessels without warning;

Attacks on undefended towns;

Mistreatment of prisoners of war;

Destruction of property without military justification;

Etc., etc., etc.

II.

Belgium and the occupied areas of France, Roumania, Serbia and Montenegro to be physically restored to a condition as near as possible to that which would have existed had war not occurred; such restoration to be accomplished when practicable by a return of actual property abstracted, otherwise compensation to be made in money or goods.

Unless reparation is due in accordance with clearly recognized principles of international law, it cannot be exacted except as specifically agreed to by the enemy. Principles II, III and IV are accordingly based on the Fourteen Points, as qualified by the Allies, which were accepted by Germany as an agreed basis of peace.

Principle II, set out above, flows directly from the original statement in the Fourteen Points relative to restoration. It is to be noted that restoration in Points VII, VIII and XI is coupled with evacuation and appears clearly to contemplate a physical, territorial restoration. The thought is that certain areas must be freed from enemy presence and restored to the condition which they would have been in had enemy invasion never occurred.

It might be argued that the complete restoration of Belgium and the occupied territories contemplated by the President's original statement is limited in scope or at least changed in point of view by the "Interpretation" placed thereon by the Allies; to-wit; "that compensation will be made by Germany for all damage done to the *civilian* population of the Allies and *their* property by the *aggression* of Germany by land, by sea, and from the air." (Italics ours.)

The inherent improbability of the Allied statement being intended to operate as a limitation or as anything but an addition is so great that we take the view that the words of the Allies: "by it they understood that compensation will be made" should be construed as though they were "they understand that compensation also will be made."

Accordingly, we regard, in the first instance, President Wilson's language and derive therefrom our Principle II which implies a complete physical restoration of the territory of Belgium, and the occupied areas of France, Roumania, Serbia and Montenegro. While such reparation would, in a large part, flow also from Principle III, it is not now clear that this latter principle would cover every case for reparation coming under Principle II and for this reason, as well as for the fact that Principle II embodies a somewhat special point of view, it is stated separately.

III.

Compensation to be made for all physical damage to property of a civilian (i.e., non-military) character, wherever located, provided such damage has been directly by German military operations.

We have seen that the qualification by the Allies of President Wilson's Points VII, VIII and XI is to be regarded not as an interpretation of, but as an addition to, the reparation provided for by these points. We have also seen that Points VII, VIII and XI provide for adequate reparation for damage to property located in Belgium and the invaded areas of France, Roumania, Serbia and Montenegro. The addition of the Allies, however, extends the right of reparation to property located *outside* the areas covered by Points VII, VIII and XI. The only apparent qualifications are (1) that the property at the time of the damage be that of "the civilian population" and (2) that the damage be the result of "aggression of Germany" by land, sea or air. While the language of the Allied qualification thus refers clearly to damage to the civilian population and "to *their* property," we attribute "civilian" to the character of the property, rather than the character of the owner. The test of the character of the owner is a purely arbitrary and unreasonable one. The test of the character of the property and the use to which it is devoted is sound and in accord with international practice.

It is also necessary to give some definite and limited construction to the words "damage" and "aggression." Otherwise all war costs might be included in clear defiance of the spirit pervading the bases of settlement. We accordingly construe "damage by aggression" to mean physical damage to property resulting directly from military operations of the enemy, including defensive, or counter-offensive, operations of the Allies. Under this construction would be covered damage to civil property resulting directly from air raids, long-range bombardments, attack by sea, etc.

IV.

Compensation to be made for all damage directly caused by injuries to civilians directly due to German military operations; this to include death, personal injury, enforced labor, and loss of opportunity to labor or to secure a just reward for labor.

The qualification of the Allies to Points VII, VIII and XI introduces the further element of reparation for injury to civilians. By this is to be understood violations of personal rights as distinct from damage to property. Adopting the same construction of the words "damage by aggression," as is outlined above, this Allied addition means that reparation must also be made for damage caused by injuries to civilians resulting directly from the military operations of Germany (this to include defensive and counter-offensive operations of the Allies). It is not, however, as easy to determine what is injury to a person as it is to determine what is damage to property. It is possible, of course, to limit damage to person to a physical injury occasioned directly, as a rifle wound. Damage to person should be given a more liberal construction than this. In view of the rather adequate provision made for damage to property, particularly in the invaded areas, it is both wise and just to construe damage to person in a liberal sense which will not invite the charge of according a special sanctity to property as distinguished from life and labor. We construe, therefore, damage to the civilian population to include damage resulting through injury to civilians in the way of death, personal injury, enforced labor and loss of opportunity to labor or to secure a just reward for labor.

Printed copy (J. F. Dulles Papers, NjP).

Charles Seymour to His Family

Dear people: Paria [Paris], February 8, 1919.

. . . Wedensday [Wednesday][1] morning I was busy getting ready for the secret session of the Premiers and Foreign Ministers in the afternoon which I was told to attend. Benes and Kramarz were to present the Czech case. We had lunch with Benes before we went over to the Quai d'Orsay. He is a delightful little chap, just as friendly and as moderate as one could wish. The only question is whether he will be able to last, for he is caught at home between the extreme chauvinists who want to grab everything in sight and have been making bad trouble with the Poles, and the socialists and labor leaders. We went over to the Quai d'Orsay right after lunch. I sat immediately behind Wilson and Lansing, having discovered that it is convenient to prompt them when the man talking is making absurd statements and to give them maps and statistics explanatory of the matter that is being discussed. I had been warned that they did not like to have too much told them, but I found them very grateful for ev[e]rything that I said and very genial. Once Wilson got up and called me into a corner to explain a point; Lansing turned around several times to ask me questions. Once it was very humorous for he asked me to point out something on the map before him; I had to stand between him and Wilson, and Lloyd George leaned over and said: "I say, what's that?" So I had to repeat in fairly lound [loud] voice: there was Benes talking to the commission and there was I, six feet away from him explaining to Wilson, Lansing, and Lloyd George. You would have been amused. I have as good a souvenir of the secret sessions as one could want: Lansing draws all the time the session goes on, with his left hand; caricatures and grotesque figures, really very well done. When one is finished he drops it on the floor and begins another. I picked up a couple and gave one to Dulles, who is Lansing's nephew, to get him to sign it as done during the conference. Lloyd George was filled with admiration for the drawings: "I say," he said, "could I have one of those; they're awfully good." So Lansing gave him one and he folded it carefully and put it in his pocket with gratitude. Lloyd George is really the best fun of these conferences; very alert, not knowing very much about things, and generally, I think, not understanding things very exactly; passing comments in a loud undertone without cessation, regardless of whether they are complimentary or not. He reminds me of a very business like bird. He is much shorter and fatter than I had realized. Balfour is very diplomatic in manner, rather "sweet," apt to be very sleepy. Of course the translator, Mantoux, is always a joy. He puts more spirit into his translations than the principal puts into his original speech. Mantoux never says: "Mr. Benes claims this territory on the ground of historic rights." He says "*We* feel that by virtue of our noble history, etc," with his voice shaking with emotion and fervour. Benes presented his case very well, I thought, but it took three hours, and poor Kramarz, who wanted to speak was not allowed to. When he asked for half an hour, Clemenceau said, "O, we'll appoint a special commission and you can talk to them for a couple of hours. Now, we had better have a cup of tea." Of course this rather irritates the delegates of the little Powers. Bratiano said to me: "The fact that our case is of the greatest importance does not prevent the big men from going to sleep, and the fact that they go to sleep will not prevent them from judging." . . .

TLI (C. Seymour Papers, CtY).
  [1] February 5, 1919.

From Josephus Daniels

[Washington] 8th February 1919

For The President.

VERY CONFIDENTIAL.

From every standpoint I wish to suggest the wisdom of selecting Mitchell Palmer as Attorney General. He has confidence of the country as a sterling patriot, is a lawyer of ability, has served in Congress and will have touch with our friends in the Legislative body, and in addition to his fitness in departmental work, has the resolve in court and in forum to make argument and uphold nation's policies. I know his appointment would be hailed with pleasure by all who were in the 1912 struggle, and he would be peculiarly welcomed by the members of the cabinet. Moreover he comes from the right part of the country particularly when consideration *Mitchel had to be recent appointments able* 16007.   Secnav.

T telegram (WP, DLC).

From Joseph Patrick Tumulty

The White House, February 8, 1919

No. 43. I hope you will consent to march at head of parade for returning soldiers on your arrival in Washington. Aside from this, there will be no public reception. Fear boys and their relatives and friends would feel hurt if you refuse to do this. In view of your desire to reach Washington as soon as possible, think you could land at New York, reserving Boston for next time.

Tumulty.

T telegram (WP, DLC).

From the Diary of Dr. Grayson

Sunday, February 9, 1919.

The President attended church on the Rue de Berri.[1] In the afternoon accompanied by Mrs. Wilson and myself he went for a long auto ride. He rested the entire day.

[1] That is, the American Presbyterian Church, the Rev. Dr. Chauncey William Goodrich, pastor.

To Lee Slater Overman

Paris, 9 February, 1919.

VERY URGENT

I hope that you will pardon me if I again express my deep anxiety about the vote on the Suffrage Amendment. It assumes a more important aspect every day, and the fortunes of our party are of such consequence at this particular turn in the world's events that I take the great liberty of again urging upon you favorable action. Please be kind enough to show this to Senator Williams.

Woodrow Wilson

CC telegram (WP, DLC).

To Joseph Patrick Tumulty

[Paris, c. Feb. 9, 1919]

Of course I will march at the head of a parade for returning soldiers when I reach Washington. All that I want to avoid is a demonstration arranged for me personally. I am thinking of coming direct to Hampton Roads. Consider demonstration premature.

T transcript (WP, DLC).

From William Harrison Short

New York, 9 Feb. 1919.

Thirty five hundred delegates representing New York, New Jersey, Maryland, Virginia, Delaware, Pennsylvania, West Virginia and District of Columbia, at League to Enforce Peace Atlantic Congress for League of Nations presided over by Mr. Taft unanimously adopted and directed me cable you following quote: "The purposes of the war can be effected and the objects of the treaty of peace about to be drawn can be achieved only by the creation of a League of free nations to safeguard the peace now won by the Allies and the United States and to maintain the settlement of international differences and disputes by reason justice and conciliation rather than by war and thereby to promote the free orderly peaceful development of the world stop. This league should have behind it the united force of these nations stop. The League to Enforce Peace stands by and upholds the President in his efforts to secure an agreement between the powers covering the details of organization the definition of functions and the formulation of the joint obligations which the great nations would assume for maintaining the authority of such a league and carrying out its purposes stop. We are convinced that the public opinion of the United States is in favor of a league to maintain the peace of the world and will sustain and justify the President and his colleagues at the peace conference in approving in terms consonant with the constitution of the United States and the spirit of the American people the assumption by this country of its proportionate burden in company with the great nations for maintaining the authority of such a league unquote."

William H. Short.

T telegram (WP, DLC).

From Ellison DuRant Smith

Washington, D. C. Feb. 9th [1919]

At a meeting of Senators and Representatives in Congress from cotton growing states a resolution was unanimously adopted instructing me as chairman of the meeting to advise you that the retention of cotton upon the embargo list is depriving cotton owners of a large market with neutral countries to the serious injury of merchants, ba[n]ker[s] and farmers in one fourth of our country and to the financial commercial injury of our entire country and while it was believed the blockade should be removed on cotton shipments to enemy countries the immediate removal of cotton from the embargo list that it may be sold without restrictions to neutral countries is the least that should be done to relieve disastrous conditions now existing please reply earliest moment possible.

E. D. Smith.

T telegram (WP, DLC).

Robert Lansing and Vance Criswell McCormick
to Frank Lyon Polk

Paris, February 9th, 1919.

658. Urgent and confidential. From Lansing and McCormick. Department's 568, February 4, 6 p.m.

In view of situation which you report[1] the President withdraws the suggestion with reference to presenting to Congressional Committees our proposed action with reference to Siberian railway. The President further authorizes the following,

One. That you formally accept the plan on behalf of the United States with reservations as to financial responsibility which shall be the subject of further discussion and that you notify the Japanese in this sense.

Two. That you request Secretary Baker to see that instructions are given General Graves as contemplated by plan.

Third. That the Wartabord [War Board] Russian Bureau, Incorporated, advance such funds as it can spare in amounts approved by the Department for the temporary support of Stevens as proposed in Mission's 521, January 31, 8 p.m.[2]

Four. That you give immediate instructions to Ambassador Morris to inaugurate negot[ia]tions for a definite plan for operating the railroad.

While in deference to your views and those of the Cabinet the President withdraws his suggestion as to placing this matter frankly before Congress, it is desired that you keep this possibility in mind and avail of any opportunity which may seem to you to be appropriate to keep Congress advised as to our policy with reference to the Siberian railroad. It is felt this matter can be treated entirely apart from the general Russian problem, as, irrespective of what our policy may be towards Russia, and irrespective of future Russian developments, it is essential that we maintain the policy of the open door with reference to the Siberian and particularly the Chinese Eastern railway.

This cable has been seen and approved by the President.

T telegram (WP, DLC).
[1] FLP to RL and V. C. McCormick, Feb. 4, 1919, Vol. 54.
[2] RL to FLP, Jan. 31, 1919, *ibid.*

William Sowden Sims to William Shepherd Benson

Paris 9 February, 1919.

The following is a paraphrase of a message received from Admiral Sims.

From: Admiral Sims.

To: Admiral Benson.

"The following is quoted from a despatch received from Admiral McCully:[1]

'I reached Archangel on February 5th. Although there is continuous ice two or three feet thick at the entrance to the White Sea, with the help of ice breakers it is possible for well built merchant vessels to get through. At present conditions in Archangel are quiet. There is no need for immediate anxiety. Reinforcements of reliable disciplined troops have not been designated. It is realized that the situation may become critical very suddenly.' "

T MS (WP, DLC).
[1] Rear Adm. Newton Alexander McCully, commander of United States naval forces in Russian waters.

From the Diary of Edith Benham

February 9, 1919

The President spoke of an amusing incident last night which he thought would appear in today's paper's account of the proceedings of the Supreme War Council and the consideration of the extension of the Armistice. Foch was speaking of the request of the German Government that certain prisoners with large families dependent on them be repatriated. This he considered within certain limits a very reasonable request and one which could be granted. Clemenceau objected for with good French thrift he said these men were used in clearing the roads and tearing down the ruins of Northern France and the civil authorities want to keep them at this work. Then as the President said occurred the extraordinary spectacle of the French Secretary of War and his General having an altercation. After "spitting at each other like cats for several minutes," the President not understanding French well enough to follow, Foch got up and walked with great dignity out of the room, his aide looked bewildered, gathered up the papers the Marshal had left, and followed after him. "Consider," as the President said, "if Baker had summoned Pershing and they had gotten into a squabble like that before an audience of the kind." He said what struck him most was the absolute unconcern of everyone. Clemenceau went about his work after Foch had stalked out as though nothing had happened and every other face was quite as imperturbable.

He was very much annoyed over Wemyss, the British Admiralty Lord, whom he said appeared with a long proposition which relates really to the Peace Conference and not to the Supreme War Council and the Armistice. It was the neutralization of the German colonies, the internationalization of the wireless station at Nauen and elsewhere in Germany, the destruction or handing over to the Allies of all submarines. It was in essence the substance of a memorandum prepared by Benson and his aides here in conference with the allies. Benson had dissented entirely from the idea of presenting this recommendation now, and had no part in it, it was simply the British Government, or Navy, I should say, trying to put over as Mr. Wilson said additional and harder terms in renewing the Armistice. He said the French Minister of Munitions read a long paper showing that Germany is manufacturing so many machine guns and other guns. Mr. Wilson asked on what these figures were based and found they were based on theoretical figures, what she had done during the war, the output of the French munitions works, and not supported in any way by facts from the German factories. You see, the French have gone quite mad over the idea that Germany is arming

again and they are terrified naturally for they have nothing left to
fight with. Mr. Wilson believes firmly that this is a scare and a very
natural one, that the German people are tired of war and even if
they were not, the Allies control three-fourths of their resources of
raw material and they couldn't manufacture arms even if they wanted.
He said he was annoyed by this unsportsmanlike wish to impose
new and harder conditions each time the armistice is renewed. He
told the council that when he read the original terms of the Armistice to Congress that the one opinion expressed there and elsewhere was "this is not an armistice but a surrender" and it was
supposed then that the terms were the most drastic that could be
imposed and based on an accurate estimate of Germany's military
resources. He asked how it would seem now to the world and if
the Council would not be entirely discredited if they admitted they
had been mistaken and month by month added new conditions.

It seems curious about Clemenceau. Mrs. Wilson said to the
President that he had been the man in whom he had been mistaken,
that Colonel House had told him he is reactionary but could be
trusted!

T MS (Edith B. Helm Papers, DLC).

From the Diary of Dr. Grayson

Monday, February 10, 1919.

The President spent a busy day at the Peace Conference and in
the evening said to me:

"The French people are the hardest I ever tried to do business
with."

The President characterized Mr. Bourgeois, who made a speech,
as a man of many words. Practically the entire day was wasted in
talking chiefly by the French.

Minutes of a Meeting of the Commission on the League of Nations

SEVENTH MEETING, FEBRUARY 10, 1919, AT 10:30 A.M.
President WILSON *in the Chair.*

ARTICLE 20.

President Wilson read Article 20 of the Covenant.

Mr. Hymans observed that Belgium was a free-trade country,
whose economic position at the present moment was most serious.
She would be gravely threatened by "dumping" at the hands of the

Germans; and, during the whole reconstruction period, she would in all probability have to ask for favoured treatment from her Allies.

President Wilson remarked that Germany would not be a member of the League during this period; and that he inclined to the idea of preferential rights for Belgium.

Mr. Larnaude made a similar claim for France; and *Lord Robert Cecil* expressed himself as favouring some special system during the reconstruction period.

Mr. Larnaude: Until the debts of war are liquidated, it would be contrary to the principles set forth in President Wilson's Fourteen Points if the nations who have suffered from the war should not be indemnified.

Mr. Orlando: There are two matters to consider: first, the question of the principles involved in Article 20, with which everyone appears to agree; second, the proposal of Messrs. Hymans and Larnaude, which has reference to the present period, and which looks toward a special system for the period.

Mr. Larnaude: There is a separate Commission now considering these matters of reparation and reconstruction, and we cannot here come to any decisions, which run the risk of conflicting with the conclusions of this Commission.

President Wilson remarked that the Covenant would form an integral part of the Treaty of Peace; but that there would be other arrangements, which would deal with the reconstruction of devastated countries.

Mr. Hymans: The Commission on Reparation and Damages is reckoning the indemnities to be required from Germany; but, in order to retrieve her lost wealth, Belgium will have to enter into relations with various Allied Powers in order to build up close commercial connections. Belgium has lost her market and her factories, and will have to protect herself by special measures during the period of transition. The word "equitable," which is proposed, does not perhaps sufficiently take this necessity into account.

But Mr. Hymans supported the idea of laying down a lasting principle, at the same time adding a temporary modification of that principle.

Mr. Larnaude could not subscribe to the compromise suggested by Mr. Hymans. He opposed the very idea of it. The plan of a Covenant was the outcome of the war, and of the condition of distress created in Poland, Belgium, and many other countries by Germany. So long as this situation remained unrelieved, we could not talk of "equitable" commerce; the word would not be understood. Throughout a period of uncertain length, it would be just to ask that we be permitted to take restrictive precautions, which would protect us from the invasion of enemy goods.

Mr. Bourgeois, reverting to Mr. Orlando's view, said that everyone was fundamentally in agreement; but that it was necessary for it to be clearly understood that the general principle would not govern during the reconstruction period, when a succession of measures would be necessary in order to regain economic life.

Mr. Batalha Reis pointed out that although Portugal had not been devastated by the war, she had nevertheless suffered severe economic loss. He therefore considered his country entitled to the benefits of any special arrangements which might be made in pursuance of Article 21. He further desired that the interpretation given by the Commission to the word "equitable" should be placed on record in the Minutes.

President Wilson proposed to take the foregoing views into account by adding the following words:

"Having in mind, among other things, special arrangements with regard to the necessities of the regions devastated during the war of 1914-1918."

This article was thereupon adopted as amended.

ARTICLE 21.

After reading the article, *President Wilson* proposed to add the following words:

"And no treaty or international engagement shall be operative until so registered."

On the motion of *Mr. Vesnitch,* the words "by a State member" were substituted for the words "between States members."

In the course of the discussion it was agreed that this article referred only to new treaties.

It was agreed that the word "any" in the English text should be changed to "every."

Subject to the two amendments and the verbal change noted above, the article was adopted.

ARTICLE 22.

Mr. Larnaude: This article contains a clause in which the idea of abrogation is implicit; in other words, whatever is inconsistent with this text is abrogated. What authority will pass upon the question of inconsistency? Some Tribunal? The Executive Council? In private law it rests with tribunals to make the decision.

President Wilson: It is probably impossible to fix in advance the authority which should decide this question. If a nation finds itself embarrassed by a treaty, it is possible for it at any time to carry the question to the League. The sanctions of this principle lie in public opinion. If the treaty is discovered to conflict with the general principles laid down in the Covenant, it would be morally impossible to sustain such a treaty. Every public declaration constitutes a moral obligation, and the decision of the court of public opinion will be much more effective than that of any tribunal in the world, since it is more powerful and is able to register its effect in the face of technicalities. Frequently the law decides one way and public opinion gives judgment in a manner that is broader and more equitable.

Mr. Larnaude: Doubtless we are all controlled by public opinion, but I am talking of countries where the idea of equality has gone a long way—I mean America and England. Would they give to public opinion power to decide questions regarding their customary law or their written law? There are technical matters, the interpretation of which only a constituted tribunal can decide.

Mr. Orlando: This 22nd Article is very important for it sets a limitation upon the freedom of Governments to enter into engagements. Is it the spirit of the Covenant to admit of alliance[s] between States? Mr. Veniselos has told us that he believes defensive alliances to be admissible, but, as a matter of fact, one never makes an "offensive" alliance. Who will pass upon their nature? A tribunal seems too rigid a body; while, on the other hand, the Executive Council seems admirably qualified to decide the question.

There is also the question of now existing treaties. It might happen that one of the contracting parties applied to the League to be relieved of its obligations thereunder. There ought to be some Power which can decide whether this treaty is in effect. If the article read, "The parties will agree to abrogate the treaty," the difficulty would disappear.

Mr. Batalha Reis: I believe that alliances between any of the members of the League of Nations may, in certain cases, be useless without necessarily becoming inconsistent or incompatible with the existence of the League. On the other hand, some ancient Treaties of Alliance, though formulated in what are now obsolete terms, are of an essentially permanent nature.

President Wilson: Matters which relate to the good faith of nations are extremely delicate; in such a case the only sanction is that of public opinion. The Courts of Justice make their decisions according to the rules of law, and in such a matter as this the moral judgment of peoples is more accurate than proceedings before a tribunal.

Mr. Vesnitch: It may well happen that public opinion will be guided by powerful currents whose direction it is difficult to foresee. Suppose that a small Power were in conflict with a great Power, public opinion might be influenced by the great Power through means which would direct it in a way contrary to the interests of the small Power. Public opinion is pliable and fluid and of such a nature that propaganda can mould it. It would appear to me wiser to submit questions under Article 21 to the consideration of the Executive Council of the League of Nations. This committee is really a body composed of all the members of the League, and each nation may be represented in its meetings and have every opportunity to be heard.

Mr. Veniselos: If there is any disagreement upon the interpretation, there is Article 21 which covers the case. If I should make a defensive agreement, I would submit it to the Chancellor of the League, and if he believed it contrary to the laws of the League he would request its consideration by the Executive Committee. In this connection Article 9 may be referred to.

Lord Robert Cecil: The Chancellor will lay the treaty before the Executive Council, and it will have the power to decide.

Mr. Hymans: There seems to be a general agreement that defensive alliances are not inconsistent with the principles of the League, but there is one case in which even offensive alliances seem permissible. Where there is a dispute, and where the Council has not given an unanimous decision, each side may make war. In this case, is not one of the parties justified in seeking allies among the nations which share its point of view and wish to support its just claims?

Mr. Orlando expressed the wish that this discussion might be included in the minutes, inasmuch as it gives a restrictive interpretation to Article 21. If this were done, he would accept the text.

Mr. Kramar: Even defensive alliances, as Mr. Orlando interjected, are not in accordance with the idea of the League. A separate alliance cannot be allowed if it is not agreed to by the Executive Council. It might be useful for small nations to conclude a defensive alliance, but it would have to be submitted to the Executive Council and validated by it.

President Wilson: That is the thought of the article,—an alliance shall not be held valid unless it is recorded.

Mr. Bourgeois: The obligation of recording appears adequate so far as new treaties are concerned, but what will be the status of treaties recorded in the past?

President Wilson: It does not rest with us to send a search-warrant into the politics of the past, though it is clear that they have taken a dangerous trend. It rests with the nations themselves to decide whether they wish to be relieved of their imprudent obligations, and to consider whether some of them should not be abrogated. For my part, I would hesitate a long time before visiting myself upon the past. Each nation will wisely and prudently attend to that. Our task is primarily to build for the future.

This article was then adopted.

Report of the Drafting Committee on Articles 13, 15, 17, *and* 19.

President Wilson read the amendments proposed by the Drafting Committee (Annex 1). Those amendments were adopted with the exception of the new draft of Article 19. A discussion followed with regard to this article.

President Wilson proposed to adopt the following substitute for Article 19:

"The High Contracting Parties agree that they will make no law prohibiting or interfering with the free exercise of religion, and they resolve that they will not permit the practice of any particular creed, religion, or belief, whose practices are not inconsistent with public order or with public morals, to interfere with the life, liberty or pursuit of happiness of their people."

Mr. Bourgeois: This only confirms the principle laid down in our declaration of the Rights of Man: "No one shall be persecuted because of his opinions or beliefs." The amendment was adopted.

Report of the Secretariat on Article 10.

President Wilson read the amendment submitted by the Secretariat (Annex 2). This amendment was adopted.

Responsibilities.

Mr. Larnaude: The Covenant embraces many things which in the beginning did not seem to be a part of the programme of the League of Nations. One of those things was pointed out by Lord Robert Cecil in his statement reprinted by the "Times" of the 26th February, 1918. According to his view, the League of Nations will be a joke or farce unless at the outset it insists upon the punishment of those responsible for this war.

This is one of the first duties of the Commission on the League of Nations. We must, therefore, decide first of all whether the League of Nations will take upon itself to judge and punish those who have been to blame. If the answer is in the affirmative it will be possible to include in the preamble some reference to this important matter.

It was agreed that the amendments offered by Mr. Vesnitch to Article 11, as well as the amendments presented by Mr. Bourgeois to Articles 6, 8, and 14, should be distributed and considered at the beginning of the next meeting, which would take place on Tuesday morning, the 11th February, at 10:30.

Articles 13, 15, 17, 19, 20, 21, and 22, as adopted, are contained in Annex 3.

(The Meeting adjourned.)

Annex 1 to Minutes of Seventh Meeting.
REPORT OF THE DRAFTING COMMITTEE.
ARTICLE 13.

Second paragraph, 3rd sentence.—Substitute the following:

"If the report is unanimously agreed to by the members of the Council other than the parties to the dispute, the High Contracting Parties agree that none of them will go to war with any party which complies with its recommendations, and that, if any party shall refuse so to comply, the Council shall consider what steps can best be taken to give effect to their recommendation."

(A similar addition would then be desirable to Article 11 as follows:

"If not, the Executive Council shall consider what steps can best be taken to give effect to the award or the decision.")

Third paragraph, 2nd sentence.—Substitute the following:

"The dispute shall be so referred at the request of either party to the dispute, provided that such request must be made within fourteen days after the submission of the dispute."

ARTICLE 15.

First paragraph, 3rd line.—Substitute:

"* * * The High Contracting Parties agree that the State or States not members of the League shall be invited to accept the obligations of membership in the League, for the purposes of such dispute, upon such conditions as the Executive Council may deem just."

ARTICLE 17.

For the first words of the new draft, substitute:

"To those colonies and territories which in consequence of the late war have ceased to be under the sovereignty of the States which formerly governed them, and which are inhabited by peoples * * * *"

ARTICLE 19.

Substitute:

"Recognising religious persecution as a fertile source of war, the High Contracting Parties solemnly undertake to extirpate such evils from their territories, and they authorise the Executive Council, wherever it is of opinion that the peace of the world is threatened by the existence in any State of evils of this nature, to make such representations or take such other steps as it may consider that the case requires."

Annex 2 to Minutes of Seventh Meeting.
REPORT OF THE SECRETARIAT.

Add to Article 10 as a new paragraph:

"In any case under this article, the award of the arbitrators shall be made within a reasonable time, and the recommendation of the Executive Council shall be made within six months after the submission of the dispute."

Annex 3 to Minutes of Seventh Meeting.

ARTICLE 13.

If there should arise between States members of the League any dispute likely to lead to a rupture, which is not submitted to arbitration as above, the High Contracting Parties agree that they will refer the matter to the Executive Council; either party to the dispute may give notice to the Chancellor of the existence of the dispute, and the Chancellor will make all necessary arrangements for a full investigation and considerations thereof. For this purpose the parties agree to communicate to the Chancellor, as promptly as possible, statements of their case with all the relevant facts and papers, and the Executive Council may forthwith direct the publication thereof.

Where the efforts of the Council lead to the settlement of the dispute, a statement shall be prepared for publication indicating the nature of the dispute and the terms of settlement, together with such explanations as may be appropriate. If the dispute has not been settled a report by the Council shall be published, setting forth with all necessary facts and explanations the recommendations which the Council think just and proper for the settlement of the dispute. If the report is unanimously agreed to by the members of the Council other than the parties to the dispute, the High Contracting Parties agree that none of them will go to war with any party which complies with its recommendations and that, if any party shall refuse to so comply, the Council shall consider what steps can best be taken to give effect to their recommendations. If no such unanimous report can be made, it shall be the duty of the majority and the privilege of the minority to issue a statement indicating what they believe to be the facts and containing the recommendations which they consider to be just and proper.

The Executive Council may in any case under this Article refer the dispute to the Body of Delegates. The dispute shall be so referred at the request of either party to the dispute, provided that such request must be made within 14 days after the submission of the dispute. In any case referred to the Body of Delegates all the provisions of this Article relating to the action and powers of the Executive Council shall apply to the action and powers of the Body of Delegates.

ARTICLE 15.

In the event of disputes between one State member of the League and another State which is not a member of the League, or between

States not members of the League, the High Contracting Parties agree that the State or States not members of the League shall be invited to accept the obligations of membership in the League for the purpose of such dispute, upon such conditions as the Executive Council may deem just, and upon acceptance of any such invitation, the above provisions shall be applied with such modifications as may be deemed necessary by the League.

Upon such invitation being given the Executive Council shall immediately institute an enquiry into the circumstances and merits of the dispute and recommend such action as may seem best and most effectual in the circumstances.

In the event of a Power so invited refusing to accept the obligations of membership in the League for the purposes of such dispute, and taking any action against a State member of the League which in the case of a State member of the League would constitute a breach of Article 10, the provisions of Article 14 shall be applicable as against the State taking such action.

If both parties to the dispute when so invited refuse to accept the obligations of membership in the League for the purposes of such dispute, the Executive Council may take such action and make such recommendations as will prevent hostilities and will result in the settlement of the dispute.

ARTICLE 17.

To those colonies and territories which in consequence of the late war have ceased to be under the sovereignty of the States which formerly governed them and which are inhabited by peoples not able to stand by themselves under the strenuous conditions of the modern world, there should be applied the principle that the well-being and development of such peoples form a sacred trust of civilisation, and that securities for the performance of this trust should be embodied in the constitution of the League.

The best method of giving practical effect to this principle is that the tutelage of such peoples should be entrusted to advanced nations who by reason of their resources, their experience or their geographical position, can best undertake this responsibility, and that this tutelage should be exercised by them as mandatories on behalf of the League.

The character of the mandate must differ according to the stage of the development of the people, the geographical situation of the territory, its economic conditions and other similar circumstances.

Certain communities formerly belonging to the Turkish Empire have reached a stage of development where their existence as independent nations can be provisionally recognised subject to the rendering of administrative advice and assistance by a mandatory

Power until such time as they are able to stand alone. The wishes of these communities must be a principal consideration in the selection of the mandatory Power.

Other peoples, especially those of Central Africa, are at such a stage that the mandatory must be responsible for the administration of the territory subject to conditions which will guarantee freedom of conscience or religion; subject only to the maintenance of public order and morals, the prohibition of abuses such as the slave trade, the arms traffic and the liquor traffic, and the prevention of the establishment of fortifications or military and naval bases, and of military training of the natives for other than police purposes, and the defence of territory, and will also secure equal opportunities for the trade and commerce of other members of the League.

There are territories, such as South-West Africa and certain of the South Pacific Islands, which, owing to the sparseness of their population, or their small size, or their remoteness from the centres of civilisation, or their geographical contiguity to the mandatory State, and other circumstances, can be best administered under the laws of the mandatory State as integral portions thereof, subject to the safeguards above-mentioned in the interests of the indigenous population.

In every case of mandate, the mandatory State shall render to the League an annual report in reference to the territory committed to its charge.

The degree of authority, control, or administration to be exercised by the mandatory State shall if not previously agreed upon by the High Contracting Parties in each case be explicitly defined by the Executive Council in a special act or Charter.

The High Contracting Parties further agree to establish at the Seat of the League a Mandatory Commission to receive and examine the annual reports of the Mandatory Powers, and to assist the League in ensuring the observance of the terms of all mandates.

ARTICLE 19.

The High Contracting Parties agree that they will make no law prohibiting or interfering with the free exercise of religion, and they resolve that they will not permit the practice of any particular creed, religion or belief, whose practices are not inconsistent with public order or with public morals, to interfere with the life, liberty or pursuit of happiness of their people.

ARTICLE 20.

The High Contracting Parties agree that provision shall be made through the instrumentality of the League to secure and maintain freedom of transit and equitable treatment for the commerce of all States, members of the League, having in mind, among other things, special arrangements with regard to the necessities of the regions devastated during the war of 1914-1918.

ARTICLE 21.

The High Contracting Parties agree that every Treaty or international engagement entered into by any State, a member of the League, shall be forthwith registered with the Chancellor and as soon as possible published by him, and that no Treaty or international engagement shall be operative until so registered.

ARTICLE 22.

The High Contracting Parties severally agree that the present Covenant is accepted as abrogating all obligations *inter se* which are inconsistent with the terms thereof, and solemnly engage that they will not hereafter enter into any engagements inconsistent with the terms thereof.

In case any of the Powers signatory hereto or subsequently admitted to the League shall, before becoming a party to this Covenant, have undertaken any obligations which are inconsistent with the terms of this Covenant, it shall be the duty of such Power to take immediate steps to procure its release from such obligations.

Printed copy (WP, DLC).

Hankey's Notes of a Meeting of the Supreme War Council[1]

Quai d'Orsay, February 10, 1919, 3 P.M.

BC-27, SWC-5

1. M. CLEMENCEAU called upon M. Klotz to explain the conclusions reached by the Inter-Allied Commission on the subject of the Financial Clauses to be added to the Armistice when next renewed.

M. KLOTZ said that since the last renewal of the Armistice the Germans had sought to elude the financial clauses of the Armistice, or have executed them with the greatest ill-will:

(1) They had only handed over an insignificant quantity of bonds and securities stolen by them and deposited in Germany in the *Kriegs Kassen*[2] and public banks.

(2) They had prevented the operation of the financial control over their foreign securities and only nominated the Commissioners, who were to be put into touch with the Allies, a few days ago.

(3) They had refused, contrary to their undertaking made in the same protocol, to examine, together with the Allies, measures tend-

---

[1] The complete text of these minutes is printed in *PPC*, III, 945-56.
[2] That is, war-loan funds.

ing to the restitution of property sequestered by them to the detriment of Allied subjects.

(4) The attitude adopted by them in the Financial Commission at Spa, and the tone in which their notes to the Allies were framed, were deliberately aggressive and should not be tolerated.

Taking these facts into consideration, the Inter-Allied Financial Commission had proposed that the following clauses should be added to the Armistice when next renewed:

(1) The German Government will, for the restitution of the property taken from the nationals of the Allied nations, follow, in all its conditions, the provisions which have been made by a common agreement by the Allied Delegations at the Financial Sub-Committee of the Spa Armistice Commission, and which will be notified by the Commander-in-Chief.

(2) This will also apply to the carrying-out of the obligations referred to in paragraph 3 of the Trèves financial clauses of December 13th, 1918.

PRESIDENT WILSON asked that the terms of the financial clauses referred to might be read.

M. KLOTZ then read paragraphs III and IV of the Financial Clauses of the Agreement for the prolongation of the Armistice, dated Trèves, December 13th, 1918, as follows:

"III. The German Government binds itself to pay at maturity and in conformity with current legislation to the natives of Alsace-Lorraine (Alsaciens-Lorrains) all debts or bills of exchange which have fallen due or which may fall due during the armistice and connected with German public funds, such as Treasury Bonds, bills of exchange, money or other orders, transfers, acceptances, etc., the corresponding transactions not being limited to those enumerated in the above recital.

The German Government binds itself not to place any special obstacle in the way of free disposal and enjoyment by Alsace-Lorrainers of all property, securities, shares and monies belonging to them and situate or being in Germany.

IV. The German Government binds itself to consider, in agreement with the Allied Governments, the steps to be taken for the speedy restitution of property sequestrated to the prejudice of nationals of the Allied countries."

PRESIDENT WILSON said that on Friday [Saturday] last an Inter-Allied Economic Commission[3] had been formed to report on all financial and economic matters. He suggested, therefore, that this question should be referred to that Commission.

---

[3] About which, see the minutes of the Supreme War Council printed at Feb. 8, 1919.

M. KLOTZ stated that a unanimous decision had been arrived at by the Inter-Allied financial experts, sitting at Spa, on the question now before the Council. He did not think, therefore, that any useful purpose would be served by again referring the matter to a similar Inter-Allied body.

PRESIDENT WILSON pointed out that although the proposed resolution had been agreed to by the Inter-Allied Financial Commission, the manner of ensuring its enforcement had not yet been considered, and he suggested that that question be referred to the Inter-Allied Economic Commission.

MR. BALFOUR said he had no objections to oppose to the question of the enforcement of the financial clauses of the Armistice being referred to the Inter-Allied Economic Commission. But he wished to suggest that the manner in which the Germans could be compelled to carry out all the agreed conditions of the Armistice should also be referred to that Commission. He had that day received a report from the Inter-Allied Naval Armistice Commission, sitting in London, to the effect that the Germans had not as yet carried out their engagements relating to the surrender of submarines and mercantile shipping. Furthermore, there were no signs that they intended to surrender the latter. Consequently, if the Armistice were renewed, it would be essential in the first place to see that the conditions already accepted were duly being complied with. He thought, therefore, that a body was required to decide how the Germans could be compelled to comply with the accepted terms of the Armistice. He could express no definite opinion in regard to the financial question, but in regard to the Naval terms he felt that a very serious situation had arisen. The Germans had promised things, but had failed to carry them out even when in a position to do so.

PRESIDENT WILSON expressed his entire agreement with Mr. Balfour, but he thought it would be necessary to have expert advice in each case. For instance, he understood that some difference of opinion existed between the Allied experts in regard to the correct interpretation of certain of the financial clauses. Therefore, he thought it was a proper question to be referred to the Inter-Allied Economic Commission. He did not know whether the Naval experts had expressed any views as to how the Naval clauses could be enforced.

MR. BALFOUR said that he would have agreed, without hesitation, to accept President Wilson's proposal, were it not for the fact that Admiral Hope had expressed the view that no further means were available for the enforcement of the Naval conditions of the Armistice. Therefore, the Army should come to the aid of the Navy to exert the necessary pressure.

PRESIDENT WILSON expressed the view that the employment of force would mean the end of the Armistice.

MR. BALFOUR explained that he had meant to suggest the use of threats and not the actual employment of force.

PRESIDENT WILSON asked Admiral Hope to say what sort of military action would, in his opinion, be necessary and practicable.

ADMIRAL HOPE said that his instructions were that no suitable naval penalties existed. Consequently, the penalties to be imposed must be of a military character, and for this reason it had been agreed that the question should be referred to the Supreme War Council. The Naval Authorities offered no suggestions.

PRESIDENT WILSON enquired whether Admiral Hope could, as an individual, suggest any line of action.

ADMIRAL HOPE replied in the negative.

PRESIDENT WILSON said that he would put a hypothetical case to Admiral Hope. On the supposition that the Germans refused to surrender the submarines under construction, would it be Admiral Hope's idea that the military should go and seize them?

ADMIRAL HOPE replied that this would mean the occupation of dockyards and some of the larger ports such as Bremen, Hamburg, etc., which would not be possible. He thought that the naval authorities had in view the employment of some other form of pressure.

M. CLEMENCEAU pointed out that two questions were being discussed, namely, a financial question and a Naval question. He suggested that the former question should first be settled, and asked M. Klotz to reply to the statement which President Wilson had made to the effect that disagreement existed between the French and American experts on the interpretation of the financial clauses.

M. KLOTZ admitted that there had been some disagreement as to the interpretation of Clause 1 of the Armistice of the 13th December, 1918, but in regard to Clauses 3 and 4 there had been complete unanimity, and all the financial experts had subscribed to the resolution which he had placed before the Council. Therefore, whilst he agreed that Clause 1 should be referred to the Inter-Allied Economic Commission, he thought that the resolution which referred to Clauses 3 and 4 should be accepted without further reference.

PRESIDENT WILSON held that this Council was not competent to decide the means of enforcing the clauses of the Armistice, and he urged that that question be referred to the Inter-Allied Economic Commission for report.

MR. BALFOUR pointed out that whilst it was quite true that no two questions were more different than a Naval and a financial question, yet the method of enforcing the conditions agreed on would probably be the same in each case. He did not think that a Financial Council was the best body to decide the method of enforcing the clauses of the Armistice. In his opinion, the military would be the best body for the purpose.

PRESIDENT WILSON said that the Germans required means of purchasing in foreign countries. There was, therefore, an economic method as well as a military method of exerting pressure. He did not ask the Economic Commission to recommend the military means but the economic means; the latter were manifold and could be applied gradually.

MR. BALFOUR agreed, and suggested that the Inter-Allied Economic Commission should be asked to report also on the economic means of enforcing acceptance of the Naval Clauses. He thought it was essential that the Germans should be made to carry out their promises, and he fully believed that the economic method would probably be found to be the best, and he concurred in the view that the Economic Commission would be the best body to decide what kind of economic pressure should be brought to bear.

M. CLEMENCEAU said that he accepted the proposal, provided immediate action was taken. The matter, in his opinion, was a very serious one. The Germans were getting very haughty, and had given insolent replies to the Allies' demands. For instance, in the case of Poland, they had refused to comply with the Allies' request to stop their attacks. From the Allies' point of view the Weimar Assembly had selected the very worst candidate as President,[4] and the same remark applied to the newly appointed Chancellor, M. Rantzau.[5] "Deutschland über Alles" had been sung at the conclusion of the last Meeting of the Constitutional Assembly. Consequently, he fully agreed with President Wilson's view that economic pressure should be applied, but a decision should be reached without delay, as the Armistice would expire on the 17th of this month.

MARSHAL FOCH said that, as a matter of fact, the Armistice would have to be signed on the 16th. The negotiations would therefore have to be begun on the 14th and completed on the 15th.

M. CLEMENCEAU agreed that a conclusion would have to be reached by the 14th, and proposed that each of the Great Powers should appoint one expert, either naval, economic or financial, to report in two days' time on the best methods of applying pressure on Germany to obtain compliance with the conditions of the Armistice,

[4] Friedrich Ebert, elected President of Germany by the Constituent Assembly at Weimar on February 11.

[5] Clemenceau was either misinformed or confused. The Chancellor of the new government which took office on February 13 was Philipp Scheidemann. Ulrich Karl Christian, Count von Brockdorff-Rantzau, was Minister of Foreign Affairs.

already accepted. Should the Commission report that economic means would give the desired result, so much the better.

PRESIDENT WILSON declared himself ready to act on any plan that would throw sufficient light on the subject. But he was also aware that the Allies were about to take a very serious decision, because they found themselves confronted by a momentous situation which might force them to a renewal of the war, since a refusal to renew the Armistice meant a renewal of war. The work done would have to be done over again, and he wondered what would be the reaction in the minds of the people of the world. Their choice on Wednesday would be very serious and solemn. No nation of the world would forgive them if hostilities were renewed for any but the most imperative reasons. It could not be foreseen what might be brought upon them by an insufficiently considered action. He could not help feeling that if, on Wednesday, they were not perfectly clear as to the steps they were going to take, it would be better to renew the Armistice on its present terms for a very short period, say one or two weeks, until they could reach a well-considered decision.

M. CLEMENCEAU asked whether Marshal Foch had any statement to make on President Wilson's proposal.

MARSHAL FOCH agreed that a very grave decision had to be taken, for if the Armistice were not renewed, it would mean war. The heavier, the more important and the more precise the new conditions to be inserted in the Armistice, the more likely would the enemy be to hesitate and to show disinclination to accept. But, not knowing the whole of the new conditions to be imposed on the enemy, it was impossible for him to say what was the chance of their being accepted. On the other hand, the non-execution of the clauses already agreed on gave serious cause for reflection, and on this account he was inclined to favour the idea of renewing the Armistice for a short period only.

PRESIDENT WILSON said that he did not wish to delay matters, but it might have a very important effect on the enemy if the Armistice were renewed only for two weeks, the enemy being told that the reasons which rendered this necessary were that the Allies were considering the action to be taken in order to enforce compliance with their conditions. The Germans would doubtless employ the short period of time so accorded to them in profitable thinking.

MR. BALFOUR thought that President Wilson's warning would no doubt be most impressive. He wished, however, to suggest a procedure which did not possess all the gravity of a refusal to renew the Armistice. It was open to the Allies to tell the German[s] at any time that they were not fulfilling their engagements, and that any further failure to do so would result in serious economic measures being taken which would entail serious consequences. He thought that in the economic blockade the Allies possessed a weapon which was conceded by the Armistice and yet did not involve war.

M. PICHON expressed the view that it might be dangerous to renew the Armistice, even for a short period, as long as the Germans failed to fulfil the conditions already agreed to. He did not think the Germans would be likely to fulfil, during the short period of extension, the conditions which they had refused to fulfil during the period of the Armistice, especially when they realised that at the end of the extended period additional serious conditions would be imposed. He thought that the proposal merely meant a temporary postponement of their difficulties. The Germans would realise that the Allies hesitated to give orders, and they would thereby be encouraged to further resistance.

PRESIDENT WILSON admitted that M. Pichon's remarks were very just, but the right solution had still to be found. M. Pichon was concerned with the effect the action contemplated would have on the German mind, but the effect which a renewal of the war would have on the minds of the Allied peoples must not be lost sight of. In his opinion, a renewal of the war would require the most extraordinary justification.

M. CLEMENCEAU suggested that the further consideration of the question be adjourned to Wednesday morning next (February 12th). No decision would have to be reached before Wednesday evening next, so that, if necessary, two meetings could be held that day. Furthermore, by Wednesday next the promised report on the situation in Poland would have been received, and that might assist them in arriving at a decision. He agreed that nothing hasty or precipitate should be done. By an adjournment, 36 hours for thought would be obtained, and by then more information bearing on the problem would have been received.

PRESIDENT WILSON agreed, on the understanding that during the interval the question would be referred to a Committee consisting of a military and an economic adviser representing each of the four Great Powers, who would report on Wednesday next as to the wise and practical means of bringing pressure to bear on the enemy for the enforcement of the clauses of the Armistice.

M. CLEMENCEAU asked that the Committee be instructed to submit their report on Wednesday morning next and that the Commanders of the Allied Armies be invited to attend the Meeting on that date.

MR. BALFOUR said that the Commanders of the Allied Armies

should not be the military advisers on President Wilson's Committee: They should merely be present at Wednesday's meeting to assist in the consideration of the whole question.

M. CLEMENCEAU agreed, and suggested that Marshal Foch should be asked to call together the Chiefs of the Allied Armies on Tuesday next in order to have a preliminary discussion of the whole question.

(It was agreed that a Committee consisting of a Military and an Economic adviser representing each of the four Great Powers should be appointed, to report on Wednesday next as to the wise and practical means of bringing pressure to bear on the enemy for the enforcement of the clauses of the Armistice. It was also agreed that the Chiefs of the Allied Armies should meet on Tuesday next, under the Presidency of Marshal Foch, for a preliminary discussion, and that they should attend the meeting on Wednesday next to assist in the consideration of the whole question.)

PRESIDENT WILSON enquired whether it would be possible for the Governments forthwith to nominate the representatives to serve on the Committee.

M. CLEMENCEAU suggested that the Meeting should be adjourned for five minutes in order to carry out President Wilson's suggestion.

(When the Meeting resumed, the following names were announced:

America	Mr. Norman Davis and
	General Bliss.
British Empire	Lord Robert Cecil and
	General Thwaites.[6]
France	M. Clementel and
	General Degoutte.[7]
Italy	M. Crespi[8] and
	General Cavallero.[9]

It was decided that the Delegates should hold their first meeting at 6 p.m. that evening at 4 bis Boulevard des Invalides.)

2. M. CLEMENCEAU said that since the discussion of the Armistice had been adjourned, he thought that the question relating to the insertion of additional clauses relating to Poland should also be postponed.

(This was agreed to.)

---

[6] Maj. Gen. William Thwaites, Director of Military Intelligence of the War Office since 1918.

[7] Gen. Jean Joseph Marie Degoutte, commander of the French Sixth Army and technical adviser on military questions in the French delegation to the peace conference.

[8] That is, Silvio Benigno Crespi.

[9] Brig. Gen. Ugo Cavallero, Italian military representative on the Supreme War Council.

3. M. BALFOUR said that the suggestions he had to make arose from a discussion he had had with the British Solicitor-General,[10] who was making up the case of inhumane breaches of international law. Many of the members of the Committee were in favour of its being made a condition of the Armistice that all those against whom a prima facie case could be made should be given up. In the clause of the Armistice dealing with this question, no names would be given, but a condition would be entered to the effect that any person asked for would in due course be surrendered. It was felt that if this were not done, there would be no use in setting up a tribunal, because when the names of the guilty people became known, they would have disappeared. He himself thought that the question was important, but that it might not be right to make it a condition of the Armistice. The question, however, required careful consideration. He understood that Mr. Lansing did not think this was a proper question to put into the Armistice, and he himself did not dissent from that view. He would even go further and say that were this clause to be put into the Armistice, no great advance would have been made. The clause would merely state that the Germans should give up a number of people whose names would be communicated at a later date. The Germans would already know who the people were, and they would resent these men being taken away to be tried before a foreign tribunal. The Germans would express their willingness to deal with criminals and to try them themselves. Consequently, he was in some doubt whether the method suggested would prove effective in the long run, and he saw no reason for introducing anything so novel into the Armistice. But by what other means could these guilty people be brought to justice? It would obviously be very lamentable, after all the expectations raised in the public mind, if when the time came, after the tribunal had been established, none of the criminals could really be brought to trial. Whether his proposal was relevant or not to the renewal of the Armistice, he had felt it his duty to bring this question to the notice of the assembly. He had no definite proposal to make, and he personally felt profoundly perplexed.

PRESIDENT WILSON agreed that the proposal would be futile at present. When the terms of peace were made it would be possible to know the names of the guilty people, and a demand could then be made for their surrender. Meanwhile the criminals might endeavour to conceal themselves, but it was not likely that they would even try to leave Germany. Consequently, the difficulty would be no greater then than at the present moment. On the contrary it

[10] Sir Gordon Hewart, also M.P. for Leicester.

would be less, because the names of the people wanted would then be known.

(It was decided to postpone the further consideration of this question.)

4. M. CLEMENCEAU said that the Council had agreed to refer all questions relating to the Blockade to the Inter-Allied Economic Commission. M. Klotz had no objections to offer, but he wished to discuss a document which revealed the fact that the Germans had drawn up a systematic plan for the destruction of French industries in the occupied territories.

M. KLOTZ said that the Conference had referred to a technical Committee all questions relating to finance, blockade and raw materials. But these questions frequently had a direct bearing on the general policy affecting the renewal of the Armistice. The question of food supplies concerned the general policy of the Armistice just as the question of the supply of raw materials concerned the general policy of the Peace Terms. Since a Commission had been formed to consider the best means of bringing economic pressure to bear on the enemy, he would confine himself merely to the question of the supply of raw materials, which had not yet been brought under discussion. The Allies had never agreed to supply raw materials to Germany. The devastated countries would never agree to raw materials being supplied to Germany, where the factories were still intact, until their own industries had been re-established. To do so would be contrary to President Wilson's third point, which prescribed "the removal so far as possible of all economic barriers, and the establishment of an equality of trade conditions among all nations consenting to the Peace and associating themselves for its maintenance." In order to bear out his contention, he would read some extracts from a German pamphlet which had been published in Munich by the German General Staff in February, 1916, at the time when the Verdun offensive was being launched.

PRESIDENT WILSON enquired what was the object M. Klotz had in view.

M. KLOTZ replied that the pamphlet in question would afford evidence of the premeditated and systematic character of the destruction of industries in France by the German official authorities.

PRESIDENT WILSON expressed the view that this evidence might no doubt affect their frame of mind, but what effect would it have on their plans?

M. KLOTZ said that in his opinion it would not in fairness be possible to consider the supply of raw materials to Germany, unless the facts contained in this document were given due weight. The Inter-Allied Economic Commission would study the question from a purely technical point of view, but there was also a political aspect of the case, which could not be ignored by the Conference. It was the latter point which he wished to bring forward.

(M. Klotz then read extracts from the work entitled "Die Industrie im Besetzten Frankreich," published in Munich under the direction and by order of the German Great General Staff in February, 1916. Copies of this publication may be obtained from the Secretariat-General.)

M. KLOTZ, in conclusion, expressed the view that a Technical Committee having been appointed to deal with the supply of raw materials, it was its bounden duty in the first place to consider and to give an absolute priority to the needs of the industries of the occupied territories, which had been destroyed by the enemy during the course of the war. To do otherwise would be to permit the aggressor to gain what he had hoped for at the expense of the victim. Subject to these observations, he had no objections to offer to the whole question being referred to the Inter-Allied Economic Commission.

5. M. CLEMENCEAU said that the next question to consider was the report submitted by the Military Representatives at Versailles.[11]

LORD MILNER remarked that he came new to the question. There might, therefore, be arguments which would account for a report which, at first sight, had somewhat surprised him. As he understood the case, the reason for the reference to the Military Representatives was that there was a desire to discover whether the military forces occupying the Turkish Empire were not excessive and whether they could not be reduced. In his opinion, that was quite a proper question to remit to the Military Representatives, namely: the amount of force required to occupy those territories. But not only had a most startling reduction in forces been proposed, but the report went on to specify the particular nature of the forces. It did not merely say that so many forces were required to hold Palestine, or Syria, or Trans-Caucasia, but it went on to show that the forces holding each of those places should be either British, or French, or Italian, as the case might be. In his opinion that was a big political question and not a military one, and very large issues had thereby been raised. For instance: he thought that the suggestion that Italy should occupy the Caucasus not only implied very serious operations, but raised the question very directly of the future political problem of this country, a problem which had not yet been before this Conference. Consequently, it was a question which he might have thought should not be discussed before the audience there

---

[11] For a summary, see the memorandum by T. H. Bliss printed at Feb. 8, 1919.

present. In one word, it was not a question for the Supreme War Council, but for the Peace Conference.

PRESIDENT WILSON explained that it was only fair to the Military Representatives to say that they had not gone further than they had been authorised to go. Mr. Lloyd George had expressed anxiety as to the number of forces the British Empire was compelled to keep in these territories and the Military Representatives had been asked to estimate the number of troops actually needed and to advise on an equitable distribution of the burden amongst the Allies, it being understood that this distribution would not prejudice any arrangement that the Peace Conference might subsequently make. Mr. Lloyd George had, at the same time, expressed the hope that the United States of America would share the burden. He (President Wilson) had replied that whilst agreeing with this sentiment, he doubted his authority to order American troops into the territory of a country with which the United States was not at war. He agreed with Lord Milner that the recommendation made by the Military Representatives tied in so closely with the possible future of these areas that it was not a matter for the Supreme War Council but for the Peace Conference to decide.

LORD MILNER, whilst disclaiming any intention of criticising the action of the Military Representatives, desired to maintain his contention that the decision of the question appertained more to the Peace Conference than to the Supreme War Council.

M. CLEMENCEAU said the solution was a simple one. The representatives of the Great Powers need only convert themselves into a Peace Conference today. Otherwise, the question could be adjourned to the following day.

(It was agreed to adjourn the further consideration of the question to the following day.

It was also decided to place the following questions on the Agenda Paper of the meeting to be held on Tuesday, the 11th February, 1919, at 3 p.m.:

1. Belgian territorial claims.

2. Occupation of territories in the Turkish Empire and Trans-Caucasia.)

T MS (SDR, RG 256, 180.03101/34, DNA).

From Albert, King of the Belgians

Dear Mr. President,   Brussels, February the 10th 1919.

On the eve of your departure from Europe, the deep concern I feel for the restoration of my country prompts me to address to you a pressing appeal in favour of Belgium.

In common with my government I have undertaken a close study of the anxious problems on which our future depends. This study has made me realize more and more the situation in which we stand, and it has brought me to the conclusion that the economical reconstruction of Belgium is materially impossible unless the enormous damages which the country has suffered are promptly and completely made good to her.

The situation of Belgium is not the same as that of other European states whose capacity of production and sources of revenue have been maintained if not increased during the war. Not only has Belgium been prevented by the almost complete invasion of her soil from preparing stocks of finished goods or provisions of raw materials; but she has not even been able to preserve the instruments of production which would have made her capable of resuming her activities immediately after her liberation. Therefore, unless the Allies promptly come to her aid, she is threatened to see her ruin brought to completion by the loss of her markets at home and abroad.

If your grave duties had not prevented you from visiting Belgium now, I would have shown you to what extent the destruction of our means of production has been systematically effected. We have nothing left us except our energies—we want to be given a chance of exerting them.

Doubtless it is possible by temporary loans and various other devices, to obtain some raw materials which would give the country an apparent and delusive economic activity, but no programme of national restoration can be set on a firm basis as long as Belgium's claims to indemnification have not been given first rank, so as to make it certain that all the damages she has sustained will be repaired. Only this will make it possible to discount the annual instalments of the indemnities which Germany will have to pay us. To this priority of rank, my country feels that it has a particular title.

One must not forget that the war between the Central Powers and Belgium was inaugurated by a violation of Belgium's neutrality which Prussia and Austria had guaranteed in a solemn covenant.

The crime against public faith which these Powers have committed has roused the world's conscience and this conscience cannot be satisfied unless the conditions of peace ensure Belgium's complete restoration.

As you have very justly said: "No other single act will serve as this will serve to restore confidence amongst the nations in the laws which they have themselves set and determined for the government of their relations with one another. Without this healing act the whole structure and validity of international law is for ever impaired."

Thus the aggression suffered by Belgium has, from the beginning, assumed a particularly immoral and hateful aspect which does not permit her cause to be placed on the same level as the causes—however just they doubtless are—of the other nations which the Central Powers have attacked and injured.

I trust that by the help of our great Allies, which have given us so many tokens of their friendship, first rank will be secured for the indemnification of all damages Belgium has sustained in defence of the cause of right. Such privilege alone will make her integral restoration possible.

To this end I address a special and solemn request to the President of the United States whose intervention on Belgium's behalf would crown his great effort to favour the reign of Order and Right in the World.

I remain, dear Mr. President

Yours very faithfully   Albert

ALS (WP, DLC).

From John Joseph Pershing

Personal.

Dear Mr. President: [Chaumont] February 10, 1919

Fully appreciating the tremendous burden resting upon your shoulders, and not wishing to encroach upon a single minute of your time, I sent word, expressing my wish to accompany you to Brest if, for any reason, you should desire it. But I can very well understand that you would want to be relieved of any formalities in taking your temporary departure from France for America. However much I should have been pleased to accompany you, I should of course abide by your wishes.

In view of certain newspaper criticisms regarding conditions at Brest, in which it has been pointed out that you did not visit the embarkation camp and military arrangements at that port, might I suggest that you spend a couple of hours in looking over our plans and preparations there for handling troops awaiting embarkation? While I do not attach any special importance to this visit, yet it might serve to answer criticism, and you could also see how our plans are being carried forward, and give our men there the pleasure of seeing you.

Please accept my very best wishes for a safe journey both ways across the Atlantic, and allow me to extend to you the greetings of the entire Army.

With warm personal regards to you and Mrs. Wilson, I remain as ever,   Yours very faithfully,   John J. Pershing.

TLS (WP, DLC).

From William Howard Taft and Abbott Lawrence Lowell

Boston, Mass. February 10th [1919]

We believe the country to be in favor of a strong league of nations and that the people are willing to make an agreement to contribute their share of economic and if need be of military force to maintain the authority of league tribunals which would be given real compulsory jurisdiction stop. We earnestly hope that before you complete the structure of the league finally and make it public you will return to the United States and yourself test public opinion upon these points before giving up the features of the league that shall make it really effective stop. We are sure that on your return to Paris you would carry with you the conviction that the American people will support you in a really effective league.

William Howard Taft,   A. Lawrence Lowell.

T telegram (WP, DLC).

From James Watson Gerard and Others

New York [c. Feb. 10, 1919]

Three American Committees for the Independence of Armenia gathered to voice Americas deep interest in the welfare of Armenia at Banquet held at Hotel Plaza New York on February 8th, 1919, after having heard Charles Evans Hughes and William Jennings Bryan unanimously adopted following resolution:

"Resolved that in the opinion of the American Committee for the Independence of Armenia, including the six vilayets in (Turkish Armenia and Cicilia) Russian Armenia and Persian Armenia should be constituted into a separate and independent state and that it is earnest hope of this Committee that the Peace Conference will make requisite arrangements for helping Armenia to establish an independent republic."

          For the Committee: James W. Gerard, Chairman
                                 Henry Cabot Lodge
                                 John Sharp Williams.

T telegram (WP, DLC).

From the Diary of Edith Benham

February 10, 1919

Sundays are always uneventful enough both conversationally and otherwise. I stay in my room nearly all morning. The President and Mrs. Wilson went to church and in the afternoon took a drive. I went for a walk with H.S.K.,[1] the first one I had had for five or six days, for I am practically never able to get out. I really could not have dreamed I would live with so little exercise and I wonder the President stands the strain. He has grown very thin for he is busy all day and many nights.

The French papers are behind the Government and are adopting the most obstructive methods.[2] I think the French Government is inspiring it. Anyway, the President asked Dr. Grayson today to drop a hint to the American newspaper men to say in their despatches that if these tactics continued it might be necessary to remove the conference from Paris to a neutral country. I think Lloyd George was to drop such a hint to the English papers. There has been trouble all along with the French press. There is leakage of news to the French papers and the English and American newspaper men have been blocked in their efforts to get news.

As the President said tonight, it was very difficult to continue to treat France sympathetically when he had the kindliest feelings, when she persisted in regarding him with suspicion. At the conference today Klotz (Minister of Finance, I think) read a long paper in which it was stated as something new that Germany had destroyed ultimately all the French industries and that this was an economic war. As the President said, he had known and everyone had known this all along and it didn't need a final note from Balfour "This is for you" to let him see it was directed against him. In summing up the situation he spoke of the selfishness of the French who feel they are the only nation which has suffered, forgetting Belgium, with all the machinery gone from her factories, no economic life left, Serbia and Poland. He said because he had said in one of his speeches that those countries must be treated justly as those we wanted to treat justly, the French had the idea he had come over as the partisan of Germany and were suspicious of him for [so?] that it was so difficult to be a friend to France.

[1] That is, Rear Adm. Harry Shepard Knapp.
[2] About this matter, see George Bernard Noble, *Policies and Opinions at Paris, 1919: Wilsonian Diplomacy, the Versailles Peace, and French Public Opinion* (New York, 1935), *passim*, particularly pp. 82-83.

From the Diary of David Hunter Miller

Tuesday, February 11th [1919]

Colonel House showed me another proposal of the Japanese,[1] of which I did not get a copy, but I expressed the opinion that it would [not] be acceptable to us.

I handed to Colonel House a list of the pending amendments but did not give him a copy of the memorandum on questions of form, prepared last evening, as I had no opportunity.

Colonel House asked me my opinion on Bullitt's revised proposal.[2] I told him that I thought it was hardly practicable.

I handed the President a copy of the list of pending amendments.

I attended the meeting of the Commission on a League of Nations, from 10:30 to 1:30. During the meeting the President asked me if the British amendments adopted at the previous meeting had been incorporated in the text before him, as he thought they had not been. I pointed out to him that they were in. I also gave him two opinions on the constitutionality of proposals made, both of which are set out in my notes.

Colonel House instructed me to attend the meeting tomorrow of the Committee on Revision, at 10:30 o'clock at the Hotel Majestic.

In the evening I got up the English and French text of the two additional amendments adopted at the meeting, and did some general work at my office.

David Hunter Miller, *My Diary at the Conference of Paris, with Documents* (21 vols., New York, 1924), I, 118-19.
[1] For its text, see the minutes of the Commission on the League of Nations printed at Feb. 13, 1919, 3:30 p.m.
[2] See W. C. Bullitt to D. H. Miller, Feb. 12, 1919, printed in Miller, *My Diary at the Conference of Paris*, V, 238-39. Bullitt proposed two amendments to the draft covenant of the League of Nations which provided for an "Assembly of Representatives" to be selected from each member nation of the league "in such a way that they will reflect the views of the more important political parties represented in its legislative assembly." The Assembly of Representatives was to consider and vote upon "measures for promoting international co-operation" and might "submit proposals embodying such measures to the Body of Delegates or the Executive Council" of the league.

A Memorandum by David Hunter Miller

February 11th, 1919.

LIST OF PENDING AMENDMENTS.

Annexed is an English text of each of these amendments.

Article VI, by M. Bourgeois.

Article VIII, by M. Bourgeois.

Article XI, by M. Vesnitch. (It was suggested that this amendment go over to the second reading.)

Article XIV, by M. Bourgeois.

Article XVII, by M. Bourgeois. (This amendment seems to be still pending as the French requested that it be distributed.)

Article XXIII, additional Article proposed by Lord Robert Cecil.

Article XXIV, additional Article proposed by Lord Robert Cecil.

AMENDMENT TO ARTICLE VI.

The second paragraph to be modified so as to read as follows:

"Furthermore no nation can be admitted into the League if it is not provided with representative institutions which permit it to be considered as itself responsible for the acts of its own Government; if it is not in a position to give effective guaranties of its faithful intention of observing its obligations; if it does not conform to the principles which the League may establish concerning its naval and military forces as well as its armaments."

AMENDMENT TO ARTICLE VIII.

After the phrase: "The Executive Council shall formulate plans for effecting such reduction," insert the following paragraphs:

"It shall institute an international control of military forces and armaments of the High Contracting Parties, which agree to submit thereto in all good faith.

"It shall determine the conditions which are necessary for assuring the permanent existence and the organization of an international force."

PROPOSAL OF M. VESNITCH.

Article XI.

The High Contracting Parties agree that whenever any dispute or difficulty shall arise between them which they recognize to be suitable for submission to arbitration and which cannot be satisfactorily settled by diplomacy, they will, *in accordance with the provisions of the Convention of the Hague for the Pacific Settlement of International Disputes*, submit the whole subject matter to arbitration, and will carry out in full good faith any award or decision that may be rendered.

Proposition de M. Vesnitch.
Article XI.

Les Hautes Parties Contractantes conviennent que, lorsqu'il s'élevera entre elles un differend ou une difficulté, susceptible d'être soumis a l'arbitrage et ne pouvant être reglé par la diplomatie, conformément *a la Convention de la Haye relative a la solution pacifique des conflits internationaux*, elles soumettront la question pleine et entière a l'arbitrage, et s'entiendront de bonne foi au jugement rendu où a la decision qui sera prisé.

AMENDMENT TO ARTICLE XIV.

After the words of the second paragraph: "to be used to protect the covenants of the League," insert the two following paragraphs:

"In the case that one of the parties to the dispute, after having followed the procedure imposed by Article X, should not accept the sentence of the arbitration, or a unanimous decision of the Executive Council, or of the Body of Delegates, the Council will propose to the associated Governments the application of appropriate penalties selected from those propounded in the first paragraph of this article.

"In the case of a recommendation made by the majority only, concerning a dispute which could involve a recourse to arms by the interested parties, the Executive Council will refer the question to the Governments themselves."

PROPOSED AMENDMENT

by M. LEON BOURGEOIS TO ARTICLE XVII
AT THE SIXTH SESSION OF THE COMMISSION
OF THE LEAGUE OF NATIONS

February 8, 1919.

In accordance with the decisions of the Conference of the Allies, the League of Nations considers itself as having assumed a moral protectorate over the populations referred to in the treaty of peace, which have not yet attained a complete development.

The character of this protectorate must differ according to the degree of the development of the people concerned, the geographical situation of their territory, their economic condition and other similar circumstances.

The rules and regulations of this protectorate are determined by international conventions. The Council of the League of Nations will cause new conventions to be called if it deems them necessary for assuring the welfare and the development of the populations concerned.

ARTICLE XXIII.

Amendments to the constitution and functions of the League can be made by a unanimous vote of the Executive Council confirmed by a majority of the Body of Delegates.

ARTICLE XXIV.

The body of delegates shall make provision for the periodic revision of treaties which have become obsolete and of International conditions, the continuance of which may endanger the Peace of the world.

CC MS (WP, DLC).

Minutes of a Meeting of the Commission on the League of Nations

EIGHTH MEETING, FEBRUARY 11, 1919, AT 10:30 A.M.
President WILSON *in the Chair.*

President Wilson opened the meeting with a discussion of the amendment proposed by the British Delegates as Article 23 of the Covenant, as follows:

"The Body of Delegates shall make provision for the periodic revision of treaties which have become obsolete and of international conditions, the continuance of which may endanger the world."

This amendment gave rise to the following comment:

Mr. Kramar observed that, if the Body of Delegates were to become the judge of all treaties, it would have powers like those of an international Parliament.

Lord Robert Cecil said that since the Body of Delegates could not act except by unanimous vote, there could be no objection on that score.

Mr. Bourgeois thought that there was no other practicable way in which to make the principle effective. It is the duty of the Body of Delegates from time to time to give publicity to treaties. In this fashion it builds the *Corpus Juris* of international life. If it discovers objectionable features it may require an explanation from the Government concerned before registering the treaty. This plan of procedure would protect the independence of States.

Mr. Batalha Reis asked whether the Executive Council or even the Body of Delegates would have the right to refuse to register a treaty. This question was answered in the negative.

President Wilson proposed the following wording:

"It shall be the right of the Body of Delegates from time to time to advise the reconsideration by the States, members of the League, of treaties which have become inapplicable, and of international conditions, the continuance of which may endanger the peace of the world."

This article was adopted.

ARTICLE 24.

Lord Robert Cecil read a proposed new article connected with the preceding article:

"Amendments to the constitution and functions of the League can be made by an unanimous vote of the Executive Council confirmed by a majority of the Body of Delegates."

Mr. Veniselos thought that it should not be made too difficult to modify the statutes of the League of Nations. It was here proposed to require an unanimous vote in the Executive Council, and to be content with a bare majority in the Assembly. In such a case it would follow that a Power in the minority might withdraw. In order to escape such an eventuality, would it not be better to provide for a three-fourths majority?

Mr. Larnaude said that the question was whether or not we wanted a League in which the long-standing rules of international law would apply in full force. Were we setting up nothing more than a treaty, or were we indeed making a permanent constitution, creating a real institution higher than States? The Covenant, by analogy, resembled the scheme of the Confederation. This being so, we were on diplomatic ground. But if we were talking about a constitution, we were in the sphere of a super-State.

President Wilson observed that when the nations subscribe to the Covenant, they will clearly be bound by the new text.

Mr. Orlando was of the opinion that a State in the minority would be forced to remain in the League. New laws should be made to accord with new facts.

Mr. Larnaude said that the Delegates would be officials whose position was like that of judges who cannot be divested of office at pleasure. They must have the international point of view and a kind of independence.

Mr. Vesnitch thought that if the nine Powers of the Executive Council should agree in proposing a change, and this change were approved by two-thirds of the nations represented in the Body of Delegates, no State could think that it was directed against its peculiar interests. This procedure ought to give complete satisfaction.

Mr. Veniselos supported it equally, but suggested that a three-quarters majority be required.

Mr. Pessoa made the same suggestion.

Baron Makino expressed his own view of the matter and commented upon the considerations which were involved in the new Article 24.

Mr. Rolin Jacquemyns[1], who had replaced Mr. Hymans, supported the view expressed by Mr. Vesnitch, Mr. Veniselos, and Baron Makino on the understanding that this should apply only to the "fundamental clauses."

President Wilson then read the following text:

ARTICLE 24.

"Amendments to this Covenant will take effect when ratified by the States whose representatives compose the Executive Council, and by three-fourths of the States whose representatives compose the Body of Delegates."

The article was then adopted.

Mr. Bourgeois then read the following note, and asked that it be inserted in the minutes:

"I had thought of asking the Drafting Committee to reconsider the text of Article 14. Then I was told that our mandate was limited to only three articles, and I was convinced that this was so. Nevertheless, I ask that I may record the following observations:

"It was understood that in this first reading we would not consider ourselves bound by what had been provisionally adopted before, and that is all the more necessary since there are certain articles whose import cannot be measured without discussing the provisions of certain later articles.

"According to the Draft which has just been adopted for Articles 12 and 13, even in case of an unanimous agreement, if a Power, acting in bad faith, and being the possessor of the thing in dispute, refuses to abide by the judgment of the arbitrators or the decision of the Executive Committee, the League of Nations is not legally bound to ensure the fulfilment of the decree. In view of the necessary consequences, it is imperative that stronger provisions be introduced in order to protect a State acting in good faith against a State which is acting in bad faith.

"Otherwise it would happen that nations faithful to their international obligations would suffer as the result of an organisation effective in appearance, but in reality a trap for nations of good faith.

"Our Commission certainly does not want this, and indeed it would be too much in conflict with the principles of justice so forcibly expressed by President Wilson.

"I feel all the more impelled to offer these observations now for

---

[1] Édouard Gustave Marie Rolin-Jacquemyns, Secretary General of the Belgian delegation to the peace conference and technical adviser on legal questions.

the reason that since we have been working here a trend of opinion has developed revealing a spirit of uneasiness to which I must call your attention.

"Our colleagues representing Great Britain and the United States have very justly called attention to the serious consideration which they must give to the public opinion of their nations, and to the necessity that their Governments should not be involved in sacrifices beyond those which are at the same time demanded and delimited by the very principles of the League of Nations.

"In the presence of these evidences of uneasiness, shall we not together examine carefully the articles which we adopted at the time of the first reading? In this way we can make whatever changes are necessary in order to secure the unqualified approval of the public opinion of our respective countries. I shall deal with the following three points:

"1. Article 14, as it is now drawn, limits the application of its sanction to violations of Article 10. It therefore does not make any provision to secure the execution of the decrees of arbitration contemplated in Article 11, nor for the unanimous decisions of the Executive Council referred to in Article 13.

"Yesterday, Articles 11 and 13 were sent back to us for re-drafting. Article 14, however, was not sent; yet the new draft of these two articles calls for a corresponding change in Article 14.

"In order that the provisions of Articles 11 and 13 may be rendered effective beyond all doubt, it is necessary that, under some form to be agreed upon, they should be backed by sanctions.

"And so I propose to add to Article 14, after these words in the second paragraph, 'To be used to protect the Covenants of the League,' the two following paragraphs:

" 'In case one of the contesting parties, after having followed the procedure prescribed under Article 10, should not accept the verdict of the tribunal, or a decision unanimously rendered by the Executive Council or by the Body of Delegates, the Council shall ask the Associated Governments to apply appropriate sanctions from among those enumerated in the first paragraph of this article.

" 'In the case of a recommendation made by majority vote, where the dispute might terminate in a resort to force by the interested parties, the Executive Council shall submit the question to the Governments themselves.'

"2. The observations which precede must likewise involve a re-examination of the text of Article 8, relating to the reduction of armaments. The substitution of the words 'national safety' for the words 'domestic safety,' which was adopted at the suggestion of the Japanese Delegate, ought to involve certain modifications with a view to insuring a practical realisation of the words of President Wilson:

" 'A force must be created, a force so superior to that of all nations or to that of all alliances, that no nation or combination of nations can challenge or resist it.'

"In order that the international force should be what President Wilson desires, it must be so great that no single force can defeat it. And so, I believe that we must organise a control of troops and armaments of such a kind as definitely to put a stop to preparation for fresh wars on the part of nations acting in bad faith, and to protect honest nations against every sudden attack; for such a thing would indicate a real failure in the organisation of law.

"In Article 8 then, the following words should be inserted after the words, 'The Executive Council shall formulate plans for effecting such reduction':

" 'It will establish an international control of troops and armaments, and the High Contracting Parties agree to submit themselves to it in all good faith. It will fix the conditions under which the permanent existence and organisation of an international force may be assured.'

"I may recall that at the meeting of the 6th February, in respect to this Article 8, I insisted that in the determination of what troops and what armaments each nation should have, on the one hand to preserve its national security and on the other hand to bear its share in maintaining an international force, it would be necessary to introduce two distinct elements, and that with the factor of power in the case of each State should be considered also the factor of risk which each State may have to run by reason of its geographical situation and the nature of its frontier.

"President Wilson clearly recognised this necessity when, speaking from the platform of the French Chamber of Deputies, he pronounced those splendid words, for which I here thank him: 'The frontier of France is the frontier of the world's liberty.' I ask then, that following the words 'The Executive Council shall formulate plans for effecting such reduction,' this clause be added:

" 'Having due regard, in determining the number of troops, not only to the relative strength of the different States, but also to the risks to which they are exposed by their geographical situation and the nature of their frontiers.'

"I offer this as a new amendment to Article 8.

"3. My third amendment, which concerns Article 6, goes back to quite a different thought. I mentioned it to you when first we discussed this Article. It relates to the conditions which shall govern the admission of a new State into the League of Nations. To my mind the veto of one nation would not be desirable, providing the majority be two-thirds. We have all stated here that mutual good faith ought to be the basis and constitute the strength of an international organisation. Guarantees of uprightness are indispensible. The associated States ought to be free States, fortified with institutions which will safeguard them in the enjoyment of liberty.

"If they have previously committed acts in defiance of law, acts of violence, acts of barbarity or crimes, they must first be required to make reparations and to pay the price which justice demands. Briefly, it is necessary that every one of the associated States be at the same time cleansed of its past and free for the future. That is the spirit of the following amendment, which will give to the League of Nations its high moral position in the eyes of the world.

"I would modify the second paragraph as follows:

" 'Furthermore no nation shall be admitted into the League unless it has representative institutions which permit of its being considered as itself responsible for the acts of its own Government; unless it is in a position to give effective guarantees of its sincere intention to abide by its agreement; and unless it conforms to those principles which the League shall formulate regarding naval and military forces and armaments.'

"The French Senators and Deputies who compose the parliamentary group of arbitration, consisting of members favourably disposed toward the League of Nations, have already taken steps to acquaint us with their anxiety regarding those matters of which I have just spoken. If we should not take formal precautions in the matter of controlling armaments, this group of men would feel that we were exposing our country to grave risks unless guarantees were given on that point, and it would oppose the plan all the more vigorously."

Mr. Larnaude supported these views, and held that they could not create difficulties. He insisted on the idea of the geographical risk, which is of such great importance for nations like Poland, the Czecho-Slovak Republic, Roumania, Belgium, France, &c. The control of munitions of war, and of other manufactures which might conceal potential preparations for war, lay at the very basis of the League of Nations, unless one wished the nations of good faith to be the victims of the others.

President Wilson: We must make a distinction between what is possible and what is not. No nation will consent to control. As for us Americans, we cannot consent to control because of our Constitution. We must do everything that is possible to ensure the safety of the world. Some plan must be worked out by which every country shall have a sufficient force, firstly, to maintain its national security, secondly, to contribute to international safety.

It may be admitted that France should maintain a force proportionately more considerable than other nations, on account of the geographical risk that has been mentioned, but as to the construction of an unified military machine in time of peace, that is quite another question. This war made apparent the absolute necessity of the unity of command, and this unity of command constituted an immense advantage which had a decisive influence on the very issue of the war, but the unity of command only became possible because of the immediate and imminent danger which threatened civilisation. To propose to realise unity of command in time of peace, would be to put forward a proposal that no nation would accept. The Constitution of the United States forbids the President to send beyond its frontiers the national forces. If the United States maintained an army, there would always be a certain inevitable delay in sending it to the States where it might be required. And it is possible that the Germans may gather together once more their military power. If the militarist madness has not been destroyed in Germany by this war, a new menace may threaten us, but this menace will not develop suddenly. The economic condition of Germany will make that impossible.

As for us, if we organise from now onwards an international army, it would appear that we were substituting international militarism for national militarism. Some eminent Frenchmen have already told me that they would not accept what the American Constitution forbids me to accept. I know how France has suffered, and I know that she wishes to obtain the best guarantees possible before she enters the League, and everything that we can do in this direction we shall do, but we cannot accept proposals which are in direct contradiction to our Constitution.

The argument which has been most employed against the League of Nations in America is that the army of the United States would be at the disposal of an international council, that American troops would thus be liable to be ordered to fight at any moment for the most remote of causes, and this prospect alarms our people. There is therefore no other course open to us but to accept some system compatible at once with our Constitution and with the views of our public opinion.

Mr. Bourgeois said that he need not add that France was ready to become a member of the League of Nations, the principles of which, as laid down in the draft Covenant, were in accordance with those which she herself had always fought for, but she required the organisation of international action to be considered and clearly defined. He thought there was a misunderstanding with regard to the word "control." President Wilson had alluded to the command of an international army, and to the difficulties that would be raised as to the admission of a single chief placed at the head of all the armies of the nations in the League. But what was most important of all was to have some means of verifying the quantities of armaments produced by each nation, and that could only be done if every State in the League undertook not to surpass certain limits, and to allow that the extent of its manufactures should be verified. This verification was indispensible in order to avoid that a State should secretly produce arms and munitions. He used the word control, therefore, only in the sense of the French words "surveillance" or "vérification."

So far as the international army was concerned it was not a question of a permanent army, but simply of making some provision for a military organisation to be given to national contingents so that they could be rapidly co-ordinated against an aggressive State. If one could not do that the League became nothing but a dangerous façade. France held the frontier of the Rhine, which President Wilson had called the frontier of liberty. She was therefore obliged to maintain a considerable force even in time of peace, and she could never be tranquil unless it were certain that, in case of attack, she could count on the effective help of the other members of the League, and that she would not have to wait for their support for months, or perhaps for years; unless this were certain France would be again exposed to a sudden attack and would think that the League was nothing but a trap.

It appeared, therefore, necessary for the safety of the members of the League who were particularly exposed to attack to provide some organisation for the international forces which would be ready to come into operation whenever affairs took a critical turn. He did not hold in any way to his wording, but simply to the double idea which he had expressed of the verification or surveillance of armaments and of a certain organisation to provide for cases in which the utilisation of national contingents might be required. He asked, therefore, for the insertion in the convention of a formula which would give public opinion the sense of security which it demanded. It was necessary that the idea of the League of Nations should engender a feeling of confidence in order to obtain universal acceptance.

President Wilson: In this discussion we have so far left on one side an essential element. Our principal safety will be obtained by the obligation which we shall lay on Germany to effect a complete disarmament. It is said that she will be able to prepare again in secret, but I ask, what part of the German military preparation was secret before this war? We knew the number of their soldiers, their plan of attack, and the extent of their armaments. In reality no serious preparation for war can be made in secret. There is nothing to be feared from a large number of men; the danger lies rather in the quantity of machines and of munitions which have been manufactured, and these things cannot be accumulated in secret. I am convinced that we shall carry out the effective disarmament of Germany, and in that case we shall enjoy on that side a period of safety, for it will be impossible for Germany to accumulate anew reserves of munitions and of the machinery of war.

Lord Robert Cecil observed that the French proposals seemed to be summed up in three principal points:

1. National security must be considered in relation to the geographical position of States. One could meet this preoccupation by adding to the article words of this sort: "Having special regard to the situation and circumstances of certain States." This was a matter which could be put right by the draughtsmen.

2. The word "control" might lead to a misunderstanding. It might be preferable to use the word "inspection." In any case the French amendment had for its object to make certain of two things: (*a*) that no State should have an army greater than a permitted maximum, and (*b*) that every State should have a force equal to the minimum imposed by the League. The second of these points seemed to him extremely delicate, and the people of Great Britain would have many objections to accepting a control which insisted on a certain number of British soldiers being maintained under arms. He did not think that this proposal could be adopted.

3. The French amendment indicated the necessity of an organisation which would permit of the immediate utilisation of the military forces of the members of the League. In this form the proposal departed from our conception of the League, which did not include an international force, but some less strict arrangement might be adopted which would permit of the preparation of agreements on the subject whenever the need for it should be felt. Thus a result could be obtained if we were content to accept some provisions such as the following: "A permanent Commission shall be established to advise the League of Nations on naval and military questions."

Mr. Larnaude: Several nations which have taken part in this war are afraid of having made sacrifices in vain. The protection which results from the existence of a League of Nations will perhaps become a guarantee of safety, but within what period of time?

Perhaps within a hundred years. By that time the militarist spirit will no doubt have disappeared, but at the present moment we are emerging from a terrible war. Can it be thought that we shall pass immediately from the state of intensive militarism in which we live to a state of practical disarmament?

To-day we are in a period of transition. We must have national contingents always ready to reassure the State within the League. The sacrifice which is asked of each State will be negligible beside this. The idea of an international force is bound up with the very idea of the League of Nations, unless one is content that the League should be a screen of false security.

President Wilson: It must not be supposed that any of the members of the League will remain isolated if it is attacked, that is the direct contrary of the thought of all of us. We are ready to fly to the assistance of those who are attacked, but we cannot offer more than the condition of the world enables us to give.

Mr. Larnaude: If the Treaty of Peace gives us absolute guarantees that Germany will be virtually disarmed, and will not be able to build up her armaments again, then we shall feel safer.

Mr. Bourgeois: The dilemma has been put to us in the following manner: Is France prepared to enter into a League of Nations such as is defined in the Covenant, that is to say, without the organisation of an international army, or would she prefer to stand alone?

We must equally call your attention to the fact that we are ourselves disposed to submit to the corresponding obligations, that is to say, to our armies, and our military preparations being controlled by the League. Other nations say they cannot consent to this control. Nevertheless, there can be no rule of justice and of safety among the different nations of the world if every State can at its will prepare an attack. Opposition to the essential principles of the League of Nations does not therefore come from our side.

President Wilson: The only method by which we can achieve this end lies in our having confidence in the good faith of the nations who belong to the League. There must be between them a cordial agreement and goodwill. Take a new State which is going to enter this League, Poland. We have confidence in Poland, we hope that she will co-operate willingly in our efforts, and that she will take the necessary measures to secure her safety, and also to make the principles of the League respected. I therefore ask the French Delegation to consider this question again, for I think that any control, by whatever name it may be called, will be too offensive to be adopted. All that we can promise, and we do promise it, is to maintain our military forces in such a condition that the world will feel itself in safety. When danger comes, we too will come, and we will help you, but you must trust us. We must all depend on our mutual good faith.

Mr. Bourgeois: France is ready to accept some system of control, and considers that in accepting it she would surrender no portion of her dignity. It is a common measure of mutual guarantee which has nothing offensive in it, since it would apply equally to all the Great Powers, and since it is made by common accord amongst them all. We are dealing with everyone on the footing of perfect equality, and we do not think that this step would involve any sacrifice of independence. I ask therefore with insistence that something should be done in this matter, which cannot be left outside our Covenant; something that will give to public opinion the feeling of safety which it demands. Without that any scheme for a League of Nations will simply arouse general distrust.

It was agreed that the matter should be considered again by the Drafting Committee.

(*The Meeting was adjourned.*)

Printed copy (WP, DLC).

From the Diary of Lord Robert Cecil

Feb. 11 [1919]

Next morning the League of Nations again, and the French developed a demand for an international army, the President and I resisting vigorously, I warning the French that if they destroyed the League of Nations they would destroy a good deal besides, and telling one of them privately after the meeting that the League of Nations was their only means of getting the assistance of America and England, and if they destroyed it they would be left without an ally in the world.

T MS (R. Cecil Papers, Add. MSS, PRO).

To Boghos Nubar

My dear Sir: Paris, 11 February 1919.

I am very much indebted to you for your letter of the 6th of February with its accompanying maps and memorandum.[1] It is what I greatly desire and I shall study the whole matter, I need not assure you, with the warmest friendliness for the Armenian peoples to whom my sympathy goes out most heartily.

Cordially and sincerely yours,   [Woodrow Wilson]

CCL (WP, DLC).
  [1] B. Nubar to WW, Feb. 6, 1919, Vol. 54.

To Howard Sweetser Bliss

My dear Doctor Bliss: Paris, 11 February, 1919.

I value your letter of February 7th.[1] I was very anxious that you should give your views to the Conference at the Quai D'Orsay when Prince Feisul appeared before it, but there was some misunderstanding about it and the invitation was not conveyed to you, as Mr. Lloyd George and I had requested it should be. I am still hoping that it will be possible for you to be there and to give us the benefit of your views before I return temporarily to the United States.

Cordially and sincerely yours,   [Woodrow Wilson]

CCL (WP, DLC).
  [1] H. S. Bliss to WW, Feb. 7, 1919, Vol. 54.

From Newton Diehl Baker

Washington, February 11, 1919.

Confidential. For the President from the Secretary of War.

QUOTE: I have received your cablegram of February eighth with regard to the use of our overseas troops to garrison portions of the Turkish Empire. I have no doubt as to the legality of sending American troops to those areas. The present emergency for which you have been authorized to use the Army plainly involves the preservation of order until permanent peace arrangements can be made, and disorder in the Turkish Empire might have consequences which would thwart the whole effort of the Peace Conference.

PARAGRAPH. The other aspects of the problem are much more grave. Public opinion here is very insistent upon the return of our troops. This appears not only in the Senate and House, but in the newspapers and in the enormous correspondence of the War Department on that subject. It would, therefore, be very much better if our troops could relieve Great Britain of some part of her duty on the Western Front and thus do our share in France and Germany, for which the reasons would be obvious to our people even though our forces greatly outnumbered the British contingent. If the decision can be postponed until your return, it would be most fortunate, both because you could act with fuller knowledge of home conditions and also could guide public opinion by your statements. If, however, the question must be decided now, and you feel obliged by your situation to participate, our troops should in no case go beyond Turkey proper and Armenia, as to which countries American opinion is already well formed and would tend to favor the protection of Christians, while Mesopotamia is known here only as a field of British influence and ambition. What the feeling of our soldiers would be I cannot say. Should any be sent to Turkey and Armenia they would have a pleasanter climate than is possible in the winter and spring months in France. General Pershing could learn for you what the probable attitude would be, and it may be possible for him to permit volunteering or allowing organizations in some way to decide for themselves upon their willingness to go. If this is not impracticable, such consultation of their wishes would be very popular, and if the soldiers could feel that they were being given an opportunity for a distinction and a compliance with your personal wishes, or helping to preserve the quiet of the world in order to enable you to gather the fruits of their victory, it would undoubtedly help greatly.

PARAGRAPH. Public opinion at home has been restless about our troops in Russia on three grounds: first, fear that the force is insufficient for its own safety; second, desire to have the soldiers all brought home; third, fear lest our forces may find themselves in opposition to popular government in Russia and in alliance with reactionary opinion. None of these grounds would apply to Turkey or Armenia. It seems certain that the disptach of our troops to Turkey without some effort to prepare public opinion here in advance, would be unwise. Could the question be postponed until your return, it would be much easier. If it cannot be, it is possible that Polk and I with a few days notice could predispose some influential persons and thus secure outspoken approvals at the first announcement, with a view to directing public thinking on the subject. The situation in Congress is such that I feel assured that the Committees on Foreign Relations ought to be consulted with before the step is taken. I would like, also to talk with Mr. Taft, who at present is touring the country making very strong speeches in favor of the League of Nations idea. I think if I talk with him he would be willing to approve such a step in his public speeches as being an illustration of the helpful action of the League to prevent other and worse troubles. In any case, should you decide to send our troops we should have a cabled statement from you showing the common interest of the United States with the Allies in maintaining the peace of Europe until the treaties can be perfected, and pointing out that this action is peaceful in character and will not prolong the stay of our soldiers in Europe. UNQUOTE.

Polk. Acting.

T telegram (SDR, RG 59, 763.72/12770, DNA).

From Charles Homer Haskins

My dear President Wilson: [Paris] February 11, 1919.

In considering the Belgian territorial problems[1] a delicate question of procedure arises. Belgium demands a revision of the treaties of 1839, to which the only other accessible signatories are England, France, and Holland. Unless the matter is taken up by the signatories as such, Holland, not being a party to the Peace Conference, may decline to enter into the discussion and thus render matters difficult. On the other hand, the question interests the whole Conference as a phase of the restoration of Belgium's sovereignty (Point VII), and in particular the United States as a friend of Belgium. An ultimate appeal to the Conference is also a wholesome prospect for Holland.

It is suggested that these difficulties can be harmonized by the following procedure:

(1) The Conference should take cognizance of Belgium's request for a revision of her international and territorial status as fixed by the treaties of 1839.

(2) The Conference should then ask England and France to invite Holland to join with Belgium and them in a discussion of the matters involved,

(3) in the interest of reaching a satisfactory settlement which shall be submitted to the Conference for final action.

Without committing itself in advance to any particular proposal, the United States should, at all stages of the procedure, help Belgium to secure the fullest opportunity for ample consideration of her case. In the second stage, however, we could appear directly only if requested to act as an *amicus curiae*.

Sincerely yours,   Charles H. Haskins

TLS (WP, DLC).
[1] The Council of Ten, at its meeting at 3 p.m. on February 11, 1919, discussed Belgian territorial claims at some length. Wilson asked only three questions, and Lansing asked one. The minutes of this meeting are printed in *PPC*, III, 957-69.

From Thomas Nelson Page

Personal

My dear Mr. President: Rome, February 11, 1919.

I hope very much that this letter will reach you before you leave Paris. It takes with it all of my congratulations on the great work which you have accomplished there, and my profoundest good wishes for the future accomplishment of those things which I know are dear to your heart for the establishment of the Peace that shall be a true World Peace.

My most earnest hope is that you will return to take your place in the Peace Conference at the earliest possible moment, for I believe that your personal presence there will have an immense effect, not only in moulding the work of the Conference in the form best adapted to carry out the principles which you have enunciated to the world and which have brought us so far forward toward Victory, but in hastening the coming of the Peace which America, under your guidance, has made possible.

The papers appear this morning for the first time after several days intermission, caused by a strike of the printers of all except the Vatican and the Socialist journals, and one other journal which was printed by non-union printers. They reveal a situation here very interesting and somewhat curious; first, in that it indicates a drawing closer to France on the part of the present Italian Government, and, incidentally, a manifest satisfaction in declaring that strong dissensions exist between France and America. One paper, indeed, speaks of it as the establishment of two distinct views, one the Anglo-American and the other the French-Italian. Secondly, in that there is an apparent lull in the press of the diatribes against Jugo-Slavia, and a substitution therefor of reports on the widening breach between Croatia and Serbia. A third curious revelation in the point of view here is that Italy, having turned her mind towards the expansion of her influence along the shores of the eastern Mediterranean, the press is beginning to speak of this as her right. It spoke originally of her right to compensation. Now it begins to speak of her right to have all war debts pooled, and all compensation pooled likewise, and apportioned according to the losses and sacrifices incurred. This apportionment, the press speaks of as something that is essential. It claims as her right the apportionment of regions which shall furnish her materials of prime necessity, and a proper outlet for her great factor of wealth consisting in her work emigrant population.

A morning paper speaks of the report of a secret arrangement having been made by France, England and Russia in 1916 by which those countries, unknown to other Allies, had delimited the respective spheres of influence and the respective territorial acquisitions in Asia Minor and had established the confines of a proposed Arabic State. The article ends with an attack, by implication, on secret treaties made during the war by a group of the Allies without informing other Allies, and expresses the hope that the Peace Conference will, in regard thereto, assume an attitude of complete liberty of action and of decision.

All of which is rather singular in a representative of the press which has hitherto been insisting on the inviolability of the secret Treaty of London.

There is great anxiety here lest the Germans should, in face of the released pressure on them, compose their own defenses and turn on the Allies, or, as the phrase goes, "come back" on them. And I confess that I myself have great anxiety about this. According to figures which I have seen, Germany has under arms—or in a condition to be under arms with little or no delay—not less than a million and three-quarters troops, the greater part of them in good condition, with abundant artillery and commanded by a great General with an experienced and capable staff. The greater part of these troops are in sufficiently good spirits to undertake a Spring campaign with a prospect of even the possibility of looting rich spoils in France, and of what spoils they might find in Italy. This army could be increased in two or three months to nearly double the forces mentioned above, for there are 12,000,000 Germans in Austria who consider themselves now substantially united with Germany, and under the present conditions I think it within the bounds of possibility that Jugo-Slavia might think it a good time to effectuate her aspirations—about which their extremists already talk—for the redemption of the Frioli Plains this side of the Isonzo.

I do not believe that there will be absolute security against some attempt on the part of the Germans without substantially disarming them, that is, without taking from them all arms which could possibly leave them under temptation to fight again, and without putting absolutely out of commission the great arms-making factories.

I recall, in my childhood, the heart-burning that existed throughout the South at the sequestration of all arms in the South, but my maturer experience has led me to the conviction that, although the means employed might, with great advantage, have been different, the sequestration of military arms was the only thing which prevented outbreaks in the South which might have given serious trouble to the Government. There were many occasions during Reconstruction times when, had the South not been disarmed and had she not recognized the parole accepted by Generals Lee and Johns[t]on, there might have been renewal of hostilities, at least in some places.

Germany is far more hostile to the Allies than any important element of our people ever was to the Union after General Lee's surrender, and she has none of the restraint which our people placed on themselves. We were resentful of certain things but not revengeful; but Germany is profoundly revengeful, and if she should see the least possibility of success she would not hesitate a moment to fling herself on us, should we be off our guard.

I should be far more anxious if I did not feel that you have been at the center of things and will know exactly what the conditions are, and will act with absolute knowledge of those conditions and their relations to the Cause of an early, a just and a durable Peace.

Believe me, with every wish for a pleasant voyage home, and the success of your devotion to the Cause of Peace, always,

Yours most sincerely, Thos. Nelson Page

TLS (WP, DLC).

From Prince Faisal

Dear Preside[n]t Wilson   Paris, le 11 Feb 1919.

I hear that you are leaving very soon for America: and I must ask you, if possible to see me for a few minutes before you leave. The position of my people is very different for the moment, and I am in great need for your advise.

Believe me   Yours very sincerely   Faïssal

ALS (WP, DLC).

From Howard Sweetser Bliss

My dear Mr. President: Paris. February 11th, 1919.

May I express the hope, most respectfully and yet most earnestly, that the consideration of the question of Syria, appointed for yesterday but postponed, may be taken up by the Peace Conference before your departure.

If an Inter-Allied Commission of Inquiry is to be sent to Syria— a most desirable arrangement—no time should be lost in sending it.   Yours very truly,   Howard S. Bliss

TLS (WP, DLC).

From Herbert Clark Hoover

Dear Mr. President: Paris, 11 February 1919.

I have just returned from Brussels where I have had several conferences with the Belgian Ministry and the King. They are, of course, naturally disappointed at your inability to visit Belgium as they had been reserving a number of important matters for discussion with you at your visit. The Belgian Prime Minister[1] asks me if it will be possible for you to make an occasion of half an hour to see him on Friday. As I will have to notify him tomorrow morning at the latest in order for him to get here in time, I am wondering if I can trouble you for an early reply.

The Belgian situation is very serious, and I feel requires some indication from you to the American Peace Mission as to their relation to Belgian problems.

Faithfully yours,   Herbert Hoover

TLS (WP, DLC).
[1] That is, Léon Delacroix.

From George Lansbury[1]

My dear President Wilson   London 11.2.19

I am very sorry indeed it was not possible to see you before leaving Paris, but of course quite understand how pressed with work you are & am grateful for your promise to see me on your return.

May I say that my only object in desiring to see you & your friend Colonel House is just this. I am editor of the most widely read labour socialist paper in England[2] it will be published as a daily at end of March. We have been backing your policy very strongly & are very much pledged to see the whole business of Peace through on your lines, in order to do this it is very important to know clearly as possible all there is to know about the policy & what difficulties there are to be overcome.

I am certain your fight is always easiest the more publicity it receives & am confident that an understanding democracy would back you through every difficulty, but understanding only comes from knowledge & this we do not get as we should.

I hope you will have a good voyage home & come back heartened & strengthened to make a genuine peoples peace.

Truly   G Lansbury

ALS (WP, DLC).
[1] That is, the British Labour party leader.
[2] The London *Weekly Herald*. The *Herald* had been a daily newspaper from its founding in 1911 until September 1914, when it became a weekly for the duration of the war. See Raymond William Postgate, *The Life of George Lansbury* (London, 1951), pp. 118-85 *passim*.

From Nikola Pašić and Others

Mr President,   Paris, 11th February 1919.

Inspired by the fullest confidence in the lofty spirit of justice which you have displayed in regard to all questions appertaining to the Peace Settlement, and desirous of contributing to the friendly solution of the territorial differences pending between the Kingdom of Serbs, Croats and Slovenes and the Kingdom of Italy, the Delegation of the Kingdom of Serbs Croats and Slovenes desires to bring to your knowledge its readiness to submit those differences to your arbitration. It has received full authority to this effect from its Government.

With the assurance of our profound esteem, We are, Mr President,   Respectfully   Nik. P Pashitch.
                                                      Dr. Ante Trumbić
                                                      Dr Ivan Zolger
                                                      Mil. R. Vesnitch[1]

TLS (WP, DLC).
    [1] That is, Ante Trumbić, Ivan Žolger, and Milenko R. Vesnić, all of whom were still not yet fully accredited delegates of Serbia to the peace conference, since the Allies had not yet recognized the Kingdom of Serbs, Croats, and Slovenes. Robert Lansing, on behalf of the United States, had granted recognition to the new kingdom on February 7. On the problem of recognition of the new nation by the great powers and the peace conference, see Ivo J. Lederer, *Yugoslavia at the Paris Peace Conference: A Study in Frontiermaking* (New Haven, Conn., 1963), especially pp. 109-13, 147-48, and 203-205.

From the Diary of Colonel House

February 11, 1919.

There was great excitement this afternoon. Admiral Grayson came in to say the President had asked him to see Ray Stannard Baker and to tell him to let the newspapers have a story to the effect that if the French continued their propaganda against the Governments assembled here, that the Conference would probably be moved elsewhere. Grayson went into Baker's office, told him the President's wishes, and when he came out, Baker told the newspaper men of the rumor.

Of course they connected it directly with Grayson. I sent for Grayson and told him to see the President at once and advise him to have Baker and Rogers kill the story and not permit it to be cabled home. The President, however, insisted upon letting it stand.[1] Grayson told me afterward that the President said that he, Lloyd George and Orlando had decided to do this. The story went around Paris like wildfire and soon the reporters were plying me with questions. The British rang me up and said they were trying to get Lloyd George to deny from London that the British had any intention of joining in the movement to change the place of the Conference. They could not get Lloyd George by telephone, therefore they did not know what his attitude was. They were not conscious of the fact that he had already agreed with the President.

To my mind, it was a stupid blunder. What the President and the two Prime Ministers should have done was to have gone directly to Clemenceau and read the riot act to him. In the first place, the threat is childish. The Conference could not be moved until at least a preliminary peace has been signed. So why make the threat?

This morning the Paris Herard [Herald] and Tribune undertook to publish the rumors and the blank spaces in the papers indicate the Censor's pencil. The French Foreign Office immediately sent Aubert around to see me, but by some mischance, he did not get in. However, he came later and we had a full and frank discussion upon the subject, which I asked him to repeat to the Prime Minister. I said to Aubert practically everything the President said, but I said it in a way which did not give offence, in fact, I obtained a person[al] promise from him.

T MS (E. M. House Papers, CtY).
    [1] There were many such reports in the American press. See, e.g., the *New York Times*, Feb. 12, 1919, and the New York *World*, Feb. 11, 1919.

To Sir Ludovic James Grant[1]

My dear Mr. Grant: Paris, 11 February, 1919.

I am greatly honored by the invitation of the Senatus Academicus of the University of Edinburgh to receive at the hands of the University the honorary degree of Doctor of Laws,[2] and it causes me very deep and genuine regret to be obliged to say that I do not see how I can conscientiously leave my duties here, except to take a hasty journey back to my own country to perform imperative duties there. I should feel most highly honored to receive an honorary degree from the University of Edinburgh and am denying myself very deep gratification. I hope therefore that the members of the Senatus will accept the expression of my very profound regret and my very deep appreciation of the honor they have paid me.

Cordially and sincerely yours,   [Woodrow Wilson]

CCL (WP, DLC).
    [1] Regius Professor of Public Law and Secretary of the University of Edinburgh.
    [2] Wilson was responding to L. J. Grant to WW, Feb. 5, 1919, TLS (WP, DLC).

From Carter Glass

Washington February 11, 1919.

For the President from Glass.

I desire to bring to your attention the importance of taking steps to reduce the cost of living and to remove dissatisfaction growing out of the feeling that prices of food commodities are being artificially maintained by governmental action. I have just received a strong letter urging importance of this from the Director General of Railroads,[1] the largest employer of labor, and from this and other evidence I am convinced that a situation exists which calls for prompt action.

As labor becomes unemployed or only partly employed, the situation becomes more pressing in Europe. Mr. Hoover is naturally impressed with the international phases of the food question and with the problem of fulfilling the moral obligations he feels he is under to food producers and securing the best possible prices for our food products in foreign markets. I am convinced that the broader national aspects of the question are far more important and that the ultimate loss which we shall sustain through maintenance of artificial prices, as for instance in the cases of wheat, pork, and sugar, will far exceed the amount which would be necessary to compensate all those to whom the Government is under any moral or legal obligation. I believe some members of the Food Administration think food prices would in some cases increase if restrictions were removed, but I think this would not happen to any relatively important extent, and that in any event it is highly desirable that all prices should be allowed to find, as promptly as possible, their economic level, and that there should be no grounds for a claim that high prices are due to governmental restrictions.

I have submitted this cable to the Cabinet and they unanimously recommend immediate removal of artificial food prices.

Polk,   Acting.

T telegram (WP, DLC).
    [1] W. D. Hines to C. Glass, Feb. 8, 1919, TCL (WP, DLC).

From Bernard Mannes Baruch

My dear Mr. President: Paris, February 11, 1919

Referring to the cables of Secretary Redfield,[1] I have had a consultation with the various heads, and they are in agreement with me that the measure suggested by Secretary Redfield is a good one. Personally, I feel that the only objection to it is that it may be in contravention of the Sherman Anti-trust Law. In the memorandum relating to the transitory period, which I submitted as Chairman of the War Industries Board,[2] this was one of the suggestions that I made; but we did not adopt the plan for the reason that it did contravene the Anti-trust Law; but my scheme went somewhat further than this.

Referring to the use of Mr. Peek, I shall certainly raise no objection if Mr. Peek desires to do this work.

Of course you realize that although this may be called a stabilization of prices, it is a fixing of minimum prices; and Mr. Hoover suggests that in case prices are so stabilized, a representative of the farming interests, like Governor Stewart,[3] should be on the committee that does it.

Very sincerely yours, Bernard M Baruch

TLS (WP, DLC).
[1] That is, W. C. Redfield to WW, Feb. 6 and 7, 1919, Vol. 54.
[2] See B. M. Baruch to WW, Nov. 19 and 27, 1918, Vol. 53.
[3] That is, Henry Carter Stuart (not Stewart), former Governor of Virginia (1914-1918) and a former member of the price-fixing committee of the W.I.B. and the National Agricultural Advisory Committee.

From Royal Meeker

My dear Mr. President: London, Feb. 11, 1919

Secretary Wilson has sent a Commission of Employers to study Industrial Reconstruction in England and France. Much interest is manifested in the United States in the Whitley Committees and the other means for adjusting labor disputes in Gt. Britain[1] and it is believed that a report from a body of employers will carry great weight in our country. It is for that reason that the Commission was made up of employers only. At the last moment I was attached to the Commission as Economic Advisor. We are meeting with cordial helpfulness in our work here in London.

It occurred to me that it is of vital importance to guarantee certain minimum standards as to working conditions and a living wage in the international agreements now being formulated at Paris. I am quite familiar with labor conditions both at home and abroad. If I can be of any service to you and the American representatives at the Peace Conference, please command me. So far as I am aware, no one connected with the American delegation has any special knowledge of labor conditions at home, or the vital importance of providing in the League of Nations for a body having jurisdiction over the all important question of labor conditions.

With best wishes for your health and success I am as ever,

Yours sincerely, Royal Meeker

ALS (WP, DLC).
[1] The most influential of the various schemes for improved postwar industrial relations in Great Britain was the "Interim Report on Joint Standing Industrial Councils" by the Committee on Relations between Employers and Employed of the Ministry of Reconstruction, which became known as the "Whitley Report." The committee, which was headed by John Henry Whitley, a Liberal M.P. for Halifax and the Deputy Speaker of the House of Commons, and was composed of leading employers, trade unionists, economists, and social workers, had been appointed in October 1916 and had presented its report in March 1917. The report proposed the creation of National Industrial Councils, known as "Whitley Councils," in each of the more highly unionized industries, with district councils and works' committees operating under them. The councils and com-

mittees would be composed of union and employers' representatives, who would meet regularly and frequently to discuss industrial problems, such as the conditions of employment, wages and hours, regular methods of negotiation, technical education and training, industrial research, and legislation affecting the industry. The government enthusiastically endorsed the idea of the "Whitley Councils," and, by 1920, fifty-six national councils covering three and a quarter million workers had been established. However, the industries affected were mostly small, and the workers in the larger industries refused to participate in the scheme. Even in industries with national councils, the district and local machineries were seldom created, and many of the councils ceased to exist after a few years. For a detailed discussion and the text of the "Whitley Report," see John Barton Seymour, *The Whitley Councils Scheme* (London, 1932). A brief description and criticism of the report, as well as of other proposals for improved industrial relations, can be found in *The Labour Year Book, 1919* (London, [1919]), pp. 245-56.

From Robert Lansing, with Enclosure

My dear Mr. President: Paris February 11th, 1919

In response to your letter of February 1st,[1] enclosing original of a telegram from Adolph Germer, concerning refusal to issue passports to Socialist Party Delegates to the International Socialist Congress, Berne, I have just received the enclosed telegram from Mr. Polk giving detailed information in reference to the matter.

I return herewith the original telegram from Adolph Germer.

Faithfully yours,   Robert Lansing

TLS (WP, DLC).
    [1] WW to RL, Feb. 1, 1919, with Enclosure, Vol. 54.

ENCLOSURE

Washington, February 10, 1919.

Your 597 February 5th. Passport applications to attend Socialist Conference in Switzerland were received from Algernon Lee, John M. Work, and James O'Neal,[1] also application to have passport amended made by Lewis Gannett[2] now in Paris. Swiss Minister intimated that he would be better satisfied if we should not grant them passports. I told him that if his Government did not want them he could refuse visas. Department delayed issuing passports, however, until we could find out whether Conference actually be held or not. Legation in Switzerland took some time in sending desired information and message only received on February 3rd that Conference would be held. Gannett's passport had already been amended and passports were immediately issued to Algernon Lee and James O'Neal. Passport refused to John M. Work as his record was extremely bad. Now think we made a mistake in granting passport to Lee, as he was connected with many disloyal movements, but as long as passport was granted it was considered wiser to let it stand.   Polk,   Acting.

T telegram (WP, DLC).

[1] Algernon Lee, journalist, writer, and editor, president and educational director of the Rand School of Social Science, former chairman of the Socialist party, and a member of the New York City Board of Alderman; John McClelland Work, a founding member of the Socialist party and its former national secretary, at this time editorial writer of the *Milwaukee Leader*; and James Oneal (not O'Neal), one of the leading publicists of the Socialist party.

[2] Lewis Stiles Gannett, at this time a correspondent for *The Survey* at the peace conference.

From Robert Lansing

My dear Mr. President: Paris, February 11, 1919

Pursuant to telegram 643 from Mr. Polk,[1] I am transmitting to you information from the Secretary of War that, though anxious about the Archangel situation, the War Department is not considering the questions of actual danger to the troops or their need of reinforcement since it understands that the American units there are operating under command of Marshal Foch and the Supreme War Council.

I am enclosing also telegrams which throw light on the military situation there at present,[2] which may be of interest to you in this connection.   Faithfully yours,   Robert Lansing

TLS (WP, DLC).

[1] FLP to RL, No. 643, Feb. 8, 1919, T telegram (WP, DLC). Lansing summarizes its contents below.

[2] Col. James A. Ruggles, Military Attaché at Archangel, to Brig. Gen. Marlborough Churchill, No. 16, Jan. 31, 1919, and No. 20, Feb. 4, 1919, and DeWitt Clinton Poole, Jr., to RL, No. 540, Feb. 1, 1919, T telegrams, all in WP, DLC. The three telegrams described the "critical" military situation in Archangel which, according to Brig. Gen. (William) Edmund Ironside, commander in chief of Allied troops in Archangel, was due to overextension of the Allied forces, the poor quality of the British officers, the homesickness and low morale of the French troops, and the inexperience of the American forces. The failure of the latest Allied offensive had made possible a Bolshevik counteroffensive. Thus, Ironside had given orders to evacuate the region of Shenkursk, which was second in importance only to Archangel itself, and he believed that, without immediate reinforcements from Murmansk, much of the occupied area would eventually have to be evacuated. However, as Ruggles pointed out, it was practically impossible to evacuate men and stores from the Archangel region at this time of the year, since the port could only be reached by icebreakers or semi-icebreakers, which had a very small troop-carrying capacity. The alternative would be an evacuation overland, but it would involve a march of 500 miles for some of the more advanced detachments. Moreover, the only means of transportation were horse-drawn or reindeer-drawn sleds, and it would be impossible to assemble anywhere near sufficient numbers of them to evacuate the 56,000 tons of military and naval supplies stored in the area. Should the Bolshevik military operations continue, Ruggles believed, most of the population would flock to them in order to save themselves from "bolshevik barbarities" once Allied protection was withdrawn.

From Joseph Patrick Tumulty

The White House, February 11, 1919.

Please cable me as soon as possible exact date and time your arrival in Washington so that parade of returned soldiers may be arranged accordingly.

Suffrage amendment defeated by one vote—55 to 29.

Tumulty.

T telegram (WP, DLC).

From the Diary of Dr. Grayson

Wednesday, February 12, 1919.

The Supreme War Council met and took up the matter of the renewal of the armistice terms. The French were particularly emphatic in their demands that the armistice terms, as originally planned, be changed and made much more drastic, along strongly French lines. The President refused to accept these suggestions and a very lively controversy resulted. Meanwhile, it had been called to the President's attention, that a special campaign of propaganda against his ideas was being carried on in the French newspapers. In this connection, it developed that the French newspaper proprietors had been tipped off by the Government that it would be a good thing for them to play up to the skies all of the Republican opposition in the United States to the President's plans, to indicate, as much as possible, that he had a very serious opposition at home to overcome.[1] As a result of this propaganda, the suggestion was put forth from American sources, that it might be necessary to move the conference from Paris to Geneva or to some other neutral point. It only required the suggestion of this to compel a change in the French attitude. As a result, the President was able to put through a motion, whereby there was added to the Supreme War Council two civilian economic experts from each of the five big nations and three additional to represent the smaller forces.

[1] About this matter in greater detail, see W. E. Rappard to H. Sulzer, Feb. 13, 1919.

Hankey's Notes of a Meeting of the Supreme War Council[1]

Quai d'Orsay, February 12, 1919, 11 A.M.

BC-29, SWC-6

1. M. CLEMENCEAU having declared the meeting opened, called for the report of the Committee which had assembled at Marshal Foch's Headquarters in accordance with the decision of the Supreme War Council, dated 10th February, 1919.

(GENERAL WEYGAND then read the conclusions of the Committee assembled in accordance with the decision of the Supreme War Council of the 10th February, 1919. For full text, see Annexure "A.")

M. CLEMENCEAU inquired whether it was thought advisable by the Conference to discuss the report at once.

PRESIDENT WILSON thought the sooner this was done, the better.

(It was agreed that the report should be discussed forthwith.)

M. ORLANDO expressed the desire to ask a question in regard to the report just read. The concluding paragraph of the Committee's report contained the following declaration: "The members of the Committee are of the opinion that naval and military terms of peace should be drawn up immediately by a Commission appointed for the purpose, and shall be imposed on the enemy." He understood that "the naval and military terms of peace" therein referred to were not the same as the conditions contained in the body of the report, which were purely provisional. The two sets of conditions constituted, in fact, two entirely separate propositions.

MR. BALFOUR agreed that there were evidently two quite different questions to be decided, namely: First, how should the execution by the Germans of the unfulfilled promises be assured. Second, what was to be the future policy of the Associated Governments in regard to the renewal of the Armistice: should the Armistice constantly be renewed, with new clauses and new conditions, or were the final Naval and Military Terms to be drawn up immediately and imposed on the enemy? The two questions should be kept quite distinct.

M. ORLANDO remarked that that was exactly the distinction he had meant to emphasise.

M. CLEMENCEAU held that the final peace terms must not now be discussed. The Committee had certainly made that suggestion; but this report contained no indication as to what the naval or

[1] The complete text of these notes, including Annexure A and its annexes, is printed in *PPC*, III, 970-99.

military terms of peace should be. The question would no doubt eventually have to be referred to the Committee for advice. But the Council was not in a position that day to discuss peace terms. On the other hand, the first of Mr. Balfour's two points, namely, the enforcement of the conditions already accepted by the Germans, called for an immediate decision, as Marshal Foch would have to confer with the Germans almost immediately for the renewal of the Armistice.

MARSHAL FOCH pointed out that the armistice would expire at 5.0 a.m. on the 17th February next, and the renewal would have to be signed on the 16th. He would therefore be obliged to leave Paris on the 14th or 15th.

M. CLEMENCEAU resuming said that only two days would therefore be available for a decision to be reached. Obviously, more than two days would be required to decide the final naval and military clauses to be included in the Treaty of Peace. Consequently, the consideration of that question would have to be postponed, but the conditions for a renewal of the armistice must at once be decided.

MR. BALFOUR agreed that it was impossible to discuss then and there the final peace terms; but the general policy which should govern their arrangements in regard to the renewal of the armistice, in view of arriving at the final peace terms, was quite another question. Doubts had been expressed as to the advisability of using the renewal of the armistice each month as a means of getting new terms out of the Germans. From time to time some slight modifications might be desirable and necessary. For instance, the question of Poland was one which called for immediate action, but many of the members of the Council held the view that it was inexpedient to introduce new terms every time the armistice was renewed. No satisfactory end could, however, be put to that method of procedure until the conditions of the final peace terms had been decided, and, he agreed, that a decision on that question could not be reached on that day. His proposal, therefore, was that only inevitably small changes, or no changes whatever, should be made in the armistice until the Allies were prepared to say to Germany: "These are the final naval and military terms of peace, which you must accept in order to enable Europe to demobilise and so to resume its life on a peace footing and re-establish its industries."

PRESIDENT WILSON said that Mr. Balfour's proposal for the first time seemed to suggest to him a satisfactory solution. All along his difficulty had been that little and irritating secondary demands were continually being added to the armistice conditions whilst at the same time reports were being received to the effect that the previously accepted terms had not been fulfilled. Each time he had asked the question "What will be the result of adding these new conditions? How can the enforcement of the unfulfilled conditions be secured?" And he had been conscious of the fact that either might involve a renewal of hostilities. He was perfectly prepared to renew the war if the Germans refused to accept the final terms of peace, decided upon by the Allies. But he was not prepared to renew hostilities because the Germans might refuse to accept some little portion of the eventual peace terms. Each time something was asked for which, if not accepted, meant the renewal of the war; but each condition by itself was not worth the renewal of the war. On the other hand, a refusal to accept the Allies' final terms of peace would be worth renewing the war, and ultimately the Allies would have to insist on the acceptance of their peace terms. Moreover, renewal of the armistice, with certain small additional conditions merely meant a repetition and a continuance of endless debates with the Germans as to the reason why they had been unable to comply with the accepted conditions: close technical distinctions being raised in regard to the meaning of these conditions. It seemed to him that this procedure placed the Allied Governments in the undignified position of debating with the Germans, while conscious all the time that a stop could be put to the debate by a renewal of hostilities. There could be no desire to debate with the Germans and, therefore, the final conditions to be imposed must be decided upon. That was business, as compared with the present policy which meant asking for things that formed only a part of the programme and not the whole programme. Personally he was deeply interested in the fulfilment of the entire programme, and he was ready to employ the whole strength of the American army to obtain the acceptance of the whole of the naval and military terms of peace: but he was not prepared to make use of that Army for the little pieces. It was reported that Germany had failed to fulfil part of the terms of the Armistice. What was to be done? It was suggested that more conditions should be imposed on the enemy at the next renewal of the Armistice. The enforcement of the new conditions would, however, inevitably lead to more debates and further discussions with the Germans. Would it not be better, as had been suggested, to go to Spa and to say to the Germans: "The present situation is altogether unsatisfactory. You have failed to keep your promises. You have failed to carry out the terms of the Armistice. The Armistice will be renewed, on the present terms, for a period which will be terminated on a few days' notice. Meanwhile the final Military and Naval terms of peace will be drawn up and presented to you for acceptance on the understanding that non-acceptance of the whole of the terms would mean an immediate resumption of hostilities."

The proposal he had just made had been suggested to him that morning and it appeared to him as a thoroughly sound and states-manlike idea.

M. CLEMENCEAU protested that yet once more, in his long career, he felt compelled with great regret to state that his views differed very considerably from those he had just heard. It had been stated that the Germans had not carried out the terms of the Armistice, but that it would merely be irritating to the Germans if difficulties were constantly raised about the non-fulfilment of secondary de-mands.

MR. BALFOUR remarked that M. Clemenceau should have said: "future secondary demands."

M. CLEMENCEAU accepted the correction and said that he had a great many remarks to make on that point. He proposed to begin his argument at the end, by referring to the proposals put forward by the Economic and Military Committee.

According to President Wilson's proposal, the Allies would con-descend to explain to the Germans that the Naval and Military terms of peace would be drawn up and presented to them for ac-ceptance as soon as possible. But the military terms depended largely on the other terms. If the differences existing between the thirty odd nations represented at the Conference were settled; if the cre-ation of the League of Nations gave the guarantees that were ex-pected from it, the military terms would be different from what they would be if no agreement were reached on these various points. Consequently, he believed the military terms could not be separated from the political, economic and financial terms.

Next, President Wilson had said: "I am ready to employ the whole strength of the American Army to obtain acceptance of the final conditions of peace. As to secondary questions—well, let them go. For vital questions, I am ready to renew the war, if necessary." If President Wilson would allow him to say so he thought that would be putting the question in an academic, theoretical and doctrinal light. In practice the question would present itself quite differently, for the final conditions of peace would only be settled after a large proportion of the troops had been sent home, when the Americans, the English and the Italians had gone. What would be the Allies' military situation when the present accepted demobilisation schemes had been carried out? The scheme relating to the forces to be maintained in the occupied territories until the signature of peace provided for the employment of 51 French, 10 British and 10 American divisions. After the frightful losses suffered by the French nation both materially, financially and in men, when it still had sufficient strength to maintain 51 divisions at the front, was that the moment to say to the Germans: "If you are not in an accommodating humour, we shall start fighting again?" The final military conditions to be imposed might be extremely difficult, and it might be that the enemies, having been left free to act on the other side of the frontier, a great deal of blood would have to be shed to conquer them a second time. He thought that problem had not received sufficient consideration. In his opinion, it had been presented in too theoretical, too academic a form. But the fact must be faced that during 4 years of war the countryside of France had been devastated and subjected to the worst kind of savagery. At the end of that time, the enemy had been forced to surrender at discretion. But, left to themselves, the Germans had created order, just as the Russians had created disorder. The Germans had succeeded in forming a Government, and the first words spoken in the National Assembly had been: "Deutschland über Alles." The second thing done had been to place all power in the hands of the accomplices of William II. News had been received that morning that Scheidemann, one of William's most direct agents, was to govern Germany.[2] Could it be imagined that *he* would alter his views though he might speak in favour of the League of Nations and of universal brotherhood? No, he did not think his hearers would allow themselves to be deceived. Let them read the German newspapers. It would be seen that they breathed nothing but threats. Ebert had said: "We will not accept terms which are too hard." And why was all this done? To exercise a detrimental influence on our moral[e], to frighten us, to make us fear that, if the Germans were angered, the war might begin again, Nobody was less desirous than himself of seeing the war begin again, but it must not be forgotten that we were still at war. War continued in the minds of men; the same minds that had made the war of 1914. The German nation had not suffered from invasion, its aggressive moral[e] had been preserved intact. On the other hand, the Allied Conference could not have acted differently, nor more quickly, than it had done. Vital preliminary work had to be done. It had, however, been accused of impotence by the press, and probably the Germans had come to think that the Allies were quarreling and that they were incapable of action. He would implore the Council not to confirm the Germans in that idea. The Germans must not be allowed to think that they would be able to face successfully France's 51 divisions after the Allied troops had dispersed.

[2] See n. 4 to the minutes of the Supreme War Council printed at Feb. 10, 1919, 3 p.m.

Returning to his starting-point, complaints had been made that the Germans were not carrying out the armistice terms. But they must be compelled to carry them out; as to that, all were agreed. Then it had been said, (it was the echo of a sentiment he had read in German newspapers), that there must be no fresh terms, otherwise, the Germans would get angry, would start discussions. That argument might hold good if the new conditions to be imposed were either frivolous or due to the sudden impulse of the moment. But, in reply, he need only draw attention to the Polish question, to which Mr. Balfour very rightly attached great importance, even though it was a new question, only a few days old. Now, provided the wishes of the Allies were plainly expressed, it would be impossible for the Germans to rise. Marshal Foch and Marshal Pétain would agree that the Germans could not at the present moment embark on an offensive against the Allies. Would the Polish question be worth an offensive? He thought so. But if the Germans were told that an attack on Poland would be followed by an immediate advance of the Allied troops along the entire Western front, Germany would at once comply with the Allies' conditions. He would here recite his *mea culpa*, for the matter concerned him directly. He wished to repeat what he had already said, namely, that the fortune of war had been such that neither American nor British territories had suffered, whilst the territory of France had been so ravaged that it would seem as though recovery would be impossible. The first wish of the French frontier peasants had been to get back the cattle which had been stolen from them by the hundred and by the thousand, and which they could watch grazing on the German side. These peasants kept on saying "We have been victorious, of course, but could not the Germans be asked to give us back our cattle?" Well that was not a question of world-wide importance. The world would still continue to go round, even if the unhappy peasants were not granted the means of making good—(and in how fragmentary a fashion)—the disasters caused by the war. Nevertheless Mr. Balfour would not, as a philosopher, contradict him when he said that there was such a thing as a philosophy of war, when events accumulated in the human brain and put it out of gear, destroying the balance of entire nations. The barbarians of whom history spoke took all that they found in the territories invaded by them, but destroyed nothing; they settled down to share the common existence. Now, however, the enemy had systematically destroyed everything that came in his way. As M. Klotz had said in his report,[3] nothing had been left standing. France would

[3] That is, in his oral report during the meeting of the Supreme War Council on February 10, 1919, 3 p.m.

be unable to compete against Germany for two years. It had been stated that Germany would be supplied with raw materials; but the industries of France had been scientifically destroyed, not for military reasons, but in order to prevent France from recovering in peace time. That was how matters stood. It was true that Italy had also suffered a great deal, but no comparison was possible, as it was the richest districts of France that had been destroyed. France had lost 3,000,000 men, either killed or mutilated, and it is truly necessary that some compensation should be obtained.

The Conference had worked conscientiously up to the present and had dealt with questions of the highest order. The purest idealism had been represented there, as well as more material interests; but the world was waiting. The Supreme Council would meet again in a fortnight or three weeks; by that time no one must be able to say: "The Associated Governments will not make up their minds to give us that satisfaction to which we are entitled."

This state of mind must not be allowed to develop. It could not be said that the French people were concerned with material interests to the exclusion of all others. If the French people deserved any reproach it was rather for erring in the opposite direction; for they are apt to be carried away by ideas, regardless of terrestrial affairs. But the people of France were attached to the soil, they were accustomed to work on the soil, and they now implored the representatives of the Allied and Associated peoples to consider this respect of the question. If no heed were given to such requests, a time would come when small, supposedly secondary, questions would accumulate and create a state of mind which would drive the people to insist on their demands with an amount of energy such as he should not like to see. Indefinite postponements would appear to the Germans as a proof of weakness. He was aware that President Wilson considered the Armistice to be a threat continually hanging over the heads of the Germans. But he (M. Clemenceau) knew the Germans better, and he would assure the Council that they will not take it thus. The Germans must, of course, be spoken to with moderation and equity, but also with firmness and decision; otherwise the Council would be obliged to meet again in a fortnight's time under less favourable conditions.

In speaking at such length—a proceeding justified by the importance of the question—he had not contradicted any arguments either of President Wilson or Mr. Balfour. He had merely wished to convey his own opinions which coincided with those of the entire French nation. France would suffer most from this indefinite prolongation of the Armistice. He was continually being assailed with requests for a speedy conclusion of peace, and that was the reason why he had been somewhat emphatic in his suggestions. He should like a decision to be reached as soon as possible. The Germans would be compelled to give satisfaction for the violation of the Armistice terms, described at length in General Weygand's report.

The Allies should remain firm on these points, including also the terms rendered necessary by the Polish question and such other questions that might arise, seeing that, on President Wilson's own proposal, an Economic Committee had been attached to Marshal Foch. He urged that the policy so far followed should be continued. The degree of pressure to be exerted would be made to fit each case as it arose. But the Germans must not be told: "Go on, Do as you like, Perhaps we shall some day threaten to break off relations; but just now we will not be firm." Germany would continue her preparations, and after the Allied troops had dispersed, Marshal Foch might perhaps find himself confronted by more German troops than might have been anticipated.

In conclusion he wished to apologise for having spoken at such length, but it was necessary to say these things.

MR. BALFOUR said that M. Clemenceau had made a speech which everybody would regard as most impressive, even though it must inevitably have lost by translation. He thought, however, there was a real misunderstanding, not on all, but on most of the points raised, which he hoped to remove. All were agreed that in regard to the past the Germans must be compelled to carry out the engagements. The wishes of the Allies in regard to Poland must also be complied with. M. Clemenceau had, however, been greatly moved (and not unnaturally) by the declaration made by Marshal Foch's Committee at the end of their report. That report had only been distributed in the Council Chamber that morning; and he himself had not seen it when he had drawn up his proposals.

M. Clemenceau apparently wished to introduce into the armistice certain conditions which would compel the Germans to restore cattle, sheep, etc., which had been stolen from the unhappy peasants in the ravaged districts of France. In his opinion, that proposal belonged to the general question of reparations, which would be included in the final peace terms and it could not be separated from similar questions, such as reparations due for the destruction of spindles and weaving machinery. But even if it were decided that the question should not be postponed until the general peace treaty came to be drawn up, such proposals should, he thought, be discussed separately with the Germans, who should be informed that the supply of raw materials would be made conditional on the return of the cattle. He need only assure M. Clemenceau that everybody felt most deeply for the general suffering which France had had to endure.

The fundamental misunderstanding which existed lay, however, in the fact that M. Clemenceau believed that the policy suggested was one dictated by a desire to put off a decision and to yield to the Germans until such time as the British and American troops had been withdrawn from France. That was not only not the policy proposed, but the whole object of his proposal was to hasten the time when the Germans would have been compelled to demobilise their forces to such a degree as to render them helpless. Speed and thoroughness was what they were aiming at. The long succession of months spent, not in bringing about a peace, but in settling small additional conditions to the terms of the armistice, was postponing the final settlement in a dangerous manner. It was, therefore, with the object of reaching a complete and a rapid end that his proposals had been put forward. Consequently when M. Clemenceau pointed to the small number of American and British troops which would be left when the final solution would come—that was the very reason why he wished to hasten the settlement so that demobilisation of the Allied forces could be carried out without fear and misgiving, after the Germans themselves had been compelled to demobilise.

His plan might be good or it might be bad, but its object was to get over the danger which M. Clemenceau foresaw, so that Germany would no longer be able to resist, and the Allies would then be in a position to exact those reparations which might be thought to be just.

He wished, therefore, to submit the following resolution for discussion at the meeting to be held that afternoon. It embodied the general policy, which he thought did not in reality differ in substance from M. Clemenceau's, though differing in form:

"The Supreme War Council agree that:

(1) The armistice with Germany shall be renewed on the present terms for an undefined period terminable by the Allied and Associated Powers at [blank] days' notice.

(2) Detailed and final naval, military, and air conditions shall be drawn up at once by a Committee to be presided over by Marshal Foch and submitted for the approval of the Supreme War Council: These, when approved, will be presented for signature to the Germans.

(3) After the signature of these preliminaries of peace Germany will be permitted to receive such controlled quantities of food, and raw materials for the rehabilitation of her industry, as shall be deemed just, having regard to the prior claims of Allied countries, especially those on whose industries Germany has deliberately inflicted damage.

(4) The question of the quantities of food and raw material to be

allowed to Germany after the signature of the preliminaries of peace shall be referred to the Economic Council for examination and report."

(It was agreed to adjourn the discussion until 3.0 p.m. that afternoon. The technical, Military and Naval Advisers were requested to be in attendance at 5.0 p.m.)

T MS (SDR, RG 256, 180.03101/36, DNA).

Hankey's Notes of Meetings of the Council of Ten and of the Supreme War Council[1]

Quai d'Orsay, February 12, 1919, 3 and 5 P.M.

BC-30, SWC-7

1. M. CLEMENCEAU, in opening the Meeting, suggested that the discussion should be continued from the point at which it left off in the morning.

PRESIDENT WILSON said that after reflecting on the morning's proceedings he had come to the conclusion that the difference of opinion was reduced to one point. That point was one of great importance. Mr. Balfour had made the difficulty quite clear by saying that we should not delay until our forces were so reduced that we could not compel the Germans to accede to our demands. This was the point that he had himself sought to make clear. By reducing our forces month by month, and by renewing the armistice month by month, we might be led to a stage at which Germany could resist with some prospect of success. He wished to be sure the danger point was past before reducing the Allied forces to the extent mentioned in the morning. Should trouble arise, he would be quite willing to re-mobilise the American forces, but this might be difficult, and it would certainly be a lengthy process, as the troops would have scattered to their homes. The longer we dealt with the Germans on this plan, the longer their hopes would have to grow. This might lead them to a false sense of self-confidence, and the German Government's forces might consolidate in a way which it was not at present possible to forecast, and the ancient pride and boastfulness of Germany might gain a new lease of life. The point under discussion in the morning concerning which no agreement had been reached was the question whether the military terms of peace could be isolated from the other conditions of peace. Peace, it had been said, was one fabric with one pattern. The plan of general disarmament, which had been alluded to, seemed to

[1] The complete text of these notes is printed in *PPC*, III, 1000-12.

render it difficult as a provisional measure to prejudge what should be the relative strengths of national forces. Disarmament contained two elements—(1) the maintenance of an adequate force for internal police; (2) the national contribution to the general force of the future League of Nations. At present we did not contemplate that Germany should make any contribution to the latter force. We need therefore not take that element into consideration. All we need contemplate was the amount of armed force required by Germany to maintain internal order and to keep down Bolshevism. This limit could be fixed by the military advisers. In general, he felt that until we knew what the German Government was going to be, and how the German people were going to behave, the world had a moral right to disarm Germany, and to subject her to a generation of thoughtfulness. He therefore thought it was possible to frame the terms of Germany's disarmament before settling the terms of peace. He was encouraged in this belief by the assurance that the military advisers could produce a plan in 48 hours. It might take more than 48 hours for the heads of Government to agree on this plan. It was not his idea that the armistice should be protracted very much longer, but a definite term could not be fixed until the Governments had matured their judgment concerning the disarmament of Germany. Once this point was settled, the Germans could be given short notice to accede to our demands under pain of having the armistice broken. The main thing was to do this while our forces were so great that our will could not be resisted. The plan he proposed would make safety ante-date the peace. He thought that this brought the two views into accord as regards the purpose in the minds of both parties to the morning's debate.

Before concluding, he wished to draw M. Clemenceau's attention to a statement made by the papers that the French Government had stopped demobilisation.

M. CLEMENCEAU said that this was not true.

PRESIDENT WILSON said that the rumour was general throughout France, and some of his friends on their way to the front had found people much alarmed at the prospect of a renewal of the war. This feeling rendered people uneasy about re-starting their ordinary lives, and these rumours were very much to our disadvantage. He thought it important to put a stop to mischief of this kind. He was himself convinced that the rumours were unfounded but after all the world was full of accomplished liars, and he wished to spoil their game.

He regretted that he had not put his views in the morning in so complete a manner.

M. CLEMENCEAU said that the purpose pursued by President Wilson was exactly the same as his own. He was therefore prepared to accept his proposal. Before doing so, however, he would like more precise information on certain points. We were to ask the experts to state as quickly as possible the conditions of the disarmament of Germany. The American experts, President Wilson had said, were ready. The French were also ready.

MR. BALFOUR remarked that the English were ready, too.

M. CLEMENCEAU said that in these conditions their report could be obtained very soon. But the thought struck him that President Wilson was going away in a few days, and the date of his return was uncertain. Though the report of the experts might be received in a short time, he would not like to discuss a matter of such importance in the absence of President Wilson. Doubtless President Wilson would be away for a month. The delay therefore would be of considerable extent. There would be a further month of demobilisation, and a critical diminution of our forces. He was not discussing the question in principle, but only seeking a way out of the difficulty. At present the armistice was being renewed month by month, but the Allies had a right to break it at any moment after 48 hours' notice. There was not therefore a very great difference between the two systems, save that the one at present enforced was established for a slightly longer period. If the President had been staying, he would have raised no objection to the indeterminate prolongation of the armistice, but, as he was going, the difficulty arose, as he was quite unwilling to discuss the matter while President Wilson was away. He would therefore suggest that things should be left as they were, and that the armistice should be renewed as heretofore. This would not prevent us from giving a stern warning to the Germans at the next renewal that severer conditions would be made at the end of the month. This modification of President Wilson's proposal did not mean any disagreement. It was quite clear that the five Governments were united. In dealing with the Germans, we must be careful not only of the substance, but also of the form. The slightest appearance of hesitation would be immediately interpreted by them as a sign of weakness and an encouragement to make use of it. President Wilson's plan he again wished to repeat satisfied him completely. He only wished to get more precision as to the date.

PRESIDENT WILSON said that M. Clemenceau had paid him an undeserved compliment. In technical matters most of the brains he used were borrowed: the possessors of these brains were in Paris. He would, therefore, go away with an easy mind if he thought that his plan had been adopted in principle. He had complete confidence in the views of his military advisers. If the military experts were to certify a certain figure as furnishing a marginal safety, he would not differ from them. The only other question was to decide whether this was the right time to act. On this point, he was prepared to say yes. In another month's time, the attitude of Germany might be more uncompromising. If his plan were agreed on in principle, he would be prepared to go away and leave it to his colleagues to decide whether the programme drafted by the technical advisors was the right one. He did not wish his absence to stop so important, essential and urgent work as the preparation of a preliminary peace. He hoped to return by the 13th or 15th March, allowing himself only a week in America. But he did not wish that, during his un-avoidable absence, such questions as the territorial question and questions of compensation should be held up. He had asked Colonel House to take his place while he was away.

M. CLEMENCEAU said that he was completely satisfied.

M. PICHON asked whether it would not be possible to obtain the report of the experts before the departure of President Wilson.

LORD MILNER pointed out that the question had already been studied and the figure of 25 divisions had been laid down as the maximum Germany should maintain.

M. ORLANDO said that he was extremely glad of this agreement. He had felt that the difference was rather in the form than in the substance. It remained, however, to decide whether the Armistice should be renewed *sine die* or with a fixed term.

M. CLEMENCEAU said that this question remained open.

M. ORLANDO said it must also be decided whether the Germans were to be given a warning that the reduction of their forces was to be imposed on them. He, himself, had asked Marshal Foch whether the reduction to 25 divisions corresponded to the maximum force which could safely be left to Germany as its final establishment. Marshal Foch had replied in the affirmative. Italy, before the war, had 25 divisions on a peace footing. Germany was a far larger country, and he was therefore inclined to think that 25 divisions must be the minimum required for internal order.

M. SONNINO asked whether there should not be in the Armistice a clause enabling the Allies to exercise some supervision over the disarmament required, and to force the Germans to accept an or-ganisation of this kind.

PRESIDENT WILSON said that the military experts appeared to have means of obtaining knowledge.

M. SONNINO said that Marshal Foch appeared to have doubt on this subject. We should be in a position to obtain week by week, or even day by day, knowledge of the measures taken by Germany to fulfil our demands.

PRESIDENT WILSON said that it might not be possible for the

Governments to make a decision in 48 hours. For instance, the naval programme put up on the previous occasion contained some very "large orders." It would need very careful consideration. The Governments, therefore, could not be ready in time for the next renewal of the Armistice, but unless the Germans were told to be ready for something more drastic on the next occasion, they would think that the Allies were weakening. It would, therefore, he thought, be more prudent to renew the Armistice indefinitely and say that final terms would be put forward at the next renewal. It might not be possible for the Governments to be ready in a month. He, therefore, advocated a renewal *sine die*, coupled with the warning suggested above. The Armistice would then be ended by the formulation of definite preliminary terms of peace on military conditions. The question of the Kiel Canal and the question of the cables, included in the naval report, would have to be dissociated from the purely naval conditions to be imposed at the close of the Armistice. These matters concerned the ultimate peace.

MR. BALFOUR said that, before lunch, he had circulated a series of resolutions which he thought might, perhaps, bring the discussion to a head and meet, perhaps, all the objections raised. Since listening to the discussion, he had re-drafted these resolutions and he proposed to read them, as amended, to the Meeting. Mr. Balfour then read the following:

The Supreme War Council agree that:

(1) As a condition of the renewal of the armistice Marshal Foch shall stipulate that the Germans shall desist from all offensive operations against the Poles, whether in Posen or elsewhere.

(2) The Armistice with Germany shall be renewed for a short period terminable by the Allied and Associated Powers at three days' notice.

(3) Detailed and final naval, military, and air conditions of the preliminaries of peace shall be drawn up at once by a Committee to be presided over by Marshal Foch and submitted for the approval of the Supreme War Council; these, when approved, will be presented for signature to the Germans, and the Germans shall be at once informed that this is the policy of the Associated Governments.

(4) After the signature of these preliminaries of peace, Germany will be permitted to receive such controlled quantities of food, and raw materials for the rehabilitation of her industry, as shall be deemed just, having regard to the prior claims of Allied countries, especially those on whose industries Germany had deliberately inflicted damage.

(5) The question of the quantities of food and raw material to be allowed to Germany after the signature of the preliminaries of peace

shall be referred to the Economic Council for examination and report.

PRESIDENT WILSON questioned whether it would be good policy to forewarn the Germans at the next renewal of the Armistice of the intentions embodied in paragraphs (4) and (5).

M. CLEMENCEAU said that, for his part, he would be very unwilling to do so, as the Allies would seem to be offering the Germans an inducement.

MR. BALFOUR then suggested that only Clauses (1), (2) and (3) should be given to Marshal Foch for communication to the Germans; Clauses (4) & (5) could be accepted by the Governments as fixing their future policy when the military terms of a preliminary peace had been accepted by Germany,

(The above Clauses were then accepted, with the reservation that only Clauses (1), (2) and (3) should be communicated by Marshal Foch to the Germans.)

M. CLEMENCEAU suggested that the military advisers should be summoned and that these clauses should be communicated to them. He pointed out that it would not be sufficient to tell the Germans to reduce their forces to a fixed number of divisions. Napoleon had done this and the Prussians had passed the whole population through the formations allowed them. It was, therefore, essential that the military experts should lay down what was to be Germany's military law. It might, further, be necessary to control those operations by means of High Commissioners appointed by the Allies.

MR. BALFOUR added that a similar provision must be made concerning munitions.

(It was, therefore, decided that, after a short adjournment, the military experts should be summoned.)

2. MR. BALFOUR said that, before adjourning, he wished to draw the attention of the Meeting to two subjects, the first of which was the commission arising out of M. Hymans' statement. He had framed a draft resolution on this subject, which he proposed to read. Mr. Balfour then read the following:

A. That an expert Commission, composed of two representatives each of the United States of America, the British Empire, France, Italy and Japan, be appointed to consider and advise on the following questions arising out of the statement made at the Quai d'Orsay on February 11th., by the Belgian Minister of Foreign Affairs on the claims of Belgium, namely:

(1) The proposed transfer of the town and district of Malmedy to Belgium.

(2) The definite incorporation in Belgium of the town of Moresnet.

(3) The possible rectification in favour of Holland of the German-Dutch frontier on the lower Ems, as a compensation to Holland for meeting Belgian claims in regard to sovereignty over the mouth of the Scheldt and the southern part of Dutch Limburg.

B. That the question of securing for Belgium in times of peace the full rights and liberties which, according to the statement made at the Quai d'Orsay on February 11, by the Belgian Minister of Foreign Affairs, the claims in regard to:

(a) the navigation and control of the waters of the Scheldt in its entire course.

(b) the Ghent-Terneuzen canal, and

(c) the communication by canals and railways between Antwerp and the Rhine and Meuse and Dutch Limburg

be referred to the Commission on the International Control of Ports, Waterways and Railways.

(This resolution was accepted without discussion.)

3. MR. BALFOUR, continuing, said that the second subject to which he wished to draw the attention of the Meeting was the method of dealing with reports sent by the Polish Commission. He proposed to institute a Committee of Experts representing the five Great Powers to follow the work of the Commission and to study the results obtained. This Committee would only send up to the Supreme Council big questions requiring their decision. If all the reports were separately sent to each of the Capitals, confusion would ensue. If all communications came direct to the Council, the Council would be overwhelmed by a quantity of unnecessary material. It was, therefore, desirable to have a Committee to sift this material, to answer the bulk of the correspondence and only refer when necessary to the Council.

(The following resolution was then adopted:

It is agreed that a Committee, composed of one representative each of the Governments of the United States of America, the British Empire, France, Italy and Japan (?), be appointed to deal with all reports and requests for instructions from the Commission sent to Poland. On matters of high policy, the Committee will refer to the Conference of the Associated Powers.)

4. It was further decided that the nominees of the various Governments should be certified to the Secretary-General as soon as possible.

(5) M. CLEMENCEAU said that he had received a demand from the Poles that at the next renewal of the Armistice the Germans should be required to return agricultural implements stolen from the Poles. He felt that as a similar provision had been made in

favour of the French and Belgian peasants, this request could not in fairness be refused.

PRESIDENT WILSON said that, even at the risk of seeming hard-hearted, he thought it would be best not to undertake this. The Poles were technically on German territory. The Allies might have moral right on their side, but the Germans would have the law on theirs.

MR. BALFOUR asked whether it would not be possible to put pressure on the Germans outside the Armistice and say to them: "You cannot expect us to assist you as long as you keep goods stolen from our friends."

PRESIDENT WILSON suggested that this should be referred to the Economic Council.

(6) M. CLEMENCEAU agreed to this provided the question of the return of French cattle should also be referred to that Council.

(It was therefore decided that the question of the return of agricultural implements to the Poles, and the question of the return of French cattle should be referred to the Economic Council.

For recommendations on these subjects see Annexures "A" and "B.")[2]

(7) M. CLEMENCEAU said that there were now Civil Commissioners attached to Marshal Foch. He wished to know whether it was understood that these Civil Commissioners were not to meet the Germans independently. The war was not yet over, and he felt that only soldiers should have direct intercourse with the enemy. The Governments could give orders to Marshal Foch, but on technical questions it would be difficult to give orders to civilian experts.

PRESIDENT WILSON said that he would agree provided that it were well understood that Marshal Foch consulted the Civil Commissioners whenever economic questions arose.

(8) On M. CLEMENCEAU'S proposal it was agreed, without discussion, that the Allies should resume commercial relations with Turkey and Bulgaria.

(The meeting then adjourned for a short time and was resumed on the entry of the military advisers.)

M. CLEMENCEAU read the first 3 clauses of the Resolution concerning the renewal of the Armistice.

(9) MARSHAL FOCH asked whether the first clause should not be made more definite. The expression "or elsewhere" made it difficult to put a stop to offensive operations by the Germans. They might, for instance, undertake movements not directly against the Poles, but in such a manner as to make the position held by the Poles untenable.

[2] These annexures are printed in *ibid.*, pp. 1010-12.

Marshal Foch explained this with the help of a map.

(It was then agreed that Marshal Foch be authorised to settle a line of demarcation between the German and Polish Armies without prejudice to the future frontiers of Germany and Poland.)

PRESIDENT WILSON pointed out that the Poles complained of German action against the civil population as well as against the armed forces.

M. CLEMENCEAU said that this matter could not be settled by Marshal Foch and suggested that if further complaints arose the question should be reconsidered by the Council.

(This was agreed to.)

(10) M. CLEMENCEAU explained the intentions of the Governments in connection with clause 2, and asked the military and naval experts to get to work immediately and to keep in close touch with himself.

(11) PRESIDENT WILSON proposed that the members of the Committee to advise on the disarmament of Germany should be named at once.

(It was decided that the Naval, Military and Air Advisers should sit together in one Committee, which should be composed, in addition to the Commanders-in-Chief, of three representatives from each of the Great Powers.)

The following nominees were then appointed:

United States of America.
> General Bliss.
> Admiral Benson.
> General Mason N. [M.] Patrick.[3]

British Empire.
> General Sir H. H. Wilson
> Admiral Wemyss.
> General Sykes.
> (Or their representatives)

France.
> General Degoutte.
> Admiral de Bon.
> General Duval.[4]

Italy.
> General Cavallero
> Admiral Grassi.
> (& a third to be nominated later)

---

[3] Maj. Gen. Mason Mathews Patrick, Chief of the Air Service, A.E.F., and an adviser on military questions to the A.C.N.P.

[4] Brig. Gen. Marie Victor Charles Maurice Duval, Adjutant General of the French Army and Inspector General of Aviation, at this time an adviser on military questions to the French delegation at the peace conference.

Japan.

(The Japanese delegates remain to be chosen.)

(12) It was agreed that Marshal Foch should obtain from M. Clemenceau the text for the renewal of the Armistice, which should be presented to the Germans.)

(The Meeting then adjourned.)

T MS (SDR, RG 256, 180.03101/37, DNA).

From Norman Hezekiah Davis, with Enclosure

My dear Mr. President: Paris, 12th February, 1919.

In compliance with your message, through Mr. McCormick, a conference was arranged with Messrs. Crespi and Stringher,[1] the Italian Ministers of Food and Treasury. Apparently, the situation is as follows:

1. Italy is not collecting enough taxes to cover fixed charges. This is an internal problem beyond our control.
2. The American Treasury is advancing to Italy all the dollars required to cover approved purchases in the United States. Notice was given last November that on January 1, a monthly allowance of $10,000,000 to cover purchases in neutral countries would be suspended, and this was done on January 1.
3. The British Treasury has discontinued advances to the Italian Government.
4. Italy's pressing requirements are now apparently for the purpose of covering charter hire of neutral and British tonnage and coal and other commodities to be purchased in the United Kingdom, and certain purchases in neutral countries, which, I am led to believe, can, to a great extent, be now met through purchases in the United States.

Their request to us is for advances to cover purchases in neutral countries for the purpose partly of making those purchases and partly of maintaining exchange rates until their export trade in some measure is revived. If this is not done, there will be, they claim, a break in their rate of exchange which would be fatal to a 10,000,000,000 lira domestic loan they propose to issue within the next few months. They also propose to use any advance that we may agree to make for neutral purchases as an argument with the British to get them to continue financial assistance for a short time.

The Secretary of the Treasury has been extremely reluctant to advance funds to any government for purchases out of the United States, among other reasons on account of the attitude of Congress in relation to such loans. He has, however, expressed his willing-

ness to make such advances if you deem them of compelling necessity. Attached hereto is an extract from a cable of the Secretary
of the Treasury, setting forth his position in regard to this matter.

As you are aware, the Secretary of the Treasury desires to have
all matters dealing or connected with advances, other than for relief,
to foreign governments discussed and handled in Washington. This
was explained to the Italian Ministers and they have wired their
representative in Washington to present the entire matter to the
Secretary there. We informed the Italian Ministers that we would,
however, explain the situation to you as they presented it to us so
that, if you felt it desirable, you might cable to the Secretary of the
Treasury such views as you entertain in the matter.

In our opinion, the removal of the blockade in southeastern Europe should assist Italy's export trade. Mr. McCormick has no doubt
explained to you the difficulties that have arisen in the raising of
the blockade in various quarters of the globe. Mr. Hoover's representatives, who have just returned from the southeastern part of
Europe, report that the Italian Army is not demobilized, and that
they are using their funds to make trouble in that region. I would
respectfully suggest, therefore, that before giving the weight of your
support to the Italian request, you may wish to make representations in regard to the demobilization of the Italian Army. It is probably important that the exchange rate should be maintained so that
there may be no break until Italy can revive her export trade, particularly not while they are bringing out their loan, but our granting
assistance in this respect may easily be made the occasion, if you
so desire, of compelling reasonable action by them in connection
with political matters. The Italians state they will be perfectly satisfied if we agree to advance the sum of $25,000,000 for neutral
purchases. This, however, would be of little practical assistance to
them, unless the British credit is restored to cover some very essential purchases, such as coal from the British Empire and the
payment for ships which would even be required to carry the commodities they wish to purchase with the funds received from us. I
am therefore suggesting to Secretary Glass the advisability of making such an advance, conditional upon the British assistance.

To facilitate your consideration of the matter, I enclose a draft
cable from you to the Secretary,[2] in case you desire to recommend
the matter.

Cordially and respectfully yours,   Norman H. Davis

TLS (WP, DLC).
[1] Bonaldo Stringher.
[2] This enclosure is missing; however, see WW to C. Glass, Feb. 19, 1919.

ENCLOSURE

Extract of a cable from Secretary Glass to Mr. Davis, relative to Treasury's policy as to advances for expenditures without the United States:

Jan. 21 1919
Treasury 727

"Second. While Treasury has authority to make advances to Allied Governments for expenditures without the United States I consider it very inadvisable to confer that authority. At the outset Congressional committees were informed our loans were to be expanded in the United States. Later when exigencies of war required relaxation of that rule they were informed that relatively small proportion of our loans represented purchases without United States. Present policy of Treasury to loan only for United States expenditures is generally understood in Congress. A departure from this policy might be serious, our expenditures having reached a tremendous amount and monthly cash disbursements are higher than ever before. To raise amounts that Treasury must obtain is requiring the greatest effort particularly as patriotic stimulus afforded by active prosecution of war is now lacking. I cannot approve increasing heavy burdens of Treasury by making loans for expenditures without United States except under most compelling urgency. To do so would likewise imperil legislation. We are seeking to authorize making loans for the United States for reconstruction purposes. This legislation is most important in interests of United States, as it will enable establishment of Government credits with which to move our surplus production to extent. It is found impossible to provide private credits for that purpose and thus avoid disturbance of our industrial and commercial balance.

"Third. I regard it as important that President should be fully informed of reasons why Treasury is most reluctant to make loans for expenditures without United States. If other considerations determine President to adopt policy requiring Treasury to make such advances Treasury to fullest extent of its legal powers will heartily cooperate."

T MS (WP, DLC).

From Alfred George Gardiner

Dear Mr. President,   London, E. C. Feb. 12/19

I am greatly flattered by your kind appreciation of the suggestions I offered in regard to the Covenant.[1] It was a high privilege that you permitted me to exercise & I need not say that I have no more sincere wish than to do anything in my power, either now or later, to forward the great task you have in hand. I trust you will not regard some of the manifestations in this country in regard to that task as representing the feeling of the overwhelming body of the plain people of this, or, I believe of any other country. That feeling is behind you in mingled hope & gratitude. I am, dear Mr. President,   Yours gratefully   A G Gardiner

ALS (WP, DLC).
¹ See A. G. Gardiner to WW, Feb. 1, 1919, Vol. 54. Wilson's reply is missing.

From Lord Curzon

My dear Mr President   [London] Feb. 12 1919

The University authorities and I are extremely loth to abandon the hope of seeing you at Oxford this summer and we are presumptuous enough to think that you may yourself share the feeling.

Further, regarding the prospect of your return to France as very bright, I venture myself to ask your permission to let the matter stand over till then

No doubt your return journey will not admit of a visit to England on the way. But when the labours of the Conference are over, I cling to the belief that you may be both able and willing to come again to our shores.

It will be for you to say whether you can then find time to address us—a task as Asquith and I endeavoured to point out, of no great burden. But in any case we shall hope to see you at Oxford for the Degree   I will therefore take the liberty of addressing you again at some date after your return.

I am   yours very sincerely   Curzon

ALS (WP, DLC).

Two Letters from Herbert Clark Hoover

Dear Mr. President: Paris, February 12, 1919.

I enclose herewith a proposed Executive Order under the recent Food Relief Bill creating the American Relief Administration. I have not yet received from the United States the full title or date of the passage of this Food Relief Bill and it is therefore necessary to ask you to sign the order with these blank, to be filled in as soon as cable advices can be received from the United States.

I am particularly anxious that the order specifically authorize the use of the Food Administration Grain Corporation as an agency for relief because I feel certain that the use of an existing organization will eliminate the necessity of establishing a complicated machinery relating to relief only.

I should therefore be obliged if you would sign the enclosed Executive Order and return to me either the original or the duplicate.   Faithfully yours,   Herbert Hoover.

TLS (WP, DLC).

Dear Mr. President: Paris, 12 February 1919.

The feeding of the Czecho-Slovenes, Viennese and Serbians all revolves around the use of port facilities and a single railway running out of Trieste. The Italians have taken such an attitude towards these other peoples that the operation of the railway is practically hopeless for the distance that it traverses Italian occupied territory. They have also stopped all communication through to Trieste from these territories and we are not even able to send the most commonplace telegrams with regard to food. They are apparently driving all of the other races than Italians out of Trieste and the consequence is that we have little reliable labor for discharging ships.

We have used every argument possible with the Italian authorities and there is in my view but one solution; that is, that the operation of such docks and railways as we need for feeding these interior people shall be placed under the direction of the Interallied Food Commission sitting at Trieste and the actual executive control vested in the American member. Their attitude on this question and many others is such that I want to protest most strongly against any further Treasury advances to the Italian Government until this matter of fearful injustice is put right. If you approve, I will ask Mr. Davis to make it a condition of further advances with the Treasury that this situation shall be straightened out to my satisfaction.
                    Faithfully yours,   Herbert Hoover

CCL (WP, DLC).

From Charles Michael Schwab

My dear Mr. President,   Paris, February 12th 1919

As an American manufacturer and business man, and as one in entire sympathy with your policies and plans, I presume to write you. In my opinion, which is shared by most of my associates, the business situation at home is critical and some co-operative methods of conducting manufacture and business is necessary during this transition period, otherwise I fear disaster. Mr. Baruch who so ably conducted the War Industries Board and as its Chairman won the confidence of American manufacturers could do more than any other man to help organize some co-operative method of procedure. I hope you can see your way to temporarily relieve him of his important duties here and allow him to return to America for conference with our manufacturers with the above object in view. I cannot too strongly state to you how important I regard this step.

Permit me, Mr. President, to congratulate you upon the wonderful work you are doing for the United States and Humanity. You have the approval of American businessmen and confidence in your policy is growing daily in all directions. Needless to say you have no stronger supporter than the undersigned.

Sincerely yours   C. M. Schwab

TLS (WP, DLC).

From the Diary of David Hunter Miller[1]

Wednesday, February 12th [1919]

After getting ready my papers I went to the meeting of the Committee of Four—Lord Robert Cecil, Veniselos, Vesnitch, and Larnaude.

The Committee considered and went through the draft during the morning but reached difficulties with the French, who proposed amendments regarding an international armed force. Finally, Cecil, saying that he was speaking very frankly but in private, said: that America had nothing to gain from the League of Nations; that she could let European affairs go and take care of her own; the offer that was made by America for support was practically a present to France, and that to a certain but to a lesser extent this was the position of Great Britain which, while vitally interested in continental affairs, yet to a certain extent could stand apart. Accordingly, he wished to say very frankly to the French delegates that in his view they were saying to America, and to a lesser extent to Great Britain, that because more was not offered they would not take the gift that was at hand, and he warned them very frankly that the alternative offer which we have made, if the League of Nations was not successful, was an alliance between Great Britain and the United States. He asked them to consider this before they made any final conclusion. At this the meeting adjourned for lunch.

I stopped to see Colonel House about the whole situation as it seemed to me of considerable importance, but as he was not in I went to the Quai d'Orsay to see President Wilson, who had a meeting there at three o'clock. President Wilson came in with M. Pichon, and I tried to see him then, not knowing that it was a ceremonial entry, but the President said that he would come out in a moment and talk to me, which he did. I then told the President very briefly what Lord Robert Cecil had said, and I told him also that it was proposed to amend the Preamble very extensively and asked him his view on that, to which he replied that he did not favor it. He thought that it would be a mistake, and I told him that I would communicate that to the Committee of Four. I told him also that I had taken the responsibility of disapproving the suggestion in the morning of dividing the covenant into chapters and articles, and he approved of my course. I then told him that the question of time was very pressing and asked him what plans he wished regarding the presentation of the final text. He said that if possible he would like to have it tomorrow morning but that he did not intend to go before the Plenary Conference but rather to ask for the appointment of a sub-commission to lay the matter before the Neutrals. I told the President that I would do my best to see that his wishes were carried out, and then proceeded again to the meeting of the Committee of Four, at which I was late. The Committee proceeded with its revision and I informed them of the view of the President regarding the Preamble and also of his intentions regarding the sub-commission.

At 5 o'clock the Committee rose and requested that Mr. Hurst and myself should confer as to clerical changes, which accordingly we did in Mr. Hurst's rooms until 8 o'clock, arriving at a final agreement at 8 o'clock. Mr. Hurst pressed me to agree to changes in Article new number XIX, old number XVII, which I refused to do. I then proceeded to have the draft printed.

Lord Eustace Percy telephoned me as to some changes which I agreed to and made a note of. He said they were desired by Lord Robert Cecil, and I made one or two trifling changes in reading the proofs.

Professor Shotwell came in to my office during the evening and read some of the proof to me.

I wrote a formal letter to the President,[2] sending him six texts, another letter to Mr. Hurst, sending him six texts, and I also wrote a memorandum to the President giving the comparison with the draft as adopted by the Commission up to the close of its previous meeting.

I left the printing office at 5:15 A.M. with 103 copies of the draft.

Miller, *My Diary at the Conference of Paris*, I, 119-21.
[1] The following entry seems to have been written early in the morning of February 13 principally about events of the day before.

From the Peace Conference Diary of Florence Haskell Corliss Lamont[1]

Paris Feb 12 [1919]

It was reported on good authority, that W.W. called the representatives of the Press together, & said that he was dead sick, fed up, etc. with the intense anti Wilson propaganda that was going on. He felt that if it did not stop, another city or country would have to be found for the Peace Conference. This was to have appeared in the morning papers, but was censored out. There was a large, white, empty space in the Herald. We are told that it did get over to England & America.

Hw MS (T. W. Lamont Papers, MH-BA).
[1] Mrs. Thomas William Lamont.

From the Diary of Dr. Grayson

Thursday, February 13, 1919

Today President Wilson went to the Hotel Crillon in the morning to attend the league of nations committee session. In the afternoon he attended the war council session while the league committee continued its sessions in his absence, finally cleaning up the draft of the covenant which was unanimously approved by the committee, thus making President's lucky 13th score again. Incidentally the league articles number twice 13 or 26. This completes the second month in France, the President having landed on December 13, at Brest.

Minutes of Two Meetings of the Commission on the League of Nations

NINTH MEETING, FEBRUARY 13, 1919, AT 10:30 A.M.
President WILSON *in the Chair.*
Second Reading of the Covenant.

The Covenant, as reported back from the Drafting Committee, appears as Annex 2.

Mr. Bourgeois asked if the second reading was about to begin, and if the articles would be put to the vote. If this were the case, then it would be in order to offer amendments, and the outcome of the voting should be indicated in the Minutes.

This procedure was agreed upon.

Lord Robert Cecil read the Preamble.

Mr. Larnaude suggested that the Preamble should be amended, to begin with the following words: "The Powers signatory to the present Covenant, unanimous in condemning those who visited upon the world the war just ended, firmly resolved to determine the issue of responsibility therefor, yet at the same time desiring to formulate the rules of an international order, whose primary object shall be that of preventing the resurgence of armed force save in the defence of right, desiring likewise to establish the reign of justice throughout the world and to maintain a scrupulous regard for international engagements, continuing and enlarging upon the work begun by The Hague Conference."

Mr. Batalha Reis said that the League of Nations, being a work of union and concord between peoples, which should prepare a future of peace, he would not like to see its Covenant begin by words of condemnation and punishment. Other nations would soon join the League. How could those nations which remained neutral during the war accept the Preamble of our Covenant if it were in the terms proposed by the French Delegates?

With regard to the reference to The Hague Conference Mr. Batalha Reis wished to insert the following declaration in the Minutes:

The Portuguese Delegate regrets that the Commission did not think it advisable to make international arbitration obligatory at least for cases of a judicial order, thus continuing the work of The Hague Conference of 1899 and 1907. This was proposed by the Portuguese Delegation in 1907, and is virtually contained in Article 73 of the Portuguese Constitution, which says:

"The Portuguese Republic, without prejudice to what is established in its Treaties of Alliance, proclaims the principle of arbitration as the best for the resolution of international conflicts."

Lord Robert Cecil felt that the question of responsibility for the war was an extremely controversial one, which should not be introduced into the text. As far as The Hague Conference was concerned, he thought that the League of Nations might better stand by itself and not bear the burden of the criticisms which have been levelled against international conventions however highly the whole world might regard them.

President Wilson, noting that the portion of the amendment which dealt with the question of responsibilities had been withdrawn, called for a vote on that part which referred to the work of The Hague.

The amendment was rejected by a vote of ten to five.

It was understood that this vote in no wise indicated that the Commission was opposed to the two ideas elaborated in Mr. Larnaude's amendment; merely that the Commission considered it inexpedient to write them into the Covenant.

The preamble was adopted.

ARTICLE 1.

This article was adopted.

ARTICLE 2.

General Smuts proposed the following amendment with a view to satisfying that element of public opinion which desired that the Body of Delegates might include representatives of the leading social groups:

"At least once in four years, an extraordinary meeting of the Body of Delegates shall be held, which shall include representatives of national parliaments and other bodies representative of public opinion, in accordance with a scheme to be drawn up by the Executive Council."

Lord Robert Cecil believed that it would be better, before making such a departure, to wait until public opinion had expressed its desires a little more clearly, and until the Covenant had been read to the Conference in plenary session.

Mr. Larnaude remarked that since Article 2 put no restriction upon the manner of choosing representatives, General Smuts' point was covered.

President Wilson was likewise of the opinion that it would be inadvisable to modify the article, since it was sufficiently flexible to permit of the later introduction of a system wholly satisfactory to public opinion.

Mr. Hymans emphasised the necessity of deciding upon the maximum number of representatives from each State. Unless this was done, he said, some States would be represented by Delegations whose number and influence in the Assembly would be wholly out of proportion to those of certain other States. More than that, if too many representatives were admitted, dissensions would arise within each Delegation itself. If there were a great number of Delegates, the League would find itself saddled with an universal parliament, so to speak, before which every man of political aspirations would be eager to deliver an oration. Furthermore, certain countries, like Belgium for example, exhibited very distinct groups, such as the agricultural class and the industrial class. If representation were given to one of these social groups, it would be necessary to give it to all the others. The only way to avoid offending anyone would be to have a small number of competent representatives chosen irrespective of party affiliations.

Lord Robert Cecil said that each Power might be represented as it saw fit. He thought it likely that England, for example, might send a leader of the Labour Party, someone who would be the spokesman of religious interests, and, he hoped, a woman.

President Wilson observed that representatives would be chosen by the State which should, in choosing, make a point of satisfying public opinion. The Government's representatives would thus be true representatives of the people at large.

Mr. Bourgeois was of the opinion that the Delegates would certainly represent the prevailing opinion of the majority of their fellow citizens. The Government would be responsible for its choice, and if it was mistaken it would promptly be advised of that fact by public opinion.

Mr. Hymans felt that Lord Robert Cecil's plan was an ideal one. He also felt that if a beginning was made of giving representation to social groups it would end up with an international parliament holding yearly meetings. Presently the custom would grow up of bringing all sorts of questions before the League of Nations, and in that way its scope of action would be too widely extended. Last of all, elections would take place and the international parliament would no longer bear any relation to the present conception of the Body of Delegates.

Mr. Orlando believed that it was necessary that each State should have the right to send the same number of representatives. As far as the issue raised by General Smuts was concerned he thought that it would be preferable to let it work itself out within the Body of Delegates.

After an exchange of opinion in which Senator Scialoja, Lord Robert Cecil, Mr. Batalha Reis, Mr. Bourgeois, Mr. Vesnitch, and Mr. Larnaude took part, a proposal that the maximum number of representatives for each High Contracting Party be fixed at five was put to the vote by President Wilson. It was rejected. Three was agreed upon as the maximum number of Delegates to be attributed to each State.

It was agreed that the following words should be added at the end of the article: "Each of the High Contracting Parties shall have one vote but may not have more than three representatives."

The article was then adopted.

ARTICLE 3.

Mr. Pessoa declared once again that he could not accept the organisation of the Executive Council in the way shown in the present article. After extending the considerations made at the time of the first reading of the draft, he added that it was clear that the question could not be settled entirely by the rigorous principles of law. The injunctions of political reason must also be considered. But it was neither equitable nor just that nations which were not considered Great Powers should have a representation which did not amount even to one Delegate per continent. Mr. Pessoa therefore suggested that the original draft, at least, should be adopted, since it allowed five Delegates for the Great Powers and four for the others.

Mr. Veniselos urged the Commission to accept four as the number of representatives to be given to States with special interests.

Lord Robert Cecil accepted four as the number, but insisted that this decision should be unanimously supported before the Conference by all the States represented on the Commission.

Mr. Batalha Reis accepted for the time being the number of four representatives, but he could not pledge his Government to this view.

Mr. Pessoa observed that it was not reasonable that the Delegates of the Great Powers should be appointed directly by them, while those of the small nations were elected by the Assembly of Delegates, that is to say, under the influence and with the collaboration of the great States. The executive power of the League must come from one single source. It could not be conceived that some of its members should be chosen by the States themselves, while others were chosen by the Assembly. Such an organisation would be an hybrid one.

Mr. Hymans likewise agreed; he foresaw complications, however, on the day when States, which might be called "intermediate," should be admitted into the League, since this would lead toward the exclusion of the small Powers.

Lord Robert Cecil was of opinion that it would be advisable to leave a certain elasticity in the text, so that the difficulties to which Mr. Hymans referred might be avoided. Certainly if the Executive Council were too large the League of Nations would be handicapped. The Body of Delegates would choose the small States which were to be represented on the Executive Council, and these States would name their own Delegates.

Mr. Bourgeois remarked that nine as the number of representatives on the Council might be changed under certain circumstances, but that the chief thing was to maintain due proportion between the Great and Small Powers, as expressed in the relation of five to four, *i.e.* a majority of one.

Mr. Hymans thought that it would be better if they were not bound by a principle or by a rule fixed in advance.

Mr. Veniselos accepted the principle of a majority of one for the Great Powers.

President Wilson remarked that the League would be qualified to deal with questions which should arise in the future. He then called for a vote on Article 3.

This article was adopted.

It was understood that the Peace Conference would name the

four States whose representatives were to be the original members of the Executive Council.

ARTICLE 4.

President Wilson read Article 4.

This article was adopted.

ARTICLE 5.

President Wilson read Article 5 (formerly Article 4), in which the word "Secretary-General" was substituted for the word "Chancellor."

This article was adopted.

ARTICLE 6.

President Wilson read Article 6 (formerly Article 5).

This article was adopted.

ARTICLE 7.

President Wilson read Article 7 (formerly Article 6).

Lord Robert Cecil observed that the draft of the French amendment had been adopted in the second paragraph of this article.

A discussion then took place upon the meaning of the words "pays libres."

Mr. Larnaude remarked that this expression was employed by writers on constitutional law to describe a State whose institutions were democratic or liberal. In any case it was used in regard to the internal constitution of the State, and was less accurate than the English expression "self-government," which was commonly used.

Any French translation of this expression would have to be paraphrased as "countries whose institutions are founded on political liberty."

Mr. Orlando agreed with the observations of Mr. Larnaude, and said that in Italian law the expression "pays libres" was used in the same sense—its meaning being clear, and understood to refer to the internal freedom of States.

The expression "fully self-governing countries" was admitted to be the most exact. Its French equivalent would be "pays de self-government total."

Lord Robert Cecil accepted the article on the understanding that India would be admitted to the League as a signatory to the Covenant.

President Wilson replied that this interpretation had already been put upon the article.

General Smuts asked whether or not neutral Powers which should adhere to the Covenant would be considered on the same basis as the original signatories?

President Wilson replied that the League was formed solely by the Allied and Associated Powers, but that the conditions of admission of other States would not be such as to exclude those who sincerely desired to join the League of Nations.

He then read the suggestion made in this connection by Lord Robert Cecil, that there be added at the end of Article 7, after the words "the admission to the League of States not signatory to the present Covenant," the words "and not named in the Protocol hereto as States to be invited to adhere to the Covenant."

Mr. Bourgeois remarked that it would be a very delicate matter to draw up a list of invitations of this sort, and that such a procedure would necessarily involve a classification of neutral Powers. On the other hand it might be imagined that some neutrals, such as Switzerland, would not accept the invitation of the Conference. So it would appear advisable not to draw up a list of those to be invited, but hold to the general conditions of admission as set forth in the article.

Following an exchange of views between Mr. Hymans, Mr. Larnaude and Mr. Orlando, *Mr. Bourgeois* recalled the fact that the scheme of the League embraced three stages: First, the organisation of the League by the Allies; second, the inclusion in the Treaty of Peace of special conditions, such as disarmament; finally, after peace, the convocation of an international conference, including all nations admitted into the fellowship of the League of Nations.

Mr. Larnaude stated that the essential thing was the imposition of severe conditions on those nations which could not be trusted. Such nations as these would have to secure a two-thirds vote in order to be admitted. As for neutral Powers, the question of their admission would have to be considered in a broad way, and distinctions could hardly be drawn between them.

Following these observations, the amendment proposed by Lord Robert Cecil was put to the vote and adopted.

President Wilson regretted that he would be unable to attend the next meeting since it conflicted with a meeting of the Council of Ten which he had to attend.

He asked the Commission to continue its work that afternoon under the chairmanship of Lord Robert Cecil.

(*The Meeting adjourned at 1 o'clock to resume its discussions at* 3:30 *P.M.*)

Annex 1 to Minutes of Ninth Meeting.
REPORT OF THE DRAFTING COMMITTEE.
ARTICLE 2.

For the words "the Ambassadors or Ministers" substitute the word "representatives." Omit the words after "High Contracting Parties."

ARTICLE 3.

Omit the word "the" before "representatives" (seventh word of the article).

For the words "together with * * * representatives of the other States" substitute the words "together with representatives of * * * other States."

ARTICLE 4.

In this article and throughout the Covenant for the word "Chancellor" substitute the words "Secretary-General."

After the words "Secretary-General of the League" change the wording as follows:

"Who shall be chosen by the Executive Council. The Secretariat shall be appointed by the Secretary-General, subject to confirmation by the Executive Council."

For the words "distribution among members of the Universal Postal Union" substitute the word "apportionment."

The Committee considered the question of the Seat of the League, and contemplated the possibility of locating the Seat at Geneva.

ARTICLE 6.

Substitute the following draft:

"Admission to the League of States not signatories of the Covenant shall require the assent of not less than two-thirds of the States represented in the Body of Delegates, and shall be limited to free countries, including dominions and colonies.

"No State shall be admitted, unless it is able to give effective guarantees of its sincere intention to observe its international obligations, and unless it shall conform to such principles as may be prescribed by the League in regard to its naval and military forces and armaments."

The Committee considered whether it would be possible to bring the League into more direct relations with the peoples of the States members of the League. They found great difficulty in devising any satisfactory plan for the purpose, and they do not recommend the inclusion in the Covenant of any article of this kind at the present moment. If, when the scheme is laid before the public, there should be manifested a strong feeling that something of the kind should be done, the matter might be reconsidered. It is suggested that reference to the point might be made when the Convention is proposed to the plenary Conference.

ARTICLE 7.

After the words "in case of any such aggression" insert the words "and in case of any threat or danger of such aggression."

For the words "the plan and" substitute the word "upon."

ARTICLE 8.

After the word "obligations" in the first sentence, insert the words "having special regard to the geographical situation and circumstance of each State."

For the second paragraph substitute the following draft:

"The High Contracting Parties further agree that the manufacture by private enterprise of munitions and implements of war lends itself to grave objections, and direct the Executive Council to advise how the evil effects attendant upon such manufacture can be prevented.

"The High Contracting Parties further undertake, by means of a full and frank publicity, in no way to conceal either the condition of such of their industries as are capable of being adapted to warlike purposes, or the scale of their armaments, and of their military and naval programmes."

Add a new article after article 8, as follows:

"A permanent Commission shall be constituted to advise the League on all military and naval questions."

ARTICLE 9.

Insert after the word "anywhere" the words "concerning international intercourse."

ARTICLE 10.

For the words "armed forces," in both places where they occur, substitute the words "any act of war."

ARTICLE 11.

After the words "the whole subject matter to arbitration" insert a full stop. Then insert the last paragraph of the article, "for this purpose * * * between them." Then conclude as follows:

"The High Contracting Parties undertake that they will carry out in full good faith any award or decision that may be rendered. In the event of any failure to comply with this undertaking, the Executive Council shall propose what steps can best be taken to give effect to the award or decision."

Similarly, the word "propose" should be substituted for the word "consider" in the third sentence of the second paragraph of Article 13.

ARTICLE 16.

For the words "entrust to the League" substitute the words "agree that the League should be entrusted with."

ARTICLE 17.

First paragraph, for the words "in consequence of" substitute the words "as a consequence of."

For the words "not able" substitute the words "not yet able."

ARTICLE 18.

For the word "commission" substitute the word "bureau."

ARTICLE 19.

The Committee feel that, in view of the complications of this question, it would be preferable to omit this article altogether. If, however, there is a strong feeling in the Commission that some such provision should be inserted, they suggest the following drafting:

"The High Contracting Parties agree that they will not prohibit or interfere with the free exercise of any creed, religion or belief whose practices are not inconsistent with public order or public morals, and that no person within their respective jurisdictions shall be molested in life, liberty, or the pursuit of happiness by reason of his adherence to any such creed, religion, or belief."

ARTICLE 21.

For the words "every treaty" substitute the words "every future treaty."

For the word "operative" substitute the word "binding."

ARTICLE 24.

For the words "a three-fourths' majority" substitute the word "three-fourths."

The Committee suggest the addition of the following new article:

ARTICLE 25.

"The High Contracting Parties agree to place under the control of the League all international bureaux already established by general treaties if the parties to such treaties consent. Furthermore, they agree that all such international bureaux to be constituted in future shall be placed under the supervision of the League."

Annex 2 to Minutes of Ninth Meeting.

COVENANT.

Preamble.

In order to promote international co-operation and to secure international peace and security by the acceptance of obligations not to resort to war, by the prescription of open, just and honourable relations between nations, by the firm establishment of the understandings of international law as the actual rule of conduct among governments, and by the maintenance of justice and a scrupulous respect for all treaty obligations in the dealings of organized peoples with one another, the Powers signatory to this Covenant adopt this constitution of the League of Nations.

ARTICLE I.

The action of the High Contracting Parties under the terms of this Covenant shall be effected through the instrumentality of meetings of a Body of Delegates representing the High Contracting Parties, of meetings of more frequent intervals of an Executive

Council, and of a permanent international Secretariat to be established at the Seat of the League.

ARTICLE 2.

Meetings of the Body of Delegates shall be held at stated intervals, and from time to time as occasion may require for the purpose of dealing with matters within the sphere of action of the League. Meetings of the Body of Delegates shall be held at the Seat of the League, or at such other place as may be found convenient, and shall consist of representatives of the High Contracting Parties.

ARTICLE 3.

The Executive Council shall consist of representatives of the United States of America, the British Empire, France, Italy and Japan, together with representatives of [blank] other States members of the League, appointed by the Body of Delegates on such principles and in such manner as they think fit. Pending the appointment of these representatives of the other States, representatives of [blank] shall be members of the Executive Council.

Meetings of the Council shall be held from time to time as occasion may require, and at least once a year at whatever place may be decided on, or failing any such decision, at the Seat of the League, and any matter within the sphere of action of the League or affecting the peace of the world may be dealt with at such meetings.

Invitations shall be sent to any Power to attend a meeting of the Council at which matters directly affecting its interests are to be discussed, and no decision taken at any meeting will be binding on such Power unless so invited.

ARTICLE 4.

All matters of procedure at meetings of the Body of Delegates or the Executive Council, including the appointment of Committees to investigate particular matters, shall be regulated by the Body of Delegates or the Executive Council, and may be decided by a majority of the States represented at the meeting.

The first meeting of the Body of Delegates and of the Executive Council shall be summoned by the President of the United States of America.

ARTICLE 5.

The permanent Secretariat of the League shall be established at [blank] which shall constitute the Seat of the League. The Secretariat shall comprise such secretaries and staff as may be required, under the general direction and control of a Secretary-General of the League, who shall be chosen by the Executive Council; the Secretariat shall be appointed by the Secretary-General, subject to confirmation by the Executive Council.

The Secretary-General shall act in that capacity at all meetings of the Body of Delegates or of the Executive Council.

The expenses of the Secretariat shall be borne by the States members of the League, in accordance with the apportionment of the expenses of the International Bureau of the Universal Postal Union.

ARTICLE 6.

Representatives of the High Contracting Parties and officials of the League when engaged on the business of the League shall enjoy diplomatic privileges and immunities, and the buildings occupied by the League or its officials, or by representatives attending its meetings, shall enjoy the benefits of extraterritoriality.

ARTICLE 7.

Admission to the League of States not signatory of the Covenant requires the assent of not less than two-thirds of the States represented in the Body of Delegates, and shall be limited to free countries, including Dominions and Colonies.

No State shall be admitted to the League unless it is able to give effective guarantees of its sincere intention to observe its international obligations, and unless it shall conform to such principles as may be prescribed by the League in regard to its naval and military forces and armaments.

ARTICLE 8.

The High Contracting Parties recognize the principle that the maintenance of peace will require the reduction of national armaments to the lowest point consistent with national safety and the enforcement by common action of international obligations, having special regard to the geographical situation and circumstances of each State; and the Executive Council shall formulate plans for effecting such reduction. The Executive Council shall also determine for the consideration and action of the several governments what military equipment and armament is fair and reasonable in proportion to the scale of forces laid down in the programme of disarmament; and these limits, when adopted, shall not be exceeded without the permission of the Executive Council.

The High Contracting Parties agree that the manufacture by private enterprise of munitions and implements of war lends itself to grave objections, and direct the Executive Council to advise how the evil effects attendant upon such manufacture can be prevented (due regard being paid in such recommendations to the necessities of those countries which are not able to manufacture for themselves the munitions necessary for their safety).

The High Contracting Parties undertake in no way to conceal from each other the condition of such of their industries as are capable of being adapted to war-like purposes or the scale of their armaments, and agree that there shall be full and frank publicity as to their military and naval programmes.

ARTICLE 9.

A permanent Commission shall be constituted to advise the League on military and naval questions.

ARTICLE 10.

The High Contracting Parties undertake to respect and preserve as against external aggression the territorial integrity and existing political independence of all States members of the League. In case of any such aggression, or in case of any threat of danger of such aggression the Executive Council shall advise upon the means by which this obligation shall be fulfilled.

ARTICLE 11.

Any war or threat of war, whether immediately affecting any of the High Contracting Parties or not, is hereby declared a matter of concern to the League, and the High Contracting Parties reserve the right to take any action that may be deemed wise and effectual to safeguard the peace of the nations.

It is hereby also declared and agreed to be the friendly right of each of the High Contracting Parties to draw the attention of the Body of Delegates or of the Executive Council to any circumstances affecting international intercourse which threaten to disturb international peace or the good understanding between nations upon which peace depends.

ARTICLE 12.

The High Contracting Parties agree that should disputes arise between them which cannot be adjusted by the ordinary processes of diplomacy, they will in no case resort to war without previously submitting the questions and matters involved either to arbitration or to inquiry by the Executive Council, and until three months after the award by the arbitrators or a recommendation by the Executive Council; and that they will not even then resort to war as against a member of the League which complies with the award of the arbitrators or the recommendation of the Executive Council.

In any case under this Article the award of the arbitrators shall be made within a reasonable time, and the recommendation of the Executive Council shall be made within six months after the submission of the dispute.

ARTICLE 13.

The High Contracting Parties agree that whenever any dispute or difficulty shall arise between them which they recognize to be suitable for submission to arbitration, and which cannot be satisfactorily settled by diplomacy, they will submit the whole matter to arbitration. For this purpose the Court of arbitration to which the case is referred shall be the court agreed on by the parties or stipulated in any Convention existing between them. The High Contracting Parties agree that they will carry out in full good faith any award that may be rendered. In the event of any failure to carry out the award, the Executive Council shall propose what steps can best be taken to give effect thereto.

ARTICLE 14.

The Executive Council shall formulate plans for the establishment of a Permanent Court of International Justice, and this Court shall when established, be competent to hear and determine any matter which the parties recognize as suitable for submission to it for arbitration under the foregoing Article.

ARTICLE 15.

If there should arise between States members of the League any dispute likely to lead to a rupture, which is not submitted to arbitration as above, the High Contracting Parties agree that they will refer the matter to the Executive Council; either party to the dispute may give notice of the existence of the dispute to the Secretary-General, who will make all necessary arrangements for a full investigation and consideration thereof. For this purpose the parties agree to communicate to the Secretary-General, as promptly as possible, statements of their case with all the relevant facts and papers, and the Executive Council may forthwith direct the publication thereof.

Where the efforts of the Council lead to the settlement of the dispute, a statement shall be published indicating the nature of the dispute and the terms of settlement, together with such explanations as may be appropriate. If the dispute has not been settled, a report by the Council shall be published, setting forth with all necessary facts and explanations the recommendation which the Council think just and proper for the settlement of the dispute. If the report is unanimously agreed to by the members of the Council other than the parties to the dispute, the High Contracting Parties agree that they will not go to war with any party which complies with the recommendation, and that, if any parties shall refuse so to comply, the Council shall propose the measures necessary to give effect to the recommendation. If no such unanimous report can be made, it shall be the duty of the majority and the privilege of the minority to issue statements indicating what they believe to be the facts, and containing the recommendations which they consider to be just and proper.

The Executive Council may in any case under this article refer the dispute to the Body of Delegates. The dispute shall be so referred at the request of either party to the dispute, provided that such request must be made within fourteen days after the submission of the dispute. In any case referred to the Body of Delegates all the provisions of this article relating to the action and powers of the Executive Council shall apply to the action and powers of the Body of Delegates.

ARTICLE 16.

Should any of the High Contracting Parties break or disregard its covenants under Article 12, it shall thereby *ipso facto* be deemed to have committed an act of war against all the other members of the League, which hereby undertake immediately to subject it to the severance of all trade or financial relations, the prohibition of all intercourse between their nationals and the nationals of the covenant-breaking State, and the prevention of all financial, commercial, or personal intercourse between the nationals of the covenant-breaking State and the nationals of any other State, whether a member of the League or not.

It shall be the duty of the Executive Council in such case to recommend what effective military or naval force the members of the League shall severally contribute to the armed forces to be used to protect the covenants of the League.

The High Contracting Parties agree, further, that they will mutually support one another in the financial and economic measures which are taken under this article, in order to minimize the loss and inconvenience resulting from the above measures, and that they will mutually support one another in resisting any special measures aimed at one of their number by the covenant-breaking State, and that they will afford passage through their territory to the forces of any of the High Contracting Parties who are co-operating to protect the covenants of the League.

ARTICLE 17.

In the event of disputes between one State member of the League and another State which is not a member of the League, or between States not members of the League, the High Contracting Parties agree that the State or States not members of the League shall be invited to accept the obligations of membership in the League for the purposes of such dispute, upon such conditions as the Executive Council may deem just, and upon acceptance of any such invitation, the above provisions shall be applied with such modifications as may be deemed necessary by the League.

Upon such invitation being given the Executive Council shall immediately institute an inquiry into the circumstances and merits of the dispute, and recommend such action as may seem best and most effectual in the circumstances.

In the event of a Power so invited refusing to accept the obligations of membership in the League for the purposes of such dispute, and taking any action against a State member of the League, which in the case of a State member of the League would constitute a breach of Article 12, the provisions of Article 16 shall be applicable as against the State taking such action.

If both parties to the dispute, when so invited, refuse to accept the obligations of membership in the League for the purposes of such dispute, the Executive Council may take such action and make such recommendations as will prevent hostilities and will result in the settlement of the dispute.

ARTICLE 18.

The High Contracting Parties agree that the League shall be entrusted with the general supervision of the trade in arms and ammunition with the countries in which the control of this traffic is necessary in the common interest.

ARTICLE 19.

To those colonies and territories which, as a consequence of the late war have ceased to be under the sovereignty of the States which formerly governed them, and which are inhabited by peoples not yet able to stand by themselves under the strenuous conditions of the modern world, there should be applied the principle that the well-being and development of such peoples form a sacred trust of civilization, and that securities for the performance of this trust should be embodied in the constitution of the League.

The best method of giving practical effect to this principle is that the tutelage of such peoples should be entrusted to advanced nations, who, by reason of their resources, their experience, or their geographical position, can best undertake this responsibility, and that this tutelage should be exercised by them as mandatories on behalf of the League.

The character of the mandate must differ according to the stage of the development of the people, the geographical situation of the territory, its economic conditions, and other similar circumstances.

Certain communities formerly belonging to the Turkish Empire have reached a stage of development where their existence as independent nations can be provisionally recognized subject to the rendering of administrative advice and assistance by a mandatory Power until such time as they are able to stand alone. The wishes of these communities must be a principal consideration in the selection of the mandatory Power.

Other peoples, especially those of Central Africa, are at such a stage that the mandatory must be responsible for the administration of the territory subject to conditions which will guarantee freedom of conscience or religion, subject only to the maintenance of public order and morals, the prohibition of abuses such as the slave trade, the arms traffic and the liquor traffic, and the prevention of the establishment of fortifications or military and naval bases and of military training of the natives for other than police purposes and the defence of territory, and will also secure equal opportunities for the trade and commerce of other members of the League.

There are territories, such as South-West Africa and certain of the South Pacific Islands, which, owing to the sparseness of their population, or their small size, or their remoteness from the centres of civilization, or their geographical contiguity to the mandatory State, and other circumstances, can be best administered under the laws of the mandatory State as integral portions thereof, subject to the safeguards above-mentioned in the interests of the indigenous population.

In every case of mandate, the mandatory State shall render to the League an annual report in reference to the territory committed to its charge.

The degree of authority, control, or administration to be exercised by the mandatory State shall, if not previously agreed upon by the High Contracting Parties, in each case be explicitly defined by the Executive Council in a special Act or Charter.

The High Contracting Parties further agree to establish at the seat of the League a Mandatory Commission to receive and examine the annual reports of the Mandatory Powers, and to assist the League in ensuring the observance of the terms of all Mandates.

ARTICLE 20.

The High Contracting Parties will endeavour to secure and maintain fair and humane conditions of labour for men, women and children both in their own countries and in all countries to which their commercial and industrial relations extend; and to that end agree to establish as part of the organization of the League a permanent Bureau of Labour.

ARTICLE 21.

The High Contracting Parties agree that they will not prohibit or interfere with the free exercise of any creed, religion or belief whose practices are not inconsistent with public order or public morals, and that no person within their respective jurisdictions shall be molested in life, liberty, or the pursuit of happiness by reason of his adherence to any such creed, religion or belief.

ARTICLE 22.

The High Contracting Parties agree that provision shall be made through the instrumentality of the League to secure and maintain freedom of transit and equitable treatment for the commerce of all States, members of the League, having in mind, among other things, special arrangements with regard to the necessities of the regions devastated during the war of 1914-1918.

ARTICLE 23.

The High Contracting Parties agree to place under the control of the League all international bureaux already established by general treaties if the parties to such treaties consent. Furthermore, they agree that all such international bureaux to be constituted in future shall be placed under the control of the League.

ARTICLE 24.

The High Contracting Parties agree that every treaty or international engagement entered into hereafter by any State member of the League shall be forthwith registered with the Secretary-General, and as soon as possible published by him, and that no such treaty or international engagement shall be binding until so registered.

ARTICLE 25.

It shall be the right of the Body of Delegates from time to time to advise the reconsideration by States members of the League, of treaties which have become inapplicable, and of international conditions of which the continuance may endanger the peace of the world.

ARTICLE 26.

The High Contracting Parties severally agree that the present Covenant is accepted as abrogating all obligations *inter se* which are inconsistent with the terms thereof, and solemnly engage that they will not hereafter enter into any engagements inconsistent with the terms thereof.

In case any of the Powers signatory hereto or subsequently admitted to the League shall, before becoming a party to this Covenant, have undertaken any obligations which are inconsistent with the terms of this Covenant, it shall be the duty of such Power to take immediate steps to procure its release from such obligations.

ARTICLE 27.

Amendments to this Covenant will take effect when ratified by the States whose representatives compose the Executive Council and by three-fourths of the States whose representatives compose the Body of Delegates.

TENTH MEETING, FEBRUARY 13, 1919, AT 3:30 P.M.
Lord Robert Cecil *in the Chair*.

. . . *Lord Robert Cecil* read Article 21.

Colonel House wished to make known to the Commission the importance which President Wilson attached to the inclusion of this article.

Mr. Larnaude, while appreciating the importance which might attach to a proclamation of the inviolability of the human conscience and the exercise of religion, nevertheless thought it difficult to include a clause on the matter. In any case, the anxieties of President Wilson related to countries which were not members of the actual League.

Baron Makino read the following note:

"The additional clause I am about to propose, I consider as coming appropriately under Article 21. It is not necessary to dwell on the fact that racial and religious animosities have constituted a fruitful source of trouble and warfare among different peoples throughout history, often leading to deplorable excesses. This article, as it stands, attempts to eliminate religious causes of strife from international relationship, and as the race question is also a standing difficulty which may become acute and dangerous at any moment in the future, it is desirable that a provision should be made in this Covenant for the treatment of this subject. It would seem that matters of religion and race could well go together. I wish to add the clause:

"The equality of nations being a basic principle of the League of Nations, the High Contracting Parties agree to accord, as soon as possible, to all alien nationals of States members of the League, equal and just treatment in every respect, making no distinction, either in law or fact, on account of their race or nationality."

directly after the end of the article as it stands. That race discrimination still exists, in law and in fact, is undeniable, and it is enough here simply to state the fact of its existence. I am aware of the difficult circumstances that stand in the way of acting on the principle embodied in this clause, but I do not think it insurmountable if sufficient importance is attached to the consideration of serious misunderstanding between different peoples, which may grow to an uncontrollable degree, and it is hoped that the matter may be taken in hand at such an opportunity as the present. What was deemed impossible before is about to be accomplished. The creation of this League itself, which the efforts of many generations of the best minds failed to accomplish, is a notable example. If this organisation can open a way to the solution of the question, the scope of the work will become wider and enlist the interest of a still greater part of humanity.

"It must be admitted, at the same time, that the question of race prejudice is a very delicate and complicated matter, involving play of deep human passion, and therefore requiring careful management. This consideration has not been overlooked from a practical point of view, and an immediate realisation of the ideal equality of treatment between peoples is not proposed. The clause enunciates the principle of equality, and leaves the working out of it in the hands of the responsible leaders of the States members of the League, who will not neglect the state of public opinion. This clause, in a way, may be regarded as an invitation to the Governments and peoples concerned to examine the question more closely and seriously, and to devise some acceptable means to meet a deadlock which at present confronts different peoples.

"As the result of this war, the wave of national and democratic spirit has extended to remote corners of the world, and has given additional impulse to the aspirations of all peoples; this impulse, once set in motion as part of the universal movement with renewed strength, cannot be stifled, and it would be imprudent to treat this symptom lightly.

"There are other considerations of a more direct nature which merit earnest thought. The future States members of the League, comprising all kind of races, constitute a great family of nations. It is in a sense a world organisation of insurance against aggression and war. If one member's independence and political integrity is menaced by a third Power, a nation or nations suitably placed must be prepared to take up arms against the aggressor, and there are also cases of enforcing common obligation which would entail contribution of armed force. These are indeed serious obligations to which each State member, in accordance with its capability and power, mutually pledges itself, and must be prepared to fulfil them for the benefit of their brother nations. This means that a citizen of one nation must be ready to share the military expenditure for the common cause and, if need be, defend other peoples by his own person. Seeing these new duties arising before him as the result of his country's entering the League, each national would like to feel and in fact demand that he should be placed on an equal footing with people he undertakes to defend even with his life.

"In this war, to attain the common cause, different races have fought together on the battlefield, in the trenches, on the high seas, and they have helped each other and brought succor to the disabled, and have saved the lives of their fellow men irrespective of racial differences, and a common bond of sympathy and gratitude has been established to an extent never before experienced. I think it only just that after this common suffering and deliverance the principle at least of equality among men should be admitted and be made the basis of future intercourse."

Lord Robert Cecil remarked that this subject had been dealt with in long and difficult discussions. It was a question which had raised extremely serious problems within the British Empire. It was a matter of a highly controversial character, and in spite of the nobility of thought which inspired Baron Makino, he thought that it would be wiser for the moment to postpone its examination.

Mr. Koo stated that the Chinese Government and people were deeply interested in the question brought up by Baron Makino, adding that he was naturally in full sympathy with the spirit of the proposed amendment. But pending the receipt of instructions from his Government, he would reserve his right of discussion for the future, and request that the reservation be recorded in the Minutes.

Mr. Veniselos was of the opinion that questions of race and religion would certainly be dealt with in the future by the League of Nations, but that it would be better for the moment not to allude to them.

Several members of the Commission agreed with this view.

Colonel House said that he would inform President Wilson of the opinion of the Commission on this matter, and that in any case he would reserve the right of the President to raise the question again at the Conference.

With this reservation, Article 21 was dropped from the Covenant. . . .[1]

Printed copy (WP, DLC).
[1] Cecil continued reading the balance of the articles, and the entire Covenant, with the exception of Article 21, was approved and spread upon the minutes. Wilson read the Covenant verbatim in his address to the plenary conference printed at February 14, 1919, hence it is not printed here.

Hankey's Notes of a Meeting of the Council of Ten[1]

Quai d'Orsay, February 13, 1919, 3 P.M.

BC-31

[The names were announced of members of the Committee on Poland and the Committee on Belgium.]

2. M. ORLANDO asked permission to make a statement in connection with the decision taken yesterday on the subject of the immediate disarmament of Germany. The import of that decision would be to anticipate the final disarmament of Germany, for it was not intended to renew the Armistice but to draw up and accept the military terms of the eventual peace treaty. The decision reached in regard to Germany raised the analogous question of Italy and Austria-Hungary, the question which was of particular importance to Italy. He quite realised that the two cases were not altogether analogous, especially as the old Austro-Hungarian Empire no longer existed and had been replaced by a number of nationalities, some

[1] The complete texts of these minutes and of the statement by Chekri Ganem are printed in *PPC*, III, 1013-38.

friendly, and some hostile to the Allies. But, as a question of form, Italian public opinion might not passively accept the situation, which was open to the interpretation that on the Western front peace had been declared, whereas on the Italian front, a state of war still existed. He was anxious to prevent the spread of such an impression. He wished, therefore, to suggest that the Inter-Allied Military Commission, appointed to draw up the military terms of peace with Germany, should be instructed also to study the similar question as between Italy and Austria-Hungary. He did not suggest that the decision in regard to the German terms should in any way be altered or delayed; but he did ask that the Italian military advisors should be authorised to bring the question of the Austrian military terms before the Inter-Allied Military Commission.

PRESIDENT WILSON expressed the view that M. Orlando had made a reasonable and right request; the suggestion had already occurred to him and he gladly accepted M. Orlando's proposal.

(It was agreed:

That the conditions of the Armistice with Austria-Hungary should be examined by the military Inter-Allied Committee, assembled under the Presidency of Marshal Foch, in accordance with the decision of the Supreme War Council, dated 12th February, 1919, with a view to determine what changes, if any, were necessary in order to arrive at the final military terms of peace with Austria-Hungary, following the procedure adopted in the case of Germany.)

(At this stage Dr. Bliss[2] entered the Council Chamber.)

3. M. CLEMENCEAU welcomed Dr. Bliss and called on him to make his statement.

Dr. Bliss then read the following statement:

"Mr. President, Gentlemen,

I shall not detain you long. My deep interest in the people of Syria, irrespective of race, creed or condition, bred from a long residence among them—in fact I was born on Mt. Lebanon—is my only excuse for detaining you at all.

First, a preliminary word as to the people themselves. They are intelligent, able, hospitable and lovable, but with the sure defects of a long oppressed race: timidity, love of flattery, indirectness. They also have the defects characteristic of people who are face to face with the results of civilisation without having passed through the processes of modern civilisation. They lack balance, they are easily discouraged, they lack political fairness, they do not easily recognise the limitations of their own rights. They must therefore be ap-

[2] That is, Howard Sweetser Bliss.

proached with sympathy, firmness and patience. They are capable of nobly responding to the right appeal. And they will grow into capacity for self-determination and independence.

My plea before this body on behalf of the people of Syria is this: that an Inter-Allied or a Neutral Commission, or a Mixed Commission, be sent at once to Syria in order to give an opportunity to the people of Syria—including the Lebanon—to express in a perfectly untrammelled way their political wishes and aspirations, viz: as to what form of Government they desire and as to what power, if any, should be their Mandatory Protecting Power.

My plan is based upon the ground that the 12th point of President Wilson's 14 points and the declarations made by France and Great Britain in November, 1918, have committed the Allies and the United States to the granting of such an opportunity of self-expression to the people freed from the Turkish yoke to so express themselves. The declaration is as follows:

'The aim which France and Great Britain have in view in waging in the East the war let loose upon the world by German ambition is to ensure the complete and final emancipation of all those peoples so long oppressed by Turks, and to establish national Governments and Administration which shall derive their authority from the initiative and free will of the peoples themselves. To realise this France and Great Britain are in agreement to encourage and assist the establishment of Native Governments in Syria and Mesopotamia, now liberated by the Allies, as also in those territories for whose liberation they are striving and to recognise those Governments immediately they are effectively established. Far from wishing to impose on the peoples of these regions this or that institution they have no other care than to assure, by their support and practical aid, the normal working of such governments and administrations as the peoples shall themselves have adopted: to guarantee impartial and even justice for all, to facilitate the economic development of the country by arousing and encouraging local initiative, to foster the spread of education, to put an end to those factions too long exploited by Turkish policy—such is the part which the two Allied Governments have set themselves to play in liberated territories.'

I maintain that such an opportunity for self expression has not as yet been given. Up to the time I left Beirut, viz: January 9th, 1919, the stringency of the censorship of the Press and of the Post Office, the difficulty of holding public or private meetings for the discussion of political problems, and the great obstacles in travelling, had made it practically impossible for the people, suffering from centuries of intimidation, and now timid to a degree, to express their opinions with any sort of freedom. It is true that a Lebanese delegation has succeeded in reaching Paris and is here to-day. I know these gentlemen, several of whom are my pupils, but there are many other groups besides this particular delegation, including other groups from the Lebanon, who would have gladly been here to speak for themselves and others had they been as fortunate as this group in being able to organise themselves and to find the means of travelling hither.

The point is this. Up to January 9th (the date of my leaving) no notice of any arrangements had been published anywhere in Syria, so far as I know, looking to anything like a general poll of the people of Syria (always including the Lebanon) or even anything like an attempt had been made to secure a widespread knowledge of public sentiment. I did hear more or less of a list of names that was being made up attached to various petitions in favour of this or that programme, but although in a position to hear of any Official or thorough or systematic general plan to ascertain the wishes of the people, no such report came to my knowledge. Many interested citizens of Beirut and the Lebanon were never approached for the purpose of ascertaining their political desires.

I therefore plead that the above mentioned Commission should be sent out as soon as possible by the Peace Conference with ample powers given to them and of course with the wholehearted support granted to them by the French and British authorities now in Syria. The ascertaining of the desires of the people should proceed either without the presence of any foreign Power (and this is impracticable) or in the presence of both French and British Authorities under whom Syria has been living for the past four months.

The people are easily frightened and intimidated even where there is nothing to fear from any source; hence these precautions. The advantage of knowing what the people wish would be a boon to the power eventually becoming the Mandatory power as well as to the people of Syria. One word as to the work of the Commission. Their task will not be an easy one. They must approach it, in my opinion, in the spirit of large sympathy, infinite patience, frankness and goodwill. In the hands of fair and openminded men, resourceful, shrewd and generous—men who can make clear their honest purpose to a timid but intelligent people—very valuable results can be secured. The result of this enquiry will be, I am convinced, the discovery of the desire for the erection of a state or states looking eventually to complete independence but at present seeking the guardianship of a Mandatory Power.

Both the state or states and the Mandatory Power should be under the control of the League of Nations. Unless in this state or states there should be an absolute separation between religion and the state, most serious results must inevitably arise. The Government on the one hand, religion on the other, can best pursue their majestic tasks apart. Surely Oriental if not general history is making that abundantly clear.

One word more. Unless the Mandatory Power working under the League of Nations approaches its great task in the spirit of lofty service, her splendid opportunity to lead an aspiring people to independence will be for ever lost. But once let the same superb spirit sustain her and the League of Nations as has animated the Allies and the United States in working together for the establishment of freedom in the world, the task, though difficult, will be accomplished."

[In response to questions by Pichon and Balfour, Bliss said that he thought that similar considerations applied to other populations and religions which had been living under Ottoman rule, but that he could speak from personal knowledge only of Syria. Balfour and Milner then asked about the effects of the British censorship.]

DR. BLISS replied that the facts were that those—the bolder men among the people—who tried to express their opinions were not able to do so on account of the stringency of the censorship. Consequently, if a Commission were sent to Syria to ascertain the wishes of the people, it should pursue its work freed from the preventive force due to the censorship of press and post-office. He himself was present at that meeting simply to plead for a principle; the determination of the wishes of the people. He did not ask that his own word should be taken, or that of anybody else; but in view of the fact that no opportunity had yet been given to the people to express their views, he thought the only solution would be the appointment of an Inter-Allied Commission, whose duty it would be to find the true opinion of the people. Those who lived in Syria would gladly accept a Mandatory Power, feeling that they had thereby been given an opportunity; and they would honestly work with the Mandatory Power, whether French, American or British, in the best possible way, feeling confidence in the fact that the promise held out to the people to express themselves had been fulfilled. Otherwise, if the opportunity, which the people had a right to claim in view of President Wilson's 12th Point and the Franco-British Declaration of 1918, were not given, the probable outcome would be discontent, sullenness, resentment and even bloodshed.

MR. BALFOUR pointed out that anybody reading the evidence given by Dr. Bliss would suppose that the British censorship had been exercised to prevent opinions unfavourable to Great Britain being expressed. If this was a correct interpretation of Dr. Bliss' statement an enquiry should be held. On the other hand, if the statement was incorrect, it should be contradicted.

DR. BLISS replied that the censorship of the papers published in Beirut was exercised by the French military authorities, and he presumed that the censorship arrangements had been carried out by the local authorities with the approval of General Allenby. But the effect of the censorship was that the people did not feel that they had a free opportunity of expressing themselves and his plea was that something should be done to enable them to have that free opportunity.

LORD MILNER said that he still felt some uneasiness as to what had been said, especially as a matter of national honour was involved. The impression left in his mind was that the British censorship was being used to suppress the expression of pro-French or other non-British sympathies.

DR. BLISS replied in the negative. The censorship was being used to suppress the expression of all opinions.

LORD MILNER agreed but insisted that the point was whether he, Dr. Bliss, thought the censorship had the effect of suppressing one opinion rather than another. Great Britain was, for the moment, the predominant military power in Syria and exercised the right of censorship. Did Dr. Bliss consider that the British Military Authority had used its powers in order to influence opinion in a special pro-British direction?

DR. BLISS replied that quite the contrary was the case. The existence of the censorship, however, made it difficult for the people to give proper expression to any views.

(Dr. Bliss having completed his evidence was invited to remain in the Council Chamber during the discussion of the Syrian question.)

[The members of the Syrian Commission[3] entered the chamber and were introduced. Clemenceau called on Chekri Ganem to make his statement. It was then agreed to adjourn the further hearing of the Syrian question to a later date.]

(5) PRESIDENT WILSON asked permission to make a statement on the question of women representation. He had recently received a visit from a group of ladies, representing the suffrage associations of the Allied countries who had assembled here in Paris, under the Chairmanship of Mrs. Fawcett of Great Britain.[4] These ladies had brought him a resolution, and had asked him to bring it to the

[3] Chekri Ganem, Anis Schenade, Jamil Mardam Bey, Georges Samne, Nejil Bey Maikarzel, and Tewfik Farhi.

[4] Millicent Garrett (Mrs. Henry) Fawcett, former president of the National Union of Women's Suffrage Societies. In her autobiography, *What I Remember* (London and New York, 1925), pp. 253-55, she very briefly describes her group's meetings with Wilson and other Allied leaders in Paris but does not provide any dates. The meetings probably took place in early February. For other very brief accounts of the group's activities, see the *New York Times*, Feb. 13, 14, 15, and 18, 1919.

notice of the Conference. The resolution contained a proposal to the effect that a Conference of women should be appointed to consider the conditions of children and women throughout the world. He sincerely desired to give effect to the views expressed by the representatives of the Suffrage Associations of the Allied countries. He wished, therefore, to enquire whether the Conference would agree to the appointment of a Commission consisting of one representative of each of the five Great Powers and four representatives of the Smaller Powers to report on the conditions and legislation concerning women and children throughout the world, and to determine whether any international regulations should be issued. This Commission to be entitled to invite the suffrage associations of the Allied countries to nominate some of its members to attend in an advisory and consultative capacity.

M. CLEMENCEAU enquired whether the question could not be referred to the existing Inter-Allied Commission on International Labour Legislation.

PRESIDENT WILSON thought that M. Clemenceau's proposal would hardly give satisfaction to the Suffrage Associations, as they asked for recognition. He did not wish to urge this against the opinion of the Conference, but in his judgment recognition should be given.

MAHARAJA BIKANER expressed the view that the question raised by President Wilson would present considerable difficulties in all oriental countries, for reasons which it would be unnecessary for him to explain at the present moment.

PRESIDENT WILSON agreed that the enquiry should be restricted to European countries and America.

M. CLEMENCEAU said he had no objections to offer to an enquiry being carried out into the conditions of woman and child labour; but he would strongly object to any enquiry being held into the political status of women.

PRESIDENT WILSON pointed out that the women were chiefly interested in the latter question.

MR. BALFOUR said he had long been in favour of woman suffrage, but he felt considerable alarm at the thought that the Peace Conference should extend its activities to a consideration of that question.

BARON MAKINO remarked that there had been a suffrage movement in Japan, but it was insignificant.

BARON SONNINO pointed out that the Inter-Allied Commission on International Labour and Legislation had already enquired into matters relating to women and children, with the exception of the Suffrage question. He, personally, was in favour of woman suffrage, but he did not think it would be good politics to take up this question at the present moment. He thought interference by the Peace Conference would hardly lead to good results.

PRESIDENT WILSON said that he did not wish to press the matter unless there was a chance of obtaining practical unanimity. Under the circumstances, therefore, he would withdraw his proposal.

(President Wilson's proposal regarding women's position in the world was withdrawn.)

(6) PRESIDENT WILSON reported that the Committee to formulate plans for the League of Nations hoped to complete their labours that night. He wished to suggest, therefore, that a call be prepared for a Plenary Conference to be held tomorrow afternoon for the submission of the scheme and in order that full explanations might be given. The conclusions reached by the Commission would very quickly become generally known, and, therefore, in his opinion, the final draft should be placed at once before the Plenary Conference. He asked, therefore, that a notice be prepared for issue on the following morning, if the Commission's report were then found to be ready for submission to the Plenary Conference.

M. CLEMENCEAU enquired whether it was not intended that the report should, in the first place, be submitted for consideration to the Conference of the Great Powers. According to President Wilson's proposal the Plenary Conference would receive the report before it had been examined by the present meeting.

PRESIDENT WILSON replied that in the ordinary course of events the best plan would perhaps have been to circulate the Commission's report in the first place to the Conference of the Great Powers. He would point out, however, that the League of Nations Commission was not a Commission of the Conference of the Great Powers but of the Plenary Conference. Consequently, the first report ought, as a matter of fact, to go to the Plenary Conference. In accordance with his proposal the Plenary Conference would be asked to receive the report, and the Chairman of the Commission would then give the necessary explanations. That is to say, the report would be submitted by himself, and some of his colleagues on the Commission would subsequently give additional explanations.

MR. BALFOUR thought that it would be a great advantage if President Wilson could explain the scheme to the Plenary Conference before he left for the United States of America. He would do this as Chairman of the League of Nations Commission and not as a member of the Conference of the Great Powers. The members of the latter Conference would not be committed to the scheme in any way. He, therefore, saw no objection to President Wilson's proposal.

M. CLEMENCEAU understood the proposal to be that the report of the League of Nations Commission would be presented to the Plenary Conference by its chairman (President Wilson), who would give certain explanations, after which the Conference would adjourn.

PRESIDENT WILSON agreed that this was his proposal, though he did not quite know how other members of the Plenary Conference could be stopped from making speeches if they wished to do so. But in any case no decision would be taken.

(It was agreed that a Plenary Conference should, if possible, be held at 3:30 p.m. on the afternoon of Friday, 14th February, 1919, in order to place before it the report of the League of Nations Commission. It was agreed that individual notices to this effect should be issued to each of the Delegates to the Peace Conference.)

(The Meeting then adjourned.)

T MS (SDR, RG 256, 180.03101/38, DNA).

From David Hunter Miller

Paris, February 13th, 1919.

MEMORANDUM FOR THE PRESIDENT:

Last Saturday the Supreme War Council set up the "Supreme Economic Council" to deal with questions of Finance, Food, Blockade Control, Shipping and Raw Materials.

Our representatives here in Europe dealing with these matters are the following:

1. Finance—Norman H. Davis;
2. Food—Herbert Hoover;
3. Blockade Control—Vance C. McCormick;
4. Shipping—Edward N. Hurley—in his absence Mr. Robinson;[1]
5. Raw Materials—Bernard M. Baruch.

I suggest that you designate these gentlemen to represent the United States on the Supreme Economic Council, each to be Chairman of that particular branch of the work of the Council as he represents.

CC MS (D. H. Miller Papers, DLC).
[1] That is, Henry M. Robinson.

To Raymond Poincaré

My dear Mr. President: Paris, 13 February 1919.

I do not feel that I can leave France for home without expressing to you my appreciation of the many courtesies which I have received, and I am writing to ask if you will not accept the enclosed autographed photograph as an evidence of my deep appreciation.

Cordially and sincerely yours,   [Woodrow Wilson][1]

CCL (WP, DLC).
[1] Wilson wrote similar letters on this date to Georges Clemenceau, Henri Philippe Benoni Omer Joseph Pétain, Stéphen Jean Marie Pichon, Joseph Jacques Césaire Joffre, Georges Jean Claude Leygues, and Richard William Martin, the chief of protocol of the French Foreign Ministry. All are CCL (WP, DLC).

To Robert Lansing

My dear Lansing: Paris, 13 February, 1919.

I do not think that it would be wise for me to intervene in this, but I do think it desirable that you should advise Polk to keep up the utmost pressure to see that this thing is not acted on at this Congress.[1]

Cordially and faithfully yours,   [Woodrow Wilson]

CCL (WP, DLC).
[1] About this matter, see the two documents printed as addenda in this volume.

To John Joseph Pershing

My dear General Pershing: Paris, 13 February, 1919.

Thank you very warmly for your letter of February 10th. I should feel guilty if I drew you away from your duties to accompany me to Brest, although I know your willingness to do anything of that kind that would be courteous and generous.

As for the criticisms about conditions at Brest, I have received one newspaper cablegram which I am having referred to you. I have no doubt you will know how to handle it in making your report to the War Department. I rather hesitate to take a hasty glance at the conditions in Brest because it would have to be so hasty that I could not really give any valuable testimony with regard to it, but you may be sure that I am depending on you with perfect confidence to making everything right there, if there is anything wrong.

My cordial best wishes. I hope not to be gone very long.

Cordially and sincerely yours,   Woodrow Wilson

TLS (J. J. Pershing Papers, DLC).

Tasker Howard Bliss to Newton Diehl Baker and Peyton Conway March

Paris [Feb. 13, 1919][1]

Number 309. Confidential. For the Secretary of War and Chief of Staff. The President directs me to cable you the following. The British Government is very anxious to send to Murmansk a force of about 2400 troops. These will comprise one operating company and one maintenance company and necessary detail of railway troops amounting to a total of 720 men; 688 engineers, ordinance, medical and other technical troops; and about 1000 pioneers. They have asked President Wilson to contribute the two companies of railway troops amounting to 720 men. The British will furnish the rest of the force. They say that this force is necessary to immediately put the railway south from Murmansk in reasonably efficient condition and to operate it. This railway is built largely over a bog and work on it can be done only when it is frozen as is the case now. Supplies and reenforcements for Archangel during the winter have to go by the railroad south from Murmansk to a point near southern extreme of White Sea. There they have to be freighted overland to Archangel. The improvement and operation of this railroad is stated by the British to be absolutely necessary to guarantee prompt movement of reenforcements to Archangel and for the more comfortable supply of allied troops south of Archangel. The British apparently do not feel any apprehension as to the military situation at Archangel. A most important object gained by the improvements of the railroad will be the greater facilities for the withdrawal of the expedition in the spring. The President has approved the sending of two American railway companies to Murmansk for the following objects: First, to assure greater safety during this winter of the allied forces both along Murmansk and at Archangel and south of Archangel; second, the much better supply and if necessary the reenforcement from Murmansk of the advanced detachments south of Murmansk and Archangel; third, to facilitate the prompt withdrawal of American and Allied troops in North Russia at the earliest possible moment that the weather conditions in the spring will permit. The President has directed me to communicate the foregoing to the heads of the Allied Governments which I have done. A copy of the memorandum approved by him goes to you by courier tomorrow. The President desires that his action and the reasons for it to be communicated to the Military Committees of the Senate *and House* for their information.   Bliss.

TC telegram (WDR, RG 407, World War I Cablegrams, DNA).
    [1] This cablegram was sent from Paris on February 14 and was received at the War Department in the morning of February 15, 1919.

Gilbert Fairchild Close to John Joseph Pershing

My dear General Pershing: Paris, 13 February, 1919.

The President asks me to send you the enclosed cable message received from the New York Evening Telegram with regard to conditions existing at the camp at Brest.[1] The President asks if you will not be kind enough to have a report on this matter made to the Secretary of War, explaining that it is in response to a request from the New York Evening Telegram.

Sincerely yours,   Gilbert F. Close

TLS (J. J. Pershing Papers, DLC).
[1] New York *Evening Telegram* to WW, Feb. 12, 1919, T telegram (J. J. Pershing Papers, DLC). The writer said that "hundreds of complaints" had been received about filthy conditions and poor treatment of soldiers at the United States Army camp at Brest and urged Wilson either to inspect the camp and remedy the abuses "costing the lives of many American soldiers" or to have the camp abolished altogether.

Gilbert Fairchild Close to Herbert Clark Hoover

My dear Mr. Hoover: Paris, 13 February, 1919.

The President asks me to acknowledge your note of February 11th,[1] and to ask if you will not be kind enough to suggest to the Belgian Prime Minister that he take these questions up with Secretary Lansing. The President would wish to give them the most mature consideration and that is really out of the question during these last busy days before he leaves for America.

Sincerely yours,   [Gilbert F. Close]

CCL (WP, DLC).
[1] HCH to WW, Feb. 11, 1919.

A Translation of a Letter from William Emmanuel Rappard to Hans Sulzer

My dear Minister: Paris, February 13, 1919.

. . . The Rhine question, which is equally under discussion here, will be, I fear, also settled out of hand without our official intervention. The most that we could hope to attain would be for us to make our views known to the interested commission by the instrumentality of some experts. President Wilson, in the course of a conversation of forty minutes which I had with him yesterday evening, told me how much he was resolved on this question in a sense favorable to our interests. But he rejected my proposition that we be authorized to be represented on the commission on navigable waterways by a member of our government. It would not be appropriate, he told me, that one of our ministers should appear here before the bar of a tribunal composed of judges who for most part would be of a rank inferior to his own. He urged me to see once more Mr. Lansing and Mr. White on this subject on his behalf and thus to see to it that a federal commission of experts should be at least convened in Paris in order to be heard on the subject of the Rhine.

3d This question of the Rhine, so far as I have been able to ascertain here, is as follows:

The French, in order to mine the potash beds of Alsace, dream of building a dam between Basel and Strasbourg and thereby to capture the hydraulic force of the stream. This project, contrary not only to the principle of our free access to the sea, but also to the treaties of 1815 and 1868, is not well viewed by the English and Americans, insofar as I have been able to determine. I fear, however, that this is one of those points on which the Anglo-Americans will resign themselves in order to give satisfaction to their allies. It will be necessary to do everything to prevent it. . . . President Wilson has not revealed to me his sentiment in this matter. . . .

4th Colonel House, in a very confidential way, has permitted me to read the plan relative to the League of Nations, which will be published within a few days. This plan will without doubt be a deception of all the partisans of an international order truly new and pacific. It is infinitely less radical and less complete than the one which we drew up at Territet[1] and the text of which will be sent to you, I think, by this same courier.

The Allied plan has, however, a very great advantage for us. It would permit Switzerland to enter the League of Nations without renouncing its traditional military neutrality. President Wilson told me yesterday evening that he did not doubt that if, in asking to be admitted to the League, we should ask at the same time, in exchange for the international services which Switzerland could render to the League, to be exempted from participation in offensive military operations against a recalcitrant, this double request could not be rejected. I pass over the question whether the federal government would want to ask for membership in a league so unfinished in structure. On all sides, it is a question of Switzerland, and notably Geneva, being the seat of the capital of the League. President Wilson repeated to me once more yesterday that this would be his preference. . . .

As you will no doubt have been apprised in the United States, the great surprise at the conference has been the Anglo-American *entente cordiale*, on the one side, and the very strong Franco-Amer-

ican tension, on the other. The reciprocal animosity between French
and American is truly very profound and very general. The Americans complain of a narrowness of view, of a national egotism, of a
passivity, and of an economic weakness among the French whose
idealism has become for them a myth.

For their part, the French do not hide their bad humor at the
preponderant influence which the Anglo-Americans exercise at the
conference. It is difficult to be precise in explaining their grounds
of complaint. They speak a great deal about the high cost of living
which, they say, is due to their guests from overseas. They reproach
the latter for having an attitude much too kindly toward their ancient enemies, and one even sees reborn among them the old leg-
ends of the Germanophiles, according to which the United States
would have entered the war only in order to look after its own
interests.

At the bottom, I attribute the bad humor of the French essentially
to their desire, still not avowed in official circles, to use their victory
in order to make annexations. . . .

President Wilson is personally completely beside himself. "Stupid, petty, insane"—such are the epithets by which he characterized their attitude in my conversation with him. France, he says to
me, must be the most bureaucratic country in the world; in this
regard, it is worse than Prussia was. Wilson is particularly indignant
over the efforts made by the French government to stir up public
opinion against his policy. Concerning this, he showed me a paper
containing the confidential instructions which the French government had given to the large newspapers. Here are the three points
which the French government had insisted upon in this curious
document which Wilson said he had received from an absolutely
reliable source:

a) Insist upon the power of Republican opinion in the United
   States.
b) Exaggerate the impression of chaos in Russia.
c) Pretend to believe in a renewed offensive by Germany.

Mr. Wilson's voice vibrated with indignation while showing me
this document. I do not wish yet to publish this, he tells me; but
I am accumulating my ammunition, and if they push me to the
wall, they will see very well who has the last word in the debate.
His great preoccupation seems to be French public opinion. To
what point the opinion of his policies is confined to governmental
spheres, to what point is it shared by the French nation itself?

He asked me this question several times, and it was very difficult
to respond. It is certain that the sector of the extreme left are still
favorable to Wilson, although I fear that the publication of the plan

of the League of Nations can only have the effect of chilling their enthusiasm a little. But everyone whom one meets in Paris no longer hides their opposition to President Wilson. . . .

Always Yours, cordially and sincerely

[William E. Rappard]

CCL (J.1.149 Mission Paris 1919 [I-III], Swiss Federal Archives).
¹ A village near Montreux.

From the Diary of David Hunter Miller

Thursday, February 13th [1919]

There were two meetings of the Commission on the League of Nations today, both of which I attended, from 10:30 A.M. to 1:00 P.M., and from 3:30 P.M. to 7 P.M. The President did not preside at the second meeting but Lord Robert Cecil did.

At the close of the afternoon session the draft with amendments was finally adopted unanimously, subject to Article XXI being reserved to see what the President's wishes were, the meeting being almost unanimous against including it, the only states in favor being Brazil, China and Roumania.

Subsequently, Colonel House told me that Article XXI was to be omitted by direction of the President, and I so notified Lord Eustace Percy, who said he would tell M. de Lapradelle¹ of the French, who was with him. This was about 9 o'clock in the evening. In the meantime I had corrected the proofs and ordered 1,000 copies printed for the next day when the text is to be made public and presented to the Plenary session of the Conference at 3 P.M.

In the morning as I came downstairs to go to the office I met Mr. Rappard, who said that he had had a talk for forty minutes with the President yesterday and that the President had told him that he could say to Secretary Lansing and Mr. White, in his name, that he would like Switzerland to be heard about the Rhine.

Rappard also told me that when he was talking to the President about the Rhine the President asked him who the other member of the Commission was besides Mr. White. Rappard said that it was Mr. Miller; whereupon the President remarked that Miller was a bright fellow, which Rappard jokingly called me.

Miller, *My Diary at the Conference of Paris*, I, 121-23.
¹ Albert Geouffre de Lapradelle, Professor of the Faculty of Law at the University of Paris and Assistant Legal Adviser to the Foreign Ministry.

From the Diary of Colonel House

February 13, 1919.

This has been a memorable day. We finished the Covenant for the League of Nations. The President sat with us in the morning from 10.30 until shortly after one in order to have a second reading of the draft. We got through with about a quarter of the Covenant, or to be precise, with six of the articles. The President could not come in the afternoon, and I asked Lord Robert Cecil to take the chair. At my suggestion, we agreed to try and make a record and, much to our gratification, we finished the other twenty-one articles by half pasy [past] six o'clock.

I did not realize how much time the President took up in talking. Another things [thing], the President was always averse to taking a vote, while Lord Robert, at my insistence, took several votes this afternoon and in this way stopped discussion.

We had arranged to have another meeting tonight at 8.30. When I telephoned the President at seven o'clock that we had finished he was astounded and delighted.

We passed Article 21 of the old draft because Baron Makino was insistent upon the race clause going in if the religious clause was retained. I would not agree to eliminate the religious clause without first giving the President a chance to express himself, but I tentatively promised that it should be withdrawn in which event Baron Makino promised to withdraw, for the moment, the race amendment which neither the British nor I could take in the form in which he finally presented it.

Makino and I agreed upon a form the other day which the President accepted and which was as mild and inoffensive as possible,[1] but even that the British refused. The result is that the Japanese have expressed to me their profound gratitude and have assured me that their Government would be equally appreciative. It has taken considerable finesse to lift the load from our shoulders and place it upon the British, but happily, it has been done. This ought to make for better relations between Japan and the United States. I understand that all the British Delegation were willing to accept the form the President, Makino, Chinda and I agreed on excepting Hughes of Australia. He has been the stumbling block.

Bourgeois tried in every way possible to get in some clause by which we should have an international army under the direction of the League. Failing that, he tried for an international staff. Lord Robert and I steadily opposed this. Lord Robert was willing to accept the insidious staff proposal made by Bourgeois and Larnaude. I objected to it, and Lord Robert sustained me by making a talk against it. Then Bourgeois and his confrere insisted upon putting in something about the Hague Tribunal. They have the greatest reverence for that institution. I think they are the only people left in the world who have. Again I objected and reference to it was eliminated.

In talking to the President afterward, he agreed to my proposal to eliminate Clause 21 after I had explained the trouble, and after I had told him that an informal vote was taken which resulted in practical unanimity against it.

Perhaps for the President's *penchant* for the number 13, his attention was called to the fact that the Covenant was finished on the 13th of the month and that the number of Articles were double that number.

I am curious to know, and I shall sometime examine to find out, how much of the original draft of the Covenant which I made at Magnolia² remains in this document. Of course, we have added a great many clauses since its revision was undertaken, but we have added them from the Wilson-Cecil-Miller document. In speaking to the President about the matter, he said that as far as he was concerned he preferred the original draft as he and I had agreed upon at Magnolia last summer. Certainly, our document was more human and a little less legal. I think it has been unfortunate that we have had so many professional lawyers on the Committee dealing with this question. They are nearly always technical and unsatisfactory.

¹ This draft is printed at Feb. 5, 1919, Vol. 54.
² See the Enclosure printed with EMH to WW, July 16, 1918, Vol. 48.

To William Cox Redfield

[Paris] 2/13/19.

After conferring with Mr. Baruch and others here I give my approval to plans suggested for appointment of Committee to deal with problem of industrial situation.¹ Only possible objection it may be in contravention of Sherman Anti-Trust Law. Mr. Baruch is quite willing that Mr. Peek should undertake this work if he wishes to do so.   Woodrow Wilson.

T telegram (WP, DLC).
¹ Wilson was responding to WCR to WW, Feb. 6 and 7, 1919, Vol. 54.

To Samuel McCune Lindsay

My dear Lindsay: Paris, 13 February, 1919.

Mr. Lamont has placed in my hands your two letters of January 23rd,[1] and I am mighty sorry to send you a disappointing answer, but it really is out of the question for me to promise to make such addresses as you suggest. It is only too evident now that our labors here will be long drawn out and, at each stage, of the most difficult and critical character, and therefore I cannot predict when I will be back with anything like what I could call leisure for such addresses as you kindly suggest.

I am sure that you will understand and will feel that this reply is justified.

With best wishes,

Cordially and sincerely yours,   [Woodrow Wilson]

CCL (WP, DLC).
[1] S. M. Lindsay to WW, Jan. 23, 1919, TLS, and S. M. Lindsay to T. W. Lamont, Jan. 23, 1919, ALS, both enclosed in T. W. Lamont to WW, Feb. 10, 1919, TLS, all in WP, DLC. Lindsay, on behalf of the Academy of Political Science in the City of New York, invited Wilson to deliver an address "dealing with the ethical and humanitarian aspects of the new international order which has already begun under your leadership and which means new international obligations and opportunities for the United States." He suggested that the academy could arrange for Wilson to speak either at a dinner meeting in a New York hotel or at a more general meeting in the Metropolitan Opera House. Lindsay's letter to Lamont discussed the time and manner of presenting his invitation to Wilson. After his arrival in Paris from the United States, Lamont sent both letters to Wilson with a covering note.

To H. Arthur Morgan[1]

[Paris] 2/13/19.

Insofar as our domestic regulations are concerned, cotton may now be exported without limit to associated countries and to all neutral countries, in amounts adequate for their needs.[2] Further exports to or for account of enemy countries raise important questions of policy which are the subject of attentive consideration by associated governments. The question of limitation of cotton imports into France and Italy is, you will understand, primarily a domestic matter for these governments, but I have every confidence that these governments will treat the situation with a sound appreciation of the mutual advantage of cordial trade relationships.

Woodrow Wilson.

T telegram (WP, DLC).
[1] In one of the telegrams cited in n. 2 below, Morgan identified himself as "Secy. Association State Farmers Union." The telegram was sent from New Orleans.
[2] Wilson was responding to H. A. Morgan to WW, Jan. 31, 1919, two T telegrams (WP, DLC).

From Merlin Hull[1]

My dear Sir: Madison, Wisconsin   February 13, 1919.

As directed, I have the honor to herewith transmit a copy of Joint Resolution No. 4, S., recently passed by the Wisconsin Legislature, relating to the establishment of a league of nations.[2]

Very truly yours,   Merlin Hull.

TLS (WP, DLC).
[1] Secretary of State of Wisconsin.
[2] Printed resolution signed by Riley S. Young, Speaker of the Assembly, and others (WP, DLC). It reads as follows:
"Whereas, The war, now brought to a victorious close by the associated power of the free nations of the world, was above all else a war to end war and protect human rights, Therefore, be it
"*Resolved, by the senate, the assembly concurring,* That we favor the establishment of a league of nations of which the United States shall be a member. We believe that such a league should aim at promoting the liberty, progress and orderly development of the world; that it should clinch the victory won at such terrible sacrifice by having the united potential force of all its members as a standing protection for the world against any nation that seeks to upset the peace of the world. Be it further
"*Resolved,* That copies of this resolution properly attested by the presiding officers be sent to the president of the United States, to the presiding officers of both branches of congress and to each of the United States senators and representatives from Wisconsin."

From Felix Cordova Davila

My dear Mr. President: Washington, D. C.   February 13, 1919

On January 9th last I presented to the Honorable, the Secretary of War, a list of elegibles, all natives of Porto Rico, for consideration in connection with the filling of the vacancy now existing in the office of Attorney General of the Island, and I take pleasure in enclosing herewith, for your information, a copy of the letter I wrote to the Secretary on this occasion.[1]

The matter, I have been assured, will receive consideration by the proper officials of the Department concerned, but it is of such importance and, to my mind, has such a large bearing upon the problem involved in the relations between the people I have the honor to represent and the great people of the United States proper, that I have felt it incumbent upon me to address myself directly to you on the subject.

It is obviously unnecessary for me, Mr. President, to point out to you, the champion of popular rights and democracy everywhere, that the appointment of a native to this important office would not only be fully in accord with the liberal spirit of American institutions and with the enlightened thought permeating your repeated utterances and efforts in the past in behalf of the people of Porto Rico, particularly those resulting in the passage of the Organic Act now in force in the island, for the adoption of which the Porto Ricans feel especially grateful to you, but also most opportune and peculiarly significant at this time when, in view of recent international events and the triumph of democratic ideals throughout the world, my countrymen feel, as if though strengthening within themselves and gathering still more vigor, their faith in the righteousness and justness of the American people and their hope that the liberal tendency manifesting itself in the policies of the Central Government as regards the island, is to receive new impulse and acceleration in the immediate future.

My duty impels me, however, to emphasize the importance of the concesson involved in this question, and to earnestly express the hope that the demand voiced in this connection by my countrymen, who are eager to see a native of the island occupying this Office, will receive full recognition. We regard this grant as being entirely in consonance with the policy which pervades and inspired the basic features of the Organic Act of March 2, 1917, and it would be a source of great disappointment to us if our expectation in this instance were not to be satisfied.

I trust, therefore, Mr. President, and confidently hope that such a conclusion will be reached in this matter as, besides rendering my countrymen debtors once more to you for your personal efforts in behalf of their just political aspirations, will confirm them in the never-failing confidence with which they look for guidance and support in their development, to the noble people of the United States.

I take advantage of this opportunity to offer to you the testimony of my best wishes for your personal welfare, together with my congratulations upon your great achievements and immortal work at the Peace Conference, and to wish you a speedy and happy return to the United States.

I am, my dear Mr. President,
                    Very sincerely yours,   Felix Cordova Davila

TLS (WP, DLC).
    ¹ F. Cordova Davila to NDB, Jan. 9, 1919, TCL, enclosing a T MS with a list of candidates, both WP, DLC.

From the Diary of Dr. Grayson

Friday, February 14, 1919.

The plenary session of the Peace Conference was held in the afternoon at the Quai D'Orsay. President read the articles of the initial league covenant and made a speech explaining them. The entire document was laid on the table pending the President's return from the United States. The President held a conference with Swope, Oulahan, Hood,[1] Bender and other correspondents just before leaving home for train. In the morning he had a conference with the bulk of the correspondents from the United States.

The President saw the newspaper men in the morning and afternoon before leaving Paris, giving them his views of various subjects taken up during the conference and expressed himself as highly pleased with the completion of the League of Nations covenant. Among the anecdotes he told was one regarding a private conversation between himself and Clemenceau, in which Clemenceau accused him of having a heart of steel to which the President replied, "I have not the heart to steal." He told of his difficulties with Premier Hughes of Australia, who is deaf, indicating plainly that he regarded Hughes as one of the troublesome obstacles at the conference—reactionary. Hughes always neglected to read the program of the next day's events and when in conference he would be unfamiliar with the subject and no one could tell him what it was about. He said the whole conference problem, particularly that portion regarding territorial questions was interwoven with secret agreements entered into during the progress of the war by the large powers and involving a territory which since is claimed by smaller nationalities. For instance he said France and England had an understanding regarding Syria,[2] and he mentioned also the pact of London, which involved the turning over to Italy of Dalmatia, Fiume and other territories. This agreement he said should never have been entered into and now all the nations except the ones immediately interested are anxious to get out of them. He said the League of Nations was, of course, the biggest thing he had accomplished in his trip to France. In this connection he said he discovered, and described it as a joke on himself, that the freedom of the seas question was automatically disposed of with the formulation of the league, because freedom of the seas involved primarily the rights of neutrals during a war and with the establishment of the league there would be no belligerents and hence no neutrals.

We left on the train for Brest at 9:20 P.M. Among those at the station to bid us goodbye were Poincaré, Clemenceau, Tardieu, Lord Derby, General Pershing, General Bliss, Colonel House and other prominent officials together with a big crowd. The station was decorated with flags and palms. Tardieu, Jusserand and General Leorat accompanied the President on the train.

[1] Edwin Milton Hood of the Associated Press.
[2] That is, the Sykes-Picot Agreement.

A News Report of A Press Conference

[Feb. 14, 1919]

FEED WORLD AND THEN TALK PEACE SAYS MR. WILSON
PEOPLE MORE ANXIOUS TO KNOW ABOUT NEXT MEAL
THAN WHO RULER WILL BE.

BY TRUMAN H. TALLEY, Special Correspondent of the Herald.

Paris, Friday.

The first interview President Wilson has granted to American newspaper representatives since he has been in Europe took place to-day. It lasted an hour. The President was most cordial and frank and expressed his regret that it had not been possible for him to see the correspondents every day while he was here. He added laughingly, however, that every one else had had his ear.

The President emphatically and gravely declared that the most tremendous issue in the world to-day concerns the economic situation.

He declared that even the peace treaty and the League of Nations could wait, if necessary, while the wheels of industry were being started up again; until the world's commerce had again been re-established.

He declared the people were more interested in knowing where their day's food is coming from, more interested in work, than they are in who will be their rulers.

The latter question, he said, is one of negotiation and it might prove difficult of solution, but the first constitutes a primary condition for the restoration of order and the blocking of the progress of Bolshevism.

He insisted that the lifting of the blockade is imperative unless we desire to see Germany become another Russia.

"You can't talk government with a hungry people," he declared.

When he was asked about Russia he shook his head and said it was almost an insoluble problem. He said the Allies' invitation to a conference on Prinkipo Island had attracted the factions least desirable, to the exclusion of those which might restore order. He regarded the Soviet reply to the Allies' as rather insulting, because their intimation of a willingness to make good the Russian debt apparently revealed the Bolshevik desire to split the loot between them and buy recognition.

All the Allies want to help the worthy Russian factions which are seeking to establish a stable government in Russia, he said.

Summarizing the world situation, he declared that economic conditions in Germany and Russia, as well as in other parts of the world which are stagnant because of war restrictions, constituted a greater crisis than any possible future wars.

The President looked weary and admitted that the tedious conferences were fraught with tension. Then, in a rather despairing way, he remarked that Mr. Tumulty had just sent a cable message to him saying that enough work had accumulated in Washington to keep him busy for six months.

Mr. Wilson humorously described how the tiresome translations in the conferences often served to cool temper[s] and to relieve strained nerves, as during the second readings all had a chance to take second thought. During these translations, also, there was a chance for wearied members to rest. He told how he surreptitiously got even a few winks of sleep yesterday while a Syrian poet[2] recited in French for two hours. He awoke in ample time to get the full gist of the remarks when they were translated.

After he had analyzed in detail the various principles of the League of Nations he was asked if the freedom of the seas was involved.

"I am glad you asked me about that," he said. "I have a joke to tell on myself. I admit that I did not realize until I arrived here that with the League of Nations there will be no neutrals. By abolishing neutrality we automatically eliminate the question of neutral rights during war. Then there is no issue over naval or sea rights. The League of Nations will promulgate the rules for naval regulation and disarmament; so, as they say, 'there ain't no such' issue as freedom of the seas."

He was asked if the British had suggested this new line of argument. He laughed heartily and said:

"No; I came to that conclusion in the privacy of my own soul."

The President hopes to present an accounting to Washington by March 4 and to leave the United States again on March 6 for Europe, where many grave issues are awaiting determination. He described intimately, but not for publication, how the League of Nations Commission worked and spoke confidently about the society's prospects. He said there was virtually unanimity of purpose among the workers for the league, but often differences of judgment—sometimes serious.

He carefully described the delicate French situation, which, he said, would readily be comprehended when it was remembered that for a generation France had lived under the dread of Germany; that to-day France's only fear was of a recurrence of the horrors from which she has just emerged.

Hence, he said, her zealousness in the peace conference.

On the other hand, the President believed, the rest of the world will be able to reassure France and to show her that what she has just gone through never will occur again.

President Wilson explained how the boundary issues are being considered. Decisions will not be announced piecemeal. That is to say, one day's adverse decision against a nation might bring an outbreak before the next day's favorable one was announced. He cited the Teschen controversy, and said it would not do to announce that either the Poles or the Czechs were deprived of that strip until it was possible to tell each of them what they had gained as well as lost.

He intimated that there are new negotiations pending which will require longer and more careful consideration than anything that has gone before. He mentioned the German boundary disputes as proof of the gravity of some of these questions.

The President was undecided how he will render an accounting to the people and to Congress when he gets home. He said he would wait and see how things looked when he reached Washington. He intimated that he might do considerably more than simply tell Congress what had been arrived at in the peace conference. He recalled that Congress must ratify the United States' actual participation in the new international code, but declared he was empowered to promise our general acquiescence.

He was confident the peace conference will reach an early and unanimous decision on the various questions before it, although with sufficient time to permit delegates like himself to consult the law and treaty making agencies at home.

Printed in the *New York Herald*, Feb. 15, 1919.

[1] G. V. Chicherin to the governments of Great Britain, France, Italy, Japan, and the United States of North America, Feb. 4, 1919, *FR 1919, Russia*, 39-42. Chicherin stated that, although the Soviet government had not received a direct invitation to the proposed Prinkipo conference, it was accepting the invitation in order to prevent the absence of any Soviet answer from being interpreted as a refusal. The note said that, as a basis for negotiation, the Soviet government was willing to make major concessions to the Allies. It proposed to recognize Russia's foreign debts and to guarantee the payment of the interest on those debts with Russian raw materials; to grant mining, timber, and other concessions to Allied business interests; to discuss a territorial settlement, including possible Soviet cession of all territories then held by Allied troops; and, in view of frequent complaints about Russian revolutionary propaganda, to agree not to interfere in the internal affairs of the Allied nations. Chicherin warned, however, that the extent of the concessions finally agreed upon would depend upon the military and internal position of the Soviet government at the time of the negotiations. This position, he insisted, was improving every day. He cited a long list of Russian cities recently taken by the Soviet armies and noted that the Mensheviks had protested against the Allied military intervention in Russia and that several former members of the Constituent Assembly had just begun talks with the Soviet government.

Several phrases in Chicherin's note were rather abrasive in tone. At one point he commented on "the great inclination which foreign capital has always displayed to exploit Russia's natural resources for its own advantage." "The Russian Soviet Government," he also said, "attaches such great value to the conclusion of an agreement which would bring hostilities to an end, that it is ready immediately to enter into negotiations for this purpose, and even—as it has often said—to purchase such agreement at the price of important sacrifices, with the express reservation that the future development of the Soviet Republic will not be menaced." As one historian has pointed out, however, the Soviet note failed to accept, or even to mention, the precondition of the Prinkipo proposal—a cease-fire by all the warring parties in Russia. See John M. Thompson, *Russia, Bolshevism, and the Versailles Peace* (Princeton, N. J., 1966), pp. 114-15.

[2] That is, Chekri Ganem.

An Address to the Third Plenary Session of the Peace Conference[1]

February 14, 1919.

Mr. Chairman: I have the honor and as I esteem it the very great privilege of reporting in the name of the commission constituted by this conference on the formulation of a plan for the league of nations. I am happy to say that it is a unanimous report, a unanimous report from the representatives of fourteen nations—the United States, Great Britain, France, Italy, Japan, Belgium, Brazil, China, Czecho-Slovakia, Greece, Poland, Portugal, Roumania, and Serbia. I think it will be serviceable and interesting if I, with your permission, read the document as the only report we have to make.

COVENANT

PREAMBLE

In order to promote international co-operation and to secure international peace and security by the acceptance of obligations not to resort to war, by the prescription of open, just and honorable relations between nations, by the firm establishment of the understandings of international law as the actual rule of conduct among governments, and by the maintenance of justice and a scrupulous respect for all treaty obligations in the dealings of organized peoples with one another, the Powers signatory to this Covenant adopt this constitution of the League of Nations.

ARTICLE I.

The action of the High Contracting Parties under the terms of this Covenant shall be effected through the instrumentality of meetings of a Body of Delegates representing the High Contracting Parties, of meetings at more frequent intervals of an Executive Council, and of a permanent international Secretariat to be established at the Seat of the League.

ARTICLE II.

Meetings of the Body of Delegates shall be held at stated intervals and from time to time as occasion may require for the purpose of dealing with matters within the sphere of action of the League. Meetings of the Body of Delegates shall be held at the Seat of the League or at such other place as may be found convenient and shall consist of representatives of the High Contracting Parties. Each of the High Contracting Parties shall have one vote but may have not more than three representatives.

---

[1] Wilson's commentary, but not the text of the Covenant, is printed in *PPC*, III, 209-15.

ARTICLE III.

The Executive Council shall consist of representatives of the United States of America, the British Empire, France, Italy and Japan, together with representatives of four other States, members of the League. The selection of these four States shall be made by the Body of Delegates on such principles and in such manner as they think fit. Pending the appointment of these representatives of the other States, representatives of [blank] shall be members of the Executive Council.

Meetings of the Council shall be held from time to time as occasion may require and at least once a year at whatever place may be decided on, or failing any such decision, at the Seat of the League, and any matter within the sphere of action of the League or affecting the peace of the world may be dealt with at such meetings.

Invitations shall be sent to any Power to attend a meeting of the Council at which matters directly affecting its interests are to be discussed and no decision taken at any meeting will be binding on such Power unless so invited.

ARTICLE IV.

All matters of procedure at meetings of the Body of Delegates or the Executive Council including the appointment of Committees to investigate particular matters shall be regulated by the Body of Delegates or the Executive Council and may be decided by a majority of the States represented at the meeting.

The first meeting of the Body of Delegates and of the Executive Council shall be summoned by the President of the United States of America.

ARTICLE V.

The permanent Secretariat of the League shall be established at [blank] which shall constitute the Seat of the League. The Secretariat shall comprise such secretaries and staff as may be required, under the general direction and control of a Secretary-General of the League, who shall be chosen by the Executive Council; the Secretariat shall be appointed by the Secretary-General subject to confirmation by the Executive Council.

The Secretary-General shall act in that capacity at all meetings of the Body of Delegates or of the Executive Council.

The expense of the Secretariat shall be borne by the States members of the League in accordance with the apportionment of the expenses of the International Bureau of the Universal Postal Union.

ARTICLE VI.

Representatives of the High Contracting Parties and officials of the League when engaged on the business of the League shall enjoy diplomatic privileges and immunities, and the buildings occupied by the League or its officials or by representatives attending its meetings shall enjoy the benefits of extraterritoriality.

ARTICLE VII.

Admission to the League of States not signatories to the Covenant and not named in the Protocol hereto as States to be invited to adhere to the Covenant requires the assent of not less than two-thirds of the States represented in the Body of Delegates, and shall be limited to fully self-governing countries including Dominions and Colonies.

No State shall be admitted to the League unless it is able to give effective guarantees of its sincere intention to observe its international obligations, and unless it shall conform to such principles as may be prescribed by the League in regard to its naval and military forces and armaments.

ARTICLE VIII.

The High Contracting Parties recognize the principle that the maintenance of peace will require the reduction of national armaments to the lowest point consistent with national safety and the enforcement by common action of international obligations, having special regard to the geographical situation and circumstances of each State, and the Executive Council shall formulate plans for effecting such reduction. The Executive Council shall also determine for the consideration and action of the several governments what military equipment and armament is fair and reasonable in proportion to the scale of forces laid down in the programme of disarmament; and these limits, when adopted, shall not be exceeded without the permission of the Executive Council.

The High Contracting Parties agree that the manufacture by private enterprise of munitions and implements of war lends itself to grave objections, and direct the Executive Council to advise how the evil effects attendant upon such manufacture can be prevented, due regard being had to the necessities of those countries which are not able to manufacture for themselves the munitions and implements of war necessary for their safety.

The High Contracting Parties undertake in no way to conceal from each other the condition of such of their industries as are capable of being adapted to war-like purposes or the scale of their armaments, and agree that there shall be full and frank interchange of information as to their military and naval programmes.

ARTICLE IX.

A permanent Commission shall be constituted to advise the League on the execution of the provisions of Article VIII and on military and naval questions generally.

ARTICLE X.

The High Contracting Parties undertake to respect and preserve as against external aggression the territorial integrity and existing political independence of all States members of the League. In case of any such aggression or in case of any threat or danger of such aggression the Executive Council shall advise upon the means by which this obligation shall be fulfilled.

ARTICLE XI.

Any war or threat of war, whether immediately affecting any of the High Contracting Parties or not, is hereby declared a matter of concern to the League, and the High Contracting Parties reserve the right to take any action that may be deemed wise and effectual to safeguard the peace of nations.

It is hereby also declared and agreed to be the friendly right of each of the High Contracting Parties to draw the attention of the Body of Delegates or of the Executive Council to any circumstances affecting international intercourse which threaten to disturb international peace or the good understanding between nations upon which peace depends.

ARTICLE XII.

The High Contracting Parties agree that should disputes arise between them which cannot be adjusted by the ordinary processes of diplomacy, they will in no case resort to war without previously submitting the questions and matters involved either to arbitration or to inquiry by the Executive Council and until three months after the award by the arbitrators or a recommendation by the Executive Council; and that they will not even then resort to war as against a member of the League which complies with the award of the arbitrators or the recommendations of the Executive Council.

In any case under this Article, the award of the arbitrators shall be made within a reasonable time, and the recommendation of the Executive Council shall be made within six months after the submission of the dispute.

ARTICLE XIII.

The High Contracting Parties agree that whenever any dispute or difficulty shall arise between them which they recognize to be suitable for submission to arbitration and which cannot be satisfactorily settled by diplomacy, they will submit the whole subject matter to arbitration. For this purpose the Court of arbitration to which the case is referred shall be the court agreed on by the parties or stipulated in any Convention existing between them. The High Contracting Parties agree that they will carry out in full good faith any award that may be rendered. In the event of any failure to carry out the award, the Executive Council shall propose what steps can best be taken to give effect thereto.

ARTICLE XIV.

The Executive Council shall formulate plans for the establishment of a Permanent Court of International Justice and this Court shall, when established, be competent to hear and determine any matter which the parties recognize as suitable for submission to it for arbitration under the foregoing Article.

ARTICLE XV.

If there should arise between States members of the League any dispute likely to lead to a rupture, which is not submitted to arbitration as above, the High Contracting Parties agree that they will refer the matter to the Executive Council; either party to the dispute may give notice of the existence of the dispute to the Secretary-General, who will make all necessary arrangements for a full investigation and consideration thereof. For this purpose the parties agree to communicate to the Secretary-General, as promptly as possible, statements of their case with all the relevant facts and papers, and the Executive Council may forthwith direct the publication thereof.

Where the efforts to the Council lead to the settlement of the dispute, a statement shall be published indicating the nature of the dispute and the terms of settlement, together with such explanations as may be appropriate. If the dispute has not been settled, a report by the Council shall be published, setting forth with all necessary facts and explanations the recommendation which the Council think just and proper for the settlement of the dispute. If the report is unanimously agreed to by the members of the Council other than the parties to the dispute, the High Contracting Parties agree that they will not go to war with any party which complies with the recommendation and that, if any party shall refuse so to comply, the Council shall propose the measures necessary to give effect to the recommendation. If no such unanimous report can be made, it shall be the duty of the majority and the privilege of the minority to issue statements indicating what they believe to be the facts and containing the recommendations which they consider to be just and proper.

I pause to point out that a misconception might arise in connection with one of the sentences I have just read—"If any party shall refuse so to comply, the Council shall propose the measures necessary to give effect to the recommendation." A case in point, a purely hypothetical case, is this: suppose that there is in the possession of a particular power a piece of territory or some other substantial thing in dispute to which it is claimed that it is not entitled. Suppose that the matter is submitted to the Executive Council for a recommendation as to the settlement of the dispute, diplomacy having failed; and suppose that the decision is in favor of the party which claims the subject matter of dispute as against the party which has the subject matter in dispute. Then, if the party in possession of the subject matter in dispute merely sits still and does nothing, it has accepted the decision of the Council, in the sense that it makes no resistance; but something must be done to see that it surrenders the subject matter in dispute. In such a case, the only case contemplated, it is provided that the Executive Council may then consider what steps may be necessary to oblige the party against whom judgment has gone to comply with the decisions of the Council.

The Executive Council may in any case under this Article refer the dispute to the Body of Delegates. The dispute shall be so referred at the request of either party to the dispute, provided that such request must be made within fourteen days after the submission of the dispute. In any case referred to the Body of Delegates all the provisions of this Article and of Article XII relating to the action and powers of the Executive Council shall apply to the action and powers of the Body of Delegates.

ARTICLE XVI.

Should any of the High Contracting Parties break or disregard its covenants under Article XII, it shall thereby *ipso facto* be deemed to have committed an act of war against all the other members of the League, which hereby undertake immediately to subject it to the severance of all trade or financial relations, the prohibition of all intercourse between their nationals and the nationals of the covenant-breaking State, and the prevention of all financial, commercial, or personal intercourse between the nationals of the covenant-breaking State and the nationals of any other State, whether a member of the League or not.

It shall be the duty of the Executive Council in such case to recommend what effective military or naval force the members of the League shall severally contribute to the armed forces to be used to protect the covenants of the League.

The High Contracting Parties agree, further, that they will mutually support one another in the financial and economic measures which are taken under this Article, in order to minimize the loss and inconvenience resulting from the above measures, and that they will mutually support one another in resisting any special measures aimed at one of their number by the covenant-breaking

State, and that they will afford passage through their territory to the forces of any of the High Contracting Parties who are co-operating to protect the covenants of the League.

ARTICLE XVII.

In the event of disputes between one State member of the League and another State which is not a member of the League, or between States not members of the League, the High Contracting Parties agree that the State or States not members of the League shall be invited to accept the obligations of membership in the League for the purposes of such dispute, upon such conditions as the Executive Council may deem just, and upon acceptance of any such invitation, the above provisions shall be applied with such modifications as may be deemed necessary by the League.

Upon such invitation being given the Executive Council shall immediately institute an inquiry into the circumstances and merits of the dispute and recommend such action as may seem best and most effectual in the circumstances.

In the event of a Power so invited refusing to accept the obligations of membership in the League for the purposes of such dispute, and taking any action against a State member of the League which in the case of a State member of the League would constitute a breach of Article XII, the provisions of Article XVI shall be applicable as against the State taking such action.

If both parties to the dispute when so invited refuse to accept the obligations of membership in the League for the purposes of such dispute, the Executive Council may take such action and make such recommendations as will prevent hostilities and will result in the settlement of the dispute.

ARTICLE XVIII.

The High Contracting Parties agree that the League shall be entrusted with the general supervision of the trade in arms and ammunition with the countries in which the control of this traffic is necessary in the common interest.

Let me say before reading Article XIX, that before being embodied in this document it was the subject matter of a very careful discussion by representatives of the five greater parties, and that their unanimous conclusion in the matter is embodied in this article.

ARTICLE XIX.

To those colonies and territories which as a consequence of the late war have ceased to be under the sovereignty of the States which formerly governed them and which are inhabited by peoples not yet able to stand by themselves under the strenuous conditions of the modern world, there should be applied the principle that the well-being and development of such peoples form a sacred trust of civilization and that securities for the performance of this trust should be embodied in the constitution of the League.

The best method of giving practical effect to this principle is that the tutelage of such peoples should be entrusted to advanced nations who by reason of their resources, their experience or their geographical position, can best undertake this responsibility, and that this tutelage should be exercised by them as mandatories on behalf of the League.

The character of the mandate must differ according to the stage of the development of the people, the geographical situation of the territory, its economic conditions and other similar circumstances.

Certain communities formerly belonging to the Turkish Empire have reached a stage of development where their existence as independent nations can be provisionally recognized subject to the rendering of administrative advice and assistance by a mandatory power until such time as they are able to stand alone. The wishes of these communities must be a principal consideration in the selection of the mandatory power.

Other peoples, especially those of Central Africa, are at such a stage that the mandatory must be responsible for the administration of the territory subject to conditions which will guarantee freedom of conscience or religion, subject only to the maintenance of public order and morals, the prohibition of abuses such as the slave trade, the arms traffic and the liquor traffic, and the prevention of the establishment of fortifications or military and naval bases and of military training of the natives for other than police purposes and the defense of territory, and will also secure equal opportunities for the trade and commerce of other members of the League.

There are territories, such as South-West Africa and certain of the South Pacific Islands, which, owing to the sparseness of their population, or their small size, or their remoteness from the centers of civilization, or their geographical contiguity to the mandatory state, and other circumstances, can be best administered under the laws of the mandatory state as integral portions thereof, subject to the safeguards above-mentioned in the interests of the indigenous population.

In every case of mandate, the mandatory state shall render to the League an annual report in reference to the territory committed to its charge.

The degree of authority, control, or administration to be exercised by the mandatory State shall if not previously agreed upon by the High Contracting Parties in each case be explicitly defined by the Executive Council in a special Act or Charter.

The High Contracting Parties further agree to establish at the seat of the League a Mandatory Commission to receive and examine the annual reports of the Mandatory Powers, and to assist the League in ensuring the observance of the terms of all Mandates.

ARTICLE XX.

The High Contracting Parties will endeavor to secure and maintain fair and humane conditions of labor for men, women and children both in their own countries and in all countries to which their commercial and industrial relations extend; and to that end agree to establish as part of the organization of the League a permanent Bureau of Labor.

ARTICLE XXI.

The High Contracting Parties agree that provision shall be made through the instrumentality of the League to secure and maintain freedom of transit and equitable treatment for the commerce of all States members of the League, having in mind, among other things, special arrangements with regard to the necessities of the regions devastated during the war of 1914-1918.

ARTICLE XXII.

The High Contracting Parties agree to place under the control of the League all international bureaux already established by general treaties if the parties to such treaties consent. Furthermore, they agree that all such international bureaux to be constituted in future shall be placed under the control of the League.

ARTICLE XXIII.

The High Contracting Parties agree that every treaty or international engagement entered into hereafter by any State member of the League, shall be forthwith registered with the Secretary-General and as soon as possible published by him, and that no such treaty or international engagement shall be binding until so registered.

ARTICLE XXIV.

It shall be the right of the Body of Delegates from time to time to advise the reconsideration by States members of the League, of treaties which have become inapplicable, and of international conditions, of which the continuance may endanger the peace of the world.

ARTICLE XXV.

The High Contracting Parties severally agree that the present Covenant is accepted as abrogating all obligations *inter se* which are inconsistent with the terms thereof, and solemnly engage that they will not hereafter enter into any engagements inconsistent with the terms thereof.

In case any of the Powers signatory hereto or subsequently admitted to the League shall, before becoming a party to this Covenant, have undertaken any obligations which are inconsistent with the terms of this Covenant, it shall be the duty of such Power to take immediate steps to procure its release from such obligations.

ARTICLE XXVI.

Amendments to this Covenant will take effect when ratified by the States whose representatives compose the Executive Council and by three-fourths of the States whose representatives compose the Body of Delegates.

It gives me pleasure to add to this formal reading of the result of our labors that the character of the discussion which occurred at the sittings of the commission was not only of the most constructive but of the most encouraging sort. It was obvious throughout our discussions that, although there were subjects upon which there were individual differences of judgment, with regard to the method by which our objects should be obtained, there was practically at no point any serious difference of opinion or motive as to the objects which we were seeking. Indeed, while these debates were not made the opportunity for the expression of enthusiasms and sentiments, I think the other members of the commission will agree with me that there was an undertone of high resolve and of enthusiasm for the thing we were trying to do, which was heartening throughout every meeting; because we felt that in a way this conference had entrusted to us the expression of one of its highest and most important purposes, to see to it that the concord of the world in the future with regard to the objects of justice should not be subject to doubt or uncertainty; that the cooperation of the great body of nations should be assured from the first in the maintenance of peace upon the terms of honor and of the strict regard for international obligation. The compulsion of that task was constantly upon us, and at no point was there shown the slightest desire to do anything but suggest the best means to accomplish that great object. There is very great significance, therefore, in the fact that the result was reached unanimously. Fourteen nations were represented, among them all of those powers which for convenience we have called the great powers, and among the rest a representation of the greatest variety of circumstance and interest. So that I think we are justified in saying that it was a representative group of the members of this great conference. The significance of the result, therefore, has that deepest of all meanings, the union of wills in a common purpose, a union of wills which cannot be resisted, and which I dare say no nation will run the risk of attempting to resist.

Now, as to the character of the document. While it has consumed some time to read this document, I think you will see at once that it is, after all, very simple, and in nothing so simple as in the structure which it suggests for the League of Nations—a Body of Delegates, an Executive Council, and a Permanent Secretariat. When it came to the question of determining the character of the representation in the Body of Delegates, we were all aware of a feeling which is current throughout the world. Inasmuch as I am stating it in the presence of official representatives of the various governments here present, including myself, I may say that there is a universal feeling that the world cannot rest satisfied with merely official guidance. There reached us through many channels the feeling that if the deliberative body of the League was merely to be a body of officials representing the various governments, the peoples of the world would not be sure that some of the mistakes which preoccupied officials had admittedly made might not be repeated. It was impossible to conceive a method or an assembly so large and various as to be really representative of the great body of the peoples of the world, because, as I roughly reckon it, we represent as we sit around this table more than twelve hundred million people. You cannot have a representative assembly of twelve hundred million people, but if you leave it to each government to have, if it pleases, one or two or three representatives, though only a single vote, it may vary its representation from time to time, not only, but it may originate the choice of its several representatives, if it should have several, in different ways. Therefore, we thought that this was a proper and a very prudent concession to the practically universal opinion of plain men everywhere that they wanted the door left open to a variety of representation instead of being confined to a single official body with which they might or might not find themselves in sympathy.

And you will notice that this body has unlimited rights of discussion—I mean of discussion of anything that falls within the field of international relationship—and that it is specially agreed that war or international misunderstandings or anything that may lead to friction and trouble is everybody's business, because it may affect the peace of the world. And in order to safeguard the popular power so far as we could of this representative body, it is provided, you will notice, that when a subject is submitted, not to arbitration, but to discussion by the Executive Council, it can upon the initiative of either one of the parties to the dispute be drawn out of the

Executive Council on to the larger forum of the general Body of Delegates, because throughout this instrument we are depending primarily and chiefly upon one great force, and that is the moral force of the public opinion of the world—the cleansing and clarifying and compelling influences of publicity—so that intrigues can no longer have their coverts, so that designs that are sinister can at any time be drawn into the open, so that those things that are destroyed by the light may be properly destroyed by the overwhelming light of the universal expression of the condemnation of the world.

Armed force is in the background in this program, but it *is* in the background, and if the moral force of the world will not suffice, the physical force of the world shall. But that is the last resort, because this is intended as a constitution of peace, not as a league of war.

The simplicity of the document seems to me to be one of its chief virtues, because, speaking for myself, I was unable to foresee the variety of circumstances with which this League would have to deal. I was unable, therefore, to plan all the machinery that might be necessary to meet differing and unexpected contingencies. Therefore, I should say of this document that it is not a straitjacket, but a vehicle of life. A living thing is born, and we must see to it that the clothes we put upon it do not hamper it—a vehicle of power, but a vehicle in which power may be varied at the discretion of those who exercise it and in accordance with the changing circumstances of the time. And yet, while it is elastic, while it is general in its terms, it is definite in the one thing that we were called upon to make definite. It is a definite guarantee of peace. It is a definite guarantee by word against aggression. It is a definite guarantee against the things which have just come near bringing the whole structure of civilization into ruin. Its purposes do not for a moment lie vague. Its purposes are declared and its powers made unmistakable.

It is not in contemplation that this should be merely a League to secure the peace of the world. It is a League which can be used for cooperation in any international matter. That is the significance of the provision introduced concerning labor. There are many ameliorations of labor conditions which can be effected by conference and discussion. I anticipate that there will be a very great usefulness in the Bureau of Labor which it is contemplated shall be set up by the League. While men and women and children who work have been in the background through long ages, and sometimes seemed to be forgotten, while governments have had their watchful and suspicious eyes upon the maneuvers of one another, while the thought of statesmen has been about structural action and the large transactions of commerce and of finance, now, if I may believe the picture which I see, there comes into the foreground the great body of the laboring people of the world, the men and women and children upon whom the great burden of sustaining the world must from day to day fall, whether we wish it to do so or not; people who go to bed tired and wake up without the stimulation of lively hope. These people will be drawn into the field of international consultation and help, and will be among the wards of the combined governments of the world. There is, I take leave to say, a very great step in advance in the mere conception of that.

Then, as you will notice, there is an imperative article concerning the publicity of all international agreements. Henceforth no member of the League can claim any agreement valid which it has not registered with the Secretary-General, in whose office, of course, it will be subject to the examination of anybody representing a member of the League. And the duty is laid upon the Secretary-General to publish every document of that sort at the earliest possible time. I suppose most persons who have not been conversant with the business of foreign offices do not realize how many hundreds of these agreements are made in a single year, and how difficult it might be to publish the more unimportant of them immediately—how uninteresting it would be to most of the world to publish them immediately—but even they must be published just so soon as it is possible for the Secretary-General to publish them.

Then there is a feature about this Covenant which to my mind is one of the greatest and most satisfactory advances that have been made. We are done with annexations of helpless people, meant in some instances by some powers to be used merely for exploitation. We recognize in the most solemn manner that the helpless and undeveloped peoples of the world, being in that condition, put an obligation upon us to look after their interests primarily before we use them for our interest; and that in all cases of this sort hereafter it shall be the duty of the League to see that the nations which are assigned as the tutors and advisers and directors of those peoples shall look to their interest and to their development before they look to the interests and material desires of the mandatory nation itself. There has been no greater advance than this, gentlemen. If you look back upon the history of the world you will see how helpless peoples have too often been a prey to powers that had no conscience in the matter. It has been one of the many distressing revelations of recent years that the great power which has just been happily defeated put intolerable burdens and injustices upon the helpless people of some of the colonies which it annexed to itself; that its interest was rather their extermination than their development; that the desire was to possess their land for European purposes, and not to enjoy their confidence in order that mankind might be lifted in those places to the next higher level. Now, the world, expressing its conscience in law, says there is an end of that. Our consciences shall be applied to this thing. States will be picked out which have already shown that they can exercise a conscience in this matter, and under their tutelage the helpless peoples of the world will come into a new light and into a new hope.

So I think I can say of this document that it is at one and the same time a practical document and a humane document. There is a pulse of sympathy in it. There is a compulsion of conscience throughout it. It is practical, and yet it is intended to purify, to rectify, to elevate. And I want to say that, so far as my observation instructs me, this is in one sense a belated document. I believe that the conscience of the world has long been prepared to express itself in some such way. We are not just now discovering our sympathy for these people and our interest in them. We are simply expressing it, for it has long been felt, and in the administration of the affairs of more than one of the great states represented here—so far as I know, of all the great states that are represented here—that human impulse has already expressed itself in their dealings with their colonies whose peoples were yet at a low stage of civilization. We have had many instances of colonies lifted into the sphere of complete self-government. This is not the discovery of a principle. It is the universal application of a principle. It is the agreement of the great nations which have tried to live by these standards in their separate administrations to unite in seeing that their common force and their common thought and intelligence are lent to this great and humane enterprise. I think it is an occasion, therefore, for the most profound satisfaction that this humane decision should have been reached in a matter for which the world has long been waiting and until a very recent period thought that it was still too early to hope.

Many terrible things have come out of this war, gentlemen, but some very beautiful things have come out of it. Wrong has been defeated, but the rest of the world has been more conscious than it ever was before of the majesty of right. People that were suspicious of one another can now live as friends and comrades in a single family, and desire to do so. The miasma of distrust, of intrigue, is cleared away. Men are looking eye to eye and saying; "We are brothers and have a common purpose. We did not realize it before, but now we do realize it, and this is our Covenant of fraternity and of friendship."[2]

Printed in *Addresses of President Wilson on First Trip to Europe December 3, 1918 to February 24, 1919* (Washington, 1919).

[2] Further speeches by Cecil, Orlando, Bourgeois, Makino, George Nicoll Barnes, Vénisélos, Wellington Koo, and Rustum Haidar are printed in *PPC*, III, 215-30. Following the speeches, Hughes asked whether the conference would have an opportunity to discuss the text of the Covenant. Clemenceau said that it was available at the bureau of the conference for examination and discussion by all the interested powers and that the bureau would lose no time in summoning the conference as soon as it was in a position to bring the report up for a discussion. The session adjourned at 6:55 p.m.

From Edward Mandell House

Dear Governor,   [Paris] Feby 14/19

Your speech was as great as the occasion, I am very happy.

E.M.H.

Bless your heart. Thank you from the bottom of my heart.

W.W.

ALI (E. M. House Papers, CtY).

Hankey's Notes of a Meeting of the Supreme War Council[1]

Quai d'Orsay, February 14, 1919, 6:30 P.M.

BC-32, SWC-8

1. M. CLEMENCEAU declared the meeting open.

MR. BALFOUR said that he was sorry to be responsible for calling together a meeting at that unusual hour. He had, however, two urgent matters to put before the Council which he thought required solution before President Wilson's departure. The first related to the passage of troops and supplies through Holland.

Mr. Balfour said all his Military advisers assured him that there were no means of maintaining the British forces on the Rhine other than transit of troops and stores through Dutch territory. The reason for this was the extreme congestion of the railways in Belgium and Northern France. He did not feel, however, that Great Britain should act alone on such a question and he therefore wished to ask the Council to approve the joint action suggested in the following identic telegram:

"The 5 allied and associated Powers consider it of vital importance to the interests of the general Peace which they are ear-

[1] The complete text of these minutes is printed in *PPC*, III, 1039-44.

nestly striving to conclude at the earliest possible moment, that the preliminary arrangements already entered into with the enemy to this end, shall be effectually carried out.

Those arrangements provide, among other things for the occupation of the German territories left of the Rhine by allied and associated troops, and necessarily cover all measures which are essential for the purpose of effecting and maintaining such occupation, including the actual transport of the troops and supplies to their destination.

Owing to the extreme congestion of the railways in Belgium and Northern France the most serious difficulties are being encountered in carrying out the arrangements which have been agreed upon by both parties and which cannot be allowed to fail except at the risk of gravely imperilling the early establishment of a satisfactory peace.

A ready means exists to meet this difficulty; and that is the utilisation of the communications by rail and by water across Holland.

The German Government having assented to the arrival of the troops on German territory cannot be, and in fact are not, interested in the routes to be followed in journeying to the Rhine, and no question of an infringement of any rule of neutrality therefore arises out of the transit of the troops across Dutch territory.

In these circumstances, the 5 Powers, sensible of the solemn duty which lies upon them to see that their efforts directed to the speedy conclusion of a durable peace for the benefit of the whole community of nations, call upon the Netherlands Government to co-operate with them to this end by facilitating in every way the movements of troops and supplies across Dutch territory strictly for the purposes agreed upon with the German Government under the terms of the Armistice.

The matter is so grave and so urgent that the 5 Powers must press upon the Netherlands Government the necessity of immediate action, failing which the responsibility for the state of things which may ensue and which may endanger both the general peace and the flow of food and supplies into the countries of Western Europe, will fall upon the Netherlands Government."

GENERAL ALBY[2] said that an agreement had been reached with the Dutch concerning the passage of food, but not, as far as he knew, to the passage of troops.

GENERAL BLISS, in reply to an enquiry from President Wilson, said that he had been trying to get into communication with General

---

[2] Gen. Henri Marie Camille Edouard Alby, Chief of the General Staff of the French army.

Pershing but had not succeeded. However, he had been told during the afternoon that an assistant to General Mosely[3] who had been charged with the negotiations for General Pershing had stated that the matter had been arranged with the Dutch Government at the Hague. According to this account, permission had been obtained for the creation of an American base at Rotterdam and for the conveyance of troops and supplies on the Rhine for the use of the American Army of Occupation.

MR. BALFOUR asked whether he might be authorised to wait until the news was confirmed. He assumed that the Dutch would be ready to do for the British what they had done for the Americans.

PRESIDENT WILSON pointed out that the news was still unofficial.

MR. BALFOUR thought that if it turned out to be correct no joint action need be taken. If, on the other hand, the Dutch were still unwilling, he asked them whether the joint action proposed in the identic telegram would be approved.

SIR HENRY WILSON pointed out that the Dutch allowed troops to pass down the Rhine away from Germany, but not up towards Germany.

BARON SONNINO asked what the Allied and Associated Powers could do if the Dutch should refuse.

M. CLEMENCEAU said that means of pressure would be found.

(It was decided that the joint action proposed by Mr. Balfour should be taken if the Dutch Government had not already conceded the principle of free passage.)

2. MR. BALFOUR said that the second point to which he wished to draw the attention of the Council was that of the proposed Meeting with the various Russian Governments at Prinkipo. He only wished to introduce the subject, and he asked Mr. Winston Churchill, who had come over for the purpose, to explain the present views of the British Cabinet.

MR. CHURCHILL said that on the previous day there had been a Cabinet Meeting in London, at which great anxiety had been manifested concerning the Russian situation, particularly in respect to the policy of the Prinkipo meeting. In view of the imminent departure of President Wilson, the Cabinet had asked him to go over and obtain some decision as to the policy on this matter. Mr. Lloyd George had expressed a wish to know whether the Allied policy which had led to the suggestion of the meeting at Prinkipo was to be pursued or, if not, what policy was to be substituted for it. If it were possible to go on with the original policy, so much the better; but if only the Bolsheviks were to attend the Conference, it was

---

[3] Brig. Gen. George Van Horn Moseley.

thought that little good would come of the meeting. The military aspect of the case must be considered. Great Britain had soldiers in Russia who were being killed in action.[4] Their families wished to know what purpose these men were serving. Were they just marking time until the Allies had decided on policy, or were they fighting in a campaign representing some common aim? The longer the delay continued, the worse would be the situation of the troops on all the Russian fronts. The Russian elements in those forces were deteriorating rapidly because of the uncertainty of the support they might expect from the victorious Allies. The Allied troops were intermingled with these Russian troops, which were weakening and quavering, and they were themselves becoming affected. If the Prinkipo meeting were not going to procure a cessation of arms, this unsatisfactory condition might last an indefinite time.

M. CLEMENCEAU expressed the opinion that a matter of such importance could not be settled at a short and unexpected meeting.

PRESIDENT WILSON said that since Mr. Churchill had come over specially to anticipate his departure, he felt that he should express what his personal thoughts on the subject were. Among the many uncertainties connected with Russia, he had a very clear opinion about two points. The first was that the troops of the Allied and Associated Powers were doing no sort of good in Russia. They did not know for whom or for what they were fighting. They were not assisting any promising common effort to establish order throughout Russia. They were assisting local movements, like, for instance, that of the Cossacks, who could not be induced to move outside their own sphere. His conclusion, therefore, was that the Allied and Associated Powers ought to withdraw their troops from all parts of Russian territory.

The second related to Prinkipo. The policy tending to a meeting at Prinkipo had been instituted in order to find out what the people in Russia were thinking and purposing to do. As far as he was concerned, he would be quite content that informal American representatives should meet representatives of the Bolsheviks. In their reply the Bolsheviks offered a number of things which had not been asked for, such as repayment of debts, concessions and territorial compensations. This answer was not only uncalled for, but might be thought insulting. What the Allies had in mind was the establishment of peace in Russia as an element of the world's peace. The first condition of the meeting asked for by the Allies was the

[4] For a detailed discussion of the activities of British troops in various parts of Russia following the Armistice, see Richard H. Ullman, *Anglo-Soviet Relations, 1917-1921: Britain and the Russian Civil War, November 1918-February 1920* (Princeton, N. J., 1968), pp. 5-58.

cessation of attacks by Russian troops on the communities outside their borders. If the other Russian Governments would not come to Prinkipo to meet the Allies, why should the Allies not imitate Mahomet, and go to them? What we were seeking was not a *rapprochement* with the Bolsheviks, but clear information. The reports received from Russia from various official and unofficial sources were so conflicting that it was impossible to form a coherent picture of the state of the country. Some light on the situation might be obtained by meeting the Russian representatives.

MR. CHURCHILL said that complete withdrawal of all Allied troops was a logical and clear policy, but its consequence would be the destruction of all non-Bolshevik armies in Russia. These numbered at the present time about 500,000 men and though their quality was not of the best, their numbers were nevertheless increasing. Such a policy would be equivalent to pulling out the linch-pin from the whole machine. There would be no further armed resistance to the Bolsheviks in Russia, and an interminable vista of violence and misery was all that remained for the whole of Russia.

PRESIDENT WILSON pointed out that the existing forces of the Allies could not stop the Bolsheviks, and that not one of the Allies was prepared to reinforce its troops.

M. SONNINO asked whether the Allies might not continue to supply arms to the non-Bolshevik elements?

PRESIDENT WILSON observed that they made very little use of them when they had them.

MR. CHURCHILL agreed that none of the Allies could send conscript troops to Russia. He thought, however, that volunteers, technical experts, arms, munitions, tanks, aeroplanes, etc. might be furnished.

PRESIDENT WILSON understood the problem was to know what use would be made of these forces and supplies. In some areas they would certainly be assisting reactionaries. Consequently, if the Allies were asked what they were supporting in Russia they would be compelled to reply that they did not know. Conscripts could not be sent and volunteers probably could not be obtained. He himself felt guilty in that the United States had in Russia insufficient forces, but it was not possible to increase them. It was certainly a cruel dilemma. At present our soldiers were being killed in Russia. If they were removed many Russians might lose their lives. But some day or other the Allied troops would have to be withdrawn; they could not be maintained there forever and the consequence to the Russians would only be deferred.

LORD MILNER pointed out that the only troops that could at present be removed were those in Siberia. The troops on the Archangel

Front were ice-bound and could not, for the time being, be removed. Should the Allies proceed to remove their troops immediately from Siberia there might be an overwhelming concentration of Bolsheviks on the Archangel Front.

PRESIDENT WILSON thought that there were no considerable Bolshevik forces in Siberia.

MR. LANSING observed that the Bolsheviks had a large army in Eastern Russia at the point of contact with the Anti-Bolshevik Siberian Forces.

MR. CHURCHILL said that he would like to know whether the Council would approve of arming the Anti-Bolshevik forces in Russia should the Prinkipo Conference prove a failure.

PRESIDENT WILSON said that he hesitated to express any definite opinion on this question. He had explained to the Council how he would act if alone. He would, however, cast in his lot with the rest.

(The meeting adjourned and it was agreed that the subject should be considered again at the conversation to be held the following afternoon.)

T MS (SDR, RG 256, 180.03101/39, DNA).

To Prince Faisal

My dear Prince Faissal: Paris, 14 February, 1919.

You may be sure that I would have responded at once to your request for another interview[1] if it had been at all possible for me to do so. The request caught me, however, just as I was in a last rush preparatory to leaving for a short visit to America, and therefore I have no choice but to beg that you will seek an interview with my fellow American Commissioners and that I will have the pleasure of seeing you when I come back.

I am deeply interested in this whole Arabian question and have been giving it very close and thoughtful attention.
                    Sincerely yours,   [Woodrow Wilson]

CCL (WP, DLC).
    [1] See Faisal to WW, Feb. 11, 1919.

To Millicent Garrett Fawcett

My dear Mrs. Fawcett: Paris, 14 February 1919.

I did not fail to take up with my colleagues at the Quai d'Orsay your suggestion about a Commission of Women. I found practically all of the conferees entirely sympathetic with the cause of woman suffrage, but if I may say so confidentially, very much embarrassed by the objections raised by representatives of India and Japan to a world wide investigation, which would raise questions most unacceptable to them. It was evident that to press the matter would lead to some unpleasant controversies and I concluded that I might be doing the cause more harm than good by insisting.

I am extremely sorry and I hope and believe that the cause can be advanced in other ways.

In unavoidable haste,

Sincerely yours,   [Woodrow Wilson]

CCL (WP, DLC).

Two Telegrams to Joseph Patrick Tumulty

[Paris] February 14, 1919

For Tumulty from the President.

Please deliver to each Member of the Foreign Affairs Committee the following message from me.

"Last night the Committee of the Conference charged with the duty of drafting a constitution for the League of Nations concluded its work and this afternoon before leaving for the United States it is to be my privilege and duty to read to a Plenary Session of the Conference the text of the twenty six Articles agreed upon by this Committee.

The Committee which drafted these Articles was fairly representative of the world. Besides the representatives of the United States, Great Britain, France, Italy and Japan, representatives of Belgium, Serbia, China, Greece, Roumania, Czecho-Slovakia, Poland, Brazil and Portugal actively participated in the debates and assisted materially in the drafting of this Constitution. Each Article was passed only after the most careful examination by each member of the Committee. There is a good and sufficient reason for the phraseology and substance of each Article. I request that I be permitted to go over with you Article by Article the Constitution reported before this part of the work of the Conference is made the subject of debate in Congress. With this in view I request that you dine with me at the White House as soon after I arrive in the United States as my engagements permit. I have asked Mr. Tumulty to fix the date of this dinner."

Please arrange this dinner for a date as soon as practicable after my arrival.

TC telegram (E. M. House Papers, CtY).

[Paris, Feb. 14, 1919]

Sailing for Boston tomorrow morning. Notify officials there will make address but desire no elaborate entertainment. Stay must be brief as possible. Must hurry to Washington. Will let you know as soon as possible from ship when (arrival) Boston is known. Arrange for train extra baggage car. Hope you will meet me in Boston (although) not essential. Notify Mrs. Grayson and other families interested.   Woodrow Wilson.

T telegram (J. P. Tumulty Papers, DLC).

To Robert Lansing

My dear Mr. Secretary: Paris, 14 February, 1919.

I am sorry that the Copenhagen government is getting irritated about our delay to appoint a Minister there in Egan's place and yet I do not know that I can blame them, and therefore write to ask if you do not think that Mr. Norman Hapgood would be a good nominee for that post?

If you do approve of that suggestion I would be very much obliged to you if you would have him sounded out (for I believe he is on this side of the water) and send me a wireless message about it on my way home.   Sincerely yours,   Woodrow Wilson

TLS (R. Lansing Papers, DLC).

To Arthur Hugh Frazier

My dear Frazier: Paris, 14 February, 1919.

Will you add another obligation to my debt to you for the many kindnesses you have rendered? Will you not see Mr. Gompers and explain to him that he is quite mistaken about my receiving any other labor delegation and that it has been a cause of genuine distress to me that during these last days of hurry it has been literally impossible for me to make an appointment of more than five minutes for the very important comparison of views which he desires?

Will you not beg him in my name to present his views to the other commissioners and assure him of my great regret that I should have been so situated.

                    Sincerely yours,   [Woodrow Wilson]

CCL (WP, DLC).

Two Letters to Herbert Clark Hoover

My dear Hoover: Paris, 14 February, 1919.

I think this may be a very useful piece of advice to give Mr. Davis in advising him how he is to handle this exceedingly important matter.[1]

In great haste,   Faithfully yours,   Woodrow Wilson

[1] See HCH to WW, Feb. 12, 1919 (second letter of that date).

My dear Mr. Hoover: Paris, 14 February, 1919.

This seems to me to contain a very grave and serious matter[1] and I would be very much obliged if you would consider it very carefully.

In haste.   Always faithfully yours,   Woodrow Wilson

TLS (Hoover Archives, CSt-H).
[1] See C. Glass to WW, Feb. 11, 1919.

To Bernard Mannes Baruch

My dear Baruch: Paris, 14 February, 1919.

The course you suggest in the last part of this important letter,[1] which I am returning in order that it may remain in Paris pending my return, had already been made to me in substance by Mc-Cormick, and I had already authorized McCormick, as I now authorize you, to make such intimations as you indicate in order that the air might be cleared. You might let Davis and Strauss see this.

Cordially and sincerely yours,   [Woodrow Wilson]

CCL (WP, DLC).
[1] Either B. M. Baruch to WW, Feb. 14, 1919, or B. M. Baruch to WW, Feb. 11, 1919; most likely the latter.

To William Harrison Short

[Paris] 2/14/19.

Your message[1] from the 3500 delegates representing the League to Enforce Peace has reached me and has given me just the assurance of support which I desire and which I most value and beg to express to all concerned my deepest appreciation for such support in the great cause.   Woodrow Wilson.

T telegram (WP, DLC).
[1] W. H. Short to WW, Feb. 9, 1919.

To George Lansbury

My dear Mr. Lansbury: Paris, 14 February, 1919.

It is a matter of sincere regret to me that I had to postpone the pleasure of seeing you, but shall look forward with genuine pleasure to having the opportunity to do so when I come back to France.

Admiral Grayson has told me how considerate you have been and I am very much obliged to you for your kindness. These have been truly distracting days when I have done what I found it absolutely necessary to do and not what I wanted to do.

With cordial regards,

In haste.   Sincerely yours,   Woodrow Wilson

TLS (British Library of Political and Economic Science, LSE).

To William Howard Taft

[Paris] 2/14/19

The cable in which you and President Lowell were kind enough to join[1] gives me very great and valuable reassurance and I beg to express my warmest thanks. I wish to thank you also for the message from Chicago[2] containing resolutions adopted by the Great Lakes Division for League of Nations.   Woodrow Wilson.

T telegram (WP, DLC).
  [1] W. H. Taft and A. L. Lowell to WW, Feb. 10, 1919.
  [2] W. H. Taft and Edgar Bancroft to WW, Feb. 12, 1919, T telegram (WP, DLC).

From Henry White

Confidential

Dear Mr. President: Paris 14 February 1919

In a letter from my son,[1] who is Chargé d'Affaires at Bangkok, in Siam, which I found on my desk upon getting home from the Conference this evening, he tells me that one of the secretaries from our Embassy at Tokio was then on a visit to him, upon the former's return from a trip with Ambassador Morris to Siberia. The following is a quotation from my son's letter:

"He tells me that the British failed at first to cooperate with us, out of jealousy, in plans for reorganizing the Siberian Railroad (the British General, Knox, even going so far as to indulge in anti-American propaganda), with the result that they were painfully surprised to find the strides made by the Japanese, who got securely in the saddle and sent freight cars with Japanese merchandise attached to military trains."

I have thought this bit of intelligence might be of interest to you during one of the moments of leisure which you may have on the "George Washington"; if indeed you should have any.

Again let me congratulate you, dear Mr. President, upon your great achievement here, and particularly upon the success of to-day's meeting of the Conference; and, with best wishes for a speedy voyage and a return to Paris as soon as it may be possible, I am, dear Mr. President,   Very sincerely yours,   Henry White

TLS (WP, DLC).
   [1] John Campbell White.

Gilbert Fairchild Close to Charles Michael Schwab

My dear Mr. Schwab: Paris, 14 February 1919.

The President received your very kind letter of February 12th just as he was in the final rush of preparation to return to America and he has asked me to reply to it for him, saying that he appreciates very deeply the importance of the business situation at home and has already consulted with Mr. Baruch and others here, as well as with the Secretary of Commerce and the men in the War Industries Board at home.

A plan has been worked out under the direction of the Secretary of Commerce which it is expected will relieve the situation a good deal and to which both the President and Mr. Baruch have given their approval.

The President asks me to thank you especially for your very kind personal words about his work and to say that letters such as yours give him the greatest satisfaction and reassurance in the difficult and perplexing problems which are now before him.

               Sincerely yours,   [Gilbert F. Close]

CCL (WP, DLC).

Tasker Howard Bliss to Newton Diehl Baker, with Enclosure

No. 46

My dear Mr. Secretary: Paris, February 14, 1919.

I sent you a telegram last night, by direction of the President,[1] informing you of the latter's decision in regard to sending two American railway companies to Murmansk, and the reasons for his action. I enclose, herewith, a copy of the memorandum which he approved.

I find among British military men an apparently universal sentiment in favor of withdrawing the expedition from North Russia as soon as the spring weather conditions permit. That has been my own view for a long time. The time has come when we must decide the purpose for which we are in Russia. It is no longer to get possession of certain military stores which otherwise might fall into the hands of the Germans; nor is it to help the Czecho-Slovaks. No other purpose is left except that of fighting the Bolsheviks. If we are going to do that, we must not only stay with our present force (if we can) but we must also send a very large additional force. No one favors that. Even the British seem to have entirely revised their former attitude in regard to military intervention to suppress Bolshevism. When the President approved the memorandum, I told him that it committed him to having a formal understanding with his colleagues on the Supreme War Council on the subject. He told me that it would be impossible for him to see Lloyd George and that substantially what was desired would be accomplished if I transmitted copies of the memorandum with his action on it to the governments concerned. I accordingly addressed a letter on the subject to each of the Military Representatives at Versailles (British, French and Italian), and at the same time sent through the British Mission here a copy to the British War Cabinet in London. This, as I see it, commits us irrevocably to withdrawal of American troops the moment the weather conditions in the spring will permit. The sending of the railway companies in question will greatly facilitate their prompt withdrawal. . . .[2]

We have a meeting of the Plenary Conference in the course of the next hour to hear Mr. Wilson present the draft for the constitution of a League of Nations, on which the committee appointed some time ago by the Peace Conference has agreed. The French will probably precipitate a hot discussion, although the President hopes to avoid it. What the French really want is not a League of Nations for the maintenance of general peace, but an armed alliance of infinite duration against Germany.

Hastily but cordially yours,   [Tasker H. Bliss]

CCL (T. H. Bliss Papers, DLC).
   [1] T. H. Bliss to NDB and P. C. March, Feb. 13, 1919.
   [2] The War Department, in a statement in the *Official Bulletin*, III (Feb. 18, 1919), 1, 3, announced that the President had approved the sending of two American railway companies to Murmansk for the three reasons detailed in (a), (b), and (c) in No. 4 of Bliss' memorandum printed as an Enclosure below. The balance of the War Department's statement briefly paraphrased Bliss' memorandum.

ENCLOSURE

Versailles February 12, 1919.

MEMORANDUM FOR THE PRESIDENT.

1. The general situation of the Allied forces in Northern Russia is as follows: Based on Archangel, there is a total Allied force of about 16,230, of which the Americans number 5,100, the British 6,200, the French 1,650, the Italians 25, the Russians 3,325. Of the American force about 1,200 are stationed at Archangel, and the remainder is scattered in small detachments, in some cases amounting to only one platoon, over a wide area extending from Pinega, about 80 miles to the eastward of Archangel, to the southeastward along the Dwina and Vaga Rivers, about 150 miles from Archangel, to the southward, along the Vologda Railroad, to about 100 miles from Archangel, and to Onega, about 80 miles to the westward of Archangel.

Based on Murmansk, there is a total Allied force of 16,200. This force includes no Americans, 6,650 British, 700 French, 1,250 Italians, 12 Serbians, 6,450 Russians. This force is scattered in detachments extending from Petchenga, on the Arctic Ocean, to Soroka, on the White Sea, about 250 miles south of Murmansk.

Archangel is entirely closed to sea communication until late May, while Murmansk is to a certain extent an open port throughout the year. Allied troops based on Archangel are then, throughout a large part of the year, entirely dependent for outside assistance on the railroad from Murmansk to a point on this railroad approximately due west of Onega and thence by road eastward. Allied troops based on Murmansk depend upon the railroad and to some extent on roads. All roads and the railroad are now in extremely bad condition. The Murmansk Railroad, in the sector where it is most essential for the maintenance of the Allied troops, is built on bog and due to this fact repairs, except in the frozen season, are almost impossible. At present the supply and maintenance of the Allied and American troops in Northern Russia due to the condition of the railroad is rendered extremely difficult and the comfort of the troops is therefore greatly affected. Should the troops in the Archangel sector continue to be hard pressed by hostile forces during the present closed season, there will be danger for their safety unless reinforcements can reach them from the Murmansk sector, and this will be possible only if the Murmansk Railroad in the White Sea sector is properly maintained and operated.

Because of the dependence that must be put upon the Murmansk Railroad for supply and maintenance of troops in the Murmansk

sector, and possible reinforcement purposes in the Archangel sector, as well as the great need for this railroad in the best possible
condition for early withdrawal purposes, which British sentiment
now favors, the British are very anxious to send to Murmansk the
following technical troops:

Railway troops, 2 Companies and details, (1 operating Company and 1 mainte- nance Company)	720 men
R.E. (1 Works Company	150 "
(Signals	240 "
(Electric Lighting	40 "
Royal Army Service Corps, Royal Army Ordnance Department, Royal Army Medical Corps	258 "
Total	1408 "

The British now make a request that the United States assist in
furnishing these technical troops to the extent of supplying the
railway troops amounting to approximately 720 men.

2. It is recommended that American railway troops, 2 Companies,
(1 for operating the railroad and 1 for its maintenance, together
with necessary details; approximately 720 men) be sent to reinforce
the Allied and American troops in Russia. The immediate object of
this reinforcement should be to assist in providing for the safety,
supply, and comfortable maintenance of the Allied and American
troops in Northern Russia during the present closed season, the
ultimate object being to place the railroad in serviceable condition
for the prompt withdrawal of the troops from Northern Russia as
soon as the season permits.

3. No doubt the idea of sending American troops, even though
they be technical troops, to Russia at this time will raise in the
United States the following questions, and similar questions with
respect to our present force in Russia even now are undoubtedly
in the minds of people in general:

First: Are additional American troops being sent to Russia to
assist in penetrating further into Russian territory? If so, how
much further and why?

Second: Are these troops to assist in maintaining the Allied
line where it now is? If so, for how long and why?

Third: Or, is this force to assist in the withdrawal of troops
from Northern Russia at the earliest opportunity?

4. I believe that the third of the foregoing questions should be
answered in the affirmative, and without delay.

I, therefore, think that the President should now have a clear understanding with his colleagues on the Supreme War Council that the sending of additional troops to North Russia is for the purpose of

a) Assuring the greater safety during this winter of the Allied forces now there;

b) The better supply and, if necessary, the reinforcement from Murmansk of the advanced detachments south of Murmansk and Archangel, by improved military facilities resulting from the sending of American Railway troops; and

c) Facilitating the prompt withdrawal of these troops as soon as the weather conditions in the spring will permit.

It is with the foregoing understanding that I recommend assent to the request of the British government for the dispatch of the American Railway troops specified above.   T. H. Bliss

Entirely approved:
Woodrow Wilson
A true Copy:
W B. Wallace
Lieutenant Colonel, General Staff.

T MS (SDR, RG 256, 861.0146/6, DNA).

From the Diary of David Hunter Miller

Friday, February 14th [1919]

In the morning I sent up to Sir Maurice Hankey 30 copies of the Covenant, to Lord Eustace Percy 20 copies. 500 copies were delivered to me at the Meurice at 4 A.M. by Captain Peacock.[1] Keeping out a few copies for myself, I took the remainder to the Crillon. I gave some to Colonel House and to Mr. Auchincloss and sent 10 up to the President with a letter, and delivered the remainder to Mr. Harrison. I also arranged that the other 500 which were to be delivered during the day were to be delivered to Mr. Harrison and that the printer should then go on printing 500 more.

In the afternoon I went to the Plenary Session of the Peace Conference, which lasted from 3 to 7. Mr. Balfour made two side remarks of some interest. At the close of the President's speech he turned and said to the President: "That was a great performance"; and when Hughes of Australia got up to speak he said in French, apparently to Clemenceau: "Que je le déteste."

When I handed the Covenant to Colonel House he asked me if I would not get up a sort of history of changes in the paper occurring in Paris.

Miller, *My Diary at the Conference of Paris*, I, 122-23.
[1] Unidentified.

From the Diary of Colonel House

February 14, 1919.

The President came down this morning at ten and did not leave until one. We sat in my private study for twenty minutes together and during that time we settled all the important questions I had on my mind to take up with him before he left for America. I outlined my plan of procedure during his absence. I told him I thought we could button up everything during the next four weeks. He seemed startled and even alarmed at this statement. I therefore explained that my plan was not to actually bring these matters to a final conclusion but to have them ready for him to do so when he returned. This pleased him.

I thought one of the main things we should do was to fix a program regarding what was necessary to make a preliminary peace with Germany. I enumerated these as follows:

1. A reduction of their army and navy to a peace footing.
2. A delineation of the boundaries of Germany. This is to include the cession of the Colonies.
3. The amount of money to be paid for reparation and the length of time in which to pay it.
4. An agreement as to the economic treatment of Germany.

I asked him if he had anything else to suggest in addition to these four articles. He thought they were sufficient.

The French Government are unable to get the Hotel Murat any longer and the President asked me to confer with them and arrange for another residence for him. I suggested that we insist upon paying them for the next house. He told me to use my judgment about this.

I asked him to bear in mind while he was gone that it was sometimes necessary to compromise in order to get things through. Not a compromise of principle, but a compromise of detail, and I called his attention to the fact that he had made many since he had been here. I did not wish him to leave expecting the impossible in all things.

We discussed the appointment of an Attorney General in place of Gregory. He had about made up his mind to Mitchell Palmer. I objected and proposed Sherman Whipple of Boston as a substitute. Neither one of them seems to me satisfactory but I thought Whipple better than Palmer. In the first place he comes from a section unrepresented in the Cabinet while Pennsylvania already has one member. On the other hand, Pennsylvania is overwhelmingly republican and New England has occasionally relapsed into democracy. In connection with this, I suggested that he land in Boston rather than in New York or Hampton Roads as he had in mind. I thought if he landed in New York there would be some unpleasant complication with the Hylan-Hearst Reception Committee.[1] On the contrary, he had treated New England with scant consideration. Boston had a democratic Mayor[2] and they were eager to do him honor. I thought it would make a good impression in Europe for him to have a great welcome from that part of the United States. He reluctantly assented and will have cables sent following out this plan.

I had Gordon write a cable to Tumulty for the President's approval, inviting the Foreign Relations Committee of both the Senate and the House to dine with him as soon as practicable after his arrival, and requesting them to refrain from comment in Congress upon the League of Nations until he had an opportunity to discuss it with them. When I first proposed this several days ago he declared he would not do it, and that the most he would do would be to make an address to Congress. This I thought wholly inadequate, because it would not please Congress since they would take it that he had called them together as a school master, as they claim he usually does. There would be no chance for discussion, consultation or explanation, and they would not regard it as a compliment but rather the contrary.

He read the cable that had been prepared and changed only one word. I had it sent immediately.

He has definitely given the Paris Ambassadorship to Hugh Wallace and Copenhagen to Norman Hapgood following my suggestion in both cases.

I asked him about cables and he expressed a wish that no one should know of the cables between us, and that they should be sent through our private code. In some ways this is preferable, but I can see many opportunities for trouble with my fellow Commissioners.

I told him I had instructed Rogers[3] to send the text of the League of Nations throughout the world, and that I had also instructed him to get a verbatim report of the speech which he, the President, delivered this afternoon, and send it along with the text of the Covenant.

And this reminds me, that as far as I can recall, I was the first to use and have adopted the word "Covenant" rather than "Constitution" or any other term. I used it first at Magnolia when I submitted a draft to the President and he followed the suggestion all through.

[1] About this matter, see NDB to WW, Jan. 1, 1919, n. 1, Vol. 53.
[2] That is, Andrew James Peters.
[3] That is, Walter Stowell Rogers, director of the Division of Foreign Cable News Service of the C.P.I., at this time also an adviser to the A.C.N.P.

After we had finished these matters which took about twenty minutes, we called in the other Commissioners. He talked to them for about an hour but there was nothing of importance said or done. I had him meet the Belgian Prime Minister for a moment, and also Oscar Straus who is helping us to form a favorable public opinion at home regarding the League.

The newspaper men sent in a request for a five minute interview with the President. He wished to put them off until after the meeting at the Quai d'Orsay but I suggested that he see them at once and get it off his mind, since there was no telling how late he would be. He consented reluctantly and then, to my astonishment, went into the other room and talked to fifteen or twenty American correspondents for nearly an hour—all of them standing. He spoke in the pleasantest and frankest way to them. I cannot understand how a man as busy as he is, and upon the day he is leaving for the United States, could do such a thing. It is to be remembered that he did not want to see them, and yet when he got to talking, he was so enthused with what he had to say that it looked as if he would never stop. It was one o'clock when he left for his luncheon.

At 3.30 there was a Plenary Meeting of the Peace Conference at the Quai d'Orsay. I had arranged most of the program. It is astonishing how easy it is to do this if one takes the initiative. Clemenceau is not interested in the League of Nations, therefore it was a matter of unconcern to him who spoke or did not speak.

After some discussion with the President and Lord Robert Cecil I sent word to Clemenceau through Frazier that the order of the afternoon would be that the President, acting as Chairman for the Committee to prepare a Covenant for the League of Nations, would make a report and read the Covenant which had been constructed, and that he would make a speech upon the subject. That Lord Robert Cecil would follow with a speech, then Orlando and perhaps Venizelos. This program was literally carried out with the exception that Bourgeois also spoke for France.

We tried to get Bourgeois not to mention any of the reservations he had made concerning the Covenant, but our efforts were futile. He promised to say nothing but a sentence or two if Cecil did not speak. After consultation with the President, we declined to make any concession because it seemed necessary for Great Britain to approve.

I received word from Wiseman after we got to the Quai d'Orsay asking whether I thought it would be well to have Barnes,[4] the labor leader Member of the British Cabinet, say a word in behalf of the Cabinet. I advised his doing so.

[4] That is, George Nicoll Barnes, Minister without Portfolio and a plenipotentiary delegate of Great Britain at the peace conference.

It was a notable and impressive occasion. I will not go into details because it is a matter of history and will be better written by others. After the President's speech I wrote on a slip of paper:

"Dear Governor: Your speech was as great as the occasion" He returned the slip with this on it: "Bless your heart. Thank you from the bottom of my heart."

The President also wrote me, "Is Venizelos going to speak?" I replied to this: "If the Prime Minister has not notified Venizelos, then he may not be prepared." The President replied on the same slip, "Suppose you send him word." I did this, saying:

"Dear Prime Minister: I think M. Clemenceau will call on you to make an address if you do not object. Will you not let me know. Sincerely, E.M.H." To which Venizelos replied on the same slip, "Je suis a la disposition de le President, M. Clemenceau."

I therefore notified M. Clemenceau to call on him, which he did. I wrote a note to Orlando after his speech saying:

"I congratulate you, my dear friend and distinguished colleague." He sent me his card in reply upon which he had written "Thanks, my dear friend, for your kind congratulations. Leaving today. I present you my best respects."

Bourgeois made his usual tiresome speech. After he had finished I did not wait to hear it translated since it was already six o'clock and I was weary of so much talking. I dislike seeing time wasted the way it is here by talking that is so perfectly useless. The President himself talks entirely too much but he does it so much better than anyone else that he always interests me. I cannot emphasize too strongly his accomplishment in this direction. It amounts to genius, and as far as I know, he is in a class unto himself.

When I returned to the Crillon, I saw the newspaper correspondents as usual and after dinner I went to the Hotel Murat to bid the President and Mrs. Wilson goodbye and go with them to the station. I was surprised to see practically all official France at the station. From the curb to the train itself, a distance of many hundred feet, a beautiful red carpet was spread with palms and other evergreens on each side, making a corridor of some fifteen or twenty feet wide and extending several hundred feet. The President and Madame Poincaré, M. Clemenceau and his entire Cabinet, the British Ambassador and everybody else of prominence was there. The President bade me a fervent goodbye, clasping my hand and placing his arm around me. The entire occasion was a fitting tribute to him and was an appropriate act to a very memorable visit. He looked happy, as well indeed he should.

From the Diary of Dr. Grayson

Saturday, February 15, 1919.

We arrived at Brest at 10:30, the train pulling up to the pier. . . .[1]

We boarded the tug and accompanied by French officials and saluted by shore batteries were taken out to the U.S.S. GEORGE WASHINGTON, which after boarding and saying the usual formal adieus, sailed for Boston, Massachusetts.

[1] Here follows a copy of the statement printed as the next document.

A Statement Upon Leaving France

[[Feb. 15, 1919]]

I cannot leave France without expressing my profound sense of the great hospitality of the French people and the French Government. They have received and treated me as I most desired to be treated, as a friend, a friend alike in spirit and in purpose.

I am happy to say that I am to return to assist with all my heart in completing the just settlements which the Peace Conference is seeking and I shall carry with me during my absence very happy memories of the two months I have spent here.

I have been privileged to see here at first hand what my sympathies have already conceived—the sufferings and problems of France—and every day has deepened my interest in the solution of the grave questions upon whose proper solution the future prosperity of France and her associates and the whole world depends. May I not leave my warm and affectionate farewell greetings?

Printed in the *New York Times*, Feb. 16, 1919.

From Joseph Patrick Tumulty

[The White House, Feb. 15, 1919]

Will go to Boston myself to arrange details of your visit so as to make it as easy as possible. Have arranged for Foreign Relations dinner.

Have waited before cabling you to ascertain opinion of country as to attitude toward League of Nations. Majority of leading papers favorable. Minority take *technical* view but present no strong case against it. Public Ledger, Republican paper says "Document bristles with _____ [teeth][1] and in this regard is wholly dissimilar to any panacea for peace ever devised by recognized authorities. Program probably grounded on reality. It is able, frank, and historically

_____ [concrete]. The President's triumph in the incorporation of his [many] planks is marked. This [Its] superb achievement crowns his home coming with sweeping victory. The world is in sight of the genuine (?) [solid] and concrete foundations of great redemption."

Republicans in the Senate and House silent as usual and waiting to see how *a few members* (?) [cat] will _____ [jump]. Hitchcock gave out admirable statement. Personally consider your achievement remarkable. Plain people throughout America for you. You have but to ask their support and all opposition will melt away. Warmest regards.   Tumulty

T radiogram (WP, DLC).
    ¹ Corrections and additions in radiograms and telegrams between Wilson and Tumulty from the "telegrams sent" in the Wilson and Tumulty Papers, DLC.

Joseph Patrick Tumulty to John Sharp Williams

My dear Senator: The White House February 15, 1919.

I send you herewith copy of a cable message which the President has directed me to have delivered to each member of the Foreign Relations Committee of the Senate and the Foreign Affairs Committee of the House of Representatives.¹

Will you not be good enough to let me know if you can dine with the President at eight o'clock Wednesday evening, February 26th?
                         Sincerely yours,   J. P. Tumulty

TLS (J. S. Williams Papers, DLC).
    ¹ For the text, see WW to JPT, Feb. 14, 1919 (first telegram of that date).

From William Harrison Short

                    Minneapolis Minn February 15 1919

Twenty two hundred registered delegates composing northern congress for a league of nations unanimously adopted following resolution stop To America has come a supreme opportunity in the reconstruction of a world order. She must rise to the high demand of the hour stop She must not forget that the war cannot be kept won until the free nations are organized to safeguard the peace won at such sacrifice of blood and treasure stop The sanctity of international and moral law must be completely reestablished stop To that end Germany must be made to pay the full penalty for every offense that she has committed stop She and all other nations must be made to understand that violation both of moral and of international law will be followed by swift and inexorable punishment stop We believe the only guarantee that international relations will hereafter rest upon the basis of law and justice is the creation of a league of free nations to maintain peace with all the moral economic and physical forces they possess stop The great free nations France, Great Britain, Italy, Japan, and the United States have been working together for great ends stop This is the stren[u]ous hour stop We call upon all those in authority to use their utmost endeavor to prevent the opportunity from being lost stop The league of free nations should be composed of selfgoverned and lawabiding peoples stop No unrepentent no unregenerate Germany should be admitted to fellowship in such a league stop Germany must be on probation until she has proved to the satisfaction of the league her right to communication with free nations stop Our fathers were wise in that they looked the facts of their day in the face stop We should follow their example by doing the same in our day stop The time has come for their sons to take part in a league of nations to maintain an enduring peace to promote the liberty progress and orderly development of the world stop We believe the overwhelming public opinion of the United States is in favor of such a league and will sustain the President and the Senate of the United States in assuming for this country any burden it may involve stop With faith in her purpose with constancy in effort with sagacity in action America should finish the work she has begun and thus help build a structure that so far as human wisdom can reach, will banish the scourge of war from among men stop To this constructive plan of statesmanship we pledge our fullest efforts and we dedicate ourselves to carry the program to the people of the four states here represented to secure for it their thoughtful consideration and an opportunity to record their earnest support   Wm H Short

T radiogram (WP, DLC).

From Edward Albert Filene

Spokane, Wash. [Feb. 15, 1919]

The gratitude of men like myself is unexpressible. The verdict of history will be that this is the greatest deed done by its greatest man stop Taft, Van Dike[1] Lowell myself and others are crossing the country to focus support for league stop Everywhere with better understanding comes determined support stop When you come home lead and clinch and you will have won the greatest victory in history.   Edward Filene

T radiogram (WP, DLC).
[1] That is, Henry van Dyke.

A Memorandum by Henry White

Mr. Delacroix,[1] President of the Council of Ministers of Belgium, came to see me today in reference to an interview he had had with the President yesterday, at which I was present. He had come specially from Belgium on short notice in order to see the President before his departure, to explain to him the uneasiness felt in Belgium lest she should have no funds at her disposal wherewith to restore the devastated parts of that country, and to express the hope to the President that some sort of priority for Belgium in the receipt of financial assistance might be promised by him before he left for the United States.

The President, of course, told the Minister that he was unable to make any such promise, and Mr. Delacroix came to see me today in the hope that some method might be found for Belgium to obtain a credit "in the United States" (really from the Treasury) wherewith to purchase raw materials to be used in starting up Belgian industries once more. He said that it is not difficult to *buy* boots, but what they want is leather to be used by Belgian workmen in making boots, and so on, in respect to raw materials for numerous other Belgian industries.

Mr. Delacroix had conceived the idea during the twenty-four hours which had elapsed since his interview with the President that perhaps the next Liberty Loan in the United States might be increased by one billion of dollars for Belgium, his idea being that the success of the loan would be greatly enhanced by the knowledge among our people that one-fifth or one-sixth of it was to be placed at the disposal of Belgium.

I replied that this suggestion did not seem a practical one to me, but that not being a financier I was unable to speak with authority in such matters, and I suggested that he confer with Mr. Davis or Mr. Strauss of the Treasury, which he said he would do.

It is evident that Belgium is somewhat alarmed lest the lion's share in whatever is obtained from Germany in the way of restitution, will go to France, and that she may find herself rather left out; and in any case that the amounts which Germany will be able to pay down immediately in the way of restoration either to France or to Belgium will be very far from sufficient to defray the cost of the restorations and reparations which ought immediately to be carried out, and the President of the Council is therefore looking for some means of finding the amount required, which he placed at five billions of francs, and the United States appears to him the only such source of supply.

T MS (R. Lansing Papers, DLC).
¹ That is, Léon Delacroix.

From the Diary of Dr. Grayson

Sunday, February 16, 1919.

The President went to church, and rested in the afternoon. He was very tired and at my suggestion agreed to rest during most of the voyage.

From Edward Mandell House

[Paris] Feb 16 9 PM [1919]

Davison giving dinner to diplomatic and press representatives in Paris on Friday February 21 to announce plans for coordinating work of Red Cross societies.¹ He would greatly appreciate a message from you to be read at dinner. I know that you wish to support this movement in every practicable way and accordingly I suggest that you authorize me to communicate to Davison substantially the following from you so that he may read at the dinner.

"I sincerely regret I cannot be in Paris to join in expressing support and approval of the plans announced for coordinating and extending the efforts of the Red Cross societies of the world. I had been familiar with these plans from their inception. They contain great possibilities for lessening and preventing distress among all peoples. This would be enough amply to justify the utmost effort but there is the promise that the joint efforts of Red Cross societies acting in concert will hasten and broaden the spread of fraternal feeling among peoples. For these two reasons I am heartily in accord with the steps now being taken to bring together the Red Cross societies of the world, all those forces which in this way can be directed toward lessening the sufferings and burdens of all humanity wherever and in whatever form they may exist. I sincerely trust that the plans which are to be announced may have the support and active assistance of all governments and all peoples before whom they may be brought."

Edward House

T radiogram (WP, DLC).
¹ About which, see S. Axson to WW, Nov. 27, 1918; the memorandum by S. Axson printed at Dec. 2, 1918; and WW to H. P. Davison, Dec. 3, 1918, all in Vol. 53.

From the Diary of Dr. Grayson

Monday, February 17, 1919.

The President rested and remained in his room throughout the day except for a short walk on deck.

To Edward Mandell House

U.S.S. George Washington, February 17, 1919.

Thank you for your message about the Red Cross. Would be very glad if you would give the message you suggest. All going well with us.   Woodrow Wilson

CC radiogram (WP, DLC).

From Robert Lansing

[Paris, Feb. 17, 1919]

The discussion on the Russian question was continued at the meeting this afternoon at the Quai D'Orsay.[1] Mr Winston Churchill submitted a resolution directing the military representatives of the Supreme War Council at Versailles, with whom might be associated as required representatives of the general staffs of the navies of the allied and associated powers, to examine and report at an early date as to the practicability possible joint military action by the associated powers to enable the Russian armies called into being by these powers during the war with Germany, to maintain themselves against Bolshevist coercion, and as to what measures and precautions might be necessary or possible to safeguard Finland, Esthonia, Livinia,[2] Poland and Roumania. The American representatives opposed the adoption of this resolution, and after considerable discussion it was agreed particularly to ensure secrecy at this stage of the discussion, that each delegation would consult its military representatives at Versailles on the points mentioned in Mr Churchill's resolution, that the military representatives would talk the matter over in confidence with each other, and that they would then report to their respective delegation as soon as possible. The matter would then come up again for discussion with a view to determining upon policy.

Marshal Foch reported that the armistice had been signed exactly as given to him on the twelfth, except for a slight modification in the southern line of boundary between the Poles and the Germans. The Marshal also reported that Erzberger had delivered to him a communication from Scheidemann, in which the latter claimed that Germany had complied with the terms of the armistice up to the exhaustion of their commerce and the collapse of their transportation. Scheidemann also complained because the new armistice ignored the creation of a government in Germany based on popular will and required the evacuation of two important towns in favor of the Poles, moreover they had given no guarantees that the Poles would abstain from attacks or treat fairly the Germans who were within the territory now controlled by them, set free the German hostages, or maintain the supply of food which Germany counted on receiving from the territory which the Poles now controlled.

Admiral Browning[3] reported that he had been able to complete satisfactory arrangements with the Germans regarding the delivery and destruction of the submarine boats.

In regard to the suggestion which had been made by the Servian delegates that you be asked to arbitrate between them and Italy,[4] Baron Sonnino stated that his government regretted that they were unable to submit arbitration questions for the readjusting which Italy had entered the war and which had already been submitted to the examination of the conference. Lansing.

T radiogram (WP, DLC).

[1] For the minutes of this meeting of the Council of Ten, see *PPC*, IV, 22-43. The minutes do not include the discussion of Russian policy mentioned by Lansing because the participants agreed to delete it. See also the House Diary, Feb. 17, 1919, not printed, and Thompson, *Russia, Bolshevism, and the Versailles Peace*, pp. 143-44.

[2] Actually, Livonia or Livland, a Russian province which is now divided between Latvia and Estonia.

[3] That is, Vice-Adm. Sir Montague Edward Browning, president of the Allied Naval Armistice Commission.

[4] See Nikola Pašić *et al.* to WW, Feb. 11, 1919.

From Edward Mandell House

[Paris, c. Feb. 17, 1919]

(Did not) see the telegram reporting meeting until after it had been sent. It does not allude to _____ atmosphere of the meeting. Churchill not only wished question as to what military action by the associated governments was practicable with respect to Russia to be referred to a military commission, but also a public statement to be made of this reference. George had wired his Secretary to show me cables—instructions sent to Churchill by George and I had read them just before meeting. They did not justify extreme position taken by Churchill. I opposed formal reference to military commission of the question and stated that General Bliss was prepared to state at once the view of the United States on the military situation _____ the United States could not employ any of her

resources against Russia for we are not at war with Russia. Plenipotentiaries further drew attention to recent tie vote in the Senate
on the resolution demanding withdrawal of all American troops
from Russia.[1] I suggested that the civil representatives of respective
governments present confer with their military advisors and that
the military men confer informally among themselves so that at a
later meeting the matter could again be discussed. Balfour supported me and in particular insisted on no press article of any kind
be made of discussion. Clemenceau made an excited speech which
Balfour considered offensive and accordingly he answered it rather
sharply. I believe that the matter has been adjusted for the time
being. There is some chance of George coming to Paris.[2] It will be
more satisfactory to deal with him than with Churchill. Wednesday
Balfour and I see Clemenceau privately in an endeavor to accelerate
work of conference.

T radiogram (WP, DLC).
    [1] S. Res. 411, about which see FLP to RL, Jan. 24, 1919 (first telegram of that date),
n. 3, Vol. 54. The proposed resolution was debated on February 14. A motion to lay the
resolution on the table resulted in a tie vote of thirty-three senators for and thirty-three
against, with thirty not voting. Vice-President Marshall broke the tie with the vote which
tabled the resolution. *Cong. Record*, 65th Cong., 3d sess., pp. 3334-42.
    [2] Lloyd George had left Paris on February 8 to return to London to deal with serious
labor unrest in various parts of England and Scotland, especially among coal miners,
railwaymen, and transport workers. He returned to Paris on March 5. For a discussion
of the labor situation in Great Britain and the government's efforts to deal with it at this
time, see Arno J. Mayer, *Politics and Diplomacy of Peacemaking: Containment and
Counterrevolution at Versailles, 1918-1919* (New York, 1967), pp. 604-22.

From Eleanor Randolph Wilson McAdoo and William Gibbs McAdoo

Dearest Father,   Montecito, California February 17th, 1919

    We wish so much that we were there in Washington to welcome
you home. It is hard, from this distance to tell you how glad we
are that you are back and how unspeakably proud we are of the
great things you have accomplished in Europe. You are so wonderful, Father darling, and everything that you do and say is done
with such skill and such genius that we are thrilled beyond measure
every time we read or think of you. It is a great happiness to hear
every day words of love and praise for you from the people out here.

    We love you very, very much—I can't tell you how much, and
we want dreadfully to see you now.

    Edith has been so lovely about writing to me. I don't see how on
earth she had time for it, but she is always perfectly sweet about
it. We have been very proud of her, too, and of the impression she
has made over there. We are so glad that you both had some fun

out of it, for it must have been desperately hard work, too, all the time, and you must both be very tired, indeed. How I wish we could hear all about every thing from you both.

We are having a beautiful time and are enjoying every moment of this glorious sunlight and warmth. Mac is very much rested and, as for Ellen and I—we are terribly fat!

Mac sends his best love—he is as proud and thrilled over you as I, and that's saying a very great deal.

With my devoted love as always, darling Father,

your loving daughter   Nell.

Dear Governor,

Welcome to you and Edith and warmest congratulations on your great triumphs and achievements in Europe. No man in our history has done so much for humanity and the world. We shall have to fight the visionless elements in the Senate to ratify the League of Nations but I believe it can be done, as I am sure the sentiment and opinion of the country is with you. I am gratified to find that the very partisan republican Los Angeles Times is strongly supporting your League of Nations as also is the local republican daily, the Press, of Santa Barbara. I made some speeches for the League of Nations on the way out and found the sentiment favorable.

I hope you are well. Have felt concerned about you under such severe strain. I am better but have been feeling very much used up. I did not decide on a complete rest too soon. My best love for Edith and yourself. Sorry we are not to see you this time.

Affectionately Yours   W G McAdoo

ALS (WP, DLC).

From the Diary of Dr. Grayson

Tuesday, February 18, 1919.

The President and Mrs. Wilson went to the bridge to watch the escort of destroyers struggle through the high seas, remaining there until forced to return below by an unusually venturesome wave spray which was thrown over the bridge and dampened the spirits of the party.

Two Radiograms from Joseph Patrick Tumulty

[The White House] 2/18/19

On assumption that you will arrive Boston Monday, committee suggests program as follows: Met at wharf by committee and guests and taken to Copley Plaza Hotel. Lunch either privately or with Committee and guests as you may prefer. Receive Governor and Mayor.[1] Motor ride or rest in afternoon. Dine privately or with committee and guests as you prefer. Evening address at Mechanics Hall, after which your train leave[s] for Washington. Boston committee think you may arrive Sunday. Is there possibility this? Think it would be mistake.   Tumulty

[1] Calvin Coolidge and Andrew James Peters.

                          The White House, February 18, 4 p.m. [1919]
Rumored here that you will call extra session March eleventh. Causing great uneasiness. Hope you will authorize me to deny. Think it would be better to wait until you arrive and can ascertain exact situation.   Tumulty

T radiograms (WP, DLC).

From Vance Criswell McCormick

My dear Mr. President: Paris, February 18, 1919.
    I am sorry that I did not have an opportunity to discuss with you further the several appointments which I believe to be of great interest to the Party, particularly the Attorney-Generalship. While you said that you would talk to me about this matter before coming to a definite conclusion, I feared that the pressure of the last few days may have prevented you from doing so, and therefore I am taking the liberty of writing you. I sincerely hope that you can see your way clear to appoint Palmer to the Attorney-Generalship, as it will be a most popular appointment as far as the organization is concerned. It will be a recognition of most valuable service to the Party, and will hearten the organization men over the entire country. He is an excellent lawyer, and his recent experience as Alien Property Custodian peculiarly fits him for the handling of the large amount of legal work which is sure to be thrown upon the Attorney-General's office in the settlement of war claims. He was, as you know, a conspicuous figure in Congress for six years, and a leader in party conventions, standing always for your progressive ideals, and his appointment would be looked upon not as an appointment from any particular state, but as an appointment at large. It would be especially gratifying to me personally, if this appointment could be made.
    I should also like to strongly recommend to you Mr. Albert B. Nortoni,[1] of St. Louis, Missouri, a member of our Progressive cam-

paign committee in 1916, for appointment to a vacancy about to occur in the office of the United States District Judge in St. Louis, as I am convinced that Judge Nortoni could fill this office most acceptably, and I believe that his appointment would be acceptable to all our friends in Missouri, and I believe that there would be no objection from the present Senators. Judge Nortoni is entitled to some recognition, as he was one of our most helpful progressive supporters in 1916, and is man of excellent character, and he would, I am sure, fill the position to the satisfaction of every one concerned.

Very Sincerely,   Vance C. McCormick

TLS (WP, DLC).
   [1] Albert Dexter Nortoni, about whom see EMH to WW, Nov. 24, 1914, Vol. 31.

From the Diary of Dr. Grayson

Wednesday, February 19, 1919.

We encountered very high seas and strong winds almost from the start of the present voyage. Yesterday and today the seas were rising very fast. The result was that the Battleship New Mexico, which was a new vessel, just out of the dock, and which had never been given a shaking-down run, was unable to make speed. We were constantly dropping behind. The NEW MEXICO has a new type of electric-drive engines, and these engines were constantly getting out of commission. Today we lost about four hours while the NEW MEXICO was trying to make repairs to her machinery. As a result of the rough seas Captain McCauley told me that if the NEW MEXICO was to continue retarding our speed, we would not be able to arrive in Boston according to schedule. I told this to the President and he told me that if conditions did not improve within the next twenty-four hours the NEW MEXICO would have to abandon us, and we would go on our way regardless of the escort. The seas were so high that they were breaking clear over the top of the escorting destroyers' stacks, and one wave carried away a Lieutenant and a Quartermaster from one of the destroyers, throwing another seaman against the stanchion and breaking his leg. As there did not seem to be any chance of the weather moderating, Assistant Secretary of the Navy Roosevelt, after consultation with myself, issued orders to the destroyers to abandon their escort and to proceed to the Azores. The heavy seas did not in any way trouble the President, who is a wonderfully good sailor, and he came on deck for the usual exercise. After dinner we attended the movies.

To the American Commissioners

U.S.S. George Washington, 19 February, 1919

Am greatly surprised by Churchill's Russian suggestion. I distinctly understood Lloyd George to say that there could be no thought of military action there and what I said at the hurried meeting Friday afternoon[1] was meant only to convey the idea that I would not take any hasty separate action myself but would not be in favor of any course which would not mean the earliest practicable withdrawal of military forces. It would be fatal to be led further into the Russian chaos.   Woodrow Wilson

CC radiogram (WP, DLC).
[1] See Wilson's closing remarks quoted in the minutes of the Supreme War Council printed at Feb. 14, 1919.

To William Harrison Short

U.S.S. George Washington 19 February, 1919.

Your impressive message received and deeply appreciated.
                                        Woodrow Wilson

CC radiogram (WP, DLC).

To Carter Glass

U.S.S. George Washington, 19 February, 1919.

I am impressed with the financial difficulties of the Italian Government and the importance of their obtaining certain food and other primary requirements for existence during this trying readjustment period.[1] Davis and Strauss, who, at my suggestion, discussed matter with Italian Ministers who approached me on the subject, will, I understand, cable you more in detail. I sympathize with your reluctance to make any advances for requirements outside of the United States, but I consider it of public interest and necessity that the situation in Italy be not allowed to grow worse and if you can see your way to do so, I would approve of your advancing to Italy, upon such conditions as you may determine, up to $25,000,000 towards meeting her current neutral purchases which may appear to be otherwise unobtainable during the next [few weeks?]   [Woodrow Wilson]

CC radiogram (WP, DLC).
[1] This radiogram was prompted by N. H. Davis, to WW, Feb. 12, 1919.

From Robert Lansing

[Paris, Feb. 19, 1919]

While motoring, as usual, to the office of the Ministry of War, about nine fifteen this morning, M. Clemenceau was shot by a young Frenchman about twenty two years of age, born at Treves, by the name of Cottin,[1] an anarchist with a police record, but not identified with any particular political group. Five shots were fired four of which lodged in the body of the automobile or piercing M. Clemenceau's clothing. The fifth bullet passed through his neck without severing any important arteries, and lodged in his shoulder. He was taken back to his residence. He was seen shortly after the attack by M. Tardieu, who stated that he was cheerful and made light of the whole matter. At four oclock this afternoon, his condition is reported unchanged. An official bulletin will be issued at five P.M. Cottin has been taken into custody by the police.

Lansing

Hw radiogram (WP, DLC).
   [1] Émile Cottin.

To Robert Lansing

U.S.S. George Washington, February 19, 1918 [1919]

Please convey to Monsieur Clemenceau my heartfelt sympathy and my joy at his escape. I sincerely hope that the report that he was only slightly injured is altogether true. I was deeply shocked by the news of the attack.   Woodrow Wilson

CC radiogram (WP, DLC).

From Robert Lansing and Others

[Paris, Feb. 19, 1919]

For the President

From Lansing, House, Baruch, Davis, McCormick:

The discussions of the reparation commission during the past two weeks have developed a definite and fundamental difference of opinion on whether war costs are to be included in the bill against enemy countries. By war costs are meant not a punitive indemnity but repayment of the extraordinary governmental expenses in maintaining military establishments during the war. The American delegation adhering to what it believes to be a correct interpretation of the *initial tentative draft*? and in accordance with the principles which McCormick showed you and which you approved in Paris[1] has stated that it cannot agree to the principle of admission of war costs although making a reservation in favor of Belgium whose position is such by reason of her neutralization and Germanys admission of liability to make complete reparation for the illegal act of violating this neutrality. Belgium will support the American position but probably no other countries represented on the commission will adhere to the American principles; primarily for fear of the political consequences of failing to insist on what is referred to as complete reparation and also because unwillingness to oppose Great Britain and France which are the most active advocates of the inclusion of war costs. The American position is based on the necessity of adherence to the statement of agreed terms of peace. The Allied declaration of Nov. 4 18. which was accepted by you and communicated to Germany reads as follows in so far as is relevant. "The Allied governments have given careful consideration to the correspondence which has passed between the President of the United States and the German Government subject to the qualifications which follow. They declare their willingness to make peace with the German government on the terms of peace laid down in the Presidents address to Congress of January 1918 and the principles of settlement enunciated in his subsequent addresses." One of the qualifications which then follows relates to reparation and reads as follows: "By it (restoration) they understand that compensation will be made by Germany for all damage to the civilian population of the Allies and their property by the aggression of Germany by land, sea and air." We feel and in this there seems to be general agreement that war costs are not properly included in this language. The general argument of those insisting on including war costs is that this language only refers to specific and immediate reparation and does not preclude war costs which are justifiable under the

general principles of justice enunciated in other portions of your
address and which are likewise to be considered as forming part of
terms of peace. They argue that justice requires all the associated
governments be put back in as near as possible the same position
as if the war had not occurred. They also point out that Allied
acceptance applies only in terms to Germany leaving Austria-Hungary Bulgaria and Turkey and these considerations likewise state
that such reparation as we contend for would be inadequate if
confined to physical reparation since any amount received by individuals in payment of such reparation would be largely absorbed
in taxes to pay war debts. An effort was made today Wednesday by
those favoring war costs to bring about a vote on the (apparent
omission here) to govern determination of amount of reparation
due. Since it was apparent that in any such vote only Belgium and
the United States would refrain from voting for inclusion of war
costs we secured the adoption of amendatory resolution referring
this matter back to the gentlemen who discussed and drew up the
statement of Nov. 4 and who consequently should be able to give
an authoritative interpretation of its meaning. We fear that Lloyd
George, Clemenceau and Orlando will oppose the view which we
have been defending. Accordingly it would be very useful if we
require [receive] from you a statement suitable for use in this connection giving your understanding with reference to war costs. *We
personally* ? are disposed to adopt as liberal construction of the
agreement of this reparation as is possible as our opponents make
a strong popular argument difficult to answer without appearing
to be bound to legal technicalities. We have refused however to
accept the principle of inclusion of war costs feeling that the adoption of this principle in the treaty opens the way to a complete
departure from the agreed terms of peace based on your 14 points
and subsequent addresses. You will understand however that the
political situation in almost all countries will make it most difficult
for their delegates to take any attitude other than insistence upon
the complete reparation which they have promised their people and
which all our inquiries show the people of the Allied countries feel
to be just and due them. While the representatives of the Allied
governments generally recognize and privately admit that it will be
impractical to secure actual repayment of war costs on account of
limited ability of the enemy to pay they seem determined upon
recognition in principle of complete reparation.   Lansing.

CC radiogram (WP, DLC).
  [1] See the declaration printed at Feb. 8, 1919.

Two Radiograms from Edward Mandell House

[Paris, Feb. 19, 1919]

Secret for the President from Col. House:

The following memorandum by the Chief of the British General Staff[1] has just been sent me:

"I had an interesting interview with Marshal Foch this morning in which he expressed the following views:

As a result of his recent discussion with the German Representatives at Treves, he is of the opinion that under existing conditions we can dictate terms of peace to Germany. The Germans will agree to whatever terms we exact. But he says there is no time to lose.

At present Germany has only one thought and that is peace, the reasons being that her government is insecure and wants peace in order to consolidate its position and the people fear above all things a renewal of hostilities. Further fighting would take place on German soil and the Germans are afraid of the devastation of their territory.

In the opinion of the Marshal Germany has at present no military forces with which she could hope to dispute the advance of the Allied armies.

For these reasons Germany will agree to our terms if we are prompt, but no one can say how long the existing conditions will last. Delay is dangerous.

The Marshal therefore strongly advocates the settling at once of the three principal conditions of the peace that the Allies intend to impose upon Germany:

1. The strength of her armed forces.
2. Her frontiers.
3. The indemnity she is to pay.

He considers that if these matters could be settled by the Peace Conference during the next few days, and if he could be entrusted with the mission of proceeding again to Treves with the Allied terms, this day week, he would guarantee that the Germans would accept the terms on the following day. The world would then pass from a state of war to a state of peace for which the French Government [it][2] longs so arderously [ardently], and there would be universal rejoicing.

As regards the three points mentioned above, the intermediary [Marshal] Foch anticipates no difficulty in coming to an agreement during the next 48 hours as to the strength of Germanys peace army and navy.

He is strongly in favor of saying to the Germans in this preliminary peace treaty that, whatever may be the fate of the Rhine [Rhenish] provinces and whatever form of government for these provinces the Allies may decide in favor of, under no circumstances will the German Empire extend beyond the Rhine. That in his governments[3] opinion is essential for the security of France, and makes the settlement of the western frontier a simple matter. He also considers that there should be no insuperable difficulties in settling a frontier between Germany and Poland, which would be capable of modification in detail later.

The Marshal would settle on a lump sum for Germany to pay and suggested hundred milliards of francs. It is unconditional surrender[4] he says, not his business to consider the actual sum, but he speaks forcibly for the principle of including a lump sum by way of indemnity in the terms to be presented to Germany the next time he goes to Treves.

If the conditions of a preliminary peace treaty can be imposed on Germany, the Allies can then turn their attention to the Russian problem which must take time to solve. The Marshal thinks the Allies may lose the war if they do not arrive at a satisfactory solution of the Russian question either by Germany settling it in her [own] interests or by the spread of anarchy. He favors the solution of helping of all the Anti-Bolshevik elements in Russia and all the neighbors of Russia will be given (apparent ommission) [who are] resisting Bolshevik encroachment. He would go so far as to accept German cooperation after the signing of the preliminary treaty of peace, and thinks it might be very valuable.["]

Ammission

[1] That is, Gen. Sir Henry Hughes Wilson.
[2] Corrections from the copy sent in the R. Lansing Papers, DLC.
[3] "governments" not in the "original" copy.
[4] "unconditional surrender" not in the "original" copy.

[Paris] February 19, 10 p.m. [1919]

You know that the memorandum I received containing account of conversation between British Chief of Staff and Foch was sent in regular cipher on account of its length.

Clemenceau, Balfour and I were to have conference at _____ [10][1] o'clock this morning to discuss plans of speeding up work of conference. Clemenceau was shot at nine (five?) o'clock so conference had to be abandoned. French have changed their position (and now) desire to hurry up signing of the (peace treaty). I believe their change of position may be explained by realization that their _____ [army] is becoming demoralized. Amount of compensation mentioned by Foch is far less than sum contended for by French

Treasury which is demanding that cost of war be (met by) Germany. I am (trying) to hasten work of conference so that when you return terms of preliminary peace will be ready for your (consideration)

Edward House

T radiograms (WP, DLC).
[1] This and the following corrections from the copy of this telegram in the Diary of Gordon Auchincloss, T MS (G. Auchincloss Papers, CtY), Feb. 19, 1919.

From Joseph Patrick Tumulty

[The White House, Feb. 19, 1919]

Number 50 Hitchcock and *McClain* [friends] embarrassed to know what their attitude should be toward *answering* Borah and other leaders of opposition to *League* of Nations. Do you think discussion now by Democrats would be helpful if Republicans insist upon discussion.   Tumulty

T radiogram (WP, DLC).

Tasker Howard Bliss to Arthur James Balfour, with Enclosure

My dear Mr. Balfour: Paris, February 19, 1919.

I and my colleagues have been asked so many times, especially in recent days, why the American People seem to be so indifferent to the Russian situation, that it occurred to me to draw up a brief statement showing what, as I conceive it, the American attitude of mind is and the reason for that attitude. On showing this statement to my colleagues, they one and all said that they thought that it was a fair statement of the case.

I venture to enclose you a copy of it.

Cordially yours,   Tasker H. Bliss.

TLS (Balfour Papers, Add. MSS 49742, British Library).

E N C L O S U R E

Paris, February 17, 1919.

MEMORANDUM

It is quite certain—and it will be the part of wisdom for all of us to take note of the fact—that the Government and the people of the United States will be radically opposed to taking part in any hostile action in Russia so long as the present general conditions elsewhere continue to exist. That Government and people will not engage in a new war of unknown extent and duration until the present war is ended by a declared and settled peace.

One reason of the American indisposition to take positive action with the respect to the situation in Russia is their inability to focus their undivided attention on Russia so as to enable them to realize what is going on there and what it may mean to the peace of the world.

To them, Bolshevism in Russia is one of the many confused blotches which disfigure the map of Europe. To them, everything here seems in an intolerable confusion, Russia no more than some other States.

If we could make final and definitive peace *at once*; if we could say to Germany and Poland and Czecho-Slovakia and other States: "These are your definitive boundaries, stay inside of them and stop fighting your neighbors and trying to acquire their territory by force"; if we could now accomplish that, thereby bringing that part of Europe into the first stages of an orderly peace which is praying for that peace, then the conditions of Russia would stand out in clear and glaring relief from this general level of peace. Then, and then only, the people of the United States might come to see that peace in Russia is the only thing necessary to secure universal peace; that her present condition is the only thing that menaces the peace of the world. It is possible that then the United States might be willing to take a part in the pacification of Russia. But it is certain that it will not lift a hand to do this so long as we maintain the state of war with the Central Powers; so long as we continue to dispute—not with Germany but among ourselves—about the terms of peace that we will impose on Germany; and so long as the United States sees each day bringing us nearer to a possible resumption of hostilities.

Finally, it is worth noting that, as many Americans think quite possible, the resumption of a state of peace elsewhere in Europe may, directly and indirectly, go a long way of itself in removing or diminishing the menace of Bolshevism. The latter lives and thrives in the murky waters of confusion and strife that still engulf Europe. When it shall stand out in the full view of the United States and of all the world without their attention and scrutiny being diverted by many other evils in many other places Bolshevism, like other disease-breeding microbes, will be weakend and perhaps die in the light.   Tasker H. Bliss.
                                          General U. S. Army,
                                  Commissioner Plenipotentiary
                                          to Negotiate Peace.

TS MS (Balfour Papers, Add. MSS 49742, British Library).

From Alfred Emanuel Smith

Albany, N. Y., February 19, 1919.

On behalf of the People of the State of New York, I have the honor to invite you to meet with the People of this State at some convenient time in the near future to be selected by you, at the Metropolitan Opera House, or some other suitable place, to discuss with them the events which have transpired at the Paris Peace Conference and also with reference to the League of Nations. The People of this State, as well as the People of the whole country, are eagerly awaiting a message from you with reference to these events of so great importance to the whole world.

Alfred E. Smith.

T telegram (WP, DLC).

From Jessie Woodrow Wilson Sayre[1]

Jefferson Hospital (by night)
Acorn Club 1618 Walnut (by day)
Darling, darling, adored Father,   Feb. 19, 1919.

Isn't it too, too bad that I cannot be in Boston to welcome you home. To think that you are to land right at my door and that I am marooned here. It makes me very sad.

It would be amusing if it were not so maddening the way the days have rolled by and the end of February finds me *still* here, and yet no little new grand child of yours has come to keep me company. Of course we made a mistake somehow, somewhere, but that doesn't make it any easier to be away from my blessed family all this time. Frank has come down for over Washington's birthday and last week he brought Francis down, and that gave me a new fund of courage and cheerfulness. He gets back to Boston on the Federal Monday morning. I wonder whether you will be there then! Meanwhile if our house in Cambridge can be of the slightest use to you, for rest or refreshment or refuge please, please, use it. The children are there with Sarah Scott,[2] who has turned out to be the most wonderful trump and they are all at your disposal. It is a nice old house, built by John Fiske, roomy and comfortable—so I am told—22 Berkeley St, Cambridge—Telephone no. Cambridge 7659.

Frank loves his work and teaching and finds it stimulating and interesting at every turn.

Please don't think that I am a miserable lonely wretched creature down here, as upon reading this letter over I find that is the probable

impression I have made. I am having a very pleasant, quietly so-
ciable time, and I have never in all my life been so well. I could
run an ambulance with ease and live on walrus hides.

Dearest, dearest, love to Edith and to your beloved self,

From your loving daughter   Jessie.

ALS (WP, DLC).
    [1] She was in Philadelphia awaiting the birth of her third child. She was under the
care of Dr. Edward P. Davis.
    [2] Of Princeton, daughter of Professor William Berryman Scott of Princeton University.

From the Diary of Dr. Grayson

Thursday, February 20, 1919.

This morning the NEW MEXICO signalled for us to proceed and
dropped out of line, saying that she would try to catch us as soon
as she was able to make necessary repairs to her machinery. Her
condition, however, was such that we never again saw her, although
we were in wireless touch with her for a matter of twelve hours.
The President after talking the matter over with me decided that
it would be just as well to allow Captain McCauley to head directly
for Boston. To do this would give us an advantage of some four
hundred miles, and in view of the poor coal which was on the
GEORGE WASHINGTON we needed all of that advantage in order to
maintain our schedule. The most annoying part of the breaking
down of the NEW MEXICO's machinery was the fact that it necessitated us getting out of wireless touch. Under ordinary circumstances, this would not have amounted to so very much but with
the President of the United States as a passenger it was a serious
proposition. The wireless of the GEORGE WASHINGTON had a carrying
radius of less than two hundred miles, and the idea of having a
battleship to act as a convoy was that we should be at all times in
constant communication with the shore. After we lost the NEW
MEXICO we picked up signals from the Cruiser NORTH CAROLINA,
which was some two hundred miles away and headed towards
Europe. I issued orders to Captain McCauley to have the NORTH
CAROLINA head directly for us and to remain with us until we picked
up either the land wireless or the escort that would be sent out
from Boston to meet us. The NORTH CAROLINA arrived late in the
afternoon and took up a position a thousand yards astern, and we
were able then to resume touch with the American shore.

The President, unfortunately, caught cold as a result of a prom-
enade about the deck, so I persuaded him to remain in his stateroom
and proceeded to give him the usual treatment. His cold was not

particularly deep-seated and speedily yielded to treatment. But it was unfortunate that he contracted it at this particular time when he needed all of his strength.

Joseph Patrick Tumulty to Cary Travers Grayson

[The White House, Feb. 20, 1919]

Please send me word at earliest possible moment how much of following program the President will approve:

Escorted from pier to Copley Plaza Hotel. Lunch with small committee. Call on legislature Governor and Mayor. During the time President is making these calls ladies committee desire to give tea to Mrs. Wilson. Dine privately or with committee as President prefers. Meeting at 8 oclock at Mechanics Hall. Leave Boston at conclusion of meeting.

Sec. Baker suggests President review parade of ninth one hundred [nine thousand] troops under Maj Gen Edwards[1] after arrival at hotel. Have told him would submit matter without giving him any encouragement.

My own suggestion is that after being escorted to hotel Pres and Mrs Wilson be left entirely free until the evening meeting lunching privately taking motor ride or resting in afternoon and dining privately. Meeting at 8 at Mechanics Hall. Leaving Boston at conclusion of meeting.

Also please send me complete list of party accompanying President so that hotel auto and train arrangements may be adequate.

Also let me know if Pres. will speak extemporaneously or if address has been prepared. Boston and surrounding country enthusiastic and will give wonderful welcome.   Tumulty

T radiogram (WP, DLC).
[1] That is, Maj. Gen. Clarence Ransom Edwards, commander of the Department of the Northeast.

Two Radiograms to Joseph Patrick Tumulty

U.S.S. George Washington, 20 February, 1919

Fear repeated messages have not reached you. Cannot make evening speech at Boston. It is my duty to leave early in the evening of Monday so as to be in Washington early Tuesday morning. Hope that the Boston authorities will make the programme of my reception as brief and informal as possible. Hope to be in President's Roads by noon on Monday. Suggest no formal lunch and an afternoon speech with perhaps the additional feature of a reception by the Massachusetts legislature, if that is their desire as intimated to me in dispatch from Boston. Do not understand the suggestion of my calling on the Governor and Mayor. Supposed that that was not the obligation of the President, but do not wish to omit any customary courtesy. Address will be extemporaneous.

Woodrow Wilson

Please get acknowledgement.

CC radiogram (WP, DLC).

[U.S.S. George Washington, c. Feb. 20, 1919]

Referring to your letter of January 30[1] with regard to the many important matters to be dealt with at home, am sorry to say present prospect is that I cannot remain at home more than eight days. I would be obliged if you would ask Secretary Lane to have his reclamation projects in the most practicable form for action if possible by the time I reach Washington. Ask Houston also for suggestions for action, advising him also that I think it would be well for Logan Page to call the heads of the Roads Departments of the several States to Washington and urge constructive action upon them, at the same time asking Houston if he does not think it would be well to have an early conference with all the Secretaries of Agriculture of the States. I shall not have the time to seriously discuss with the Governors such plans as you speak of, but if you think it wise, I would be very glad to have you invite the Governors of the States in my name to come together for such a conference, say on the third of March, in order that I might at least have the pleasure of being with them at their opening sitting. You will yourself be able to judge how they would relish being summoned and then immediately left to their own resources. You could speak in your invitation of the constructive work which it might be possible to do in the way of stimulating employment and promoting public works.

Woodrow Wilson

T radiogram (WP, DLC).
  [1] JPT to WW, Jan. 30, 1919, Vol. 54.

To Wilhelmina

U.S.S. George Washington,

Her Majesty Queen Wilhelmina: February 20, 1919.

I trust that Your Majesty has understood why my reply to your gracious letter handed me by Mr. Loudon has been so long delayed.[1]

I know that your own sense of public duty will render it easy for you to believe that I merely yielded from day to day to the immediate demands of what was evidently pressing public duty.

I would not have you think that I was ungrateful for your courtesy and kindness. I begged Mr. Loudon to express to you the warm appreciation I felt, and it is a pleasure now to avail myself of my first days of release from hourly engagements to assure Your Majesty of my sincere friendship and the sincere friendship of the people of the United States for the people of Holland, and my hope that it may often be possible for us to prove that friendship in action.

It would have been a great pleasure to visit Holland if it had seemed feasible for me to visit any of the neutral countries in the present circumstances, but I have felt that it was not possible and can only thank Your Majesty for your kind and hospitable thought of me.

Cordially and respectfully yours,   [Woodrow Wilson]

CCL (WP, DLC).
  ¹ Wilhelmina to WW, Dec. 12, 1918, HwLS (WP, DLC).

To Albert, King of the Belgians

U.S.S. George Washington,
His Majesty King Albert: February 20, 1919.

Your Majesty's letter¹ brought to me at Paris by your personal representative has confirmed the impressions I had already formed of the singular situation and special necessities of Belgium arising out of this terrible war, which has meant for her almost the necessity of beginning her industrial life all over again, and you may be sure that it will be a matter of constant interest and concern with me to do everything that it may be possible for me to do for her relief and assistance.

I think Your Majesty would be reassured if you could know how much this is in the minds of those with whom I am brought into contact in Paris. The plans being made there mature slowly but in a very enlightened spirit, I think, and Belgium has many friends who will be happy to consider her interests to the utmost.

Building up from the ground will be a slow and discouraging process, but we must do all that it is humanly possible to do to promote it.

I am still confidently looking forward to the pleasure of visiting Brussels and am only sorry that the pleasure has had to be deferred because of duties which were plainly imperative.

With warmest regards,

Sincerely yours,   [Woodrow Wilson]

CCL (WP, DLC).
  ¹ Albert to WW, Feb. 10, 1919.

From Edward Mandell House

[Paris, c. Feb. 20, 1919]

Newspapers announce you are to make an important speech about the conference upon landing at Boston. When you left I understood that you had no such intentions however in view of the dinner you are to give to the members of the foreign relations committees of Congress. I hope you will compliment them by making your first explanation of affairs over here to them and confine your Boston remarks to generalities.　　　　Edward House.

T radiogram (WP, DLC).

From the Diary of Dr. Grayson

Friday, February 21, 1919.

Today the President had practically recovered from his cold and was able to go on deck. At luncheon at which Probert, Nevin and Bender¹ were present, the President told the following interesting story which he attributed to French Ambassador Jusserand:

"I must confess that there is one phase of the German character now being displayed that puzzles me. It is hard to define. It is their utter servility. Just before we left Paris Ambassador Jusserand told me a typical incident which illustrates what I mean. It seems that the French after the armistice had been signed about six weeks sent several French Officers to Berlin to look after the French embassy there. Christmas Eve they were invited to a cafe to dine where the Germans were sitting around tables, eating, drinking and listening to the music. There was no hostility in evidence anywhere. Finally, a lady came over to the table and, holding a wine glass in her hand, asked the officers to drink a toast to France. They told her they could not do so because they could not reciprocate. This of course, was a nice way to get out of an apparent difficulty. The lady retired in confusion but returned a few minutes later and said to the Officers: 'Well if you can't drink that toast will you not join me in a toast to Paris, the most beautiful city in the world.' The officers naturally drank the toast. Now if this had been someone who wanted to curry favor I could understand it but this woman came from a far corner of the room and seemingly knew no one who knew these officers."

Bender asked the President what Ambassador Jusserand thought about this, to which the President replied: "He thought it indicated German servility."

Nevin asked the President whether he did not believe that this attitude was due to the fact that the commercial interests in Germany are now supreme and that it indicated they were willing to do anything to get back their former commercial supremacy. The President said he did not think this entirely explained it. It was then suggested that the present German attitude properly represented that of the ordinary bully after he had been licked. The President said: "Yes, brutality usually goes with servility when the brute gets the worst of it."

[1] That is, Lionel Charles Probert, John Edwin Nevin, and Robert Jacob Bender, representatives of the Associated Press, the International News Service, and the United Press, respectively.

Two Radiograms to Joseph Patrick Tumulty

[U.S.S. *George Washington*] February 21, 1919.

Number one. Arrangements for parade moving [involving?] returned soldiers entirely acceptable.

Please say to Democratic Senators that of course I wish them to feel at liberty to answer criticisms of the league of nations. The whole world is looking to America to lead in this matter and any holding back will disappoint the hopes of half the nations of the world.

Am convinced that Sherman Whipple is the right man,[1] *but would be* obliged if you would have the nomination ready to (discuss?) with me.   Woodrow Wilson.

T radiogram (J. P. Tumulty Papers, DLC).
[1] That is, for the attorney generalship.

[U.S.S. *George Washington*, Feb. 21, 1919]

Hope to reach outer harbor Boston Monday by noon and feel that it is imperative that I should be in Washington by not later than nine o'clock Tuesday morning. I assume that this would mean leaving Boston early in the evening. The programme suggested from Boston therefore is clearly impossible. Please see my earlier message for my own suggestions.

I have no idea of calling extra session at an early date. I see no necessity for it until I can make a complete report of the work at Paris. I hope you will make any announcement you think wise to quiet rumors.   Woodrow Wilson

T radiogram (WP, DLC).

From Joseph Patrick Tumulty

The White House, February 21, 1919.

Your two messages and Grayson's message received. Have notified Boston authorities. May I suggest reconsideration as to evening address? You could leave Boston ten o'clock Monday evening and reach Washington at ten or before Tuesday morning. Hope you will consent to this. Tumulty.

CC radiogram (J. P. Tumulty Papers, DLC).

From Edward Mandell House

[Paris, c. Feb. 21, 1919]

This morning at the request of the French foreign office I went over a house which the French authorities suggest you occupy upon your return. It is situated on the Place des Etats Unis just across the street from the apartment house occupied by Lloyd George and Balfour. The house is a beautiful one. It has a small garden but this does not completely surround it and on one side the house faces directly on the street. The only objection to it so far as I can discover is that your bedroom and that which would be occupied by Mrs Wilson are on the ground floor which is slightly elevated from the street. Your bedroom faces entirely on the garden. Mrs Wilson's salon faces on the garden and the street and her bedroom faces on the street. There is a room on the ground floor suitable for your use as a study. The hallway and staircase leading to the second floor are very handsome. The second floor is devoted entirely to the dining room and a number of handsome salons. There are five comfortable bedrooms and four baths on the third floor and plenty of rooms for secretarial work. There are at least twelve servants rooms. If it were not for the fact that your bedrooms are on the ground floor I believe the house is more comfortable than the Murat residence. I spoke to Sharp today at lunch and he believes it a very suitable house for your occupancy. To sum it up: the location, the house is very desirable and convenient and I think that if nothing better is offered it would be advisable for you to take this house rather than inconvenience Sharp by making it necessary for him to move out of his house. Besides the situation of Sharp's house is rather inconvenient. I should very much like to have your views about this matter at an early date   Edward House

T radiogram (WP, DLC).

Albert De Silver[1] to Joseph Patrick Tumulty

My dear Mr. Tumulty: New York Feb. 21, 1919

During the week of Lincoln's Birthday, mass meetings demanding the release of political prisoners and urging the repeal of the Espionage Act were held under the auspices of this Bureau in various cities throughout the country. Meetings were held in New York, Boston, York, Pa., Chicago, San Francisco, Los Angeles and in other places. As a result of this demonstration, a delegation of citizens bearing the message of these meetings wishes to wait upon the President and to lay before him their earnest request that the President declare a general amnesty for all political prisoners and that he use his great influence for the repeal of the Espionage Act.

We are of course mindful of the great matters which claim the President's time and attention at this crisis in the affairs of the world, and it is only because of our conviction of the necessity of repairing the damage which the administration of the Espionage Act has caused to our democratic institutions, that we take the liberty of requesting a personal conference with the President.

Will you not be good enough to advise me of the date and hour when we may have an appointment with the President.

         Sincerely yours,   Albert De Silver.

TLS (WP, DLC).
[1] Lawyer of New York, director of the National Civil Liberties Bureau.

From the Diary of Dr. Grayson

         Saturday, February 22, 1919.

At noon a salute of twenty-one guns fired in honor of Washington's birthday and the President wrote a letter to "The Hatchet," the ship's paper commemorating the first anniversary of the publication and paying a tribute to the soldiers.[1] This will be run over the editorial column of every issue hereafter. The President had at luncheon, Ambassador Francis, Assistant Secretary and Mrs. F. D. Roosevelt, Captain McCauley, Miss Benham and me. As usual the President entertained the company with many interesting stories and anecdotes of the conference. Ambassador Francis said that he believed the people of the United States would support the League of Nations and the President said it would be a great pity if the people of the United States did not do so. "The failure of the United States to back it," he said, "would break the heart of the world, for the world considers the United States as the only nation represented in this great conference whose motives are entirely unselfish."

When told that Senator Borah was going on a forty-day tour of the country, to oppose the League, the President said that Borah was an able man, but he has not had international experience and did not have an international viewpoint—in fact, he was too provincial to analyze the influence and get the effect he desires.

The President said that last summer, representatives of the League to Enforce Peace, an organization headed by Ex-President Taft, called upon him at the White House, to urge him to support the programme of the League.[2] As a strange coincidence, while this delegation was talking with him in the Blue Room, there was a loud crash in the hall and an investigation revealed that the huge picture hung there of Ex-President Taft had fallen from its hanging. Fortunately, the magnificent painting, by Zorn,[3] was uninjured.

[1] The "article," as quoted in the *New York Times*, Feb. 26, 1919, reads as follows:
"I congratulate The Hatchet on the completion of the first year of its publication. I have been a constant reader while on board, and have taken pleasure in keeping a file of the numbers issued, which I shall regard as one of the most interesting souvenirs of a voyage which everybody has seemed to unite in trying to make one of the pleasantest voyages I have ever taken. I shall always remember the George Washington as a sort of home, and its officers and crew as a body of friends.
"May I take this opportunity to extend a heartfelt greeting to the soldiers on board who are returning home? My heart goes out to them for the great things they have done, and I shall be all my life proud that I was permitted to be their Commander in Chief. WOODROW WILSON."
[2] A reference to the conversation between Wilson and William Howard Taft and A. Lawrence Lowell on March 28, 1918, about which see the memorandum by William Howard Taft printed at March 29, 1918, Vol. 47.
[3] Anders Leonard Zorn, a Swedish artist.

Two Radiograms to Joseph Patrick Tumulty

George Washington, New Brunswick, 10:41 a.m., Feb. 22, 1919.

Please explain to Boston authorities that my first and immediate duty is to get to Washington and take hold of my work there and ask them to make their arrangements accordingly. My request is that they arrange no formal reception or exercises, but make the whole thing informal and incidental to my passing through the city. Any speech I may make should be made at some natural stop, as for example, at the station, at the landing place, or at some convenient stopping place between the landing place and the station. It is not my wish to feature *the conference*, but to make the whole country realize that I know my immediate duty to be to get to Washington. I am sure the Mayor will understand and cooperate.

Woodrow Wilson.

U.S.S. George Washington, February (4:55 p.m.) 22, 1919.

My objection to (evening?) speech at Boston is that it would give the whole visit the appearance of an arrangement for a premeditated address, whereas I am anxious that it should have no such appearance and should (appear?) [seem][1] what it is—just an informal greeting on reaching home. I am thinking, in short, of the impression on the hill. If the Boston authorities (cannot make?) satisfactory afternoon arrangement, I would yield rather than insist upon an impossible thing, but believe and hope that it will be possible for them to arrange it. The address (will be?) extemporaneous and will be much more certain to get out to the morning papers if delivered before evening.   Woodrow Wilson.

T radiograms (J. P. Tumulty Papers, DLC).
[1] Correction from the copy in the Wilson Papers.

From Joseph Patrick Tumulty

Sent from Copley-Plaza 2:00 pm—22 February 1919

In accordance with your message February fourteenth and subsequent messages asking me to arrange for address, arrangements have been made whereby upon your arrival at pier in Boston, you will be driven immediately a short distance to Copley-Plaza Hotel for private luncheon for yourself and Mrs. Wilson. From there to hall four minutes away for short address. Thereafter leaving on four-thirty train for Washington, arriving there between six and seven o'clock Tuesday morning. Any substantial change of this arrangement would disappoint many thousands who are assembling from all over New England to greet you on your return, including Governors and other officials of all New England states. It will be especially embarrassing to Mayor Peters who has made the arrangements based upon your cables to me, particularly the cable of February 14th[1] in which you say quote notify officials Boston will make address end quote. Furthermore, a change of programme at this time would be open to mischievous misconstruction. Your arrival awaited in Boston with splendid and entirely non-partisan enthusiasm.   Tumulty

T radiogram (J. P. Tumulty Papers, DLC).
[1] WW to JPT, Feb. 14, 1919 (second telegram of that date).

From Walker Downer Hines

[Washington] Feb. 22 10 P.M. [1919]

Walker D. Hines requests following be sent you by cable.

"I wish to lay before you a critical situation as to the appropriation of seven hundred and fifty million dollars sought by the Railroad Administration. The House has passed this appropriation bill yesterday with only fifteen opposing votes, after several hours debate, and after thorough investigation by the House Appropriations Committee. The Senate Appropriations Committee now evinces an unwillingness even to take the bill up for consideration on the ground that there is no time to pass it and that the supply bills must be given pr[e]cedence. The appropriations provided by the supply bills will not be effective or needed until July first next because the various departments have appropriations to carry them for the intervening period. But the Railroad Administration has no available appropriation whatever and needs at once the appropriation sought. The general deficiency bill carries appropriations needed promptly by various departments, but the bill is not yet out of the House Committee so it cannot serve as an excuse for the Senate Committee refusing to consider promptly the railroad bill. Failure to pass this railroad appropriation will render the Railroad Administration unable to discharge obligations aggregating about seven hundred million dollars which are already largely due in the next three months to railroad corporations and to equipment corporations and which have been incurred under the express agreement authority of the Federal Control Act and in accordance with the recognized policy involved in taking possession of the railroads. The railroad appropriation differs from most government appropriations because it will be repaid in the future. It is anticipated that the entire one billion and two hundred and fifty million dollars which would be appropriated if the present appropriation is granted will all be returned eventually to the government with the exception of approximately two hundred million dollars loss which was incurred on account of war conditions in operating the railroads during the calendar year 1918. The failure to grant the appropriation will force the Railroad Administration practically to suspend payment early in March and this in turn will cause widespread embarrassment to railroad corporations and equipment corporations, disabling them from meeting their obligations. This will have disastrous effect on the Liberty Loan. An additional result will be that the Railroad Administration will be forced to curtail in every possible way its purchases of materials and supplies and its improv[e]ments program. This will greatly accentuate existing industrial conditions whereas the prompt granting of this appropriation will materially aid in improving both financial and industrial conditions. Secretary Glass heartily agrees with me in these views and has joined me in urging the Senate Committee to act at once. He and I are to confer with Senators Martin and Underwood at ten o'clock Monday morning February 24th to urge this matter further but both of those gentlemen make it plain that they are distinctly unfavorable to consideration of the matter. I believe the appropriation, if reported by this Committee, will be passed by the Senate. The action of the House shows that it is not a partisan matter and that the Republicans are willing to support it. The crisis is so grave that I feel it should be laid before you at once."   Tumulty.

T radiogram (WP, DLC).

From the Diary of Dr. Grayson

Sunday, February 23, 1919.

We attended divine services and the President invited for lunch Mr. and Mrs. Thomas J. Spellacy and Mr. and Mrs. Perry Francis.[1] At luncheon the President discussed his visit to England and especially his impressions of King George. He said that one noticeable thing about the King was his extreme hatred for his German relatives, the Kaiser being his cousin. Passing into Buckingham Palace the King suddenly turned to the President and, pointing to the wonderful marble statue of Queen Victoria in the big square near the Palace said, "Just to think that only a few short years ago I should have unveiled that statue and beside me stood that unspeakable Kaiser whose crimes have scandalized the entire world."

Passing to the discussion of home affairs Mr. Spellacy asked the President whether he did not believe that the direct election of United States Senators by the people had weakened the strength of the Senate itself. In reply the President said that apparently this was so yet it had its compensations in that it had relieved the Senate from control by the vested interests. As a matter of fact the President said it was rather too early to debate the good value of the new plan. It had certainly made possible the election of a senator who was not the choice of the interests in control of financial affairs. One bad feature of the popular election of senators, the President pointed out, was that in those states which were close politically, a candidate for Senator had to make his run first in the primaries, then if successful, he found it necessary immediately again to engage in a spirited campaign for actual election with his political rivals. This placed a double burden upon the aspirant for the office.

However, the President thought that in the long run the present system of electing United States Senators has proved the ideal one.

Shortly after 2:30 in the afternoon, while the GEORGE WASHINGTON, escorted by four destroyers sent out from Boston Navy Yard was steaming toward Boston harbor one of the destroyers swerved from the column and crossed our bow, at full speed ahead signalling to our bridge to reverse our engines. The fog was very dense and before the manouvre was completed land loomed up directly ahead and only some 300 yards distant. It had not been discerned from the bridge of the GEORGE WASHINGTON and only the quick work of the destroyer had prevented the big transport from going on the beach. Had she done so under the headway that we were making she would have stuck hard and fast, if not completely wrecked. The GEORGE WASHINGTON backed away and finally stopped while soundings were taken to ascertain the depth of the water in the vicinity. Anchors were dropped to a safe distance in order to prevent the transport from drifting on the shore. Meanwhile the destroyers circled about in vain effort to find some familiar land mark so that the exact location might be determined. After about half an hour's wait the fog lifted for a few seconds and the twin lighthouse of Thatcher's Island loomed directly ahead. This disclosed that the GEORGE WASHINGTON had gone some seventeen miles off her course and directly to the north of Boston harbor. It was 4:15 when the fog lifted sufficiently to allow the navigator to get his direction. The afternoon however cleared up beautifully, and the run to Boston was made before 5:45. The President's ship anchored within the harbor in what is known as President's Roads at 6:30 and remained there all night. About midnight Mr. Tumulty came on board. He was filled with the latest news regarding the complex political situation that had developed since the President went to Europe. He came to my room and remained until 4:00 the next morning. He returned about 8:00 and had the temerity to ask me whether I had rested well.

[1] Thomas Joseph Spellacy, Nellie Walsh Spellacy, John D. Perry Francis, and Emelie De Mun Smith Francis. Spellacy, the United States District Attorney for Connecticut, was at this time a legal adviser to Franklin D. Roosevelt in the settlement of the affairs of the United States Navy in Europe. Francis, a son of David Rowland Francis, was a banker of St. Louis.

Two Radiograms to Edward Mandell House

[*U.S.S George Washington*, c. Feb. 23, 1919]

Hope you will be very plain and decided to the effect that we are not at war with Russia and will in no circumstances that we can now foresee take part in military operations there against the Russians. I do not at all understand why Churchill was allowed to come to Paris on such an errand after what Lloyd George had said with regard to the British sending troops to Russia. Have just read the memorandum given you by the Chief of the British General Staff of an interview with Marshal Foch.[1] It seems to me like an attempt on the part of the French to hurry us into an acquiescence in their plans with regard to the Western bank of the Rhine, a plan to which I could, as I now see the matter, in no case accede. I know that I can trust you and our colleagues to withstand such a program immovably, except that I am of course willing to have the strictly military and naval terms promptly decided and presented to the Germans. I am not willing to have anything beyond the military and naval terms decided and believe that the Conference of Ten would be going very much beyond its powers to attempt anything of the sort. The determination of the geographical boundaries of Germany involves the fortunes and interests of many other peoples and we should not think of being hurried into a solution arrived at solely from the French point of view. I beg that you will hold things steady with regard to everything but the strictly naval and military terms until I return. Marshal Foch is acting in this matter I am sure under exterior guidance of the unsafest kind. Warm thanks for full information you are sending.[2]

T radiogram (WP, DLC).
    [1] See EMH to WW, Feb. 19, 1919 (first radiogram of that date).
    [2] The text of this radiogram, as decoded and read by House, follows:
"Hope you will block plan decided to the effect that we are not at war with Russia and will in no circumstances that we can now foresee take part in military operation there against the Russians. I do not at all understand why Churchill was allowed to go to Paris on such an errand after what Lloyd George had said with regard to the British sending troops to Russia. I have just read the memorandum given you by the Chief of the British General Staff of an interview with Marshal Foch. It seems to me like an attempt to use the good offices of the French to hurry us into and acquiesce in their plans with regard to Western bank of Rhine. Proposition for your consideration and in the light in which I see the matter in no case accede. I know I can trust you and our colleagues to withstand such a programme immovable except of course I am willing to have the strictly military and naval terms promptly decided and presented to the Germans. I am not willing to have anything beyond the military and naval terms and believe that the conference of ten would be going very much beyond its powers to attempt anything of this sort. The determination of the geographic boundaries of Germany involves the fortunes and interests of the other peoples and we should not risk being hurried into a solution arrived at solely from the French official viewpoint. I beg that you steady with regard to everything to the strictly military and naval terms until I return. Marshal Foch is acting in this matter I am sure under exterior guidance of the most unsafe kind. Warm thanks for full information you are sending. W. Wilson. Opnav." WW to EMH, received Feb. 24, 1919, T radiogram (E. M. House Papers, CtY).

[*U.S.S. George Washington*, Feb. 23, 1919]

Your radio about house on Place des Etats Unis received. We are willing and pleased to take the house suggested. What arrangements do you suggest about servants? Are the French authorities still insistent we should accept the house at their hands or are they to permit us to rent it? In the latter event the question of servants becomes very important.   Woodrow Wilson

T radiogram (E. M. House Papers, CtY).

To Robert Lansing

USS George Washington February 23rd, 12 Noon [1919].

For Secretary Lansing.[1] I feel that we are bound in honor to decline to agree to the inclusion of war costs in the reparation demanded. The time to think of this was before the conditions of peace were communicated to the enemy originally. We should dissent and dissent publicly if necessary not on the ground of the intrinsic injustice of it but on the ground that it is clearly inconsistent with what we deliberately led the enemy to expect and can not now honorably alter simply because we have the power.

Woodrow Wilson.[2]

T radiogram (J. F. Dulles Papers, NjP).
[1] Wilson was replying to RL *et al.* to WW, Feb. 19, 1919.
[2] There is a copy of this radiogram in the House Papers.

To Joseph Patrick Tumulty

Received at Boston at 1:21 PM—23 Feb 1919.

Programme suggested entirely satisfactory for a speech in Mechanics Hall at two-thirty. I had never thought of disappointing Boston authorities in matter of an address. We are encountering a slight fog which may somewhat delay us but will certainly go ashore at eleven o'clock as the Mayor suggests, if we can make it.

Woodrow Wilson.

T radiogram (J. P. Tumulty Papers, DLC).

To Oscar Wilder Underwood

[*U.S.S. George Washington*] 23 February, 1919.

On the way home I have been reading very carefully reports from the Railway Administration and have grown very anxious lest by some unfortunate combination of circumstances the absolutely necessary appropriation of seven hundred and fifty million dollars sought by the Railway Administration might fail of action or be sidetracked.

I therefore take the liberty of asking most earnestly for your co-operation in securing this appropriation, which I learn has already been passed by the House of Representatives by a very large majority. The consequences of a failure to make this appropriation would be so serious to the Railway Administration and to the industrial and financial conditions throughout the country at this critical time of transition that I feel justified in making a direct appeal for your invaluable assistance and cooperation in this matter.

Woodrow Wilson

CC radiogram (WP, DLC).

To James Harry Preston[1]

U.S.S. George Washington,
My dear Mr. Mayor: 23 February, 1919.

I am ashamed to have been so long in complying with your wish to have a few words to put upon the Lafayette monument.[2] I am sure you will forgive me in the circumstances. I suggest the following and hope that it will seem to you suitable.

Lafayette, immortal because a self-forgetful servant of justice and humanity. Beloved by all Americans because he acknowledged no duty more sacred than to fight for the freedom of his fellow-men.[3]

With all best wishes, and thanks for your last message,

Sincerely yours,   [Woodrow Wilson]

CCL (WP, DLC).
    [1] Mayor of Baltimore.
    [2] The correspondence relating to this subject is J. H. Preston to WW, Nov. 9, 14, and 18, 1918, all TLS (WP, DLC); WW to J. H. Preston, Nov. 12, 1918, TLS (Letterpress Books, WP, DLC); and J. H. Preston to WW, [Feb. 12, 1919], T telegram (WP, DLC).
    [3] There is a WWT copy of this inscription in WP, DLC.

From the American Commissioners

Paris. February 23rd, 1919.

876. For the President.

Your telegram February 19th. Churchill's project is dead and there is little danger that it will be revived again by the Conference. General Bliss explained to Churchill that he must have misunderstood your views, since you could not have made the statement which he attributed to you regarding military action in Russia.

Ammission.

T telegram (WP, DLC).

Two Telegrams from Edward Mandell House[1]

[Paris] February 23rd, 1919.

Serial Number 2. For President from House. George will not arrive in Paris until Friday, February twenty-eighth. STOP. No action will be taken respecting Russia until after his arrival. STOP. I have ascertained his views respecting this question and they are substantially as follows: QUOTE. No foreign intervention in Soviet Russia and no foreign troops to be sent to aid of non-Bolshevik Russia unless volunteers choose to go of their own accord but material assistance to be supplied to these governments to enable them to hold their own in the territories which are not anxious to submit to Bolshevik rule. Russia must save herself. If she is saved by outside intervention she is not really saved. We are bound to give moral material and if necessary full military support to protect Poland, Finland and other such States against Bolshevik invasion. The military party in France and England both favor intervention but have absolutely declined to commit themselves as to how the expense thereof would be met. France surely cannot pay and I am sure we cannot either. Will America bear the expense. UNQUOTE. I do not think we shall have any difficulty reaching an agreement respecting our Russian policy after George arrives inasmuch as his views apparently coincide with ours.   Edward House.

T telegram (E. M. House Papers, CtY).
  [1] There is a garbled version of this telegram in WP, DLC, which Close was unable to decipher. The White House asked for a repetition, which House sent on February 28, 1919. T telegram (WP, DLC). There is no decoded version of House's No. 2 in WP, DLC, but presumably it was decoded, and Wilson read it.

[Paris] February 23 [1919][1]

Number 3. At his request I had a conference with Clemenceau yesterday.

(1) He is anxious now to speed up and make an early peace with Germany. He at last realizes the danger of delay.

(2) He is insistent upon the question creation of a Rhenish republic. There will be about four millions of Germans segregated in this way. He desires that this republic should be exempted from the payment of any indemnity; that they should have no armed force; that everything should be done to make them prosperous and contented so that they will not want to join the German federation and if they have such a desire they will not be permitted to do so.

(3) (Word omitted) [On the][2] East Clemenceau thinks that Danzig should go to Poland. Our experts also think this to be the best

solution and they are joined (I) understand (in this) belief by the British experts, but the British government disagree this point.

(4) Clemenceau says that German Austria will not join the German federation if they receive an intimation from the allies that they do not wish them to do so. He is insistent that this intimation be given them.

(5) He thinks the entire terms should be given at once and that the military terms should not be made now as at first (planned). There was afterwards (common agreement?) on this point at our meeting at the Quai D'Orsay.

(6) He thought that he would be able to attend meetings in a few days. I doubt it. I feel that he is by no means out of danger.

(7) I assume that you get full report of meetings at the Quai.[3]

Edward House.

T telegram (WP, DLC).
   [1] Received at the White House on February 25, 1919.
   [2] Corrections and additions in square brackets in Wilson's and House's telegrams from the "telegram sent" in the Wilson and House Papers, unless otherwise noted.
   [3] See WW to EMH, Feb. 27, 1919.

From Francis Bowes Sayre

Philadelphia, Penna., February 23, 1919.
Woodrow Wilson Sayre[1] and Jessie send love.   Frank.

T radiogram (WP, DLC).
   [1] Wilson's grandson was born on February 23, 1919.

David Rowland Francis to Robert Lansing and Others

Boston Mass. February 23, 1919.
For Lansing, House, Bliss and White.

Had a thorough talk with the President[1] concerning Russia. Presented plan that Allied Missions return to Petrograd to occupy domiciles accompanied by 100,000 Allied troops and abundant food; also suggested Prinkipo investigation be transferred to Petrograd and all professed Russian governments be summoned there and their statements confined to replying to questions asked. Allied Missions would issue address to Russian people disclaiming intentions of interfering in internal affairs stating that still considered Russians as Allies and object in re-occupying domiciles was to assist Russia in her misfortunes and difficulties and to afford unawed opportunity for free election and fair count for election constitutional convention to select form of government by majority. In order to accomplish this, order would necessarily be restored. President said would give plan consideration; admitted that withdrawing Allied forces from Russia would mean deplorable slaughter of Russian friends of Allies but repeated George and Clemenceau statement concerning ordering British French troops to Russia.[2]

I expressed opinion that army of 200,000 composed of American, British, French and probably Italian soldiers would volunteer when appeal made to them to go to Russia to protect representatives of their governments but stated that I thought 100,000 would be ample.

Radios indicate Secretary of War Baker has said that Allied troops would be withdrawn from Northern Russia end of Spring; my judgement is that such policy would be mistake and would delay peace negotiations because no peace treaty would be effective with Russia left out. If treaty signed with Bolsheviks dominating Russia or disorder prevailing there Germany will so utilize Russia's immeasurable resources and so organize Russian man-power as to convert defeat into victory in ten years or shorter time. Furthermore, Bolshevism prevailing in Russia would extend its baneful influence to other countries and become more potential menace than it is now, not only to organized governments but to society itself. Bolshevik doctrines destroy family relations and if predominate will mean wanton barbarism.

I must not return with the President but shall keep in touch with State Department and can be in Paris on 2 weeks notice. Disembark with the President Boston going thence Washington arriving on the 25th.   Francis.

T telegram (SDR, RG 256, 861.00./291, DNA).
    [1] Aboard *U.S.S. George Washington.* For Francis' account of his return to the United States and his interview with Wilson, see David R. Francis, *Russia from the American Embassy, April, 1916-November, 1918* (New York, 1921), pp. 306-12.
    [2] That is, if British and French soldiers were ordered to Russia, they would refuse to go and mutiny.

From the Diary of Dr. Grayson

Monday, February 24, 1919.

This was a crowded day. About 10:30 the official reception committee, headed by Mayor Peters, General Clarence R. Edwards, Commanding the Department of the Northeast, Governor Coolidge and Rear Admiral Wood,[1] with their respective staffs came on board to escort the President to the shore. They met him in his office on C deck.

Before the President left the ship he went down among the returning troops to say good bye to them. The President told the men the deep satisfaction it had given him to have them accompany him home. He said that while they might have lost a day through his coming to Boston he had no doubt their welcome home would be all the warmer because of that fact. His appearance among them was apparently very pleasant to the soldiers.

We left the GEORGE WASHINGTON at 11:30 on the Coast Guard Cutter Ossipee. As we steamed towards the South Boston dock a large fleet of excursion vessels circled about but were driven back to a respectful distance by our escorting destroyers and submarine chasers. Every steam craft we passed in the harbor had its whistle tied down and the din at times was deafening. Approaching Commonwealth Pier, where we landed, an enormous crowd which had gathered at every point of vantage cheered the President. The landing was made just at noon. The President was escorted to a freight elevator and taken to the street level of the pier, where automobiles were in waiting. There were more than fifty automobiles in the procession which passed through the heart of Boston en route to the Copley Plaza Hotel. The President's welcome was far more enthusiastic than had been thought possible. The streets were jammed with people. The arrangements, however, were perfect. Some twelve thousand troops, aided by blue jackets and marines from the Boston Navy Yard, lined the entire route. All streets were roped off, while two blocks of narrow streets through which the procession had to pass were completely closed, no one being allowed in the streets or the houses adjacent. As a precautionary measure soldiers with loaded rifles were stationed on the roof of every block of buildings over the entire route from Commonwealth Pier to the Hotel. There were no incidents however. The police made one arrest, that of a Polish subject on whom they found a revolver, a box of cartridges and a black jack. He was simply a crank however and it is doubtful if he had any evil designs. One of the features of the parade was the massing on the temporary grandstand in front of the capitol, on the Beacon Street side, of four hundred wounded soldiers brought over from the receiving hospital to have a look at the Commander-in-Chief as he went by. It was noticeable that at least a score of them wore the American Distinguished Service Cross, while others had the French War Cross. They applauded very warmly as the President passed by.

Following luncheon at the hotel the President was driven to Mechanics Hall, where he delivered his first address since leaving France. In it he accepted the challenge of the opponents of the league of nations and announced that if America did not lead the way in adopting this plan for permanent peace the world would be deeply disappointed.

The demonstration was altogether a very pleasing one. John McCormack, the noted tenor, sang the Star Spangled Banner with a vim and touch that well nigh carried the audience off its feet. Mayor Peters made a flamboyant address directed chiefly at the President. Governor Coolidge, who followed, pledged himself to any plan or scheme which the President would devise or design to end war for all time. This was rather remarkable in view of the fact that the Governor is a Republican, but it could be explained when it was remembered that the Governor entertained senatorial ambitions and Senator Lodge was an opponent of the league plan as well as a fellow Republican.

Following the speech we were escorted to South Station where a special train was in waiting to take us to Washington. The exit from Boston was marked by very friendly demonstrations from people of every class who gathered along the route to cheer the passing train.

The first stop was Providence, Rhode Island. Here a large and happy crowd gathered to cheer the President until he finally was compelled to make a few remarks of appreciation of the warm welcome. Again he assured his hearers that the whole world was waiting on America and would be disappointed should America fail in her duty at this critical time.[2]

Another brief halt at New London found another large crowd that cheered and applauded wildly. At New Haven an enormous crowd had gathered up the main street just before the depot was reached. The Mayor[3] and the City Council, who were at the station, were not anxious that the President should greet this crowd so they caused the train to be run by some distance down into the station yard. Fortunately, however, Secret Service Agent Murphy saw the crowd waiting and told the President who at once asked the conductor to back the train. The Mayor, discovering that his little scheme was known then volunteered to the President to tell the crowd that the President was sorry the train had run past. I told the conductor to back the train up, which was done, and the President was able to wave greetings to the many people who had waited in the cold for a long time to cheer him as he passed. There were at least ten thousand people in this crowd. It is needless to say that the Mayor and Council were Republicans.[4]

At 6:55, just before the train reached New London the President affixed his signature to the six billion revenue bill, the biggest tax measure ever enacted in the United States and probably the greatest in the history of any nation in the world.

The signing of the Revenue Bill carried with it a rider which made the District of Columbia bone-dry. Word of the signing, while not officially given out from the President's train, was telegraphed ahead to Washington and the authorities seized very large quantities of liquor in shipment to residents in the District of Columbia.

The President was asleep when the train passed through New York, and although there was a good crowd in the Pennsylvania Station he was not awakened.

[1] Spencer Shepard Wood, commandant of the 1st Naval District, with headquarters at Boston.

[2] Wilson's remarks were as follows: "You are no more happy to meet me than I am to see you. It is a fine thing to be home again. The thing that has pleased me most in my contact with the peoples of Europe is that they trust the people of America, and all I have to say is that if America disappoints them, the heart of the world will be broken." "Speech of President Wilson at station at Providence," [Feb. 24, 1919], T MS (WP, DLC).

[3] David Edward Fitzgerald.

[4] Grayson was in error. Fitzgerald had been chairman of the Connecticut Democratic State Central Committee since 1914. Whatever antipathy he may have felt toward Wilson probably derived from the fact that he was the son of an Irish immigrant. Although the Editors have been unable to determine the political affiliation of each member of the New Haven Board of Aldermen, it seems safe to assume that a substantial number of them were also Democrats, since the city had voted Democratic in recent elections.

An Address in Boston

February 24, 1919.

Governor Coolidge, Mr. Mayor, fellow citizens: I wonder if you are half as glad to see me as I am to see you. It warms my heart to see a great body of my fellow citizens again because in some respects during recent months I have been very lonely, indeed, without your comradeship and counsel, and I tried at every step of the work which fell to me to recall what I was sure would be your counsel with regard to the great matters which were under consideration.

I do not want you to think that I have not been appreciative of the extraordinarily generous reception which was given me on the other side, in saying it makes me very happy to get home again. I do not mean to say I was not very deeply touched by the cries that came from greater crowds on the other side. But I want to say to you in all honesty, I felt them to be the call of greeting to you rather than to me. I did not feel that the greeting was personal. I had in my heart the overcrowning pride of being your representative and of receiving the plaudits of men everywhere who felt that your hearts beat with theirs in the cause of liberty. There was no mistaking the tone in the voices of these great crowds. It was not the tone of mere greeting, it was not the tone of mere generous welcome, it was the calling of comrade to comrade, the cry that comes from men who say we have waited for this day when the friends of liberty should come across the sea and shake hands with us to see that the new world was constructed upon a new basis and foundation of justice and right.

I cannot tell you the inspiration that came from the sentiments that came out of these simple voices of the crowd. And the proudest thing I have to report to you is that this great country of ours is trusted throughout the world. I have not come to report the proceedings or results of the proceedings of the peace conference—that would be premature. I can say that I have received very happy impressions from this conference, the impression that, while there are many differences of judgment, while there are some divergencies of object, there is nevertheless a common spirit and a common realization of the necessity of setting up a new standard of right in the world. Because the men who are in conference in Paris realize as keenly as any American can realize that they are not masters of their people, that they are servants of their people, and that the spirit of their people has awakened to a new purpose and a new conception of their power to realize that purpose, and that no man dare go home from that conference and report anything less noble than was expected of it.

The conference seems to you to go slowly; from day to day in Paris it seems to go slowly. But I wonder if you realize the complexity of the task which is undertaken. It seems as if the settlements of this war affect, and affect directly, every great, and I sometimes think every small, nation in the world. And no one decision can prudently be made which is not properly linked in with the great series of other decisions which must accompany it, and it must be reckoned in with the final result if the real quality and character of that result is to be properly judged.

What we are doing is to hear the whole case, hear it from the mouths of the men most interested, hear it from those who are officially commissioned to state it, hear the rival claims, hear the claims that affect new nationalities, that affect new areas of the world, that affect new commercial and economic connections that have been established by the great world war through which we have gone. And I have been struck by the moderateness of those who have represented national claims. I can testify that I have nowhere seen the gleam of passion. I have seen earnestness, I have seen tears come to the eyes of men who plead for downtrodden people whom they were privileged to speak for, but they were not tears of anger, they were tears of ardent hope. And I do not see how any man can fail to have been subdued by these pleas, subdued to this feeling that he was not there to assert an individual judgment of his own but to try to assist the cause of humanity.

And in the midst of it all, every interest seeks out first of all, when it reaches Paris, the representatives of the United States. Why? Because—and I think I am stating the most wonderful fact in history—because there is no nation in Europe that suspects the motives of the United States. Was there ever so wonderful a thing seen before? Was there ever so moving a thing? Was there ever any fact that so bound the nation that had won that esteem forever to deserve it? I would not have you understand that the great men who represent the other nations there in conference are disesteemed by those who know them. Quite the contrary. But you understand that the nations of Europe have again and again clashed with one another in competitive interest. It is impossible for men to forget these sharp issues that were drawn between them in times past. It is impossible for men to believe that all ambitions have all of a sudden been foregone. They remember territory that was coveted, they remember rights it was attempted to extort, remember political ambitions which it was attempted to realize, and, while they believe men have come into different temper, they cannot forget these things, and so they do not resort to one another for dispassionate view of matters in controversy.

They resort to that nation which has won enviable distinction, being regarded as the friend of mankind. Whenever it is desired to send a small force of soldiers to occupy a piece of territory where it is thought nobody else will be welcome, they ask for American soldiers. And where other soldiers would be looked upon with suspicion and perhaps met with resistance, the American soldier is welcomed with acclaim. I have had so many grounds for pride on the other side of the water that I am very thankful that they are not grounds for personal pride, but for national pride.

If they were grounds for personal pride, I would be the most stuck-up man in the world. And it has been an infinite pleasure to me to see these gallant soldiers of ours, of whom the Constitution of the United States made me the proud commander. Everybody praises the American soldier with the feeling that in praising him he is subtracting from the credit of no one else. I have been searching for the fundamental fact that converted Europe to believe in us. Before this war, Europe did not believe in us as she does now. She did not believe in us throughout the first three years of the war. She seems really to have believed that we were holding off because we thought we could make more by staying out than by going in. And all of a sudden, in a short eighteen months, the whole verdict is reversed. There can be but one explanation for it. They saw what we did—that is, without making a single claim, we put all our men and all our means at the disposal of those who were fighting for their homes in the first instance, but for the cause—

the cause of human right and justice—and that we went in, not to support their national claims, but to support the great cause which they held in common. And when they saw that America not only held the ideals but acted the ideals, they were converted to America and became firm partisans of those ideals.

I met a group of scholars when I was in Paris. Some gentlemen from one of the Greek universities[1] who had come to see me and in whose presence, or rather in the presence of the traditions of learning, I felt very young, indeed. And I told them that I had had one of the delightful revenges that sometimes come to men. All my life I have heard men speak with a sort of condescension of ideals and of idealists, and particularly of those separated, encloistered persons whom they choose to term academic, who were in the habit of uttering ideals in a free atmosphere when they clash with nobody in particular. And I said I have had this sweet revenge. Speaking with perfect frankness in the name of the people of the United States, I have uttered as the objects of this great war ideals, and nothing but ideals, and the war has been won by that inspiration.

Men were fighting with tense muscle and lowered head until they came to realize those things, feeling they were fighting for their lives and their country. And when these accents of what it was all about reached them from America, they lifted their heads, they raised their eyes to heaven when they saw men in khaki coming across the sea in the spirit of the crusaders. And they found that these were strange men, reckless of danger not only, but reckless because they seemed to see something that made that danger worthwhile. Men have testified to me in Europe that our men were possessed by something that they could only call religious fervor. They were not like any of the other soldiers. They had a vision; they had a dream, and they were fighting in that dream; and, fighting in that dream, they turned the whole tide of battle, and it never came back.

An American humorist, meeting the criticism that American soldiers were not trained long enough, said: "It takes only half as long to train an American soldier as any other, because you only have to train him one way"—and he did only go one way, and he never came back until he could do it when he pleased.

And now do you realize that this confidence we have established throughout the world imposes a burden upon us—if you choose to call it a burden. It is one of those burdens which any nation ought to be proud to carry. Any man who resists the present tides that

---

[1] Wilson presumably met these men at the time of his address at the University of Paris printed at Dec. 21, 1918, Vol. 53. There is no record of any separate meeting with Greek academics.

run in the world will find himself thrown upon a shore so high and barren that it will seem as if he had been separated from his human kind forever.

The Europe that I left the other day was full of something that it had never felt fill its heart so full before. It was full of hope. The Europe of the second year of the war—the Europe of the third year of the war—was sinking to a sort of stubborn desperation. They did not see any great thing to be achieved even when the war should be won. They hoped there would be some salvage; they hoped that they could clear their territories of invading armies; they hoped that they could set up their homes and start their industries afresh. But they thought it would simply be a resumption of the old life that Europe had led—led in fear, led in anxiety, led in constant suspicion and watchfulness. They never dreamed that it would be a Europe of settled peace and justified hope. And now these ideals have wrought this new magic that all the peoples of Europe are buoyed up and confident in the spirit of hope, because they believe that we are at the eve of a new age of the world, when nations will understand one another; when nations will support one another in every just cause; when nations will unite every moral and every physical strength to see that right shall prevail. If America were at this juncture to fail the world, what would come of it?

I do not mean any disrespect to any other great people when I say that America is the hope of the world. And if she does not justify that hope, the results are unthinkable. Men will be thrown back upon bitterness of disappointment, not only, but bitterness of despair. All nations will be set up as hostile camps again; men at the peace conference will go home with their heads upon their breasts, knowing they have failed—for they were bidden not to come home from there until they did something more than sign the treaty of peace. Suppose we sign the treaty of peace and that it is the most satisfactory treaty of peace that the confusing elements of the modern world will afford, and go home and think about our labors? We will know that we have left written upon the historic table at Versailles, upon which Vergennes and Benjamin Franklin wrote their names, nothing but a modern scrap of paper, no nations united to defend it, no great forces combined to make it good, no assurance given to the downtrodden and fearful people of the world that they shall be safe. Any man who thinks that America will take part in giving the world any such rebuff and disappointment as that does not know America. I invite him to test the sentiments of the nation.

We set this nation up to make men free, and we did not confine our conception and purpose to America, and now we will make men free. If we did not do that, all the fame of America would be gone, and all her power would be dissipated. She would then have to keep her power for those narrow, selfish, provincial purposes which seem so dear to some minds that have no sweep beyond the nearest horizon. I should welcome no sweeter challenge than that. I have fighting blood in me, and it is sometimes a delight to let it have scope, but if it is challenged on this occasion it will be an indulgence. Think of the picture, think of the utter blackness that would fall on the world. America has failed. America made a little essay at generosity and then withdrew. America said, "We are your friends," but it was only for today, not for tomorrow. America said, "Here is our power to vindicate right," and then next day said, "Let right take care of itself and we will take care of ourselves." America said, "We set up light to lead men along the paths of liberty, but we have lowered it—it is intended only to light our own path."

We set up a great ideal of liberty, and then we said: "Liberty is a thing that you must win for yourself. Do not call upon us." Think of the world that we would leave. Do you realize how many new nations are going to be set up in the presence of old and powerful nations in Europe and left there, if left there by us, without a disinterested friend? Do you believe in the Polish cause, as I do? Are you going to set up Poland, immature, inexperienced, as yet unorganized, and leave her with a circle of armies around her? Do you believe in the aspirations of the Czecho-Slovaks and Jugo-Slavs, as I do? Do you know how many powers would be quick to pounce upon them if there were not guarantees of the world behind their liberty? Have you thought of the sufferings of Armenia? You poured out your money to help succor Armenians after they suffered. Now set up your strength so that they shall never suffer again.

Arrangements of the present peace cannot stand a generation unless they are guaranteed by the united forces of the civilized world. And if we do not guarantee them, can you not see the picture? Your hearts have instructed you where the burden of this war fell. It did not fall upon national treasuries; it did not fall upon the instruments of administration; it did not fall upon the resources of nations. It fell upon the voiceless homes everywhere, where women were toiling in hope that their men would come back. When I think of the homes upon which dull despair would settle if this great hope is disappointed, I should wish for my part never to have had America play any part whatever in this attempt to emancipate the world.

But I talk as if there were any question. I have no more doubt of the verdict of America in this matter than I have doubt of the blood that is in me. And so, my fellow citizens, I have come back to report progress, and I do not believe that progress is going to stop short of the goal. The nations of the world have set their heads now to do a great thing, and they are not going to slacken their purpose. And when I speak of the nations of the world, I do not speak of the governments of the world. I speak of peoples who constitute the nations of the world. They are in the saddle, and they are going to see to it that, if their present governments do not do their will, some other governments shall. The secret is out, and present governments know it. There is a great deal of harmony to be got out of common knowledge.

There is a great deal of sympathy to be got of living in the same atmosphere, and, except for the differences of languages, which puzzled my American ear very sadly, I could have believed I was at home in France or Italy or in England when I was on the streets, when I was in the presence of crowds, when I was in great halls where men were gathered irrespective of class. I did not feel quite as much at home there as I do here, but I felt that now, at any rate after this storm of war had cleared the air, men were seeing eye to eye everywhere, and that these were the kind of folks who would understand what the kind of folks at home would understand— that they were thinking the same things. I feel about you as I am reminded of a story of that excellent wit and good artist, Oliver Herford, who one day, sitting at luncheon at his club, was slapped vigorously on the back by a man whom he did not know very well. He said: "Oliver, old boy, how are you?" He looked at him rather coldly, and said: "I don't know your name; I don't know your face; but your manners are very familiar." I am going to say that your manners are very familiar, and delightful. It is a great comfort, for one thing, to realize that you understand the language that I speak. A friend of mine said that, to talk through an interpreter, was like witnessing the compound fracture of an idea. But the beauty of it is, that, whatever the impediments of the channel of communication, the idea is the same, that it gets registered, and it gets registered in responsive hearts and receptive purposes.

I have come back for a strenuous attempt to transact business for a little while in America, but I have really come back to say to you, in all soberness and honesty, that I have been trying my best to speak your thoughts. When I sample myself, I think I find that I am a typical American, and if I sample deep enough and get down to what probably is the true stuff of a man, then I have hope that it is part of the stuff that is like the other fellow's at home. And, therefore, probing deep in my heart and trying to see things that are right without regard to the things that may be debated as expedient, I feel that I am interpreting the purpose and the thought of America; and in loving America, I find I have joined the great majority of my fellow men throughout the world.[2]

Printed in *Addresses of President Wilson Boston, Mass., February 24, 1919 New York, N. Y., March 4, 1919* (Washington, 1919), with additions and corrections from the transcript by F. E. Brown, T MS (WC, NjP).
[2] There is a WWT one-page outline of this address, dated "24 Feb'y, 1919," in WP, DLC.

From Edward Mandell House

[Paris, Feb. 24, 1919]

Number 4. You have no doubt received the texts of the (separate) resolutions adopted to-day regarding the preparation of (preliminary) peace terms with Germany Austria-Hungary Bulgaria and Turkey.

(1) General Bliss is working with the (omission) military court authorities [military authorities] and their report will be cabled when the same has been prepared.

(2) Our territorial experts are in substantial agreement with the British and the French respecting the boundaries of Germany. Tardieu who since attack on Clemenceau has become more or less (omit) [prominent] said to me yesterday that France would be willing to have the Rhenish republic set up only for a limited period of years, at the end of which the population would be permitted to decide for themselves what the future should be. He said that in this way (a breathing) space would be given us all (and France) would secure protection (until she) had recovered from the present war. The principle of self-determination would be in this way safeguarded.

(3) (It now) seems possible that we shall arrive at a solution of the reparation matter which we can accept without abandoning the principle accepted by Germany (and the) allies at the time of the (armistice). In the event, however, that this principle is seriously threatened with repudiation by the allies (it may be) wise for us to intimate that as we do not wish to impair in any way the agreement between the associated governments and Germany at the time of the armistice we would prefer to withdraw from any participation in any recovery [from] Germany except to the extent of our own claims for reparation which we (qokef) [can] satisfy (Nezyw) [out of the] funds in the hands of the (Alien Property Custodian). If this intimation is given it may be necessary that the allies will reconsider their position.

(4) The statement of the economic conditions to be accorded Germany (will) necessarily have to be made in general terms.

(5) At the present time the plan we are pursuing is as follows: The giving of priority to the work of committees involving matters essential in the preparation of peace treaty with Germany. Reports from these committees should be available by March eighth and should, upon your arrival, be in shape so that you can consider them without delay. After you have (it would seem) that [have approved them] they should be submitted to a plenary session of the conference and an agreement of all the powers (Pazip) [reached] respecting them. If this [procedure] is followed it ought to be possible (to supercede) [to summon] the peace conference [for] a date not later than (Razap Huses) [the first week] of April.

(6) It is probable that French Government will insist that you be their guest. I will cable instructions definitely about this and the (Pamav Sehod) suggestion [question of servants] tomorrow.

Edward House.

T telegram (WP, DLC).

From Walker Downer Hines, with Enclosure

Dear Mr. President: Washington February 24, 1919.

I take the liberty of enclosing a memorandum which endeavors to state my view of various facts and conditions bearing upon the railroad situation, with reference to the developments which have taken place since I wrote you on the 31st ult.[1] The statement is fragmentary and in itself may not prove especially helpful, but if, in the midst of the many matters pressing upon you, there is an opportunity for you to discuss these problems with me, I think the memorandum may prove helpful as a part of the basis for the discussion.

I also enclose for your convenience memorandum[2] which summarises relevant portions of your address of December 2nd to Congress and some excerpts from Mr. McAdoo's letter to Senator Smith and Judge Sims.[3]   Sincerely yours,   Walker D Hines

TLS (WP, DLC).
    [1] W. D. Hines to WW, Jan. 31, 1919, TLS (WP, DLC). In this letter, Hines discussed the sentiments in Congress, the Interstate Commerce Commission, and the business community with regard to continued governmental control of the railroads. This discussion was substantially the same as that in numbered paragraphs 1 to 6 of the Enclosure printed as the next document.
    [2] T MS (WP, DLC). Not printed.
    [3] That is, Ellison DuRant Smith and Thetus Willrette Sims, members of the Senate Interstate Commerce Committee and the House Committee on Interstate and Foreign Commerce, respectively.

ENCLOSURE

Memorandum.   February 24, 1919.

The developments and status in respect of railroad legislation (apart from the Appropriation) are as follows:

1. The Senate Committee on Interstate Commerce has conducted almost daily hearings throughout the session up to and including Friday, February 21st. It is generally understood that it will not propose any permanent solution or any extension of the present control beyond the 21 months period, the time being admittedly too short for such legislation to receive consideration. The House Committee on Interstate and Foreign Commerce has had no hearings upon the subject and about a week ago announced that it would have none, thus indicating its view that there could be no such legislation at this session.

2. There is widespread and outspoken opposition to Government ownership and operation as a permanent policy. This seems to be the prevailing and, as far as I can see, the almost universal sentiment in the present Congress, and the sentiment of the shipping, commercial and business and banking organizations generally throughout the country. Labor appears to be in favor of permanent Government ownership and operation. There is nothing to indicate that the farming element has anything approaching solidarity of position on the subject. I get the distinct impression that even the ardent supporters of permanent Government ownership and operation feel partially eclipsed and at a disadvantage now because of the vociferous reaction against such a solution. This reaction in my opinion does not grow entirely or principally out of the Administration of the railroads, but is largely a reaction from Government control in general, during the war, of business and industrial matters, including the telephone and telegraph service.

3. There is nothing to indicate any centering of support upon any particular plan of return to private management. The Interstate Commerce Commission has recommended a return to private management with various modifications of the law which I do not regard as fundamental and which, among other things, leave the intrastate rate-making power in the hands of the State Commissions. The railroad executives have recommended a plan which goes further and vests all rate-making power in the Federal authorities and creates a Secretary of Transportation to handle administrative functions and to control questions of rate suspension, leaving quasi-judicial matters and rate-making matters to the Interstate Commerce Commission. Mr. S. Davies Warfield,[1] representing a se-

[1] Solomon Davies Warfield, financier of Baltimore, who specialized in railroad and utilities

curity owners' association, has recommended a plan whereby the Government will undertake to see that rates are sufficiently high to pay 6 per cent upon the railroad investment as a whole, leaving it to each company to get what business it can and to prosper or fail on the rates thus allowed. Labor has proposed a plan of Government ownership with a lease to a single corporation owned and controlled by the officials and employes.[2] Senator Cummins, who will be the next Chairman of the Senate Committee, favors a plan of consolidation of railroads into a few large systems, probably competitive rather than regional, with a Government guaranty of a participation in the profits in excess of the guaranty. Mr. Victor Morawetz of New York favors much the same solution. Mr. Paul Warburg's ideas are in the same direction. Personally, I do not believe that anything short of such a plan will really meet the fundamental difficulties. With all these plans before it for solution through private management, I am not able to form a reliable estimate as to the leaning of the Senate Committee or as to the leaning of Congress. My instinctive feeling is that the tendency is more in the direction of a return to old conditions with a few modifications than it is in the direction of any really effective reform.

4. The prevailing sentiment in Congress is against any extension of the 21 month period. The same sentiment is widely manifest throughout the country, although I believe many thoughtful people who oppose permanent Government control believe that the extension is desirable and eventually will become necessary as an incident to an effective permanent solution. But at the moment that sentiment is not strong enough to produce action at this Congress. Labor favors the extension. The reasons generally expressed in opposition to the extension is that it would mean permanent Government ownership and operation. This is a mistaken view in my opinion, but it has caught the fancy of a large part of the public.

5. I believe the sentiment is very strong in Congress and in the country that there ought to be a permanent solution of the railroad problem at the earliest possible time; that the country is thinking about it and will give more intelligent attention to the subject now than the subject will receive if consideration is postponed; and that Congress ought to proceed vigorously to this end at its next session. I do not believe that any substantial support could be gained in any

---

consolidation; president of the Continental Trust Co. and chairman of the board of the Seaboard Air Line.

[2] This was the so-called Plumb plan, named after the railroad and labor lawyer, Glenn Edward Plumb. About this plan, see Glenn E. Plumb, "Labor's Solution of the Railroad Problem," New York *Nation*, CIX (Aug. 16, 1919), 200-201, and K. Austin Kerr, *American Railroad Politics, 1914-1920: Rates, Wages, and Efficiency* (Pittsburgh, 1968), pp. 160-78.

quarter for a plan of postponing permanent action and holding that matter in abeyance until we can have a further test of the present control.

6. My best judgment is that there is a strong sentiment in Congress and in the country against any relinquishment of the railroads in the next few months prior to a permanent solution. I believe the general thought is that Congress ought to be given a reasonable opportunity to legislate before there is relinquishment; and also that the operating revenues now fall so short of paying operating expenses and interest and dividends that the immediate throwing of the railroads back on their own resources would be disastrous from a financial standpoint. At a recent meeting of the Railroad Committee of the United States Chamber of Commerce, selected to consider railroad legislation and consisting of about forty representative bankers, business men, economists and labor men, I am told a unanimous vote was passed in opposition to the early return of the railroads prior to the adoption of a permanent solution, and that the labor men were especially strong in this opinion.

7. Broadly, the present situation as to operation is this: December is the only month since the signing of the armistice for which we have the operating results. They were most disappointing. The operating costs were very high and the operating revenues had begun to fall off. We will not have the results for January until about March 10th. But I am satisfied that the results will be unfavorable. We are incurring heavy increases in costs due to the large (but necessary) increases of wages and to the increases in cost of coal and other materials and supplies. Indeed, we shall be compelled, even yet, to increase the wages of a few remaining classes of employes, notably the train and engine men, to put them on a parity with classes of employes who were increased last year. These remaining classes applied last year for corresponding increases but their cases are only now maturing for disposition. Such additional increases will complete the "cycle" of increases to which the Railroad Administration committed itself last year and which must be completed to secure relative justice among employes without which successful operation will be an impossibility. At the same time we are having a falling off in business. The increased costs and the reduced business would make it impossible at the moment, if the railroads were immediately returned to private control, to pay their interest and dividends, and I believe any return now would precipitate serious financial difficulties. We are going through a period of careful readjustment of operating costs, seeking to obtain greater efficiency, and eliminate overtime and unnecessary hours of employment. Our Federal Managers are actively at work in this

direction. We cannot, however, know what will be the result of a thorough readjustment until several months shall have elapsed, and even then the situation will be largely dependent upon the volume of business, which in turn will depend upon the general financial situation. I am, therefore, of the opinion, and my entire staff concurs in that view, that no relinquishment should be contemplated until we shall have reasonably completed this process of readjustment.

8. If a permanent solution shall not be adopted during the present calendar year, I look with concern on the matter of railroad operation during the calendar year 1920. The problem, being unsolved, is likely to be debated vigorously throughout the presidential campaign. Much partisan criticism will inevitably be directed toward the Railroad Administration. At the same time Federal control will be nearing its end (assuming there has been no definite extension) and this will impair the effectiveness of the organization. In such circumstances railroad operation under the President's direction is bound to involve embarrassment rather than comfort and is not likely to be satisfactory to the public. With such difficulties in prospect, I believe the choices (if we have any) which will prove least unattractive will be either relinquishment of the railroads near the end of the calendar year 1919 (assuming there has been a reasonable opportunity to legislate and it has not been availed of) or an extension which will carry the period well beyond the presidential election. Any thoroughgoing permanent solution even if adopted in this calendar year will in all likelihood contemplate retention of the railroads in Federal control for a considerable period during which the necessary transition shall be worked out. Therefore it is not unlikely that the extension will turn out to be obtainable and desirable rather than the relinquishment.

9. I am without advice in the matter of an extra session, but if the question whether an extra session shall be called is not yet decided and if the factors for it and against it are still being weighed, it occurs to me that a factor that would weigh in favor of it would be that thereby Congress would be given a reasonable opportunity to legislate on the railroad problem. If, with such opportunity, a solution should not be forthcoming the justification for relinquishment would be very strong (assuming that by that time the earning capacity of the railroads is sufficient to justify that course). If a solution should be adopted it would probably involve either an early relinquishment or a definite statutory extension upon such terms as would put the Railroad Administration in better position to weather the presidential campaign without impairment of the service.

T MS (WP, DLC).

From Walker Downer Hines

Dear Mr. President: Washington February 24, 1919.

Doctor Garfield tells me he wishes to submit to you some suggestions relative to the governmental dealing with prices of coal, probably with special reference to the policy of the Railroad Administration. The matter involves from the standpoint of the Railroad Administration some vital considerations which I do not think Doctor Garfield has had occasion to consider fully, and indeed it is not his business to consider them. I hope very much, however, that before taking any action on Doctor Garfield's suggestions, if he presents them, you will find it convenient to give me an opportunity to present the matter from the standpoint of the Government's interest in the operation of the Railroads.

Sincerely yours, Walker D Hines

TLS (WP, DLC).

From Herbert Clark Hoover

Dear Mr. President: Washington February 24, 1919

I have the honor to transmit the following to you at the request of Mr. Hoover:

"I have received your request for my view upon the cablegram of Mr. Glass, recommending the immediate abandonment of all control of prices by the Food Administration.[1]

I feel that there must be some misunderstanding as to the amount and nature of the control outstanding. By the end of this month, control of all but four or five commodities will have been entirely demobilized. These four or five commodities comprise from twenty-five to thirty percent of the nation's food bill.

It is my understanding of the suggestion of the Cabinet, that Congress should undertake the compensation of all those who become losers from the alteration of Congressional or moral guarantees. In order to do this, Congress would have to make provision in advance for liquidated payment to probably fifteen million individuals in the United States. Unless this advance provision were made, there would ensue the most disastrous financial collapse in certain trades. Furthermore, taking a world view over the next four months, while some drop in prices might follow removal of control, the world situation on the few remaining commodities is such that even higher prices than the present might rule.

In order that you may see more clearly something of the situation and the difficulties, I set out below some of the circumstances surrounding the commodities which are under some measure of control.

Firstly, as to wheat; I would be obliged if you would consult Mr. Barnes who will inform you how impossible it is to reach the loser by any form of direct payment to the producer, in the event of abandonment of the Congressional guarantee. Furthermore, the farmer who raises wheat would be subject, more acutely than in the case of any other commodity, to the present 'world control' of wheat which covers 80 percent of the world export and which 'world control' could make any price at will. We would thus have to fix some price at any event. In view of the spread of famine in India, the demand in Europe, the total supplies, etc., I am convinced that in a free market, the price would not be appreciably changed from the present level, but there can be no free prices before next harvest and any relaxation in our control would simply mean a gift to the 'international wheat control.' All this is, of course, aside from the technical difficulties of compensating the farmer.

Secondly, as to sugar; the price of this commodity is being retained even now at ten and eleven cents retail and has been prevented from advancing during the war to twenty-five or thirty cents a pound by various measures adopted by the Food Administration. The price today ranges from fourteen to twenty cents per pound in the blockaded countries. We have the cheapest sugar in the world today, with the exception of a few small countries producing a surplus of sugar, and who at the same time, restrain exportation. The present stabilization is based not only on a moral guarantee to our beet and Louisiana cane producers, but also on a binding contract between the United States and Cuba for the purchase of two-thirds of the Cuban crop. Any change would require either; (A) the consent of the Cuban Government to cancel this contract, or; (B) a direct appropriation by Congress to meet the losses on reduction of the Cuban price. This would imply the abandonment of the moral guarantee given to the beet and Louisiana sugar producers. If the contract fixing the Cuban price were rescinded and stabilization withdrawn, it is possible that during the next two or three months of restricted shipping and blockaded trade outlet, there might be a drop of one or even two cents a pound in the value of raw sugar, but thereafter, to all appearances, there would develop a world shortage. It is extremely unlikely that a drop in raw sugar price would ever be reflected to the consumer in the face of the speculation and profiteering that would ensue and much higher prices would probably maintain later in the year.

Thirdly, cottonseed and rice products were placed under control to restrain profiteering and high prices and are now subject to the

uncertainties of domination of foreign buying agencies and blockade and are still subject to some degree to moral assurance to the
producers until next summer. The prices of cottonseed and rice
products bear a very small relation to the cost of living and the
great proportion of these products remaining in the United States
should go for export.

To sum up, it seems to me impossible even by Congressional
appropriation, to reach the many millions of farmers, manufacturers, and tradesmen who would be losers by the abandonment of
the control of wheat and sugar, and a period of speculation and
possibly even higher prices would follow. As to the cottonseed and
rice production, these can be terminated at once if advisable and
you consider it justifiable. The resulting losses would be local.

I recognise that the tide of criticism is now turning from that of
the producer who has felt that prices were unduly restrained, to
that of the consumer who feels prices are unduly maintained in
these few commodities. I feel deeply the necessity of lowering food
prices for the consumer and of freeing the distributive trade from
all control as not only a necessity for the United States, but as a
movement towards fundamental stability of the world. The unemployed in the United States give more emphasis to this, but I
feel that in pressure to secure these desirable results, we cannot
justly disregard the other factors which enter into the demobilization of our war measures, lest the evils we create are greater than
those we remedy." Signed, Hoover.

I have the honor to remain,

Always faithfully yours,   Theo F Whitmarsh

TLS (WP, DLC).
    [1] C. Glass to WW, Feb. 11, 1919.

From Edward William Bok

My dear Mr. President: Philadelphia February 24 1919

A hearty welcome home from a full heart! And to greet you I
enclose an editorial from to-day's Public Ledger which reflects the
sane thinking of intelligent people.[1] One has only to sit at a large
gateway of public sentiment to realize that the people are absolutely
with you. One can trust the people to think clearly, despite the
vaporings of certain Senatorial ossified minds. They don't seem to
enjoy the fact that *you* are doing this.

Very heartily always   Edward Bok

ALS (WP, DLC).
    [1] "WILSON WILL FIGHT LEAGUE FOES ANYWHERE," Philadelphia *Public Ledger*, Feb.

24, 1919. The editorial declared that Wilson had returned home prepared to fight a "battle royal" on two fronts—for a just peace and a league of nations. He would fight against the opponents of his policies both at home and in Paris. "He sees," the writer said, "that if idealistic, detached and disinterested America repudiates the league, we cannot expect cruelly scarred, chronically suspicious and ever-imminently menaced Europe to trust it with her very life." The writer predicted that Wilson would win his battle at home because he would be supported by "all real Americans who simply will not believe permanently that gun-play is the proper way to settle differences between individuals or nations." Fortified by this support at home, Wilson would return to the peace conference at Paris, where he would be supported by the peoples of the world in his renewed struggle for peace and international organization.

From the Diary of Dr. Grayson

Tuesday, February 25, 1919.

Arriving in Washington this morning at 5:00 o'clock, the President did not leave the train until 8:15. He went directly to the White House, where he had breakfast. Immediately after breakfast he proceeded to his office to pick up the accumulation of business that awaited him there. The President signed a large number of documents, and in the afternoon presided over a regular Cabinet meeting, at which reports were made by the members of the Cabinet touching on the general political situation and the mix-up in Congress.

In the evening the President conferred with Senator Martin, Majority Leader of the Senate, and with Senator Simmons, Chairman of the Senate Finance Committee. The Senators reported to the President that the Republican Senate leaders were desirous of forcing a special session in order that they would be able to debate all of the peace proceedings, but especially the conditions and constitution of the League of Nations during the time that the President was in Paris, following the adjournment of the 65th Congress. The President told Senator Martin that he would not call a special session until the work of the Peace Conference was completed. On leaving the White House Senator Martin issued a public statement to that effect.

To Joseph Patrick Tumulty, with Enclosure

Dear Tumulty: [The White House, c. Feb. 25, 1919]

I would be very much obliged if you would tell me your own judgment about this suggestion of Gavit's.   The President

TL (WP, DLC).

ENCLOSURE

From John Palmer Gavit

Dear Mr. President: [New York] February 24, 1919.

I do not believe that in the press of the enormous burdens that you have had to carry, you have fully realized the extent or the enormity of the things that have been done under cover of war and under stress of the psychology inseparable from war, in defiance and denial of the fundamentals of American freedom. It is in my judgment for that very reason that you are not having now the liberal backing that is your right. The reasonable moderates are largely dumb—muzzled or bullied into silence. Just now, with every reason and need for utmost freedom of speech and candor of sane counsel, utterance is heard only from the ultra-conservatives, jingoes and militarists on the one end, and the ultra-daring advocates of violence on the other.

There seems to me a golden opportunity, while you are here these few days, to declare immediate and unconditional amnesty for all those persons who have been convicted for expression of opinion. I can think of nothing that would so uplift and electrify the liberal forces in this and other countries, or have, in the end and on the whole, a more salutary or far-reaching political effect.

I have nothing to ask for those found guilty of acts of violence or conspiracy thereto. What I do desire is to show our people by this signal act of Americanism, that they can speak and be heard; that those are liars who assert that redress and progress are to be had only through acts of violence.

My heartiest congratulations upon your great work so far, and my hearty wish for your further success. What I am urging you to do *now* will greatly attest the sincerity of your service to the cause of the world's liberty.   Sincerely,   John P. Gavit

TLS (WP, DLC).

To Theodore Elijah Burton

[The White House] February 25, 1919.

Your message[1] greatly appreciated. Am myself confident that the people of the country will rally with practical unanimity to the support of a plan in which the whole world is looking to them to be the leaders.   Woodrow Wilson.

T telegram (Letterpress Books, WP, DLC).
  [1] T. E. Burton to WW, Feb. 24, 1919, T telegram (WP, DLC).

To Carter Glass

Dear Mr. Secretary: [The White House] 25 February 1919.

I am sending herewith a recommendation from the National Advisory Committee for Aeronautics suggesting legislation placing the licensing and regulation of aerial navigation in charge of the Department of Commerce, and also an estimate of an appropriation for carrying the same into effect.

I fully approve the suggested legislation and estimate for transmission to the Congress.

Very sincerely yours,   Woodrow Wilson

TLS (Letterpress Books, WP, DLC).

To Joseph Swagar Sherley

Dear Mr. Sherley: [The White House] 25 February 1919.

I have approved a recommendation and estimate of the National Advisory Committee for Aeronautics that the licensing and regulation of aerial navigation in the United States and its dependencies be placed in charge of the Department of Commerce, and have transmitted it to the Congress through the Secretary of the Treasury.

In view of the situation that has been developed by the signing of the armistice and the cessation of most of the war activities in this country, it is very desirable that provision should be promptly made for the licensing of aeronautical pilots and air craft, and that suitable rules and regulations should be established governing national aerial navigation.

The question of international rules and regulations for aerial navigation is now under consideration by a special international commission in Paris, and I deem it of the utmost importance that there should be established as soon as possible rules and regulations governing our national aerial navigation.

Very sincerely yours,   Woodrow Wilson

TLS (Letterpress Books, WP, DLC).

Two Telegrams from Edward Mandell House

[Paris] February 25, 2:00 p.m. [1919]

Number 5. French authorities insist that you be (their) guest. They see no objections, however, to your bringing White House servants. Please cable me as soon as possible if this is satisfactory and how many servants you will bring and the exact duties of (Gyhen) [each] servants [servant]. Edward House.

[Paris] February 26 [25] 1919.

Number 6. I suggest that you ask [Mr.] Taft (to come) and see you. He is (omission) [the] leader of those (in the United States) who are trying to sway [sustain] you in your fight for a League of Nations.

Sincere congratulations on your admirable speech at Boston. It is commended here in the highest terms. Edward House.

T telegrams (WP, DLC).

From Walker Downer Hines

Dear Mr. President: Washington February 25, 1919.

I submit the following as information relative to the railroad appropriation:

This morning the Senate Appropriations Committee gave Secretary Glass and me a hearing on this appropriation. Senator Martin expresses the opinion that the Committee will support the appropriation and the further opinion that the only possibility of securing its passage at this session of Congress will be for the Senate Committee to report it as an Amendment to the General Deficiency Bill which has not yet been passed by the House and Senator Martin intends to try to accomplish this result. He is exceedingly anxious to get the General Deficiency Bill reported by the House Committee and passed by the House at the earliest possible moment, and contemplates asking you to make a request on Chairman Sherley to this effect.

Senator Cummins of the Interstate Commerce Committee and Senator Kenyon of the Appropriations Committee are both insistent that there shall be attached to the railroad appropriation an amendment which will prohibit the relinquishment of the railroads until the expiration of the 21-months period and a further amendment which will give the Interstate Commerce Commission the power to suspend rates initiated by the President during Federal control. You will recall that under private management the Commission has the power to suspend for a period of ten months the rates initiated by the railroad companies. The Federal Control Act does not give the Commission any such power of suspension in respect of rates initiated by the President, although it does give the Commission the power to pass upon and modify these rates after they shall have gone into effect. These two Senators are insistent that the same power of suspension must be attached to rates initiated by the President. Senator Martin is exceedingly anxious to avoid the possibility of delay which will arise if these amendments are attached to the appropriation, and to avoid also the danger of other amendments being proposed and debated. This is why he wishes to get the appropriation attached to the General Deficiency Bill. He wishes to discuss with you at the earliest possible time these and perhaps other phases of the situation which he thinks have an important bearing on the passage of the railroad appropriation.

Further consideration confirms the opinion I expressed to you in my wireless message of last Saturday[1] to the effect that it is of the highest importance, both from the financial standpoint and from the industrial standpoint, to get this entire appropriation made before the end of the present session.

                    Sincerely yours,   Walker D Hines

TLS (WP, DLC).
  [1] W. D. Hines to WW, Feb. 22, 1919.

From William Gibbs McAdoo, with Enclosure

Personal

Dear Governor: Santa Barbara, Cal., February 25, 1919.

This Congress is going to do nothing about the railroads. The Republicans are playing politics, as usual, and have had the aid of some reactionary Democrats who are not astute enough to see the game of the Republican politicians and the selfish interests behind them. I have never seen a more vicious and persistent propaganda of misrepresentation nor one more effectively carried on than that conducted by the railroad owners and executives with the aid of the Republican political machine. The country has been made to believe every conceivable sort of unfair and unjustifiable thing about Federal control of the railroads for the past year, and there is not time nor are the means at hand to combat the effects of this propaganda successfully before the new Congress assembles in December next. I believe that the country has been seriously prejudiced against Federal control of the railroads by this propaganda as well as by the very strong sentiment and prejudice which exist against the control of the telephones and telegraphs.

What the owners of the railroads and their Republican political allies want to bring about is a continuation of Federal control for the twenty-one months under the present law with their earnings guaranteed so that they would be absolutely safe, while at the same time they are left free to make the Administration a target of continuous attack and to render Federal control odious as well as unsuccessful. With their rentals guaranteed, they are safe to conduct this form of guerilla warfare. The public discontent is so easily aroused by blaming every trifling detail of mismanagement or of inconvenience on the Government that the retention of the railroads will, in my judgment, not only be harmful to the public interest, but distinctly injurious to the Party. If you return the railroads to private control, the Congress will still be as free to legislate on the railroad problem, while at the same time the public will not be able to blame the Administration for the faults and defects of private management which will again be brought glaringly to the public consciousness by the return of private control.

There are in our own Party a great many timid and easily alarmed people who may urge that the railroads be retained because some of them may fail if restored to their owners and that the general financial situation may be so upset that the Liberty Loan may be affected, etc., but I attach no importance to these things. Certainly we are not justified in holding the railroads and paying a high rental for them out of the public treasury merely because some weak railroads may go into the hands of receivers unless supported at the public expense. If you wait until after the next Liberty Loan to relinquish the railroads, ample time will be allowed for readjustment and the roads could be returned June 30, 1919, or at any time thereafter. Announcement of your intentions need not be made unless you care to do so until after the next Loan is out of the way.

The Republican machine and the railroads working in concert, made the people believe that the two hundred million dollar railroad deficit in 1918 was due entirely to incompetent Government management, which is, of course, untrue, and they have also made the public believe that if Federal control is continued for the year 1919 the deficit will be even greater. If this be true, why should the Federal Government incur this loss in 1919 when the railroad owners, by necessary implication from their argument, could prevent it through their more efficient management of the properties, if returned to them? For the good of the country, prompt relinquishment of Federal control is to my mind essential in the circumstances, and politically speaking, it is greatly to the advantage of the Administration to be relieved of the railroads.

If the Republicans succeed in the effort they are making to amend the railroad appropriation bill so as to deprive you of the discretion you now have to relinquish the railroads before the end of the twenty-one months period, I should, if I were you, not hesitate to veto the bill. Some inconvenience might result in paying promptly claims against the railroads, but it would not be serious. The next Congress would have to take care of that situation and the blame would be upon the Republicans for all intermediate inconvenience. If you return the railroads promptly to their owners, you have the whip hand of the situation. If you hold them, you give it to the Republicans. They are determined to make this the big issue in the next campaign and they can make it a most effective issue against the Administration if it is at that time holding the railroad bag.

Please forgive me for intruding my views, but the whole sinister plot is so clear to my mind that I cannot help feeling a deep interest in defeating it, not only for the sake of the country, but for the success as well of your Administration.

Affectionately yours,   W G McAdoo

P.S. If the Republicans succeed in depriving you of your discretion to return the railroads to their owners at any time, they will take away the only remaining weapon through which you may exercise some sort of restraint upon the railroad corporations. I enclose copy of my reply to a letter from Mr. Hines asking my views about the relinquishment of the railroads.

TLS (WP, DLC).

E N C L O S U R E

William Gibbs McAdoo to Walker Downer Hines

My dear Hines: Santa Barbara, Cal., February 25, 1919.

Your letter about railroad control duly received.

My judgment is absolutely against any attempt to hold the railroads if the Congress refuses, as now seems certain, to extend the period of Federal control. The roads ought to be returned promptly to their owners, and I should think about June 30 would be an excellent time, but the President does not have to decide this point immediately. He will have ample time to make up his mind and he can take action when the conditions are most favorable.

With the railroads in the hands of their owners, you will find that the problem of legislation will be much simplified. So long as the Government retains them and guarantees the owners a high rental, leaving them free to attack Government control with impunity and to make it both odious and unsuccessful, the greater will be the difficulty to secure proper legislation. Moreover, the public mind has been so poisoned by misrepresentation about the discomforts, inconveniences and inefficiencies of Government control that a return to private ownership is necessary as a corrective and to restore a properly balanced public opinion upon which legislation for a permanent solution may be based. I have never seen a more vicious and effective propaganda of misrepresentation than that which the railroad executives and their allies have carried on for the past two months.

I have reviewed this problem from every conceivable angle and I can see absolutely no advantage in retaining public control in view of the failure to grant the reasonable extension asked for. The very difficulties you mention in your letter, the five year control was intended to obviate. But the various interests which are most concerned have refused to listen to reason and ought now to take the consequences.

If an extra session should be called, it cannot be assembled before next summer and it will not be able to legislate before the Presidential election. If while that legislation is under way, the Government is trying to run the railroads and is the target for all the unfair attacks, of which there has been such an ample demonstration for the past two months, you will find that progress will be impossible along any just and reasonable lines. Let the railroad owners have the responsibility of operating the railroads while the legislative solution is being worked out and you will find the situation not only greatly clarified, but when it comes it will more likely be in the public interest.

My plan for the five year extension never at any time precluded legislation for a permanent solution before the end of the extension. The opponents of the extension seemed to me particularly obtuse, if not intentionally so, in refusing to see that even if the extension was granted, the next Congress was in no way handicapped or interfered with in an effort to secure at the earliest possible moment a permanent solution of the problem.

We are face to face with one of those situations where the Government must act with decision and courage. That, to my mind, dictates only one course and that is the prompt return of the properties to their owners at the earliest possible moment. Let the railroads go back to their owners and then let us all pull together and get a wise solution of this problem.

Cordially yours,   W. G. McAdoo

CCL (WP, DLC).

From Frank Morrison and Samuel Gompers

Sir: Washington, D. C. February 25, 1919.

As you are aware, President Gompers is now in Paris. With him are four members of the Executive Council of the American Federation of Labor, three of them executive officers of the building trades organizations. Speaking for his four colleagues as well as for himself, President Gompers has cabled me as follows:

"Five members Executive Council in Paris urge you lay before the Congress and President Wilson when he arrives the following:

Our investigation and findings on European countries show that unrest and unhealthy conditions now prevailing among laboring classes are due mainly to after war conditions; that there is danger to the public weal in some of the efforts that are being put forward by the discontented masses and that to prevent growth of similar condition in America Congress must take such action as will put governmental affairs into constructive rather than a passing or questionable position.

We recommend that project to defer building construction for governmental purposes until February first, 1920, be abandoned and that individual enterprises in building industry be encouraged.

We also strongly urge that action be taken towards completion of ships now twenty five per cent or more finished, thus giving employment to those now idle and likely to become idle, and with the additional advantage of avoiding the loss which would otherwise occur if ships were not completed, even if necessary to sell ships at less than normal prices if not needed by the government."

I am not unmindful of the fact that questions of tremendous importance press upon your consideration for every hour of your stay in Washington, but yet, I am persuaded that the vital importance of the above will commend itself to your, I hope, favorable consideration.   Respectfully yours,   Frank Morrison

TLS (WP, DLC).

From Thomas James Walsh

My dear Mr. President: Washington February 25, 1919.

The recent discussions in the Senate and the study which individual members have made of the draft of the constitution for the League of Nations has disclosed not a little in the language employed that is obscure and more, the wisdom of which is seriously questioned by the earnest friends of the project. I believe incalculable good would result if you could devote just one day of your brief stay to a conference with, say, six members of the Senate and six members of the House, who would sit down with you at the table and go at the draft as one of our committees is accustomed to do with important bills. You will appreciate what excellent work was done in that way in perfecting the federal reserve bill. I have in mind subjecting the draft to real constructive criticism, an expression that has been much abused recently. I venture to propose the following among the Senators: Swanson, Pittman, Wolcott, Robinson, Hitchcock, Walsh.

Hitchcock is genuinely in favor of the League, and for obvious reasons it would be wise to include him, notwithstanding past differences. I do not venture to make any recommendations in respect to the House members, but suggest for consideration Scott Ferris and Cordell Hull.

Senator Knox is to speak on Saturday. We have all heard him once and could go on that day without losing much.

I appreciate that the demands on your time will be tremendous, but you have no other duty that compares in importance with this, and I believe you will find that the time will have been profitably spent.

Hitchcock and I have been sounding out the friendly Republican Senators, most of whom have some criticism to make of particular provisions of the draft. These could be made the subject of consideration. You doubtless would be glad to know their views. The meeting this evening may,[1] in some measure, contribute to the result I have in mind, but obviously discussion can not be as free as under the plan I propose, with much diffidence, but with much earnestness.   Cordially yours,   T. J. Walsh

P.S. I have conferred with Swanson and Hitchcock on the suggestion herein made which is warmly approved by both
                                                    T.J.W.

TLS (WP, DLC).
  [1] He must have meant the dinner meeting at the White House on February 26, about which see the news report printed at that date. Or perhaps Walsh's letter was misdated.

From Josephus Daniels

My Dear Mr. President: Washington. Feb. 25. 1919.

A short time after the Attorney General resigned I sent you a brief cable expressing the hope that you would feel that your administration would be strengthened and the public good subserved by the appointment of Mitchell Palmer.[1] You know him as well—better no doubt—that [than] I do, but I feel you always wish the views of those whose advice is prompted only for the common good. In addition to his recognized ability and high character his appointment would be pleasing alike to the bar and to the Old Guard of Democrats, particularly those who won the fight at Baltimore and conducted the campaign.

Sincerely yours,   Josephus Daniels

It was my purpose to speak to you about this after cabinet meeting but did not have the opportunity

ALS (WP, DLC).
¹ JD to WW, Feb. 8, 1919.

From Felix Cordova Davila

My dear Mr. President: Washington, D. C. February 25, 1919

I have the honor to refer to my letter of the 13th instant¹ in regard to the proposed filling of the vacancy now existing in the Attorney Generalship of Porto Rico.

I realize that the extraordinary pressure of the questions awaiting your decision and the briefness of the period elapsed since your return to the United States has prevented your consideration thus far of the subject-matter of my previous letter. I am writing again, however, to say that it is my impression that the Governor of Porto Rico,² who has just arrived from the Island and is now in Washington, has taken a decided stand against the appointment of a native to this Office. This attitude, Mr. President, as I had occasion to state to the Governor in the course of an interview with him today, involves an unjustifiable disregard of the views and expressed desires of the people of Porto Rico who are asking with insistence the selection of a native.

I beg further to say in this connection that strong hostility has developed in the Island to the proposed re-appointment of the present incumbent.³ This is illustrated by the fact that recently a resolution was adopted by the Insular House of Representatives declaring its opposition to his recommission.

I have not the least doubt, Mr. President, that your decision in this matter, as in the case of all others requiring the intervention of your high Office, will be a just one, and, therefore, I feel confident that the wishes of my countrymen in this question will not fail to merit and receive your friendly and attentive regard. However, should circumstances of which I am not aware, or other considerations make you feel unjustified in reaching the conclusion I took the liberty to suggest in my former letter, I beg to request that I be given, at your convenience, an opportunity to be heard in the matter, with a view to explaining further my position therein.

With warmest personal regards and most cordial congratulations upon your happy return to the United States, I am,

Very sincerely yours,   Fel. Cordova Davila

TLS (WP, DLC).
[1] F. Cordova Davila to WW, Feb. 13, 1919.
[2] That is, Arthur Yager.
[3] Howard Lewis Kern.

From Cleveland Hoadley Dodge

My dear President   New York February 25th 1919

Welcome home! and hearty congratulations.

Your talk to dear old Boston was superb. You have the fight of your life on your hands, but I firmly believe the people are with you. God bless you and give you wisdom & courage to win out

Grace joins me in love & best wishes to Mrs Wilson and yourself

Ever devotedly yours   Cleveland H Dodge

P.S. Many thanks for your letter from Paris[1] & for all that you have done to help us in our efforts to help the suffering in the Near East[2]   CHD

ALS (WP, DLC).
[1] WW to C. H. Dodge, Jan. 25, 1919, CCL (WP, DLC). Wilson explained briefly that he had not sent a message to the banquet of the American Committee for the Independence of Armenia because he had felt that it probably would be unwise for him to say anything "which might prejudice a question which the Peace Conference is to consider."
[2] In response to C. H. Dodge to WW, Jan. 7, 1919, T telegram (WP, DLC), Wilson had sent the following telegram in support of a campaign for $30,000,000 for near eastern relief: "The appropriation asked of Congress for handling food relief is not intended in any way to take the place of the subscription being asked for relief and rehabilitation in the near East. I hope that this subscription will not in any way be interrupted or reduced. The need is immediate and very great." WW to C. H. Dodge, Jan. 7, 1919, T telegram (WP, DLC).

From Ellen Duane Davis

My very dear Friend,   Philadelphia 25. Feb. 1919

I cannot let tonight pass without writing to tell you E.P. allowed me to go to Jefferson Hospital today to see, not only Woodrow Wilson Sayre, but also your dear Jessie. Without *any* exception you have the handsomest baby for a grandson I have ever seen. Jessie was very bright and glad to see me & I think the boy was too, because I took him from Jessie & laid him on his "tummie" across my knee & after looking at me very wisely and "sizing me up" went to sleep.

This is also a note to welcome The Greatest Man on Earth home. We have fairly dogged your footsteps since you have been gone and longed for your safe return. Now I suppose you will be going again and we *know* what you do is for the best. Your speech in Boston was simply fine & it is so good to know you belong to us. E.P. would be sending his love to you and Mrs Wilson with mine, but he has gone to New York tonight to a dinner to arrange about the International Med. Congress to be held in the U. S. in Sept. 1920. They have made him Chairman of an important Comm. on Foreign Affairs & it means a lot of work & possible help from you. You may be sure he is doing everything he can for Jessie and will always for you & yours. Please tell Mrs Wilson from me that she never did a kinder act in her life than by sending for our niece Kate Boyd when she was in London. When *shall* we ever get a chance to hear all about it? E.P. has been and is terribly busy and needs rest which he does not get, and says he cannot get it in this country. However I am hoping like Mr. Micawber, for something to turn up & have been fairly well myself. The Baby has your hands such nice long fingers & thumbs only yours are not as dimpled as his hands are tonight. Tell Mrs Wilson that she has our loving admiration too. Always,   Most sincerely yours   Ellen Duane Davis

If you come to Phila. to see Jessie wont you both take lunch with us? You shall have a welcome if not as great as those you have have [*sic*] had but a loving one any way & a bite to eat.

ALS (WP, DLC).

From the Diary of Josephus Daniels

February Tuesday 25 1919

At Cabinet meeting WW detailed story of Paris Conference with many incidents. French resolved & British wish cost of war to be borne equally by all engaged. Would mean that this country would renounce all British, French & Italian debts & then some. He fenced to keep this direct proposition from coming to a head.

He thought Venezelos the biggest man he met. Smuts he called "a brick" Lloyd George practical man but no idealist.

Told of gunner of Plunketts guns:[1] "Kills everybody within 100 mi & hunts up his next of kin & kills them.

At first Press of Paris were to [be] told to do three things[2]

1. Magnify Rep. opposition to Wilson
2. Make it appear conditions in Russia worse than they are
3. Cause it to appear that Germany is able to renew the war

Wilson presents the Covenant of the League of Nations to the Third Plenary Session of the Peace Conference, February 14, 1919. Painting by George Sheridan Knowles

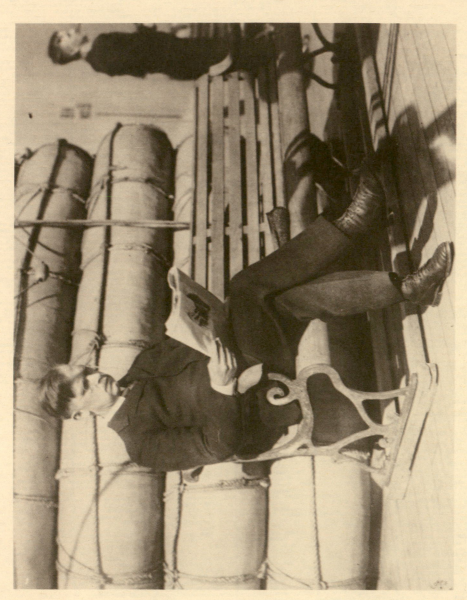

Ray Stannard Baker aboard the U.S.S. *George Washington*

David Hunter Miller and Major James Brown Scott

Irwin Hood (Ike) Hoover

William Christian Bullitt

From left to right: Charles C. Wagner, Gilbert Fairchild Close, and Charles Lee Swem

On the bridge as the U.S.S. *George Washington* arrives in Boston Harbor

In Mechanic's Hall, Boston, on February 24, 1919

Extra session talk. Reps. will not pass appro. bills. Would he agree to call extra session within 30 days of his return from [Paris].

Hw bound diary (J. Daniels Papers, DLC).

[1] That is, the five 14-inch naval guns mounted on railway cars which were in action in France from September 6 to November 11, 1918, under the command of Rear Adm. Charles Peshall Plunkett, U.S.N. The "gunner" was exaggerating the power of his weapons: the guns had a maximum range of about twenty-four miles. See United States Navy Department, Office of Naval Records and Library, Historical Section, *Publication Number 6: The United States Naval Railway Batteries in France* (Washington, 1922), especially pp. 1-23.

[2] About this matter, see W. E. Rappard to H. Sulzer, Feb. 13, 1919.

From the Diary of Dr. Grayson

Wednesday, February 26, 1919.

The President devoted all of today to meeting various individuals with whom he had previously arranged appointments, to signing a number of bills that had been passed and sent down from the Capitol. In the evening he had as his guests at dinner the members of the Senate Foreign Relations Committee and of the House Foreign Affairs Committee. The absentees were Senators Borah and Fall and Representative [Dorsey W. Shackleford].[1] Borah had previously announced that he would not attend because he believed his presence would bind him to refrain from using the information given him by the President. However, before the dinner had even started the President let it be known that there was nothing confidential in the information which he was furnishing to members of the two Committees, and that they could use such information in any manner they saw fit. The dinner and following conference lasted until nearly midnight. The conference itself was held in the East Room, with the members of the two Committees sitting in a semi-circle about the President. He explained to them at some length the various difficulties he had encountered in Paris and related in detail the steps by which the tentative constitution of the League of Nations finally was arrived at. The meeting was more or less of a free and easy character inasmuch as the President invited questioning, and his invitation was taken advantage of by many of those present, chiefly Senators Lodge and Hitchcock and Representative Cooper.[2] Following the conference no official statement was issued from the White House, and the various Senators who were interviewed by the newspaper correspondents failed to agree in their stories of what actually transpired.

[1] Democrat of Missouri.
[2] Henry Allen Cooper, Republican of Wisconsin.

A News Report

[*Feb. 26, 1919*]

PRESIDENT EXPOUNDS LEAGUE OF NATIONS
TO DINNER GUESTS, URGES THAT PRESENT
DRAFT BE NOT RADICALLY AMENDED; SOVEREIGNTY
DIMINISHED, HE SAYS, FOR THE WORLD'S GOOD

Washington, Feb. 26.—President Wilson, in tonight's dinner and conference at the White House with members of the Senate Foreign Relations Committee and the House Foreign Affairs Committee not only made his own statement of the situation as he views it but submitted himself to the very widest range of questions and was remarkably frank in his replies.

The temper of those present was everything that could be expected. There was no attempt by Republican Senators or Representatives to embarrass or heckle the President, and when questions were in order they showed by their attitude, as did the Democrats present, that they realized the momentous character of the occasion and approached the issues and problems involved as serious men seeking enlightenment.

Nothing could have been freer than the interchange of views that took place. There was no limitation on the asking of questions and the President did not restrain himself in the replies that he made. This was very evident when he was asked whether it was true that the formation of a League of Nations with the United States as one of its constituent members would involve any surrender of sovereignty on the part of this nation?

The President minced no words in his answer. He told the Senator who asked this question, very frankly, that in his opinion this nation would relinquish some of its sovereignty, but asserted that every other nation in the League would make a similar surrender and sacrifice, but for the good of the world, as he and the others with whom he conferred at Paris viewed it.

The President in reply to other questions, dealt with the Monroe Doctrine, disarmament, the situation in Europe, and other vital matters.

Probably the most important point that he made in reply to questions was his statement that the provision of the charter for disarmament would not involve any surrender of the right of Congress to fix and determine our armament.

The President said that, while it did not so appear in the text of the charter as published, it was the unanimous understanding of those who framed the charter that every proposal relating to the fixing of the size of armaments would have to be unanimously approved by each of the powers represented in the Executive Council—that is, by England, the United States, France, Japan, and Italy—before the plan for fixing armaments could be put into effect. This was a wholly new idea relative to the covenant.

The President's guests met him promptly by appointment at 8 o'clock. For the first time in two years the White House was illuminated as for a State dinner or reception, outside as well as within, and the guests were first escorted to the State dining room, where covers for thirty-six were spread. Those present besides the President were Mrs. Wilson and the thirty-four members of Congress. Mrs. Wilson, following the dinner, was escorted into the East Room by Senator Lodge of Massachusetts.

The President and the members of the committees strolled into the East Room, where the conference was held following the dinner. Mrs. Wilson remained in the East Room only long enough to exchange greetings with those with whom she had dined.

For about ten minutes the Senators and Representatives stood about chatting informally. Meanwhile chairs had been arranged by ushers in the form of an oval. The President asked his guests to be seated and then took a seat himself. He sat at the apex of the oval with Senators and Representatives sitting around in the oval—one line of chairs only.

There was nothing formal about the affair. The committee members present did not sit according to seniority, but each took the nearest chair. The President seemed perfectly at ease and was in a happy humor. His guests were in equally good humor.

When the men had taken seats, the President first made his own statement of the situation as he viewed it. The President told his guests that if he could be permitted to make his statement he would answer any question asked. He asked that these questions be frank. He said that he wanted to meet every point of view if possible, and was desirous that no one keep anything in the back of his head.

The President in his preliminary statement said that the statesmen assembled at Paris were agreed upon the need and the importance of forming a League of Nations, of doing something practical to bind the nations together in an effort to prevent a new breaking out of the present war and to stop future wars, if possible. They had all found this to be a huge task, but were seriously seeking to accomplish it.

He said that no man could visit Europe as he had done without being tremendously impressed with the desire of both statesmen and people there that repetition of this war be prevented by some concerted action of the nations. He said that the people of Europe had suffered so much from the war that they were determined that the old system of things must cease. Statesmen abroad were convinced, he had found, that there must be united action to eliminate war.

After making this general statement, in which he briefly explained some of the statements he had made in Paris and in his Boston speech, the President told his guests that he was satisfied that the better way to get at the matter in hand was over the question and answer route.

"Ask anything you want to know, gentlemen, and ask it as freely as you wish," said the President. "I will answer you very frankly."

Questions were asked by most of the Senators and Representatives present. Among those prominent in asking questions were Senators Lodge, Brandegee, Knox, Swanson, Williams, Hitchcock, and Representatives Flood and Cooper.

One of the first questions put was as to the President's construction of Article VIII of the charter of the League of Nations, a provision of the Constitution as first drafted which has been the subject of much debate in the Senate and elsewhere. This deals with disarmament and was dealt with at length in the speeches of Senators Borah and Reed. It has been argued that this article would take away from Congress its constitutional right to fix the size of our own army and navy.

The construction, given to this article by President Wilson in his replies to questions, threw new light on the project for a League of Nations. The President said, in discussing this article, that no order could be issued by the Executive Council of the proposed League of Nations, and made binding, unless that order was issued as the result of unanimous action by the Executive Council.

Moreover, said the President, before any such order relative to the size of armaments could be issued by the Executive Council and made effective it must be submitted to each of the Governments having representation on the Executive Council; and, as this nation was one that would be permanently represented on the Executive Council, it meant that any project for disarmament would have to be submitted to this country before it could be adopted.

Even after it had been so submitted to each of the nations represented on the Executive Council, it would have to be approved unanimously by the Council. In this way the United States would pass on the size of England's army and navy. England would pass on the size of the German army and navy, France on the size of Japan's army and navy, the United States on the size of Italy's army and navy, and all the members of the Executive Council of the League would have to approve the disarmament project, making it unanimous so far as the council and the nations having votes in that council were concerned, before any order for disarmament or fixing the size of armies and navies could be approved, or made binding on this country.

The Monroe Doctrine, which has been to the forefront in Senate debate, was not forgotten at tonight's conference. The President said that the Monroe Doctrine was one that was announced to the world many years ago to the effect that we would not permit foreign aggression on this hemisphere. Now, he stated, those who were preparing to set up the League of Nations were recommending that the Monroe Doctrine be extended to cover the world.

As far as the Monroe Doctrine was concerned, the President insisted, the United States was making all nations a party to the Doctrine and proposing thereby to broaden its scope and strengthen its application.

Another question put to the President related to the right of the proposed League to take notice of any act that might threaten the peace of the world. The President was told by his conferees that this provision of the charter had not been clearly understood, and, as the discussion proceeded tonight, the President frankly admitted that he saw how that provision had been misunderstood. The President said that this part of the charter could well be amended in the interest of clarification.

The President explained that it was the idea of those framing the charter for the League that if a dispute should arise between two nations they should agree to arbitrate, if each thought the matter a fit subject for arbitration. The President said that the idea of those behind the project was that if these two nations did not consider the dispute a fit subject for arbitration they would then submit it to the League of Nations for consideration.

The Executive Council of the League, he explained, would then seek to bring about an adjustment of the dispute. But, the President objected, the intention was that if both nations involved desired to disregard the suggestion of the League of Nations, then they would be left to their own resources in the matter, but if one nation involved in the dispute should accept the decision of the League of Nations, that acceptance would throw no burden on the power not accepting the decision of the League excepting in one instance.

That one exception, the President explained, was that the nation not accepting the award would agree not to attack the nation that did accept the award. Even in this exception, the President went on to explain, in response to questions, there was a safeguard, and this was that the recommendation of the League of Nations in acting on the dispute must be unanimous before these conditions could arise.

So far as the United States was concerned, the President went on to say, as we would have representation on the Executive Council, the decision could not be unanimous in a dispute in which we might be involved, unless our representative on the Executive Council should also agree to it.

These statements were made by the President when asked by members of the committee to show that the application of this article of the charter of the League was only limited.

The President said that when he spoke at Paris, explaining the charter for the League, he explained this feature, but it seemed to have been overlooked or forgotten in the debates here. He said that when he made this explanation at Paris, he had done so by special request of the members of the committee which had framed the charter.

The next phase, taken up in questions to the President, related to the statements that England, by reason of the representation of its colonies in the League, each with a vote, would have five votes, while the most the United States would have would be one vote. The President stated that so far as England's four extra votes (the four votes of her main dominions) were concerned, it was next to impossible for England to have at any time more than one vote in the Executive Council of Nine.

The President pointed out that the Executive Council would be composed of representatives from nine nations only. Five of these nations would be permanently represented on the Executive Council of Nine—the United States, England, France, Italy, and Japan.

The other four members of the Executive Council remained to be picked, the President explained. He called attention to the fact that the four places would probably go to four of the smaller or lesser nations. He said this would be the case because, under the charter proposed, the four nations which would be represented on the Executive Council would be named by the body of delegates. This body of delegates was to be composed of delegates of all the nations in the League of Nations.

The President said that those who framed the plan for the League did not conceive of a situation in which the smaller nations, with their overwhelming votes in the proposed body of delegates, would ever vote to give England two votes in the Executive Council of Nine. The understanding at Paris, the President explained, was that the smaller nations, voting in the body of delegates, would take the four unnamed places on the Executive Council for four nations from among their own number.

At this stage the question of the surrender of American sovereignty was raised, and it was then, when he was asked whether he did not think that the League would call on us to surrender some of our sovereignty, that the President frankly admitted that some of our sovereignty would be surrendered.

Then he stated that it was inconceivable that any concert of action of the nations to eliminate war from the world could be taken without some surrender of sovereignty, without some sacrifice, and that these sacrifices would not only be necessary, but warranted by the effort to protect the weak against the strong, each nation yielding something to accomplish such an end.

The President also asserted his belief that the project for a League of Nations would never be carried out successfully if the objection of sovereignty was insisted upon by the Senate.

Then the President was asked what would happen to the League of Nations scheme if the United States should, through action of the Senate, refuse to go into the League. The President replied he believed that in such a contingency the project for the League would fail.

He was asked what would be the effect if no League of Nations were created. He stated his belief, saying it was the belief of others with whom he had conferred abroad, that if no League of Nations were formed the whole of Europe would be thrown into turmoil, and that the horrors resulting would be beyond description.

The President was asked whether he thought the proposal for agreements to participate in furnishing forces to go into some foreign nations, under the concerted action of the League, would be a usurpation of the authority of Congress itself, under the Constitution, to declare war.

The President said that he did not think that it would involve any such usurpation, that it would be merely carrying out the agreement, made under the treaty for the League of Nations, which would not be effective so far as this nation was concerned unless the Senate should ratify the project for a League of Nations.

The President asserted that the United States was sacredly bound by its treaties, and that the violation of pledges under any of our treaties might create situations which, under the old order of things, were calculated to compel us to declare war to enforce the broken pledges. But, he asserted, the fact that such violations might force us to declare war was not a usurpation of the power of Congress to declare war.

The President sought the questioning tonight and it was stated after the conference by men who were present that he had answered the questions so frankly that Senators who had disagreed with him, and probably still disagreed with him, went away at least satisfied with the fullness of the statements made of the situation as he viewed it.

The course of the President tonight seemed to have removed from the minds of some of those who were present the idea that he was trying to push the campaign for the League without the advice and consent of the Senate.

One thing which is said to have helped along the conference at the beginning was a statement the President made soon after he began to speak, that he was much surprised over the furore raised over his message, asking that the Senate not discuss the charter for the League until after tonight's dinner.

He said that he had not intended to interfere with the right of the Senate to debate the charter freely, but merely made that suggestion because he desired to make a statement to the representatives of the Senate and House and answer their questions before they went on with the debate of the matter.

After the conference was over members of the two committees stood around for ten minutes in the East Room, talking over the conference with the President and one another.

That President Wilson hoped that the present draft of the League covenant would become effective without radical changes in its construction was the idea brought away from the White House by the Senators and Representatives.

The President, it is said, asserted that in his opinion it would be very difficult to make amendments to the draft, as fourteen nations already had accepted it in its present form.

Another view which he is said to have put forward is that the United States would feel that it should at least take a prominent part in the policing of Armenia until proper conditions could be restored there.

The conference ended at 11:45 o'clock. Most of those who attended were unwilling to talk at length about the conference before they had had time to think over carefully the statements made by Mr. Wilson. It was stated, however, that President Wilson did not in any way attempt to bind those who attended the dinner to secrecy and did not expect them to refrain from using in debate the explanations he gave.

In connection with the view held by some of the Republican Senators that the terms of the League would force the United States to participate if occasion arose by sending armed forces to Europe, it is reported that the President took the stand that this would be a matter for the United States to decide and that such contribution was not mandatory upon it.

One impression which got out also was that the drafters of the proposal of a League of Nations felt that the extent of disarmament was a matter which would be a subject of debate in the United States.

In this connection, it was pointed out also that the control, which was exercised through the League over the manufacture of munitions of war, would play a prominent part in controlling armament.

After the conference Senator Hitchcock said to THE NEW YORK TIMES:

"The President laid strong emphasis on the despair that would come over the world if the League of Nations should fail. He declared that the war would have been fought in vain. The President cleared up one doubt, concerning the right of a member of the League to withdraw. He talked at length on this phase of the League and said that any member of it could withdraw, by taking the proper step, at any time it wished. The steps to be taken, he explained, are those that pertain to abrogation of treaties.

"The President answered questions very freely as to whether the Monroe Doctrine would be done away with in the League project. The League, the President said, would have the same purpose as the Monroe Doctrine and that it would be an extension of that doctrine to the whole world. The United States, he said, would not sacrifice anything in the Monroe Doctrine in going into the League."

Senator Brandegee said:

"The President talked freely about the League of Nations, and when he was through he asked if there were any questions the Senators wished to ask. He spoke of the suppositious queries raised in the lobby of the Senate and in the cloak rooms.

"For myself, I can say that nothing the President said changed my opinion about the League of Nations. I am against it, as I was before.

"One point raised at the conference concerned the question whether any member of the League would be able at any time to withdraw if it felt so disposed. The President said that that was a fact."

One Senator, who would not allow himself to be quoted, told THE NEW YORK TIMES correspondent that the President had indicated that he did not expect that the League project would go through without change. The President, he said, told the conferees that he expected that there would have to be changes made in some of its phases, but that they would not touch the vital features of it.

The Senators, he said, were all impressed with the idea that the President did not impose secrecy upon them, but that, rather, he was disposed to have the whole country know his ideas, as conveyed to them. The President, he said, indicated that what he had said was merely for the guidance of the Senators in debating the League project, and that he was not trying to impress his own will upon them.

One of the Republican Senators, who would not be quoted, stated that President Wilson was asked, flatly, whether Germany would immediately be allowed representation in the League of Nations, and particularly in the Executive Council. The President replied, he stated, that none of those who participated in the framing of the draft was in favor of recognizing that Germany had any immediate right to a place in the League. They were especially opposed, he stated, to giving Germany a place on the Executive Council, now or at any other time, unless the League was to increase the membership of the Council.

This Senator said that he understood the President's viewpoint was that Germany would, under no circumstances, become a member of the League within the next few years. Germany's acceptance at any time thereafter, he said, would be dependent upon whether the other members of the League were convinced that the Germans had undergone a thorough political reform. If this were true, the Senator remarked, in his opinion, the proposed League could not be made a part of the treaty of peace—a document to which Germany must subscribe.

Printed in the *New York Times*, Feb. 27, 1919.

To Thomas Watt Gregory

My dear Gregory: [The White House] 26 February, 1919.

I have been thinking, and thinking hard and in many directions, about the appointment of your successor, and each time my mind comes back to Mitchell Palmer. I think that on the whole he is my most available man. I have looked into some of the matters you mentioned to me in our last talk and think that they clear themselves up quite satisfactorily.

I cannot tell you with what grief I think of your leaving the Cabinet. I have never been associated with a man whose gifts and character I admired more, and my admiration has grown into very deep and genuine affection. I shall feel robbed of one of my chief supports when you are gone, and I wish with all my heart that it were possible for you to remain. I know that you will be generous enough to advise me after you break your official connections with the administration, but that will not be the same thing and I shall miss you sadly.

Always,   Affectionately yours,   [Woodrow Wilson]

CCL (WP, DLC).

To Walker Downer Hines

My dear Mr. Hines: [The White House] 26 February, 1919.

I have your letter of yesterday and am glad to say that I have been doing all that I could to promote the matters of which you speak.

In haste,
                    Cordially and sincerely yours,   Woodrow Wilson

TLS (Letterpress Book, WP, DLC).

To Joseph Swagar Sherley

My dear Mr. Sherley: [The White House] 26 February, 1919.

If I begin to trouble you right away, I am afraid you will be sorry that I have returned, but there are some matters which I dare not neglect to help in as far as I can.

One of these matters is the $750,000,000 appropriation urgently needed by the Railway Administration and which has already passed the House but, if pressed as a separate bill in the Senate, is in danger of coming to grief in the hurried last days of the session. I am therefore writing to express the hope that it will be possible to get the General Deficiency Bill over to the Senate at the earliest possible hour. Senator Martin feels confident that he could get the Railway appropriation attached to the General Deficiency Bill in the Senate, if there were a little time after the Deficiency Bill is received by his committee. This appropriation is absolutely essential as I am sure you yourself feel, to the Railway Adminiistration, and I contemplate with great uneasiness any possibility of losing a chance to pass it.

There is another matter which I take the liberty of begging you will include in the Deficiency Appropriations, and that is $5,000,000 for the State Department to cover contingent expenses connected with the Peace Conference. I can personally testify that this appropriation is absolutely necessary if the very complicated work to be done by Commissions in connection with the peace settlements is to be properly participated in by the United States, and I beg that you will urge this appropriation as in the public interest.

I wish I had time to go into details in the matter, but I have really summed up the thing in what I have already said. It is evident that there is going to spring out of the Peace Conference a whole process of adjustment which will be elaborate and will run through many months, and in which in justice to ourselves and every interest involved the United States must play a full, if not a leading, part.

With warmest regard,

Cordially and sincerely yours,   [Woodrow Wilson]

CCL (WP, DLC).

To Joseph Patrick Tumulty, with Enclosure

Dear Tumulty: [The White House] 26 February, 1919.

Please thank Mr. Burton very warmly for this and express my great appreciation of the work which the League of Nations Society is undertaking, and express my hope that when I get back to stay I may have the pleasure of cooperating with them.

The President

TL (WP, DLC).

ENCLOSURE

Theodore Elijah Burton to Joseph Patrick Tumulty

My dear Mr. Tumulty: New York. February 24, 1919

The New York Peace Society and the World's Court League have recently incorporated under the name of "The League of Nations" the object being to support the new League of Nations Covenant. The organization starts under the most excellent auspices and with the cooperation of very prominent persons.

I am reluctant to ask it because I know how much the President has to do, but if he should feel that during his present stay in this country he could address a meeting here in New York, just before leaving perhaps, we would organize a most enthusiastic gathering. It has seemed to me that possibly he might wish to convey a message to the citizens of New York.

May I ask you to present this to him and to obtain if possible a favorable answer?   Very cordially yours,   Theo. E. Burton

TLS (WP, DLC).

To Georges Clemenceau

[The White House] 26 February, 1919.

It delights me and it delights us all to hear what rapid progress you are making towards recovery. It will be delightful to see you well again when I get back.   Woodrow Wilson

T telegram (Letterpress Books, WP, DLC).

To Carter Glass

My dear Glass: [The White House] 26 February, 1919.

Here is a letter[1] which is really a reply to a cablegram of yours and which I submit for your consideration. It seems to me that Hoover gives some pretty convincing reasons.

          Cordially and faithfully yours,   Woodrow Wilson

TLS (Letterpress Books, WP, DLC).
  [1] HCH to WW, Feb. 24, 1919.

To Breckinridge Long

My dear Mr. Long: The White House 26 February, 1919.

I appreciate very much your letter of yesterday[1] and particularly your generous wish to be of service in supporting the League of Nations. There was certainly no impropriety in what you did at the banquet at which you replied to Senator Reed. His ignorance and passion render it necessary to check him wherever he utters his erroneous opinions, and such attacks as his could not properly be allowed to go by unnoticed.

I am in doubt whether the time has come for a systematic campaign on this subject, but I have been discussing that very matter with Tumulty recently and would appreciate it very much if you would get into conference with him and see what between you you can work out as desirable in the way of systematic discussion and instruction of public opinion as to the real facts and the real purpose and character of the proposed league.

          Your fine spirit in the matter excites my very genuine admiration.
          Cordially and sincerely yours,   Woodrow Wilson

TLS (B. Long Papers, DLC).
  [1] B. Long to WW, Feb. 25, 1919, TLS (WP, DLC).

To Frank Morrison

My dear Mr. Morrison: [The White House] 26 February, 1919.

Thank you for your letter. I appreciate the importance of the recommendations you quote from Mr. Gompers and his colleagues who are with him on the other side, and my own judgment concurs with theirs. I hope it will be possible for me incidentally to do something to further the realization of their advice.

Cordially and sincerely yours,   Woodrow Wilson

TLS (Letterpress Books, WP, DLC).

To Thomas James Walsh

My dear Senator: [The White House] 26 February, 1919.

Your letter of February 25th is very generous and makes a suggestion of great importance. If I can find a time when it will be possible for me to do what you suggest, I will of course do so. My trouble is that deliberate conferences seem this time impossible.

I realize that there are many parts of the proposed Covenant of the League of Nations which could with advantage be clarified and rewritten, but on the whole I think that its reasonable interpretation is clear and that it is a thoroughly workable instrument not only, but entirely consistent with the reasonable independence of the nations who are to constitute the League. If I could tell you of the processes through which it was put, I think I could convince you that a rewriting of it would be a work of extreme difficulty if indeed it would be possible at all. But I would not only welcome but would find very serviceable indeed any suggestions that you or any of the gentlemen you name might be willing to make, in order that I might take advantage of any opportunity that should arise for bringing them to the consideration of those with whom I have been working on the other side of the water.

Would it be taxing your kindness too much to ask you to suggest to the gentlemen you name in your letter how much I would value any memoranda and comments they might be willing to send me?

Cordially and sincerely yours,   Woodrow Wilson

TLS (Letterpress Books, WP, DLC).

To Anna Howard Shaw

My dear Dr. Shaw: [The White House] 26 February, 1919.

I have your letter of February 24th[1] and need hardly tell you that I entirely agree and sympathize with the position you take about the provisions in the Census Bill. The trouble is this. There are just a few days of the session remaining, so that it would be practically impossible to get an alteration of the bill, and if no bill becomes law the whole census operation is hopelessly delayed to the great detriment of many functions of the government. I am deeply distressed about the whole thing, but feel that I have been caught in a corner.

It was very delightful to hear from you and I hope that you have been well throughout these strenuous months. Mrs. Wilson and I are delighted to get home and wish with all our hearts that we could stay.

Thank you very warmly for your personal words of greeting, which I deeply appreciate.

Cordially and sincerely yours,   Woodrow Wilson

TLS (Letterpress Books, WP, DLC).
[1] Anna H. Shaw to WW, Feb. 24, 1919, TLS (WP, DLC). She called Wilson's attention to an amendment to the bill to provide for the Fourteenth and subsequent Censuses (H.R. 11984) which gave preference in all civil-service appointments to honorably discharged members of the armed services and to widows of such men. She observed that this rider appeared "to exclude all civilians from appointment to any position in the various departments or branches of government service so long as there are men on the register who have done military duty, and all women except widows of soldiers, regardless of their personal service." She urged that two principles should be applied in the government's service at all times:

"(1) That all service for the United States Government should be performed by those persons who are best fitted, selected by standards of efficiency at the time the service is required, and not as a reward for work done in the past if such service was rendered in a different field of activity which does not usually equip people for new duties to which they may be assigned.

"(2) That if privilege and preferment are given by the Government as a reward for service in time of war, they should not be denied to women who performed war service in many cases as dangerous and in all cases as essential to the success of the war as that required of men."

She urged Wilson to veto the entire census bill because of the provision to which she objected.

To William Howard Taft

My dear Mr. Taft: [The White House] 26 February, 1919.

I have your letter of February 1st in reply to my letter of January sixth.[1] As usual, you act with disinterested public spirit in the matter of the Red Cross chairmanship, and I want to express my great appreciation.

Will you not permit me to add a word to say how great a service I think you are doing the country in championing so actively the cause of the League of Nations, with which you have so long been identified.

Cordially and sincerely yours,   Woodrow Wilson

TLS (Letterpress Books, WP, DLC).
    [1] W. H. Taft to WW, Feb. 1, 1919, TLS, and WW to W. H. Taft, Jan. 6, 1919, CCL, both in WP, DLC. Both letters concerned Wilson's nomination of Livingston Farrand as chairman of the Central Committee of the American Red Cross.

To Frederic Yates

My dear Fred: The White House 26 February, 1919.

Your letter gave me a pang,[1] because it spoke of an immediate operation, but its date, the fourth of February, encourages me to believe that by this time you have not only come through but are beginning to feel a bit normal again. My heart goes out to you. It was generous of you to write me, and you may be sure that it touched me very much. I want you to know how deeply you have established yourself in my admiration and affection. Please give my love to the dear ones,[2] and above all things take care of yourself and get strong.[3]   Affectionately yours,   Woodrow Wilson

TLS (F. Yates Coll., NjP).
    [1] F. Yates to WW, Feb. 4, 1919, Vol. 54.
    [2] His wife, Emily Chapman Martin Yates, and his daughter, Mary Yates.
    [3] As H. D. Rawnsley to WW, March 2, 1919, reveals, Yates had died on February 11.

To Thomas L. Snow[1]

My dear Mr. Snow: The White House 26 February, 1919.

It was a real pleasure to see your letter of January 31st[2] and I am glad that it was brought to my personal attention because it gives me great pleasure to send you a message of the warmest greeting. My thoughts often turn back to the delightful old days at the Bluff,[3] and I am not without hope that some day I may come back to you, if you are still there, and enjoy that quiet again.

My Secretary has shown me your letter of February 13th[4] asking if I was at all disposed to dispose of any of the property on Muskoka which I own. I must say that I am not. I suppose it is useless to hope that I can some day establish a little summer home up there, but I have not given up the hope and therefore do not want to cut myself off.

Was I not rightly informed that your sons were both in the service? If so, I hope with all my heart that you are to have them back again with the added distinction which their service will give them.

Cordially and sincerely yours,   Woodrow Wilson

TLS (photostat in RSB Coll., DLC).
  [1] About whom, see the index references in Vols. 11, 12, 15, and 17 of this series.
  [2] T. L. Snow to WW, Jan. 31, 1919, TLS (WP, DLC).
  [3] A lodge at Judd-Haven in the Muskoka Lake district of Ontario.
  [4] T. L. Snow to the Secretary to the President, Feb. 13, 1919, TLS (WP, DLC).

To William Gibbs McAdoo and Eleanor Randolph Wilson McAdoo

[The White House] 26 February, 1919.

Warmest love from Edith and me. It was delightful to get your message and we are very happy to know what fine rest and refreshment you are both getting. We expect to sail again on the fifth of March.   Woodrow Wilson

T telegram (Letterpress Books, WP, DLC).

From Edward Mandell House

[Paris] February 27 [26], 1919.[1]

Number 7.

(1) George is desirous of arranging his engagements so that he can be in Paris (JEHON) at a time most advantageous from your standpoint. He can either come the latter part of this week and remain here for about a week or he can be here on about March fourteenth and remain here for approximately ten days. His labor committee is expected to report on March twentieth, but he can probably put off receiving this report for five or six days at the most, provided he is engaged in conference in Paris during that time. I suggest that you (GYCAT) [authorize me to] express to him your hope that he arrive in Paris on March fourteenth and stay as long as practicable. Please cable me as soon as possible respecting (this matter).

(2) Last Monday night Pichon and Klotz called on me. They were very much disturbed over the French financial situation and stated that unless England furnished France (VIPYB) [some] sterling exchange almost immediately there will be a serious break in (the price of) the French franc with disastrous results. They stated that the British chancellor of the exchequer would come to Paris if he could see me for a conference respecting this matter. I agreed to see him at any time he came. On Tuesday [Thursday] at noon Klotz, Tardieu and other French treasury officials called on me and asked me (to intervene) at once with England so that France would be furnished immediately with a few million pounds sterling exchange

to tide them over until the chancellor of the exchequer could come to Paris for conference. I promised to do what I could. I at once took steps to point out to Lloyd George the (unfortunate) effect which would be caused by French financial difficulties at this time and I urged that some sterling exchange be given the French to tide them over (Hegof) [their difficulties.] George directed that this be done. Klotz expressed deep gratification of French [cabinet] for this assistance. British chancellor of the exchequer will come to Paris early (next week) for conference.

(3) Tardieu has submitted memorandum on French position respecting left bank of Rhine.[2] I will cable you about this (fully) when I have had an opportunity of studying it.   Edward House.

T telegram (WP, DLC).
   [1] This telegram was received in the White House on February 27.
   [2] About which, see n. 1 to the memorandum printed at March 11, 1919.

From Franklin Knight Lane, with Enclosure

My dear Mr. President: Washington February 26, 1919.

I enclose a copy of the Smith-Bankhead[1] Americanization Bill[2] which we hope is about to be reported favorably by the House Committee and which the Senate Committee has today favorably reported. Yesterday I suggested that you speak to Senator Smith. Today I beg to make the suggestion, if agreeable to you, that you send a line to Mr. Bankhead of the House, who has introduced this bill in that body, urging upon him that it be passed. Some of the facts which would move towards its adoption are presented in the enclosed digest. The press of the country is very strongly for it, so are the industries and the American Federation of Labor, and I believe if you would give it a good shove we could get it over even at this late time.

                Cordially and faithfully yours,   Franklin K. Lane

TLS (WP, DLC).
   [1] Senator Hoke Smith of Georgia and Representative William Brockman Bankhead of Alabama.
   [2] Printed copy of S. 5464, WP, DLC.

E N C L O S U R E

IN RE: SMITH-BANKHEAD AMERICANIZATION BILL
SENATE NO. 5464—HOUSE NO. 15402.

"A Bill to promote the education of native illiterates, of persons unable to understand and use the English language, and of other resident persons of foreign birth; to provide for cooperation with the States in the education of such persons in the English language, the fundamental principles of government and citizenship; the elements of knowledge pertaining to self-support and home making and in such other work as will assist in preparing such illiterates and foreign-born persons for successful living and intelligent American citizenship."

DIGEST

This bill directs the Secretary of the Interior through the Bureau of Education to cooperate with the several States in the education of above-mentioned persons and the preparation of teachers for this work.

For the present fiscal year ending June 30th, $5,000,000 is provided, and annually thereafter until 1926, $12,500,000.

For the purpose of cooperating with the several States and preparing teachers, supervisors and directors, there is immediately appropriated for the use of the several States for the fiscal year ending June 30th, 1919 $250,000, and thereafter $750,000 annually.

To secure the benefits of this act each State shall equal its Federal appropriation.

No State shall participate until it has required the instruction for at least 200 hours a year of illiterate and non-English speaking minors of sixteen and over.

Federal money shall be used solely for salaries and training of teachers and no Federal money shall be used by the States for the purchase or upkeep of buildings or land or equipment or for the support of religious or private schools.

Each State receives money in proportion to the number of its illiterates and of persons unable to speak, read or write English.

$250,000 is provided for the fiscal year ending June 30th, 1919, and $1,000,000 annually thereafter to administer and enforce the provisions of this act, for cooperative work hereunder, for investigations, studies and reports, salaries, office and incidental expenses, equipment and for the stimulation of national unity.

According to the last census report, there are of native illiterates or persons above ten years of age living in America who do not speak our tongue and cannot read or write our language over eight and a half millions. Five and a half millions were born here. The majority of those who do not know English are uneducated in any language. (See Tabulation by States: Exhibit "A.")[1]

Eight million who can't read the laws of this country! More people who can't read our language or understand it than Canada's whole population. More than the whole population of the South in the Civil War.

This total exceeds the combined populations of Nevada, Wyoming, Delaware, Arizona, Idaho, Mississippi, Vermont, Rhode Island, North Dakota, South Dakota, Oregon, Maine, Florida, Connecticut and Washington. More of these than all the men, women and children of all the cities in the United States west of the Mississippi except one.

The South leads in illiteracy but the North leads in non-English speaking. Over seventeen percent of the persons in the east-south-central States have never been to school:—approximately sixteen percent of the people of Passaic, New Jersey, must deal with their fellow workers and employers through interpreters. And thirteen percent of the folk in Lawrence and Fall River, Massachusetts, are utter strangers in a strange land.

The extent to which our greatest industries are dependent upon this labor is perilous to all standards of efficiency. Their ignorance not only retards production and confuses administration, but constantly piles up a junk heap of broken humans and damaged machines which cost the nation incalculably.

A letter from the Director of the Bureau of Mines[2] indicates the situation in practically every great national enterprise where illiterates and principally non-English speaking aliens are employed. Accompanying this communication is a statement of facts which would justify the enactment of this law for our mining states alone.

Among other figures contained in his statement are statistics which show that the non-English speaking races in the anthracite regions are twice as liable to death and injury as the English speaking workers. This is equally true in the bituminous fields of West Virginia; it is approximately so wherever we use such labor in hazardous enterprises. (See Exhibit "B" for quotations from this letter.)

It is our duty to interpret America to all potential Americans in terms of humanity, in terms of protection as well as of opportunity; and neither the opportunities of this continent nor that humanity which is the genius of American Democracy can be rendered intelligible to these eight millions until they can talk and read and write our language.

Steel and iron manufacturers employ 58% of foreign born helpers; the slaughtering and meat packing trades 61%; bituminous coal mining 62%; the silk and dye trade 34%; glass making enterprises 38%; woolen mills 62%; cotton factories 69%; the clothing business 72%; boot and shoe manufacturers 27%; leather tanners 57%; furniture factories 59%; glove manufacturers 53%; cigar and tobacco trades 33%; oil refiners 67% and sugar refiners 85%.

One quarter of the above workers are so benighted that they cannot even read or write their own language.

Of foreign-born wage earners (in this country five years or more) who were of adult age on arrival, only 31% are naturalized and only 14% have first papers.

If we except the Northern Italians, hardly 10% of recent immigrants residing in this country from five to nine years have adopted citizenship. Among such Russians only 8% have been naturalized; 5% of Portugese and 4% of Greeks.

In all history no country ever before held so many aliens or permitted such an unallegianced multitude to share equality with and enjoy all the privileges of its own people.

These folk have little or no knowledge of the history or ideals of the republic. We have suffered them to retain many misconceptions and pernicious theories with which they came to us. As they exist today they are not fit melting pot metal and if they were ready to be, we, the native-born, have generally forgotten our duty as fire tenders.

The making of America cannot proceed faster than the making of Americans—else we sophisticate the quality of the future with perilous elements.

The making of America cannot proceed faster than the making of minds trained to share our visions and of consciences fit for our purposes.

If a hundred million of us must stand together we must think together, and think without a foreign accent.

Democracy did not down its last enemy when militarism was ended. A monstrous evil still persists in the world, a gibbering, blind, unreasoning thing, incapable of measuring the values of liberty,—IGNORANCE.

And with eight million persons in America practically beyond the reach of inspiration and conference, unable to read an American document or newspaper, we tempt the disorganizer, the anarchist, and all the agents of disruption to seduce and exploit this vast influence which we have neglected to win for intelligence and citizenship.

The Secretary of the Interior has graphically painted the accusatory situation in his annual report. He reminds us that our illiteracy problem is not confined to alienism. He shows us an army of illiterates marching past the White House in double file at the rate of twenty-five miles a day for more than two months,—an army of which fifty eight per cent are white and one and a half million are native-born whites.

He begs you to consider the economic loss rising out of this multitude; he estimates that if the productive labor of an illiterate is less by one fifty cents a day than that of an educated worker, the country is losing $825,000,000 a year through illiteracy.

But we can safely figure that the labor of an illiterate is worth five dollars a week less than that of a man who can read. And that of eight million will yield the nation $2,000,000,000 annually in excess of present earnings from this class—which $2,000,000,000 annually would not only pay the interest on our war debt but will soon amortise it as well.

Secretary Lane reminds us the Federal Government and the States expend millions every year to help our farmers make better crops and better homes, yet three million seven hundred thousand, or 10% of our rural folk can't read an agricultural bulletin, a farm journal, a thrift appeal, a newspaper, the Constitution of the United States, their Bibles, answer an income tax questionnaire or keep business accounts.

He is right when he says "an uninformed democracy is not a democracy, that people who have no access to the mediums of public opinion, the messages of Presidents and the Acts of Congress" can't be expected to understand why they all must contribute in due share of energy or property or lealty (loyalty)[3] to the ideals of this country.

CC MS (WP, DLC).
[1] Lane apparently did not enclose this exhibit and the other exhibit mentioned below.
[2] Vannoy Hartrog Manning.
[3] WWhw.

From Henry Morgenthau

My dear Mr. President: New York February 26th, 1919.

Hearty Welcome Home! Sincerest congratulations to your great success in Europe.

I returned this evening after participating in the very successful Congresses that have been organized by the League to Enforce Peace.

The method they adopted of holding Congresses of delegates from large surrounding districts of the various meeting places, gave the gatherings much greater value than mere meetings would have done.

The men and women were representative, and when convinced, became emissaries of the Cause to their many constituencies.

You would have rejoiced at the applause your name and achievements received everywhere.

I feel all doubters could be convinced that this is a non partisan question, if you would have Mr. Taft appear with you, before some representative audience in New York, Washington or elsewhere and expound your views. The place is immaterial, as the message would reach all parts of the world.

Taft coming back fresh from direct contact with nine congresses and many additional audiences, could authoritatively state how the public feels. All Americans and Europeans would be electrified and uplifted by the spectacle of having you and Taft the only living men that have been honored with the Presidency, and representing the two great political parties, unite on one platform in recommending and urging the adoption of your program.

What a fine demonstration of harmony, and how it would lift our international relation[s] out of party politics!

The Republicans want to share the credit and responsibility of our approval of a League of Nations. Invite them to do so—and there will be no need of force; they will flow to it. They have their pride, and should it not be considered?

Am ready to arrange for meeting and attend to all details—and if you desire it, shall be happy to call on you and give you fuller account of our trip and the sentiment of the people we met.

With affectionate greetings,

Yours most devotedly,   Henry Morgenthau

TLS (WP, DLC).

From Joseph Patrick Tumulty

Dear Governor: The White House February 26, 1919

I have canvassed the situation with reference to your making a speech in New York and have reached the conclusion that it would not be safe for us, because of the peculiar character of the membership and the objects of the various League of Nations Societies that have invited you, to accept any of these invitations. I have gone over the situation with Frank Polk, and we both join in putting before you this suggestion, which has the backing of Governor Smith of New York:

A meeting either at the Carnegie Hall or the Metropolitan Opera House, presided over by Governor Smith, at whose invitation as Governor of New York you are present. Arrangements for the meeting to be handled by a committee, non-partisan in character, appointed by Governor Smith. In addition to your address, an addressed [address] to be delivered by Mr. Taft. Mr. Elkus, representing Governor Smith, telephoned Mr. Polk that Mr. Taft's attendance could be procured through Mr. Herbert Houston,[1] who represents one of the League of Nations Societies. Mr. Elkus said that the prominent men of all the societies would be members of the committee, so that all of the societies that have invited you would be represented.

My own idea is that this would be an ideal plan and have a fine effect upon the country.

What do you wish me to do?   Tumulty

All right, if Taft can be got   W.W.

TLS (J. P. Tumulty Papers, DLC).
   [1] Herbert Sherman Houston, vice-president of Doubleday, Page & Co.; editor of the Spanish edition of *World's Work*; treasurer of the League to Enforce Peace.

From Charles Mills Galloway and Others

The President: Washington, D. C.   February 26, 1919.

The Census Bill provides that preference shall be given to veterans and their widows in making appointments. The conference committee at first rejected the Senate amendment conferring the preference. In the House, however, the conference report was rejected and the conferees were instructed to accept the Senate amendment. A second report has been made by the conferees, which is now in the Senate.

We invite your attention to the inclosed memorandum of objections to this sweeping preference as being fatal to the efficiency of the civil service,[1] and we are constrained to urge that you veto the bill unless the preference shall be modified. The views of the Commission as to a proper preference are contained in the inclosed draft of a bill[2] which was considered by the House Committee on Reform in the Civil Service but rejected.

We have the honor to be,

Very respectfully,   Chas M Galloway
                     H. W. Craven
                     John A McIlhenny

TLS (WP, DLC).
   [1] T MS (WP, DLC). Not printed.
   [2] *Idem.*

Two Letters from William Bauchop Wilson

My dear Mr. President: Washington February 26, 1919.

Referring to the Conference of Governors and Mayors called for the 3d of March, I am inclosing you a copy of statement made by me before the Committee on Rules of the House of Representatives on December 11th last,[1] which, if you can find time to read it, will give you an outline of the problem as I see it. In the statement I attempt to deal only with the immediate problem without reference to the problems of social reconstruction, which I take it can be worked out more methodically and to better advantage with our people busy than if we have large numbers of unemployed.

Faithfully yours,   W B Wilson

[1] *Employment of Soldiers and Sailors: Statement of Hon. W. B. Wilson, Secretary of Labor, before the Committee on Rules, House of Representatives, Sixty-fifth Congress, Third Session, on H. Res. 452 and H. Res. 463, December 11, 1918* (Washington, 1918).

My dear Mr. President: Washington February 26, 1919.

As intimated by Secretary Redfield yesterday, the Appropriations Committee of the House has failed to make any appropriation for the United States Employment Service of this Department for the next fiscal year. That means that the Service will not only terminate on June 30th but will immediately begin to disintegrate and lose its value for the balance of the current fiscal year.

The Employment Service has been, in my judgment, a very successful experiment. It has been one of the important factors in mobilizing labor during the past year and a half, and since the signing of the armistice has done a splendid piece of work in finding places for the demobilized soldiers and war workers. Paragraphs 4 and 14 of the inclosed memorandum[1] will give more specific information. The Service should be continued for piece [peace] time purposes, but in any event it would be a serious mistake to put it out of existence before the termination of the readjustment period, which will not occur until all of our soldiers are back from France.

For many months there has been carried on a systematic and underhanded propaganda against the Employment Service by the remnants of the Manufacturers Association and a few other small organizations of reactionary employers, which is responsible in a great measure for the attitude of the Committee. The vast majority of employers, as well as working men, throughout the country realize and acknowledge the value of the service being rendered by this Division of the Department of Labor.

A battle is now going on on the floor of the House to secure a reversal of the action of the Committee and the insertion of an appropriation of $10,000,000. I feel that the continuance of this Service during the readjustment period is of vital importance, and therefore ask you, if you can possibly find time, to bring such influence to bear on the members of the House and Senate as will secure the needed appropriation.

Faithfully yours,   W B Wilson

TLS (WP, DLC).
    [1] "U. S. EMPLOYMENT SERVICE: WAR AND POST-WAR ACTIVITIES AND ITS PLACE IN THE NATIONAL PROGRAM," T MS (WP, DLC). Paragraphs 4 and 14 discussed the numbers of persons registered with and placed in jobs by the service since January 1, 1918.

From Norman Hapgood

New York, February 26, 1919.

The League of Free Nations Association[1] began its statement of principles issued November twenty seventh, nineteen eighteen, with this sentence: Quote: The object of this Society is to promote a more general realization and support by the public of the conditions indispensable to the success at the Peace Conference and thereafter of American aims and policy as outlined by President Wilson. Unquote. Our appeal then closed with this sentence Quote: At a time when deep-seated forces of reaction would hamper a democratic solution and assert the old schemes of competitive militarism of economic wars after the war of division and bitterness and unhealed sores such as will breed further wars and rob this one of its great culmination, we call on all liberal minded men to stand behind the principles which the President has enunciated and we invite them to join in fellowship with us for their realization. Unquote.

Your brilliant leadership has more than justified our appeal. We are renewing with constantly increasing enthusiasm this appeal to liberals everywhere to support your ideals for a League of Nations.

Norman Hapgood.

T telegram (WP, DLC).
    [1] About its organization and subsequent activity, see Wolfgang J. Helbich, "American Liberals in the League of Nations Controversy," *Public Opinion Quarterly*, XXXI (Winter 1967-1968), 568-96.

From Samuel Walker McCall

To The President: Atlantic City, N. J. February 26th, 1919.

I hesitate to trouble you with suggestions, but among those that have occurred to me in reading the plan for the society of nations,

I should like to bring one or two to your attention. The Monroe Doctrine is now only our national policy. Why not by recognizing it in the treaty make it part of the public law of the world. Every independent government upon this hemisphere is modeled upon our own. Our Republic is the mother of them all. If the relation of England to her colonies is to be unaltered, why should we sever that even more intimate tie based upon the primary political interests of our group of nations and supplant the special protection of our Monroe Doctrine, put forward in the interest of our peace and safety, by the authority of a body which may be dominated by the representatives of monarchi[c]al governments. I believe the elevation of this doctrine to a place in international law instead of its abrogation will add strength to the league of peace. There certainly seems nothing to be gained by throwing it away.

Then it occurs to me that it would be well, seriously to reconsider the administrative mechanism of the League. Our solidarity, power, and comparative isolation make us the natural arbiter of the world. Our moral influence for peace is greater than the net combined influence of the European nations with their so many points of contact and collision sure to be increased by the new near-Balkan States with their serrated boundaries and by the other States to be established. The giving of only one representative in nine to America does not seem to put a proper appraisal upon her value as a pacific force. The greatest gift that we can transmit to the future will be a concert of nations designed to do away with war just as slavery and cannibalism have been done away with. But a concert may be made which would not utilize the resources of the world for peace and might even contain in itself the germ of a future war. I know of the infinite difficulty of your task to secure an agreement among so many nations and I profoundly hope that under your leadership mankind may be emancipated from servitude to war.

Yours respectfully,   Samuel W McCall

TLS (WP, DLC).

Robert Lansing to Frank Lyon Polk

Paris. February 26, 1919.

Very secret. In January, February and March 1917, Japan asked Great Britain, France, Italy and Russia separately to give assurance that each would support Japanese at the time of peace negotiations in demanding from Germany the cession of its territorial rights and special interest possessed before the war in Shantung and in the islands north of the Equator in the Pacific Ocean.

Great Britain gave such assurance on February sixteenth referring to an oral request preferred on January (*) 1917, and asked
in return the support of Japan for Great Britain's claims to the
islands south of the Equator, formerly belonging to Germany. Japan
on February twenty first promised such support.

France was (*) on February 19th and March first gave promises
to support Japan's claims asking in return that Japan would give
its support to an effort to persuade China to break off diplomatic
relations with Germany, which has to include handing of passports
to German diplomatic and consular officers, the expulsion of German subjects from China, the sequestration of German shipping
and commercial establishments and the forfeiture of German settlement concessions. To this Japan agreed on March sixth. Russia
was asked on same day as France and gave assurance on March
fifth. A confidential memorandum citing these agreements was
handed the Italian Minister for Foreign Affairs on March 28th and
similar assurance asked of Italy. The Minister replied orally that
he had no objection. The texts of these agreements will be sent to
the Department by mail. Give copy to President.[1] Lansing.

Ammission.

(*) Apparent omission
Repetition for omissions requested.

T radiogram (WP, DLC).
  [1] "Confidential DOCUMENTS Relative to the Negotiations between JAPAN AND THE ALLIED
POWERS . . . ," T MS (SDR, RG 59, 793.94/766, DNA). A copy was undoubtedly given
to Wilson, but it cannot be found in WP, DLC.

From the Diary of Dr. Grayson

Thursday, February 27, 1919.

The appointment of A. Mitchell Palmer of Pennsylvania as successor to Thomas W. Gregory of Texas to be Attorney General was
announced this morning and the nomination sent to the Senate in
the afternoon. The President also conferred with Harry A. Garfield,
formerly Fuel Commissioner, and with a number of Senators and
Representatives, who explained to him the jam in which the Senate
had found itself. In the afternoon the President led a welcome-
home parade in honor of the District of Columbia soldiers, marching
from the Peace Monument to the White House, where he entered
a specially prepared grandstand and reviewed the column as it
passed. Congregated in seats in the Lafayette Park, directly opposite, were a number of wounded soldiers from Walter Reed Hospital,
while other wounded soldiers rode in automobiles in the procession.

Immediately after the parade ended the President went to the Capitol and conferred with members of both Houses. He again made it very plain that his mind was fully made that there would be no special session of the new Congress until the work of the Peace Conference was completed.

A News Report

[*Feb. 27, 1919*]

PRESIDENT HOLDS LEVEE AT CAPITOL;

OPPOSITION SENATORS UNCONVERTED

Washington, Feb. 27. . . . President Wilson will not call an extra session of Congress upon his return from Europe, unless he considers such a step necessary. The President will not speak to Congress upon the League of Nations. These two facts became known during a visit made by the President this afternoon to his room at the Capitol.

During the two hours he spent at the Capitol, the President saw many Senators and Representatives, and for the first time in many months talked to a group of Washington newspaper correspondents. He appeared to be in the best of spirits and health.

The impression was strong about the Capitol, following the President's visit, that he hoped that the matters now being dealt with in Paris would be concluded by August or September, if not sooner. It appears, at present, impossible for the delegates to the Paris Conference to approximate more exactly the period at which they will conclude their negotiations. It is understood, however, they do not expect to remain in session until the end of 1919. The economic life of many nations is hanging in the balance, and the conferees are anxious to settle the great questions as well and as speedily as possible.

The American delegation and the President do not consider that the Constitution of the League of Nations, as now framed, in any fashion violates the Constitution of the United States. It is not thought by them that there is a single conflict. Great attention has been paid to this, and whenever danger of such a conflict became apparent the League Constitution was changed so this would be impossible.

At the Capitol the President maintained firmly that the Monroe Doctrine was not impaired at all, but that the League of Nations so enlarged and strengthened the Monroe Doctrine as to make the doctrine, as one might express it, a Monroe Doctrine of the world.

Senators and Representatives learned that the President was much gratified that representatives of the various nations at Paris differed not as to the objects of the League, but merely as to its details.

The final draft of the Constitution of the League is understood to be nearly complete, and word was received here today from the American delegation that the commissioners from the fourteen nations were practically unanimous in believing it practical. There may be amendments in a few particulars. The delegates have discussed each phase so carefully, it was explained, and have made up their minds so firmly that to change them would be extremely difficult and would hardly be worth attempting unless the object in view were very great.

There may be a change in one of the sections—that applying to a case where the Executive Council of the League has made a decision on a question submitted to it for arbitration and one of the parties has accepted, but the other has not. The further procedure in such a case will be studied by the conferees, as it has not yet been fully worked out.

The President is anxious to return to Paris in order to participate in the settlement of pressing territorial questions. Already the general principles of adjustment have been reached, but the detailed settlements are yet to be made. It is definitely understood in Washington that a complete agreement upon territorial adjustment will be arrived at before it is offered for the consideration of the various countries. This would follow the procedure of the conferees who framed the constitution of the League of Nations. That document was made public intact, and not piecemeal.

The fact that the President would not necessarily call an extra session of Congress upon his return from abroad came as a surprise to members of Congress. When announcement was made a day or so ago that he would not call Congress together until he returned from Europe, it was believed that an extra session would be called at that time. It may be stated as a fact, however, that Mr. Wilson does not now believe it will be absolutely necessary that Congress be convened during the Spring or Summer.

His decision not to appear before Congress and speak upon the League of Nations is understood to be because he takes the position that work upon the League is still in progress and he has, at this time, no final report to make.

A steady stream of callers visited Mr. Wilson at the Capitol. He arrived with his usual punctuality at 3:30 P.M., and left at 5:30.

The first persons who waited upon him were Senator Martin of Virginia, the Democratic leader of the Senate, and Senator Simmons of North Carolina, Chairman of the Finance Committee. Following these came Senator James Hamilton Lewis of Illinois, the

Democratic whip, and Senator Kirby of Arkansas.[1] An earnest conversation ensued between the President and Senator Nugent of
Idaho.

The Missouri delegation, headed by Speaker Clark, saw the President in an endeavor to have its National Guard divisions come back
from overseas in as intact shape as possible. Senator Overman of
North Carolina, Chairman of the Judiciary Committee, had a short
conversation, it is understood, concerning some papers in the State
Department dealing with Bolshevist conditions, which Senator
Overman wished to use in connection with the subcommittee now
investigating Bolshevist propaganda in the United States.[2]

Senator Swanson of Virginia, Chairman of the Naval Affairs Committee; Senator Thompson of Kansas,[3] Senator Morris Sheppard of
Texas, and Senator Jones of New Mexico, Chairman of the Committee on Woman Suffrage, all paid their respects.

The next visitors were Southern Democrats, interested in having
the embargo on cotton repealed. These included Senators Smith of
Georgia, Fletcher of Florida, Smith of South Carolina, who seemed
to act as the spokesman; McKellar of Tennessee, Overman, Sheppard, Gay of Louisiana, Ransdell of Louisiana, and Representatives
Heflin of Alabama, Garner of Texas, Garrett of Tennessee, Venable
of Mississippi, Wingo of Arkansas, Eagle of Texas, Young of Texas,
Candler of Mississippi, Ragsdale of South Carolina, Jones of Texas,
Harrison of Mississippi, and Oldfield of Arkansas.[4]

The President sent for Representative Sherley of Kentucky,
Chairman of the Appropriations Committee, and had a long talk
with him.

Throughout the President's visit to the Capitol today both Senate
and House continued engaged at high pressure on their congested
calendars, and much headway was made during the day. Ultimate
failure of several important measures, however, still was regarded
by leaders as almost certain.

From 3:30 o'clock to 5:30 o'clock a constant stream of callers
filed into the Chief Executive's private room off the Senate chamber, while the President, almost standing entirely throughout, gave
and received suggestions on a multitude of subjects.

During his conferences the President emphatically reiterated his
determination not to call the new Congress in extraordinary session
until he returned from France, and asked administration leaders
to so inform the Republicans, who were represented by the Democrats as determined to defeat the Victory Loan bill and thus force
an extra session.

President Wilson, it was said, set his jaws, and with emphatic
gestures told the Democratic leaders to tell the Republicans that

they would be responsible for failure of the bill, and that, regardless of their attitude, he would not call Congress together until he returned.

In his conferences the President was told by Administration leaders that all important legislation could not be passed because of Republican opposition. The President was said to have especially urged passage of the navy and other appropriation bills, and the "Victory Loan" measure.

Many Republican members passed through the crowd outside the room, but none called on or were called by the President. The Executive earnestly conversed with the seventy-odd visitors, but signed no bills, merely giving and receiving counsel. Occasionally the President, apparently tired, leaned or sat upon a marble topped desk, and when his last caller, Representative Sherley, was received, he sat on a lounge.

The President's conferences were held in full view of tourists and other spectators passing by his door, and his animated gestures in his discussions were closely watched by the callers.

President Wilson and Senator Chamberlain of Oregon, Chairman of the Military Committee, met today for the first time since their controversy of more than a year ago, when the President wrote a letter sharply criticising the Senator for his New York speech in which he said certain Government bureaus had "almost ceased to function."[5]

Senator Chamberlain called to pay his respects to the President, who was at the Capitol conferring with Senators and Representatives. The President shook Senator Chamberlain's hand once, and the smile on his face disappeared. Gravely bowing, the President released Mr. Chamberlain's hand and without speaking turned to greet another Senator.

Senator Overman of North Carolina, Chairman of the Senate subcommittee investigating radical propaganda, asked the President to approve the committee's receipt from the State Department of consular reports bearing on the subject. The President agreed, but, it was said, stated that he had read them all and believed there would be found little of value to the committee in its work. The President also was said to have expressed the view that the committee should not receive hearsay testimony.

Appointment of an American Minister to Czechoslovakia and other new nations was discussed with the President by Representative Sabath of Illinois, who, it was understood, was informed that the representative to Czechoslovakia probably would be some American now in the Diplomatic Service in a nearby country.

Printed in the *New York Times*, Feb. 28, 1919.
  [1] William Fosgate Kirby.
  [2] Between September 27, 1918, and February 11, 1919, a subcommittee of the Senate Committee on the Judiciary, headed by Senator Overman, had investigated the alleged connection between American brewing and liquor interests and German propaganda efforts in the United States. See G. Squires to WW, Jan. 30, 1919, n. 1, Vol. 54. On February 4, 1919, the Senate had adopted a resolution (S. Res. 439), introduced by Senator Walsh, which extended the authority of the Overman committee to inquire into Bolshevik propaganda activities in the United States and alleged efforts to overthrow the American government. The committee conducted hearings on this matter from February 11 to March 10 and heard the testimony of twenty-six witnesses, among them John Reed, Louise Bryant, Raymond Robins, David R. Francis, and Col. Vladimir S. Hurban. See *Bolshevik Propaganda: Hearings Before a Subcommittee of the Committee on the Judiciary . . . Pursuant to S. Res. 439 and 469* (Washington, 1919). On June 6, Overman submitted the committee's final report on both the German and the Bolshevik propaganda activities to the Senate. *Cong. Record*, 66th Cong., 1st sess., pp. 1132-47. The report, together with the full testimony and other related documents on German and Bolshevik propaganda efforts, was also published as *Brewing and Liquor Interests and German and Bolshevik Propaganda: Report and Hearings of the Subcommittee on the Judiciary . . . Pursuant to S. Res. 307 and 439*, 66th Cong., 1st sess., Sen. Doc. No. 62 (3 vols., Washington, 1919).
  [3] That is, William Howard Thompson.
  [4] The representatives mentioned were James Thomas Heflin, John Nance Garner, Finis James Garrett, William Webb Venable, Otis Theodore Wingo, Joe Henry Eagle, James Young, Ezekiel Samuel Candler, Jr., James Willard Ragsdale, Marvin Jones, Pat (Byron Patton) Harrison, and William Allan Oldfield.
  [5] About this matter, see WW to G. E. Chamberlain, Jan. 20, 1918; G. E. Chamberlain to WW, Jan. 21, 1918; and the press release printed at Jan. 21, 1918, all in Vol. 46.

To Edward Mandell House

The White House, 27 February, 1919.

Sorry to say new means of communication so far so unsatisfactory that I really do not clearly know anything that you are trying to tell me. Am not in touch with your proceedings and unable to advise. The new code is extremely complicated, is imperfectly transmitted, and of such a character that when one word is lost it throws out all that follows.   Woodrow Wilson

STRAIGHT GREEN CODE

T telegram (WP, DLC).

To Anna Howard Shaw [1]

My dear Doctor Shaw: [The White House] 27, February 1919.

The Secretary of War has presented to me your letter of February seventeenth, setting forth a copy of the resolution of the Woman's Committee tendering the resignation of its members, and effecting the dissolution of the Committee. [2] This action, I understand, is taken because, in the opinion of the Committee, its distinctive work is at an end, and so much as remains to be done is covered by the Field Division of the Council of National Defense.

In accepting these resignations and consenting to the dissolution of the Committee, it would be invidious to make any assessment of its work by way of comparison with that of any other agency organized in the great emergency through which the country has just passed. But surely you and the members of the Committee must be confident that the women of America responded in this war with service and patriotic enthusiasm which were at once an invaluable aid to the nation's cause and a wholesome demonstration of the solidarity of opinion and feeling among our people. In the midst of sacrifice the women of America found their consolation in service. The organization of this work was entrusted to many agencies of specialized kinds, but the centralization of the impulse was largely the work of the Woman's Committee.

It would be difficult to over-estimate the importance of the function the Committee has served in being both a vast bureau for the dissemination of information, and itself a well-spring of inspiration and zeal. I beg you to accept for yourself and the members of the Committee this expression of my deep appreciation of the service they have rendered the nation.

Cordially and faithfully yours,   Woodrow Wilson

TLS (Letterpress Books, WP, DLC).
  [1] The following letter was composed by Newton D. Baker: a CC MS enclosed in NDB to WW, Feb. 27, 1919, TLS (WP, DLC).
  [2] Dr. Shaw's letter is missing in WP, DLC.

To Frank Lyon Polk, with Enclosures

My dear Polk: The White House 27 February, 1919.

Will you not be kind enough to ask the Italian Charge d'Affaires[1] to transmit the following reply to the generous message from Mr. Orlando:

"Your message has made my heart very warm, and it is the more singularly generous because you have yourself played so great and influential a part in bringing about the consumation which we are about to realize in the formation of the League of Nations. It has been altogether delightful to be associated with you and to witness the spirit and purpose of unselfish public service which you have manifested in all our counsels. I send you heartfelt greetings of genuine friendship and admiration."[2]

Cordially and sincerely yours,   Woodrow Wilson

TLS (SDR, RG 59, 763.72119/3982, DNA).

¹ Baron Pietro Arone di Valentino, Secretary of the Italian embassy in Washington.
² Wilson's message was transmitted in W. Phillips to Baron di Valentino, Feb. 28, 1919, CCLS (SDR, RG 59, 763.72119/3982, DNA).

ENCLOSURE I

From Frank Lyon Polk

Dear Mr. President: Washington February 25, 1919.

Acting under instructions from the Italian Premier, Mr. Orlando, the Italian Chargé d'Affaires in Washington has transmitted to the Department for communication to you, a personal message from the Premier, on the occasion of your return to the United States. This message has an extract from a personal report which the Premier submitted to the King of Italy recommending the granting of a general amnesty for military and political offenses, and is that portion of the report having particular reference to the League of Nations. The amnesty recommended by Mr. Orlando was granted by the King on February 22nd.

In pursuance of the request of the Italian Chargé d'Affaires I have the honor to send you enclosed, the Italian copy of Mr. Orlando's message¹ together with a translation into English, which was made by the Italian Embassy.

Faithfully yours,   Frank L Polk

TLS (WP, DLC).
¹ T MS (WP, DLC).

ENCLOSURE   II

REGIA AMBASCIATA D'ITALIA

Personal Message of H. E. Orlando to H. E. President Wilson.
Free Translation

"In Paris, the heart of heroic France, through the high and persevering desire of a great Leader of a great people, the nations who have fought together for the liberty and the justice of the world, have also determined together in the sanctity of a solemn covenant, and in the name of liberty and justice of all peoples, to establish a peace which shall reign supreme over the future destinies of the world.

To this covenant, which shall be the intangible charter of Humanity, Italy, who in the past and in the present has always championed the cause of right, and proclaimed and consecrated it with her laws and with her blood, brings the contribution of her assent with fervid expression and deep conviction.

Our hearts, with sincere faith, celebrate this event which is and will remain one of the most memorable in human history; and it is fitting that the whole Italian people comprehend and acclaim with joy its high value and its everlasting significance."

Washington, D. C. February 24, 1919.

T MS (WP, DLC).

To William Brockman Bankhead

My dear Mr. Bankhead: [The White House] 27 February, 1919.

Perhaps it is idle to hope for the passage of any but the most immediately essential measures at this session, but I have been so much impressed with the importance of the so-called Americanization Bill that I am writing to ask if you see any chance of getting it through without interfering with the supply bills.

Cordially and sincerely yours,   Woodrow Wilson

TLS (Letterpress Books, WP, DLC).

To Bainbridge Colby

My dear Colby: The White House 27 February, 1919.

I had intended to look you up when I got to Washington, but am hurried hour by hour from one thing to another and am driven to write you instead.

I wanted to tell you how grieved I felt at the idea that you must leave your work at the Shipping Board where it has been of the greatest value and assistance to us all,[1] and yet I knew I was bound to add that I had no right to ask you to stay at such a sacrifice as you have been making. I can only tell you how anxious I am to serve your interest in some true way as well as the interest of the Government. I therefore want you to feel perfectly free to regard your resignation as accepted, if you think it necessary that it should be.

This is a very informal way of doing a thing which has, in my mind at any rate, the greatest public importance (for I know of no public servant whose attitude and ability I more admire than your own), but I am doing it in this way just to show you my personal and affectionate regard.

Cordially and sincerely yours,   Woodrow Wilson

TLS (B. Colby Papers, DLC).
  [1] Colby had tendered his resignation on December 14, 1918, to take effect at Wilson's

convenience, in order to be able to devote more time to his business and personal affairs. B. Colby to WW, Dec. 14, 1918, TLS (WP, DLC). However, at that time, Hurley had persuaded Colby to stay on at least until the return of Commissioner Raymond Bartlett Stevens from Paris. On February 26, 1919, Hurley told Wilson that Colby was very anxious to receive his formal release as soon as possible. Colby felt it necessary to return to New York, because his large law practice had suffered greatly in his absence and because he wished to spend more time with his family and his invalid daughter, who had to remain in New York close to her physicians. Since Stevens had returned from France, Hurley now asked Wilson to accept Colby's resignation and to let him know how much his remarkable ability and his loyal cooperation had been appreciated. E. N. Hurley to WW, Feb. 26, 1918, TLS (WP, DLC).

To Edward William Bok

My dear Mr. Bok: The White House 27 February, 1919.

Your letter of February twenty-fourth has cheered me mightily. It is very delightful to get such messages and I value your support in every way.

I must say that the press of the country has been giving the League of Nations splendid support and I am very much cheered because I believe with you that the people are absolutely with the purposes and plan of the thing.

With most cordial regards, in haste,

Sincerely yours,   Woodrow Wilson

TLS (WP, DLC).

To Cleveland Hoadley Dodge

My dear Cleve: The White House 27 February, 1919.

Your little note welcoming me home cheered me up mightily. It was delightful merely to see your handwriting on the outside of the envelope, and the message inside has made my heart very warm. Bless you both. Mrs. Wilson joins in sending most affectionate greetings.   Your affectionate friend,   Woodrow Wilson

TLS (WC, NjP).

To Allen Schoolcraft Hulbert

My dear Allen: [The White House] 27 February, 1919.

I have your letter of February 24th[1] and am writing to the Secretary of War, asking him to give you a chance to bid on the trucks to whose sale you refer. You will no doubt get some communication from the War Department. To tell the truth, I do not "know the ropes" myself.

It was very nice to hear from you. Do I draw the right inference in thinking that you are permanently in New York now, or are you just there temporarily? Please give my best regards to your mother and say how often I think of her. I sincerely hope that she has entirely recovered from the accident to her foot.

In unavoidable haste,

Sincerely yours,   Woodrow Wilson

TLS (Letterpress Books, WP, DLC).
¹ It is missing. However, as WW to NDB, Feb. 27, 1919, TLS (Letterpress Books, WP, DLC) reveals, Hulbert had written to Wilson about a contract which the War Department was offering for the disposal of about ten thousand surplus trucks. Hulbert had told Wilson that he had a partner with ample means, organization, and ability to handle this contract in accordance with the department's requirements, but that he hardly knew where to begin in order to make a bid.

To Ellen Duane Davis

My dear Friend: [The White House] 27 February, 1919.

Just a line to say how much and what deep pleasure your letter gave us both.

I am hoping of course to stop to see Jessie, but just how it can be managed doth not yet appear.

With most affectionate messages to you both,

Your grateful friend,   Woodrow Wilson

TLS (Letterpress Books, WP, DLC).

Three Telegrams from Edward Mandell House

[Paris] February 28 [27], 1919.

We repeat our Number 8. February 27, 10:00 p.m.

I suggested to Balfour and Cecil this morning that we make an effort to start the League Nations functioning at once. They (approved) my plan, which is this:

[Let the] Members of the committee which formed the covenant act as the provisional executive council proposed in the covenant; have the council of ten which sits at the Quai D'Orsay or the plenary conference refer certain matters to the League; have the League report back to the council of ten or the plenary conference, as the case may be, with recommendations. In the meantime it is our purpose call in the neutrals and explain the covenant to them and say that an invitation is soon to be extended to them to become members. We will not call the committee together unless the French Japanese and others agree not to offer any amendments to covenant until you return. I anticipate no difficulty in this. The British would like to have Hankey appointed secretary general of the League. I approve for the reason that he has done this sort of work since the beginning of the war and because it would make George and his confreres, who are not strong believers in the League, more enthusiastic[.] having an English speaking secretary general will lessen our difficulties and not put us at such disadvantage as would (a French) or Italian secretary general. It would also enable us to take the chairmanship of the executive council if we so desire. Please give me your views.[1]   Edward House.

[1] Was this House's way of suggesting subtly to Wilson the idea of separating the Covenant from the peace treaty itself? Such might, indeed, have been the case. At least since February 24, 1919, the American commissioners in Paris had been discussing the feasibility and wisdom of such a plan, more specifically, to make the Covenant an "annex" to the treaty of peace. For example, on February 24, Lansing said that he had heard of such a plan, and the minutes of the meeting of the commissioners on that day record House as saying: "Colonel House considered this an excellent idea and hoped that Mr. Lansing would develop it further." PPC, XI, 73. Or, again, the commissioners, at their meeting of March 11, agreed that the treaty of peace would "become ridiculously long and unwieldy" if the Covenant was included along with all the other terms of the treaty. However, at this point, the commissioners equivocated by agreeing that the Covenant, although an annex to the peace treaty, would have to be recognized by Germany as constituting an "integral and inseparable" part of the peace treaty. Ibid., p. 113. (To our knowledge, the minutes of the meetings of the American commissioners were never communicated to Wilson.) For the evidence, which strongly indicates that House on his own had abetted the efforts to separate the Covenant from the treaty, see n. 2 to the extract from the Diary of Dr. Grayson printed at March 13, 1919, and the extract from that same diary printed at March 15, 1919.

[Paris] 28 [27] February 1919.

Number 9. Everything is going well except the Italian Jugoslav situation which is [grows] worse. If you were here I would favor an immediate decision on the questions affecting it [them]. We could bring them to reason by shutting off our financial and economic help but that would create bad feeling and might cause a revolution in Italy. If Orlando were neutral [here] I think I could do something, but Sonnino is hopeless. The French and Italians have gotten closer together recently. Both they and the British are disinclined to bring pressure or to bring to an issue the Italian claims as to the pact of London.   Edward House.

[Paris] 28 [27] February 1919.

Number 10. At the request of the Belgians I am trying to get the French and English to agree to give Belgium a priority claim of five hundred million dollars so that she can negotiate a loan and immediately begin industrial activities. Balfour says the British will be sympathetic to the plan. I shall present it to the French tomorrow. Balfour and I also have agreed to talk with Clemenceau within a few days concerning Luxemburg. We shall ask him to keep hands off and let Luxemburg determine (for herself) whether or not she wishes an economic or even closer union with Belgium.

Edward House.

T telegrams (WP, DLC).

From Carter Glass and William Cox Redfield

My dear Mr. President: Washington February 27, 1919.

As you were orally informed yesterday at the meeting of the Wednesday Afternoon Conference, the War Trade Board has removed all export price regulations on pork products effective March 1. Following this the Food Administration has asked your authority for conforming to this action. This letter is written with the knowledge of the Food Administration and of the War Trade Board to state our views on this important matter and to ask that the authority desired be given.

At the request of the War Trade Board, the Secretary of Commerce attended their meeting when this matter was discussed and there entered earnest protest against the continuance of price maintenance on pork products. The Secretary of the Treasury presented his protest to like effect through his representative on the War Trade Board, Mr. May.[1] You will recall that the entire Cabinet cabled you strongly recommending removal of the price restrictions.[2] At the meeting of the War Trade Board the matter was also discussed by the Industrial Board of the Department of Commerce, appointed with your approval to consider readjustment of industrial prices.[3] It seems to them obvious that the government cannot properly invite industry to make sacrifices by reducing prices while the government is itself acting to maintain abnormal prices on other products.

The Food Administration say there is a normal obligation to maintain the high prices of pork products until all the pigs farrowed in the spring of 1918 have been actually marketed. They agree, however, that there is no contract or money guaranty but that the moral obligation still holds. The high price of pork was fixed to stimulate the production of hogs for fats as a war measure. The war necessity has passed. Whatever the moral obligation was it is, in our view, satisfied by the extension of a month that has already taken place, to wit. the month of February itself, and we feel that substantial notice was thus given that there was, to say the least, uncertainty as to whether it would be renewed.

Two considerations, however, seem to us to outweigh any possible remainder of a moral obligation that may be alleged to exist. The peace necessities of the people of the country are now supreme. This is a time of serious and growing unemployment, of grave social unrest, of definite and avowed attempts at social revolution. There can exist no moral obligation to do an immoral thing, and to maintain now under existing public conditions by the deliberate act of the government an unnecessarily high price on food seems to us distinctly to do wrong to the people as a whole and not to be now justifiable.

But there is another consideration not alone of morality but of humanity. Through the continuance of the high price of pork, the suffering peoples who look to us for food have been made and will be made, if the high prices continue, to pay an excessive price for the foods they need. The means wherewith to pay for this food they must get by borrowing from us and our people are thus forced into the position of furnishing money to starving peoples which they are in substance compelled to pay back to us for food at a price artificially maintained above the normal by the government. We respectfully urge that there can be no moral justification for such a condition.   Yours very truly,   Carter Glass.
                                                    William C. Redfield

TLS (WP, DLC).
    [1] George Oliver May, an expert on tax matters and a senior partner of Price, Waterhouse & Co., public accountants of New York. May, who later became known as the "dean of American accounting," had been appointed as an additional representative of the Secretary of the Treasury on the War Trade Board on January 23, 1919, since the Treasury's regular representative, Albert Strauss, was at this time in Paris as an adviser on financial questions to the A.C.N.P.
    [2] See C. Glass to WW, Feb. 11, 1919.
    [3] See WCR to WW, Feb. 6, 1919, Vol. 54, and WW to WCR, Feb. 13, 1919.

From Edgar Rickard

My dear Mr. President: Washington February 27, 1919

We have been furnished with a copy of a letter addressed to you by the Secretary of the Treasury and the Secretary of Commerce with a statement in the opening paragraph as follows:

"As you were orally informed yesterday at the meeting of the Wednesday Afternoon Conference, the War Trade Board has removed all export price regulations on pork products effective March 1. Following this the Food Administration has asked your authority for conforming to this action. This letter is written with the knowledge of the Food Administration and of the War Trade Board to state our views on this important matter and to ask that the authority desired be given."

This statement is misleading. The Food Administration has not asked any such authority. We insisted that the agreement which we had with the producers of hogs must be carried out until the 31st of March when we felt that our moral obligation to them would be discharged, and we insisted that the War Trade Board should continue in effect, their rule that licenses for exportation of pork products should continue to be subject to the approval of the Food Administration as to price, until the 31st of March unless you directed us to discontinue all regulations of the price of hogs and pork products. We stated very clearly the position of the Food Administration in accordance with direction from Mr. Hoover.

We have not asked authority to discontinue our regulations as to pork products but we simply stated to the Chairman of the War Trade Board[1] and to the Secretary of Commerce that we felt it our duty to continue through March, the regulation as to hogs and pork products unless we were directed by you not to do so. The facts about this matter are clearly set forth in Mr. Hoover's cabled letter to you of February 24th.

If you, however, approve the views expressed by the Secretary of the Treasury and the Secretary of Commerce, we ask that you advise us. On the other hand, if you approve our continuing the present regulations as to price of hogs and pork products until March 31st, we respectfully ask that the War Trade Board be advised to continue their present rule that licenses for exportation of pork products should continue to be subject to the approval of the Food Administration as to price until March 31st.

Yours faithfully,　Edgar Rickard
Acting for Herbert Hoover
United States Food Administrator

TLS (WP, DLC).
[1] That is, Clarence Mott Woolley, vice-chairman of the War Trade Board and acting chairman in McCormick's absence.

From the Diary of Dr. Grayson

Friday, February 28, 1919.

The President conferred with Hugh Wallace, the newly appointed Ambassador to France, and was host at luncheon to the members of the Democratic National Committee, who had met in Washington for the purpose of reorganizing and electing Homer Cummings of Connecticut chairman in succession to Vance McCormick, resigned. This was a very crowded day and the President worked hard until about five o'clock, when he and Mrs. Wilson left the White

House and went for a brisk walk through the downtown section of Washington. He was recognized and cheered by many of the pedestrians, traffic finally becoming so congested that it became necessary for the police reserves to clear the sidewalks. The President remained at his desk until nearly midnight.

Remarks to Members of the Democratic National Committee

February 28, 1919.

I cannot let this occasion go by without saying how very glad Mrs. Wilson and I are to see you and how welcome it is to have a few words of conference with you, for we do not have time for more. I am glad that my return home coincided with your meeting so that this happy thing could occur. I have been saying to a great many that I never knew how good America felt until I got back to it, or how great a sacrifice it was to leave it. Because, of course, not only the natural intricacies of politics—local politics—center in Paris at present, but all the intricacies of the politics of the world, and, while there are many gyrations and complexities in our politics, I could not help feeling that the air was more wholesome on this side of the water than it was on the other.

And yet I ought to hasten to say that I have acquired a real admiration for the men that we have been trying to cooperate with. They have many varied interests, they represent peoples who have sometimes had mighty little friendship for each other, and whom it is difficult to bring to a common agreement; and yet I think their sincere object is to bring about a common view and a settlement which will last because it is the right settlement as nearly as may be. I would not be doing them justice if I did not express the pleasure I have experienced in working with them and the pleasure I have received in coming in contact with their minds and the bodies of information and experience which they represent.

But what I wanted to talk about a little was not what is happening on the other side, but rather the proper attitude of our own great party in this country. Personally, I am not the least discouraged by the results of the last congressional election. Any party which carries out, through a long series of years, a great progressive and constructive program is sure to bring out a reaction, because, while in the main the reforms that we have accomplished have been sound reforms, they have necessarily in the process of being made touched a great many definite interests in a way that distressed them, in a way that was counter to what they deemed their best and legitimate interest. So that there has been a process of adaptation in the process of change. There is nothing apparently to which the human mind is least hospitable than change, and in the business world that is particularly true, because if you get in the habit of doing your business in a particular way and are compelled to do it in a different way, you think that somebody in Washington does not understand business, and, therefore, there has been a perfectly natural reaction against the changes we have made in the public policies of the United States. In many instances, as in the banking and currency reform, the country is entirely satisfied with the wisdom and permanency of the change, but even there a great many interests have been disappointed and many of their plans have been prevented from being consummated. So that there is that natural explanation. And then I do not think that we ought to conceal from ourselves the fact that not the whole body of our partisans are as cordial in the support of some of the things that we have done as they ought to be. You know, I heard a gentleman from one of the southern states say to his senator (this gentleman was himself a member of the state legislature)—he said to his senator: "We have the advantage over you because we have no publication corresponding with the Congressional Record and all that is recorded in our state is the vote, whereas the Congressional Record records all that happens before the vote; and, while you have always voted right, we know what happened in the meantime because we read the Congressional Record." Now, with regard to a great many of our fellow partisans in Congress, the Congressional Record shows what happened between the beginning of the discussion and the final vote, and our opponents were very busy in advertising what the Congressional Record disclosed. And to be perfectly plain, there was not in the minds of the country sufficiently satisfactory evidence that we had supported some of the great things that they were interested in any better than the other fellows. The voting record was all right and the balance in our favor, but they can show a great many things that discount the final record of the vote.

Now, I am in one sense an uncompromising partisan. Either a man must stand by his party or not. Either he has got to play the game or he has got to get out of the game, and I have no more sufferance for such a man than the country has, not a bit. Some of them got exactly what was coming to them, and I haven't any bowels of compassion for them. They did not support the things they pretended to support. And the country knew they didn't; the country knew that the tone of the cloakroom and the tone of the voting were different tones. Now, I am perfectly willing to say that

I think it is wise to judge of party loyalty by the cloakroom, and not by the vote, and the cloakroom was not satisfactory. I am not meaning to imply that there was any kind of blameworthy insincerity in this. I am not assessing individuals. That is not fair. But in assessing the cause of our defeat we ought to be perfectly frank and admit that the country was not any more sure of us than it ought to be. So that we have got to convince it that the ranks have closed up and that the men who constitute those ranks are all on the war path and mean the things that they say and that the party professes. That is the main thing.

Now, I think that can be accomplished by many processes. Unfortunately, the members of Congress have to live in Washington, and Washington is not part of the United States. It is the most extraordinary thing I have ever known. If you stay here long enough, you forget what the people of your own district are thinking about. There is one reason on the face of things. The wrong opinion is generally better organized than the right opinion. If some special interest has an impression that it wants to make on Congress, it can get up thousands of letters with which to bombard its senators and representatives, and they get the impression that that is the opinion at home, and they do not hear from the other fellows; and the consequence is that the unspoken and uninsisted-on views of the country, which are the views of the great majority, are not heard at this distance. If such an arrangement were feasible, I think there ought to be a constitutional provision that congressmen and senators ought to spend every other week at home and come back here and talk and vote after a fresh bath in the atmosphere of their home districts and the opinions of their home folks.

But that brings me to what I wanted to speak of: the function of the national committee not only, but of the state committees, with which the national committee is in touch. Surely it is the proper function to make the general body of opinion at home visible to the men who represent the district in Congress. They can do that without any offense, without seeming to try to dictate in any way, by seeing to it that the real bodies of opinion are felt where action is taken. It is our present malady, you know, that Congress sits all the time. I call it a malady, not because it is in the least tiresome for me, but because it prevents the members of Congress from getting into frequent contact with their constituents with these continuous sessions of Congress. Congress has been practically continuous ever since I came here and was continuous for six or eight years before that. In these circumstances, party representatives owe it to their representatives in the House and the Senate to see to it that they are informed of the real opinion of the country.

The other evening we had a dinner at which the senior senator from Massachusetts had the honor of sitting next to Mrs. Wilson. Innocently she dwelt upon the magnificent reception we had gotten in Boston. And I think she was acting as I would wish the committeemen to act—apprising their representatives innocently of the real state of opinion. And I understand that if not that, at any rate something, had an interesting effect upon the speech that was delivered today by the senior senator from Massachusetts.[1] He was

[1] On February 28, Republican senators had resumed their assault on the Covenant of the League of Nations which they had temporarily abandoned when Wilson had asked them to refrain from criticism of the League until he had conferred with them on the matter. The first blow of this renewed attack was delivered in a long speech by Senator Lodge, who began by assailing the "really evil suggestion" that any criticism of the proposed Covenant was synonymous with an opposition to permanent peace. The proponents of the present scheme, Lodge argued, had to meet objections with something more than rhetoric, personal denunciations, and "shrill shrieks" that virtue was to be preferred to vice and that peace was better than war. "Glittering and enticing generalities will not serve," he declared. "We must have facts, details, and sharp, clear-cut definitions."

The constitution of the League, Lodge maintained, in order to serve as a foundation for permanent peace, had to be so plain and so explicit that it could not possibly be misunderstood. However, the proposed draft was characterized by such "crudeness and looseness of expression" that almost every clause was already being subjected to differing interpretations. Thus, there was a serious danger that the very nations which signed the Covenant would soon quarrel about the exact meaning of the various articles, and that the Covenant itself, instead of promoting international agreement and harmony, would become a source of controversy and dissension.

Lodge then addressed some of the implications of American membership in the League. He pointed out that membership would entail nothing less than a fundamental change in the established foreign policy of the United States. It would mean the abandonment of the revered principles of Washington's Farewell Address and of the Monroe Doctrine, which had served the nation well for more than a century. Perhaps, Lodge continued, the time had come when it was necessary to give up these great policies, but it should not be done "in the twinkling of an eye" and without considering fully the "profound gravity" of this step. "Very complete proof must be offered of the superiority of any new system," Lodge stated, "before we reject the policies of Washington and Monroe." Lodge directed his sharpest criticism at Article X of the Covenant and its "very perilous promise" to guarantee, by force, if necessary, the political independence and territorial integrity of all members of the League. The American people, he argued, would do well to consider carefully whether they were willing to have the United States forced into a war by decision of the League and against their own will. Moreover, by agreeing to submit "every possible international dispute" to the League for decision, the United States would relinquish its right to control immigration and leave it to other nations to determine whether America should admit "a flood of Japanese, Chinese, and Hindu labor." "We are asked," Lodge declared, "to give up in part our sovereignty and our independence and to subject our own will to the will of other nations, if there is a majority against our desires. We are asked, therefore, in a large and important degree to substitute internationalism for nationalism and an international state for pure Americanism. Certainly, such things as these deserve reflection, discussion, and earnest thought. I am not contending now that these things must not be done. . . . What I ask, and all I ask, is consideration, time, and thought."

Lodge then discussed the Covenant article by article, commented favorably on some of the provisions, and opposed others. He specifically suggested amendments to exclude immigration from the jurisdiction of the League, to protect the Monroe Doctrine, to provide for a possible withdrawal from the organization, and to clarify the question of the creation and the composition of the proposed international army. He concluded: "Unless some better constitution for a league than this can be drawn, it seems to me . . . that the world's peace would be much better, much more surely protected, by allowing the United States to go on under the Monroe doctrine, responsible for the peace of this hemisphere, without any danger of collision with Europe as to questions among the various American States, and if a league is desired it might be made up by

feeling around and suggested not so much that he was opposed to the League of Nations as that it might be in need of amendments— of bad amendments as well as good amendments.

Now, the real issue of the day, gentlemen, is the League of Nations, and I was just saying to our colleagues who sit near me here that I think we must be very careful to serve the country in the right way with regard to that issue. We ought not, as I know you already feel from the character of the action you have just taken²—we ought not even to create the appearance of trying to make that a party issue. And I suggested this to Mr. Cummings and the others who sat by me: I think it would be wise if the several national committeemen were to get in touch with their state or- ganizations upon returning home and suggest this course of ac- tion—that the Democratic state organizations get into conference with the Republican state organizations and say to them: "Here is this great issue upon which the future peace of the world depends; it ought not to be made a party issue or to divide upon party lines; the country ought to support it regardless of party (as you stated in your resolution); now we propose to you that you pass resolutions supporting it, as we intend to do, and we will not anticipate you in the matter if you agree to that policy; let us stand back of it and not make a party issue of it." Of course, if they decline, then it is perfectly legitimate, it seems to me, for the Democratic organiza- tion, if it pleases, to pass resolutions, framing these resolutions in as nonpartisan language as is possible, but nevertheless doing what citizens ought to do in matters of this sort. But not without first making it a matter of party record that it has made those approaches to the Republican organizations and has proposed this similarity of action. In that way we accomplish a double object. We put it up to them to support the real opinion of their own people and we get instructed by the resolutions, and we find where the weak spots are and where the fighting has to be done for this great issue. Because, believe me, gentlemen, the civilized world cannot afford to have us lose this fight. I tried to state in Boston what it would mean to the people of the world if the United States did not support this great ideal with cordiality, but I was not able to speak when I tried to fully express my thoughts. I tell you, frankly, I choked up; I could not do it. The thing reaches the depth of tragedy. There is a sense in which I can see that the hope entertained by the people of the world with regard to us is a tragical hope—tragical in this

the European nations whose interests are chiefly concerned, and with which the United States could cooperate fully at any time, whenever cooperation was needed." *Cong. Record*, 65th Cong., 3d sess., pp. 4520-28.

² That is, the adoption of the resolution Wilson mentions below.

sense, that it is so great, so far-reaching, it runs out to such depths that we cannot in the nature of things satisfy it. The world cannot go as fast in the direction of ideal results as these people believe the United States can carry them, and that is what makes me choke up when I try to talk about it—the consciousness of what they want us to do and of our relative inadequacy.

And yet there is a great deal that we can do, and the immediate thing that we can do is to have an overwhelming national endorsement of this great plan. If we have that, we will have settled most of the immediate political difficulties in Europe. The present danger of the world—of course, I have to say this in the confidence of this company—but the present danger in this world is that the peoples of the world do not believe in their own governments. They believe these governments to be made up of the kind of men who have always run them, and who did not know how to keep them out of this war, did not know how to prepare them for war, and did not know how to settle international controversies in the past without making all sorts of compromising concessions. They do not believe in them, and, therefore, they have got to be buttressed by some outside power in which they do believe. Perhaps it would not do for them to examine them too narrowly. We are by no means such ideal people as they believe us to be, but I can say that we are infinitely better than the others. We do purpose these things, we do purpose these great unselfish things. That is the glory of America, and, if we can confirm that belief, we have steadied the whole process of history in the immediate future; whereas if we do not confirm that belief I would not like to say what would happen in the way of utter dissolution of society.

The only thing that that ugly, poisonous thing called Bolshevism feeds on is the doubt of the man on the street of the essential integrity of the people he is depending on to do his governing. That is what it feeds on. No man in his senses would think that a lot of local soviets could really run a government, but some of them are in a temper to have anything rather than the kind of thing they have been having; and they say to themselves: "Well, this may be bad, but it is at least better and more immediately in touch with us than the other, and we will try it and see whether we cannot work something out of it."

So that our immediate duty, not as Democrats, but as American citizens, is to concert the most powerful campaign that was ever concerted in this country in favor of supporting the League of Nations and to put it up to everybody—the Republican organizations and every other organization—to say where they stand, and to make a record and explain this thing to the people.

In one sense it does not make any difference what the constitution of the League of Nations is. This present constitution in my
judgment is a very conservative and sound document. There are
some things in it which I would have phrased otherwise. I am
modest enough to believe that the American draft was better than
this, but it is the result of as honest work as I ever knew to be
done. There we sat around the table where there were representatives of fourteen nations. The five great powers, so-called, gave
themselves two delegates apiece, and they allowed the other nine
one delegate apiece. But it did not count by members—it counted
by purpose.

For example, among the rest was a man whom I have come to
admire so much that I have come to have a personal affection for
him, and that is Mr. Vénisélos, Prime Minister of Greece, as genuine
a friend of man as ever lived and as able a friend as honest people
ever had, and a man on whose face a glow comes when you state
a great principle, and yet who is intensely practical and who was
there to insist that nothing was to be done which put the small
nations of the world at the disposal of the big nations. So that he
was the most influential spokesman of what may be called the small
powers as contrasted with the great. But I merely single him out
for the pleasure of paying him this tribute, and not because the
others were less earnest in pursuing their purpose. They were a
body of men who all felt this. Indeed, several of them said to us:
"The world expects not only, but demands of us that we shall do
this thing successfully, and we cannot go away without doing it."
There is not a statesman in that conference who would dare go
home saying that he had merely signed a treaty of peace, no matter
how excellent the terms of that treaty are, because he has received,
if not an official, at least an influential mandate to see to it that
something is done in addition which will make the thing stand after
it is done; and he dare not go home without doing that. So that all
around that table there was cooperation—generous cooperation of
mind to make that document as good as we could make it. And I
believe it is a thoroughly sound document. There is only one misleading sentence in it—only one sentence that conveys a wrong
impression. That can, I dare say, be altered, though it is going to
be extremely difficult to set up that fourteen-nation process again
as will have to be done if any alteration is made.

The particular and most important thing to which every nation
that joins the League agrees is this: that it won't fight on any
question at all until it has done one of two things. If it is about a
question that it considers suitable for arbitration, it will submit it
to arbitration. You know, Mr. Taft and other serious advocates of

this general idea have tried to distinguish between justiciable and nonjusticiable subjects, and, while they have had more or less success with it, the success has not yet been satisfactory. You cannot define expressly the questions which nations would be willing to submit to arbitration. Some question of national pride may come in to upset the definition. So we said we would make them promise to submit every question that they considered suitable to arbitration and to abide by the result. If they do not regard it as suitable for arbitration, they bind themselves to submit it to the consideration of the Executive Council for a period not exceeding six months, but they are not bound by the decision. It is an opinion, not a decision. But if a decision, a unanimous decision, is made, and one of the parties to the dispute accepts the decision, the other party does bind itself not to attack the party that accepts the opinion. Now in discussing that we saw this difficulty. Suppose that Power B is in possession of a piece of territory which Power A claims, and Power A wins its claims so far as the opinion of the Executive Council is concerned. And suppose that the power in possession of the territory accepts the decision but then simply stands pat and does nothing. It has got the territory. The other party, inasmuch as the party that has lost has accepted the decision, has bound itself not to attack it and cannot go by force of arms and take possession of the country. In order to cure that quandary, we used a sentence which said that in case—I have forgotten the phraseology but it means this—in case any power refuses to carry out the decision, the Executive Council was to consider the means by which it could be enforced. Now that apparently applies to both parties but was intended to apply to the nonactive party which refuses to carry it out. And that sentence is open to a misconstruction. The commission did not see that until after the report was made, and I explained this to the general conference. I made an explanation which was substantially the same as I have made to you, and that this should be of record may be sufficient to interpret that phrase, but probably not. It is not part of the Covenant and possibly an attempt ought to be made to alter it.

But I am wandering from my real point. My point is that this is a workable beginning of a thing that the world insists on. There is no foundation for it except the good faith of the parties, but there could not be any other foundation for an arrangement between nations.

The other night after dinner, Senator Thomas, of Colorado, said: "Then, after all, it is not a guarantee of peace." Certainly not. Who said that it was? If you can invent an actual guarantee of peace you will be a benefactor of mankind, but no such guarantee has been found. But this comes as near being a guarantee of peace as you can get.

I had this interesting experience when the Covenent was framed. I found that I was the only member of the committee who did not take it for granted that the members of the League would have the right to secede. I found there was a universal feeling that this treaty could be denounced in the usual way and that a state could withdraw. I demurred from that opinion and found myself in a minority of one, and I could not help saying to them that this would be very interesting on the other side of the water—that the only Southerner on this conference should deny the right of secession. But nevertheless it is instructive and interesting to learn that this is taken for granted; that it is not a covenant that you would have to continue to adhere to. I suppose that is a necessary assumption among sovereign states, but it would not be a very handsome thing to withdraw after we had entered upon it. The point is that it does rest upon the good faith of all the nations. Now the historic significance of it is this.

We are setting up right in the path that German ambition expected to tread a number of new states that, chiefly because of their newness, will for a long time be weak states. We are carving a piece of Poland out of Germany's side; we are creating an independent Bohemia below that, an independent Hungary below that, and enlarging Rumania, and we are rearranging the territorial divisions of the Balkan states. We are practically dissolving the empire of Turkey and setting up under mandatories of the League of Nations a number of states in Asia Minor and Arabia which, except for the power of the mandatories, would be almost helpless against any invading or aggressive force, and that is exactly the old Berlin-to-Baghdad route. So that when you remember that there is at present a strong desire on the part of Austria to unite with Germany,[3] you have the prospect of an industrial nation with seventy

---

[3] The Provisional Assembly of German Austria, in its proclamation of November 12, 1918, which established German Austria as a democratic republic (see n. 3 to the memorandum by W. C. Bullitt, Nov. 2, 1918, Vol. 51), had declared that German Austria was to be "a constituent part of the German Republic." On November 15, Otto Bauer, the newly appointed Secretary of State for Foreign Affairs, had appealed to Wilson to support the right of self-determination for all peoples of the former Austro-Hungarian Empire and to endorse the proposed union of German Austria with Germany. Bauer's note was transmitted in W. A. F. Ekengren to RL, Nov. 16, 1918, TLS (SDR, RG 59, 763.72119/2676, DNA). In his reply, Wilson had stated that he would take the question "under the most serious consideration in the conferences to be held in Paris." WW to W. Phillips, Nov. 30, 1918, TLS, and FLP to W. A. F. Ekengren, Dec. 7, 1918, CCL, both in SDR, RG 59, 763.72119/2877, DNA. For a detailed discussion of the *Anschluss* movement in Austria in 1918 and 1919, see Herbert Steiner, "Otto Bauer und die 'Anschlussfrage' 1918/19," in Richard G. Plaschka and Karlheinz Mack, eds., *Die Auflösung des Habsburgerreiches: Zusammenbruch und Neuorientierung im Donauraum* (Munich, 1970), pp. 468-82, and M. Margaret Ball, *Post-War German-Austrian Relations: The Anschluss Movement, 1918-1936* (Stanford, Calif., and London, 1937), pp. 8-25.

or eighty millions of people right in the heart of Europe, and to the southeast of it nothing but weakness, unless it is supported by the combined power of the world.

Unless you expect this structure built at Paris to be a house of cards, you have got to put into it the structural iron which will be afforded by the League of Nations. Take the history of the war that we have just been through. It is agreed by everybody that has expressed an opinion that, if Germany had known that England would go in, she never would have started. What do you suppose she would have done if she had known that everybody else would have gone in? Of course she would never have started. If she had known that the world would have been against her, this war would not have occurred; and the League of Nations gives notice that if anything of that sort is tried again, the world will be against the nation that tries it. And with that assurance given that such a nation will have to fight the world, you may be sure that, whatever illicit ambitions a nation may have, it cannot and will not attempt to realize them. But if they have not that assurance and can in the meantime set up an infinite network of intrigue such as we now know ran like a honeycomb through the world, then any arrangement will be broken down. This is the place where intrigue did accomplish the disintegration which made the realization of Germany's purposes almost possible. So that those people will have to make friends with their powerful neighbor, Germany, unless they have already made friends with all the rest of the world. So that we must have the League of Nations or else a repetition of the catastrophe we have just gone through.

Now if you put that case before the people of the United States and show them that, without the League of Nations, it is not worthwhile completing the treaty we are making in Paris, then you have got an argument which even an unidealistic people would respond to, and ours is not an unidealistic people but the most idealistic people in the world. Just let them catch the meaning which really underlies this and there won't be any doubts as to what the response will be from the hearts and from the judgments of the people of the United States.

I would hope, therefore, that, forgetting elections for the time being, we should devote our thought and our energies and our plans to this great business, to concert bipartisan and nonpartisan action, and, by whatever sort of action, to concert every effort in support of this thing. I cannot imagine an orator being afforded a better theme, so trot out your orators and turn them loose, because they will have an inspiration in this that they have never had before, and I would like to guarantee that the best vocabulary they can mobilize won't be equal to the job. It surpasses past experience in the world and seems like a prospect of realizing what once seemed a remote hope of an international miracle. And you notice the basis of this thing. It guarantees the members of the League, guarantees to each their territorial integrity and political independence as against external aggression.

I found that all other men around the conference table had a great respect for the right of revolution. We do not guarantee any state against what may happen inside itself, but we do guarantee against aggression from the outside, so that the family can be as lively as it pleases, and we know what generally happens to an interloper if you interfere in a family quarrel. There was a very interesting respect for the right of revolution, it may be, because many of them thought it was nearer at hand than they had supposed, and this immediate possibility breathed a respect in their minds. But whatever the reason was, they had a very great respect for it. I read the Virginia Bill of Rights very literally but not very elegantly to mean that any people is entitled to any kind of government it damn pleases, and that it is none of our business to suggest or to influence the kind that it is going to have. Sometimes it will have a very riotous form of government, but that is none of our business. And I find that that is accepted, even with regard to Russia. Even conservative men like the representatives of Great Britain say it is not our business to dictate what kind of government Russia shall have. The only thing to do is to see if we can help them by conference and suggestion and recognition of the right elements to get together and not leave the country in a state of chaos.

It was for that reasonable purpose that we tried to have the conference at a place I had never heard of before—a place called Prinkipo. I understand it is a place on the Bosporus with fine summer hotels, and so forth, and I was abashed to admit that I had never heard of it. But having plenty of house room, we thought that we could get the several Russian elements together there and see if we could not get them to sit down in one room together and tell us what it was all about and what they intended to do. The Bolshevists had accepted, but had accepted in a way that was studiously insulting.[4] They said they would come and were perfectly ready to say beforehand that they were ready to pay the foreign debt and ready to make concessions in economic matters, and that they were even ready to make territorial readjustments, which meant, "we are dealing with perjured governments whose only interest is

[4] For a summary of the Bolshevik note, see n. 1 to the press conference printed at Feb. 14, 1919.

in striking a bargain, and if that is the price of European recognition and cooperation, we are ready to pay it."

I never saw anybody more angered that Mr. Lloyd George, who said: "We cannot let that insult go by. We are not after their money or their concessions or their territory. That is not the point. We are their friends who want to help them and must tell them so." We did not tell them so, because to some of the people we had to deal with the payment of the foreign debt was a more interesting and important matter, but that will be made clear to them in conference, if they will believe it. But the Bolshevists, so far as we could get any taste of their flavor, are the most consummate sneaks in the world, I suppose, because they know they have no high motives themselves, they do not believe that anybody else has. And Trotsky, having lived a few months in New York, was able to testify that the United States is in the hands of capitalists and does not serve anybody else's interests but the capitalists'. And the worst of it is, I think he honestly believes it. It would not have much effect if he didn't. Having received six dollars a week to write for a socialistic and anarchistic paper, which believed that and printed it, and knowing how difficult it is to live on nothing but the wages of sin, he believes that the only wages paid here are the wages of sin.

But we cannot rescue Russia without having a united Europe. One of my colleagues in Paris said that we could not go home and say we had made peace if we left half of Europe and half of Asia at war, because Russia constitutes half of Europe and Siberia constitutes half of Asia. And yet we may have to go home without composing these great territories, but if we go home with a League of Nations, there will be some power to solve this most perplexing problem.

And so, from every point of view, it is obvious to the men in Paris, obvious to those who in their own hearts are most indifferent to the League of Nations, that we have to tie in the provisions of the treaty with the League of Nations because the League of Nations is the heart of the treaty. It is the only machinery. It is the only solid basis of masonry that is in the treaty, and in saying that I know that I am expressing the opinion of all those with whom I have been conferring. I cannot imagine any greater historic glory for the party than to have it said that for the time being it is thinking not of elections, but of the salvation of the plain people of the world. And the plain people of the world are looking to us who call ourselves Democrats to prove to the utmost point of sacrifice that we are indeed democrats, with a small "d" as well as a large "D," that we are ready to put the whole power and influence of America at the disposal of free men everywhere in the world, no matter what the sacrifice involved, no matter what the danger to the cause.

And I would like, if I am not tiresome, to leave this additional thought in your mind. I was one of the first advocates of the mandatory. I do not at all believe in handing over any more territory than has already been handed over to any sovereign. I do not believe in putting the people of the German territories at the disposition, unsubordinated disposition, of any great power, and therefore I was a warm advocate of the idea of General Smuts—who by the way is an extraordinary person—who propounded the theory that the pieces of the Austro-Hungarian Empire and the pieces of the Turkish Empire and the German colonies were all political units or territorial units which ought to be accepted in trust by the family of nations, and not turned over to any member of the family, and that therefore the League of Nations would have as one of its chief functions to act as trustee for these great areas of dismembered empires. And yet the embarrassing moment came when they asked if the United States would be willing to accept a mandatory. I had to say offhand that it would not be willing. I have got to say offhand that, in the present state of American opinion, at any rate, it wants to observe what I may call without offense pharisaical cleanliness and not take anything out of the pile. It is its point of pride that it does not want to seem to take anything, even by the way of superintendence. And of course they said, that is very disappointing, for this reason (the reason they stated in as complimentary terms as I could have stated it myself): you would be the most acceptable mandatory to any one of these peoples, and very few of us, if any, would be acceptable. They said that in so many words, and it would greatly advance the peace of mind in Europe if the United States would accept mandatories. I said, I am perfectly willing to go home and stump the country and see if they will do it, but I could not truthfully say offhand that they would, because I did not know.

Now what I wanted to suggest is this: personally, and just within the limits of this room, I can say very frankly that I think we ought to. I think there is a very promising beginning in regard to countries like Armenia. The whole heart of America has been engaged for Armenia. They know more about Armenia and its sufferings than they know about any other European area; we have colleges out there; we have great missionary enterprises, just as we have had Robert College in Constantinople. That is a part of the world where already American influence extends—a saving influence and an educating and an uplifting influence. Colleges like Beirut in Syria have spread their influence very much beyond the limits of Syria, all through the Arabian country and Mesopotamia and in the distant parts of Asia Minor. And I am not without hope that the people of the United States would find it acceptable to go in and be the trustees of the interests of the Armenian people and see to it that the unspeakable Turk and the almost equally difficult Kurd had their necks sat on long enough to teach them manners and give the industrious and earnest people of Armenia time to develop a country which is naturally rich with possibilities.

But the place where they all want us to accept a mandate most is at Constantinople. I may say that it seems to be rather the consensus of opinion there that Constantinople ought to be internationalized. So that the present idea apparently is to delimit the territory around Constantinople to include the Straits and set up a mandate for that territory which will make those straits open to the nations of the world without any conditions and make Constantinople truly international—an internationalized free city and a free port. And America is the only nation in the world that can undertake that mandate and have the rest of the world believe that it is undertaken in good faith, that we do not mean to stay there and set up our own sovereignty. So that it would be a very serious matter for the confidence of the world in this treaty if the United States did not accept a mandate for Constantinople.

What I have to suggest is that questions of that sort ought to be ventilated very thoroughly. This will appeal to the people of the United States: are you going to take the advantages of this and not any of the burden? Are you going to put the burden on the bankrupt states of Europe? For almost all of them are bankrupt in the sense that they cannot undertake any new things. I think that will appeal to the American people: that they ought to take the burdens, for they are burdens. Nobody is going to get anything out of a mandatory of Constantinople or Armenia. It is a work of disinterested philanthropy. And if you first present that idea and then make tentative expositions of where we might go in as a mandatory, I think that the people will respond. If we went in at Constantinople, for example, I think it is true that almost all the influential men who are prominent in the affairs of Bulgaria were graduates of Robert College and would be immediately susceptible to American interests. They would take American guidance when they would not take any other guidance.

But I wish I could stay home and tackle this job with you. There is nothing I would like to do so much as to really say in parliamentary language what I think of the people that are opposing it. I would reserve the right in private to say in unparliamentary language what I think of them, but in public I would try to stick to parliamentary language. Because of all the blind and little provincial people, they are the littlest and most contemptible. It is not their character so much that I have a contempt for, though that contempt is thoroughgoing, but their minds. They have not got even good working imitations of minds. They remind me of a man with a head that is not a head but is just a knot providentially put there to keep him from raveling out. But why the Lord should not have been willing to let them ravel out, I do not know, because they are of no use, and if I could really say what I think about them, it would be picturesque. But the beauty of it is that their ignorance and their provincialism can be made so perfectly visible. They have horizons that do not go beyond their parish; they do not even reach to the edges of the parish, because the other people know more than they do. The whole impulse of the modern time is against them. They are going to have the most conspicuously contemptible names in history. The gibbets that they are going to be erected on by future historians will scrape the heavens, they will be so high. They won't be turned in the direction of heaven at all, but they will be very tall, and I do not know any fate more terrible than to be exhibited in that future catalogue of the men who are utterly condemned by the whole spirit of humanity. If I did not despise them, I would be sorry for them.

Now I have sometimes a very cheering thought. On the fifth of March, 1921, I am going to begin to be a historian again instead of an active public man, and I am going to have the privilege of writing about these gentlemen without any restraints of propriety. The President, if my experience is a standard, is liable some day to burst by merely containing restrained gases. Anybody in the House or Senate can say any abusive thing he pleases about the President, but it shocks the sense of propriety of the whole country if the President says what he thinks about them. And that makes it very fortunate that the term of the President is limited, because no President could stand it for a number of years. But when the lid is off, I am going to resume my study of the dictionary to find adequate terms in which to describe the fatuity of these gentlemen with their poor little minds that never get anywhere but run around in a circle and think they are going somewhere. I cannot express my contempt for their intelligence, but because I think I know the people of the United States, I can predict their future with absolute certainty. I am not concerned as to the ultimate outcome of this thing at all, not for a moment, but I am concerned that the outcome should be brought about immediately, just as promptly as possible. So my hope is that we will all put on our war paint, not as Democrats but as Americans, get the true American pattern of war paint and a real hatchet and go out on the war path and get a collection of scalps that has never been excelled in the history of American warfare.

T MS (C. L. Swem Coll., NjP).

A News Report

[*Feb. 28, 1919*]

WILSON DENIES IRISH STATEMENT
Brands as Falsehood Remark Attributed to Him at
White House Dinner.

Washington, Feb. 28.—President Wilson today authorized a denial "as a deliberate falsehood" of a newspaper statement that he had told Senators and Representatives in the famous White House dinner conference over the League of Nations on Wednesday night that the Irish question was a matter between Ireland and England to settle and that Ireland would have no voice in the Peace Conference at present. What the President was alleged to have said of the Irish question also gave rise to a lively argument in the Senate debate today.

The denial issued by direction of the President was embraced in this statement from Joseph P. Tumulty, his Private Secretary:

"In the last few days the following quotation has appeared in the press under a Washington date line, as part of the newspaper report of the dinner given by the President at the White House Wednesday evening, Feb. 26, to the members of the Committee on Foreign Relations of the Senate and the Committee on Foreign Affairs of the House:

" 'The President told the committees that the Irish question was a matter between Ireland and England, and that Ireland would not have any voice in the Peace Conference at present.'

"The President wishes me to say that this statement has no foundation in fact, and is a deliberate falsehood."

Senator Hitchcock brought the Irish question up in the Senate when he read this excerpt from a newspaper story of the conference:

"Ireland is to be left to the mercies of England."

Mr. Hitchcock took exception to this sentence.

"The President," he said, "made no statement that by any possibility could be stretched or interpreted to mean anything of the sort."

"Would it be possible," asked Senator Borah, "for the Senator to state what he did say with reference to Ireland?"

"The President practically stated nothing with reference to Ireland: the Irish question was not under consideration," replied Senator Hitchcock.

"But there were questions asked?" persisted Senator Borah.

"Oh, there was a question asked, which was greeted with laughter, and there was nothing more said about it," was Senator Hitchcock's answer. "It was not an issue in the conversation and had nothing to do with it. We were not discussing internal questions, but international questions."

"Does the Senator say the President made no response to the question which was presented to him with reference to the independence of Ireland?" asked Senator Borah.

"It was not a serious question presented; it was not presented in a serious way," Mr. Hitchcock said.

Still standing at his desk, Senator Borah interrupted again, asking:

"Pardon me, does the Senator say the President made no reply to it?"

"I do," replied Senator Hitchcock. "However," he added, "the Senator from Mississippi, Mr. Williams, corrects me. He says the President stated that the League had nothing to do with domestic and internal questions. He did state that; that he stated several times during the evening, and in stating it said it had not anything to do with the immigration question, which has been raised here as a great bugaboo against the League of Nations, the attempt being made to arouse prejudice against the League of Nations by construing it to bring the Japanese immigration question into the realms of arbitration."

"Then," asked Senator Borah, "if I understand the Senator correctly, what the President said with reference to the question, since he has raised the question himself with reference to Ireland, was that the League will have nothing to do with internal questions?"

Mr. Hitchcock replied: "The Senator from Mississippi, Mr. Williams, recollected that."

The following colloquy then occurred between the two Senators:

Mr. Borah: "And that was a matter, therefore, with which the League had nothing to do, but which must necessarily be settled by Ireland and England?"

Mr. Hitchcock: "The Senator can draw his own conclusions. It evidently and obviously is not an international question, at this time, with which the League has to do."

Mr. Borah: "Then if the League has nothing to do with it, of course it must be left where it was before, between Ireland and England."

Mr. Hitchcock: "The Senator can draw his own conclusions. I am dealing with facts. I am dealing with the fact that one of the great papers of the country has come in here and arraigned Senators of the United States as guilty of the grossest violation of a decent respect for a private conference and hospitable entertainment."

Mr. Borah: "But the Senator is attacking a piece in the paper and indirectly Senators."

Mr. Hitchcock: "No, I am defending Senators; I am not attacking Senators."

Mr. Borah: "So I observe. The Senator now admits that the question which the paper discusses was brought up, and that the President did make an answer."

Mr. Hitchcock: "The Senator from Mississippi, Mr. Williams, corrected me when I said the President made no answer. It passed so momentarily that I did not recall that he made any answer. The Senator from Mississippi states that he made the answer that domestic and internal questions were not subjects of the League's jurisdiction, and of course he did state that. He stated it repeatedly during the evening, when domestic questions were presented."

Mr. Borah: "If the Senator from Mississippi and the Senator from Nebraska are at a difference as to what the President said upon that important matter other Senators might have understood it in a different way."

Senator Hitchcock said he accepted Senator Williams' recollection as "very definite."

Printed in the *New York Times*, March 1, 1919.

To Edward Mandell House

The White House, 28 February, 1919.

One. Unless you think that I should come more immediately to Paris, I shall land at Antwerp and go from thence to Brussels and from Brussels through the devastated regions around Lille to Paris. I believe that I can be confident of reaching Antwerp by the thirteenth or fourteenth and should be in Paris some four days later. I would be obliged if General Harts would arrange for the motor transportation through the devastated regions.

Two. This however seems to conflict with Mr. Lloyd George's appointments, and I am quite willing, if he wishes me to do so, to come direct to Paris by Brest, because I hope that you will say to him that I regard it as of the highest importance that we should constantly have the benefit of his counsel and guidance. Please let me know as soon as possible whether the Antwerp plan should be given up and my visit to Brussels made later.

Three. We note what you say about the house we are to occupy and the insistence of the French Government that we should be its guests. We find that it will not be possible to bring a complete set of servants and think it on the whole unwise to attempt to bring a few. We would be very much obliged therefore if you would arrange through the French Government for reliable servants.

Four. I am glad that you were able to assist the French Government in the matter of exchange.   Woodrow Wilson[1]

T telegram (WP, DLC).
  [1] There are only a few minor differences in the decode of this telegram in the House Papers.

To Albert Sidney Burleson

My dear Burleson: The White House 28 February, 1919.

This is tough enough in all conscience, but I cannot believe that it would be wise to do any more suppressing. We must meet these poisons in some other way.

In great haste,   Faithfully yours,   Woodrow Wilson[1]

TLS (A. S. Burleson Papers, DLC).
  [1] This note may well have followed a conversation with Burleson about his continuing suppression of radical publications. Burleson wrote at the bottom of this letter: "Continued to suppress and Courts sustained me every time."

To Thomas Erby Kilby[1]

[The White House] February 28, 1919.

Various cititzens of the City of Chicago have presented to me urgently by telegram[2] the case of Sergeant Edgar Caldwell, sentenced to be hanged, this morning, for first degree murder, by the civil courts of the State of Alabama. Though a soldier and in the military service at the time of the alleged offense, Sergeant Caldwell was delivered to the civil authorities for trial. I, of course, have no means of knowing what the record in his case discloses, and have every faith that you and your legal advisers have inspected the record, but in view of the fact that this man was a soldier of the United States, would you not be willing to grant a brief reprieve in order that the Attorney General may at my request examine the record as the basis of any further suggestion which I might venture to make upon the ultimate disposition of the case?[3]

Woodrow Wilson.

T telegram (Letterpress Books, WP, DLC).
[1] Governor of Alabama, a Democrat.
[2] Louis B. Anderson *et al.* to WW, Feb. 24, 1919, T telegram (WP, DLC).
[3] Newton D. Baker drafted this telegram. It is a CC MS, enclosed with NDB to WW, Feb. 27, 1919, TLS (WP, DLC).

From Thomas Erby Kilby

Montgomery, Ala., February 28, 1919.

Your today's message, case of Sgt. Edgar Caldwell has been appealed to the supreme court of the state, thereby suspending sentence pending appeal.

Thos. E. Kilby.

T telegram (WP, DLC).

To William Howard Taft

[The White House] February 28, 1919

I am very glad to learn that you are to speak with me at the meeting in New York next Tuesday.

Woodrow Wilson

T telegram (Letterpress Books, WP, DLC).

To Samuel Walker McCall

[The White House]
My dear Governor McCall: 28 February, 1919.

I have read your letter of the twenty-sixth with the greatest interest and appreciation and acknowledge that the suggestions it contains have very great weight.

I need hardly say that I agree with you that the greatest make-weight for peace is the influence of the United States and yet after the long discussions I went through in Paris I feel confident that it would lead to some very embarrassing and serious misunderstandings if I were to ask a larger voice in the affairs of the League for the United States than it has in the proposed plan. You will note that the real working and guiding force of the League is to be the Executive Council, and in that the United States has as potent a voice as any other nation. The British Dominions are represented only in the Body of Delegates.

I never made any specific suggestion with regard to the Monroe Doctrine, and I feel that it will be worth while, when I get back, to broach and discuss the matter with my colleagues of the Commission that framed the draft of the League, and I shall be very much interested to see their reactions. I have very little doubt that they would, if they could see a way to do it consistent with the general plan, be quite willing to leave to us the single responsibility of safeguarding territorial integrity and political independence of American states.

 With warm appreciation,
          Cordially and sincerely yours,   Woodrow Wilson

TLS (Letterpress Books, WP, DLC).

To Henry Morgenthau

My dear Morgenthau: The White House 28 February, 1919.

 I warmly appreciate your kind letter of the twenty-sixth. I am happy to tell you that Mr. Taft has already generously agreed to speak with me on Tuesday night next.

 Amazing and apparently desperate efforts have been made to fill this whole situation with lies, but fortunately there is time to clear the whole case, and I believe that by concerted effort that can be triumphantly done.

 In great haste, with warm regard,
          Cordially and sincerely yours,   Woodrow Wilson

TLS (H. Morgenthau Papers, DLC).

To Robert Somers Brookings

My dear Mr. Brookings: [The White House] 28 February, 1919.

 Allow me to acknowledge your letter of February 22nd[1] relative to winding up the business of the Price Fixing Committee and to express to you the very great appreciation I have had of the conscientious and thoughtful way in which the Price Fixing Committee has performed its difficult and important duties. My own associations with them, associations too infrequent for my pleasure, have always been of the most gratifying and satisfactory sort and I hope that you will convey to your associates and accept for yourself my warm appreciation and my official thanks on behalf of the Government.

 With the best wishes,
          Cordially and sincerely yours,   Woodrow Wilson

TLS (Letterpress Books, WP, DLC).
 [1] R. S. Brookings to WW, Feb. 22, 1919, TLS (WP, DLC).

To Charles Mills Galloway

My dear Mr. Galloway: [The White House] 28 February, 1919.

In view of the resignation of Mr. McIlhenny as a member of the United States Civil Service Commission[1] I have definitely reached the conclusion that it is in the interest of the public service that the Civil Service Commission be reorganized.[2] I shall be glad, therefore, if you will send me your resignation.

Sincerely yours,   Woodrow Wilson[3]

TLS (Letterpress Books, WP, DLC).
[1] That is, John Avery McIlhenny, president of the United States Civil Service Commission. McIlhenny had tendered his resignation on February 28, and Wilson, in a gracious letter of appreciation, had accepted it on the same day. J. A. McIlhenny to WW, Feb. 28, 1919, ALS (WP, DLC), and WW to J. A. McIlhenny, Feb. 28, 1919, TLS (Letterpress Books, WP, DLC).
[2] During the war, the Civil Service Commission had come under sharp criticism, particularly from the National Civil Service Reform League, for its alleged failure to respond adequately to the increased demands which war conditions had imposed upon the administration of the civil service. Throughout 1918, the league had repeatedly called Wilson's attention to the unsatisfactory situation and had asked Wilson to replace the three members of the commission—McIlhenny, Galloway, and Hermon Wilson Craven—with more capable and experienced members. Although, as early as April 1918, Wilson had considered a "partial reorganization" of the commission, he had not changed its personnel at that time. Richard Henry Dana, president of the National Civil Service Reform League, to WW, April 8 and June 28, 1918, TLS (WP, DLC), and WW to R. H. Dana, April 10, 1918, CCL (WP, DLC). See also the *New York Times*, Nov. 28, 1918. After the Armistice, the attacks by the league on the commission intensified. In late November 1918, the league issued a report by its Committee on Investigation and Reconstruction, which charged the civil service commissioners, among other things, with mismanagement, inefficiency, neglect of their duty, and political partisanship and, again, called for their immediate dismissal. *New York Times*, Nov. 28, 1918; George Thurman Keyes, secretary of the National Civil Service Reform League, to WW, Nov. 25, 1918, TLS, enclosing R. H. Dana *et al.* to the Council of the National Civil Service Reform League, Nov. 26, 1918, T MS (WP, DLC). Sometime in late February 1919, Wilson and Burleson decided to use McIlhenny's resignation as an opportunity to reconstitute the entire commission. JPT to WW, Feb. 26, 1919, TL (WP, DLC).
[3] Wilson sent the same letter, *mutatis mutandis*, as WW to H. W. Craven, Feb. 28, 1919, TLS (Letterpress Books, WP, DLC). Craven resigned on March 11. However, as future documents will show, Galloway refused to resign at this time.

From Frank Lyon Polk

My dear Mr. President: [Washington] February 28, 1919.

The Minister of Peru[1] has informed me that he has been instructed by his Government to inquire of the American Government whether, in its opinion, the Government of Peru should now present the question of its differences with Chile[2] to the Peace Conference or if this is not considered advisable whether the Government of Peru could not at the earliest opportunity lay its claim against Chile before the League of Nations in order to obtain priority over other claimants.

I have had many conversations with the Ambassador from Chile[3] and the Ministers from Peru and Bolivia.[4] It is very evident that Peru and Bolivia are anxious that we should arbitrate their difficulties, but Chile is holding off. I do not think that Chile is holding off from any lack of confidence in the United States, but rather because they have no intentions of expediting the final determination of this question. I impressed on the Chilean Ambassador that if something was not done now, that undoubtedly the matter would be forced to the front by Peru or Bolivia, either at the Peace Conference or before some international tribunal.

I would be very much obliged if you would let me know what your opinion is as to the best line we should take. The choice seems to be:

One. Try to influence Chile to accept the United States as an arbitrator.

Two. Press them to select one or more arbitrators and intimate that they might select United States and two European countries, or even three European countries.

Three. Leave the question to be dealt with at the Peace Conference.

Four. Leave question until the League of Nations is formed.

To my mind number one is objectionable, as whatever our decision would be, it is fairly certain it would not be acceptable to any of the parties concerned and therefore we would be laying up more grounds for unpopularity for this Government in South America.

I am inclined to feel that number two is the best course to pursue. Edwards,[5] the Chilean Minister to England, who was in Washington last month, rather intimated that this line should be taken by the United States. Personally I do not see that it makes any difference to us who decides the question as long as it is settled.

To wait for the formation of the League of Nations would be quite acceptable to Chile, as that would mean further delay. I think we might intimate to Chile that unless they accept plan two, the matter might be brought up at the Peace Conference, although as to what jurisdiction the Conference would have I am not clear.

While you may not be ready to express any opinion, could you give me some sort of an answer to convey to the Peruvian Minister before you sail. I am marking this urgent as the Minister may bring up this question today when he is presented.

Faithfully yours,   [Frank L Polk]

CCL (F. L. Polk Papers, CtY).
   [1] Manuel de Freyre y Santander, who was about to be replaced, on March 1, 1919, by Don Francisco Tudela y Varela.
   [2] About this, the so-called Tacna-Arica dispute, see WW to J. L. Sanfuentes Andonaegui, Dec. 4, 1918, n. 2, Vol. 53, and n. 3 to the Enclosure printed with WJB to WW, April 3, 1915, Vol. 32.
   [3] Don Beltran Mathieu.
   [4] The Bolivian Minister was Don Ignacio Calderón.
   [5] Agustin Edwards.

Two Letters from Carter Glass

Dear Mr. President: Washington February 28, 1919.

I received your wireless message of the nineteenth, indicating your approval of advances to Italy up to the amount of $25,000,000 for the purchase of products of neutral countries. I have also received through the Italian Embassy a communication from the Italian Minister of Finance[1] on the subject and also a cable from Mr. Davis.

In my judgment there are two principles which we ought to seek to establish in connection with any arrangement for meeting such requirements of the Italian Government: first, that the arrangement by which Great Britain contributed one-half of the Italian requirements for expenditures outside the United States and Great Britain should be continued by that Government; and, second, that where needs of the Italian Government for commodities of foreign origin can be met from surplus stocks in the United States, this should be done rather than that Italy should make fresh purchases in the countries of origin.

Before the receipt of your message I requested further information from the Italian representatives regarding the purposes for which the special credit requested is to be applied, and whether and to what extent the British Treasury was prepared to continue advances to the Italian Government for the purpose of meeting its expenditures in neutral countries. I am now in receipt of advices from the Italian representatives that Great Britain has granted Italy a new credit of £5,000,000 to provide for purchases in neutral countries, to be advanced at the rate of £1,000,000 during the months from February to June.

In view of your wireless message above referred to I am advising the Italian representatives that I am prepared to establish in favor of the Italian Government a special credit in the amount of $25,000,000 for the purchase of products of neutral countries, under certain limitations set forth in my letter of even date to Mr. Alliata, of which I enclose herewith a copy.[2]

During the entire course of the war the obligations contracted by the Italian Government for the payment of which it has later requested advances from us has been a matter of concern to the Treasury. In many instances there has been an apparent disinclination on the part of the Italian Government to comply with the requirements of the Treasury that proposed contracts must be approved on behalf of our Government before they are entered into. The Treasury has been constantly asked to make advances to Italy to meet its obligations entered into without the knowledge or consent of the Treasury. I have carefully noted your letter of November

23, 1917 to Secretary McAdoo[3] calling attention to the imperative necessity of keeping very strictly to the agreements upon which our loans are based in regard to the method of purchase. In order to properly deal with the Italian situation and as well with those arising with other foreign governments, it is, in my judgment, quite necessary to adhere to the plan which you have approved that all discussions and negotiations regarding our further loans must be carried on here in Washington under my direction. I regard it also as highly important that our financial assistance to the various Allied Governments should be limited very strictly towards meeting their requirements in the United States. I believe that such limitation is required in order to preserve our own financial and commercial prosperity which is being put to a severe strain by the tremendous expenditures which the Treasury is being called upon to meet. Cordially yours, Carter Glass.

[1] Filippo Meda.
[2] C. Glass to Enrico Alliata, Financial Secretary of the Italian embassy at Washington, Feb. 28, 1919, CCL (WP, DLC).
[3] WW to WGM, Nov. 23, 1917, TLS (Letterpress Books, WP, DLC).

Dear Mr. President: Washington February 28, 1919

Adverting to my brief conversation with you over the telephone concerning the status with respect to the existing authorization for the issue of bonds and Treasury certificates, I am writing this letter in order that you may have before you a memorandum of the facts.

The amount of Treasury certificates outstanding as of today, including certificates now being offered for subscription, is about $6,000,000,000. The maximum amount of certificates authorized to be issued under existing law is $8,000,000,000. As there is no reason to hope that the current expenditures of the Government will average less than $1,500,000,000 a month, it is apparent that, after allowing for, say, $1,000,000,000 tax receipts as a result of the new revenue bill, the Treasury will have had to issue all the Treasury certificates authorized by existing law by the end of April.

Under existing law no additional bonds may be issued at a higher interest rate than $4\frac{1}{4}\%$ nor at a price less than par nor carrying exemption from supertaxes or excess profits taxes. You will, no doubt, recall that in order to make the success of the Fourth Liberty Loan possible Secretary McAdoo asked and secured the enactment of a supplemental bond bill conferring valuable exemptions from supertaxes and excess profits taxes upon subscribers for the Fourth Liberty Loan. Those exemptions do not extend to the remaining bonds authorized but unissued under existing legislation. In the meantime the rates of surtaxes and war excess profits taxes have been greatly increased by the new revenue law.[1] The outstanding Liberty Bonds are selling in the market between 94 and 95. It does not need argument to show that a bond bearing the same rate of interest and subject to heavier taxation could not be sold at par.

It takes a full month for the proceeds of a Liberty Loan to reach the Treasury after the campaign begins. The sale of War Savings Certificates is limited to $1,000 to any one person in any one year.

Under existing law, therefore, the Treasury will have exhausted all authority to borrow money by about the end of April, and the Government will by that time be obliged to suspend all payments.

This is not a matter of opinion, but of simple arithmetic. It has, of course, been my duty to bring the situation to the attention of the Committees of Congress in connection with the pending bill, and the fundamental facts are well understood by the members of the Ways and Means Committee of the House and of the Finance Committee of the Senate and are pretty fully stated in the printed testimony of myself and of other Treasury officials before those Committees.   Sincerely yours,   Carter Glass.

TLS (WP, DLC).

[1] The origin of the Revenue Act of 1918 went back as far as May 1918, when McAdoo had written to Wilson about the need for new and immediate revenue legislation, and Wilson had appealed to Congress to provide more adequate resources for the Treasury in the form of higher taxes on incomes, war profits, and luxuries. See WGM to WW, May 23, 1918 (first letter of that date), and Wilson's address to a joint session of Congress, May 27, 1918, both printed in Vol. 48. On September 3, 1918, Representative Kitchin introduced a revenue bill (H.R. 12863), drafted by the House Ways and Means Committee, which was based on McAdoo's estimate that governmental expenditures for the fiscal year 1918-1919 would amount to $24 billion, one third of which should be raised by taxes. The House adopted H.R. 12863 on September 20, but the Senate Finance Committee kept the bill bottled up for months. After the Armistice, McAdoo and the Senate Finance Committee reduced the estimated governmental expenditures for fiscal 1918 to $18 billion and the amount of tax revenues to $6 billion. The committee finally reported a heavily amended version of H.R. 12863 on December 6, and the Senate adopted it on December 23. After a protracted struggle over the numerous differences in the House and Senate versions, the conference committee reported the bill on February 8, 1919, and the House adopted it on the same day. The Senate passed the bill on February 13.

As signed by Wilson on February 24, the Revenue Act of 1918 did not essentially differ from the Revenue Act of 1917 (about which, see R. L. Owen to WW, Aug. 2, 1917, n. 2, Vol 43), but it increased the tax load by almost 250 per cent. About four fifths of the entire revenue yield of $6 billion was designed to be raised by taxes on incomes, war profits, excess profits, and estates, with the balance to be provided by taxes on luxuries and semiluxuries, excises, and imports. For the year 1918, under the Revenue Act of 1918, the normal tax on all individual incomes above the exemption of $1,000 for single persons and $2,000 for married persons was fixed at 6 per cent on the first $4,000 and at 12 per cent on the remainder. Under the same measure, for 1919, the respective rates were 4 per cent and 8 per cent. On top of the normal tax, the Act imposed, for 1918 and 1919, a graded surtax, which began at 1 per cent on incomes over $5,000 and increased proportionately to 65 per cent on incomes in excess of $1 million. Thus, for 1918, the maximum tax on individual incomes amounted to 77 per cent—an increase of 10 per cent over the previous tax rate. The normal tax on corporate incomes in excess of $2,000 was 12 per cent for the year 1918 and 10 per cent for 1919. In addition, the Act sharply increased the existing excess-profits and war-profits taxes on corporate incomes. The base for the excess-profits tax was a deduction of $3,000, plus an amount equal to 8 per cent of invested capital for the taxable year. For 1918, corporate incomes between this so-called excess-profits credit and 20 per cent of invested capital was taxed at 30 per cent, incomes over 20 per cent of invested capital at 65 per cent. For 1919, these rates were lowered to 20 per cent for the first bracket and 40 per cent for the second bracket. With regard to the war-profits tax, the Act allowed a credit of $3,000 and the average net income for the years 1911 to 1913, plus or minus 10 per cent of the difference between the average invested capital for the prewar period and the invested capital for 1918. The amount of the war-profits tax consisted of 80 per cent of the net income in excess of the war-profits credit, minus any amount paid in excess-profits tax. Thus, for example, a company which had a capital of $100,000, a prewar net income of $7,000, and a net income for 1918 of $75,000 would have to pay slightly over $52,000 in combined normal, excess-profits, and war-profits taxes. For 1919, the war-profits tax was abolished, except for a provision which taxed at the rate of 1918 all incomes of corporations deriving more than $10,000 from government war contracts. For a detailed discussion of the act, see Roy G. Blakey and Gladys C. Blakey, "The Revenue Act of 1918," *American Economic Review*, IX (June 1919), 213-43; Sidney Ratner, *Taxation and Democracy in America* (New York, 1967), pp. 389-99; and Charles Gilbert, *American Financing of World War I* (Westport, Conn., 1970), pp. 102-16.

A Translation of a Telegram from Georges Clemenceau

Paris, February 28, 1919.

Very deeply touched by your renewed mark of sympathy. I rejoice in thinking of my soon resuming with you our common work. The receipt of your photograph gave me great pleasure.

G. Clemenceau

T MS (WP, DLC).

From Newton Diehl Baker

Dear Mr. President: Washington. February 28, 1919.

Dr. Moton, President of Tuskegee Institute, call[ed] on me this morning to say that just before he left Paris Colonel House insistently urged him to return to Paris after he had straightened his affairs out here in the United States, in order that our Peace Commissioners might have the benefit of conference with him, particularly about African questions. Dr. Moton is willing to go to Paris again, but does not desire to go unless he can be of real service, and apparently he is a little fearful lest the suggestion of Colonel House was a bit generous and cordial, rather than the result of carefully matured plans. He asks me to find out from you whether you desire him to return to France, and says that perhaps you would prefer to wait until you get to Paris where, if you find him needed, you can telegraph me and he will respond to any call from you. If, on the other hand, you think it better for him to go at once, he will of course do as you wish.

Respectfully yours,   Newton D. Baker

TLS (E. M. House Papers, CtY).

From William Cox Redfield

My dear Mr. President: Washington February 28, 1919.

I have received from the Acting Food Administrator copy of his letter to you of the 27th instant. As respects what is therein said about my statement being misleading, etc., I will only say that the letter thus criticized was dictated in the presence of the Acting Chairman of the War Trade Board, who was present throughout the interview with the Food Administrator and was approved by him, the Acting Chairman of the War Trade Board, as representing the facts.

The only matter urged upon me and upon Mr. C. M. Woolley at that interview was that your authority be given. Indeed Judge Glasgow[1] went so far as, in Mr. Woolley's presence, to ask that I include in the letter to you a request that price restrictions be taken off the other commodities on which they are now maintained as well as off pork products.

Allow me two further suggestions to show the gravity of this matter:

(1) The Chairman of the Industrial Board, appointed with your approval, Mr. G. N. Peek, who was specially released by Mr. Baruch for this work, is now in conference with the steel industry in New York. He telephoned last night that if it would be possible to get favorable advice that the pork prices would be discontinued, it would have more weight in getting a satisfactory settlement with the steel industry than anything he could put forth. The one serious obstacle to a general reduction in the price of steel is the fact of the inconsistency of the government asking industry to make such sacrifices when it insists on holding up high prices on commodities which it, the government, controls.

I am sure the one general obstacle to a reduction of industrial prices today is this maintenance of food prices by the government.

(2) Consider, also, that the government had placed orders with over ten thousand manufacturers without any contracts giving the right to cancel them. On these orders manufacturers had invested largely, supposing, of course, that orders placed without qualification would be completed. Two days after the armistice, on a ruling by the Comptroller of the Treasury, these ten thousand or more contracts were stopped without notice. The Acting Chairman of the War Trade Board, himself a sufferer from these conditions, points out that these thousands of manufacturers accepted the situation without demur, save for such action as would secure for them what might actually be found to be due, believing that the necessities of the country should have supreme weight over any

moral obligation due them and any moral claim on their part against the country.

How can we make fish of industry and fowl of agriculture? Why is not the attitude taken by and toward one the proper attitude by and toward the other?

Yours very truly,   William C Redfield

TLS (WP, DLC).

[1] That is, William Anderson Glasgow, Jr., counsel for the Food Administration.

From Dudley Field Malone

Personal and Immediate.

Dear Mr. President: New York February 28, 1919.

Your fight for a two-thirds vote in the United States Senate to support the League of Nations has, it seems to me, reached a critical stage and every liberal element in the country seems necessary for victory. That you have sometimes found my political judgment sound in the past, alone prompts me respectfully to offer it now.

We all know why Republican Senators, reactionaries of both parties and bourgeois "Americans" are opposed to your leadership and the League of Nations. But just returning from abroad, you may not as clearly realize why powerful radical groups throughout the country are opposing you and the League of Nations. From my sources of information, radicals are opposing the League of Nations chiefly because they fear its combined power may be invoked to prevent the masses of a country from rising in revolution to change unresponsive institutions or Governments. Many radical groups in the United States who supported you in 1916 are opposed to your leadership now because the Government and its agents continue to act as if we were still at war. You *may* be able to convert radical support to the League of Nations by overcoming such objections; you *can* win radical support to your leadership now by a bold and generous stroke. Therefore, I respectfully suggest that before you sail for Europe next Wednesday, if it be possible, you publicly proclaim substantially the following program:

(1) Announce that you will urge upon the new Congress the repeal of the Espionage Law. It is no longer needed, Mr. President, and its enforcement, with continued prosecutions and continued acquittals, as in the recent case of Professor Scott Nearing,[1] is causing profound unrest among the poor and the working classes. When men like Nearing are prosecuted and men like James M.

Beck[2] not even indicted, the seeds of Bolshevism are freely sown. Have the new Attorney General Mitchell Palmer drop all political cases from the Court Calendars.

(2) Order the Post Office Department to cease all war-time interference with publications.

(3) Proclaim a general amnesty of *all* political prisoners. Such a generous measure is urged today in England by citizens like C. P. Scott, Editor of the Manchester Guardian, John Galsworthy and Arnold Bennett, John Burns and all the great men and women labor leaders, Viscount Bryce, Viscount Morley, and a host of others. Do proclaim this measure first for our country. This will open the steam valves so that the machinery of reconstruction may run more smoothly in the complete restoration of a free press and free speech.

(4) Urge all public and police officials, federal, state and municipal, to cease over-zealous interference throughout the country with public meetings. Do remind the nation of the right of public assembly. Most of the officials throughout the country, instead of realizing that there are deep-laid economic and political reasons for unrest, are engaged in arresting agitators who are merely speaking the grievances of the unrest.

Mr. President, if you will publicly proclaim this program now, you will, I am confident, win enthusiastic support from radicals the world over, and here at home you will win a force great and militant enough to crush the opposition to the League of Nations.

Yours respectfully,   Dudley Field Malone.

TLS (WP, DLC).

[1] Nearing, then the chairman of the radically pacifist People's Council of America for Democracy and Peace and a lecturer at the Rand School of Social Science in New York, had been indicted in April 1918, together with the American Socialist Society, which operated the Rand School, for allegedly violating Section 3 of the Espionage Act. They were charged with conspiring and attempting to cause insubordination, disloyalty, and mutiny in the armed forces of the United States and with conspiring and attempting to obstruct the draft by writing and publishing, respectively, a socialist antiwar pamphlet entitled *The Great Madness*. Nearing and the American Socialist Society were tried jointly in the Federal District Court for the Southern District of New York from February 5 to 19, 1919. During the trial, the charges of conspiracy were dropped, and Nearing was acquitted on the remaining two counts. However, the American Socialist Society was found guilty for publishing and circulating the pamphlet and was fined $3,000. See The Rand School of Social Science, *The Trial of Scott Nearing and the American Socialist Society* (New York, 1919), and Scott Nearing, *The Making of a Radical: A Political Autobiography* (New York, Evanston, San Francisco, and London, 1972), pp. 115-20.

[2] That is, James Montgomery Beck, former Assistant Attorney General (1900-1903), a conservative critic of the Wilson administration and its war policy. See Morton Keller, *In Defense of Yesterday: James M. Beck and the Politics of Conservatism, 1861-1936* (New York, 1958).

From Alexander Mitchell Palmer

My dear Mr. President: Washington, D. C. February 28, 1919.

I am deeply grateful for the high honor you have done me in naming me Attorney General. This renewed evidence of your friendship and confidence is the greatest thing which has come to my life, and I shall hope—and work—to deserve and justify it.

Thanking you, I am,

Very sincerely,   A Mitchell Palmer

TLS (WP, DLC).

From Jacob McGavock Dickinson[1]

Sir: [Chicago] Feb. 28th 1919.

I have done and am doing all I can to help establish the League of Nations. The papers stated that you said in your Boston speech that the form was that proposed by the English, or words to that effect. This has been seized on by those Republican papers who are unscrupulously playing politics and by all enemies of England to arouse a sentiment against the plan.

My own interpretation was that there had been conferences and points agreed upon and that after this drafts were made and that the English draft, embodying the result of the conferences was the one accepted. If that should be true or anything like it, or if there are any other facts which would overcome the impression now being made that the English have dictated the plan, I respectfully suggest that you give to the public an early statement on the subject. It is having a tremendous effect here and ought to be overcome, if possible. I would not take the liberty of writing to you except for my own interest in trying to sustain the work you are doing.

Respectfully,   [Jacob M. Dickinson]

CCL (J. M. Dickinson Papers, T).
[1] Secretary of War, 1909-1911; prominent lawyer of Nashville, Tennessee (1874-1899), and then of Chicago; at this time, vice-president of the American Society of International Law.

From the Diary of Dr. Grayson

Saturday, March 1, 1919.

The President today conferred with a number of newly appointed members of the Diplomatic Corps, and spent the remainder of his time working at his desk.

A Statement

[*March 1, 1919*]

A White House Denial.

Washington, March 1. (Associated Press.)—In regard to published reports that President Wilson told Democratic Committeemen who lunched with him yesterday that he would not accept nomination for a third term, it was stated today at the White House that the subject of President Wilson again being a candidate was not mentioned. It was explained that the President merely remarked to his guests that he yearned to get back to writing and that he had in contemplation the compiling of a history.

Some of those who attended the luncheon said today they gained the impression that the President meant he would retire to private life at the end of his term.

It also was stated that the President evinced deep feeling against opponents of the League of Nations. He was said to have expressed the view that the League should be an American and not a partisan issue, but that if the Republican State Committees should reject a proposal to indorse the League the Democratic State Committees then would be free to act independently.

Printed in the *New York Times*, March 2, 1919.

Two Letters to Joseph Patrick Tumulty

Dear Tumulty: The White House. 1 March, 1919.

This distresses me very much.[1] I simply cannot take the point of view of Roger Sullivan in this matter. There is a man in Illinois who is far and away superior to Lucey in qualifications and I feel that at the present juncture when the party is temporarily deprived of the confidence of the country, it would be a very serious mistake to appoint a Circuit Judge of the United States whose appointment would be known to be made in order to please Sullivan. Lucey is an able man, but his qualifications for the office do not compare with those of men who are available and who are known to the whole country for their ability, and sincerely as I should like to gratify Sullivan I cannot in conscience see my way to doing it.

The President

[1] "Dear Governor: Roger Sullivan came to me and pleaded with me to bring this letter to your attention. He said that it is the one thing that he wants and that his whole heart is set on the appointment. J.P.T." JPT to WW, Feb. 28, 1919, TL, enclosing R. C. Sullivan to WW, Feb. 17, 1919, ALS, both in WP, DLC. Roger Charles Sullivan, the Democratic boss of Chicago, called Wilson's attention to the pending appointment of a

new circuit judge for Chicago and northern Illinois, and he urged Wilson to give the post to Patrick Joseph Lucey, a lawyer of Chicago and the city's former attorney general. See also R. C. Sullivan to JPT, c. Feb. 17, 1919, ALS (WP, DLC).

Dear Tumulty: The White House. 1 March, 1919.

It is quite out of the question for me to see Mr. Brainard.[1] I wish you would tell him that I would not be at all willing to have anybody undertake to abbreviate my History or to prepare single volumes for schools and academies. Probably the house has somebody in Paris who could take these matters up with me there, but I could not in any case consent to the London programme proposed.

The President

TL (WP, DLC).
[1] Clinton Tyler Brainard, president and treasurer of Harper & Brothers and the McClure Newspaper Syndicate, president of the Herald Publishing Company and the Wheeler Newspaper Syndicate, and editor of the *Washington*, D. C., *Herald*. Brainard had told Tumulty that it was "absolutely" necessary for him to see Wilson for ten minutes. According to Brainard, Harper & Brothers could sell the duplicate plates of Wilson's ten-volume *History of the American People* to the largest London publishing house, which planned to have the work abbreviated by the "head professor" of history at the University of London into two volumes for general sale and into one volume for use in schools and academies. Moreover, Brainard had just sold the French rights to Wilson's work and had offers for the Swedish and the Spanish rights. C. T. Brainard to JPT, Feb. 28, 1919, T telegram (WP, DLC).

To Newton Diehl Baker

My dear Baker: [The White House] 1 March, 1919.

As usual, Dr. Moton, the President of Tuskegee, shows his good sense, and I am very much obliged to him for suggesting that he will await my return to Paris to get my judgment as to whether he should return to the other side of the water or not. I had had no talk with House about the matter and am entirely uninformed. I should be glad,when I get back to Paris, to send Dr. Moton an intimation of my judgment in the matter.

Cordially and faithfully yours,   Woodrow Wilson

TLS (Letterpress Books, WP, DLC).

To Edward Nash Hurley

My dear Mr. Hurley: [The White House] 1 March, 1919.

My attention has been drawn to the question of the disposition of the housing facilities created by the various agencies of the Government for war service.[1] I am afraid I do not have a very

accurate picture of the varying situations in the several Departments, but of course the Emergency Fleet Corporation has built
great numbers of houses, and in the work has sought to establish
more or less ideal industrial communities by having well-considered
plans of community development. Now that we have come to the
time when these matters are to be closed up, it would seem a distinct
loss to allow the sale of these properties without interposing such
restrictions and safeguards as will preserve the ideal industrial living conditions which we have sought to establish. As you know,
the Secretary of Labor was designated by me to carry out the housing program, and I am told that the War Department is cooperating
with the Secretary of Labor in the disposition of properties erected
by them along the lines I have here suggested. Would you not be
willing to have the Emergency Fleet Corporation also consult the
Secretary of Labor and his associates with a view to ascertaining
how far practical and beneficial restrictions could be imposed to
prevent these very modern and ideal communities from being lost
as examples of what the homes of industrial workers ought to be?
I have no very definite suggestions to make, but it would seem
clear that a uniform policy ought to prevail and that we ought, in
disposing of these properties, go as far as we can to preserve ideal
living conditions for the workers who are hereafter to occupy them.

Cordially and faithfully yours,   Woodrow Wilson

TLS (Letterpress Books, WP, DLC).
    [1] About this first federal housing project, see Roy Lubove, "Homes and 'A Few Well-
Placed Fruit Trees': An Object Lesson in Federal Housing," *Social Research*, XXVII (Jan.
1961), 469-86.

To Carter Glass

My dear Glass: [The White House] 1 March, 1919.

I am approving the suggestion contained in your letter[1] which I
return with this, and approving it without hesitation, but I assume
that this authorization will not be made public because there is a
great deal of advantage in making our loans to those governments
dependent upon their fulfillment of certain international obligations, as I am sure you also think.

Cordially and faithfully yours,   Woodrow Wilson

TLS (Letterpress Books, WP, DLC).
    [1] C. Glass to WW, Feb. 28, 1919 (first letter of that date).

To Alvan Tufts Fuller[1]

My dear Mr. Fuller: [The White House] 1 March, 1919.

Your letter of the twenty-seventh of February has interested and gratified me very much.[2] I feel as you do about the project to sink the German ships. It seems to me like the counsel of those who do not know what else to do. But I have not yet had the opportunity to discuss it with any authoritative naval men, and therefore do not like to form a final judgment about it without hearing them. I shall take it up when I get back to Paris and shall not forget that your judgment coincides with my own present conclusion.

You are very generous in your personal message and I appreciate it most deeply. Your confidence in what I am trying to do gives me the most delightful reassurance.

Cordially yours,   Woodrow Wilson

TLS (Letterpress Books, WP, DLC).
  [1] Republican representative from Massachusetts. He was Governor of Massachusetts when Nicola Sacco and Bartolomeo Vanzetti were executed on August 23, 1927.
  [2] A. T. Fuller to WW, Feb. 27, 1919, TLS (WP, DLC).

To Josephus Daniels

My dear Daniels: The White House 1 March, 1919.

I must say I cannot quite understand this policy that Benson is proposing[1] and shall have to wait until I get to Paris to learn more about it. What is your impression, I wonder?

In haste,   Faithfully yours,   Woodrow Wilson

TLS (J. Daniels Papers, DLC).
  [1] See W. S. Benson to WW, with Enclosure, Jan. 31, 1919, Vol. 54.

To William Cox Redfield

My dear Mr. Secretary: [The White House] 1 March, 1919.

I had an interview the other evening with the Secretary of Agriculture about the pork prices, and he kindly undertook to have a fresh consultation with the War Trade Board and the Food Administration, in order to come to a final decision and adjustment, and I hope the thing will be worked out, as far as it can be consistently with the obligations of the government, in this troublesome matter.

Cordially and sincerely yours,   Woodrow Wilson

TLS (Letterpress Books, WP, DLC).

Thomas Watt Gregory to Joseph Patrick Tumulty

My dear Mr. Tumulty: Washington, D. C. March 1, 1919.

I acknowledge receipt of yours of the 28th,[1] enclosing copy of a letter addressed to the President by Mr. John P. Gavit, bearing the date of the 24th.[2] You ask for my opinion in regard to Mr. Gavit's suggestion that the President "declare immediate and unconditional amnesty for all those persons who have been convicted for expression of opinion."

This Department has taken every precaution against prosecuting people for mere expressions of opinion. There is a great difference between prosecuting men for opinions and prosecuting them for making assertions or taking action intended to cause interference with the prosecution of the war in a manner forbidden by law.

After your memorandum was sent me, but before I received it, I had discussed this whole situation fully with the President. I am sending him a letter[3] expressing my views fully on this subject and indicating the procedure which I have been following with respect to certain of the cases complained of. The letter referred to will, I think, apprize you fully of my views.

                         Respectfully,   T. W. Gregory

TLS (WP, DLC).
  [1] JPT to TWG, Feb. 28, 1919, CCL (WP, DLC).
  [2] It is printed as an Enclosure with WW to JPT, Feb. 25, 1919.
  [3] Printed as Enclosure II with the following document.

From Joseph Patrick Tumulty, with Enclosures

My dear Governor: The White House 1 March 1919.

You asked my opinion with reference to Mr. Gavit's suggestion that you declare an immediate and unconditional amnesty for all persons convicted under the Espionage Act.[1] I conferred with the Attorney General regarding it because you thought whatever action you would take should have his approval and support; and I am in receipt today of a letter from the Attorney General which is attached hereunto, also certain warrants of commutation in the cases of thirty or forty prisoners.

I do not believe that in the hurry and bustle of things here at this time you ought to accept the policy outlined in the Attorney General's letter as final because once it is announced, it would look like weakness to change it. The Attorney General says in his letter that "there naturally have been some cases in which the evidence of wilful intent was indirect or circumstantial in character and that in close cases of this type injustice resulted to certain defendants because of the all-prevalent condition of intense patriotism and aroused emotions on the part of jurors." I do not know whether the cases he has sent to you for commutation are of this kind, but if they are, surely there ought to be not a commutation but a pardon.

In looking through the warrants you will find that they are simply reductions of sentences—in many cases the reductions are not at all considerable. I think it would be much better if you would keep in mind the idea of a general amnesty and not foreclose yourself from acting along a different line by taking precipitate action with reference to the policy set up by the Attorney General. The Attorney General is insistent that publicity be given to this letter today. If we do this, the country will construe the act as yours. Remember, my dear Governor, that in all these cases the Attorney General's office was really the prosecuting attorney and without taking issue with Mr. Gregory or the officers of his Department, they always feel that the proper thing to do is to insist upon the carrying out of the sentences of the court.

If you could do it without hurting Mr. Gregory's feelings, my suggestion would be that you write the Attorney General, telling him of your desire that these cases be investigated to find out if any of these convictions have been the result of what the Attorney General calls "animated patriotism and aroused emotions on the part of jurors." There ought to be some big man in the country whom the Attorney General could select for this work who could cooperate with his Department and make recommendations to you upon which you could safely base a policy in this matter.

Sincerely yours,   [J. P. Tumulty]

TL (J. P. Tumulty Papers, DLC).
    [1] See WW to JPT, Feb. 25, 1919.

E N C L O S U R E   I

From Thomas Watt Gregory

My dear Mr. President: Washington, D. C. March 1, 1919.

The annexed letter, in which I state my views on the subject of granting amnesty to so-called "political prisoners," outlines a policy for dealing with cases of conviction under the Espionage Law on which I have been proceeding for some time past.

You will recall my conversation with you on this subject prior to your going abroad.

If you see no objection, I would like very much to make public this afternoon a copy of the letter addressed to you. I will telephone Mr. Tumulty later in the day asking for your view on this request.

Respectfully,   T. W. Gregory

From Thomas Watt Gregory

My dear Mr. President: Washington, D. C. March 1, 1919.

During the past month I have received a number of communications from individuals referring to the administration of the so-called Espionage Law and demanding that I recommend a general amnesty for all persons convicted thereunder,—whom the writers of these communications describe as "political prisoners." There has also been some agitation by the press in certain quarters, making in substance the same demand.

The persons convicted and sentenced for a violation of this statute are in no sense "political prisoners," and they have not been convicted for *mere expression of opinion*. All of them have been convicted upon a trial by jury of a wilful violation of a law whose sole aim was to prevent deliberate obstruction to the prosecution of the war. The statute under which they were convicted required in every instance that proof be made of their wilfulness and of an evil intent to hinder this country in the conduct of the war; and the assertion that, as a class, these defendants are "political prisoners" is one which cannot be sustained. I cannot recommend an indiscriminate pardon of these persons.

There naturally have been some cases in which the evidence of wilful intent was indirect or circumstantial in character, and it has happened that in close cases of this type injustice resulted to certain defendants because of the all-prevalent condition of intense patriotism and aroused emotions on the part of jurors. By repeated instructions to the prosecuting officers I sought to safeguard the rights of defendants against this danger, and the members of the Federal Judiciary with substantial unanimity endeavored to protect defendants from the ill results of any such conditions. That injustice did result in certain cases of this type must be conceded:—it could hardly be otherwise. For the same reasons it is apparent that in certain individual cases the severity of the sentence imposed would sometimes be out of proportion to the intrinsic character of the offense committed.

Having these considerations in mind, some three months ago I caused a review to be instituted by several of my most trusted assistants of all cases in which men have been convicted under the Espionage Law or other so-called War Statutes. In making this review we have borne in mind the necessity for correcting any mistakes such as I have described, as well as the danger of interfering arbitrarily with that administration of the law for which our civil courts have deserved such high praise during the critical days of war.

The result of this careful analysis and review of each individual case satisfies me that in most cases of conviction substantial justice was done defendants by the conduct of the trial, the character of the evidence and the sentences imposed. In other cases, however, I am satisfied that the ends of justice do not now require that the sentences imposed by the court during the war need be enforced with full severity.

I, therefore, have the honor to submit herewith warrants of commutation embodying my recommendations to you for the exercise of executive clemency to the extent indicated in each particular case. The work of reviewing all convictions has not been completed, and I shall later take the liberty of submitting recommendations in some of the remaining cases.

The same practice of careful scrutiny and analysis is being followed out with respect to all cases now pending under the Espionage Act, in order that, so far as possible, only those cases shall be prosecuted which have substantial merit and are clearly prima facie violations of law.   Respectfully,   T. W. Gregory

TLS (WP, DLC).

ENCLOSURE   III

From Joseph Patrick Tumulty

Dear Governor: The White House. March 1, 1919

Since I talked with you about the attached, the Attorney General told me there was a Supreme Court decision coming down in these matters on Monday, next.[1] He said it would be advantageous to get his letter out before the decision was made public, and if you agree and will sign the attached warrants, I will notify the Attorney General, so that he can give out his letter tonight.[2]   J.P.T.

TL (WP, DLC).
[1] *Schenck v. United States* (249 U.S. 47), the first of six major cases involving convictions under the Espionage Act which reached the Supreme Court in the immediate postwar period. Charles T. Schenck, the general secretary of the Socialist party in Philadelphia, had been found guilty of conspiring to violate the Espionage Act, of attempting to cause insubordination, disloyalty, and mutiny in the armed forces of the United States, and of obstructing the draft by printing and distributing 15,000 antiwar leaflets. These leaflets, which were mailed to men accepted for the draft, declared conscription to be unconstitutional despotism, urged their readers to challenge this alleged threat to American liberty, and exhorted them to assert their rights and to strike down all "militarism" by joining the Socialist party in its campaign for a repeal of the draft. Schenck had appealed his conviction on the ground that the Espionage Act was unconstitutional and violated the right of free speech guaranteed by the First Amend-

ment. However, the Supreme Court unanimously upheld the constitutionality of the
Espionage Act and affirmed the verdicts of the lower courts. Moreover, in delivering
the opinion of the Supreme Court, Justice Oliver Wendell Holmes, Jr., took the opportunity to define, for the first time, the true scope of the First Amendment as it related
to political expression. Promulgating his famous "clear and present danger" test for free
speech, Holmes wrote: "The character of every act depends upon the circumstances in
which it is done. . . . The question in every case is whether the words used are used in
such circumstances and are of such a nature as to create a clear and present danger
that they will bring about the substantive evils that Congress has a right to prevent. It
is a question of proximity and degree. When a nation is at war many things that might
be said in time of peace are such a hindrance to its effort that their utterance will not
be endured so long as men fight and that no Court could regard them as protected by
any constitutional right." For a detailed discussion of the Schenck case, see Fred D.
Ragan, "Justice Oliver Wendell Holmes, Jr., Zechariah Chafee, Jr., and the Clear and
Present Danger Test for Free Speech: The First Year, 1919," *Journal of American History*,
LVIII (June 1971), 24-45; Zechariah Chafee, Jr., *Free Speech in the United States* (Cambridge,
Mass., 1941), pp. 80-82; and, most particularly, David M. Rabban, "The Emergence of
Modern First Amendment Doctrine," *University of Chicago Law Review*, L (Fall 1983),
1207-1355.
    [2] A Hw note on this letter reads: "Warrants signed & returned to Justice." Gregory's letter
was published, e.g., in the *Official Bulletin*, III (March 3, 1919), 3.

Two Letters from Joseph Patrick Tumulty

Dear Governor: The White House 1 March 1919.

You have been so busy during the past few days that you have
not been able, I think, to give sufficient thought to the importance
of the request to receive a delegation to present a resolution with
reference to Ireland's cause.

Your attitude in this matter is fraught with a great deal of danger
both to the Democratic party and to the cause you represent.

During the past few days men of all races have come to me,
urging me to request you to see this committee. Republicans are
taking full advantage of this, and will use every means to embarrass
you in this matter. You know that I am not a professional Irishman
but your refusal to see this delegation will simply strengthen the
Sinn Fein movement in this country.

                              Sincerely yours,   [J. P. Tumulty]

CCL (J. P. Tumulty Papers, DLC).

Dear Governor: [The White House, c. March 1, 1919]

My suggestion is that you see this delegation[1] in one of the reception rooms at the Metropolitan Opera House after your speech
there. I am sure it could be handled without embarrassment.

                              The Secretary

Okeh W.W.

TL (J. P. Tumulty Papers, DLC).
    [1] About this delegation and Wilson's meeting with them, see the extract from the
Grayson Diary and the news report, both printed at March 4, 1919.

Two Telegrams from Edward Mandell House

Paris (March 1, 1919)

Number 12. After receiving your number one[1] I got in communication with Lloyd George by telephone. He thinks that it is essential for you to come directly to Paris as soon as possible. His difficulties with the coal miners and other laborers culminates [culminate] around the 24th or 25th of March, and it will be necessary for him to return to England by then. If you arrive in Paris by the 13th or 14th we both believe it may be possible to settle the preliminaries of peace terms with Germany by the 23rd and name a day for the regular peace congress in which the Central Powers are to participate. I have April 2nd tentatively in mind for the assembling of the congress. The preliminary peace terms for Austria should also be ready early in April. The Brussels trip can be taken during the interim between the calling of the peace Congress and its date of assembling. I am glad you are not bringing your servants, the French government are holding those you had at the Hotel Murat intact for you.   Edward House.

[1] WW to EMH, Feb. 28, 1919.

Paris March 1, 1919.

No. 13. The French Minister of Finance has agreed to giving Belgium priority on five hundred millions provided the British will assent to the principle that valuables or their equivalent stolen from the allied countries should also have priority. I shall take the matter up with the British in a few days.   Edward House.

T telegrams (WP, DLC).

From David Rowland Francis

My dear Mr. President: Washington March 1, 1919.

Since you will not have time to receive me before your departure I write to thank you for the delightful voyage from Brest to Boston and thence to Washington, and for your many courtesies.

I am the guest of the Assistant Secretary of State, Mr. Breckinridge Long, 2829 Sixteenth Street, North West. I shall remain in Washington until noon Wednesday when I go to White Sulphur Springs where Mrs. Francis has promised to meet me; after several weeks sojourning there for rest and recuperation I shall go to Saint Louis for a short visit, having been granted a sixty-day leave of absence from February 14th. If in the meantime, however, my services are required in France, or in Russia, or in any part of Europe, or if I can serve you in any way, please command me.

I had hoped to receive a message from you concerning the plan of the Allied Missions being sent back to Petrograd to reoccupy their domiciles. The morning papers quote Doctor Andre Tardieu, one of the French delegates to the Peace Conference, as saying that the Prinkipo meeting has been dropped. You will recall that I suggested that the investigation be transferred from Prinkipo to Petrograd and be fixed for some date subsequent to the arrival there of the Allied Missions.[1]

I still think it would be possible to have thirty or forty thousand English and thirty or forty thousand French troops to volunteer to go to Petrograd in company with fifty thousand American soldiers. Today's dispatches state that Bolshevism is again raising its head in Germany; I am pleased to see that we are taking firm steps toward preventing it from making any headway in this country.[2]

I can be reached through the State Department and can be in Washington twelve hours after receiving instructions to come.

I have the honor to be, Sir,

Your obedient servant.   David R. Francis

TLS (WP, DLC).
[1] About Francis' interview with Wilson, see D. R. Francis to RL *et al.*, Feb. 23, 1919.
[2] Francis was probably referring, in particular, to the inquiry by a subcommittee of the Senate Judiciary Committee into Bolshevik propaganda activities in the United States, about which see n. 2 to the news report printed at Feb. 27, 1919.

From Frank Lyon Polk

My dear Mr. President: Washington March 1, 1919.

Mr. Lansing told me last Fall he had a conversation with you August 30, 1918 on the subject of Siberia and you then said you would provide funds for the maintenance of the Russian Railway Service Corps when the Russian funds set aside for that purpose were exhausted.[1]

The Russian funds in question are now altogether expended and the need for additional funds presses. I have an urgent telegram from Mr. Stevens asking for $75,000 for the maintenance and upkeep of the Corps in Siberia and am also informed by the Russian Embassy that the salary payroll due March first and monthly thereafter—on the existing basis of organization—will amount to $42,000.

I shall be glad to know what measures you wish to be taken in order to make the above funds immediately available to the Russian

Chargé d'Affaires[2] so that he can provide for the payment of salaries due March first and also forward at once to Mr. Stevens the $75,000 necessary to meet expenses in Siberia.

Until other arrangements may be made by the inter-Allied Committee, which will supervise the Siberian Railways, I shall also be grateful to know how you would like further calls for funds for this purpose to be met.

The actual expenses of the Russian Railway Service Corps during the seventeen months of its existence have averaged about $80,000 a month, about equally divided between monthly salaries and occasional allocations of $75,000 every few months for maintenance and upkeep in Siberia.

You will recall that when we asked the Secretary to confer with you in Paris as to the necessity of securing an emergency fund for Mr. Stevens to start operations under the plan to supervise the Siberian Railways, it was pointed out that the two purposes for which such a fund would be imperatively needed were, first, to pay Russian railway employees arrears of wages now long over due and to provide for payment of wages and salaries in the immediate future; and second, to purchase needed equipment. You then authorized Mr. McCormick to have the War Trade Board, Russian Bureau, Incorporated, advance for that purpose a sum up to $1,000,000 to Mr. Stevens, provided Japan did not object; but this authorization would not cover the maintenance of the Russian Railway Service Corps. Advances for the Corps from the current National Security and Defense Fund will be available only up to July 1, 1919.   Faithfully yours,   Frank L Polk

TLS (SDR, RG 59, 861.77/735d, DNA).
    [1] See RL to WW, Aug. 30, 1918, Vol. 49.
    [2] Serge Ughet, Financial Attaché and Director of Supplies of the Russian embassy; Chargé d'Affairs ad interim since December 3, 1918.

From Frank Lyon Polk, with Enclosure

Dear Mr. President: Washington March 1, 1919.

I look for very serious and increasing foreign and domestic pressure upon the Administration for some action in regard to Mexico.

The Mexican question is being agitated in Congress[1] and out, and the Department is in constant receipt of complaints on account of the exactions of the Carranza Government, its failure to protect the lives and property of foreigners; its seizure and retention of foreign banks and public utilities; its absolute neglect of its obligations and debt, and its general incompetence and unfriendly and unfair attitude to legitimate foreign interests.

As you will not have time during your visit to devote to this subject, I enclose a memorandum prepared by Ambassador Fletcher, showing the present state of Mexico, which I hope you may find time to read on your way back to Europe, and let me have your views.

Yours sincerely,   Frank L Polk

[1] This "agitation" in Congress manifested itself, above all, in the introduction of various resolutions concerning the Mexican situation. For example, on December 30, 1918, Senator William Henry King of Utah introduced a resolution (S. Res. 399), which directed the Secretary of State to report to the Senate whether the claims for damages suffered by American citizens in Mexico had been presented to the Mexican government and what steps had been taken to prosecute those claims. A resolution introduced by Senator Ashurst on January 2, 1919 (S. J. Res. 206), directed the Secretary of War to investigate and determine upon claims of American citizens for damages inflicted by "outlaw, revolutionary, insurgent, or Federal forces" in Mexico since December 1, 1912. On February 11, 1919, Senator Lewis introduced a further resolution (S. Res. 449). It called on the Senate Foreign Relations Committee to ascertain from the State Department whether the charges by American citizens against the Mexican government were true and to recommend to the Senate a course which the United States Government should pursue to assure the safety of lives and property of Americans in Mexico. Finally, on March 1, 1919, Norman Judd Gould, a Republican representative from New York, introduced a resolution in the House (H. Res. 618) which requested "full information" about the situation in Mexico. Except for S. Res. 399, which the Senate adopted unanimously on February 7, 1919, these resolutions never emerged from the respective committees to which they were referred. *Cong. Record*, 65th Cong., 3d sess., pp. 927, 932, 2898, 3115, 4809.

E N C L O S U R E

From Henry Prather Fletcher

CONFIDENTIAL MEMORANDUM

Dear Mr. President: [Mexico City] March 1, 1919.

At the direction of the Acting Secretary of State I beg to submit the following observations on the present state of Mexico:

The present Government is in practical, if not unchallenged, control of the country. It controls all ports of entry, and performs more or less completely the ordinary governmental functions throughout the Republic. In certain sections, however, its authority is still resisted, notably in the State of Morelos, parts of Oaxoca [Oaxaca], Vera Cruz, Guerrero and Michaocan [Michoacán]. Villa is still at large in Chihuahua and a disturbing element.

The rebels and bandits have no common leadership, plans or aims, except the embarrassment and attrition of the Carranza Government. They hold no large towns. Their activities, however, make many districts unsafe and compel the Mexican Government to expend over 80 per cent of its entire revenue in "pacification." This work of pacification has made little real progress in the past two years. Many believe that the generals in command of the various disturbed zones do not really desire, even if they could accomplish, a restoration of peace and order, because under present conditions each has great prestige and power in his district with large sums of money to spend and even misappropriate. The habits of the people have been profoundly affected by seven years of internal war and revolution, and the country under present methods will not soon settle down to peaceful pursuits.

This condition works against the resumption of industrial, mining and agricultural work. In many districts work is carried on under constant menace, tribute has to be paid to and immunity bought from the local insurgent chief and the regular greatly increased taxes paid to the Carranza Government, both state and national.

The spirit of the Revolution, of the Constitution, and of the Government is intensely, archaically nationalistic. The ordinary rights and interests of foreigners, and especially Americans, are treated by officials everywhere rather as privileges, and our representations in their behalf are heeded grudgingly—if at all, and this applies as generally to the individual American planter or small company as to the great corporation. Fifteen or sixteen Americans have been killed in the Tampico district alone since I took charge of the Embassy. The policy of "Mexico for the Mexicans," which attracts a natural support and sympathy from all fair minded people, can not be realized with the rapidity now being attempted.

Article 27[1] of the New Constitution practically closes the door to future foreign investments and threatens those already made in the country. This would be of little importance if Mexico and the Mexicans were able to keep themselves and their country going, and make it financially and economically independent. I do not see that they can. They have not the genius of industrial development, nor have they had the training required. The internal and external credit of Mexico has been destroyed by the Carranza revolution. The internal credit was destroyed by financing the revolution on paper money and immediately repudiating it, by seizing and retaining railway and other public utility properties, and by taking over the banks and appropriating their reserves. That the Carranza Government has no internal credit is proved by the fact that over a year ago it made the most strenuous efforts to raise a domestic loan by popular subscription, on patriotic grounds,—it failed dismally and completely. The attempt to establish a government bank has also so far failed.

Its foreign credit has been destroyed by its hostile attitude toward

[1] That is, the provision which vested ownership of all mineral and oil subsoil rights in the Mexican people. For Carranza's decree implementing Article XXVII, see n. 5 to the Enclosure printed with RL to WW, April 15, 1918, Vol. 47.

all foreign interests operating in Mexico, its failure to pay a cent of interest on its bonds, both state and national since 1914.

Carranza is virtually dictator. Public opinion is non-existent or voiceless. The last Congress elected was selected. The administration, including the courts, may not be more corrupt than in the days of Diaz, but I am informed and believe, is not less so. Carranza I believe to be honest. Most of his lieutenants now about him I believe to be dishonest and incompetent.

Carranza and his party were at heart pro-German and entirely out of sympathy with our ideals and struggle. Neutrality was maintained from fear rather than desire, and the triumph of Germany would have been celebrated as a revenge for '48 and the removal of the Yankee menace, and American and English methods, capital and influence generally would have been substituted by German if possible.

When you spoke in the White House last June to a group of Mexican newspaper men,[2] Carranza and the Mexican Government made no response, except to order all the newspapers in Mexico to publish in large type our Government's note of protest against confiscating American owned petroleum lands.[3] Nor could I personally secure from Carranza any corresponding expression of friendly feeling. His only reply to my question as to what he thought of your friendly speech was "Let us hope his words will be confirmed by deeds."[4]

I speak of these things at tiring length, not to create prejudice in your mind, but to show the atmosphere and spirit in Mexico so that you can judge how any suggestions or attempts at friendly counsel or assistance are likely to be received.

The attitude of the Mexican Government toward a League of Nations will be governed entirely by selfish considerations. If it may prove a shield of defense of its national rights as a weak nation, and at the same time a wall behind which it may escape from performance of its national or international duties, it will be supported. If it carries the possibility of foreign interference or assistance it may be resisted.

The present national debt of Mexico is estimated at about $350,000,000 guaranteed by the Central Government. The railways which were financed by foreign capital are also bankrupt and in need of reorganization, and refinancing. Practically all of them have been taken over and are being operated by the Government. The receipts are covered into the Government Treasury and no com-

---

[2] Wilson's remarks are printed at June 7, 1918, Vol. 48.
[3] For the text of this note and for related documents, see *FR 1918*, pp. 704-16.
[4] About Fletcher's interview with Carranza of June 12, 1918, see H. P. Fletcher to RL, June 12, 1918, *ibid.*, p. 580.

pensation for their use nor interest on their securities has been paid. This is also true of the Canadian-owned tram lines of Mexico City, and the Wells Fargo Express Company (American). The railways in the south and east are constantly attacked by bandits, and the Vera Cruz-Mexico City line is unsafe.

The present status of the petroleum question is that the decrees based on Article 27 of the Constitution, have not been enforced. The cases contesting the law are in the Courts. It is President Carranza's intention to submit the whole subject to a special session of Congress to be called in April or May. As a result of the firm stand of our Government and protracted negotiations between representatives of the petroleum companies and the Mexican Government, Mr. Carranza has promised to recommend to Congress a partial recognition by Congress of their rights, but the terms by which these rights shall be recognized in the bill are not sufficiently broad to cover, in the opinion of the oil companies, their rights legally and honestly acquired previous to the promulgation of the new Constitution.

Mr. Carranza has sent an agent to the United States[5] to sound out the financial interests as to a refunding of the national debt of Mexico. This agent has no powers to negotiate however, and no serious consideration can be given to the matter until Mr. Carranza shows some tangible interest in this question. As long as he will be allowed to go as in the past, the debt will not greatly concern him nor will the foreign owned properties which he has seized be returned.

The crux of the situation is the restoration of law and order; this besides stopping the enormous drain on the treasury will enable Mexico to enter the paths of production. Carranza claims he can pacify the country if given arms and ammunition, but I believe it will take him a long time, if indeed he can do it at all completely.

Carranza has issued a formal proclamation that he will not stand for re-election after his present term expires on December 1, 1920. He would prefer to leave office, without contracting a loan and will, I think, only consent to such a refunding of the Mexican debt as will not increase its present amount. In other words, if the bondholders will accept, say fifty cents on the dollar in new bonds, some arrangement may be made. Otherwise the adjustment will probably be left to his successor.

[5] Rafael Nieto, the Mexican Undersecretary of the Treasury and Acting Minister of Finance, had arrived in New York during the first week of February to confer with American bankers about the possibility of a loan to Mexico. About Nieto's mission, see the *New York Times*, Jan. 23, Feb. 7, 11, and 25, and March 5, 20, and 21, 1919. See also Robert Freeman Smith, *The United States and Revolutionary Nationalism in Mexico, 1916-1932* (Chicago and London, 1972), pp. 131-32.

The foreign claims for damage suffered during the disturbances of the past eight years amount to many millions. The Mexican Government has appointed a Claims Commission to pass upon them. But so far nothing has been done, nor can much be done before the end of Carranza's term. The payment of these will also be left to his successor.

The attitude of the Carranza Government is not distinguished by a desire for closer relations with the United States. No advance made by you or the Government to give Mexico special consideration has been met in a friendly spirit. Carranza considers himself the bulwark of Latin America vis-a-vis the United States, and would prefer to finish his term without particular improvement in our relations.

From present indications, without external pressure to put his house in order, he can probably finish his term, and the day of reckoning may be postponed. But no real nor substantial improvement in the situation may be looked for. Foreign interests will be subjected to threats and embarrassment and obstruction, and in many cases confiscation; life and property will continue unsafe; over 80 per cent of the revenue will be devoted to a "pacification" which fails to pacify, and little or nothing will be done to restore the internal and external credit of the country and put Mexico in her proper place in the family of nations.

Two courses are open.

First: To let matters drift in their present unsatisfactory condition, and to confront the clamor at home and abroad.

Second: To call upon the recognized Government of Mexico to perform its duties as a government internally and externally, or to confess its inability so to do and accept disinterested assistance from the United States or of an international commission to restore order and credit.

Mexico can be quickly restored if peace is established, and the government honestly and efficiently administered.

I have the honor to attach copy of a letter addressed to me by Consul General Chamberlain on this general subject,[6] with especial reference to our commercial position in Mexico.

Sincerely yours,   Henry P. Fletcher

TLS (SDR, RG 59, 812.00/23111a, DNA).
  [6] George Agnew Chamberlain, Consul General in Mexico City, to H. P. Fletcher, March 1, 1919, TLS (SDR, RG 59, 812.00/23111a, DNA).

From Frank Lyon Polk

My dear Mr. President: Washington March 1, 1919.

The Norwegian Minister,[1] I understand, has an appointment with you this afternoon for the purpose of discussing a settlement for the Norwegian ships being built in this country and taken by the Shipping Board at the outbreak of the war.

You will probably remember that you asked the Attorney General to look into this question for you and make recommendation. The Attorney General gave a hearing to the representatives of the Norwegian ship-owners and the Shipping Board some time in December, and then decided it was not wise for him to render an opinion in this matter, as it would involve the question of what was reasonable compensation, and this question is one involved in a great deal of litigation now in the hands of the Department of Justice. He had a talk with me, pointed out his objections to acting in the matter, and said he would communicate with you.

It is my impression that he felt that Mr. Whipple,[2] representing the Shipping Board, was driving rather a hard bargain with the Norwegians. This also was my view of the case at that time. I understand that Mr. Whipple has made some concessions since then, but as to whether it is a fair offer of settlement or not, I am not prepared to say.

I do not know whether you would be disposed to take the matter out of the hands of the Shipping Board, but as it is a difficult question, and one to which you can at present give no time, it might be well to refer it to some one here in Washington to hold an informal arbitration, and make recommendation to you for settlement, in case the Shipping Board and the Norwegians cannot agree. I have Mr. Lane in mind. If he should be too busy, Woolley, of the War Trade Board, or some officer of the Navy, could probably dispose of the matter satisfactorily.

Yours faithfully,   Frank L Polk

TLS (WP, DLC).
[1] Helmer Halvorsen Bryn.
[2] That is, Sherman Leland Whipple, general counsel for the United States Shipping Board and the Emergency Fleet Corporation.

From William Howard Taft

Atlanta, Ga., March 1, 1919.

I thank you for your kind telegram.[1] I am glad to have the opportunity of emphasizing the transcendental importance and the non-partisan character of the issue in respect to the proposed League of Nations by speaking with you in New York next Tuesday night.

Wm. H. Taft.

T telegram (WP, DLC).
    [1] WW to W. H. Taft, Feb. 28, 1919.

From Carter Glass

Dear Mr. President: Washington March 1, 1919.

I received your brief note of February 26th with the inclosed letter of February 24th from Mr. Whitmarsh, transmitting a communication from Mr. Hoover to you concerning the control of prices by the Food Administration. I should not venture to trouble you further with the matter were it not one to which I have given the most careful consideration and one which concerns directly the administration of the Treasury.

I am satisfied that the prevailing high prices for foodstuffs and the consequent maintenance of the cost of living at the high level established during the period of active warfare not only imperil our financial and industrial fabric but carry with them the grave risk of social unrest. This was the unanimous opinion of your Cabinet, as evidenced by my cable of February 11th to you,[1] of which a copy is enclosed herewith. Also enclosed is the letter from the Director General of Railroads dated February 8, 1919, to me referred to in that cable.[2]

These food prices were fixed in war time and are the resultant of two conflicting objects—one to prevent excessive prices, the other to stimulate production. Broadly speaking, the removal of the submarine peril and the release of a vast ocean tonnage for commercial purposes have removed the necessity for artificial stimulation of production. These prices never could have been established had there not been practically an unlimited demand on the part of the Government for itself and the allies. They could not now be maintained except for the continuance of Governmental buying. That buying is only possible as the result of heavy expenditures out of the United States Treasury. So far as these expenditures are the result of direct appropriation by Congress for the Food Administration or other Governmental agencies, they are not within my control although, since I must find the means of meeting them, I cannot be indifferent to the extent of the appropriation or the use made of it. Very largely, perhaps predominantly, however, the maintenance of these prices is made possible only by the use of the proceeds of loans made by the Government of the United States to

the allies. For making these loans the sole authority and responsibility is vested in me by the Acts of Congress, subject only to your
power of veto.

It is repeatedly argued by representatives of the Food Administration that a substantial proportion of the food for which high prices
are thus exacted is paid for by the foreigners to the advantage of
Americans. Even if that were true, I could not myself find gratification in the knowledge that we were by direct Governmental action
enabling a group of our citizens to profiteer at the expense of the
needy peoples of Europe nor could I believe that such a course
would harmonize with your desire to bring peace with mercy and
justice to the world. But for practical purposes, it is utterly untrue
that foreigners are *paying* for any important portion of these foodstuffs. I have said that the maintenance of the present high prices
would not be possible without Governmental buying. For the whole
of that buying funds must be provided by the people of the United
States in taxes or loans to the Government of the United States.
For so much of the food purchased as is resold to the Governments
of the Allies we do, it is true, receive obligations of those Governments to repay to this Government the purchase price. Predominantly the buying Governments are not now those in good credit,
but are the weaker of the warring Governments and include the
Governments of the liberated peoples. The repayment of these loans
can be looked for only at a distant future date. At the present time
of trial for the American people, the high prices maintained for
foodstuffs, which must be paid for in cash out of the Treasury of
the United States, benefit only the producers of those foodstuffs,
and add just so much to the burdens which must be imposed,
directly upon the American people as a whole in taxation and in-
debtedness, and indirectly by maintaining the present exorbitantly
high cost of living.

To these vital considerations affecting the fundamental welfare
of the American people—considerations of economics and finance
concerning which it is the business of the Secretary of the Treasury
to form and express correct opinions, presented by me with the
united support of your Cabinet—Mr. Hoover, who has been absent
from the country during practically the whole period of readjustment, interposes little more by way of answer than a non possumus.
The vital welfare of the American people is to be sacrificed to the
inability of the Food Administration to devise means of unravelling
the situation which it has created.

It is not for me to suggest the particular measures which should
be adopted by the Food Administration to restore normal conditions.
The Treasury has consistently from the moment of the armistice

urged upon the Food Administration the necessity of procuring appropriate legislation to enable it to make good its obligations, legal and moral, by direct appropriation out of the Treasury instead of by the infinitely more costly and gravely injurious method which has been pursued and is still being pursued of maintaining high food prices. It is due solely to the insistence of the Treasury that, with your approval, the necessity for an appropriation to make good the wheat guaranty was submitted by the Secretary of Agriculture and the Food Administration for the consideration of this Congress. Mr. Hoover, in his message to you transmitted by Mr. Whitmarsh under date of February 24th, appears to say that it would be as a practical matter impossible to make adequate provision for making good the wheat guaranty without maintaining the high price of wheat and says that "Congress would have to make provision in advance for liquidated payment to probably fifteen million individuals in the United States." Yet the Secretary of Agriculture two months ago, on December 27th, joined with Mr. Rickard, acting for Herbert Hoover, United States Food Administrator, and Mr. Glasgow, Chairman of the Executive Board of the United States Food Administration, in submitting to the Congress a memorandum signed by them proposing legislation to enable the United States to make good the wheat guaranty for the 1919 crop. This memorandum contains the following statement:

"In order to meet the competition from Argentina and other countries, it seems apparent that our wheat of the 1919 crop, for export, must be paid for here at the guaranteed price *and perhaps sold in competition at a price considerably below the guaranteed price. If we sell export wheat at a price below the guaranteed price there would be difficulty in holding our own prople [people] to a price for flour based on the guaranteed price of wheat, even if this were desirable.*"

Pursuant to these representations of the Food Administration and the Department of Agriculture, a bill has been introduced and, with certain differences, has passed both Houses of the Congress, which appropriates the sum of $1,000,000,000 for the purpose of making good this guaranty and which expressly authorizes the sale of guaranteed wheat at less than the guaranteed price. The thing which Mr. Hoover says is impracticable in respect to wheat is precisely the thing which was contemplated by the formal joint memorandum of the Department of Agriculture and the Food Administration two months ago. What can be done and should be done in respect to wheat of the 1919 crop could have been done and should have been done with respect to the wheat of the 1918 crop. A similar course could have been and should have been pursued in respect to sugar, rice, cotton seed, and pork if and to the extent that the Food Administration is under legal or moral obligation to the producers thereof. But notwithstanding what Mr. Hoover says in his message of February 24th to you about his recognition of the necessity of lowering food prices for the consumer and of freeing the distributive trade from all control, the Food Administration has for a period of nearly four months stubbornly persisted in the opposite course.

I should not perhaps be entitled to express myself so strongly concerning this matter if it were one which concerned solely or even primarily the administration of another Department of the Government. All these matters have a vital bearing on the problem which you have entrusted to me of financing the Government during the difficult period of readjustment. Not only am I thus generally concerned with the policy of the Food Administration, but I am directly concerned in that policy because I am being placed in the unhappy position of being obliged, by making loans for which the responsibility is mine, to make possible the continuance of a policy which I totally disapprove.

The maintenance of the present high food prices would be impossible without the maintenance also by the War Trade Board, upon which the Treasury is represented, of certain embargoes, and such action by the War Trade Board constitutes, in my opinion, an abuse of its powers and in effect taxes the American people without authority of law.

Mr. Hoover says in his letter:

"I feel deeply the necessity of lowering all food prices for the consumer and of freeing the distributive trade from all control as not only a necessity for the United States but as a movement towards fundamental stability of the world."

I respectfully advise and request that you direct Mr. Hoover immediately to take active and effective steps to accomplish this result, the necessity of which he recognizes.

I am returning herewith Mr. Whitmarsh's letter to you.

Sincerely yours,   Carter Glass.

TLS (WP, DLC).
  [1] C. Glass to WW, Feb. 11, 1919, Vol. 54.
  [2] W. D. Hines to C. Glass, Feb. 8, 1919, TCL (WP, DLC).

From Edgar Rickard

Dear Mr. President: Washington March 1, 1919.

The War Trade Board at its meeting last Wednesday passed a Resolution rescinding their agreement with the Food Administration by which export pork licenses were subject to approval of the Food Administration as to prices. We have protested and the War Trade Board have postponed putting this ruling into effect until March 5th pending the expression of your views. If this action is taken it will cause us to completely abandon our regulations for the stablization of pork prices and break faith with the producers. The War Trade Board are willing to postpone any action until March 31st should you signify your desire that the Food Administration should continue carrying out its obligation until that date. We feel that any action of this kind will justly subject the Government to the criticism of having repudiated its agreement with the swine producers, and if we can maintain this stabilization until March 31st we believe we will have fulfilled our obligations. A short note to the War Trade Board of your endorsement of our position that stabilization should be continued until March 31st will be sufficient direction to the War Trade Board to make their announcement effective March 31st.   Faithfully yours,   Edgar Rickard

TLS (WP, DLC).

From Harry Augustus Garfield

Dear Mr. President: Washington, D. C. March 1, 1919.

The relation between the three great groups of coal fields in the United States,—the Atlantic group, the Middle States group and the group west of the Mississippi,—offers an opportunity for industrial readjustment at the present juncture which we cannot afford to overlook. I venture to press it upon your attention at this time because I believe you have it in your power by a simple arrangement, both to stabilize our industrial condition and to strengthen your hands in overcoming opposition to the League of Nations' program. This is the situation.

The rich coals from the Atlantic seaport press upon the coals of the Middle States group. Those coals in turn compete with the coals beyond the Mississippi. Reverse the process, furnish an outlet through export for the Atlantic coals, and the effect will be felt throughout the extent of the coal fields. In other words, the middle and western groups will be vitally interested in the export of the coals of the Atlantic group. The entire body of more than 700,000 mine-workers will find employment, and because coal will once more move freely, the wheels of industry will be set going.

South America, Italy and France, are in dire need of coal. We can furnish it. At the present time England cannot. Is it not possible to effect an amicable arrangement with Great Britain by which we shall, at any rate for the present, furnish the coal they are not able to supply?   Cordially and faithfully yours,   H. A. Garfield

TLS (WP, DLC).

From George Creel

My dear Mr. President: Paris, 1 March, 1919.

I have been trying for two weeks to get a boat home. The latest report from Admiral Benson is that I will be able to sail from Brest on March 4th. This, unfortunately, puts me in the United States after your departure.

All the domestic work of the Committee on Public Information has been closed up. All foreign work has been discontinued save the news distribution machinery with offices in New York, Paris and London.

Aside from this force, the only paid employes left will be an accountant and his assistants in a small office in Washington, who will of necessity remain until all monies are collected and the last bills paid.

I have dismissed myself from the payroll today, March first, and will make a statement to that effect immediately upon my arrival in the United States,[1] together with the announcement that the Committee on Public Information is out of business. I think this will give the necessary effect of complete severance and yet permit me to discharge the routine duties of settlement. This connection will be infrequent and inconspicuous and I am only too glad to donate the time and services that may be required.

May I now say a word to you with regard to Ireland? In my opinion, this is one of the most important questions with which you will have to deal. I know the Irish in America. They mean to unite as never before, and they will be joined by every German in the United States eager to take advantage of the opportunity to embarrass our relations with Great Britain.

Make no mistake about the Sinn Fein. It controls Ireland absolutely, with the exception of four counties in Ulster, and in two of these counties it has forty per cent. of the voting strength. All the old Home Rule leaders have been swept out of power and are absolutely discredited. The cry today is for an Irish republic. At the present time, this cry has its base in a great anger against England and is not really believed in by the conservative leaders of Sinn Fein or by the great bulk of Irish Americans.

If Lloyd-George will put through at once a Dominion Home Rule bill, with county option in Ulster, giving these counties the right to vote on coming in or staying out, I feel convinced that this plan will be accepted as a satisfactory adjustment of the situation.

If it is not done within the next two months, sentiment in Ireland and America will harden in favor of an Irish republic.

Lloyd-George blandly dismisses the whole matter by professing his entire willingness to grant any settlement that Irish leaders will agree upon. This is buncombe. Irish leaders have agreed time and again within the last four years, and every agreement has been set aside. As a consequence, no Irish leader would dare to enter into any negotiations with the English government, as it would mean his death politically and perhaps physically.

The agitation has not really started yet in the United States, but as it gains strength it will be the dominant factor in our political situation, and the determining factor in any international arrangement involving Great Britain.

Let me thank you for a support that has always been generous and an association that has been inspiring. Please count always upon my devotion.   Respectfully,   George Creel

TLS (WP, DLC).
¹ For Creel's statement of resignation, see the *New York Times*, March 12, 1919.

From Frank Morrison

My dear Mr. President: Washington, D. C. March 1, 1919.

I earnestly urge that you grant a brief hearing before your departure for France to representatives of the several groups of organized workers under the jurisdiction of the Postmaster-General, who desire to acquaint you with facts in connection with what they term the unjust, unreasonable and oppressive labor policies of Mr. Burleson.

This situation is critical, otherwise I would not add to your present weight of affairs by broaching it. There is no one else to whom we can appeal. Mr. Burleson has steadfastly persisted in his disregard of the rights of the workers under his official direction. Both Mr. Gompers and myself have repeatedly pleaded in vain with him for a more enlightened policy toward his employes. He is obdurate. Only your intervention, I believe, can relieve and correct a serious situation.

Three organized groups of workers under Mr. Burleson's jurisdiction—the telegraphers, the telephone operators and the electrical
workers—are showing signs of unrest. He has refused to adopt the
policies of other Department heads, namely, Secretary Daniels, Secretary Baker and former Secretary McAdoo and deal collectively
with his employes.

The evidence against Mr. Burleson's administration is strong. It
comes from many sources. It can not be lightly dismissed as an
isolated mistake in judgment, nor as an unfounded complaint from
a dissatisfied subordinate. He is out of harmony with your splendid
ideals and actions.

I believe that you should know all the facts and for that reason
I express the hope that you can meet personally the men authorized
to speak for the workers whose rights Postmaster-General Burleson
has ignored.[1]   Yours very truly,   Frank Morrison

TLS (WP, DLC).
[1] For a brief discussion of the origin of this controversy, see Valerie Jean Conner, *The
National War Labor Board: Stability, Social Justice, and the Voluntary State in World War
I* (Chapel Hill, N. C., 1983), pp. 163-66.

From John Nevin Sayre

My dear Mr. President: Suffern, New York March 1, 1919.

May I congratulate you on the great progress you have so far
made with the League of Nations? I am ashamed that so many in
our country should oppose it as they do, but I hope that with the
further success which you will attain in Europe and with the educational effect of your speeches in this country, the League can
be successfully set up.

There is one thing which as I see it would greatly help to rally
the laboring classes to your support. It is the granting of general
amnesty to all prisoners sentenced under the special war time legislation, such as the draft law and espionage act. There is a deep-
ening suspicion among labor circles that in many cases this war
machinery has been selfishly used by capitalistic interests to suppress and terrorize those who are active in labor leadership. Whether
this suspicion is well founded or not, I think there can be no question but that it exists and that it tends to undermine confidence in
your proposals for a League of Free Nations.

I am sure you will agree that the American people are essentially
merciful and generous and that now since the war is over they do
not want any of their fellow countrymen to suffer in jail a moment
longer than is necessary. I think Abraham Lincoln sensed this
feeling and endeared himself to us by often acting upon it. Perhaps

you have not noticed the story related in Lamon's "Recollections of Lincoln,"[1] page 246, of an interview between General Creswell[2] and the President on the day of the latter's assassination. The General asked Mr. Lincoln if he would not pardon a friend who had been captured in the rebel army. According to Lamon, Mr. Lincoln replied:

"Creswell you make me think of a lot of young folks who once started Maying. To reach their destination, they had to cross a shallow stream, and did so by means of an old flatboat. When the time came to return, they found to their dismay that the old scow had disappeared. They were in sore trouble, and thought over all manner of devices for getting over the water, but without avail. After a time, one of the boys proposed that each fellow should pick up the girl he liked best and wade over with her. The masterly proposition was carried out, until all that were left upon the island was a little short chap and a great, long, gothic-built elderly lady. Now, Creswell, you are trying to leave me in the same predicament. You fellows are all getting your own friends out of this scrape; and you will succeed in carrying off one after another, until nobody but Jeff Davis and myself will be left on the island, and then I won't know what to do. How should I feel? How should I look, lugging him over? I guess the way to avoid such an embarrassing situation is to let them all out at once."

Mr. President, I hope you won't feel that I have intruded too much on your time with this letter. It is written solely in the interest of that freedom, justice and forgiveness which I know we both have at heart.

You will be interested to hear that my friend, Evan Thomas,[3] was set free by ruling of the Judge Advocate General. I see by the paper that you are intending to stop off in Philadelphia to see your new grandson and my nephew. I envy you the chance. Please give my love to Jessie.

With best wishes for your entire success in the League of Nations and with my highest personal regards,

I beg to remain,

Very sincerely yours,   John Nevin Sayre

TLS (WP, DLC).

[1] Ward Hill Lamon, *Recollections of Abraham Lincoln, 1847-1865,* ed. Dorothy Lamon (Chicago, 1895). A copy of this book is in the Wilson Library, WP, DLC.

[2] John Andrew Jackson Creswell, Adjutant General of Maryland (1862-1863), Republican congressman (1863-1865) and senator (1865-1867) from Maryland, and Postmaster General (1869-1874).

[3] Evan Welling Thomas, pacifist and conscientious objector, who had been imprisoned at Fort Leavenworth. He had been released on January 14, 1919, because of a technical error in the court-martial proceedings which had led to his conviction.

From the Diary of Josephus Daniels

March Saturday 1 1919

Had talk with President about French decorations. Decided, in view of their being given to Army men, to accept and confer them.

"I feel like swearing" said the President referring to the filibuster in Congress.

Weaver unseated & Britt seated.[1]

President said Great Britain would be very sore if we bought the stock in the Mercantile Marine Co[2] & we would get so little advantage (we could not get ships since Maclay[3] says he would take them) would it be worthwhile?

[1] In the congressional election of 1916, Zebulon Weaver, a Democrat of Weaverville, North Carolina, had been elected by a majority of nine votes to represent the state's tenth congressional district in the Sixty-fifth Congress. His Republican opponent, James Jefferson Britt of Asheville, who had represented the district in the previous Congress, had contested Weaver's election on the ground that the vote count had involved several flagrant irregularities. The case finally came before the House on March 1, 1919, and engendered a bitter debate. With the Republicans in a temporary majority on the floor, the House, by several close votes along strict party lines, unseated Weaver and seated Britt for the remaining three days of the Sixty-fifth Congress. However, Weaver, who had defeated Britt decisively in November 1918, resumed his seat on March 4, 1919, and continued to serve, with one brief interruption, until 1947. *Cong. Record*, 65th Cong., 3d sess., pp. 4777-4807. See also *Contested Election Case of Britt v. Weaver: Hearings Before the Committee on Elections No. 3, House of Representatives, Sixty-fifth Congress, Second Session ... May 23 and 24, 1918* (Washington, 1918), and U. S. Congress, House of Representatives, Committee on Elections No. 3, *Contested-Election Case Britt v. Weaver*, 65th Cong., 3d sess., H. Rept. No. 1115 (Washington, 1919).

[2] See the numerous documents in Vols. 53 and 54 relating to the International Mercantile Marine Corporation.

[3] That is, Sir Joseph Paton Maclay, British Minister of Shipping.

From the Diary of Dr. Grayson

Sunday, March 2, 1919.

The President attended church in the morning. He took a motor ride in the afternoon with Mrs. Wilson and conferred with Senator Martin in the evening.

From Edward Mandell House

Paris March 2 [1919].

Number 14. I notice Lodge says League Nations will make wars instead of preventing them. I would suggest that in your New York speech you use the argument that when the Federal Reserve Act was proposed the opponents said that it would make panics instead of preventing them. (Root) made notable speech in the Senate against the measure and made just such a statement. We now know what the Federal Reserve Act has done to prevent panics and we are just as confident that a League Nations will prevent future wars.   Edward House.

T telegram (WP, DLC).

From Joseph Patrick Tumulty

Dear Governor: The White House. 2 March 1919.

Mrs. Catts' friends in the suffrage movement have been to see me and told me that there is a possibility with Senator Gay's assistance of putting over suffrage. But Senator Swanson refuses to give them pairs. They have told me that if you could get Senator Swanson on the telephone and urge him to help, he might cooperate with you.   Sincerely yours,   J. P. Tumulty.

I did   W.W.

TLS (WP, DLC).

From Stephen Samuel Wise, with Enclosures

My dear Mr. President: New York March 2, 1919.

I beg to send you two memoranda which the delegation of the American Jewish Congress is formally to present to you later in the afternoon. Perhaps you will have a moment of time in which to glance over these papers, though of course you are familiar with the questions considered therein. We know, too, what your reaction naturally would be, and appreciate the helpfullness of such response as I am sure you will make. This last we can discuss when we meet at six.   Faithfully yours,   Stephen S. Wise

TLS (WP, DLC).

E N C L O S U R E   I

From Julian William Mack and Others

The President.   March 1, 1919.

As the representatives of the Jews of the United States, elected at the American Jewish Congress held in Philadelphia on December 18, 1918, and as officers of various other Jewish organizations, we respectfully direct your attention to the unhappy status of the Jews of Eastern Europe, and present a statement of the reasons which make it imperative that, before the deliberations of the Peace Conference shall end, they shall receive enforceable guaranties of full civil, religious, political, and national rights.

THE PRESENT STATUS OF THE JEWS OF EASTERN EUROPE

They constitute in the aggregate seven million souls, more than one-half of all of the Jews of the world. They and their ancestors have resided in the lands which they now inhabit for centuries. They have been peaceful, industrious and law-abiding, and loyal to their ancient faith. They have led simple and moral lives. But few of them are illiterate. Such illiteracy as exists among them has been due solely to repressive legislation. The great mass of them belong to the middle classes. Wherever the opportunity has been accorded, they have performed military duty and have sought the right of citizenship. Unfortunately, however, that right has been extended to them in exceptional cases only, and even where it has been granted, they have been subjected to discriminatory laws and regulations and have been regarded as occupying the status of an inferior people.

Russia.

Until the Russian revolutions of March, 1917, the habitations of the Jews of Russia were confined to the cities within the so-called Pale of Settlement—the territory which they were permitted to occupy constituting less than one two-thousandth part of the area of Russia. They were prohibited from owning land and from pursuing agriculture. Industrially they were limited to a comparatively few occupations. Educationally only a small percentage of them were permitted to seek higher learning; but few of them were enabled to adopt learned professions. The burden of heavy special taxes was imposed on them. They were hounded by the police, they were persecuted by the Black Hundreds, and ever and anon became the victims of massacres and were stripped of the slender possessions acquired by dint of bitter deprivations and extraordinary thrift. Statutes, ordinances, edicts, and judicial decisions directed against them ran into the thousands. The mere enumeration of them would fill a book of more than five hundred pages.

One of the first acts of the Lvoff Government was to repeal all of these laws and to grant equality of right to the Jews of Russia, but what the effect of later uprisings upon this decree of emancipation has been and will be is problematical. What the consequences of the creation of new States, such as Ukrainia, Lithuania, Finland, the Lettish Provinces and Poland, out of the former Russian Empire will be, depends entirely upon the action of the Peace Conference.

Roumania.

What has been true of Russia has been equally true of Roumania. At the present time there are approximately three hundred thousand Jews within the boundaries of what now constitutes Roumania. In large measure their ancestors settled there centuries ago. They have led a precarious existence and have been subjected to continuous oppression. Since 1878 there have been enacted in Roumania two hundred and twenty statutes operating exclusively against the Jews, and depriving them of practically every human right.

Poland.

In spite of the fact that all of the inhabitants of Poland suffered from the weight of Russian oppression, the Poles have, ever since 1912, waged incessantly an economic boycott, directed solely against the Jews, of unparalelled rancor and bitterness, deliberately conceived and carried into execution for the purpose of exterminating the Jews or driving them out of Poland, for no other reason than to punish them for refusing to elect to the Duma a pronounced anti-Semite, the exercise of this right of suffrage being denounced as a "Jewish attempt on the sovereign rights of the Poles." This fact has been boldly admitted by Mr. Roman Dmowski, the President of the National Polish Committee. A report of his avowal is appended.[1]

This boycott extended to Posen and Galicia. Its results have been disastrous. The Jews of Poland, who for the most part are industrious artisans and small tradesmen and who were already suffering under the disabilities imposed on them by Russia, were brought to the verge of starvation by hundreds of thousands. Georg Brandes and other writers have characterized the persecution as the worst ever suffered by the Jews of Eastern Europe.

The political organ of Mr. Dmowski[2] has unceasingly denounced the Jews as aliens and foreigners, taking precisely the same position as that of the Roumanians. In the organ of that party published in London as late as July 14, 1918, there appeared an article which denied the right of Polish Jews to Polish citizenship, on the ground that it was not desirable for the State to admit so large an alien element. Its concluding words are:

"The weal of the country demands above all to be relieved of the awful burden of the Jewish mass of two millions, which, owing to its excessive concentration and shop-keeping mode of life, is regularly poisoning itself and the Polish milieu."

---

[1] The report cited in L. Marshall to WW, Nov. 7, 1918, n. 1, Vol. 51.
[2] *Tygodnik Polski (Polish Weekly).*

Within the past four months there have occurred in Russian Poland and in parts of Galicia, a series of pogroms which have cost the lives of hundreds of Jews, which have involved the infliction on men and women of brutal atrocities and shameful indignities, entailing intense suffering, and which have resulted in the seizure and destruction of vast amounts of property. Within the past few weeks the London Times has published the result of a dispassionate investigation, from which it appears that, during November last, pogroms of varying gravity occurred in one hundred and ten towns and villages in Poland and Galicia. At Lemberg more than six hundred Jews were butchered, and it is estimated that nearly eighty per cent. of all of the property belonging to Jews there was completely demolished.

Czecho-Slovakia.

Even in Czecho-Slovakia there have occurred, since November last, uprisings of the populace in various towns, which have culminated in attacks upon the Jews in efforts to drive them out of the country. To his credit be it said that, when apprised of these facts, President Masaryk took prompt action to quell the disturbances and to protect the Jews against mob violence.

Galicia and Transylvania.

The Jews of these provinces, though granted rights of citizenship, have, for economic reasons, been compelled to eke out a miserable existence. Legal disabilities have not, however, been imposed upon them, nor have they suffered indignities at the hands of their fellow-citizens of other faiths.

THE EFFECT UPON THE JEWS OF THE ORGANIZATION OF NEW AND ENLARGED STATES IN EASTERN EUROPE.

While the Jews who live within these regions, as well as those of Western Europe and of the United States, sympathize with the aspirations of those who are seeking to establish a Greater Poland and Greater Roumania, Czecho-Slovakia, Jugo-Slavia, and, if it be deemed desirable, other States, and would be unwilling to do aught that would be an interference with the realization of these ambitions, it is believed that the enlargement of existing States and the creation of new States should be coupled with conditions which will enable the Jews residing in these several States to enjoy complete equality with all other residents of those States. In other words, their watchword is: "Equal rights to all men in all lands."

Without undertaking at this time to go into detail as to the entire Eastern European territory, we will for the present content ourselves with calling attention to the effect of the establishment of the New Poland and the Enlarged Roumania upon the Jews who shall dwell within the respective boundaries of these States.

The New Poland.

It is contemplated that this State shall include, not only what has hitherto constituted Russian Poland, but also Galicia and parts of Silesia and of Prussia. The number of Jews in this territory would be upwards of three millions. Those of Galicia, Silesia and Prussia have, in recent years at least, enjoyed full rights of citizenship and have been under no legal disabilities whatsoever. Poland, as a State, has had no existence for more than a century. Until, during the present war, it was overrun by the armies of the Central Powers, its laws were those of Russia, and consequently the Jews of Poland were under the disabilities to which we have adverted. During the Polish revolution of 1862, in which the Jews actively participated, the proposed Constitution, while purporting to grant to them equal rights, did so under the following condition:

"In consideration for their admission to the enjoyment of equal rights the Jews shall renounce the use of a language of their own in speech as well as in writing. * * * After the promulgation of this act, no legal act, no will, no contract or guaranty, no obligation of any sort, no accounts or bills, no books or commercial correspondence shall be written or signed in Hebrew or Yiddish. All such documents shall in that case be held to be invalid."

The significance of this enactment lies in the fact that upwards of ninety per cent. of the Jews of Poland speak and write and are deeply attached to Hebrew and to their Yiddish tongue. As is well known, their religious services are conducted exclusively in Hebrew, as they have been for centuries. This legislation, though superseded by the Russian law, is still regarded by the Polish National Committee as being in full force.

We again advert to the economic boycott, which has been stimulated by the controlling political party of Poland, by the press, and by the clergy. During the occupation of Poland by Germany and the establishment of a Municipal Council in Warsaw, which constituted the highest Polish political authority in the country, the Poles succeeded in having the shops of the Jews in eligible locations in the market halls removed, and compelled them, if they desired to avail themselves of the markets for commercial purposes, to huddle together, in a species of Ghetto, in a corner of the market hall. The Jews, though constituting thirty-eight per cent. of the population of Warsaw, were deprived of the opportunity of receiving employment on the public works and of acting in any official capacity. Though cooperative societies of a mercantile character were organized in all parts of Russian Poland, no Jews have been admitted to membership in these societies, and they have become the centres of agitation against the Jewish population.

The Polish National Committee has recently intimated that the proposed Constitution of the new Polish State would provide that "Polish citizens, without distinction as to origin, race or creed, must all stand equal before the law." Admonished by the unhappy experience of the Jews of Roumania, to which reference will presently be made, who were promised similar rights by the Treaty of Berlin of 1878, and warned by the cynical frankness of Mr. Dmowski, the head of that Committee, as to his past and present attitude toward the Jews, such a pronouncement is wholly inadequate. When it speaks of "Polish citizens," it affords the same loophole for evasion as that by which Roumania has hitherto successfully nullified the conditions of the instrument which called it into being—the lack of a definition of the term "citizen." It also significantly fails to forbid discrimination or restriction of the imposition of disabilities; and it does not confer the right to employ any language other than Polish, commercially, socially or educationally.

The leaders of this restrictive policy are and have been officially connected with the present government of Poland. They look upon the Jews, not as citizens, but as aliens, in spite of the fact that Jewish settlement in Poland began in the twelfth century and that a vast majority of the Jews have sprung from ancestors who lived in Poland before American independence was achieved.

The Enlarged Roumania.

Roumania, as now constituted, consists of Wallachia and Moldavia. It has at present two hundred and fifty thousand Jews. It is proposed to annex to it Bessarabia and Transylvania. By such annexation approximately five hundred thousand more Jews will become subjects of Roumania. These Jews at present enjoy the rights of citizenship in the countries to which they have hitherto belonged. The Jews of Roumania, however, have been officially regarded as aliens. In the eye of the law they are even without the protection of alienage, since allegiance on their part to any other Government is not recognized. They are, therefore, literally looked upon as men without a country.

Under the Treaty of Berlin, entered into in 1878, at the close of the Russo-Turkish War, Roumania became an independent kingdom. The signatories of the treaty intended that the disabilities which had rested on the Jews of Roumania should be removed, and to that end Articles XLIII and XLIV were made a part of the treaty. They read as follows:

"XLIII. The High Contracting Parties recognize the independence of Roumania, subject to the conditions set forth in the two following Articles.

XLIV. In Roumania the difference of religious creeds and confessions shall not be alleged against any person as a ground for exclusion or incapacity in matters relating to the enjoyment of civil and political rights, admission to public employments, functions and honors, or the exercise of the various professions and industries in any locality whatsoever.

The freedom and outward exercise of all forms of worship shall be assured to all persons belonging to the Roumanian State, as well as to foreigners, and no hindrance shall be offered either to the hierarchical organization of the different communions, or to their relations with their spiritual chiefs.

The subjects and citizens of all the Powers, traders or others, shall be treated in Roumania, without distinction of creed, on a footing of perfect equality."

Roumania never complied with this condition of the treaty, and so formulated its Constitution and laws as to evade compliance with the very law of its being. These provisions of the Constitution, which were adopted in 1880, are contained in Article VII and are as follows:

"Article VII. The difference of religious creeds and confessions does not constitute in Roumania an obstacle to the acquirement of civil and political rights and their exercise.

1. Every foreigner, without distinction of creed, whether enjoying any foreign protection or not, can acquire naturalization under the following conditions:

(a) By addressing to the Government an application for naturalization, in which must be declared the capital he possesses, his profession, and his wish to establish his domicile in Roumania.

(b) By residing in the country for ten years after having made this application, and by proving by his acts that he is useful to the country.

2. The following may be exempted from this delay of residence (ten years):

(a) All who shall have introduced into the country industries, useful inventions, or distinguished talents, or who shall have founded large commercial or industrial establishments.

(b) All who have been born or educated in Roumania of parents domiciled in the country, and have neither in their own case nor in that of their parents, at any time been in the enjoyment of any foreign protection.

(c) All who have served with the colours during the war of independence, and these can be naturalized collectively on the proposition of the Government by a single law without further formalities.

3. Naturalization can only be granted by a Law, and individually.

4. A special Law will determine the manner in which foreigners can establish their domicile on Roumanian territory.

5. Roumanians, and naturalized Roumanian citizens, can alone acquire rural estates in Roumania.

Rights acquired up to the present time are respected.

The International Conventions existing at present remain in force, with all their clauses, and for the term mentioned therein."

No general naturalization law such as the Powers were assured would be enacted was ever passed. Roumania, as theretofore, withheld from the Jews civil and political rights. It added to their restrictions and burdens. It deprived them of the most elemental rights. In the forty years that have elapsed since the proclamation of the treaty, not to exceed three hundred Jews have, by special enactment by the Parliament of Roumania, become naturalized.

Although the United States was not a party to the treaty, the sufferings of the Jews of Roumania having become more and more intolerable, many of them sought asylum in this country. This led Secretary Hay, on July 17, 1902, to address to the Roumanian Government a note of protest against the treatment of the Jews by Roumania, in which he declared:

"Whether consciously and of purpose or not, these helpless people, burdened and spurned by their native land, are forced by the sovereign power of Roumania upon the charity of the United States. This Government cannot be a tacit party to such an international wrong. It is constrained to protest against the treatment to which the Jews of Roumania are subjected, not alone because it has unimpeachable ground to remonstrate against the resultant injury to itself, but in the name of hymanity [humanity]. The United States may not authoritatively appeal to the stipulations of the Treaty of Berlin, to which it was not and cannot become a signatory, but it does earnestly appeal to the principles consigned therein because they are the principles of international law and eternal justice, advocating the broad toleration which that solemn compact enjoins and standing ready to lend its moral support to the fulfillment thereof by its cosignatories, for the act of Roumania itself has effectively joined the United States to them as an interested party in this regard."

This and various efforts made by publicists throughout the world, failed to ameliorate conditions. Attempts were from time to time made by some of the signatory Powers to induce action which would accomplish the objects of the treaty, but without result.

After the Central Powers had overcome Roumania during the present war, Germany pretended to enforce the provisions of Article XLIV of the Treaty of Berlin, in the Treaty of Bucharest, but in such terms as showed on their face the hollowness of the pretence, since the language employed was such as almost to invite evasion. That sham treaty no longer exists.

Recently, at the instance of Mr. Bratianu, the present Prime Minister of Roumania, who has always been a bitter anti-Semite, Roumania has promulgated a decree which, while pretending to emancipate the Jews, is couched in such phraseology as to make the grant practically valueless, because of the proofs required to establish the nativity of the Jews of Roumania and to satisfy the hostile Roumanian tribunals that these Jews have never enjoyed foreign protection; whatever this elastic phrase may mean in a country which, during the past two years, has been overrun by foreign armies.

It is at once obvious that the Bessarabian and Transylvanian Jews who have all these years under foreign protection, because the former were embraced by the Russian Empire and the latter by the Austro-Hungarian Empire, and are not of Roumanian nativity, cannot possibly bring themselves within the terms of this hastilty [hastily] enacted decree, the belated pronouncement of which coincided with the opening of the Peace Conference.

THE GUARANTIES REQUIRED BY THE JEWS TO SECURE FOR THEM FUNDAMENTAL HUMAN RIGHTS.

The facts thus far recited, all of which are either conceded or can be established by irrefragable documentary evidence, show that, if the age-long sufferings and legal disabilities of the Jews are to cease and of all the people of the earth they are not to be the only ones to be deprived of freedom, it becomes the bounden duty of the Peace Conference to emancipate them and to give to them a charter of liberty, which does not consist of mere promises, but which shall constitute a grant self-executing, indefeasible, and which cannot be evaded. This can be brought about only by avoiding a repetition of the experience which followed the deliberate breach of the Treaty of Berlin, which the signatories of that instrument were unable to enforce. Such a result can be accomplished if the Peace Conference shall, as a condition precedent to the creation of the new States or of the enlarged States, and before they shall come into existence, require them to adopt, as part of their organic laws, irrepealable clauses which shall grant to all inhabitants of these new or enlarged States these fundamental rights. At the American Jewish Congress these principles were formulated as follows:

1. All inhabitants of the Territory of (name) including such persons together with their families, who subsequent to August 1st, 1914, fled, removed or were expelled therefrom and who shall within ten years from the adoption of this provision return thereto, shall for all purpose be citizens thereof, provided however that such as have heretofore been subjects of other States, who desire to retain their allegiance to such States or assume allegiance to their successor States, to the exclusion of (name) citizenship may do so by formal declaration to be made within a specified period.

2. For a period of ten years from the adoption of this provision, no law shall be enacted restricting any former inhabitant of a State which included the territory of (name) from taking up his residence in (name) and thereby acquiring citizenship therein.

3. All citizens of (name) without distinction as to race, nationality or creed shall enjoy equal civil, political, religious and national rights, and no laws shall be enacted or enforced which shall abridge the privileges or immunities of, or impose upon any persons any discrimination, disability, or restriction whatsoever on account of race, nationality, or religion, or deny to any person the equal protection of the laws.

4. The principle of minority representation shall be provided for by the law.

5. The members of the various national, as well as religious bodies of (name) shall be accorded autonomous management of their own communal institutions whether they be religious, educational, charitable or otherwise.

6. No law shall be enacted restricting the use of any language and all existing laws declaring such prohibition are repealed, nor shall any language test be established.

7. Those who observe any other than the first day of the week as their Sabbath shall not be prohibited from pursuing their secular affairs on any day other than that which they observe; nor shall they be required to perform any acts on their Sabbath or Holy Days which they shall regard as a desecration thereof.

EXPLANATION OF THE VARIOUS GUARANTIES ADVOCATED.

It will be observed that in none of these provisions is there any reference to any particular race, nationality, or creed. They are intended to apply, without discrimination, to all men and women who live within the State, so that the American ideal may prevail in the strictest sense of the term in Eastern Europe, where hitherto the idea of equality before the law has been unknown. We shall briefly refer to the most striking features of these provisions:

(1) Citizenship is not left to be defined by the new or enlarged States arbitrarily or capriciously. The Peace Conference is to define the term. The test is inhabitancy of the State. Owing to the disturbed conditions which have prevailed there during the past four years, it is to include such persons, together with their families, who subsequent to August 1, 1914, fled, removed or were expelled therefrom, and who within a specified period after the adoption of the treaty shall return thereto. It contains the proviso that such persons as have heretofore been subjects of other States who desire to retain their allegiance to such States or to assume allegiance to their successor States, may do so by a formal declaration to be made within a specified period. So far as Roumania is concerned this will protect the residents of Bessarabia and Transylvania, who, if they desire, may retain their allegiance to Russia or Austria-Hungary. In the case of Poland the residents of Galicia, Silesia and Prussia may retain their former allegiance.

(2) For a fixed period subsequent to the enactment of the treaty no law shall be enacted which shall restrict any former inhabitant of the new State from taking up his residence therein and thereby acquiring citizenship thereof. This is obviously just, the only question being as to what period of time should be specified.

(3) The third provision is a practical adoption of the time-honored principles of liberty and equality enshrined in the Constitution of the United States and the Amendments thereto. Attention should, however, be called to the fact that, in addition to providing for equality of civil, political and religious rights, it is also asked that national rights shall be guaranteed. This calls for an explanation. By "national rights" are meant those which may be accorded in the respective States to the several racial groups which compose the population. Nothing is further removed from our purpose than to countenance the establishment of an *imperium in imperio*. Nor do the racial groups to which we refer entertain such an idea. It is to be borne in mind that we are dealing with Eastern European conditions, not those which prevail in the United States or in England, France and Italy, where the populations are practically homogenous and where the term "national" has reference to a political, as distinguished from an ethnic, unit. For the sake of illustration let us instance Galicia. Among other of the "national groups" of that territory, using the phrase according to its meaning in Galicia, are Poles, Ruthenians and Jews. It is contended by some of these groups that they are entitled to certain rights, which may be called cultural

or communal for want of a better term. It is their belief that the welfare of the State and the happiness of its people will be best promoted by the stimulation of the several racial cultures. It is not for us in the United States to determine the wisdom of that conception. It is one that has entered deeply into the consciousness of these several groups. If any of them is accorded national rights in the sense indicated, then every other group should be equally entitled to enjoy the same character of national rights. Hence were the Ruthenians, for instance, given such rights, then should the Jews desire similar rights they should have them.

Account must be taken of the newly formulated and intense desire of all of the various ethnic minorities in Eastern Europe to preserve their cultural identity. Lord Bryce has referred to that phenomenon. Practically all of the new and enlarged States which are to be organized will possess a number of such minorities. In the new Poland one-third of the population will be composed of Jews, Ruthenians, Lithuanians, Letts and Russians. The same is true of Ukrainia, Lithuania and Roumania. Most of the Jews of these lands share with their fellow-countrymen the desire for cultural autonomy, and the most advanced statesmen in these lands sympathize with this feeling and favor the granting of these rights.

(4) The principle of minority representation is incorporated in the Constitutions of several of the States of the Union, and is to be found in the charters of many of our cities. In the new States to be formed in Eastern Europe the adoption of such a principle is important for the protection of the rights of minorities, which might otherwise be invaded by one of the preponderating groups, which, by reason of its strength, might be tempted to disregard the rights of what would otherwise be a voiceless minority.

(5) The remaining provisions are self-explanatory. They are called for by the conditions which prevail in Eastern Europe, where many nationalities are intermingled, where religion and life are interwoven and traditions are regarded as sacred, and where, as a natural consequence, the utmost care must be exercised lest there be an invasion of what the several parts of the population look upon as essential to their existence. Whilst we recognize the principle that it is the right of every State to establish an official language, it is especially important in these Eastern lands that no restriction upon the use of the language of any of the minority groups shall be permitted, for there is nothing to which men so tenaciously adhere as to their ancestral tongue.

In Poland and Roumania there are many inhabitants who are unable to speak the official language, largely because they have been prevented from learning it by laws forbidding them from attending at schools where the official language is taught. Among themselves, in the family circle, and in their houses of worship, they employ the languages which to them have traditional value and which they hold in deep affection and veneration.

Moreover, it should not be forgotten that if Bessarabia and Transylvania were annexed to Roumania, there would be added to its population Poles, Russians, Ukrainians, Ruthenians and Jews, unable to speak Roumanian. To prevent them from employing their mother tongues would not only be the height of cruelty, but would prove a dead letter; yet, if not protected in the enjoyment of the right, persecution would be certain to result.

The Sabbath question is also one of great importance, especially in Poland, where it affects the economic interests of the Jews, who quite generally abstain from all labor on the seventh day and therefore find it necessary to carry on their occupation on Sunday. The conflict of economic interests which now prevails in Poland, as evidenced by the boycott, make it important that this guaranty should be contained in the organic law. Otherwise, legislation might be so shaped as to become the ready instrument for economic oppression.

THE IMPORTANCE OF FAVORABLE ACTION NOW.

For the first time in the history of the world has there been such a gathering of the Nations as that which is now witnessed at the Peace Conference. The peoples of Eastern Europe are all of them suppliants for political rights. Poland, Roumania, Czecho-Slovakia and Jugo-Slavia are suing for sovereignty and for enlarged boundaries. Nobody will begrudge them the realization of their dreams.

The Jews of Eastern Europe also come to present their cause for adjudication. They are not seeking sovereignty or special privileges, but merely justice. For twenty centuries they and their ancestors have suffered from oppression, have been deprived of every right that men hold dear, and have been fettered and burdened by disabilities of every kind. For the first time the light of hope dawns upon them. They behold in the Peace Conference their last opportunity to secure those rights which are conceded to all other men. It is inconceivable that they will be turned away from the council table without the relief which they demand. Unless they now secure what they have so long sought, in terms which cannot be evaded, they will be the only people living in supposedly civilized lands who would be deprived of the simplest, and yet the most precious, of human rights—civil, political and religious liberty.

For the first time our country will have the strictly legal right to raise its voice in their behalf. Knowing, as our fellow-citizens do,

what the three million Jews of America have contributed to our
national development in commerce and industry, and to our intel-
lectual life, knowing how they have shared in the defense of the
Nation in the great conflict which is now culminating, it will be
enabled to speak with authority concerning the blessings which
will inure to Government and subjects alike from the emancipation
of the Jews in those lands where they still stagger under the burdens
of indignity and oppression, which have made them the most unhappy beings on earth. Let it be understood that the Nations which
are seeking rights must be prepared to grant them to all of their
inhabitants. This is the grandest opportunity that has ever arisen
for proclaiming liberty throughout the world, for creating genuine
democracies, for putting an end to man's inhumanity to man. It is
inconceivable that any State shall be permitted to reduce to practical
slavery or to a state of helotism any part of its population. It would
be a travesty upon justice and a sorry awakening from that spiritual
exaltation which has won this war in the cause of humanity, if the
Jews of Eastern Europe, the descendants of the oldest of the civilized races, were to be the only ones who would have no lot or part
in a regenerated world.

   Mr. President: We look to you, in conjunction with the representatives of the Allied countries associated with you in the Peace
Conference, as the champions of humanity, to take such action as
will put an end to the intolerable conditions which have constituted
the most tragic chapter in human history.

Respectfully submitted,   Julian W. Mack
Louis Marshall
Stephen S. Wise

Bernard G. Richards[3] Secretary

   [3] Bernard Gerson Richards, editor of the New York *Maccabean* and one of the founders
of the American Jewish Congress.

E N C L O S U R E   I I

The President.   March 1, 1919.

   As representatives of the delegates elected at the American Jewish Congress, held in Philadelphia December 18, 1918, we respectfully ask that the Peace Conference recognize the aspirations and
historic claims of the Jewish people in regard to Palestine; that
such action be taken by the Conference as shall vest the sovereign
possession of Palestine in such League of Nations as may be formed
and that the Government thereof be entrusted to Great Britain as
the mandatory or trustee of the League.

Under the mandate or trusteeship, Palestine should be placed under such political, administrative and economic conditions as will secure the establishment there of a Jewish National Home, and will ultimately render possible the creation of an autonomous Commonwealth, it being clearly understood that nothing shall be done which might prejudice the civil and religious rights of existing non-Jewish communities in Palestine, or the rights and political status enjoyed by Jews in any other country. That there shall be forever the fullest freedom of religious worship for all creeds in Palestine, and that there shall be no discrimination among the inhabitants with regard to citizenship and civil rights on the ground of religion or of race.

THE HISTORIC BASIS FOR THESE CLAIMS.

Palestine is the historic home of the Jews. There they achieved their greatest development. From that center, through their agency, there emanated spiritual and moral influences of supreme value to mankind. By violence they were driven from Palestine, and through the ages large numbers of them never ceased to cherish the longing and hope of return.

Palestine is not large enough to contain more than a part of the Jews of the world. The greater portion of the fourteen millions or more scattered through all countries must remain where they now abide, and it will doubtless be one of the cares of the Peace Conference, as we have already urged upon you, to ensure for them wherever they have been oppressed, as for all peoples, equal rights. Such a Palestine would be of value to the world at large, whose happiness is in large measure derived from the healthy diversities of its civilizations.

The land itself needs rehabilitation. Its present condition is a standing reproach. Two things are necessary for its reconstruction, a stable and enlightened Government, and an addition to the present population of energetic and intelligent men and women, devoted to the country, and supported by such resources as are indispensable to development. Such a population the Jews alone, it is believed, could supply. Inspired by these convictions, Jewish activities during the last thirty years have operated in Palestine to the extent permitted by the Turkish administrative system. Large sums have been expended in the establishment of Jewish agricultural settlements, which have for the most part proven highly successful. With commendable enterprise the Jews have adopted modern scientific methods and have proven themselves to be capable agriculturalists. Hebrew has been revived as a living language. It is the medium of instruction in the schools, and is in daily use. A Jewish university has been founded at Jerusalem, and funds have been pledged for its creation and support. For the further development of the country, large sums will be required for drainage, irrigation, the building of highways, railways, harbors, and public works of all kinds.

THE ACTION OF THE BRITISH AND OTHER GOVERNMENTS.

The historic title of the Jews to Palestine was recognized by the British Government in its Declaration of November 2, 1917, addressed by the British Secretary of State for Foreign Affairs to Lord Rothschild and reading, as follows:

"His Majesty's Government view with favor the establishment in Palestine of a National Home for the Jewish people, and will use their best endeavours to facilitate the achievement of this object, it being clearly understood that nothing shall be done which may prejudice the civil and religious rights of existing non-Jewish communities in Palestine, or the rights and political status enjoyed by Jews in any other country."

The Governments of France and Italy have declared their approval of this Declaration. You, Mr. President, have expressed your sympathy with the spirit of the British Declaration,[1] and among others, the Governments of Japan, Greece, Serbia and China have added their approval.

GREAT BRITAIN AS TRUSTEE.

The resolutions of the American Jewish Congress have asked that Great Britain act as mandatary or trustee of the League of Nations for Palestine. Its selection as such mandatary or trustee is urged on the ground of the desire of the Jews, due to the peculiar relationship of England to the Jewish Palestinian problem. The return of the Jews to Zion has not only been a remarkable feature in English literature, but in the domain of statecraft it has played its part, beginning with the readmission of the Jews under Cromwell. It manifested itself particularly in the 19th century in the instructions given to British consular representatives in the Orient after the Damascus incident;[2] in the various Jewish Palestinian

---

[1] See, e.g., WW to S. S. Wise, Aug. 31, 1918, Vol. 49.

[2] On February 5, 1840, an Italian Capuchin monk, long resident in Damascus, and his Muslim servant disappeared. The Capuchins spread the rumor that Jews had murdered them in order to use their blood for the rituals of Passover. The French Consul in Syria and the Governor General of Syria collaborated in an investigation of the affair in which several Jews were arbitrarily arrested and tortured to secure "confessions" and the implication of others. Several Jews died and many others were imprisoned. Western Jewry protested against the affair vigorously, and the governments of Austria, Great Britain, and the United States intervened. Muhammad Ali, the Khedive of Egypt, was finally persuaded to order the liberation of the Jewish prisoners in Damascus who had survived the affair.

The Damascus incident was one of several factors which led Henry John Temple, Viscount Palmerston, then the British Foreign Secretary, to suggest to the Turkish

projects suggested by English non-Jews prior to 1881; in the letters of endorsement and support given by members of the Royal Family and Officers of the Government to Lawrence Oliphant;[3] and finally, in the three consecutive acts which definitely associated Great Britain with Zionism in the minds of the Jews, viz,—The El Arish offer in 1901;[4] the East African offer in 1903,[5] and lastly the British Declaration in favor of a Jewish National Home in Palestine in 1917. Moreover, the Jews who have gained political experience in many lands under a great variety of governmental systems, whole-heartedly appreciate the advanced and liberal policies adopted by Great Britain in her modern colonial administration.

THE TERMS OF TRUSTEESHIP.

In connection with the Government to be established by the mandatary or trustee of the League of Nations until such time as the people of Palestine shall be prepared to undertake the estab-

---

government on several occasions that British Consuls in the Middle East might convey complaints of Jews residing in that area to the British Ambassador at Constantinople, who would forward them to the appropriate Turkish authorities. See Frederick Stanley Rodkey, "Lord Palmerston and the Rejuvenation of Turkey, 1830-41," *Journal of Modern History*, II (June 1930), 214-16.

[3] Laurence Oliphant (1829-1888), English author, traveler, politician, and Christian mystic, became an advocate of Jewish settlement in Palestine in the late 1870s. In November 1878, he proposed a plan for settlement to Benjamin Disraeli, Earl of Beaconsfield, the British Prime Minister, and to Robert Arthur Talbot Gascoyne-Cecil, 3d Marquess of Salisbury, the Foreign Secretary. In 1879, Oliphant went to Palestine, carrying with him letters of recommendation from the Foreign Office. He decided that the best place to start Jewish settlement was the Gilead region in Transjordan. He carried on negotiations with the Turkish government to further the project, which ultimately came to nothing. He published an account of his travels and efforts on behalf of the scheme in *The Land of Gilead, with Excursions in the Lebanon* (Edinburgh and London, 1880). He later lived for a time in Haifa. See Philip Henderson, *The Life of Laurence Oliphant: Traveller, Diplomat and Mystic* (London, 1956), pp. 203-11, 223-25, 229-32.

[4] The Zionist leader, Theodor Herzl, had discussed in 1902 (not 1901) with Joseph Chamberlain, then the British Colonial Secretary, and Henry Charles Keith Petty-Fitzmaurice, 5th Marquess of Lansdowne, the Foreign Secretary, the possibility of an autonomous Jewish settlement in the area adjacent to El-Arish, a town on the Mediterranean coast of the Sinai Peninsula. Both were favorable to the idea but said that Herzl would have to secure the assent of Evelyn Baring, 1st Earl of Cromer, the British representative in Egypt, and of the Egyptian government. Herzl sent a commission to El-Arish to investigate the feasibility of the project. The commission reported favorably, but in May 1903 the Egyptian government turned down the plan on the ground that too much water would have to be diverted from the Nile River to irrigate the land around El-Arish. Lord Cromer and the British Foreign Office concurred in this decision. See Alex Bein, *Theodore Herzl: A Biography*, trans. Maurice Samuel (Cleveland, Philadelphia and New York, 1962), pp. 411-37, 439, 442-43.

[5] Chamberlain, in April 1903, had suggested to Herzl the possibility of a Jewish settlement in British East Africa as an alternative to El-Arish. Herzl at first ignored the proposal; he preferred El-Arish because it was much closer to Palestine. However, when it became clear that the El-Arish project was doomed, Herzl decided to pursue the East African alternative. The British government later proposed a portion of present-day Kenya as the site of the Jewish colony. This plan ultimately came to naught because of the death of Herzl in 1904, the opposition of English colonists already in East Africa, and the refusal of Zionists to settle anywhere except in Palestine. See *ibid.*, pp. 435-36, 439-503 *passim*.

lishment of representative and responsible Government, the following terms are deemed important.

(1) In any instrument establishing the constitution of Palestine, the declarations of the Peace Conference shall be recited as forming an integral part of such constitution.

(2) The Jewish people shall be entitled to fair representation in the executive and legislative bodies and in the selection of public and civil servants.

(3) In encouraging the self-government of localities, the mandatary or trustee shall secure the maintenance by local communities of proper standards of administration in matters of education and communal or regional activities. In granting or enlarging autonomy, regard shall be had to the readiness and ability of the community to attain such standards. Local autonomous communities shall be empowered and encouraged to combine and cooperate for common purposes.

(4) Assistance shall be rendered from the public funds for the education of the inhabitants, without distinction of race or creed. Hebrew shall be one of the official languages and shall be employed in all documents, decrees and announcements issued by the Government.

(5) The Jewish Sabbath and Holy Days shall be recognized as legal days of rest.

(6) The established rights of the present population shall be equitably safeguarded.

(7) All inhabitants of Palestine who, on a date to be specified, shall have their domicile therein, except those who, within a period to be stated, shall in writing elect to retain their citizenship in any other country, shall be citizens of Palestine, and they and all persons born in Palestine or naturalized under its laws after the day named, shall be citizens thereof and entitled to the protection of the mandatary or trustee.

We are confident, Mr. President, that in common with the representatives of the Allied Governments, you will lend to these aspirations the powerful support which through you the American people is ready to exert at this historic moment.

Respectfully submitted,   Julian W. Mack.

Louis Marshall

Stephen S. Wise

Bernard G. Richards   Secretary

TS MSS (WP, DLC).

A News Report

[*March 2, 1919*]
PRESIDENT GIVES HOPE TO ZIONISTS
Tells Delegation He Approves Plan for a
Jewish Commonwealth in Palestine.

Washington, March 2.—Approval of the plans of Zionist leaders for the creation of a national Jewish Commonwealth in Palestine was given tonight by President Wilson to a delegation of representative American Jewish leaders who spent an hour at the White House in conference with the President over the international status of Jews around the world. The delegation was headed by Rabbi Stephen Samuel Wise of New York, and also included Judge Julian W. Mack of Chicago, Louis Marshall of New York, and Bernard J. [G.] Richards of New York, members of the delegation to the Paris Peace Conference recently named by the American Jewish Congress.

Here is the word of promise that was given to the delegation by the President:

"As for your representations touching Palestine, I have before this expressed my personal approval of the declaration of the British Government regarding the aspirations and historic claims of the Jewish people in regard to Palestine. I am, moreover, persuaded that the allied nations, with the fullest concurrence of our own Government and people, are agreed that in Palestine shall be laid the foundations of a Jewish Commonwealth."

The delegation presented to the President a memorial setting forth the present status of the Jews in eastern Europe and the effect upon them of the formation of new and enlarged States—Poland, Czechoslovakia, and Jugoslavia. The delegation also presented the resolution adopted by the American Jewish Congress held in Philadelphia last December which set forth the guarantees considered necessary for securing fundamental human rights to Jews throughout the world.

After the conference the delegates stated that they had found the President, "as always, sympathetic with the incontestable principle of the right of the Jewish people everywhere to equality of status."

Printed in the *New York Times*, March 3, 1919.

From the Very Reverend Hardwicke Drummond Rawnsley[1]

Kendal March 2, 1919.

Fred Yates died after operation. Leaves widow and daughter unprovided for. We are appealing to friends to obtain annuity for widow. Will you care to help. Please cablegram answer.

Rawnsley.

T telegram (WP, DLC).

[1] Canon of Carlisle, Proctor in Convocation, and Honorary Chaplain to George V since 1912. The author of numerous books of poetry and travel literature, Rawnsley had been the vicar of Crosthwaite, Keswick, and Rural Dean from 1883 to 1917 and was an old acquaintance of Wilson's.

From the Diary of Vance Criswell McCormick

March 2 (Sunday) [1919]

At 5.00, Colonel House and Tardieu came for tea, also Aubert with Tardieu. They agreed on plan for Rhenish Republic[1] and discussed method of getting [Lloyd] George's approval, also on Saar Coal Basin.[2] Agreed Poland should have Danzig and Belgium Luxembourg, all of these, of course, with proper reservations. Agreed to push to conclusion work of committees so that reports would be ready for President upon his arrival the 4th, and Tardieu said Foch very anxious to get the Germans at conference, Versailles, 26th. Colonel agreed and they both hope it can be wound up May 1. This program is an ambitious one but I believe it can be done and should be, although I still see rocks ahead, particularly on questions of priority as to reparation payments.

[1] See the memorandum on the Rhine question printed at March 11, 1919.
[2] Presumably that France should be permitted to annex the Saar Valley.

From the Diary of Dr. Grayson

Monday, March 3, 1919.

The conference of Governors and Mayors called under the direction of the Secretary of Labor, designed to deal with the industrial problems, assembled in the East Room and the President made an address in which he emphasized that it was the duty of business generally and of the states and municipalities to handle the labor problem as a local issue.

During the afternoon a coterie of Republican Senators, who had opposed the League of Nations plan, circulated a round-robin, to which they secured 37 signatures of Republican members and members-elect, pledging them to vote against the League constitution plan.[1] During the night's session Senator Lodge introduced a resolution declaring it to be the sense of the Senate that the President on his return to France should insist on the completion of a treaty of peace that would deal only with the matters growing out of the war and permit the League of Nations plan to be taken up and dealt with separately. When Senator Lodge presented this resolution in the Senate objection was made by Senators Martin and Swanson of Virginia, which automatically killed consideration. However, Senator Lodge made public the round-robin pledging the Republican Senators. In their effort to again force the immediate calling of a special session of the new Congress, the Republican Senators killed the Urgent Deficiency Bill carrying with it a big appropriation absolutely essential for the continuation of the Government's control of the railways. They also killed a number of other important bills. The Congress remained constantly in session through the night and until noon of the next day.

[1] As early as January 1919, a group of Republican senators, who were opposed to a league of nations as an integral part of a general peace treaty, had pondered the question of how to express the antileague sentiment of a substantial minority of the Senate in a more formal and more effective way than merely through individual speeches and statements. At that time, several senators, including Senator Lodge, had already considered the possibility of having more than one third of the members and members-elect of the next Senate pledge themselves to reject any peace treaty which contained the constitution of a league of nations. To Lodge and the opponents of the league, the need for a strong statement became even more imperative after they had seen the proposed Covenant and had found it unacceptable. Moreover, since Wilson indicated that he would not call a special session of Congress while the peace conference was in progress, some declaration had to be made before the adjournment of the Sixty-fifth Congress.

On March 2, Senator Frank Bosworth Brandegee of Connecticut conferred with Lodge about the possibility of introducing a resolution in the Senate rejecting the Covenant in its present form. Although both men knew that such a resolution could not possibly be adopted, they believed that, if at least thirty-three Republican senators and senators-elect could be induced to support it, the resolution might have the desired effect. If less than the required number of senators refused to commit themselves to the resolution in advance, it would not be introduced, and its existence would not be disclosed. Thus, Lodge, with the help of Brandegee and Senator Knox, drew up an appropriate resolution, circulated it among Republican senators on the following day, and secured thirty-seven signatures.

Lodge introduced his resolution in the Senate shortly before midnight on March 3. It stated, among other things, that it was the sense of the Senate that "the constitution of the league of nations in the form now proposed to the peace conference should not be accepted by the United States"; that "the negotiations on the part of the United States should immediately be directed to the utmost expedition of the urgent business of negotiating peace terms with Germany"; and that "the proposal for a league of nations ... should be then taken up for careful and serious consideration." Although Lodge then asked unanimous consent for the immediate consideration of his resolution, he hoped, in fact, that at least one Democratic senator would raise a point of order against its introduction. Lodge realized that, if the Democrats would permit a vote on the resolution, it would be defeated by a large majority and would probably lose much of its psychological impact. Thus, when Senator Swanson objected, Lodge gladly withdrew his resolution and proceeded instead, "by way of explanation," to read the names of the thirty-seven senators who, "if they had had the opportunity, . . . would have voted for the foregoing resolution." *Cong. Record*, 65th Cong., 3d sess., p. 4974. For a detailed discussion, see also Ralph Stone, *The Irreconcilables: The Fight Against the League of Nations* (Lexington, Ky.), 1970, pp. 70-74.

An Address to a Conference of Governors and Mayors

March 3, 1919.

Mr. Secretary and gentlemen of the conference: I wish that I could promise myself the pleasure and the profit of taking part in your deliberations. I find that nothing deliberate is permitted me since my return. I have been trying under the guidance of my Secretary, Mr. Tumulty, to do a month's work in a week, and I am hoping that not all of it has been done badly. But inasmuch as there is a necessary pressure upon my time, I know that you will excuse me from taking a part in your conference, much as I should be profited by doing so. My pleasant duty is to bid you a very hearty welcome and to express my gratification that so many executives of cities and of states have found the time and the inclination to come together on the very important matter we have to discuss. The primary duty of caring for our people in the intimate matters that we want to discuss here, of course, falls upon the states and upon the municipalities, and the function of the federal government is to do what it is trying to do in a conference of this sort—draw the executive minds of the country together so that they may profit by each other's suggestions and plans, and so that we may offer our services to coordinate their efforts in any way that they may deem it wise to coordinate. In other words, it is the privilege of the federal government in matters of this sort to be the servants of the executives of the states and municipalities and counties, and we shall perform that duty with the greatest pleasure if you will guide us with your suggestions.

I hope that the discussions of this conference will take as wide a scope as you think necessary. We are not met to discuss any single or narrow subject. We are met to discuss the proper method of restoring all the labor conditions of the country to a normal basis as soon as possible, and to effecting such fresh allocations of labor and industry as the circumstances may make necessary. I think I can testify, from what I have seen on the other side of the water, that we are more fortunate than other nations in respect to these great problems. Our industries have been disturbed and disorganized—disorganized as compared with a peace basis, very seriously, indeed, by the war, but not so seriously as the industries of other countries. And it seems to me, therefore, that we should approach these problems that we are about to discuss with a good deal of confidence—with a good deal of confidence that, if we have a common purpose, we can realize that common purpose without serious or insurmountable difficulties.

The thing that has impressed me most, gentlemen, not only in the recent weeks when I have been in conference on the other side of the water, but for many months before I went across the water, was this: we are at last learning that the business of government is to take counsel for the average man. We are at last learning that the whole matter of the prosperity of peoples runs down into the great body of the men and women who do the work of the world, and that the process of guidance is not completed by the mere success of great enterprises—it is completed only by the standard of the benefit that it confers upon those who in the obscure ranks of life contribute to the success of these enterprises. The hearts of the men and women and children of the world are stirred now in a way that has never been known before. They are not only stirred by their individual circumstances, but they are beginning to get a vision of what the general circumstances of the world are, and there is for the first time in history an international sympathy which is quick and vital—a sympathy which does not display itself merely in the contest of governments, but displays itself in the silent intercourse of sympathy between great bodies that constitute great nations. And the significance of a conference like this is that we are expressing in it, and will, I believe, express in the results of this conference, our consciousness that we are servants of this great silent mass of people who constitute the United States, and that, as their servants, it is our business, as it is our privilege, to find out how we can best assist in making their lives what they wish them to be, giving them the opportunities that they ought to have, assisting by public counsel in the private affairs upon which the happiness of men depends.

And so I am the more distressed that I cannot take part in these councils because my present business is to understand what plain men everywhere want. It is perfectly understood in Paris that we are not meeting there as the masters of anybody—that we are meeting there as the servants of, I believe, it is about 700,000,000 people, and that, unless we show that we understand the business of servants, we will not satisfy them, and we will not accomplish the peace of the world, and that, if we show that we want to serve any interest but theirs, we will have become candidates for the most lasting discredit that will ever attach to men in history. And so it is with this profound feeling of the significance of the things you are undertaking that I bid you welcome, because I believe you have come together in the spirit which I have tried to indicate, and that we will together concert methods of cooperation and individual action which will really accomplish what we wish to see accomplished in steadying and easing and facilitating the whole labor processes of the United States.

CC MS (C. L. Swem Coll., NjP).

To Newton Diehl Baker[1]

[My dear Mr. Secretary:]   [The White House, March 3, 1919]

Will you please express to the gentlemen of the commission representing the Philippine Legislature my regret that I shall be unable to see them personally on their arrival in Washington, as well as my hope that their mission will be a source of satisfaction to them, and that it will result in bringing about the desirable ends set forth in the joint resolution of the Legislature approving the sending of the commission to the United States?

I have been deeply gratified with the constant support and encouragement received from the Filipino people and from the Philippine Legislature in the trying period through which we are passing. The people of the United States have, with reason, taken the deepest pride in the loyalty and support of the Filipino people.

Though unable to meet the commission, the Filipino people shall not be absent from my thoughts. Not the least important labor of the conference which now requires my attention is that of making the pathway of the weaker people of the world less perilous—a labor which should be, and doubtless is, of deep and abiding interest to the Filipino people.

I am sorry that I cannot look into the faces of the gentlemen of this mission of the Philippine Islands and tell them all that I have in mind and heart as I think of the patient labor, with the end almost in sight, undertaken by the American and Filipino people for their permanent benefit. I know, however, that your sentiments are mine in this regard and that you will translate truly to them my own feeling.

[Cordially and sincerely yours,   Woodrow Wilson]

Printed in the *New York Times*, April 5, 1919.
  [1] Baker, upon Wilson's request, read the following letter, when Baker received the so-called Independence Mission of the Philippine Islands on April 4, 1919. Headed by Manuel Luis Quezon, President of the Filipino Senate, and accompanied by Francis Burton Harrison, Governor General of the Philippines, the delegation of forty prominent Filipinos had come to Washington to present a formal memorial asking for the complete independence of the Philippines. In his accompanying remarks, Baker stated that both he and Wilson, as well as the large majority of the American people, were in favor of Philippine independence and that the day was "very close at hand" when it could be formally accomplished. For a detailed account, see the *New York Times*, April 5, 1919; see also NDB to WW, April 8, 1919, printed as an Enclosure with T. H. Bliss to WW, April 9, 1919.

To Joseph Patrick Tumulty

Dear Tumulty: The White House. 3 March, 1919.

Please thank these people but say that there is no present prospect that I shall be able to write any such sketch.[1]

The President

TL (WP, DLC).
[1] Marie Mattingly (Mrs. William Brown) Meloney to JPT, March 1, 1919, TLS (WP, DLC). Mrs. Meloney, the acting editor of *Everybody's Magazine*, had written to Tumulty to obtain for her magazine "the first serial rights for the publication of President Wilson's 'History of Eight Years in the White House,' to be released for publication on any date which may be designated by the President." Mrs. Meloney was authorized to offer Wilson $40,000 for a series of ten articles or, if Wilson decided to write less than ten articles, $5,000 an article.

Two Telegrams to Edward Mandell House

The White House. 3 March, 1919.

[Number 3.] I will come directly to Brest and Paris as you advise.

Woodrow Wilson

The White House. 3 March, 1919.

[Number 4.] Your plan about starting the League of Nations to functioning at once[1] disturbs me a little, because I fear that some advantage would be given to the critics on this side of the water if they thought we were trying in that way to forestall action by the Senate and commit the country in some practical way from which it would be impossible to withdraw. If the plans you have in mind can be carried out with the explicit and public understanding that we are merely using this machinery provisionally and with no purpose of forestalling any subsequent action, but merely for the present facilitation of the processes of peace, perhaps this danger would disappear. The people of the United States are undoubtedly in favor of the League of Nations by an overwhelming majority. I can say this with perfect confidence, but there are many forces, particularly those prejudiced against Great Britain, which are exercising a considerable influence against it, and you ought to have that constantly in mind in everything you do.   Woodrow Wilson

T telegrams (WP, DLC).
[1] See EMH to WW, No. 8, Feb. 27, 1919. Wilson obviously had discussed this matter with Gregory and had asked for an opinion from the Justice Department. For the opinion, see G. C. Todd to TWG, March 11, 1919.

Two Letters to Frank Lyon Polk

My dear Polk: The White House 3 March, 1919.

I must admit that I do not see where we can get any money to pay these expenses[1] after the thirtieth of June next, but until then I am willing to pay out of the fund for National Security and Defence the necessary amounts for the actual maintenance of our American railway corps in Siberia. I understand from the enclosed letter that the present need is for $117,000 dollars. I hope that you will use this letter as an authorization for that amount and will keep me in touch with these things from month to month.

In haste,
          Cordially and sincerely yours,   Woodrow Wilson

TLS (SDR, RG 59, 861.77/835, DNA).
  [1] See FLP to WW, March 1, 1919 (first letter of that date).

My dear Polk: [The White House] 3 March, 1919.

I have read this letter of yours[1] with closest attention and agree with its conclusion that Number Two is the best course to pursue and that we ought to pursue it with considerable energy and persistence. If Chile knows what is best for her, she will accept it.

In haste,
          Cordially and faithfully yours,   Woodrow Wilson

TLS (Letterpress Books, WP, DLC).
  [1] FLP to WW, Feb. 28, 1919.

To Edgar Rickard

My dear Mr. Rickard: The White House 3 March, 1919.

I have had a number of conferences about the termination of the control over pork exports exercised by the War Trade Board until the first of March, and I must say that my conclusion is that it would not be wise for me to request the War Trade Board to reconsider or rescind their action suspending control the first of this month.

I wish that I had time in the few hours left me to enter into the reasons which have led me to this conclusion. I can only beg you to believe that I have given the most careful and sympathetic consideration to the arguments urged by the Food Administration and am constrained to believe that there is no real legal justification for the further exercise of the restraint which the War Trade Board exercised until the first of March.

Cordially and sincerely yours,   Woodrow Wilson

TLS (Hoover Archives, CSt-H).

To Edward Nash Hurley

My dear Hurley: [The White House] 3 March, 1919.

When you were here yesterday there was a matter I omitted to take up with you and which is of very considerable importance.

I had an interview with the Norwegian Minister in which he expressed a very earnest desire to come to an agreement with the Shipping Board with regard to the compensation for the Norwegian ships.[1] I promised him that I would speak to you about it.

I think we would be justified in coming to a liberal agreement, and I gathered from such particulars as his conversation contained that they would be quite willing to come down to two hundred and twenty-five.

But my interest is not so much in the figure as in a settlement which will impress the Norwegian Government with our sincere desire to be liberal and not haggle too long over a price.

Cordially and faithfully yours,   Woodrow Wilson

TLS (Letterpress Books, WP, DLC).
  [1] See FLP to WW, March 1, 1919 (third letter of that date).

To George Carroll Todd

My dear Mr. Todd: [The White House] 3 March, 1919.

It is with genuine grief that I received your request of March first[1] that I accept your resignation as Assistant to the Attorney General. The services you have rendered have been of the finest sort, and it is with genuine and deep regret that I learn of the necessity you feel to turn to the practice of your profession. I am constrained to accept your resignation, because evidently the reasons for it are in your mind imperative, but I hope that you will carry away with you the feeling that there is in my mind, and in the mind of all who have known your work, of admiration not only, but of gratitude for the service you have rendered.

In accordance with your suggestion, I accept the resignation to take effect at the end of the present month.

With most cordial good wishes,

Sincerely yours,   Woodrow Wilson

TLS (Letterpress Books, WP, DLC).
¹ G. C. Todd to WW, March 1, 1919, TLS (WP, DLC).

To John Nevin Sayre

My dear Nevin: [The White House] 3 March, 1919.

Of course, I do not feel that there is any intrusion in your thought-ful letter of the first of March. I can only say that it is a matter which I have approached again and again without being able to satisfy myself of a wise conclusion, but I am going to keep on thinking.

With warmest regard, in unavoidable haste,

                    Faithfully yours,   Woodrow Wilson

TLS (Letterpress Books, WP, DLC).

To Eleanor Randolph Wilson McAdoo

My Darling Little Girl: [The White House] 3 March, 1919.

In these breathless days it seems as if it were necessary to deny myself everything that I want to do, and therefore I have been able to send you nothing more than the telegram I sent the other day.[1] But I must, before I get away, send a more extended message from both of us of love and constant thought of you and of Mac.

There is nothing special to say about ourselves except that we are well and that we are hurrying back to Paris only because we believe that by hurrying back we can hasten the date when we have the blessed privilege of coming home to stay.

We have followed you both as well as we could with the deepest and most constant affection, as you need not be told. We shall have a happy reunion when the work at Paris is over.

With a heartful of love,   Your devoted Father

TLS (Letterpress Books, WP, DLC).
¹ That is, WW to W. G. McAdoo and Eleanor R. W. McAdoo, Feb. 26, 1919.

From David Franklin Houston

Dear Mr. President: Washington March 3, 1919.

The day after my conference with you, in accordance with your expressed wish, I acted as an intermediary and secured a confer-ence consisting of Secretary Glass, Mr. Ritter[1] representing Sec-retary Redfield, members of the Food Administration and of the

War Trade Board, and Governor Stuart,[2] Chairman of the National Agricultural Advisory Committee. The matter of maintaining the hog price agreement until the 31st of March was discussed for more than two hours. The conferees could not agree. Mr. Glass and the members of the War Trade Board thought the agreement ought to end now. The Food Administration thought it should run through March. Governor Stuart was very strongly of this opinion. I hold the same view and strongly urged it at this meeting.

I am in favor of removing all restrictions as rapidly as possible. I recognize the importance of having the Nation return approximately to normal at the earliest moment. I do not believe, however, that this particular arrangement, which will undoubtedly have a tendency to keep up the price of hog products, should not[3] be abrogated. It is proposed to let it run only for this month. It cannot in itself hold up industry very long. I am not of the opinion that the manufacturers will effect much reduction in their commodities within that time. If the agreement is not maintained, the hog producers of the Nation will think that an injustice has been done them. They began to prepare their animals nearly a year ago at the request of the Government. They have fed them over this period corn which they could have sold at high prices. They have not been able to get to market their hogs, produced at the urgent request of the authorities, because of the great numbers of them and transportation embargoes and difficulties. They will feel especially that the agreement has been abrogated without due notice. I think they ought to have approximately a month's notice.

My judgment is that the agreement ought to continue during this month, that the War Trade Board ought to support the Food Administration, and that very clear and specific notice ought now to be given that the agreement will cease absolutely on the 31st of March. I take the position I do notwithstanding the fact that I originally advised Mr. Hoover not to enter into the agreement.

Faithfully yours,   D. F. Houston.

TLS (WP, DLC).
    [1] That is, William McClellan Ritter, a member of the Industrial Board of the Department of Commerce and chairman of its Price Conference Committee.
    [2] That is, Henry Carter Stuart, former Governor of Virginia.
    [3] *Sic!*

From Carter Glass

Dear Mr. President: Washington March 3, 1919.

I have received your letter of March 1, 1919, with your approval of the establishment of credits in favor of foreign governments recommended in my letter to you of February 27.[1]

I entirely agree that your approval of the establishment of credits should not be made public. It has never been the practice of the Treasury to make public your approval of the establishment of credits in advance of the actual establishment of the respective credits.

I am most anxious to cooperate in every way so that our advances to foreign countries will be made dependent upon their fulfillment of their international agreements.

At this stage of the war it is sometimes necessary that the Treasury should, in connection with the making of foreign loans, make general statements as to its policy and, as well, enter into firm arrangements to obtain from Great Britain and from France the currencies of those countries needed to meet our expenditures in Europe. It would therefore be of great aid to the Treasury in carrying out your wishes, if it were possible that it should receive, as far in advance as it is practicable, some indication of the conditions which must be met by specified foreign countries in order that they may continue to receive advances from the Treasury.

In order to ascertain whether any of the Departments of our Government desired any conditions to be attached respecting our future advances to foreign governments, or to the establishment of credits in their favor, about January first last I wrote the Secretary of War, the Secretary of the Navy, the Vice-Chairman of the War Trade Board, the Chairman of the United States Shipping Board, and Mr. Rickard of the Food Administration, asking whether there were any outstanding questions with any governments or any suggestions which they respectively desired the Treasury to take into account in making final arrangements with Allied Governments in regard to our foreign loans. I have not however been advised of any matters which it has been possible for the Treasury to take into account in making loans to foreign governments.

Cordially yours,   Carter Glass.

TLS (WP, DLC).
[1] Actually, of February 28.

Two Letters from Harry Augustus Garfield

Dear Mr. President: Washington, D. C. March 3, 1919.

You asked me on Saturday to give you more specific information, if possible, concerning the report that England would refuse to ship coal to the War Department for the use of our soldiers in France, if we shipped coal to Italy.

Mr. Hurley confirms the report, stating that it was given to him at Tours by a representative of Major-General Rogers',[1] now in this country. I have today been in communication with General Rogers,

who asserts that it is true, and was understood by him and the
members of his staff while in France, that the English Government
had refused to continue to ship the 300,000 tons per month to
France for the use of our troops if we shipped coal to Italy. He is
unable to give me names and dates, but tells me that Colonel
D. B. Wentz,[2] care Chief Quartermaster, A.E.F., Tours, France,
will be able to furnish them. If it becomes important to secure details
of this arrangement, I advise that General Harbord,[3] in command
at Tours, be directed to send Colonel Wentz to Paris with the
information.

With devout wishes for your safe journey, and the success of
your great mission, I remain, as always,

Cordially and faithfully yours,   H. A. Garfield.

[1] Maj. Gen. Harry Lovejoy Rogers, Quartermaster General of the United States Army.
[2] Lt. Col. Daniel Bertsch Wentz, a coal operator from Virginia.
[3] That is, Maj. Gen. James Guthrie Harbord, commander of the Service of Supply of
the A.E.F.

Dear Mr. President: Washington, D. C. March 3, 1919.

Referring to my letter of the 1st instant, concerning the relation
of export coal to industrial unrest, I met Mr. Hurley and Mr. Rossiter[1]
Saturday afternoon and, in accordance with your request, asked
how much tonnage could be put at disposal for export coal within
the next few months. We ought to have from one to two million
tons per month. Apparently the best that can be accomplished
between now and September 1 will be as follows: April 250,000
tons; May 300,000; June 350,000; July 400,000; August 500,000.
This can be materially increased if the turn-around is reduced.
Delays are now most serious, but I will not venture into the controversy between the Shipping Board and the War and Navy Departments concerning the cause. I expect further information which
I will send to you.

Will you pardon me if I again emphasize the very great importance of an amicable international arrangement by which fuel oil
will be surely supplied for our navy and merchant marine, and by
which the export of our coals to Italy, France and South America,
will be made available to meet present needs. Above all things, I
fear the return of unregulated competition. It lies at the root of
industrial and international unrest, and is almost as disturbing as
unbridled combination.

Accompanying this letter is a memorandum concerning coal,
with attached papers,[2] and another concerning oil,[3] which I trust
may be of service.

Cordially and faithfully yours,   H. A. Garfield.

TLS (WP, DLC).

¹ John Henry Rosseter (not Rossiter), vice-president and general manager of the Pacific Mail Steamship Company, vice-president of W. R. Grace & Company, and one of the leading shipping experts of the country; at this time, director of the Division of Operations of the U. S. Shipping Board and trustee of the Emergency Fleet Corporation.

² H. A. Garfield, "MEMORANDUM FOR THE PRESIDENT OF THE UNITED STATES FROM H. A. GARFIELD CONCERNING COAL," March 3, 1919, TS MS, enclosing H. A. Garfield, "A PLAN TO PROMOTE THE PUBLIC WELFARE BY MORE EFFECTIVE COOPERATION BETWEEN THE GOVERNMENT OF THE UNITED STATES AND INDUSTRY," Feb. 26, 1919, T MS, and "CONFERENCE BETWEEN DR. GARFIELD AND REPRESENTATIVES OF THE NATIONAL COAL ASSOCIATION AND THE UNITED MINE WORKERS OF AMERICA," Feb. 11, 1919, T MS, all in WP, DLC. Garfield's memorandum of Feb. 26, 1919, is summarized in H. A. Garfield to WW, March 27, 1919, n. 2.

³ H. A. Garfield, "MEMORANDUM FOR THE PRESIDENT OF THE UNITED STATES FROM H. A. GARFIELD CONCERNING THE OIL SITUATION," March 3, 1919, TS MS (WP, DLC). Garfield, in addition, enclosed the following correspondence: W. E. Perdew to B. M. Baruch, Feb. 4 and Feb. 10, 1919, TCL; W. E. Perdew to V. H. Manning, March 1, 1919, T telegram; M. L. Requa *et al.*, to H. A. Garfield, Feb. 28, 1919, TCL; and J. H. Rosseter to H. A. Garfield, March 1, 1919, TCL, all in WP, DLC.

From Newton Diehl Baker, with Enclosure

My dear Mr. President: Washington. March 3, 1919.

I think you will be very much interested to know that all of my late reports from Siberia show that General Graves has been conducting himself with discretion and good judgment, and has won the hearty commendation of Mr. Morris, American Minister to Japan, and others who have come in contact with him. At one time, you will recall, you and I were disposed to doubt his good judgment.

I put into this envelope a letter from General Graves which you may care to read on the way over to Europe, covering a good many observations about the Siberian situation as it appeared to him in December.   Respectfully yours,   Newton D. Baker

E N C L O S U R E

Vladivostok, December 29, 1918.

From: The Commanding General.
To: The Adjutant General of the Army, Washington, D. C.
Subject: Conditions in Siberia.

1. The political situation seems to be uncertain. From what I can gather from people here who receive reports from all parts of Siberia and also from people who return from Western Siberia, it seems impossible for Koltchak to continue in power unless he receives some additional assistance from the French and English. The consensus of opinion is that if it were not for Allied troops he would be quickly overthrown. It may be possible that there are not enough arms in the hands of those opposed to Koltchak to effect his overthrow. He has the support of the autocratic class which includes nearly all former Russian army officers.

2. An effort is being made by the military to organize a force for service in Siberia. Admiral Koltchak has recently issued an order directing the mobilization of officers and soldiers. This order directs all Generals, Staff, and other officers, forty-three years of age or under, to present themselves before the 1st of January to the commanders of towns or the principal military officers in command. Officers serving in technical or industrial concerns will be temporarily exempted. Officers over forty-three years of age will be retired. There is a belief in some quarters that there is danger in arming any large number of troops as the people from which enlisted men are drawn are, generally speaking, opposed to the autocratic form of Government. Reports are constantly received as to uprising of small bodies of troops west of Lake Baikal.

3. The railway situation is growing worse every day. The engines are becoming out of condition and practically all employees of the railroad are grafting. In fact this is about the only way they have to live as they are receiving no pay. I am reliably informed, and there is no doubt in my mind as to the accuracy of this, that if anyone goes to the railroad company asking for transportation, they will immediately say they have no cars. They will continue to refuse to give cars until they are paid a certain price for them. This is the rule all along the railway line. When a train of empty cars passes a small station, and the Agent has received his graft from the proposed shipper, he sends someone out to tap on the wheel of a car and finally writes on the box that the car is to be repaired. The car is left at the station, the sign is removed, and the shipper is permitted to load his stores. Colonel Emerson[1] telegraphed me yesterday that at Chita out of ninety-six engines only twelve were serviceable and these are in bad shape. This is probably due to the lack of oil.

4. The representatives in Siberia of England are undoubtedly giving their whole support to Koltchak. This is well known to the Russian people and the democratic class is not pleased with this attitude of the British representatives. General Janin is undoubtedly working with Koltchak and there is undoubtedly an agreement between Koltchak, General Janin, and General Knox, British service, as to the use of troops in Siberia. Admiral Koltchak has agreed to give General Janin command of all troops, Allied and Russian, operating in the Urals, and General Knox is to have charge of the training of troops and those on the line of communication. This arrangement was undoubtedly made with the idea that Russian troops would be armed and equipped by England. General Knox

[1] That is, Col. George H. Emerson, chief of the Russian Railway Service Corps.

showed me a paper, which purported to have been received by him from the British Government, agreeing to arm two hundred thousand Russian troops, under the agreement above quoted, provided the Russian Government consented to the plan. General Knox later informed me that England will only arm and equip one hundred thousand instead of two hundred thousand as the situation is too uncertain to justify arming all of two hundred thousand. This arrangement is further verified by Admiral Koltchak sending for Captain Schuyler,[2] who is now at Omsk, and telling him to notify me that he, Admiral Koltchak, was afraid I would misunderstand the order of the French Government and that it was not his intention that General Knox should take command of American troops. I telegraphed Captain Schuyler to see if he could get hold of the copy of the French order referred to by Admiral Koltchak. I am of the impression that this arrangement entered into by Admiral Koltchak was objected to by some of his strongest backers and he began to back-peddle. As far as I can see, the Japanese have taken steps to stop Kalmikof from committing murder. I proposed to them in writing that in view of his high-handed and unwarranted acts that General Otani inform him that Japanese and American troops would use such force as was necessary to take from him in future any man or woman he arrested without first notifying the senior Commander of the American or Japanese troops of the offense the prisoner had committed and then we would see that the accused got a fair trial; and that in case he killed anyone we would use such force as was necessary to arrest him and those committing the murder and turn them all over to civil authorities for trial according to Russian law. General Otani said that Kalmikof had promised him on November 28th that he would not kill any more people and his investigations showed that he had kept this promise. He would, however, if I desired it sign the letter I had prepared and send it to Kalmikof. I told him my only desire was to stop this murderer from running wild and if the Japanese had taken steps to stop him I was perfectly satisfied. I believe Kalmikof has stopped murdering people as I have received no complaints in the last two or three weeks. The Japanese seem to be trying to control Simeonof.[3] I am unable to determine what their object is but it seems to me they are trying to occupy a position which will enable them to jump on either side of the fence in case it is to their advantage to do so. I believe they will support Koltchak, Simeonof, or anyone that will give them what they are after in Siberia. The Czechs are apparently very much dissatisfied and want to go home. They are not working

[2] Capt. Roy L. Schuyler.
[3] That is, Grigorii Semenov.

harmoniously with Koltchak and, as I telegraphed the War Department a day or two ago, practically all Czech troops have been put in reserve. This information came from Major Slaughter,[4] who is on the ground and who is very careful in his reports. With reference to the property being sent here to the Czechs, I am convinced there is to be another great waste of property. More material is being sent in here than they need and in fact we have to unload it and put it on the dock and it will be left there unless the Russians take it and use it, which I think will be the case. A great number of automobiles and trucks are being sent over which it is absolutely impossible, with the railroad as it is, to get out to the Czech troops. This is true with a great deal of other property being sent here. I am convinced the Czechs are satisfied that they are not going to use it and these expensive Cadillac cars will remain on the dock in all kinds of weather for a long time unless the Russians take the property and use it for purposes for which it was not sent to Vladivostok. I do not know under what conditions or supervision this property was purchased in the United States.

5. Siberia seems full of profiteers. They are at times so extravagant in their demands as to make them ludicrous. They seem to think, however, that they ought to get money any way they can: as an example, when the American troops came here they went to the town authorities to get a building for our use. Colonel Styer,[5] who preceded me, had gotten the building we are now in. When I came I inquired as to the price we were paying; no arrangement had been made relative to paying for the building. I immediately detailed a Board to investigate the matter and the Agents first stated they wanted Eight Thousand Dollars Gold per month and finally came down to Six Thousand. The Board investigated and found an excellent law on the statute books which lists all buildings in Vladivostok, and I presume in other towns in Russia, showing the cost, taxes paid, and the rental that should be given in case a building is taken for military purposes. The law also forbids the payment of anything in excess of this specified amount. The amount for the building was Seven Hundred Fifty Dollars Gold per month, which I offered to pay the owner. He refused to take it for two or three months but as he finally found out that the matter had been carefully gone into by the Board he has accepted the payment. There are very few telephones in Vladivostok. The Y.M.C.A. recently found one not in use; they wanted to get it and the man who had it asked them Thirty Six Thousand rubles for the telephone.

[4] Maj. Homer Havron Slaughter, Assistant Military Attaché in Russia, at this time stationed at Omsk.
[5] Col. Henry Delp Styer, commander of the 27th Infantry, who had landed at Vladivostok on August 16, 1918, two weeks before the arrival of General Graves.

6. On the 27th I cabled to Washington relative to the designation of people in Russia as Bolsheviks. There is undoubtedly an excellent propaganda being conducted by the autocratic class to classify everyone who differs from them as Bolsheviks. This word is now being used throughout the world so that a Bolshevik is a criminal or brigand. In my judgment there are many more good people classified by the autocratic crowd as Bolsheviks than there are good people in the autocratic class in Siberia. If the people in European Russia are as determined to have some form of representative Government as are the people in Siberia, I am convinced in my own mind that they must be permitted to try some form of democratic Government before any stable Government can be established. These views are obtained from various classes of people who come from all sections of Siberia. The autocratic class practically admit this is so, but they claim the people are not sufficiently educated to justify giving them autonomous Government, but this will be done when the people are better educated and are better informed in political affairs. Along these lines I made an investigation of what appears to be an interesting inquiry relative to the composition of the Zemstvo in Vladivostok. There are between forty and fifty members of the Zemstvo; all but about ten are from the peasant class. Without exception the peasants have selected to represent them men who can read and write and are able to inform themselves as to political and other conditions throughout the world. This is an indication that in case they were given a voice in the formation of a Government that they would not select criminal or ignorant men to represent them but would choose men able to read and write.

Wm. S. Graves.

TLS (WP, DLC).

From Thomas Lincoln Chadbourne, Jr.

Dear Mr. President: New York March 3, 1919.

I am not unappreciative of the delicacy of the Irish question and of your difficulties in approaching it on the other side of the water, but I am so impressed with its importance to our party that I am taking the liberty of writing you respecting it.

I find not only among Irish democrats but among democrats generally a strong feeling that if the peace conference reaches its conclusion without an expression from us of some kind unfavorable to allowing England to settle this question in her own way, the effect upon our party will be distinctly bad.

I am not an Irishman and am no more interested, except from

the party's standpoint, in the Irish than in the Polish or the Jugo-Slav problem. Whatever you may think of my conclusions I feel that you will know that I am writing from a sincere conviction of the importance of the question to the party.

I beg to remain, with great respect,

Sincerely and cordially yours,   Thomas L. Chadbourne.

TLS (WP, DLC).

Newton Diehl Baker to Robert Russa Moton

Personal and Confidential:

My dear Major Moton: [Washington] March 3, 1919.

I send, for your information, a note which I have just received from the President,[1] covering his judgment in the confidential matter which you submitted to me. Perhaps you had better regard the President's note as entirely confidential.

Cordially yours,   Newton D. Baker.

TCL (R. R. Moton Coll., ATT).
[1] WW to NDB, March 1, 1919.

Tasker Howard Bliss to Newton Diehl Baker
and Peyton Conway March

Paris March 3d [1919]

Number 213 [313] Rush

For the Secretary of War and the Chief of Staff. Strictly Confidential.

The following is digest of the proposed final Military Terms and Military and Naval Aviation Terms of Peace with Germany. Consideration of them by the Supreme War Council late today. The American Commission ask me to telegraph them so that the President can have them before he sails. Military terms under following general headings:

Reduction of Strength,

Reduction of Armament,

Future German Military Law and Control.

Essential features under reduction of strength are: Total German Army for all purposes 200,000 men and 9 thousand officers; organizations limited to 15 divisions of Infantry and 5 of Cavalry; 5 Army Corps Staffs and 1 Army Staff maximum allowed for these divisions; any other organizations or grouping of forces or other organs of command prohibited; abolishes great German General Staff, Krieges' Academy and all Military Schools exept those sufficient to provide officers for army allowed her. All of above reductions to be made within time limit of two months.

Essential features under reduction of armament are: Provision for disposing of all armament in excess of the minimum necessary for forces allowed Germany according to a table of equipment; limited replacements of material; definite locations (to be made known to Allied and Associated Powers) of depots for storing reserves of munitions. All foregoing provisions to be complied with within a time limit of one month. Manufacture of all war equipment to be in limited number of factories name and place of which to be made known to Allied and Associated Powers; all fortifications and forts within 50 kilometers of Rhine to be disarmed and dismantled; status quo to be maintained of all fortifications on southern and eastern frontiers of Germany; armament of fortifications on land or sea authorized to be maintained never to exceed number and caliber of cannon existing at date of signature of agreement and supplies of munitions for these cannon are to be fixed; and nine new fortifications to be constructed.[1] Time limit three months. Germany is prohibited from manufacturing war equipment for foreign states or to receive same from foreign states. No military forces or establishments to be maintained on left bank of Rhine.

Following are essential features to be embodied in German Military laws within a time limit of three months. Total number of 200,000 men is to include a Cadre of enlisted or reenlisted men which are not to exceed 20,000 and number, not exceed 180,000, of those called in each class of recruits. Aside from this number no military forces to be maintained in Germany in form of militia or any other form; total duration of service of each class not to exceed one year and service to have been continuous. If service of a class or any part of a class of any year is less than one year, for the remainder of that year German Army will not exceed the strength of Cadre, or 20,000 men, plus part of class held to year's service; Officers newly commissioned must pledge themselves to serve actively for 25 years unless discharged for disability; Officers retained in the Army must serve until they are 45 years of age or if discharged because of ill health shall not be replaced until they have reached age of 45 years, or in case of new officer who has pledged himself to serve 25 years, until the 25 years have elapsed.

The proportion of officers discharged on ground of ill health shall not exceed annually 15 per cent of total strength of 9,000 officers. Reenlisted men shall be made to serve minimum of 15 years. No measures for mobilization shall be provided; Military exercises of all state employees are forbidden and all civilian associations forbidden from considering military questions or permitting instruction in use of arms of warfare.

Commission of allied and associated powers to be appointed to sit in Germany to work control over her in carrying out conditions which it is demanded she fulfill within time limit up to three months duration. Functions of this commission ceasing at expiration of that period.

Following are essential features of military and maritime Air Service terms. Reduction of material to following: No military airplanes; one hundred hydro planes or gliders until Oct. 1st only, these to be without arms, munitions or bombs; one additional motor for each hydro plane or gliders; nothing except dirigible balloons. Personnel: No personnel for land aviation; 1000 men for entire navigating and non navigating personnel of the marine aviation; no aviation grounds or dirigible hangars to be maintained or established within 150 kilometers of Rhine or within 150 kilometers of eastern or southern frontiers of Germany. Germany to permit Allies free aircraft passage over and landing on its territory until evacuation of her territory by Allied troops; manufacture of air material including motors forbidden Germany until definitive signing of treaty of peace. Excess material to be delivered to Allies. Control over Germany in carrying out these terms to be exercised by a commission similar to one heretofore mentioned and to cease its function only when Germany carries out agreements as to air terms.

Bliss.

TC and CC telegram (WP, DLC).
  [1] Obviously a garbled phrase; it does not appear in the statement of proposed terms presented to the Council of Ten by the Supreme War Council on March 6, 1919. This statement is printed in *PPC*, IV, 230-42.

Gilbert Fairchild Close to Frank Lyon Polk, with Enclosure

My dear Mr. Counselor: The White House 3 March, 1919.

The President asks me to say, with reference to the enclosed letter, that if you will be kind enough to send a mememorandum [memorandum] about this matter to Secretary Lansing, he will handle it as you suggest, but in any case the President things [thinks] we ought to refuse a passport to Judge Cohalan.

Sincerely yours,   Gilbert F. Close

ENCLOSURE

From Frank Lyon Polk

My dear Mr. President: Washington March 1, 1919.

I understand that Judge Cohalan and some others representing the "Freedom of Ireland" movement in this country have been seeking an interview with you.[1] I have reason to believe that these gentlemen desire to go to Paris for the purpose of presenting Ireland's case to the Peace Conference. The question will then come up as to whether they should receive passports, and I would like your instructions.

As the refusal of passports will cause intense irritation among the Irish in this country, it occurred to me that if you are unwilling to let them have passports, we might hold the matter until you reach France and you then might find that the French would refuse to visé the passports. I quite appreciate this is not a very bold way of meeting the situation, but in view of the fact that you will have to make a fight in this country for the League of Nations, the less opposition we create now, the better.

        Yours faithfully,   Frank L Polk

TLS (F. L. Polk Papers, CtY).
 [1] See G. Creel to WW, March 31, 1919.

Gilbert Fairchild Close to Dudley Field Malone

My dear Mr. Malone: [The White House] 3 March, 1919.

The President asks me to acknowledge receipt of your letter of February 28th and to express his regret that he cannot give a personal answer to it because of the rush of business in which he is involved, but he asks me to say that he recognizes the importance of the suggestion you so kindly make and thanks you for it.

        Sincerely yours,   Gilbert F. Close

CCL (WP, DLC).

Timothy O'Brien[1] to Joseph Patrick Tumulty

Dear Sir: Hutchinson, Minn. March 3, 1919

Voters of Irish birth or descent will not soon forget for the Democratic party the contemptuous treatment accorded by President Wilson (and by yourself, for that matter) to the delegation from the Irish Race Convention which sought an interview with him during the past week, as reported by press dispatches during the past few days.

Speaking for myself, there is one Democratic vote the less from this forward, and one opponent the more for Mr. Wilson's League of Nations as at present constituted; and I believe I have at least a little influence in this community.

Very sincerely yours,   (Rev.) T. O'Brien

TLS (WP, DLC).
¹ Pastor of St. Anastasia's Roman Catholic Church in Hutchinson, Minn.

An Unpublished Statement

[c. March 4, 1919]

The 65th Congress, now adjourning, deserves the gratitude and appreciation of a people whose will and purpose I believe it has faithfully expressed. One cannot examine the record of its action without being impressed by its completeness, its courage and its full comprehension of a great task. The needs of the Army and the Navy have been met in a way that assures the effectiveness of American arms, and the war-making branch of the Government has been abundantly equipped with the powers that were necessary to make the will and purpose of the nation effective.

I believe that it has also in equal degree, and as far as possible in the face of war, safeguarded the rights of the people and kept in mind the considerations of social justice so often obscured in the hasty readjustments of such a crisis.

It seems to me that the work of this remarkable session has not only been done thoroughly but that it has also been done with the utmost despatch possible in the circumstances or consistent with a full consideration of the exceedingly critical matters dealt with. Best of all, it has left no doubt as to the will and purpose of the nation but has affirmed them as loyally and as emphatically as our fine soldiers will affirm them on the firing line.

WWhw and WWT MS (C. L. Swem Coll., NjP).

A Statement

[*March 4, 1919*]

A group of men in the Senate have deliberately chosen to embarrass the administration of the Government, to imperil the financial interests of the railway system of the country and to make arbitrary use of powers intended to be employed in the interest of the people.

It is plainly my present duty to attend the Peace Conference in

Paris. It is also my duty to be in close contact with the public business during a session of the Congress. I must make my choice between these two duties, and I confidently hope that the people of the country will think that I am making the right choice.

It is not in the interest of the right conduct of public affairs that I should call the Congress in special session while it is impossible for me to be in Washington, because of a more pressing duty else-where, to co-operate with the Houses.

I take it for granted that the men who have obstructed and pre-vented the passage of necessary legislation have taken all of this into consideration and are willing to assume the responsibility of the impaired efficiency of the Government and the embarrassed finances of the country during the time of my enforced absence.

Printed in the New York *World*, March 5, 1919.

From the Diary of Dr. Grayson

Tuesday, March 4, 1919.

The President went to the Capitol as usual for the closing hours of the Congress. He found very little to do, inasmuch as the Re-publicans through their unorganized filibuster had completely de-moralized all pending legislation. Immediately following the final adjournment of Congress the President gave out the following state-ment in which he placed the direct responsibility for the failure of the important and much-needed legislation. . . .[1]

Tuesday, March 4, 1919, (continued)

RETURN TRIP TO FRANCE.

The President reached the Union Station at 1:56 o'clock. He was greeted on arrival by a large crowd outside of the station and another in the train-shed, who cheered him lustily as he passed through the gate and entered the special train in waiting. He left promptly at 2:00 o'clock. He was accompanied by Mrs. Wilson, Secretary Tumulty, former Attorney General Gregory (who relinquished office this day), Miss Edith Benham (Mrs. Wilson's secretary), and my-self. Others in the party were Raymond T. Baker,[2] Director of the Mint, Dr. John W. Coughlin, National Committeeman of Con-necticut,[3] Samuel Fordyce of Missouri,[4] M. Brice Clagett[5] and Oscar Price,[6] Assistant Directors of the Railroad Administration, John E. Nevin of the International News Service, Robert Bender of the United Press, and Mr. Curtis of the Associated Press.[7]

While on the train the President discussed with Mrs. Wilson, Secretary Tumulty and myself some of the details of the recent actions in Congress. After talking over the situation at length he excused himself and went to his room to prepare his speech for the evening, which was delivered without any notes or memoranda. He spent an hour in thought—which covered the preparation for his speech at the Metropolitan Opera House.

Last evening (March 3rd) I examined the President before retiring, and notwithstanding the severe physical strain he has been through in the past week I found him somewhat fatigued, but his blood pressure, blood examination and urinalysis were unusually good for a man of his years. When I revealed to him the findings of my examination he remarked that it was very gratifying because he had never been driven so hard as he had in the past three months, and that he was encouraged because I was satisfied with his *physical equilibrium* in these unusual conditions. He made his usual remark after such examination: "I thank you very much, my dear fellow."

The trip to New York was without incident until Wilmington, Delaware, was reached. Here there were gathered on the station platform a large number of men and women—munition workers—who waved a salutation as the train swept by.

Arriving at the Philadelphia Market Street Station the President and Mrs. Wilson were escorted to waiting automobiles and proceeded to Jefferson Hospital, where the President called on his daughter, Mrs. Francis Sayre, and where he had his first view of his new grandson, Woodrow Wilson Sayre, who was born on February 22d. He was greeted on his arrival at the Hospital by Dr. E. P. Davis, who was attending Mrs. Sayre. The corridors of the Hospital were crowded with nurses, attendants and patients who were able to be about—all anxious to get a glimpse of the President as he walked along to his daughter's room. The meeting with his daughter was most affectionate and touching; she was so glad to see her father—the tears welled up in her eyes. The President patted her and said to her—"My dear little girl." He inspected the new arrival with considerable curiosity and interest, and remarked "He is a bully little fellow." The baby appeared plump and well-formed, and lay there with its eyes tightly closed and its mouth wide open, which amused the President very much. The nurse remarked: "I wish he would open his eyes so you could see how beautiful they are," whereupon the President replied: "With his mouth open and his eyes shut, I predict that he will make a Senator when he grows up." His sense of humor is ever-present.

The President returned to the train and exactly one hour from the time of arrival in Philadelphia the journey to New York was resumed. We had dinner on the train, the party consisting of the President, Mrs. Wilson, Secretary Tumulty, Miss Benham, former Attorney General Gregory and myself.

We reached New York at 8:15 o'clock. The President was greeted at the station by his classmate and close personal friend, Cleveland H. Dodge, as well as a reception committee, headed by Governor Al Smith of New York. Mr. Abram I. Elkus had charge of the arrangements of the meeting. The President made a quick run to the Metropolitan Opera House with Mrs. Wilson, Mr. Dodge and Mr. Elkus. The streets were crowded with people, all of whom cheered lustily as the auto carrying the President went by. He was forced to stand uncovered responding to the cheers almost the entire distance. In the reception room underneath the stage in the Opera House, the President met former President William H. Taft, who was to make a speech. The Opera House was jammed, the police saying that the crowd was the largest that had ever been allowed inside of it. The only space unfilled was in the corridors and even that would have been occupied if the fire authorities had granted permission. Outside of the Opera House there was a crowd of 15,000 people, held back in the side streets by the police.

The President was given a warm reception when he arose to speak. Despite the fact that he was very tired as the result of his strenuous labors since his return, he was in excellent voice and his speech made a very good impression everywhere.

Following the formal speech the President returned to the offices of the Opera House, where he held a conference with Governor Smith while the theatre was being emptied. Upstairs, in what is known as the club room, had gathered a committee of twenty-five, which had been appointed by the Irish Race Convention which met in Philadelphia on Sunday, February 23d. This committee had been in Washington and endeavored to force itself upon the President, but he had been unable to find time in which to listen to it, and announced his willingness to meet them tonight. However, before he would consent to meeting this committee, the President insisted that Daniel F. Cohalan, a Justice of the Supreme Court of the State of New York, be eliminated from the committee. In the presence of some Irish policemen who surrounded him, the President remarked: "I will not attend the meeting if Cohalan is there because he is a traitor." Cohalan is a brother-in-law of Jeremiah O'Leary, a noted pro-German agitator, who was indicted and placed on trial for treason as a result of his activities against the Government during the war. Cohalan had been especially obnoxious in attacking the President and had been a leader in the spreading of pro-German propaganda for many months. The conference itself was entirely in the nature of a general discussion, the committee endeavoring to have the President promise that he would take action along lines which would result in the formation of an Irish Republic when he arrived in Paris. The committee wanted the President to promise that he would take this matter up with the Peace Conference itself, and they also wanted him to arrange for a hearing by the Peace Conference of delegates representing the proposed Irish Republic. The President heard the committee courteously but made no promises. The President said it was a domestic affair for Great Britain and Ireland to settle themselves, and not a matter for outside interference.

Leaving the Opera House the President was escorted to the Lackawanna Ferry, at the foot of 23d Street, rushed across the North River, and speeded directly to the Hoboken Wharves, where the GEORGE WASHINGTON was in waiting. Vice-Admiral Gleaves and General McManus[8] met the President at the foot of the decorated stair-way and escorted him to the ship.

The President was very tired, showing the result of the hard campaign, but was very cheerful as he came on board, greeting the officers of the GEORGE WASHINGTON with the pleasant statement that it was "almost like coming home."

The President remained up until after midnight to sign the commissions of Attorney General A. Mitchell Palmer and Comptroller of the Currency John Skelton Williams, whose nominations had failed of confirmation in the closing hours of the Senate session.

It was considered somewhat of a coincidence that it was just thirteen weeks ago since the President came on board the GEORGE WASHINGTON for his initial departure Europeward.

[1] Here follows a copy of the statement just printed.
[2] Raymond Thomas Baker.
[3] John William Coughlin, M.D., actually of Fall River, Mass., and a member of the Democratic National Committee from Massachusetts.
[4] Samuel Wesley Fordyce (1877-1948), a lawyer of St. Louis and a former counsel of the War Finance Corporation, active in Democratic party politics in Missouri.
[5] Maurice Brice Clagett (1889-1951), White House correspondent for the Associated Press, 1914-1917; executive secretary to McAdoo, 1917. He married McAdoo's youngest daughter, Sarah (Sally) Fleming McAdoo, in 1928.
[6] That is, Oscar A. Price.
[7] Lucius Fisher Curtis.
[8] Vice-Adm. Albert Gleaves, commander of the cruiser and transport force of the Atlantic Fleet, and Brig. Gen. George Henry McManus, the troop movement officer in charge of the embarkation of American forces at Hoboken.

An Address at the Metropolitan Opera House

March 4, 1919.

My fellow citizens: I accept the intimation of the air just played. I will not come back " 'till it's over, over there." And yet I pray God, in the interest of the peace of the world, that that may be soon.

The first thing that I am going to tell the people on the other side of the water is that an overwhelming majority of the American people is in favor of the League of Nations. I know that that is true. I have had unmistakable intimations of it from all parts of the country, and the voice rings true in every case. I account myself fortunate to speak here under the unusual circumstances of this evening. I am happy to associate myself with Mr. Taft in this great cause. He has displayed an elevation of view and a devotion to public duty which is beyond praise.

And I am the more happy because this means that this is not a party issue. No party has a right to appropriate this issue, and no party will in the long run dare oppose it.

We have listened to so clear and admirable an exposition of many of the main features of the proposed Covenant of the League of Nations that it is perhaps not necessary for me to discuss in any particular way the contents of the document. I will seek rather to give you its setting. I do not know when I have been more impressed than by the conferences of the commission set up by the conference of peace to draw up a Covenant for the League of Nations. The representatives of fourteen nations sat around that board—not young men, not men inexperienced in the affairs of their own countries, not men inexperienced in the politics of the world. And the inspiring influence of every meeting was the concurrence of purpose on the part of all those men to come to an agreement and an effective working agreement with regard to this league of the civilized world.

There was a conviction in the whole impulse; there was conviction of more than one sort; there was the conviction that this thing ought to be done; and there was also the conviction that not a man there would venture to go home and say that he had not tried to do it.

Mr. Taft has set a picture for you of what a failure of this great purpose would mean. We have been hearing for all these weary months that this agony of war has lasted of the sinister purpose of the Central Empires, and we have made maps of the course that they meant their conquests to take. Where did the lines of that map lie, of that central line that we used to call from Bremen to Baghdad? They lay through these very regions to which Mr. Taft has called your attention, but they lay then through a united empire. The

Austro-Hungarian Empire, whose integrity Germany was bound to respect as her ally, lay in the path of that line of conquest; the Turkish Empire, whose interests she professed to make her own, lay in the direct path that she intended to tread. And now what has happened? The Austro-Hungarian Empire has gone to pieces and the Turkish Empire has disappeared, and the nations that effected that great result—for it was a result of liberation—are now responsible as the trustees of the assets of those great nations. You not only would have weak nations lying in this path, but you would have nations in which that old poisonous seed of intrigue could be planted with the certainty that the crop would be abundant, and one of the things that the League of Nations is intended to watch is the course of intrigue. Intrigue cannot stand publicity, and if the League of Nations were nothing but a great debating society it would kill intrigue.

It is one of the agreements of this Covenant that it is the friendly right of every nation a member of the League to call attention to anything that it thinks will disturb the peace of the world, no matter where that thing is occurring. There is no subject that may touch the peace of the world which is exempt from inquiry and discussion, and I think everybody here present will agree with me that Germany would never have gone to war if she had permitted the world to discuss the aggression upon Serbia for a single week. The British Foreign Office suggested, it pleaded, that there might be a day or two delay so that representatives of the nations of Europe could get together and discuss the possibilities of a settlement. Germany did not dare permit a day's discussion. You know what happened. So soon as the world realized that an outlaw was at large, the nations began, one by one, to draw together against her. We know for a certainty that, if Germany had thought for a moment that Great Britain would go in with France and with Russia, she never would have undertaken the enterprise, and the League of Nations is meant as a notice to all outlaw nations that not only Great Britain, but the United States and the rest of the world, will go in to stop enterprises of that sort. And so the League of Nations is nothing more nor less than the covenant that the world will always maintain the standards which it has now vindicated by some of the most precious blood ever spilt.

The liberated peoples of the Austro-Hungarian Empire and of the Turkish Empire call out to us for this thing. It has not arisen in the council of statesmen. Europe is a bit sick at heart at this very moment, because it sees that statesmen have had no vision, and that the only vision has been the vision of the people. Those who suffer see. Those against whom wrong is wrought know how desirable is the right of the righteous. The nations that have long been under the heel of the Austrian, that have long cowered before the German, that have long suffered the indescribable agonies of being governed by the Turk, have called out to the world, generation after generation, for justice, for liberation, and for succor, and no cabinet in the world has heard them. Private organizations, pitying hearts, philanthropic men and women have poured out their treasure in order to relieve these sufferings, but no nation has said to the nations responsible, "You must stop; this thing is intolerable and we will not permit it." And the vision has been with the people. My friends, I wish you would reflect upon this proposition: the vision as to what is necessary for great reforms has seldom come from the top in the nations of the world. It has come from the need and the aspiration and the self-assertion of great bodies of men who meant to be free. And I can explain some of the criticisms which have been leveled against this great enterprise only by the supposition that the men who utter the criticisms have never felt the great pulse of the heart of the world.

And I am amazed—not alarmed, but amazed—that there should be in some quarters such a comprehensive ignorance of the state of the world. These gentlemen do not know what the mind of men is just now. Everybody else does. I do not know where they have been closeted; I do not know by what influences they have been blinded; but I do know they have been separated from the general currents of the thought of mankind.

And I want to utter this solemn warning, not in the way of a threat; the forces of the world do not threaten, they operate. The great tides of the world do not give notice that they are going to rise and run; they rise in their majesty and overwhelming might, and those who stand in the way are overwhelmed. Now the heart of the world is awake, and the heart of the world must be satisfied. Do not let yourselves suppose for a moment that the uneasiness in the populations of Europe is due entirely to economic causes or economic motives; something very much deeper underlies it all than that. They see that their governments have never been able to defend them against intrigue or aggression, and that there is no force of foresight or of prudence in any modern cabinet to stop war. And therefore they say: "There must be some fundamental cause for this," and the fundamental cause they are beginning to perceive to be that nations have stood singly or in little jealous groups against each other, fostering prejudice, increasing the danger of war rather than concerting measures to prevent it. And that if there is right in the world, if there is justice in the world, there is no reason why nations should be divided in the support of justice.

They are, therefore, saying if you really believe that there is a right, if you really believe that wars ought to be stopped, stop thinking about the rival interests of nations and think about men and women and children throughout the world. Nations are not made to afford distinction to their rulers by way of success in the maneuvers of politics. Nations are meant, if they are meant for anything, to make the men and women and children in them secure and happy and prosperous, and no nation has the right to set up its special interests against the interests and benefits of mankind, least of all this great nation which we love. It was set up for the benefit of mankind; it was set up to illustrate the highest ideals and to achieve the highest aspirations of men who wanted to be free. And the world—the world of today—believes that and counts on us, and would be thrown back into the blackness of despair if we deserted it.

I have tried once and again, my fellow citizens, to say to little circles of friends or to larger bodies what seems to be the real hope of the peoples of Europe, and I tell you frankly I have not been able to do so, because when the thought tries to crowd itself into speech, the profound emotion of the thing is too much. Speech will not carry. I have felt the tragedy of the hope of those suffering peoples.

It is a tragedy because it is a hope which cannot be realized in its perfection; and yet I have felt besides its tragedy, its compulsion—its compulsion upon every living man to exercise every influence that he has to the utmost to see that as little as possible of that hope is disappointed, because if men cannot now, after this agony of bloody sweat, come to their self-possession and see how to regulate the affairs of the world, we will sink back into a period of struggle in which there will be no hope and, therefore, no mercy. There can be no mercy where there is no hope, for why should you spare another if you yourself expect to perish? Why should you be pitiful if you can get no pity? Why should you be just if, upon every hand, you are put upon?

There is another thing which I think the critics of this Covenant have not observed. They not only have not observed the temper of the world, but they have not even observed the temper of those splendid boys in khaki that they sent across the seas. I have had the proud consciousness of the reflected glory of those boys because the Constitution made me their commander in chief, and they have taught me some lessons. When we went into the war, we went into it on the basis of declarations which it was my privilege to utter, because I believed them to be an interpretation of the purpose and thought of the people of the United States.

And those boys went over there with the feeling that they were sacredly bound to the realization of those ideals; that they were not only going over there to beat Germany; they were not going over there merely with resentment in their hearts against a particular outlaw nation; but that they were crossing those 3,000 miles of sea in order to show to Europe that the United States, when it became necessary, would go anywhere where the rights of mankind were threatened. They would not sit still in the trenches. They would not be restrained by the prudence of experienced continental commanders. They thought they had come over there to do a particular thing, and they were going to do it, and do it at once. And just as soon as that rush of spirit, as well as the rush of body, came in contact with the lines of the enemy, they began to break, and they continued to break until the end. They continued to break, my fellow citizens, not merely because of the physical force of those lusty youngsters, but because of the irresistible spiritual force of the armies of the United States. It was that that they felt. It was that that awed them. It was that that made them feel if these youngsters ever got a foothold they could never be dislodged, and that therefore every foot of ground that they won was permanently won for the liberty of mankind.

And do you suppose that, having felt that crusading spirit of these youngsters who went over there, not to glorify America, but to serve their fellow men, I am going to permit myself for one moment to slacken in my effort to be worthy of them and of their cause? What I said at the opening I said with a deeper meaning than perhaps you have caught. I do mean not to come back until it's over over there, and it must not be over until the nations of the world are assured of the permanency of peace.

Gentlemen on this side of the water would be very much profited by getting into communication with some gentlemen on the other side of the water. We sometimes think, my fellow citizens, that the experienced statesmen of the European nations are an unusually hardheaded set of men, by which we generally mean, although we do not admit it, that they are a bit cynical. They say, "This is a practical world," by which you always mean that it is not an ideal world; that they do not believe that things can be settled upon an ideal basis. Well, I never came into intimate contact with them before, but if they used to be that way, they are not that way now. They have been subdued, if that was once their temper, by the awful significance of recent events and the awful importance of what is to ensue. And there is not one of them with whom I have come in contact who does not feel that he cannot in conscience return to his people from Paris unless he has done his utmost to do something more than attach his name to a treaty of peace. Every man in that conference knows the treaty of peace in itself will be inoperative, as Mr. Taft has said, without this constant support and energy of a great organization such as is supplied by the League of Nations.

And men who, when I first went over there, were skeptical of the possibility of forming a League of Nations, admitted that if we could but form it it would be an invaluable instrumentality through which to secure the operation of the various parts of the treaty. And when that treaty comes back gentlemen on this side will find the Covenant not only in it, but so many threads of the treaty tied to the Covenant that you cannot dissect the Covenant from the treaty without destroying the whole vital structure. The structure of peace will not be vital without the League of Nations, and no man is going to bring back a cadaver with him.

I must say that I have been puzzled by some of the criticisms—not by the criticisms themselves—I can understand them perfectly, even when there was no foundation for them—but by the fact of the criticism. I cannot imagine how these gentlemen can live and not live in the atmosphere of the world. I cannot imagine how they can live and not be in contact with the events of their times. And I particularly cannot imagine how they can be Americans and set up a doctrine of careful selfishness thought out to the last detail. I have heard no counsel of generosity in their criticism. I have heard no constructive suggestion. I have heard nothing except, "Will it not be dangerous to us to help the world?" It would be fatal to us not to help it.

From being what I will venture to call the most famous and the most powerful nation in the world, we would of a sudden have become the most contemptible. So I did not need to be told, as I have been told, that the people of the United States would support this Covenant. I am an American, and I knew they would. What a sweet revenge it is upon the world! They laughed at us once; they thought we did not mean our professions of principle. They thought so until April of 1917. It was hardly credible to them that we would do more than send a few men over and go through the forms of helping. And when they saw multitudes hastening across the sea, and saw what those multitudes were eager to do when they got to the other side, they stood at amaze and said: "The thing is real; this nation is the friend of mankind as it said it was." The enthusiasm, the hope, the trust, the confidence in the future bred by that change of view are indescribable. Take an individual American and you may often find him selfish and confined to his special interests; but take the American in the mass and he is willing to die for an ideal. The sweet revenge, therefore, is this, that we

believed in righteousness, and now we are ready to make the supreme sacrifice for it—the supreme sacrifice of throwing in our
fortunes with the fortunes of men everywhere.

Mr. Taft was speaking of Washington's utterance about entangling alliances, and if he will permit me to say so, he put the exactly
right interpretation upon what Washington said—the interpretation
that is inevitable if you read what he said, as most of these gentlemen do not. And the thing that he longed for was just what we are
now about to supply—an arrangement which will disentangle all
the alliances in the world.

Nothing entangles, nothing enmeshes a man except a selfish
combination with somebody else. Nothing entangles a nation, ham-
pers it, binds it, except to enter into a combination with some other
nation against the other nations of the world. And this great disen-
tanglement of all alliances is now to be accomplished by this Covenant, because one of the covenants is that no nation shall enter
into any relationship with another nation inconsistent with the
covenants of the League of Nations. Nations promise not to have
alliances. Nations promise not to make combinations against each
other. Nations agree that there shall be but one combination, and
that is the combination of all against the wrongdoer.

And so I am going back to my task on the other side with renewed
vigor. I had not forgotten what the spirit of the American people
is, but I have been immensely refreshed by coming in contact with
it again. I did not know how good home felt until I got here.

The only place a man can feel at home is where nothing has to
be explained to him. Nothing has to be explained to me in America,
least of all the sentiment of the American people. I mean about
great fundamental things like this. There are many differences of
judgment as to policy—and perfectly legitimate—sometimes profound differences of judgment, but those are not differences of
sentiment, those are not differences of purpose, those are not differences of ideals. And the advantage of not having to have anything
explained to you is that you recognize a wrong explanation when
you hear it.

In a certain rather abandoned part of the frontier at one time it
was said they found a man who told the truth; he was not found
telling it, but he could tell it when he heard it. And I think I am
in that situation with regard to some of the criticisms I have heard.
They do not make any impression on me, because I know there is
no medium that will transmit them, that the sentiment of the country is proof against such narrowness and such selfishness as that.
I commend these gentlemen to communion with their fellow citizens.

What are we to say, then, as to the future? I think, my fellow citizens, that we can look forward to it with great confidence. I have heard cheering news since I came to this side of the water about the progress that is being made in Paris toward the discussion and clarification of a great many difficult matters; and I believe that settlements will begin to be made rather rapidly from this time on at those conferences. But what I believe—what I know as well as believe—is this: that the men engaged in those conferences are gathering heart as they go, not losing it; that they are finding community of purpose, community of ideal to an extent that perhaps they did not expect; and that, amidst all the interplay of influence—because it is infinitely complicated—amidst all the interplay of influence, there is a forward movement which is running toward the right. Men have at last perceived that the only permanent thing in the world is the right, and that a wrong settlement is bound to be a temporary settlement—bound to be a temporary settlement for the very best reason of all, that it ought to be a temporary settlement, and the spirits of men will rebel against it, and the spirits of men are now in the saddle.

When I was in Italy, a little limping group of wounded Italian soldiers sought an interview with me. I could not conjecture what it was they were going to say to me, and, with the greatest simplicity, with a touching simplicity, they presented me with a petition in favor of the League of Nations.

Their wounded limbs, their impaired vitality, were the only argument they brought with them. It was a simple request that I lend all the influence that I might happen to have to relieve future generations of the sacrifices that they had been obliged to make. That appeal has remained in my mind as I have ridden along the streets in European capitals and heard cries of the crowd, cries for the League of Nations from lips of people who, I venture to say, had no particular notion of how it was to be done, who were not ready to propose a plan for a League of Nations, but whose hearts said that something by way of a combination of all men everywhere must come out of this. As we drove along country roads, weak old women would come out and hold flowers up to us. Why should they hold flowers up to strangers from across the Atlantic? Only because they believed that we were the messengers of friendship and of hope, and these flowers were their humble offerings of gratitude that friends from so great a distance should have brought them so great a hope.

It is inconceivable that we should disappoint them, and we shall not. The day will come when men in America will look back with swelling hearts and rising pride that they should have been privileged to make the sacrifice which it was necessary to make in order to combine their might and their moral power with the cause of justice for men of every kind everywhere.

God give us the strength and vision to do it wisely! God give us the privilege of knowing that we did it without counting the cost, and because we were true Americans, lovers of liberty and of the right![1]

Printed in *Addresses of President Wilson Boston . . . New York. . . .*, with corrections from the complete text in the *New York Times*, March 5, 1919.
[1] There is a WWT outline, dated March 4, 1919, of this address in EBWP, DLC.

A News Report

[*March 4, 1919*]
WILSON WON'T MEET COHALAN WITH IRISH
President Waits Until Justice Leaves Room
Before He Talks with Delegates.

After informing the delegation of the Irish race convention that he would not receive them while Supreme Court Justice Daniel F. Cohalan was one of their member, President Wilson met the committee after his speech in the Metropolitan Opera House last night and in an interview lasting twenty-five minutes outlined his views upon the Irish question in a way that was construed by his audience as being favorable to the Irish cause.

A statement giving a report of the questions asked and the answers made by the President was given out by ex-Supreme Court Justice John W. Goff,[1] Chairman of the committee. Judge Goff told of the aspirations of Ireland, and then asked the President the direct question:

"Mr. President, representing, as we do, millions of your fellow American citizens, I ask you if you will present to the Peace Conference at Paris the right of Ireland to determine the form of government under which she shall live."

President Wilson replied that he thought he ought not to be called upon to answer the question as head of the nation and official representative of this country at the Peace Conference, and added that it was his understanding that he was only to receive the committee appointed at the Irish Race Convention in Philadelphia, hear their arguments, but express no opinion.

After some discussion upon this point the statement issued by the committee continued:

"The President then stated that he was in thorough accord with the aspirations voiced by the Judge and had been for a long time;

that all he meant to say was that he should not be called upon as the head of one of the Governments taking part in the Peace Conference to state his official attitude, no matter what his personal feelings might be in the matter; that we had gathered there as friends and that he would say further that he was not unfriendly to the cause as we presented it, but that it was a very delicate and complicated situation with which he had to contend, and that with a situation like that to meet, of course, he must be allowed to meet it by methods which seemed best to him and not use a method that might injure the cause instead of helping it."

Frank P. Walsh, former joint Chairman of the National War Labor Board, then took up the discussion, according to the official statement of the Irish Committee. He asserted that the President had said in his message to Congress on April 7 [2], 1917, that the United States was entering the war for the rights and liberties of small nations, and for the freedom of the seas. Mr. Walsh said that the President had been followed with enthusiasm by the country at large, and particularly by citizens of Irish descent. According to the official statement of the Irish Committee the President interrupted to say:

"I agree with your argument. Yes, I agree with what you say."

Mr. Walsh then asked the President, stipulating that no reply was expected, that he should use his influence at the Peace Conference in favor of the reception of a delegation to be sent by Ireland to present the cause of that country. In reply to another question by the President, Mr. Walsh said that he expected no answer from Mr. Wilson. The official statement then continues:

"At this point the President turned to Judge Goff and said: 'I wish you to understand, Judge Goff, further, that the Irish question has not yet been presented to the Peace Conference, and those other countries are falling into our laps, as it were, on account of the breaking up of the powers with which we were at war, and when this case comes up I will have to use my best judgment as to how to act.' "

Bishop Muldoon[2] then presented his views on the Irish question, but the official statement of the committee records no answers from the President. After shaking hands with each member of the committee the President left the room, followed by the Secret Service men and members of the committee, who went immediately to the Hotel McAlpin to write their statement.

Printed in the *New York Times*, March 5, 1919.
[1] John William Goff, long active in reform politics in New York and a justice of the New York Supreme Court, 1906-1919. He had just retired.
[2] The Most Rev. Peter James Muldoon, Roman Catholic Bishop of Rockford, Ill.

From Edward Mandell House

No. 1.   Paris, March 4, 1919

1. We have not yet found a satisfactory way to make the League of Nations function as I suggested, and nothing will be done until [after] your arrival. In the meantime, we will try to shepherd the neutrals into the fold.

2. The situation in Germany, particularly as to [in] Bavaria,[1] is extremely critical and I have tried to impress both the British and the French with the necessity of getting food into these countries immediately. After a consultation [conference] with Clemenceau and Balfour, we agreed to bring the question of supplying Bohemia before the Council of Ten tomorrow. Clemenceau asked that he be given a short time to bring the French public to a realization of the importance of sending food into Germany, when he promises earnest cooperation with us in that direction.

3. Balfour and I also took up with Clemenceau the question of Luxemburg. He has agreed to withdraw the French troops stationed there, and [I] shall confer with Pershing on Thursday as to whether American forces shall occupy it.

4. Everything has been speeded up and I feel confident that by the time of your arrival all questions will be ready for your approval.

5. George is expected to arrive tomorrow night.

                                        Edward House.

T radiogram (WP, DLC).

[1] The Bavarian capital of Munich had been one of the most turbulent centers of revolutionary activity in Germany in late 1918 and early 1919. Spearheaded by the small Independent Social Democratic party, the only political party officially associated with opposition to the war, a relatively quiet and bloodless *coup d'état*, on November 7, 1918, had deposed the Wittelsbach dynasty and the Bavarian government, had established a Bavarian Republic, and had vested all political power in a provisional Council of Workers, Soldiers, and Peasants. As chairman of the council, the Independent Socialist leader, Kurt Eisner, had become the republic's provisional Prime Minister and the head of a revolutionary cabinet composed almost entirely of Majority Social Democrats and Independent Social Democrats. In the following months, Eisner had tried to steer a middle course beween the establishment of a parliamentary system advocated by the Majority Socialists and a government by revolutionary councils demanded by the radical left. As a result, he had come under increasing attack from both the moderates and the radicals and had gradually lost most of his authority. Under pressure from the Majority Socialists, Eisner had called elections for a Bavarian parliament on January 12, 1919, which had given the bourgeois parties 100 seats in the Landtag, as opposed to sixty-one seats for the Majority Social Democrats and only three seats for Eisner's Independent Socialists. On February 21, 1919, Eisner had finally decided to resign and to turn the political power over to the Landtag, when, on the way to the Landtag building to announce his resignation, he had been assassinated by a right-wing student, Count Anton Arco-Valley. Eisner's murder had precipitated the so-called second Bavarian revolution, which was characterized by anarchy and street fighting and which, on April 7, 1919, led to the proclamation of the first Bavarian Soviet Republic. For a detailed account, see Allan Mitchell, *Revolution in Bavaria, 1918-1919: The Eisner Regime and the Soviet Republic* (Princeton, N. J., 1965).

From Li Shengto, Wang Yitang, and the
Chinese Parliament

Peking March 4 1919.

Since the Chinese declaration of war against Germany all treaties concluded between China and Germany have become null and void. We therefore venture in the most ea[r]nest manner possible to beg you to support the demand of this country at the peace conference that the leased territory of Kiaochow be handed back to China direct by Germany as this single act will do more to convince the peoples of eastern Asia of the reality of world justice than any other measure that could be devided [devised].

Li Shengto President of Senate,
Wang Yitang Speaker of House of Representatives
and the whole 100 body of Members of
Parliament

T telegram (WP, DLC).

From Josephus Daniels

My dear Mr. President: Washington. 4th of March 1919

I have your favor of March 1st. I think your course is right in waiting to get to Paris. I would suggest, when you have the time, that you send for Admiral Benson and talk with him about it. I feel, with Admiral Benson, that no nation ought to have a force, either on land or sea, to dominate, and in military and naval strength our country ought to be ready and willing to furnish, in proportion to its wealth and commercial importance, the necessary force to maintain the world's peace.

Sincerely yours,   Josephus Daniels

TLS (WP, DLC).

From Josephus Daniels, with Enclosures

My Dear Mr. President: Washington. March 4. 1919.

Enclosed is the official report of the substance of the draft of naval peace terms submitted by naval representatives. With it are the comments of Admiral Benson. You will observe that he makes several important reservations. Inasmuch as the report and comments were received only a few minutes ago I have had opportunity only to run over them hastily and do not feel that I am fully enough informed to discuss them now.

From the first my general opinion has been against the idea of sinking the battle-ships. How could we successfully ask Congress for money to build the ships authorized if we advocated sinking so many ships? As to the submarines, I believe all should be sunk and no more should be built by any nation if and when the League of Nations becomes a fact. At the best they are stilettos and like poisonous gas should be put beyond the pale. I think, however, there is much sentiment in our Navy that with our long coast line in the case of trouble submarines would be our best protection. Certainly until the League is adopted the submarine would be a protection on both coasts particularly from Panama to Florida.

The destruction of Heligoland is the best guarantee against future German sea power, and I think it ought to be destroyed.

As to the other matters I will give them study and communicate with Admiral Benson by secret code. Of course, in the absence of the atmosphere of the discussions, I am not in a position to feel that confidence in any opinions stated as if this information was in my possession.   Sincerely yours,   Josephus Daniels

ALS (WP, DLC).

ENCLOSURE I

From: Admiral Benson.   I-Mission 318
To: Opnav.
Priority A for Secnav.

Official report substance of draft of naval peace terms with Germany as submitted by naval representatives of allies and United States and is forwarded at suggestion of commissioners in order that it may be transmitted to the President before his departure. Covering letter forwarding peace terms will not be cabled. Letter states in substance that naval clause for preliminary terms of peace are divided in two classes. First, naval subjects which include articles one to eleven as given below. Second, subjects intimately connected with naval matters on which admirals deem it essential to present their views and recommendations. This covered by articles twelve to twenty. Conditions for naval aircraft have been embodied in general air terms.

Conclusions as submitted by naval representatives follow quote Article one. Future strength of German fleet. Until such time as Germany shall have fulfilled all her obligations under the final treaty of peace, the strength of the German fleet in personnel and ships shall be restricted as follows:

(A) Personnel. subparagraph. The total personnel for naval purposes, including the manning of the fleet, coast defense, signal stations, administration and other land service, shall not exceed 15,000 ([including] officers) and recommend the adoption of all grades and corps be included.

The condition of service of naval personnel shall be based on the same principles as are laid down for the German Army in the military terms.

(B) Seagoing fleet.

Germany shall be authorized to maintain in a seagoing condition, as a maximum—battleships of the DEUTSCHLAND or LOTHRINGEN type. Six light cruisers for coast watch and fishery duty following, twelve destroyers, twelve sailing boats.

Until the completion of the mine sweeping prescribed by clause eleven, Germany will keep in commission the number of mine sweeping vessels fixed by the allies and the United States. Note. Admiral Benson does not agree [to] the limitation of the German fleet after the final treaty of peace, except as imposed by the League of Nations.

Article two. Disposing of surplus.

Personnel. Officers and men belonging to the German Navy in excess of the number authorized by clause one shall be demobilized within period of two months from the signature of the preliminary terms of peace.

Vessels of War. Vessels of war over and above the seagoing fleet authorized by clause one shall be disposed of as required by clauses three, four, five, six, and ten, or, if not specially provided for in these clauses, shall be placed in reserve or utilized for commercial purposes. Note. Admiral Benson does not agree to limitation of the German fleet after the final treaty of peace, except as imposed by the League of Nations.

Article three. Submarines.

(A) All German submarines, without exception, submarine salvage vessels, and docks for submarines, (including the tubular docks) are to be surrendered to the allies and the United States. All which can, to proceed under their own power, or which can be towed, shall be taken by the Germans into allied ports, to be there destroyed (see note below) or broken up. Note. Admiral De Bon,[1] by direction of minister of Marine of France,[2] making reservations on this point.

Germany shall inform the neutral powers concerned that she

---

[1] Vice-Adm. Ferdinand Jean-Jacques de Bon, Chief of the French Naval General Staff and French representative on the Inter-Allied Naval Council.
[2] Georges Jean Claude Leygues.

authorizes the deliverance to the allies and the United States of all German submarines in neutral ports.

(B) The German submarines which cannot be delivered in Allied ports, as well as those which are in course of construction shall be completely broken up by the Germans, under the supervision of the allied and United States commissioners.

The breaking up of these submarines shall be completed within a maximum period of three months after the signature of the preliminaries of peace.

(C) The naval commission appointed by the allies and the United States to supervise the execution of the terms of the armistice has decided as to which submarines are to proceed or are to be towed to allied ports and which are to be broken up by the Germans. The decision of this commission shall be strictly carried out.

Article four. Surface vessels of war now interned. All German surface vessels of war now interned in allied ports, in conformity with the terms of the armistice, or interned in neutral ports, cease to belong to Germany; they are definitely surrendered to the allies and the United States for the purpose of being broken up or destroyed (see note below) in the shortest possible time.

Germany shall inform the neutral powers concerned that she authorizes the delivery to the allies and United States of the German surface vessels of war in neutrality. Note. Admiral De Bon by direction of the Minister of Marine of France, makes reservations on this point.

Article five. Further reduction of surface vessels of war. The German vessels of War named below shall be sunk under the supervision of the allies and the United States within two months after the signing of the preliminaries of peace.

Commissioners of the allies and the United States shall fix the localities where these vessels should be sunk.

Vessels are to have their guns on board. In other respects they are to remain unarmed as ordered by article twenty of the armistice convention dated November 11th 1918.

With the above the German government may remove from these ships before they are sunk such material as has a commercial value. The vessels are: Battleships OLDENBURG, THÜRINGEN, OSTFRIESLAND, HELGOLAND, POSEN, WESTFALEN, RHEINLAND, NASSAU. Light cruisers, STETTIN, DANZIG, MÜNCHEN, LÜBECK, STRASSBURG, AUGSBURG, KOLBERG, STUTTGART. Forty two modern destroyers. Fifty modern torpedo boats. Note Admiral De Bon by direction of the Minister of Marine of France makes reservations on this point.

Article six. Vessels of war under construction. Germany shall stop the construction of all vessels of war, including submarines.

All German surface vessels of war now under construction shall be broken up under the supervision of allied and United States commissioners.

Article Seven. Material arising from vessels broken up. That material arising from the breaking up of German vessels of war, whether surface vessels or submarines, may be used, but solely for industrial or commercial purposes, and on no account for warlike purposes. Germany shall not sell or dispose of these materials to other countries.

Article eight. Construction of vessels of war. Until the terms of the final treaty of peace have been fully carried out, Germany shall not undertake the construction or acquire any new vessels of war, submarines included, except as follows:

(A) New vessels shall only be built to replace units of the seagoing fleet authorized by clause one.

(B) They shall be designated purely for coast defense and coast watch purposes.

(C) No new vessels shall exceed 10,000 tons displacement.

(D) Except in the case of the loss of a ship, units of the different classes shall only be replaced at the end of twenty years in the case of battleships and cruisers, fifteen years in the case of destroyers and torpedo boats. This number of years shall count from the first year in which credit is taken in the budget for the construction of the ship which is to be replaced to the year in which credit is taken in the budget for the construction of the new ship. Note. Admiral Benson does not agree to the limitation of the German fleet after the final treaty of peace, except as imposed by the League of Nations.

Article nine. Naval war material. The allowing of arms, ammunition, and all important items of naval war material for the German Navy will be fixed by a commission of the allies and the United States on the basis of the seagoing fleet and personally authorized by clause one. The reserve of naval ordnance, arms, ammunition, and war material shall be in proportion to the number and type of units of seagoing fleet.

All arms, ammunition, and naval war material, including mines and torpedoes, belonging to Germany and now in possession of the German naval authorities, in excess of the above establishment, shall be surrendered to the allies and the United States, at place to be determined, to be destroyed or made useless. The surrendering of the material under this clause shall be within a period of thirty days from the date of signing of the preliminaries of peace. The manufacturing by Germany for foreign countries of naval ordnance, ammunition, mines and torpedoes or their parts, or naval war material of any description is prohibited. Note. Admiral Benson does not agree [to] the final paragraph of this clause.

Article ten. Merchant cruisers and fleet auxiliary armed German merchant cruisers, whether in ports of the central powers or interned in neutral ports, and fleet auxiliaries which can be readily adapted for commercial purposes, or which have been converted from merchant shipping, shall be disarmed and treated as other merchant vessels.

The vessels affected by this clause are given in appendix.

Article eleven. Mine sweeping. Germany shall sweep up all mines in the areas which have been assigned to her in the agreement already entered into between the allies and the United States.

In accordance with this agreement, Germany shall be responsible for sweeping the following areas: (1) That portion of the North Sea which lies to the Eastward from Longitude four degrees no minutes east from Greenwich between the parallels of latitude 53 degrees no minutes North and 59 degrees no minutes North. (B) To the north of latitude 60 degrees 30 minutes north. (2) The Baltic Sea, excluding Russian waters. In regard to these waters further details will be given as soon as the Russian question is determined.

Article twelve. Helgoland, Germany. The fortifications, military establishments and harbors of the island of Helgoland and Dune shall be destroyed under the supervision of the allied commissioners, by German labor and at the expense of Germany, within a period to be determined by the Commissioners.

The harbor terms shall include the Northeast Mole; the West Mole; the outer and inner breakwaters and reclamation work within them; and all naval and military works, fortifications and buildings, constructed and under construction, between lines connecting the following positions taken from the British Admiralty chart number 120 of April 19th 1918;

(A) Latitude 54 10 49 North, Longitude 7 53 39 East.
(B) Latitude 54 10 35 North, Longitude 7 54 18 East.
(C) " "   54 10 14   "   "   "   7 54 00   " .
(D) " "   54 10 17   "   "   "   7 53 37   " .
(E) " "   54 10 44   "   "   "   7 53 26   " .

The disposal of the island will be decided by the final treaty of peace. Note Admiral Benson makes a reservation regarding the destruction of the harbors.

Article thirteen. Routes of Access into the Baltic.

In order to insure the free access into the Baltic to all nations, Germany shall not erect any fortifications in the area comprised between Latitude 55 27 North and 54 00 North and Long. 9 99 East and 16 00 East of the meridian of Greenwich, nor install any guns commanding the maritime routes between the North Sea and the Baltic.

The fortifications now existing shall be demolished and the guns removed under the supervision of allied commissioners.

The German government shall place at the disposal of the allies and the United States complete copies of all hydrographic information now in its possession concerning the channel and adjoining waters between the Baltic and the North Sea.

Article fourteen. Kiel Canal.

The Kiel canal shall be open at all times to all war and commercial vessels of every nation. No nation shall benefit by especial favorable treatment, and no class of vessels shall be excluded from the canal. Note Admiral Benson does not agree [with] this clause and believes it can not be justified except as a punitive measure.

Article fifteen. German colonies. The German colonies shall not be returned to Germany.

Article sixteen. Wireless telegraph. The German high-power WT stations at Nauen, Hanover, and Berlin shall not be used for the naval, military, or political purposes of Germany or of any state which has been allied to Germany in the war, without the assent of the allied powers and the United States, which will not be given until they are satisfied that the naval and military stipulations of the treaty of peace have been fully carried out. During the interval these stations may be used for commercial purposes, but only under the supervision of the Allies and the United States, who will decide the wave lengths to be used.

Germany shall not build any more high power WT stations on her own territory or that of Austria-Hungary, Bulgaria or Turkey until the Naval and Military stipulations of the treaty of peace have been fully carried out.

Paragraph Three. In the event of Germany violating the provisions of the treaty peace the Allies and United States shall be at liberty to withhold the services of their wireless stations from German stations.

Paragraph Four. Germany shall have only one vote at the next international Radio Telegraph conference, irrespective of the number of independent or semi-independent states into which Germany may be divided.

Article seventeen. Submarines cables. The German cables enumerated below shall not be returned to Germany Emden (Germany) Vigo, Emden Brest, Emden Teneriffe, Emden Azore Islands two cables, Azore Islands New York two cables, Teneriffe Monrovia, Liberia, Pernambuco, Brazil, Monrovia, Liberia, Lomé Douala, Constantinople, Turkey, Constanta, Roumania, Chifu(Hyphen)Tsingtau

(Hyphen) Shanghai, China, Yap(Hyphen) Shanghai, China, Yap Menado (Celebes). Note: Admiral Benson disagrees paragraph article 18 reparation for allied ship losses. Reparation for allied ship losses shall be made by Germany to the extent and in the method to be laid down in the permanent treaty peace. Part of such reparation shall consist in the handing over by Germany to the Allies and the United States of all merchant ships with such exception as may be laid down in the treaty now completed, launched, or under construction which were on eleven November 1918 the property of the German Government or under German merchant flag.

For the removal of doubt be deemed open to question and without prejudice to the further elucidations which may be inserted in the treaty of peace it is hereby declared that

(A) Reparation for ship losses. The reparation required from Germany for ship losses shall be based upon the total number of ships destroyed or lost constructed or actually (something omitted) through the hostile action of Germany, irrespective of the means employed for the destruction.

For the purpose of this.

The terms: "Ships" and "Shipping" shall be deemed to include fishing vessels. (Sub paragraph)

Merchant vessels captured by Germany. All Allied or neutral merchant vessels which have been condemned by the German prize courts and which were German property at the date of the German vessels for the purpose of being included in the number of German merchant vessels which may be required to be surrendered under the head of Reparation.

Salvage of allied ships and cargoes. Notwithstanding that reparation may have been paid for sunken allied ships and cargoes, the property in such ships and cargoes, if salvaged outside of German territorial waters, shall remain at disposal of allies.

Article nineteen. Commissions for execution of naval terms. All the above measures shall be carried out under control of a special naval commission appointed for purpose by allies and United States.

This commission will act under supreme direction of the Admiralties of the allies and United States, and may appoint sub-commissions or delegates as may be found necessary.

German government shall facilitate by all possible means the exercising of this control and shall furnish the fullest information demanded of it on all questions in connection with the same including designs of warships, details, and samples of war materials, guns, ammunition, torpedoes, mines, and other explosives and WT apparatus. Note. Admiral Benson disagrees as to requiring Germany to furnish designs, samples etc. of war materials and makes reservations regarding participation by naval representative of United States in commission dealing with execution of articles one, eight, nine, twelve, thirteen, and fourteen.

Article twenty. Armistice conventions. Nothing in these preliminaries of peace shall invalidate anything done or required to be done under armistice convention of November 11th or subsequent conventions for its renewal.

Appendix. Armed German merchant cruisers and fleet auxiliaries (list referred to in clause 10 of naval terms). Interned in neutral countries, three, Berlin; Santa Fe; Yorck. In Germany 28, AMMON, ANSWALD, BOSNIA, CORDOBA, CASSEL, DANIA, RIO NEGRO, RIO PARDO, SANTA CRUZ, SCHWABEN, SOLLING, STEIGERWALD, FRANKEN, GUNDOMAR, FUERST BUELOW, GERTRUD, KOGOMA, RUGIA, SANTA ELENA, SCHLESWIG, MOEWE, SIERRA VENTANA, CHEMNITZ, EMIL GEORG VON STRAUSS, HABSBURG, METEOR, WALTRAUTE, SCHARNHORST. Mission 318.

E N C L O S U R E   I I

From: Admiral Benson   I-Mission 319
To: Opnav.
Priority A for Secnav Mission 319 Section one.

At suggestion of commissioners the following extracts from memorandum submitted to our commissioners along with proposed terms for preliminary peace is forwarded with the request it be transmitted immediately to the President.

I have made reservations or disagreed in each instance with those clauses which limit naval powers of Germany after final treaty of peace.

Comment on article one. This article originally provided for permanent limitation of German fleet, but was modified upon the suggestion of the British of a limitation during period when Germany had not fulfilled all her obligations under the final treaty of peace. In addition to fact that I believe principle to be unsound of limiting the sovereignty of a country after final treaty of peace, I regard this article and other articles dealing with further limitations German naval powers as too detailed for insertion in a treaty of peace. Execution of article will require too close a supervision, a too intimate supervision of foreign commissioners over affairs that are purely German.

Comment on article two. This article is of same general nature as article one and open to same objections.

Comment on article three. I am in hearty accord with complete destruction German power in submarines. This article is drawn up so as to be inclusive of all arrangements which have heretofore been made as part of armistice terms.

Comment on article four. I am in complete accord with the provision of this article. Attention is invited to the fact that this article in its present form necessitates the destruction of, or breaking up of all those vessels. This is a step that is essential and no argument which may take place in the Supreme War Council or elsewhere should be allowed to prevail in omitting its provision. Repeated attempts were made on the part of French representatives to omit from this article the present part of it which states that quote "For the purpose of being broken up or destroyed in the shortest possible time" unquote. The same resistance will undoubtedly be encountered when this article is considered by the Supreme War Council and by the Peace Conference.

Comment on article five. I am in accord with the provision of this article. The vessels of war enumerated are still in German possession. When Germany gives them up she will be left with practically no Navy. This fact in itself will be a strong inducement towards preventing the further expansion of naval armament in Europe. Attention is invited to the provision that the vessels named shall be sunk. I consider it essential that this provision should remain unchanged despite the fact that strong pressure will be brought to bear to have it changed. The French Minister of Marine is not in favor of the destruction of the vessels surrendered by Germany. His proposition cannot be entertained by American delegates without serious injury (1) to the interest of the world; (2) to American interest.

Comment on article six. This paragraph extends the present armistice provision regarding submarine construction to all naval vessels.

Comment on article seven. The provisions of this article are necessary in order to prevent the vessels now being broken up or to be broken up, from being reassembled as soon as peace is signed thus defeating our object.

Comment on article eight. This article is designed to limit the future naval power of Germany, and is supplementary to articles one and two. It is open to the same objections as those articles.

Comment on article nine. This article was inserted towards the end of the committee's work in order to make the terms. I accepted the article in so far as it relates to the adjudicated reduction of German naval supplies, but I made a reservation regarding the future, and particularly regarding the last paragraph of this article, which would prohibit Germany from manufacturing for foreign account, naval armament, ammunition, mines, torpedoes, and so forth.

Comment on article ten. This article as originally drawn included the two ex-German vessels now commissioned in the United States Navy, namely, the USS DE KALB and USS VON STEUBEN. I maintain that the sovereignty over these vessels had been vested in the United States absolutely, and that consequently no articles of the peace terms should presume to question that. My view accepted. Have since learned unofficially that question of ownership of German merchant vessels seized in our ports will be raised in spite of fact that Congress has decided that title to them is vested entirely in the United States.

Comment on article eleven. This article asserts to Germany her proportionate share of the great task of clearing the sea of mines. This is the last of the purely naval articles.

Comment on article twelve. In my memorandum to the President[1] I pointed out that Heligoland was in my opinion defensive position and that its dismantlement would not materially alter naval power of Germany, since Germany would have no Navy which could base on Heligoland. In my discussion with the Naval Representatives I made them acquainted with my idea and stated to them that, as Heligoland was a purely European question, I would not be too persistent in my idea. In the matter of harbors I withheld my consent to their destruction. As the question of Heligoland is not purely naval, I think that the political aspect of removing the principal defenses of the principal commercial rivers of Germany should be considered by the Commissioners in its political and military aspects.

Comment on article thirteen. This clause is justified only on the basis of giving free access to vessels into Baltic Sea at all times. Attention is invited to the fact that channels which are free of German fortifications by provision of this clause are commanded by Danish fortifications. Attention is further invited to fact that demolition of fortifications proposed leaves German naval base at Kiel with east end of Kiel canal, and all the North Coast of Germany as far east as Longitude 16 degrees, without any fixed defenses whatever. This is a question which is not purely naval, and which must be decided by commissioners from its political and military aspects as well as from its naval aspects. Is it desirable to leave Baltic frontier of Germany in a defenceless state?

Comment on article fourteen. I did not agree to this article. I consider it important that any action taken concerning the Kiel canal should not be such as to permit its being quoted as a rival at some later period for action concerning water ways which are wholly

American. In a discussion regarding the proposed clause throwing open the Kiel canal, it was recognized by all the admirals that Germany, in time of war in which she was one of the belligerents, would certainly not be bound to admit her enemy to Kiel, and that she would undoubtedly be able to control the Kiel canal or destroy it if necessary.

Comment on article fifteen. This article was inserted solely to indicate that from the standpoint of naval warfare German colonies should not be returned to Germany and thus be made available to her as future bases of submarine or cruiser warfare against commerce. Political questions involved in the disposition of German colonies were not considered by naval representatives.

Comment on article sixteen. This article was inserted by British in order to prevent distribution propaganda during reconstruction period.

Comment on article seventeen. I disagree with this article entirely. Cables mentioned have in several cases been interfered with by English and French, sections of them having been taken up and moved to other places. Was of the opinion cables so taken up might be considered prizes of war, but that cables which had been left in place should, at conclusion of peace, be returned to former owner. I as a compromise proposed that question of all these cables should be submitted to the prize court of belligerent countries concerned. This proposal was first accepted but later rejected on the grounds that the prize court would probably not take cognizance of the case. Attention is invited to the fact that seizure of these cables would still further perfect the monopoly of cable communication between America and Europe to disadvantage of America. To our interest that we should be able to communicate directly by cable with all these countries with which we expect to trade. A list of cables given under article seventeen includes the only two cables, which previous to the war, connected New York direct to Germany without going through French or British offices. The growing of our merchant marine makes it a matter of considerable importance to us. Our facilities for communication and our facilities for fuelling vessels in all parts of the world should be guarded and developed.

No comment on article eighteen.

Comment on article nineteen. The original proposal was for a permanent commission to sit in Berlin, Germany, for the purpose of carrying out peace terms and for supervisory measures connected with limitation of Germany's naval power in the future. I objected to such a commission believing it to be unsound in principle and likely to provoke trouble evasive [pervasive?] in form which Commission is provided for in Article nineteen. Commission will undoubtedly be necessary to attend to execution of those parts of peace terms dealing with surrender of material and destruction of material. I make reservation in conjunction with all commissions which might have to deal with limitation of Germany's future naval power.

No comment on article twenty. Mission 319.

T telegrams (WP, DLC).
¹ See W. S. Benson to WW, Feb. 7, 1919, Vol. 54.

From Breckinridge Long, with Enclosure

My dear Mr. President: Washington March 4, 1919.

In the absence of Mr. Polk at the Capitol, and in view of your departure within an hour or so, I take the only available course and communicate with you directly to send you a copy of a memorandum just handed me by the Japanese Ambassador.¹ At ten minutes to twelve he telephoned me and I broke other engagements to receive him. He arrived just at twelve o'clock noon, and said that he had received this from his Government with instructions to request an audience with you and present it. I told him that you were at the Capitol, and could not now make any further engagements as you were proceeding directly to New York.

The importance of the communication is such that I feel you will want it. I will ask Mr. Polk to cable this text to Paris.

I take this opportunity to wish you a pleasant journey to Europe, and to hope that your work there will be crowned by the success that we all confidently expect and hope for.

Faithfully yours,   Breckinridge Long

TLS (WP, DLC).
¹ That is, Viscount Ishii.

E N C L O S U R E

3/4/19 Original text handed me
by Jap. Amb. at 12. noon
today. B.L.

The Japanese Government are much gratified to perceive the just and disinterested spirit in which the President is using his best endeavors to secure an enduring peace of the world. They also are sincerely grateful for the sympathy and support which the President and the American peace delegation were friendly enough to give to the proposition of the Japanese delegation on the question of doing away with race discriminations. In view of the fundamental spirit of the League of Nations the Japanese Government regard as of first importance the establishment of the principle that the difference of race should in no case constitute a basis for discriminatory treatment under the law of any country. Should this great principle fail of general recognition the Japanese Government do not see how a perpetual friction and discontent among nations and races could possibly be eliminated. If such be the case, they are gravely concerned that the smooth functioning of the League of Nations itself will be seriously hampered. The Japanese Government are therefore disposed to continue their efforts for the adoption of this just and equitable proposition and they permit themselves to confidently hope that the President give further friendly support to them in this matter. As for the form and wording of the proposition, the Japanese Government have no intention to insist on the adoption of the original draft and any suggestion from the President on this point will be intertained [entertained] with great pleasure.

a correct copy   B.L.

TC MS (WP, DLC).

From Gilbert Monell Hitchcock

My dear Mr. President: [Washington] March 4, 1919.

A number of republican Senators who signed Lodge's manifesto on the league of nations constitution will, in my opinion, vote for it nevertheless if it is a part of the peace treaty. A still larger number will give it support if certain amendments are made. The following I would mention as likely to influence votes in the order given:

First, a reservation to each high contracting party of its exclusive control over domestic subjects.

Second, a reservation of the Monroe doctrine.

Third, some provision by which a member of the league can, on proper notice, withdraw from membership.

Fourth, the settlement of the ambiguity in Article 15.

Fifth, the insertion on the next to the last line of first paragraph of Article 8, after the word "adopted," of the words, "by the several governments."

Sixth, the definite assurance that it is optional with a nation to accept or reject the burdens of a mandatory.

I wish you a safe journey.

Yours truly,   G. M. Hitchcock.

TCL (WP, DLC).

From Morris Jastrow, Jr.[1]

My dear President Wilson: Philadelphia, Pa. March 4, 1919.

I am sending you these few lines, in the first place to wish you a safe journey, secondly to assure you, as I took the liberty of doing on your former sailing,[2] that you carry with you again the fervent wishes and the firm confidence of all those who realize that we are entering upon a new order, which demands entirely different methods in international relationships, and above all, that outlook towards the future which you possesss [possess] in so preeminent a degree.

Thirdly, I want to say a word about the statement to the Peace Conference which I understand was handed to you by Representative Julius Kahn,[3] before you left Washington, and in which I am deeply interested, having had a share in drawing up the document and in formulating the plans for obtaining the signatures of the representative citizens from all parts of the United States which are attached to it. We could easily have obtained thousands of signatures, for there are very many American citizens of the Jewish faith who, while entirely sympathetic towards the plan of promoting the colonization of Jews in Palestine, feel that it is a serious mistake, involving a misreading of the history of the Jews, to make the attempt of setting up at any time such a thing as a Jewish State in Palestine.

I hope my dear President Wilson that you will be able to find the time on the steamer to read the statement carefully, so as to realize our point of view. The only feature of Zionism to which we are opposed is the introduction of the political factor, which is bound to work mischief in Palestine, and will endanger the position that the Jews have acquired in Western lands. Those of us who have signed this document feel strongly that the principle of self-determination of peoples should be applied to Palestine precisely as to other countries; and this would lead naturally to a Palestinian State (under such mandatory control as the Peace Conference may decide) in which all religions and all nationalities represented at present in Palestine, or that may be there in the future, shall be placed precisely on the same footing. All that we ask is that in the deliberations of the Peace Conference on this subject the views of those voiced in the statement will be taken into consideration.

I have the honor to be,

Obediently yours,   Morris Jastrow Jr.

TLS (WP, DLC).

[1] Professor of Semitic Languages at the University of Pennsylvania and the Librarian of the university. One of the most eminent orientalists of his time and a leader in the

study of the history of religion, he was the author of more than 200 books and articles on Semitic languages, religions, and literature, and on contemporary political questions.

² M. Jastrow, Jr., to WW, Dec. 3, 1918, ALS (WP, DLC).

³ It is missing in WP, DLC. However, it was printed in the *New York Times*, March 5, 1919. The petition was signed by thirty-one prominent American Jews, including Kahn, Jastrow, Henry Morgenthau, Simon Wolf, Edwin R. A. Seligman, and Adolph S. Ochs. Jastrow summarizes its main arguments well.

From Norman Hapgood

Dear Mr. President: New York City March 4, 1919.

Although I thanked you orally for the very serious responsibility you have put on me,¹ I wish to repeat my appreciation in writing. To have any part in collecting the facts about the tremendous trial that the world is going through and will be going through for a long time, is something that any man ought to be thankful for, and to take part in so big a task under such inspired leadership as you have given us multiplies many times the satisfaction.

The behavior of the Senate about the covenant is depressing, of course, but I do not think it is exactly discouraging. There are a good many of the signers who are easily affected by currents of public opinion, and if things go well with popular moods in this country between now and your return, I think a number of the Senators will be shaken into a different attitude.

With the warmest wishes in your incomparably big work,

Yours sincerely,   Norman Hapgood

TLS (WP, DLC).
¹ That is, his appointment as Minister to Denmark.

From Arthur Briggs Farquhar¹

My dear Mr. President: York, Penna. March 4, 1919.

I hope you have not been discouraged by the misconduct of the howling dervishes in the Senate (as ex-President Taft calls them). The people are with you. I have not met a single soldier who is not for the League of Nations. The Christian churches must necessarily take it up. I tell our ministers that any clergyman who does not make that the leading feature of his work is not a Christian minister. I have been deeply interested in this move for many years, and hoped for great things from the Peace Conference, but what you have done far transcends my wildest dreams. I think the opposition will not long be heard of. It will be buried under a storm of protest from all sane lovers of humanity, and with the League of Peace and the abolition of the demon alcohol, we will indeed have a world

fit to live in, and you will go down in history as its greatest benefactor.

I have been trying to stir up ex-Senator Root, Nicholas Murray
Butler and others to the importance of breaking loose from narrow
partisanship and putting in practice what they have been preaching
for years, and encouraging those connected with the movement to
use the public press. Enclose clipping of an article just published
in our leading Republican sheet,[2] as a sample of what may be done
in that direction. The vaporings of its opponents are mere cam-
ouflage, cannot be dignified as arguments.

But I have no right to take up your precious time. With regards
to Mrs. Wilson, and Miss Wilson when you meet her, I am,
Very sincerely your friend,   A B Farquhar

TLS (WP, DLC).
    [1] Prominent manufacturer, conservationist, and civic leader of York, Pa.
    [2] "Farquhar Defends League of Nations," *York Dispatch*, c. March 4, 1919, clipping,
WP, DLC. The first paragraph of the article summarizes Farquhar's letter to the editor
as follows: "The proposed league of nations does not conflict with the Constitution of
the United States, is not at variance with the Monroe Doctrine and cannot involve this
country in entangling alliances, is the opinion expressed by A. B. Farquhar."

From Anita Eugénie McCormick Blaine

Dear Mr. President: [Chicago, c. March 4, 1919]

I think even in the midst of the world questions which you carry
you would want to hear about a soldier[1] from his wife[2] and his
mother if you had the moment.

I am thinking that you might have such a moment on the ocean
and so I am sending you my word.

I want to thank you and Mrs. Wilson from the depth of my heart
for the word of your sympathy which you sent me.[3]

I know that you know better than words could convey what help
it is to have such supporting sympathy—the sympathy that understands the upholding quality of the sacrifice.

Please know my gratitude and my daughter's for words would
not tell it.

To you I want to report about Emmons' service to his country
because you were so good to speak to me about it.

He had taken up agriculture as his work after college and at first
when we entered the war it was so emphasized as a need that he
thought it might be his best service, especially as he knew that his
physique was not one for trench warfare.

He hoped he could make some especial contribution from his
farm. But he found by investigating the subject that he really could
not.

Then he felt it to be impossible to him to do—however serviceable it might be—no differently than he would have done if we had not been at war. He longed to be doing for it and he wanted to try to enter some branch of the military service.

It was then that I wanted to know that that would be of more use. His life was very precious and I wanted it to be in the best place for service. He let me ask you the question for my own satisfaction.

Your answer came—that both were of use and his feeling would be the only guide.

Your word was strengthening to us both. It gave his feelings free scope. And he determined to try to enter some engineering branch of the service, feeling—both of us—that he no doubt could be admitted there.

He had one radical fault in his physique and he consulted doctors on this score about his responsibilities in entering the army. Here his hopes were dashed and he was wholly convinced that he had no right, for the sake of the army, to attempt to put himself into the army in any real way. The idea of trying to get into some easy or nominal position for the sake of being in it was abhorrent to him. He could not tolerate it.

He wanted to go to France in some other work—possibly construction. But he was convinced equally that he should not for the same reasons do that.

So he turned to find the thing here that would give him the chance to contribute in the most direct way to the war need.

Shipbuilding seemed to him to represent that. He obtained a job on Hog Island and went to work in it.

He was warned that it would probably be an over-strenuous work for him. But he welcomed the thought that there was risk, and I think it consoled him that it was so.

There the influenza caught him and took him.[4]

I like you to know these facts because you were so good to give us your word and what you said meant so much to him—not only because you were the leader of it all but because he had such profound respect for you.

Your valuing whatever he should do went to the heart of him and I am sure it helped him when he could not do what he desired to do.

The job was little. Was his effort wasted? Was his soul's purpose for naught?

Not if the sunsets and the songs; the aspirations, the prayers and the poems of life are not wasted—not if there is need for spirit, true and pure.

I am   Yours faithfully   Anita Blaine

ALS (WP, DLC).
¹ Emmons Blaine, Jr.
² Eleanor Gooding Blaine.
³ WW to Anita E. M. Blaine, Oct. 18, 1918, TLS (Anita M. Blaine Papers, WHi).
⁴ He died of pneumonia in Philadelphia on October 9, 1918. Gilbert A. Harrison, *A Timeless Affair: The Life of Anita McCormick Blaine* (Chicago and London, 1979), pp. 170-72.

From the Diary of Dr. Grayson

Wednesday, March 5, 1919.

The GEORGE WASHINGTON backed out of her pier and headed down the North River seaward at exactly 8:15 o'clock in the morning. Despite the lateness of his retirement the President arose at 7:00 o'clock and had breakfast at 7:30. I had breakfast with him.

After breakfast the President, Mrs. Wilson and I went to the bridge to witness the departure. Thousands of people had gathered on the piers and waved good-bye.

Just as the GEORGE WASHINGTON was leaving the pier a telegram was received announcing the death of Mr. [Ferdinand de Mohrenschildt],¹ the son-in-law of William G. McAdoo. It also mentioned the grave illness of Mrs. [de Mohrenschildt], Mr. McAdoo's daughter.² The President at once sent a message to Mr. McAdoo expressing his sympathy and his wish that it were possible for him to stay back and help him in some way.³

While passing the Statue of Liberty the President told me the story of the negro, who had recently seen service in France and who was very home-sick and scared; he was recently returned to the States and while standing on the deck of the ship as he was passing the Statue of Liberty, he said: "Take a good look at me, old girl, take a good look, 'cause if you ever sees dis nigger again you sure has got to turn around."

Proceeding down the harbor the President was escorted by destroyers, flying machines and dirigible balloons. The President got a glimpse of the first moving picture he has ever seen being taken from a flying-machine. He relaxed himself by playing Canfield in his cabin, alone, remarking to me that he wanted to do something trivial that would occupy his mind and make him forget all the big problems that confronted him during the past week. By this mental relaxation he secured a much-needed rest.

After lunch we had a little talk on reminiscences. He said that when he was teaching he found much stimulation of the mind in the questions propounded in the class-room; but he said this cycle continued only about ten years. After a period of ten years he found that the same questions were being asked. Then he realized that he was advancing in years but still dealing with boys of the same age and the same questions. Now and then, however, a genius would bob up and ask a question out of the usual cycle. At first it was difficult for him to account for the fact that the same questions were being asked. I named a man whom I knew to be rather successful in his profession, but about whom there was a variance of opinion as to his ability. I asked the President what he thought of him as a student, and he replied that "he was exposed to education but it did not take."

In referring to the Irish meeting last night, at which an effort was made to get the President to promise that he would bring their cause before the Peace Conference, he said that the Irish as a race are very hard to deal with owing to their inconsiderateness, their unreasonable demands and their jealousies. He predicted that owing to the dissatisfaction among the Irish-Americans and the German-Americans with the Democratic administration, unless a decided change was brought about, it might defeat the Democratic party in 1920.

The President showed me a flag which an American woman had sent him at New York with the request that it be adopted as the League of Nations flag for the use of the world.

The President attended the moving pictures in the dining-room of the GEORGE WASHINGTON and saw a Chaplin and Fairbanks movie. The crowd was much smaller than on either of the previous voyages. This caused the President to remark smilingly, as he entered the room: "This is a somewhat select gathering."

While a transport was passing us this morning loaded with soldiers some one remarked that there were 15,000 aboard, whereupon the President asked me how my native town of Culpeper would look with 15,000 turned loose in it. I remarked that it would look like crowds on March Court day or when the circus came to town. I told him that although the Census showed but 2201 inhabitants in Culpeper, it was such a wonderful place that it could easily accommodate 15,000 additional people without embarrassment! He replied that my remarks were not very consistent, recalling that I had at one time attempted with great pride to show him my native town while passing through on a train, but he said: "To my chagrin a freight car was standing at the station and obstructed the view," making it impossible for him to see the town. The fact is that on this occasion a long freight train was running parallel with our train and did obstruct the view. He has always taken the greatest delight in telling the joke that I tried to show my native town but that a freight car prevented my doing so. He loves to tease any one he knows well, but, as he admits, it is costly to him sometimes, as the temptation is so great that he at times indulges in it at the wrong time.

The President referred to our visit to Yorktown, Virginia.[4] He and I arrived in Yorktown on the MAYFLOWER, unattended by any one at all except a Sergeant of Marines and Lieutenant Manley[5] of the MAYFLOWER. When we left Washington we did not expect to leave the MAYFLOWER, so none of the secret service men accompanied us. Upon landing at Yorktown, which has only a few hundred inhabitants, we at once went to the old Court House. We entered one of the rooms—it was in the month of July—and a man was sitting at a table writing in a deed book, with his coat off, with suspenders much in evidence, and smoking a corn-cob pipe. I inquired of him, while the President was standing by my side, if there were any old deed books or maps that we could see. He remarked that there were some in an adjoining building—which was a small one-story structure. The President asked him if we could go into his Court Room. He replied: "Yep, help yourself, walk right up-stairs." The President inquired as to who the Judge was, and he said: "D. Gardner Tyler,[6] son of the tenth President of the United States, brother to Lyon G. Tyler,[7] President of William and Mary College, about twelve miles from here; he is not only a distinguished man but a fine gentlemen." All this talking was done while he was still writing; he did not stop smoking nor did he look up. The fellow never realized the presence of his distinguished visitor. Upon entering the Clerk's Office we met a Mr. Hudgins,[8] of whom the President often speaks as a real Virginia gentleman. We did not introduce ourselves. The President asked Mr. Hudgins whether he could see any old deeds or maps which he had in the Clerk's Office. Mr. Hudgins replied: "Yes, and I shall be glad to show them to you." Thereupon he got out a number of colonial surveys and deeds, which the President examined with the deepest interest. A large campaign poster of the President was pasted on the wall, and I thought how remarkable it was that this gentleman did not recognize the President, and there he was standing beside a large picture of himself. The President asked him a number of questions; the gentleman was most obliging and his replies were most courteous. When we left the Clerk's Office I felt sure that the President had been unrecognized, but later I learned that Mr. Hudgins did recognize the President and made the statement: "I did not care to intrude by introducing myself, as the President and his friend had not introduced themselves to me."

We walked around the little town—it was a very hot July afternoon—visited the old custom-house—the first in America—and stopped in the shade of a tree near a little store, where there were two or three negroes lying on the benches half asleep. The merchant wanted to know if we did not want to buy some "pop" or ginger-ale, assuring us that he would "sell it to us right." We conversed with him for a short while but did not take advantage of his offer. In addition to being the proprietor of the store, he was also the postmaster.[9]

From here we walked down to what is known as the Nelson House, which was Cornwallis' headquarters during the American Revolution. On our way we met a little girl[10] about twelve years of age, and, as all children do, she recognized the President. She stopped and spoke to him: "Excuse me, sir, but you certainly do favor the pictures of President Wilson." The President said: "Yes, I have often been told that"; whereupon she said: "Indeed, is not this President Wilson?" And the President smiled and said: "Yes, I am guilty." She said: "Well, please wait right here until I can run and tell my mother." The news soon spread that the President was in Yorktown.

We went through the old Nelson House, observing its colonial architecture, and the damage done by the artillery in the Revolutionary War. We were guided through the building by this little girl and her mother, and as we came out of the house, the little girl's mother remarked: "Look at the crowd coming up the street to see the President." I counted seven people. In this crowd that came to greet the President was the merchant and postmaster. He inquired of the President if he might speak to him privately. The President told him to go ahead. He wanted to know if the President would not raise his salary as Postmaster, as he was only getting $30 a month.

From Yorktown we went in a motor-boat down the river to Temple Farm, which was Washington's headquarters. There was no landing at this place and we could only get the boat within ten or fifteen yards of the bank of the river, so we pulled off our shoes, rolled up our trousers, and waded ashore. We climbed up a steep embankment, through the briars and the bees. In walking across a field towards the Temple Farm, we were attracted by a vicious looking bull. He began to paw the earth and bellow. Realizing the responsibility of being alone with the President, I said: "I think we had better go around another way; that bull acts like he means business." The President here told me the story of an Irishman who was chased by a bull, and just as he got partly over the fence, the bull hit him with his horns and knocked him completely on the other side of the fence; then the bull began to paw the earth and bellow, and the Irishman remarked: "You may bow and may scrape as much as you please but I'll be damned if I don't think you meant it." And the President said: "I agree with you that this bull means it, so we will go around and be protected by this fence."

We went through the Temple Farm house and saw many old portraits and pictures and prints of General Washington; old minnie balls and rifles and swords that were collected on the farm.

[1] He had died of pneumonia on March 4. De Mohrenschildt had come to the United States as the Second Secretary of the Russian embassy in Washington. He had married Nona Hazlehurst McAdoo on May 15, 1917. Shortly after the Bolshevik Revolution in November 1917, he had resigned from the embassy staff and had taken a position with the United States Shipping Board. He and his wife had moved to New York after the Armistice.
[2] About which, see WW to E. de Mohrenschildt, March 20, 1919.
[3] It is missing in WP, DLC, and in the W. G. McAdoo Papers, DLC.
[4] On July 2, 1913. For a detailed account of Wilson's visit, see also the *New York Times*, July 4, 1913.
[5] Lieut. Matthias Evans Manly.
[6] David Gardiner Tyler, former congressman from Virginia (1893-1897), since 1904, judge of the Fourteenth Virginia Judicial Circuit.
[7] That is, Lyon Gardiner Tyler.
[8] T. T. Hudgins, county clerk of York County, Va.
[9] Unidentified.
[10] Her name was Catherine Shield.

From James Watson Gerard

[The White House, March 5, 1919]

Number one period telegram received today from James W. Gerard chairman American Committee for the Independence of Armenia one Madison Avenue New York reading as follows quote President Wilson colon following is a petition addressed to you signed by twenty-thousand Protestant ministers and Catholic priests comma seventy-five Episcopal bishops comma thirty-six governors and two hundred fifty college and university presidents colon subquote We ask you respectfully to do your utmost to secure and insure the independence of Armenia comma including the six vilayets comma Cilicia and the Littoral of Trebizonde in Turkish Armenia Russian Armenia and Persian Armenia to exert your great influence to the end that the Peace Conference may make requisite arrangements for helping Armenia to establish an independent republic and to obtain adequate reparation for the terrible losses the Armenian people have suffered during the war end quotes

Tumulty

T radiogram (WP, DLC).

From William Bauchop Wilson

[The White House, March 5, 1919]

Secretary Wilson requests following be sent by cable: "March 5; 3:00 P.M. No. 2. The General Deficiency Bill which failed of passage contained an item of $1,800,000 to carry the employment service to the close of this fiscal year. The House unanimously passed the appropriation for the service and the Senate Committee made a favorable report on the item. The employment service is the only national institution connecting demobilized soldiers and war workers with labor opportunities of the country. The discontinuance of the service at this time would be a decided disadvantage. There are no state or local agencies sufficiently organized and financed to meet the conditions, and if there were, they have no national connecting links.

"We have funds enough to continue our present organization for one month, which means that we will be compelled to begin immediately to discontinue the organization unless it is possible to secure an allotment from your National Security and Defense fund. I realize the burden that the failure of Congress to act must place upon that fund, and yet I am constrained to ask you to make an allotment to the Department of Labor to enable it to continue the employment service.

"If you desire to do so, please send wireless message to that effect so that we may make our arrangements to continue the service pending the arrival of the written authorization."

Tumulty.

T radiogram (WP, DLC).

From Edward Albert Filene

New York 3/5/1919

Heartiest congratulations on your great meeting last night stop All of us who were there realized telling effect of your parting message stop Have just returned from eight thousand mile trip across country speaking for league and know you are right in saying country behind you stop Best wishes for a safe voyage and quick return with success country knows you will achieve

Edward A Filene

Hw radiogram (WP, DLC).

Gilbert Fairchild Close to Joseph Patrick Tumulty

U.S.S. George Washington, March 5, 1919.
Please send President's bath-robe in first Department pouch.
Close.

CC radiogram (WP, DLC).

From the Diary of Dr. Grayson

Thursday, March 6, 1919.

The President spent the entire day resting. In the evening he went to the movies. He looked very much refreshed as the result of the freedom from toil.

The President commented on the admirable speech which Mr. Taft delivered at the Metropolitan Opera House Tuesday evening, the 4th. He said that he (the President) omitted to call attention in his speech to the fact that Mr. Taft in making a speech in New Jersey when the President was Governor of New Jersey had embodied many of the points that are in the League of Nations.[1] He wanted to give him credit for it but forgot to do so. He said that if the League of Nations proved to be a success, which he firmly believed it would be, and there was a division in the Republicans over it, he believed Mr. Taft would be nominated for President in 1920 and that it would be due him. He further said that he would be hard to beat, because all the money interests would rally to his support, especially Wall Street and possibly the German-Americans and the dissatisfied Irish-Americans. Of course, if it became a defined issue that the German-Americans and the Irish-Americans were back of him that would defeat any candidate they favored. If Mr. Taft should allow Wall Street to control him, he feared that it might produce a revolution.

[1] Probably Taft's address at the Methodist conference in Ocean Grove, N. J., on August 15, 1911, at which Wilson was present. It is printed in *Addresses of President Taft on Arbitration* (Washington, 1911), pp. 46-55.

From Joseph Patrick Tumulty

[The White House] 3/6/19

Number Three period At special congressional election twenty second district Pennsylvania Democrat winner by five hundred comma cutting down Republican majority approximately ten thousand[1] semicolon first democrat elected in this district in fifty

years period Everything fine period Republicans greatly worried
period Seniority rule adopted by Republican caucus semicolon Mann[2]
forces in control   Tumulty

T radiogram (WP, DLC).
    [1] In a special election on March 5, 1919, to fill the vacancy caused by the death of
the Republican incumbent, Edward Everett Robbins, who had been elected in November
by a plurality of more than 7,000 votes, John Haden Wilson, an attorney of Butler,
Pennsylvania, had defeated his Republican opponent, John Martin Jamison, a coal
operator of Greensburg, Pennsylvania, by 473 votes. During the campaign, Wilson had
asked for his election as a sign of support for the policies of President Wilson, and he
had strongly endorsed the League of Nations. Jamison, on the other hand, had taken
no stand on the question and had merely declared that he would follow the policy of
the Republican party in this matter. New York Times, March 6, 1919. See also the extract
from the Grayson Diary printed at March 7, 1919, and JD to WW, March 7, 1919.
    [2] That is, James Robert Mann, Republican congressman from Illinois and the minority
leader in the previous four Congresses. Although Mann had lost the nomination for the
speakership of the House to Frederick Huntington Gillett of Massachusetts on February 27,
1919, he had been elected, on March 5, 1919, as the chairman of the influential Committee
on Committees, and his supporters had been named as chairmen of eleven of the thirteen
most important House committees.

A Memorandum by Ray Stannard Baker

[U.S.S. George Washington]
My Dear Mr. President: March 6, 1919.

In the hope of sharpening up and making more useful our news
department of the Peace Commission I have been making some
inquiries during the past eight days regarding public opinion in
America on the League of Nations and the Peace Conference generally. You may be interested in a very brief summary of what I
found.

As you know, I have been away from America for a year and I
expected to find a very much greater lack of knowledge of the
League of Nations and of the problems before the Peace Conference
than I actually did find. I also expected to find far more of the
hostility bred of that ignorance than actually exists.

In my own town, for example—Amherst, Mass.—one may find
a typical stronghold of old-fashioned New England conservatism
with an almost impenetrable Republican following. Lodge and Weeks
are strong among our farmers and small business men. Last Saturday night I spoke at a crowded meeting of our Amherst club, the
leader of which is State Senator Churchill,[1] who is one of the king-
pins of the Republican organization in Massachusetts. I know all
these men personally and thoroughly and was greatly surprised, in
the discussion which followed my talk, to find an almost unanimous
support of the League of Nations idea and an outspoken disapproval
of the obstinate position of Senator Lodge. Knowing the strong
partisanship of many of these men, this surprised me very much.

Senator Churchill himself, who heard you in Boston, called your
address there "a perfect speech both in form and in matter" and
told me that the Republicans could not stand upon this issue against
you.

At Boston I talked with R. L. O'Brien,[2] editor of the Boston Herald,
whom I have known for many years. His paper is now, perhaps,
the most powerful Republican organ in New England but he agrees
with my conservative neighbors in Amherst. He said he had told
both Lodge and Hale[3] that they could not safely make an issue
against the League of Nations. I attach an editorial from the Boston
Herald[4] written after your Boston speech by O'Brien himself, which
expresses this point of view.

This testimony is valuable because it comes from the opposition.

Senator-elect Capper of Kansas[5] has been in New York. He refused to sign the Lodge resolution and said his people were for the
League and he did not propose to do anything to obstruct it.

I talked with Frank Cobb of the World, who is, of course, strongly
with you. He regards the senatorial protest as serious because, while
the Senators pretended to support the League of Nations idea, they
were at the old familiar game of attempting to destroy it with objections and amendments. They confused the public mind. What
was needed was strong and definite support for the Covenant practically as drawn.

I talked with a good many of our best liberals and radicals, one
of whom showed me the following statement just issued by the
chairman of the new American Labor party in New York,[6] which
closely represented the point of view I heard expressed by other
radicals:

"The American Labor party gives resolute support to President
Wilson's fourteen points and a real league of nations. The draft
which the President is bringing from Europe may be the best he
can wring from the diplomats, but it falls short of what labor everywhere expects. While others grasp for trade and territory and punitive indemnities, labor keeps its mind on the only object worth
talking about—there must be no more war. That result cannot be
obtained by half-way measures. We demand honest self-determination in Ireland as well as in all disputed territories. We demand
honest disarmament. We want the open-door policy everywhere,
open discussion and open trade. We will not help to guarantee any
imperialistic peace. At the same time we shall oppose with all our
might the jingoes like Senators Poindexter, Reed, and Lodge, who
want isolation, conscription and conquest. As between them and
Wilson we are for Wilson, but we are not behind Wilson. We are
a long way ahead of him."

As representing the other end of the scale I enclose a letter from Dwight M. Morrow[7] of Morgan & Co. who has been writing an interesting series of articles for the New York Evening Post[8] not only supporting the idea of the League of Nations but the Paris Covenant. His last article on the Covenant[9] is an excellent analysis.

Summing up I should say:

1. There is tremendous popular support throughout the country for the idea of a League of Nations, but there remains much vagueness of mind as to the expression of this idea in an actual constitution.

2. This vagueness of the popular mind is what gives the opponents of the idea their opportunity not only to attack the idea itself by destructive criticism, but to develop political capital out of their criticism.

3. The great need now is to explain and defend the Covenant as adopted by your committee, to convince people that the League of Nations as set forth in the Covenant is *the* League. I would admit the need of slight amendments to clarify certain provisions, but I would stand for the document, in its broad lines, just as it is. For I believe that if the American people could have presented to them directly all the problems and difficulties which your committee had to face, the average opinion would reach the same conclusions that are set down in the covenant as now drawn. This I say although I myself would have liked to make the Covenant a more radical instrument in several respects than it is at present. But the Covenant has "started a process," and if once it begins to function actively the liberal forces of the world will have a better chance than ever before to press forward. With this view I find Norman Hapgood, Herbert Croly of the New Republic and other liberals with whom I talked in accord.

4. Therefore it seems of paramount importance for the Peace Commission and its news department to get before our people as vividly as possible all the factors which confronted your committee and to explain and re-explain, and enforce and re-enforce the Covenant, illustrating how it applies in specific cases.

5. After the armistice there was a reaction in America toward "little Americanism"—toward getting away from "entangling alliances," as the phrase is popularly misunderstood. This was, perhaps, a natural reaction from the intense occupation with more or less ugly European problems during the war, but it is now passing away and our people are beginning to see that we must also take up our "white man's burden" for good and all. Our people showed during the war their willingness to respond to calls for real service and real sacrifice. Ask enough of America—hard enough things—

and they can be had! We must make it plain that we cannot rightly enjoy the benefits of a League of Nations without also accepting the responsibilities and making the sacrifices necessary to any true co-operative enterprise. The reactionary senators are counting upon the selfishness and jealous localism of America, and our appeal must be made, and strongly made, to the spirit of national service and national sacrifice.   Ray Stannard Baker

TS MS (WP, DLC).

  [1] George Bosworth Churchill, Professor of English Literature at Amherst College.

  [2] Robert Lincoln O'Brien, president and director of the Boston Publishing Company.

  [3] That is, Frederick Hale, Republican senator from Maine.

  [4] It is missing in WP, DLC.

  [5] That is, Arthur Capper, former Governor of Kansas, a Republican.

  [6] The American Labor party of Greater New York had been founded on January 11 and 12, 1919, by a convention of more than 800 representatives of labor unions from the New York area. Its formation was part of a nationwide movement which sought to create a national labor party and which culminated, in November 1919, in the establishment of the American Labor party. The convention appointed as temporary chairman of the new party William Kohn, a representative of the New York District Council of the Upholsterers' International Union, and it invited the Socialist party to join the movement. It adopted a platform which, among other things, included many of the traditional demands of organized labor, advocated the creation of a public-works program during the period of reconstruction, and called for the restoration of the fundamental political rights of free speech, free press, and free assemblage. The platform endorsed Wilson's Fourteen Points and proposed that the future League of Nations be supplemented by a league of workers of all nations "pledged and organized to enforce the destruction of autocracy, militarism and economic imperialism throughout the world." See the *New York Times* and the *New York Herald*, Jan. 12 and 13, 1919.

  [7] That is, Dwight Whitney Morrow, a lawyer and partner of J. P. Morgan & Co., and an adviser to the Allied Maritime Transport Council from February to December 1918. His letter was D. W. Morrow to R. S. Baker, March 4, 1919, TLS (WP, DLC).

  [8] Dwight W. Morrow, "The Society of Free Nations," New York *Evening Post*, Feb. 21, 22, 24, 25, 26, 27, and 28, and March 1, 6, and 7, 1919.

  [9] "Dwight W. Morrow Discusses the Proposed Covenant of the League," *ibid.*, March 6, 1919.

From Frank Lyon Polk, with Enclosure

My dear Mr. President: Washington March 6, 1919.

Sir Horace Plunkett sent me the enclosed letter and hoped it would reach you before you sailed. Unfortunately, it arrived the day after you left Washington. As he seemed to be very anxious to have it reach your hands, I am taking the liberty of forwarding it to Paris, as his views may be of use.

Yours faithfully,   Frank L Polk

From Sir Horace Plunkett

Dear Mr. President: Battle Creek Michigan March 2, 1919.

I came to the United States some four weeks ago with the object of getting into touch with men of influence who were interested in the Irish situation and whom I thought should know the facts from one in a position to state them accurately.

From the first day of the war I have felt that an Irish settlement, which I passionately desired for other reasons, had become urgently important as a factor in the mutual regard of the peoples in the British Commonwealth of Nations on the one hand and the great Republic over which you preside on the other. A settlement could have been reached and ought to have been reached during the war; but it is idle to speculate on the results which might have followed from such a feat of statesmanship. You may, however, perhaps agree that the peace value of an ending to the Irish Question would be at least as great as any possible war effect it might have.

Already I notice the troubles of my country are being used to embarrass you. Anticipating an organized effort to bring pressure to bear upon Congress during your brief stay at Washington with the object of urging you to demand at the peace conference the application of the principle of self determination to Ireland, I wrote to Mr. Tumulty saying that in the event of my being of any possible service, as an independent source of information about Ireland, I would come to Washington at a moment's notice. He replied, as I had expected, that it would be impossible for you to see me. Happening to meet here Mr. Richard Crane, I mentioned the matter to him. Before he left this morning for Washington he told me that Mr. Polk, with whom he had been in correspondence, had offered to put before you any communication I wished to send. I have thought it well to submit the following brief observations:

Throughout the forty years during which I have been in intimate touch with American opinion, especially in the Middle West, the interest of your people in the Irish Question has varied in its intensity but has never ceased to be keen out of all proportion to the numerical strength of the Irish people, even if the larger number of the Americans of Irish birth or lineage be thrown in. On the broad issues between England and Ireland at least ninety-five per cent of Americans seem to me to take the Irish view. I expected to find—and I believe that there *was* quite recently—bitter resentment at the failure of the Irish people to come whole-heartedly into the war when the United States took up arms. I do find an undercurrent of indignation at certain actions of the Roman Catholic hie[r]archy in Ireland and an even yet more angry feeling over the relations between the disloyal German element in America and the extreme Irish. On the whole, however, the traditional anti-British sentiment which the Irish controversy always arouses is the dominant note wherever a genuine lover of Ireland, a hater of Britain or a politician wanting a sure grindstone for his axe introduces the subject. It is early yet to say what effect of Cardinal Gibbons' rather unfortunate association with Judge Colahan [Cohalan] at the Irish Convention in Philadelphia may have but I am inclined to think that, in view of the impossibility of bringing about any general understanding of even the elementary issues involved in the present Irish difficulty, this historic disturber of Anglo-American amity will not cease to trouble in the United States unless British statesmanship realizes and acts upon the imperative need of an Irish settlement.

I am quite sure—and indeed I have so stated to every Irishman that I have met since I landed—that it is extremely improbable that you would take any action in regard to Ireland which might even have the appearance of intervention in the domestic affairs of the British Isles. You may, however, see fit to make your personal wishes and that of your people privately known to the British Government. It is notorious that the recent general election resulted in a triumph for Mr. Lloyd George and at the same time surrounded him with colleagues who on all questions of doemstic [domestic] politics (including Ireland) are what would be called over here reactionary. I will, therefore, set down the broad facts of the present Irish difficulty and point out where suggestions from you might be extremely helpful[.]

The Irish Convention[1] was a very genuine effort on the part of nearly one hundred representative Irishmen to come to agreement. Quite a number of these men earnestly desired a settlement during the war in order that their country might play a great part in it. On the 9th of April last year I handed the report of the Convention to the Prime Minister in the morning. In the afternoon he had to introduce the last military service bill. It was at the gravest crisis in the war and it was absolutely necessary to insure Irelands full participation in it, not only because Ireland's man power might be needed but the additional draft upon the man power of England, Scotland and Wales could not have been obtained if Ireland still stood out. Without going into minor details, which I admit were difficult enough, there seemed to be two courses which Mr. Lloyd George might adopt. The first was to say to the Ulster minority that since the Convention had revealed the possibility of an agreement upon the main question of Irish Government of the whole of Ireland outside the Northeast corner, Sir Edward Carson[2] and his followers ought no longer to stand in the way of an Irish settlement. He could call upon that section to state what guarantees and safeguards they required to come into an all-Ireland Parliament. He could then say that an Irish Government, necessarily somewhat provisional in character, should be set up immediately and the Irish people must do their part in the war. The other course, and the one which he actually adopted, was to tell the Irish people that the British Parliament would now have to impose conscription on Ireland. It takes but little political imagination to realize the effect this decision was bound to have. What was the use of telling the Irish people that they had no Parliament of their own to deal with the matter when that institution existed *de jure* and was interned in the British statute book? The extreme demand for an Irish Republic is the inevitable, if not very logical, consequence of this unfortunate action.

Of course the mistake, which kept Ireland more than ever out of the war, not only proved to be of no military advantage but greatly aggravagated [aggravated] the policital [political] situation. It has become far more difficult to deal with than it was before this false step was taken. I still think, however, that the only hopeful solution is to be found in an appeal to the Ulster minority to yield to the wishes of the majority. That there would be no danger to Ulster interests, that on the contrary the Irish minority would stand before their own countrymen and before the world in a far stronger position than they stand today, I think I could demonstrate to your satisfaction but not without exceeding the bounds of any proper communication.

I may have done this already, and therefore I will close with the suggestion that you hand this letter to Colonel House with whom I was in correspondence on the subject before I left Ireland and who has all the papers necessary for coming into a fair judgment upon the issue I have raised.

I also enclose a pamphlet written in July last and a leaflet written in November[3] which I think are self-explanatory, and will probably throw some light upon the recent events which have brought the Irish Question to its present impasse.

Believe me to be, with profound respect,

Very sincerely,   Horace Plunkett.

P.S. Perhaps your private secretary would have a proper copy made, as the only absolutely confidential clerical assistance available here was not very efficient & if I had the letter retyped it wd. be too late

TLS (WP, DLC).
    [1] About which, see E. Drummond to W. Wiseman, April 2, 1918, n. 1, Vol. 47.
    [2] That is, Sir Edward Henry Carson, former First Lord of the Admiralty, a member of the British War Cabinet from July 1917 to January 1918, and the longtime leader of the Ulster Unionists in the House of Commons.
    [3] Sir Horace Plunkett, *Home Rule and Conscription* (Dublin and London, 1918), and *Irish Reconstruction Association*, printed copy of a letter from Plunkett to the Dublin press of November 22, 1918, both in WP, DLC.

From Howard Duryee Wheeler[1]

My dear Mr. President: Paris, March 6, 1919.

I need hardly say that I was intensely interested, and profoundly gratified at the announcement, contained in dispatches from Washington, that you have in contemplation the writing of your own history of your administration.[2]

I had hoped to ask the honor of an interview with you in connection with this announcement, as soon as convenient to you after your return to France. But as a result of the fact that Mrs. Wheeler[3] has suffered a severe attack of pneumonia, it has become all-important that she be removed without delay to a warmer climate. Her illness has necessitated our departure for southern Italy and I shall not, in all probability, be able to return to Paris before the first week in April.

It is my earnest hope that you will not, by then, have made definite arrangements for publication, and that it will not be then too late for me to have the high privilege of laying before you certain proposals, on the part of the publishing house which I represent, in relation to the first serial publication of your work.

Very respectfully,   Howard Wheeler

TLS (WP, DLC).
    [1] Editor of *Everybody's Magazine*.
    [2] Wilson's remarks to the members of the Democratic National Committee on February 28, 1919, to the effect that he would be an historian after March 4, 1921, had been widely reported in the press.
    [3] Eleanor Josephine McPartland Wheeler.

From the Diary of Dr. Grayson

Friday, March 7, 1919.

The President and I walked around the deck, while Mrs. Wilson played cards in her apartments with her Secretary, Miss Benham. After lunch the President and Mrs. Wilson attended a movie matinee in the main dining-room. The room was very hot and the ventilation imperfect with the result that the President got the start of what later turned out to be a nasty cold. At night he also attended the movies.

The President today sent a telegram of congratulation to Congressman-elect John H. Wilson, at Greensburg, Pennsylvania, who has just been elected on the Democratic ticket, his platform calling for a complete endorsement of the President's peace program and ratification of the League of Nations covenant. The President was much gratified over this, as it is a forecast of what may be expected when the people of the United States have the opportunity to pass upon the League of Nations plan. It was especially gratifying because this is a marked Republican district, John H. Wilson being the first Democratic Congressman elected in the district for over fifty years, and the second Democrat ever elected in the district. The President said that if the Republicans insisted upon making this an issue it might be a straw as to how the 1920 election was going. He said that the political conditions in Pennsylvania really had to be viewed with alarm, because they were so corrupt and content. For instance, when Vance McCormick ran for Governor, he carried, if he recollects, every county in the State except Pittsburgh and Philadelphia. In Philadelphia they have a machine by which they can keep on counting votes as long as they like and count out any one they do not want.

From Josephus Daniels

[Washington] 3-7-19

For the first time in fifty years a democrat was elected to Congress at special election to fill vacancy in 22nd Pennsylvania district. At last election Democrat defeated by nine thousand. The successful candidate John H Wilson of Butler Pennsylvania made his campaign upon endorsement of the League of Nations and asked electorate to uphold the President. His opponent did not take any stand on the League of Nations. In answering inquiry said he would be governed by the course the Republican party decided to follow. You have won first blood in the appeal to the people.

Josephus Daniels

T radiogram (WP, DLC).

To Joseph Patrick Tumulty

[*U.S.S. George Washington*, c. March 7, 1919]

Please extend my cordial congratulations to Mr. Wilson just elected in Pennsylvania and express my gratification that he won upon the issue of the League of Nations.   Woodrow Wilson

CC radiogram (WP, DLC).

From Edward Mandell House

[Paris, March 7, 1919]

No. 2. Lloyd George, Clemenceau and I in conference this morning discussed the following subjects:

1. The distribution of the sum which Germany is to be called upon to pay. George said he could not sustain himself with his people [if] on a question [of priority] that all this sum should go to France and Belgium for reparation. He suggested that it should be apportioned as follows: Three parts for reparation and two parts for costs [of war], and that France [Belgium] and all the countries at war with Germany should participate in these two parts as well as Great Britain. I thought this proposal of George fair, but there must be no demand on Germany inconsistent with our _____ [terms of] armistice with Germany and the fourteen points. Clemenceau seemed to think the proposal just, but could not commit himself [reserved final judgment] until he could consult his financial experts.

2. [We] Took up the [question of] feeding of Germany, and Clemenceau did not disagree [agree] to the plan which George and I presented from our experts. However, Germany has refused to turn over any shipping until a satisfactory plan has been mutually agreed upon which will provide food until next harvest.[1]

3. The left bank of the Rhine was discussed, but no tentative agreement was reached because of Clemenceau's very unreasonable attitude. He wanted [wants] the Rhenish republics to be perpetually restrained from joining the German Federation. Tardieu tells me he will urge him to modify this view.

4. The naval terms declared for the dismemberment or sinking of the German ships, but the French made reservation in favor of partitioning them amongst the Allies. The British were on the point of yielding to this, but I told George that the President [we] could never consent to the British augmenting their Navy so largely; if this were done, it would surely lead to American and British rivalry in this direction. We finally agreed that the ships should be parti-

tioned but that Great Britain, the United States and Japan should sink those coming to them.

5. In discussing the dismemberment of the Turkish Empire, both Clemenceau and George expressed the wish that we acknowledge _____ [accept mandatories] for Armenia and Constantinople. I thought the United States would be willing when the proposal was brought before them.

6. George was unwilling to accept the clause in our military terms to Germany relating to conscription. He offered a substitute which Clemenceau and I accepted, which provides for a volunteer army of 200,000, the period of supplement [service to] be for the twelve years. This was afterwards adopted by the Council of Ten this afternoon. George's reason for this was largely to meet a political situation in England and because that if the _____ [principle of] conscription was _____ [forbidden in Germany] it would be _____ [soon] discontinued everywhere.

Edward House.

T radiogram (WP, DLC).

[1] At the meeting of the Council of Ten on January 13, 1919 (see the minutes of that body printed at that date in Vol. 54), the Allies and the United States had acknowledged that Germany was in desperate need of food supplies to tide her over until the autumn harvest. Thus, in accordance with Article 26 of the Armistice agreement, they had agreed to a relaxation of the blockade and to the provisioning of Germany and had decided that, if a satisfactory method of payment could be arranged, Germany would receive, in the first instance, 200,000 tons of breadstuffs and 70,000 tons of pork products. Moreover, on January 16, Article 8 of the second renewal of the Armistice stipulated that these supplies would be shipped immediately, provided Germany placed her entire merchant fleet at the disposal of the Allies and the United States for that purpose.

In the following weeks, as strikes and political unrest threatened the demise of the Ebert-Scheidemann government and numerous reports from Allied and American agents in Germany indicated the possibility of an imminent Bolshevik takeover, British and American economic experts, in particular, concluded that the German food shortage had to be alleviated as soon as possible in order to eliminate one of the supposed main causes of Bolshevism.

However, although the Allies, the United States, and Germany agreed in principle that the transfer of the German fleet, the shipment of foodstuffs, and the payment for these supplies had to be part of one and the same transaction, they were unable to work out a concrete agreement. At a series of conferences at Spa on February 6, 7, and 8 and on March 4 and 5, the German delegate adamantly opposed the use of Germany's entire merchant fleet for food shipments, unless Germany received an ironclad guarantee that the United States and the Allies would supply all of Germany's food requirements until the next harvest. If the Associated Powers could promise only a partial revictualing of Germany, the German government would, at best, release only part of its fleet. The French delegates, on the other hand, were unwilling to give any long-term assurances which would effectively emasculate the blockade as an instrument of pressure upon Germany at the peace settlement. Furthermore, in their desire to preserve Germany's gold reserves and other assets for future reparations, the French objected categorically to an Anglo-American financial plan which allowed Germany to pay for its food imports in part with securities and gold.

After the breakdown of the negotiations at Spa, the Supreme Economic Council, unable to resolve the disagreement over fundamental policy issues between the British and American economic advisers and their French colleagues in its meeting on March 7, referred the question of revictualing Germany to the Council of Ten, which took up the problem on March 7 and 8. As chairman of the Supreme Economic Council, Lord Robert Cecil introduced the discussion, and he submitted a proposal which he and

Hoover had drafted and which was similar to the original Anglo-American scheme. It provided that, in exchange for the use of her merchant fleet, Germany would immediately receive the 270,000 tons of foodstuffs already agreed upon and would be permitted to import an additional 370,000 tons of food each month until September 1. Germany would pay for these supplies with the export of commodities, credits from neutral countries, the sale of foreign holdings, and advances and loans against such collaterals as foreign investments and gold. The outright sale of gold was permitted only if the Associated Powers determined that all other means of payment should prove inadequate.

The French, however, remained adamant. In lengthy filibusters, Clémentel, Loucheur, Klotz, and Clemenceau kept insisting that Germany should only be fed a month at a time and should be allowed to pay with resources earmarked for reparations and indemnities only after all other credit resources had been exhausted. In response, Hoover and Lloyd George launched a massive attack on France's objections, asserting that Germany was teetering on the brink of anarchy and that only immediate food relief could arrest the spread of Bolshevism to Germany and possibly to other European countries. In the face of this Anglo-American front, the French finally gave up their resistance and approved Hoover's and Cecil's scheme.

An agreement with the German delegates was easily negotiated at Brussels on March 14 and 15, and the German government promptly began delivery of 700,000 tons of cargo ships. Hoover, anxious to begin the provisioning of Germany as soon as possible, did not wait for these ships to cross the Atlantic and to return with supplies from the United States and Canada. Instead, he immediately diverted several food shipments to German ports, drew heavily on British and American stocks already in Europe, and arranged for some 200,000 tons of American shipping to be loaded in American ports. On March 25, the first American provisions ship, the S.S. *West Carnifex*, arrived at Hamburg, carrying 6,600 tons of flour, and, by the end of May, Germany had been supplied with some 400,000 tons of foodstuffs. For a detailed discussion, see Mayer, *Politics and Diplomacy of Peacemaking*, pp. 504-14, and Klaus Schwabe, *Woodrow Wilson, Revolutionary Germany, and Peacemaking, 1918-1919: Missionary Diplomacy and the Realities of Power* (Chapel Hill, N. C., and London, 1985), pp. 191-207.

From Charles Mills Galloway

My dear Mr. President: Washington, D. C. March 7, 1919.

I feel absolutely sure that you have been misinformed as to my official actions in connection with the work of the Civil Service Commission.[1] I respectfully request, therefore, that I be not condemned and disgraced without a hearing, either before you or some one designated by you, and that you withdraw your request for my resignation.

Hoping that you will give me an opportunity to exonerate myself from any false accusations that have been made against me, and having the sincere belief that you will do nothing less than this, I am,   Respectfully yours,   Chas M Galloway

TLS (WP, DLC).
   [1] About this matter, see WW to C. M. Galloway, Feb. 28, 1919.

From the Diary of Dr. Grayson

Saturday, March 8, 1919.

The President was today reminiscing on Daniel Webster, Robert Y. Hayne and James Louis Petigru. He often thought on March

8th of the great speech made on this day by Daniel Webster. It was
a debate on slavery and the participants were Webster of Massachusetts and Hayne of South Carolina, the former being strongly
opposed to slavery and the latter in favor of it. Afterwards Webster
tried to make a compromise speech; his friends went back on him
because of his attitude and criticised him severely. Many thought
that it broke Webster's heart. The President commented on how
seldom it is that bosom friends could retain their friendship when
they had opposite views on political and public questions. The most
striking instance of this the President ever knew was the friendship
which existed between James Louis Petigru and Robert Y. Hayne.
Petigru was perhaps the most able man of his time. He favored the
abolition of slavery. He and Hayne opposed each other bitterly on
this question, and yet it never touched their friendship. When Petigru died he was buried at St. Michael's Churchyard, Charleston,
South Carolina, and although he was against slavery, and the feeling was bitter and intense, the bombardment around Charleston
ceased on the Confederate side at the time Petigru was buried.
Some of the most eloquent tributes ever paid man were uttered in
his behalf at that time. The following epitaph appears on his tomb-
stone:

JAMES LOUIS PETIGRU
Born at Abbeville, May 10th, 1789; Died at Charleston,
March 9th, 1863.
JURIST, ORATOR, STATESMAN, PATRIOT.
Future times will hardly know how Great a Life this simple
Stone Commemorates,—
The Tradition of his Eloquence, his Wisdom
and Wit may Fade;
But he Lived for Ends more Durable than Fame.
His Eloquence was the Protection of the Poor and Wronged.
His Learning Illuminated the Principles of Law—
In the Admiration of his Peers, in the Respect of his People,
In the Affection of his Family, His was the Highest Place;
The Just Meed of his Kindness and Forbearance.
His Dignity and Simplicity
His brilliant Genius and his unwearied Industry, Unawed by
Opinion, Unseduced by Flattery, Undismayed by Disaster,
He confronted Life with antique Courage and Death with
Christian Hope.
In the great Civil War he withstood his People for his Coun-
try, But his People did Homage to the Man who held his
Conscience higher than their Praise
And his Country heaped her Honours

on the Grave of the Patriot,
To whom, Living, his own Righteous Self-Respect sufficed,
alike for Motive and Reward.

"Nothing is here for tears, nothing to wail
Or knock the breast, no weakness, no contempt
Dispraise or blame, nothing but well and fair
And what may quiet us in a life so noble."

Petigru and Hayne lie side by side in the St. Michael's Church-yard, notwithstanding all the hostility of feeling at that time. Though they differed it never interfered with their friendship. Perhaps a like occurrence is not known in history. Petigru never gained a national reputation like Hayne, because he could not be elected to office on account of his anti-slavery views. If he could have entered public life, he would have been recognized as one of the greatest men in his day. The President said: "If he were living today, think what a big calibered man he would be!" With reference to the words—"unawed by opinion"—the President remarked: "That's a great thing; it takes real nerve and backbone to withstand it."

The President this afternoon was feeling badly, and I persuaded him to remain in bed all the afternoon. He got up for dinner but had no appetite. I took his temperature, which was found to be 102, and advised him to go to bed. About an hour afterwards he had a chill. He has a sore throat and a very sore gum as the result of a filling put in his tooth the day before he left Washington. After making him as comfortable as possible, treating his throat, and giving him other medical treatment, and after visiting him at different intervals during the afternoon and night, he expressed his usual appreciation for taking care of him and said: "Now, don't you bother to come to see me any more tonight. I will send word to you by the orderly outside of the door if I want you."

This morning the President told me a story about Daniel Webster. He said Daniel had a brother named Zeek, and they lived in a little house that had a loft to it. Both were playing in the attic and making a good deal of noise, when the father hollered up and said: "Zeek, what are you doing up there?" Zeek replied: "Nothing." "Daniel, what are you doing?" "Helping Zeek," Dan replied.

The President said that Daniel Webster was perhaps one of the few lawyers who ever influenced the Supreme Court by oratory. It was in a case in which Dartmouth College was involved—Webster's Alma Mater—and among the phrases which he used was: "It is a little college but there are those who love it." The decision in this case established a precedent and influenced the decision in a number of other cases before the Supreme Court.

From the Diary of Ray Stannard Baker

At Sea Friday the 8th [March 1919]

I had quite an interesting talk, in company with General Gregory, with the President to-day. At the Metropolitan meeting the other night he looked very much worn, his face gray & drawn, showing the strain of his heavy work at Washington—a really terrific week— but a little rest has put him in good condition again. His physical endurance is remarkable. I asked him about his interview the other night after the Metropolitan meeting with the Irish committee. No question has more dynamite in it now than the Irish question: & the Irish-Americans have been trying to "smoke out" the President upon it, & make him commit himself. They want him, quite crudely, to come out for the independence of Ireland. He said that he refused to receive the committee if Judge Cohalan was on it, & that he told the representatives of the committee who came to him immediately after the meeting was over—and in language so plain & loud that it could be heard by the Tammany policemen who stood about, that he regarded Judge Cohalan as a traitor & refused to meet him. The representatives withdrew & finally the Committee appeared without Cohalan & stated their case: "They were so insistent," said the President, "that I had hard work keeping my temper."

He believes that the Irish question is now a domestic affair of the British Empire & that neither he nor any other foreign leader has any right to interfere, or to advocate publicly any policy. He said he did not tell them so, but he believed that when the League of Nations covenant was adopted & the League came into being, a foreign nation—America if you like—might suggest, under one of its provisions, that the Irish question might become a cause of war & that therefore it became the concern of the League—but that time had not yet arrived.

The President has a good deal of the Red Indian in him—and his dislikes of certain men (like Cohalan) are implacable. Once in Paris, last month, I know he refused to receive a group of newspaper men because of one of them whom he would not, under any circumstances, meet.

In amplification of my memorandum to the President on public opinion in America on the L. of N. I argued that it was necessary to explain the problems presented to the Committee (the President's Committee) which drew up the Covenant—the idea being that the average American would come to the same compromise & the same conclusions embodied in the Covenant if he had access to the same facts. What was needed, I argued, was not so much to convince our people of the necessity for a League (the great majority are

already convinced), but to assure them that *the* League of the Paris
Covenant is the best obtainable. The President said that this specific
knowledge would be valuable in most cases, but not in all. He gave
this example. In his original draft of the Covenant[1] (a copy of which
he gave me) there was a provision (article VI of the supplementary
agreements) which provided that all new states must bind themselves "to accord to all racial or national minorities within their
separate jurisdiction exactly the same treatment & security, both
in law & in fact, that is accorded the racial or national majority of
their people." This was a very valuable provision, making for more
democracy in the world. But it was violently opposed by Dmowski,
the Polish leader, who is bitterly anti-semitic: and who feared the
Jewish issue in Poland; and it also brought up, acutely, the Japanese
question, the Japanese standing for what the president called "an
absurdly mild" recognition of the racial equality of the Japanese—
but this was opposed by the British, on account of their colonials,
particularly Australia. The whole provision was left out. He considered that publicity upon such an acute issue as this would do
more harm than good: and make the adoption of the best obtainable
Covenant more difficult.

(I cannot feel myself in agreement here. I believe the President's
original proposal was sound & right, & that with real publicity at
every step he could have carried it before the court of the world's
conscience. It is probably right now that the Covenant is before us
in black & white not to raise the issue—for the important thing
now is to *get peace*, get something started instantly, & a welter of
new discussion can only make for delay.[)] It is an odd thing that
while the President stands for "pitiless publicity" & "open covenants
openly arrived at"—a true position if ever there was one—it is so
difficult for him to practice it. He is really so fearful of it. No man
ever wanted greater publicity than he for the *general* statements
of his position: & few leaders are more secretive when it comes to
the discussion of the specific problem. He speaks to the masses in
terms of the new diplomacy, but he deals with the leaders by the
methods of the old. This may be the greater wisdom of compromise:
it may be the only present method, considering the immense ignorance of the masses of mankind, to get constructive results. What
he does is to let the crowd infer the general principles—and I
suppose no man ever lived who could do it better—and then to
compromise & dicker remorselessly with the leaders in the practical
application of those principles. Could it be done differently? I think
so: I have greater faith in the general sense of humankind, & would

[1] Printed at January 8, 1919, Vol. 53.

trust them more fully, even if it took longer to reach a decision. But the President is a very wise & a very great man—& in the long run he will be judged by results rather than by methods.

He is a good hater—& how he does hate those obstructive Senators. He is inclined now to stand by the Covenant word for word as drawn, accepting no amendments, so that the 37 of the round-robin will be utterly vanquished, will have no chance of saying afterwards "Well, we forced the amendments didn't we?" & being thus able to withdraw from their present ugly position & come to the support of the covenant.

Admiral Grayson told me to-day that the President was practically blind in one eye, the result of the rupture of a blood vessel some years ago—the kind of a rupture which, if it had been in his brain, would have killed him.[2] Grayson is one of the men who ought to have credit for a League of Nations, if ever it is established, for he has done a wonderful service in preserving & keeping in good order the precious life of the President. When the President came to the White House in 1913 he was far from being a well man. His digestion was poor & he had serious neuritis in his shoulder. It was the opinion of so good a doctor as Weir Mitchell[3] that he could not last long. To-day he is in practically perfect health & can stand no end of work & strain: and this is due, in no small degree, to the daily care of Grayson who watches him like a hawk. It is also due, of course, to the remarkable self discipline of the President himself: his complete command of both body & mind. He rests when he rests completely: & works when he works, utterly. He & Mrs. Wilson have attended the moving picture shows every evening both going & coming on these voyages: & to-day they were at the shows both afternoon & evening—in short about 4 or 5 hours of moving pictures in one day! Some of them are so inane, so utterly trashy that it is hard to understand how a man of Wilson's intellect, could bear them at all. They do not, he says, hurt his eyes, & he finds them restful. It is very curious, the *play* of his mind. He likes a pun, he loves limericks—quoting one to-day, about seasickness, & sometimes he apparently finds amusement in the most childish anagrams & puzzles. Grayson showed me the other day, to see if I could solve it, the following verbal puzzle supposed to have been used as the address on a letter, which the President had set down for him

[2] Here Grayson referred to what we have called a major stroke on May 28, 1906, which largely blinded Wilson in the left eye and which we have said had significant effects upon his personality and behavior, at least until early 1910. See, e.g., WW to J. D. Greene, May 30, 1906, Vol. 16. For a discussion of the literature on Wilson's health history, see the Introduction to Vol. 54.

[3] That is, Silas Weir Mitchell.

wood

John

Mass.

It was in the President's handwriting. You are to read it off: "John Underwood, Andover, Mass."

Surely these are about the lowest & most childish forms of humor, or wit, & yet the President relaxes in that way.

Mrs. Wilson & Grayson read aloud to the President a good deal. He has been enjoying A. G. Gardiner's books & sketches of public men: "Prophets, Priests & Kings," "War Lords" &c.

He told me to-day that he had never been sea-sick but once—crossing the English Channel.

He sees very few people & seems to have almost no intimate friends. There is no man in the world who better understands the democratic spirit in its broad manifestations: and few with less of the easy democracy of personal friendship & the give & take of intimacy. The voice of humanity reaches him with wonderful clearness: & makes him an almost infallible judge of the great ground swells of public opinion. How he gets it is the secret of his genius; at any rate he seems not to want to get it from innumerable visitors (as Roosevelt did) and it is apparently a strain to him to have people argue with him about these things. He receives delegations but keeps them at arm's length & does most of the talking himself. He does it as a duty without, I think, any particular enjoyment. Neither in Washington nor in Paris has he ever entertained much. Yet he is very dependent upon Mrs. Wilson & Admiral Grayson, & with a few people around him whom he likes he is altogether delightful. Coming over on the George Washington I was invited into his cabin one day for lunch & it was altogether a charming occasion. The President was full of good stories, interesting comments on affairs in Paris—witty & genial. I enjoyed it greatly. Mrs. Wilson is a good woman and of enormous service to the President. But the man himself lives the lonely life of the mind, & it is in his public addresses that he is most self-revealing. He is the type, par excellence, of the *public man*: and in order to be that, & do the great service he is called upon to do, he reduces his private life to the utmost simplicity. To many of those who know the true riches of friendship, those who wish to enjoy the world as they go through it, it will seem a poverty-stricken private life. It may be the price he has to pay!

The President, as one would anyway know, is a very temperate man: he smokes not at all, and infrequently, coming in wet or cold, takes a small drink of Scotch whisky. Dr. Grayson tells me that no one of the three Presidents he has known so intimately was a smoker. Roosevelt took some wine with his meals & liked champagne with big dinners but was never intemperate in this respect, though he was often charged with being. Taft was & is a total abstainer. But Roosevelt was not a temperate man by nature, but was given to extremes & excesses of all kinds—very different in temperament from Wilson. Though not an excessive user of alcohol, he sometimes drank an inordinate amount of tea—6 or 8 or even 10 cups at a time. This stimulated him violently, so that he sometimes talked & acted almost as though intoxicated. Afterwards he could not sleep & would get up the next morning fagged & worn. But he would not give up. In order to clear his head & put himself in order again he would order out his horse & invite some long-suffering diplomat or army officer & go with him for a pounding ride in the park or through the country. He would perspire tremendously, do all sorts of "stunts," such as jumping fences or riding through streams & getting himself wet through—but would come back feeling "bully." In the long run these excesses killed him: he developed rheumatism, & a kind of eczema, & his heart finally gave out & he died too young. Yet, if he had not had this determination & will power—even this extreme temperament—he probably would never have developed himself, in his earlier years, from a rather weakling youth into a manhood of unexampled robustity.

Wilson is given to no excesses whatever. He has perfect control of himself—including a hot temper. Under the most bitter & provocative attacks by Roosevelt he never once responded, never even referred to Roosevelt, treated Roosevelt & his whole campaign of opposition as though they did not exist. Nothing could have been better calculated to infuriate a man of Roosevelt's temperament more than this. It drove him wild!

Mr. Wilson made a very significant remark to me yesterday: "A high degree of education," he said, "tends, I think, to weaken a man's human sympathies."

It is remarkable & a satisfactory thing that all three of our last Presidents have been men of the highest moral character—irreproachable in their private lives, loving their families & children. All three have also been active in their religious observances—and strong in their religious convictions—Roosevelt of the Dutch Reformed Church, Taft, Unitarian, and Wilson Presbyterian. The Puritan tradition is strong in all three.

Hw MS (R. S. Baker Papers, DLC).

From Eugene Francis Kinkead[1]

My dear Mr. President: Newark, New Jersey March 8, 1919.

May I write to you frankly and to some length regarding the Irish question.

It is my judgment that every American of Irish lineage, and millions of our fellow Americans of other racial characteristics, expect you to be the spokesman at Versailles for the extension of the principle of self-determination to Ireland.

I was one of those who felt, while we were engaged in war, that no international question should be permitted to divide the American people. In May 1918, I wrote you[2] resenting a request made to you for a conference by so-called "Friends of Irish Freedom" to ascertain your views on the Irish question. I stated then, "If these men are Irish, they should return to Ireland and fight the battle there. If they are Americans, they should do as the rest of us are doing—all that lies within our power to bring success to American arms." It is true that some of those who were active in this cause while we were at war are interested in the movement today, but I have never known you to turn from a just cause on account of it being supported by some with whom you have previously differed.

May I recall that in your FOURTEEN POINTS OF PEACE you said:

"A free, open-minded, and absolutely impartial adjustment of all colonial claims, based upon a strict observance of the principle that in determining all such questions of sovereignty the interests of the populations concerned must have equal weight wiith the equitable claims of the Government whose title is to be determined." Later on February 11, 1918, in your REJOINDER TO THE CENTRAL POWERS you stated:

"That all well-defined national aspirations shall be accorded the utmost satisfaction that can be accorded them without introducing new or perpetuating old elements of discord and antagonism that would be likely in time to break the peace of Europe and consequently of the world."

At Mount Vernon, on July 4, 1918, you said:

"The settlement of every question, whether of territory, of sovereignty, of economic arrangement, or of political relationship, upon the basis of the free acceptance of that settlement by the people immediately concerned, and not upon the basis of the material interest or advantage of any other nation or people which may desire a different settlement for the sake of its own exterior influence or mastery."

In your last public utterance in New York you said:

"It is one of the agreements of this covenant that it is the friendly right of every nation a member of the League to call attention to anything that it thinks will disturb the peace of the world, no matter where that thing is occurring. There is no subject that may touch the peace of the world which is exempt from inquiry and discussion. * * *" And I find the same thought expressed in almost the same language in the Covenant of the League of Nations:

"It is hereby also declared and agreed to be the friendly right of each of the high contracting parties to draw the attention of the body of delegates or of the Executive Council to any circumstances affecting international intercourse which threatens to disturb international peace or the good understanding between nations upon which peace depends."

I believed when you spoke these words, and I believe now, that Ireland comes directly within their scope.

If we are to have lasting peace, Mr. President, the Irish question must be settled rightly. Ireland has been in rebellion at least four times in the last century and will continue to rebel as long as the Irish people are denied the right to determine for themselves the character of government under which they shall live. With the millions of our citizens of Irish blood and other millions scattered throughout the world sympathizing with the Irish claim for self-determination, it is, I think, plain that there is a vulnerable spot in the armor which is being cast to ward off future wars.

I will not take the liberty of discussing in this communication the political side of the question, except to state that a brief presentation of the question by Mr. Frank P. Walsh and myself caused the Democratic National Committee to unanimously adopt a resolution favorable to the plan,[3] and on March 4th the House of Representatives by a vote of 276 to 41 adopted a resolution expressing the hope that the right of self-determination might be given to Ireland, after the Chairman of the Rules Committee, Mr. Pou of North Carolina, said that it was absolutely impossible to consider the resolution.[4]

I need not recall to you that I have given you an affectionate loyalty from the eventful hour in August 1909 when I had the honor to be one of four who requested you to run for Governor of New Jersey[5] down to the present time, and I have written at this length in order that you may know the feelings of one who resented the introduction of the Irish question while America was at war, but who now feels that in accordance with the principles laid down by you before the war, during the war and after the war, that Ireland will have the same generous and effective efforts on your part as Poland, Czecho-Slovia, or the Jugo-Slavs, and the other smaller nationalities, in the recognition of whose freedom I rejoice. I am sure that you will never permit it to be written into the Constitution of the League of Nations that the right of self-determination shall operate in favor of the suppressed peoples of every other nation and be denied to the Irish who have fought for freedom wherever her banner was unfurled.

I, for one, believe that lack of full information alone may lead you to wrong conclusions regarding the Irish question, and I do hope, Mr. President, that you will ascertain the views of the people of Ireland which resulted on December 28, 1918 in the election of 73 representatives pledged to the cause of self-determination in 105 districts, despite the fact that the leaders of the movement were in jail, their campaign literature destroyed and the Island covered by 180,000 British soldiers intent on stifling the movement for self-determination.

While assuring you of my sympathetic understanding of at least some of the difficulties that you are faced with in endeavoring to write into actuality your well-defined principles, may I suggest that were it possible to accom[m]odate all other conterverted questions and leave the Irish question unsettled, that in my judgment the covenant of the League of Nations might not be adopted by the United States and if it were adopted the League would not long continue.

With great respect, I am, Mr. President,

Very sincerely yours,   E. F. Kinkead.

TLS (WP, DLC).

[1] President of the Jersey Railways Advertising Company and the Orange Publishing Company. A former congressman from New Jersey (1909-1915), and Sheriff of Hudson County, New Jersey (1914-1917), he had been one of the leaders of the Hudson County Democratic machine.

[2] E. F. Kinkead to WW, May 27, 1918, TLS (WP, DLC).

[3] The Editors have been unable to find this resolution or to learn anything more about it.

[4] Kinkead referred to the so-called Gallagher resolution concerning "the right to freedom, independence, and self-determination of Ireland," about which see JPT to WW, Jan. 28, 1919, n. 1, Vol. 54. The House Committee on Foreign Affairs reported the resolution on February 11, 1919. However, it changed the resolution from a joint resolution to a concurrent resolution (H. Con. Res. 68), which required the consent of the Senate. Moreover, the committee amended the resolution to the effect that it was "the earnest hope of the Congress of the United States" that the peace conference would "favorably consider the claims of Ireland to the right of self-determination." The House debated the resolution in the early hours of March 4, but a lengthy filibuster, led by Representative Mann, prevented a vote on it for several hours. Mann charged that the Democrats, who allegedly supported the resolution, had deliberately changed it to a concurrent resolution and had then delayed its consideration, in order to forestall its adoption by the Senate and to prevent it from being sent to the President as "an expression of the American people shown through their Representatives elect." The House finally voted on the resolution at 5:30 a.m., and it was adopted by a vote of 216 to forty-five. *Cong. Record*, 65th Cong., 3d sess., pp. 66, 3174, 5027-35, 5042-57.

[5] Kinkead was obviously confused. He must be referring to the so-called Lawyers' Club conference in New York on July 8, 1910, about which, see G. B. M. Harvey to WW, July 7, 1910, and the Editorial Note printed at July 8, 1910, both in Vol. 20.

From the Diary of Dr. Grayson

Sunday, March 9, 1919.

The President remained in bed all day.

Monday, March 10, 1919.

The President did not arise until noon. After lunch he went on deck for the first time and promenaded around the enclosed "B" Deck a few times. He was attracted to the shuffle board game, and he and Mrs. Wilson amused themselves playing it for a little while. The President was not very lucky, his highest score in any of the games approximating only three. He could get the blocks in the squares, but they usually landed on the line and did not therefore count in the score.

In today's issue of the HATCHET—the U.S.S. GEORGE WASHINGTON'S publication—the following despatch appeared:

BERLIN, Mar. 10,—The first break in the general strike of the German workers took place on Sunday when the subway workers and telephone operators returned to work. This was the result of the action of the government in recognizing the soldiers and workers councils and in promising that their interests shall have consideration at the hands of the government.

After reading this article the President said that this looked bad; that if the present government of Germany is recognizing the soldiers and workers councils, it is delivering itself into the hands of the bolshevists. He said the American negro returning from abroad would be our greatest medium in conveying bolshevism to America. For example, a friend recently related the experience of a lady friend wanting to employ a negro laundress offering to pay the usual wage in that community. The negress demands that she be given more money than was offered for the reason that "money is as much mine as it is yours." Furthermore, he called attention to the fact that the French people have placed the negro soldier in France on an equality with the white man, and "it has gone to their heads."

Discussing bolshevism, the President referred to the fact that its theory had some advantages but the trouble was that an attempt was being made to accomplish it in the wrong way. It is a very serious and grave question and one that will have a marked bearing on future business. And in speaking of business, he said that the employees do not seem to be satisfied with what is called a partnership or share of the profits. As to profit sharing they doubt their employers when the business concern tells them that they cannot afford to give them more than, say, 10% of the profits; they often say: "We believe they can afford to give us 20%," or sometimes they go as far as to say, even 50%, and that they (the employees) have no way of examining the books and ascertaining just what they are entitled to under this system. The President thought it might be feasible to make the workmen partners of the business to the extent of having half of the directors from the working-class, because then they could see what is going on; they would be present at the meetings and could examine the books and have their own representatives present at all times, and in that way be convinced as to the actual conditions.

The President today said: "In 1902 I was having lunch at the Everett Hotel, New York, a quiet little hotel that I used to frequent when in New York. While there at lunch Mr. Gilder,[1] editor of the Century Magazine, came over to my table and said: 'I see that some one in the Indianapolis News has nominated you for President.'[2] I said: 'President of what?' He replied: 'Why, President of the United States.' To which I exclaimed: 'That is rather a large order.' Mr. Gilder added: 'And he isn't a fool either,' I said: 'I like that.' And he then began not to take me seriously but to apologize, saying that: 'I meant to show you what a big calibered man he is and a man of good sense and great vision.' I jokingly changed the subject. I had been recently elected President of Princeton University."

[1] That is, Richard Watson Gilder.
[2] See An Old-Fashioned Democrat to the Editor of the *Indianapolis News* printed at May 1, 1902, Vol. 12.

To Edward Mandell House

[*U.S.S. George Washington*] 10 March, 1919.

Your cable March eighth [seventh], eleven A.M. just deciphered. Am made a little uneasy by what you say of the left bank of the Rhine. I hope that you will not even provisionally consent to the separation of the Rhenish provinces from Germany under any arrangement but will reserve the whole matter until my arrival.

Woodrow Wilson

CC radiogram (WP, DLC).

From Howard Sweetser Bliss

My dear Mr President: Paris March 10th 1919

I am leaving for America today and am most sorry not to see you again. For I am alarmed at the way in which the old order of the world is reasserting itself consciously and unconsciously.

The rights of Syria and similar countries are in danger.

The Peace Conference needs your wise, courageous, insistent leadership, if the declarations quoted in the enclosed sheet[1] are not to become mere "scraps of paper."

If the Conference fails to live up to these plain and fundamental declarations we shall face a calamity of the first order. Forces are busily at work seeking to evade or emasculate them. Our own American Commission, sent out to investigate has apparently done nothing if it has not actually broken down and ceased to exist. If an Interallied Commission is impracticable, our own Commission ought to be rehabilitated.

No self respecting man could face the people of Syria without shame, if a Government is imposed upon them before they have been consulted.

Syria is a little country but a big principle is involved in the settlement of its political future.

Yours very respectfully   Howard S. Bliss.

ALS (WP, DLC).

[1] DOCUMENTS UPON WHICH IS BASED THE RIGHT OF THE PEOPLE OF SYRIA TO BE CONSULTED AS TO THEIR POLITICAL FUTURE BEFORE ANY GOVERNMENT IS IMPOSED UPON THEM BY THE PEACE CONFERENCE, printed copy (WP, DLC). It quoted the following: the Anglo-French declaration of November 1918 (for which, see Lord Robert Cecil to C. A. de Rune Barclay, Oct. 31, 1918, n. 2, Vol. 51, and the minutes of the Council of Ten printed at Feb. 13, 1919, 3 p.m.); the twelfth point of Wilson's Fourteen Points Address of January 8, 1918; the second principle stated in Wilson's Address at Mount Vernon on July 4, 1918; and part of Article XIX of the Covenant of the League of Nations as presented to the peace conference on February 14, 1919.

From the Diary of Dr. Grayson

Tuesday, March 11, 1919.

The President's temperature is normal today, and when I asked him how he felt he replied: "Better, much better. I think that you made an error in my diagnosis. It is true I had a headache, neuralgia, sore-throat, tooth-ache, fever and a chill, and my equatorial zone has been on a strike, and you can diagnose it just what you please. I usually have admiration and respect for your opinion and diagnosis, but this time I have decided you are wrong. My trouble is this, and I have worked it out myself: I am suffering from a retention of gases generated by the Republican Senators—and that's enough to poison any man."

In looking at some pictures today, and commenting on the wonderful development made in photography, he expressed the wish that a good picture had been taken of his mother.

During the day he also made the following remark: "I have been advocating education most of my life. While it seems to broaden the horizon at times, with some people it narrows their sympathies."

The President worked at his desk for a part of the day, took a walk in the afternoon, and went to the movies at night. He witnessed a "fearful and wonderful" performance labeled "The Spirit of Lafayette," which was designed originally to show the influence of the French in America and that America's participation in the war was a payment for French aid in Revolutionary times. The pictures were most elaborate but decidedly badly chosen.

The following despatch appeared in the HATCHET:

"PARIS, March 9—the Sein Fein representatives here today openly made threats that unless their claims for the establishment of an Irish Republic are agreed to by the Peace Conference they will utilize Irish votes in the United States to kill the League of Nations plan there. Their threats are unanswered by the American delegates."

The President in commenting on this article said that if an attempt should be made to defeat the League of Nations plan by the Irish-American vote, he would go to the mat with them and show them where they got off in America; that the American people would not stand for an alignment with Mr. Lodge. While he would hate to see this issue brought up in America, if the Irish would resort to this method, he would gladly accept the challenge. He said he told Lloyd-George sometime ago that he thought he had the solution of the Irish question, whereupon Lloyd-George exclaimed: "My God, I hope you have." The President's proposition was to give them Home Rule and to reserve the moving picture rights. But seriously speaking, he said, it was an internal matter which should be decided not by the United States but by themselves. Lloyd-George told him that it was a matter that had given him untold sorrow and grave concern. The President said: "My advice would be, if I had anything to do with it, to give them an independent state and let them fight it out among themselves; and I venture to say it would only be a short time before they would all be on their knees asking for help. The Irish are a jealous race and difficult to satisfy." Tumulty has done his level best to play fair with all parties, the President said, and he deserves to run for any office but the Irish and the Catholics would defeat him, because he has strived to serve everybody honorably.

The President remarked that the English people—and when I say English I mean the inhabitants of Great Britain and not Americans—made it a practice to maintain friendship more than any other peoples. For instance, they constantly remember your birthdays by sending letters and notes of congratulation, and, at stated intervals, they keep up a correspondence with their relatives and friends. We as Americans so often neglect these little attentions. In America, after a man is married, he often forgets the birthday of the various members of the family or of some old and one-time intimate friend.

A Memorandum[1]

Rhine Question

[March 11, 1919]

Discussion

The discussion of the draft dealt with the familiar general considerations, and three points, viz. (1) occupation by an inter-allied force of bridgeheads East of the Rhine, (2) the occupation by an inter-allied force of the Rhine Provinces, and (3) the political independence of these provinces and the fixing of the German western frontier at the Rhine. In the course of the discussion (2) and (3) merged when Tardieu pointed out that the Provinces could not be allowed to have an army, and an international force was the necessary alternative.

SITUATION WHEN THE DISCUSSION TERMINATED

Tardieu, after seeing the Premier, yielded the bridgeheads proposal, accepting, as a substitute, rigid military inspection in Germany.

Kerr[2] was holding out *against* political independence and interallied occupation of the Rhine Provinces if intended as any more

Tardieu's Draft

WESTERN FRONTIER OF GERMANY

I. In the general interest of peace and in order to assure the effective operation of the clauses constituting the League of Nations, the western frontier of Germany is fixed at the Rhine. Consequently Germany renounces all sovereignty over, as well as customs union with the territories of the former German Empire situated on the left bank of the Rhine.

II. The line of the Rhine shall be occupied by virtue of a mandate from the League of Nations by an Inter-Allied force.

The limits and the conditions of occupation in German territory of the bridgeheads of Kehl, Mannheim, Mainz, Coblenz, Cologne and Düsseldorf, necessary for the security of the Allied forces, shall be determined by the definitive treaty of peace. Pending the signature of the aforesaid treaty, the conditions fixed in this respect by the Armistice of November 11, 1918, shall remain in force.

than a very short-lived measure winding up the war.

Tardieu was holding out for *both*, mentioning first a 15 to 20-year term, later a ten-year term, and at the end alluding to, but not accepting (*he* would), a five-year term.

Kerr's main points were (1) with Germany reduced to 100,000 men, etc., France will be safe. (2) Separating the Provinces from Germany and *keeping them separate* for any time, and the maintenance of an alien force in them, will result in irritating incidents that will inflame public opinion, in some quarters, and lead to agitation weakening to the entente, France's chief safeguard. (3) British public opinion will not tolerate, for any length of time, a British contingent in the Rhine Provinces, and the Dominions will not hear of it.

Tardieu's chief points were (1) the League, pledging the help of Great Britain and America, will protect France and Belgium from ultimate defeat, but not from sudden invasion and a war on their territory (only holding the Rhine barrier will do the latter); (2) French public opinion demands the protection of the Rhine barrier, and the French government cannot recede. (3) The unavoidable alternative, on which France

Within a zone of 50 kilometers to the east of her western frontier, Germany shall not have the right of maintaining or establishing any fortification.

III. The territories of the left bank of the Rhine (excepting Alsace-Lorraine) shall be constituted in the form of one or several independent states, under the protection of the League of Nations. Their western and southern frontiers shall be fixed by the Treaty of Peace. Germany undertakes to do nothing which might impede the aforesaid State or States in the accomplishment of the duties and the exercise of the rights devolving upon it or them in consequence of the causes and conditions of their creation.

IV. Within a period of one month from the date of the signature of the present Preliminaries of Peace, the general conditions for the evacuation of the superior German and Prussian administrative authorities, at present holding office on the left bank of the Rhine, shall be fixed by a special agreement between the Signatory Powers and the German Government.

V. Within a period of two

must insist, is worse, i.e., demanding a strategic frontier for herself, taking in some million and a third of Germans, and similar annexations for Belgium.

Just before the close of the conversation Tardieu suggested, as a possible alternative to an inter-allied force, a Franco-Belgian force under mandate for the League. Not discussed.

months from the date of the signature of the present Preliminaries of Peace, a special agreement between the Signatory Powers and the German Government shall determine, under the guarantee of the League of Nations, the general conditions of the liquidation of German economic interests on the left bank of the Rhine.

VI. The German Government undertakes to assure annually to the independent States or State, which may be created on the left bank of the Rhine, the quantity of coal necessary for their industries. This quantity shall be placed to the credit of Germany in the general account of reparations.

T MS (WP, DLC).

¹ The following memorandum was probably prepared by Sidney Edward Mezes. Either he or House must have handed it to Wilson soon after his return to Paris.

Harold I. Nelson, *Land and Power: British and Allied Policy on Germany's Frontiers, 1916-19* (London and Toronto, 1963), 198-218, is a detailed account of the background and dénouement of this document. Even before the opening of the peace conference, various high French leaders had been pressing for the dismemberment of Germany in the West by the creation of a republic on the left bank of the Rhine under French control. Colonel House had initially opposed this project very strongly, as had Lloyd George and other British leaders. At Clemenceau's direction, André Tardieu brought this question to a head on February 26 by distributing a memorandum "of the French Government." It demanded permanent inter-Allied occupation of the Rhine bridgeheads and the establishment of a "free Rhine State" to "act as a barrier and buffer between Germany and the Western Democracies." Tardieu reprints this memorandum in his *The Truth about the Treaty* (London, 1921), pp. 147-70. As Nelson, p. 207, points out, Tardieu's memorandum "appears as a possible tactical manoeuvre prompted by considerations of domestic political expediency and based on the immemorial customs of bargainers."

In his telegram to Wilson of February 26, 1919, House mentioned Tardieu's memorandum and promised to inform Wilson about it as soon as he had had an opportunity to study it. This House absolutely failed to do. Instead, as the extract from the diary of Vance C. McCormick, printed at March 2, 1919, reveals, House and Tardieu agreed on the plan for a Rhenish republic on that day; even more, they discussed ways and means of winning British approval for this project. As a result, on March 10, Lloyd George, Clemenceau, and House established a secret committee, composed of Philip Kerr, Lloyd George's private secretary, Tardieu, and Mezes, to determine the western boundaries of Germany. Tardieu submitted the plan embodied in the memorandum printed below to the secret committee on March 11. As the text printed under the rubric of "*Discussion*" reveals, only Kerr opposed Tardieu's plan. Mezes, in contrast, assured Tardieu of American concern for French security and hinted that the American government would not oppose the establishment of a buffer state under certain conditions. Nelson, p. 213. Clearly, Mezes was speaking for House. We might add that our account differs somewhat from Nelson's, because he missed the above-mentioned entry in the McCormick Diary.

Tardieu, Kerr, and Mezes met again on March 12. Much to Tardieu's surprise, Mezes asked that the decision on Germany's western frontier be postponed until Wilson's arrival in Paris. Mezes was undoubtedly acting at House's direction, and House was obviously responding to the peremptory instructions conveyed in Wilson's radiogram to him of March 10.

As House's telegrams to Wilson have shown, House had not yet informed Wilson of his independent negotiations relating to the question of a Rhenish republic. In addition, House, in the diary that he kept between February 25 and March 12, mentioned the project for a Rhenish republic only twice. On March 10 he recorded the appointment of the secret committee. On March 12 he related that Lloyd George was still strongly opposed to the plan for a Rhenish republic.

From Asbury Francis Lever

[Washington] 3/11/19.

For the President. Earnestly request suspension of judgment matter of Galloway Civil Service Commission. Your ardent friend victim of circumstances. Friend of Senator Smith and me. Before final action all angles should be known. Can not afford fundamental injustice   A. F. Lever

T radiogram (WP, DLC).

From William Bauchop Wilson

[Washington] 3/11/19

Referring to my radiogram fifth, unless can obtain allotment from your fund will have to dismiss about three thousand of employment service employees by March 15th and retain during the rest of fiscal year a skeleton organization to hold together the 2000 voluntary bureaus for returning soldiers, and direct activities of voluntary welfare organizations. Otherwise must discontinue entire organization April 1st. Service now placing 90,000 workers each week. Situation acute. Important to know your decision in order that proper notice may be given to employees affected   W. B. Wilson

T radiogram (WP, DLC).

George Carroll Todd to Thomas Watt Gregory

Washington, D. C. March 11, 1919.

While we have found no cases directly on the point, the Solicitor General[1] and myself are of opinion on principle and on analogous cases that the question of the United States becoming a party to the League of Nations is a subject falling within the treaty-making power as distinguished from the legislative power, and that therefore the United States could not be made a party by concurrent resolution of the two Houses of Congress.

G. Carroll Todd

TS radiogram (WP, DLC).
[1] Alexander Campbell King.

From the Diary of Dr. Grayson

Wednesday, March 12, 1919.

The President worked all morning on correspondence. At luncheon he had as his guests Mr. John E. Nevin of the International News Service; Mr. Charles H. Grasty of the New York Times; Mr. Carl D. Groat[1] of the United Press; Mr. L. F. Curtis of the Associated Press; and Ray Stannard Baker, well-known author under the name of David Grayson.

After luncheon the President talked at some length about golf, Grasty asking him whether he had ever played over any of the noted Scottish links. The President said: "No," and he added that he would be rather loathe to do so in view of the fact that the gray-bearded old caddies there know more about the game than any American professional. Illustrating the Scottish character he told a story of two elderly Scotchmen, who were playing around the St. Andrews links. They said nothing whatever until they reached the sixteenth hole, when one turned to the other and said: "I have you dormied." The other looked at him in disgust for a second, and then ejaculated: "Chatterbox."

Another story of the President's had to do with a graduate of Princeton who went over there to play and started around the course accompanied by an ancient caddie, who watched his game reflectively. Becoming somewhat embarrassed over the critical scrutiny, and realizing that he was not playing according to accepted Scottish standards, the Princetonian turned to the caddie and said: "I suppose you have seen worse players." The caddie made no reply, and the player assuming that he had not heard, and having made another very bad stroke, repeated his question. The Scotchman looked him squarely in the eye, and said to him: "Weel, mon, I heard ye the first time; I was just thinking."

From golf the conversation drifted to the international problems, and the President said he was sorry to see in the wireless despatches a report that the conference would decide to end the German frontier at the Rhine, making the left bank of the Rhine either a buffer

[1] Carl Diedrich Groat, the Berlin correspondent of the United Press.

state or giving France a mandatory control over it.[2] He declared that this could not be. When Germany took over Lorraine in 1870, he said, there was a substantial German population there, and the German Government had hoped that it would become really German in the course of years. This had not happened, the desire for a return to France having dominated the majority of the people. In the Rhine Basin, so-called, the President said, there were absolutely no French. The desires of the people were German in character. Taking this territory away from Germany would simply give a cause for hatred and a determination for a renewal of the war throughout Germany that would always be equal to the bitterness felt by France against Germany over the "lost provinces."

The President was none too well pleased with the statement in the wireless despatches that it was likely that Arthur James Balfour would retire and be succeeded by Earl Curzon as British Foreign Minister. The President felt it would be a mistake to lose Mr. Balfour at this time. Curzon, the President said, had never had a single *Liberal* thought in his life. Mrs. Wilson suggested that possibly his going to America for his two wives[3] might be construed as liberalism, but the President intimated that money rather than sentiment might have been the compelling nature there—the first wife having been a Miss Leiter, of the Chicago Leiter millionaire family.

There was a discussion of Lloyd-George at the table, Grasty and Baker holding that he was only an opportunist, and that he was a trimmer in that he lived from day to day, caring nothing for yesterday and less for tomorrow. Nevin took exception to this, holding that it was hardly fair; that Lloyd-George was the big outstanding figure in all British politics, and that it was almost certain that there was no man who could take his place. As a matter of fact, he (Nevin) asked the President whether he believed there was any man in England today who was as strong as Lloyd-George. The President said he did not believe so, at least there was none in sight. Nevin then asked the President if he did not believe that if anything happened to Lloyd-George a revolution in England would be certain. The President said that it would be hard to prevent it, in view of the fact that the men now in control of British affairs were Tories entirely, and that there was no liberalism in the government. Lloyd-George, he said, was the Premier of a British Tory Government.

The President said that the Irish problem was quite a very difficult

---

[2] There were numerous reports from Paris on March 12 to the effect that the peace treaty would provide for the creation of a buffer state on the west bank of the Rhine. See, e.g., the *New York Times*, March 14 (with Berlin dateline of March 12), 1919; the New York *Sun*, March 13 (with Paris dateline of March 12), 1919; and the New York *Evening Post*, March 13 (with Berlin dateline of March 12), 1919.

[3] That is, Mary Victoria Leiter and Grace Elvina Hinds (Mrs. Alfred) Duggan.

one for England to solve, and he said that if Sir Robert [Edward] Carson had been hanged for treason at the time he tried to force the division between the north and the south of Ireland, the problem would have been very materially solved.

This turned the conversation to the question of the League of Nations, and the President related how he, a Southern-born President of the United States, found himself the only man in attendance at the conference committee which framed the constitution of the League of Nations who did not believe that when a nation actually participated in this League she reserved in toto the right to withdraw from the League at any time. Although this was the doctrine of the Southern States prior to the war between the states, the President said he hardly thought it a good one in the present circumstances, as the precedent has been established in the case of the United States. He said that he had labored with the other committeemen to define this carefully but had found they were all convinced the right of secession would always exist, and he passed up the matter temporarily at least.

In the afternoon the President took a long walk about the decks with Mrs. Wilson, and later on he and I played shuffle-board on the upper deck. Although it may have bordered on lese majeste I managed to defeat him in the game we played.

Later in the day the President spoke of Rudolph Forster's life as being a part of the Executive Office; that he had given at least twenty-five years of the best of his life and ability to the welfare and efficiency of the Executive Office; and that he was thoroughly conscientious, painstaking and always dependable; in fact, the Executive Office would not run without him.

While speaking of an office as being part of one's life, he said that Abraham Lincoln spent much of his life in his office instead of his home. This was partly on account of his wife. She was a Miss Todd and had the airs of an aristocrat. Mr. Lincoln did things that were not very tidy so far as his personal appearance was concerned. He would come into the house, pull off his coat, suspenders showing, remove his shoes, and go about the house in this fashion. This irritated Mrs. Lincoln and she would "nag" at him, which seemed to hurt him. It is believed that if she had approached him in a sweeter manner she could have persuaded him to change his habits as she wished. He would often steal Tad and take him to his office-rooms, where he would talk with him and enjoy his companionship. There were certain chambers deep down in Lincoln, the President said, that no one seemed to be able to penetrate. These chambers were not communicable, even to those who knew him best. As every one knows, Lincoln was intensely human. On the contrary,

General Washington was warm inside but externally he gave the impression of being austere. For example, when he came into the presence of little children, they would invariably stop playing in fear of him—which seemed to hurt him because he loved children, loved to see them play and to play with them. He would often peep through the crack of a door and watch them play.

In speaking of men of the present day, the President said that David F. Houston (Secretary of Agriculture), a member of the President's cabinet, internally is intensely warm, brilliant and humorous, but externally he is as cold as polished marble. If he could only show externally his internal qualities, he would be one of the greatest forces in the world. When he lectures or talks in a convention of men, he speaks under the greatest stress, with an apparent impediment, and only touches his subject in a superficial way, without giving color or life to it. In private conversation he sparkles with life, is logical, has fine, common sense, is a master of details and always has a thorough knowledge of the subject under discussion, has fine vision, and an excellent sense of humor. Deep down internally he is a great man.

While aboard the GEORGE WASHINGTON the President, by way of diversion, amused himself by working out a formula as to the most available place in which to live after his terms of President expires. Five factors were involved: Freedom, friendship, literary study, variety and amusement. He named the following places, working out a percentage at the same time: New York, Washington, Boston, Baltimore, Richmond, Virginia, and the Bermudas. For instance, for literary study he would give Baltimore, say, 60%; New York he would give variety 100%; freedom in Washington 15%. The average put Baltimore first, Boston 2d, New York 3rd.

To Alexander Mitchell Palmer

U.S.S. George Washington,
My dear Mr. Attorney General: 12 March, 1919.

One cannot but have a great deal of sympathy and a great softening of heart towards persons like the petitioners in the enclosed papers,[1] and I am sending these papers to you for the purpose of requesting that you will be kind enough to have the papers carefully gone over and the matter examined sufficiently to ascertain whether they have in fact been treated justly and upon the same terms as others or not.

The terms of imprisonment are clearly excessive, but I assume that these are sentences which are being reconsidered along with all the others by the Department, with a view to scaling down to reasonable terms by commutation.

Cordially and faithfully yours,   Woodrow Wilson

TLS (A. M. Palmer Papers, DLC).
¹ "Enclosing petition from members of International Bible Society who were sentenced to 20 years in Atlanta penitentiary for violation of the Espionage Law." T note on CC of this letter in WP, DLC. It was, in fact, a petition from leaders of the International Bible Students' Association and the Watch Tower Bible and Tract Society (popularly known as Jehovah's Witnesses). They had been arrested at their headquarters in Brooklyn, New York, on May 8, 1918, and had been indicted in the Federal District Court in Brooklyn on four counts of promoting and conspiring to promote insubordination and disloyalty in the armed forces of the United States and of obstructing the draft by issuing antiwar statements in their various publications. They had been sentenced, on June 21, 1918, to four concurrent terms of twenty years in the federal penitentiary in Atlanta, and their two applications for bail pending the appeal of their conviction had been denied. Among those sentenced was Joseph Franklin Rutherford, a lawyer and former circuit judge from Missouri, and the head of the International Bible Students' Association. See the *New York Times*, May 9, June 7, 18, 21, and 22, and July 2, 1918.

To David Franklin Houston

My dear Houston: U.S.S. George Washington, 12 March, 1919.

I had to bring your letter of March third away with me, because I did not have time to answer it before leaving.

When I got into closer conference with the Treasury Department and the War Trade Board about the pork exportation business, I became convinced that it was very questionable whether the War Trade Board had the legal right to continue its restrictions, and inasmuch as it had already announced that the restrictions would be withdrawn on and after the first of March and the first of March had already passed, I saw no course open to me but to notify the War Trade Board that I would not suggest any modification of what they had done.

I have been very much puzzled by the apparent variety of counsel that obtained in the Food Administration itself about the matter. But after all, that is not the point in my mind at present, but only this: that further restriction would probably be illegal.

In haste, with the warmest regard,

Faithfully yours,   [Woodrow Wilson]

CCL (WP, DLC).

To Morris Jastrow, Jr.

My dear Professor Jastrow:

U.S.S. George Washington,
12 March, 1919.

Thank you for your letter of March fourth. You may be sure that the views of the highly responsible persons for whom you and Mr. Kahn speak will certainly receive most respectful consideration. I have time, as you will understand, just at this moment for only a line of acknowledgment, but it is one of very cordial and appreciative acknowledgment.

Cordially and sincerely yours,   [Woodrow Wilson]

CCL (WP, DLC).

To Clinton Tyler Brainard

My dear Mr. Brainard:

U.S.S. George Washington,
12 March, 1919.

I am sorry not to have been able to return those papers before I left our side of the water.

I am equally sorry not to be able to fall in with the plans you outline in your letter of March 5th.[1] The fact is that I do not feel that I would be justified in letting someone else undertake a condensation of my History or a reversioning of it, and inasmuch as it would be literally impossible for me to read and revise anything that anybody else should attempt in that line, I feel that I have no choice but to say that it is not practicable at the present time. May I not say how much I appreciate your thought of my interest in this matter and how much I regret my inability to cooperate at present. I know you will understand.

Cordially and sincerely yours,   [Woodrow Wilson]

CCL (WP, DLC).
[1] C. T. Brainard to WW, March 5, 1919, ALS (WP, DLC). About this matter, see WW to JPT, March 1, 1919 (second letter of that date), n. 1.

To Anita Eugénie McCormick Blaine

My dear Mrs. Blaine:

U.S.S. George Washington,
12 March, 1919.

Your letter[1] has given me just the information I wanted about your son who is gone. His death seems to me to have been as direct and honorable a sacrifice for the country as if he had died on the battle field, and I hope with all my heart that this thought is in your mind also and will serve as a sufficing comfort. His spirit was admirable, and I feel honored that he should have accepted my counsel as a guide. All that your letter tells me increases my sense of admiration and also makes me the more conscious of what you have lost.

Thank you for letting me see your paper read before the League to enforce Peace.[2] Apparently the only thing we can do now is to press, press, press the moral obligations and indeed the imperative necessity to accept such an arrangement as has been worked out at Paris for a League of Nations.

In unavoidable haste, with the most cordial regard,

Sincerely yours, Woodrow Wilson

TLS (Anita M. Blaine Papers, WHi).
[1] Anita E. M. Blaine to WW, March 4, 1919.
[2] It is missing.

From James Levi Barton and Others

Washington March 12th [1919]

1076. Following two telegrams from Constantinople transmitted by Admiral Bristol.[1] One. "Following for the President. March 1, 5 PM. Reports coming to the American Committee Relief Near East from civilians, as well as our own investigations here on the ground, are proof Turkey is politically, financially, morally bankrupt, and that on account of the problematical future of the country there is imminent danger social disorder and anarchy. Situation is likely to create international complications which would be most unfortunate just at the close of the war. May we express opinion only adequate way to forestall such dangers is speedy appointment of strong mandatory power with full authority to establish a stable government, and to lay foundation for prosperity and independence. Continuation of this cablegram will be sent at once." End of first section.

"Continuation of March 5th, 4:00 p.m.

For the President.

The regions involved are rich in unutilized natural resources and in manpower and need only wise direction in order to provide the means of financing a complete program of reconstruction and rehabilitation.

Believe that with independence definitely assured to each nationality as it becomes qualified to exercise self government control by a disinterested mandatory will be welcomed by an overwhelming majority of the people concerned.

For a century American capital has poured into Turkey in a constant stream founding colleges and establishing institutions of mercy to which thousands of American men and women have devoted their lives during the past three years. American men and women have stood by these investments regardless of the risk involved.

Until a just government is established it will be impossible to secure the results of this American generosity and heroism.
Signed James L. Barton, William W. Peet, Edward E. Moore, John H. T. Main, Harold A. Hatch."[2]   Polk,   Acting.

T telegrams (WP, DLC).
  [1] Rear Adm. Mark Lambert Bristol, commander of the United States naval forces in Turkey.
  [2] Persons not heretofore identified in this series were Edward Caldwell Moore, Parkman Professor of Theology and Plummer Professor of Christian Morals at Harvard University and Preacher to the University; John Hanson Thomas Main, President of Grinnell College; and Harold Ames Hatch, a member of Deering, Milliken & Co., commission merchants of New York. The senders of this telegram were all members of the American Committee for Relief in the Near East.

From the Diary of Dr. Grayson

Thursday, March 13, 1919.

The President slept late today, realizing that he would be kept up late tonight, inasmuch as the steamer was not scheduled to reach Brest until sometime after seven o'clock. He had received wireless messages giving the program and every matter needing attention had been thoroughly cleaned up long before the French shores were sighted.

The President after lunch said to me: "Before I came to Washington I was an advocate and strong admirer of General Leonard Wood. Soon after my election to the Presidency several Congressmen called at Trenton to see me and to warn me against the intrigues of General Wood. After I was sworn into office I sent for General Hugh Scott, who was an old acquaintance and upon whom I felt I could rely. I asked him to give me his candid and personal opinion about General Wood. He told me that he thought he was the ablest officer in the Army, which I was glad to hear, especially because it substantiated my impressions of General Wood. I kept him for two years as Chief of Staff with an eye on trying him out. Much to my disappointment I found that he did not ring true. I always found him exceedingly able, but I first began to doubt his loyalty when he began to criticise severely Colonel Theodore Roosevelt to me. It had all the appearances of criticising him in order to gain favor with me. I still think that he is perhaps the most able of any man in the Army, but, unfortunately, he is full of intrigue and disloyal to his superiors. I think the suggestion which you made accounts for this change in his character, which was due to the operation performed on his skull for a depression of bone and a diseased area of bone adjoining the brain.[1] This trouble was so near headquarters—the vital centers of the brain—that I can see how it would produce a change in character. I recommended to the Secretary of War that he be given an opportunity for active service abroad, and the matter was put up to General Pershing. General Pershing, however, strongly objected to having him, placing his objection on the ground that he would be disloyal and might try to undermine him and interfere with proper cooperation in the Army. You have always been a strong advocate and a great admirer of General Wood and I have had the same opinion and would have insisted on his assignment abroad but for the recommendations of General Pershing. After putting General Pershing in command, I felt that we ought to back him up in his selections."

As the GEORGE WASHINGTON anchored off the sea-wall, the American transfer boat used by the port authorities hove in sight to starboard. The President was on Deck B with Mrs. Wilson and myself when the boat appeared. He went to his office on the port side to receive the committee of welcome. There were about 35 in the reception committee, which was headed by M. Pichon, and included Ambassador and Madame Jusserand, the Army and Navy Commanding Officers at Brest, with their staffs. A large bouquet of flowers was presented to Mrs. Wilson, and they were welcomed back to France by the French official representatives. While the transfer boat was lying alongside a little French launch with two men aboard caught fire and there was a little excitement for a moment until a destroyer lying astern came over, put the fire out and rescued the imperiled men.

Little time was lost in landing. By direction of the authorities the proposed program of a parade in automobiles through Brest was abandoned. The President entered the transfer boat and went directly ashore with his party, being landed at Pier 5, where a guard of honor of American doughboys had been lined up to receive him. The special train—the same which was used on our initial arrival— had been run down directly to a point in the rear of the landing dock, and after a few words of felicitation and welcome, the President proceeded to it, first, however, passing through the big Y.M.C.A. canteen here and inspecting it.

Colonel House had come down to Brest to see the President but

[1] See C. W. Eliot to WW, March 27, 1917, n. 3, Vol. 41.

waited for him on the pier. The train was scheduled to start for Paris at 11:00 o'clock, but the schedule was advanced more than half an hour, and the start made as soon as the baggage of the party had been put on board.

Leaving Brest the President and Colonel House went into conference and Colonel House told the President of the various developments, including the apparent desire on the part of the French authorities to have the League of Nations covenant side-tracked and a preliminary peace treaty signed which would include the complete disarmament of Germany, the creation of a Rhinish Republic, and would in effect do what the President had declared on a number of occasions he would not countenance—absolutely denude Germany of everything she had and allow Bolshevism to spread throughout that country.[2]

The run out of Brest was made through double lines of American troops, every precaution having been taken to safeguard the party.

[2] House's report of this conference (see the entry from his diary for March 14, 1919, printed below) is inconsequential. The only account that sheds any direct light on the nature of the meeting is Mrs. Wilson's. As she wrote in her *My Memoir*, nearly twenty years after the event, she was "shocked" by the change in her husband's appearance when she saw him immediately after his conference with House. She continued: "He seemed to have aged ten years, and his jaw was set in that way it had when he was making superhuman effort to control himself. . . . He smiled bitterly. 'House has given away everything I had won before we left Paris. He has compromised on every side, and so I have to start all over again and this time it will be harder, as he has given the impression that my delegates are not in sympathy with me.'" Edith Bolling Wilson, *My Memoir* (Indianapolis and New York, 1938), pp. 245-46.

Although Mrs. Wilson's reminiscences are not always reliable, and her account of this meeting is inaccurate in some peripheral details, she seems to have been largely correct in her report of Wilson's consternation. For example, Ray Stannard Baker has stated in *Woodrow Wilson and World Settlement* (3 vols., Garden City, N. Y., 1922-23), I, 306-10, which he wrote in close consultation with Wilson, that, from the moment Wilson conferred with House on the train from Brest to Paris, a "coldness" began to develop between the two men which was not due to "trivial personal causes or little, mean jealousies, as popularly reported," but was based upon "far deeper failures in understanding and action." To Baker, House's main "failure" was the Colonel's compliance, out of weakness rather than conviction, with what Baker saw as a veritable plot by the Allied leaders to kill the League of Nations or, at the very least, to separate the Covenant from the peace treaty.

Grayson, in an article written in 1926 but not published until 1964, has elaborated on the reasons for the "break" between Wilson and House: "It was upon Mr. Wilson's return to France that he found to his amazement that Colonel House had consented to a plan for a separation of the Peace Treaty from the covenant of the League of Nations. He had assented to Premier Clemenceau's wishes and suggestions about this matter. He had also agreed to the establishment of a Rhenish republic that would act as a buffer state between Germany and France, the creation of which would have been in absolute contradiction to President Wilson's Fourteen Points. So President Wilson had no sooner arrived in France than he found it necessary to repudiate practically everything that had been done during his absence. . . . From that time on, the relationship between the President and the Colonel ceased to be close and confidential." Cary T. Grayson, "The Colonel's Folly and the President's Distress," *American Heritage*, XV (Oct. 1964), 4-7, 94-101. As Inga Floto has recently shown beyond reasonable doubt, it was during the conference on the train after leaving Brest that House gave Wilson a first brief account of the situation with regard to the League and the Rhineland program. Dr. Floto concludes: "It is thus to the brief talk in the train that we must assign the 'break.' After this discussion, the personal trust between the two men was broken and the friendship damaged beyond repair." Inga Floto, *Colonel House in Paris: A Study of American Policy at the Paris Peace Conference 1919* (Princeton, N. J., 1980), pp. 164-70.

After the President had retired I talked over the developments since we had left Paris with some of the newspapermen and others who had come down on the train.

While en route from Brest to Paris the President told me that the French Ambassador had said to him that every one was in favor of the League of Nations, but, of course, there were a number of changes that would have to be made. The President said: "Hold on, Mr. Ambassador. I was at the meeting of this League of Nations, and every man there gave his opinion. They swapped their opinions, matched their minds against each other, and it was largely a game of give and take. There were a great many things that I wanted to put in there that I had to leave out. For instance, the Japanese wanted free immigration, and this was something to which others could not agree. This is the result of an agreement of all parties and it is the best agreement we could arrive at in the circumstances. It did not go as far as I would like—the Covenant I drafted contained a number of things which were cut out—but I would rather accept this than nothing. If we had not accepted what we have here we would not have a League of Nations."

From the Diary of Ray Stannard Baker

At Sea, March 13 [1919].

I lunched with the President & Mrs. Wilson yesterday in their private cabin. Most interesting talk. In these informal relationships the President & Mrs. Wilson are altogether charming, friendly, simple people. The President is full of stories, not of the indigenous, homely sort that Lincoln told, but remembered anecdotes, limericks, puns of various sorts. He applies them with amazing aptness. Yesterday, he told a number of Scotch golfing stories, pleasantly imitating the Scotch burr, as he can also imitate the Negro dialect whenever he tells a Negro story. We talked of the prohibition amendment which he signed on the train the other day (with Miss Benham's fountain pen) on the way to Washington. He said with a humorous turn that the new law could cause some personal deprivation, but that, once the country became adjusted to it, that it would be of inestimable value. He believed that the masses of the people were behind it upon conviction.

He has a profound distrust of the French press: said to us that he had positive evidence of the control of many of the papers by the French government, this in the form of an order (written instructions, of which he had a copy) issued through the Maison de la Presse (given to him personally by a French editor whose name, of course, could not be disclosed) in which the papers were advised regarding three items of policy

1. To emphasize the opposition to him (Mr. Wilson) in America by giving all the news possible of Republican & other opposition

2. To emphasize the disorder & anarchy in Russia, thereby, to provoke allied intervention

3. To publish articles showing the ability of Germany to pay a large indemnity.

He thought this system abominable—an evil attempt to influence the deliberations of the Peace Conference. If worse came to worse he could publish this evidence, or suggest the removal of the Conference to Geneva.

Grasty told of the venality of many French newspapers, & how they were subsidised by various interests—especially in older times by Russia—when the Russians desired to float another loan in Paris.

The President is looking forward to strenuous days in Paris & a rather prompt conclusion of the Peace Conference.

Now that it is concluding I wish I could set down, not so much the facts, but an adequate *impression* of this voyage. It has been very quiet & simple: a small group and friendly. Coming out of strenuous days, controversies & great meetings, the President has rested. He looked worn & gray when he came aboard: I have never seen him looking wearier than at the Metropolitan speech, but he soon recuperated, under Dr. Grayson's care, so that now he looks as well as ever. He shows in these quiet & friendly relationships at his best—in a light in which I wish many Americans, who think him a cold, unamiable man, could see him. He and Mrs. Wilson were frequently on deck, once they played deck shuffle-board, & they came in quite regularly to the moving-picture shows and seemed to enjoy them greatly. Or they listened to the excellent music of the ship's orchestra. Sometimes after meals or even after the evening entertainment two or three of us would find the President & Mrs. Wilson at the bottom of the stairs near their cabin & have a good talk—very lively of the problems, but talk once, for example, of Lafayette, again of the French people & their peculiarities, again of golf & golfing—with many stories & much laughter. Mrs. W. is not one of the pleasantest of women, but possesses great good sense, and it is plain enough that the President leans heavily upon her. On two or three days the President had various members of the party in to luncheon & dinner, starting very simply with a quiet grace, said in low tones, and the meal itself passing off with the friendly give & take of every American family meal. After one of these luncheons I heard a member of the party say: "Well, I never knew that the President was that kind of a man at all—so human & so simple."

The President & Mrs. Wilson have quite won the hearts of the officers & crew of the ship. They have been passengers now for three voyages—27 days aboard. "It is getting to be a kind of house-boat," said Mrs. Wilson. It is almost like a big family! At the closing entertainment on Wednesday night, just as we were about to break up a group of seamen in the back of the hall began to sing, "God be with you till we meet again," continuing through all the verses. Then the whole company, including the President, sang together "Auld Lang Syne." I wondered among what other people in this world, there could develop just such relationships in such a spirit!

I presented a couple of volumes of David Grayson's books to Admiral Grayson with apologies for the appropriation of his name. He read several of the stories aloud to the President & Mrs. Wilson during the voyage.

From Porter James McCumber[1]

Confidential

My dear Mr. President: [Washington] March 13, 1919.

My earnest devotion to the cause of a League of Nations that shall assure the peace of the world prompts me to present to you some changes which I feel will be necessary to be made in the constitution of a League of Nations as now drawn, to assure its adoption by the Senate.

In my discussion of that instrument in the Senate on March 3rd, I sought to demonstrate how far fetched and strained were most of the criticisms aimed at the text of the agreement. In entering into this agreement we in no way surrender our sovereign powers. We simply exert those powers in conjunction with other sovereign nations to secure peaceful settlement of international disputes.

We in no way surrender our Monroe Doctrine unless we call the extension of that Doctrine or the merging of it into a world policy a surrender.

We in no way authorize either the Council or the high contracting parties themselves to interfere with the purely domestic policies or laws of any country.

And yet all the assaults made against this compact are based on the bald assertion that we do surrender our sovereign power, our Monroe Doctrine and our domestic affairs to this League; and then to clinch the case against us, it is argued that we will be out-voted in every instance fourteen to one.

While all these assertions can, in my judgment, be met and explained away to any audience by a mere reading and explanation of each article, still you know the vast majority of the people do not critically examine such documents; and therein lies the influence which can be exerted by the platform orator who deals in bold assertions for his facts and appeals to the gingoistic sentiment of his audience for his support.

There is no question but that the great majority of the American people wish a League of Nations to maintain world peace. But I am fearful that so many will be led astray by the earnest arguments and by the strong organization to defeat this project that its safety is greatly endangered unless these erroneous conclusions are met by some clear and definite declaration in the instrument itself.

To meet these assaults, may I suggest that there be inserted declarations to the effect,

First, "That nothing herein contained shall be construed to authorize the Council or the high contracting parties to assume any control over the purely domestic concerns of any nation."

Second, "That nothing herein contained shall be construed to deprive any country of its full, free and independent sovereign powers except to such an extent as any one of such powers is held in abeyance by the agreement of the country itself to effectuate the purposes of the said League of Nations, to substitute public inquiry, diplomacy and arbitration for war as a means of settling international disputes."

Third, "That nothing herein contained shall be construed to change or modify the policy of the United States, generally known as the Monroe Doctrine, which also guarantees the territorial or political integrity of every independent country in the western hemisphere."

There are a number of Senators who will be opposed to any League of Nations which may be proposed. There are, however, in my judgment others who have signed the declaration against this particular proposed constitution for the League of Nations who will vote for a League of Nations if it is clear that our sovereignty, our domestic affairs and our Monroe Doctrine are not jeopardized.

And while I am dealing with this subject will you permit me, Mr. President, to offer this suggestion of a humble American citizen:

I think there is a real danger in entirely disposing of the question of peace, and having the peace treaty presented as a separate treaty, independent of any provision for the League of Nations to preserve peace. My own judgment is that it would be far better to have the two propositions in one instrument. I am feafful [fearful] that, having once settled the peace treaty, a League of Nations compact would be delayed so long and so many specious objections made to it, that it would finally fail of confirmation.

Very sincerely yours,   P. J. McCumber

TLS (WP, DLC).
[1] Republican senator from North Dakota.

From Joseph Patrick Tumulty

The White House, 13 March 1919.

#8 Country greatly disturbed over stories appearing Paris and elsewhere under Associated Press head that League of Nations is not to be included in peace treaty.   Tumulty.

T telegram (WP, DLC).

From Pietro Cardinal Gasparri

Rome. March 13, 1919

CONFIDENTIAL.

The Rector of the American Catholic College[1] requested me to-day to forward to the President the following message:

"To His Excellency Woodrow Wilson,
         the President of the United States.

From reliable sources we have learned that the German people, especially women and children, are dying of hunger. The Holy Father makes warm and confident appeal to the sentiments of humanity of your Excellency and the Great American Republic, to obtain an immediate cessation of this hetacomb, the only means of stopping the spread of Bolshevickism in Europe. (Signed) Cardinal Gasparry."

He states that same appeal had been given to Count De Salis, British Minister to the Vatican.   Nelson Page.

T telegram (WP, DLC).
   [1] That is, Msgr. Charles Aloysius O'Hern.

Frank Lyon Polk to Robert Lansing and Vance Criswell McCormick

Washington, March 13, 1919.

1106. For the Secretary of State and McCormick.

Mr. Morris reports[1] that a somewhat acute situation is arising as between General Graves and the Japanesse military authorities because of radical divergence of policy. General Graves is holding absolutely aloof from internal conflicts between Russian factions. On this subject, he telegraphs as follows:

"200, March 5th. Secret. As I construed my original instructions, which are still in force, I was to take no part in differences between different Russian factions before Armistice. I permitted United States troops to be used in cooperation with Japanese along the Ussuri

Railroad against a force composed of German, Austrians and Russians. Since the Armistice there has been no menace from Germans and Austrians, but there is danger of serious trouble between different Russian factions which may develop at any time.

The feeling is now becoming so bitter that each faction claims if you are not with them you are against them. The Japanese have started campaign to put down an uprising in Amur province, as reported in my 197,[2] and my refusal to permit the use of United States troops in the trouble between Russian factions has enabled reactionary party to claim that Americans are Bolsheviks, and enabled the other parties to claim we cannot agree favorably to reactionary party because by our presence reactionary party is enabled to commit excesses on the people which these could not do if Allied troops were not present. No one doubts the truth of the latter contention. Japan and the United States are in Siberia with the same announced purposes, and following opposite courses relative to taking part in internal troubles. This has made it seem advisable to me to ask if my policy in considering the Bolshevik trouble in Siberia entirely an internal trouble, in which case I should take no part, is the policy the Department desires me to continue to follow. Graves"

In this connection I refer to the Department's instructions to Consul General Harris,[3] which have been repeated to London, Paris and Rome, to ascertain whether those governments are inclined to take the same position, and to you for your information.

You will recall that the firm stand taken by Ambassador Francis at Archangel, under somewhat similar circumstances, did much to clarify the situation there. My own opinion is that General Graves should be authorized to make quite clear to the Russian Military Authorities at Vladivostok, and in the Primorskaya and Amur provinces, that the power of this Government to assist Russia in Eastern Siberia will be paralyzed if any group in control reverts to arbitrary or reactionary methods, and furthermore that such a course will create public sentiment in America, which may have a far reaching effect. In other words, I think that General Graves, without employing his forces to assist one Russian faction as against another, should be authorized definitely to throw the weight of such influence as he may have through the presence of American forces to insist upon a policy of moderation, and at the same time should make perfectly clear that this Government can not lend itself to any measures which savor of counter revolution or reaction. Let me also point out the advantages of taking measures to prevent civil war in the rear of the Czechs, who are now in Central Siberia. I think it also necessary to emphasize again the fact that the support which General Graves is to lend Mr. Stevens, as provided by the plan,[4] will require him, not only to use his good offices to prevent armed conflicts between factions, but also to interfere by force where the question of communications or the safety of our own men are threatened. In the cities and towns along the railways the population should be protected from arbitrary acts, and encouraged in any orderly efforts to manage their local affairs.

In my opinion the situation is somewhat beyond General Graves, and I think he will be required to be told specifically how far he can go, as his inclination is to interpret his instructions very conservatively. This will no doubt require your discussing the question with the President. If you do so, please let me know directions he will issue to the Secretary of War. I feel confident the French and British will approve, but believe we may have difficulty in securing the cooperation of the Japanese. I would like to be in a position to place the situation strongly before them to secure unity of action. Have been informed through General Churchill last month, General Graves, after conferring with Mr. Stevens, asked for authority, first to move one battalion of American troops to Harbin, and subsequently two companies to Irkutsk, in compliance with the President's authorization for General Graves to lend Mr. Stevens the support necessary to make the railway plan effective.[5] The War Department approved General Graves request.

Polk,   Acting

T telegram (WP, DLC).

[1] R. S. Morris to FLP, March 8, 1919, T telegram (SDR, RG 59, 861.77/736, DNA); printed in *FR-1919, Russia*, pp. 475-77.

[2] Conveyed in FLP to WW, March 6, 1919 (WP, DLC).

[3] FLP to J. W. Davis, March 8, 1919, *FR-1919, Russia*, p. 478

[4] About which, see WW to RL, Jan. 20, 1919, n. 1, Vol. 54, and FLP to RL, Dec. 30, 1918, n. 4, Vol. 53.

[5] See RL and V. C. McCormick to FLP, Feb. 9, 1919.

Cary Travers Grayson to Joseph Patrick Tumulty

Dear Mr. Tumulty: U.S.S. George Washington, 13 March, 1919.

Everything has been progressing satisfactorily so far, except that the President was quite sick for two or three days. I am happy to say he is feeling fine now.

The President had the newspaper men in to lunch with him yesterday and was in fine form. His cordial reception pleased them immensely.

Your message to the President about the Pennsylvania Congressional election was exceedingly gratifying to him, and I know that, in the midst of your trials and tribulations, it was a pleasing piece of news to you.

Please don't forget to communicate freely with me, giving me any pointers and suggestions that you may see fit. Bear in mind that I am constantly in need of your advice and of your judgment. I feel that if you were only over here we could make things "hum." Of course, if there is anything in the world that I can do over here that you want me to do, don't hesitate to let me know.

I appreciate so much your kindness in sending me messages about Mrs. Grayson. Naturally, I have her constantly in mind, and I feel sure you will realize what these messages mean to me at this time.

We are due to reach Brest this evening.

I hope everything is going all right with you.

With warm regards,   Sincerely yours,   Cary T. Grayson

P.S. Regards of Ray Baker.

TLS (J. P. Tumulty Papers, DLC).

From the Diary of Dr. Grayson

Friday, March 14, 1919.

The President breakfasted in his car at nine o'clock, and after breakfast resumed his conference with Colonel House. The Colonel exhibited the various reports which had been prepared and acquainted his chief with all details in order that he might be able to cope with the situation that was to present itself immediately upon arrival at the Invalides Station in Paris.

The returning trip was noteworthy because of the large number of people who were out to see the train go by, despite the fact that this time the French authorities had very carefully guarded the schedule from the public. The outward reason for this naturally was one of safety, but it was remarked that a secondary reason, which in some official minds may have been the compelling one, was that they were none too anxious to have the popularity of the President with the French common people, especially the agriculturists, too much emphasized.

The guards about the various stations were for the most part women and children and old men, bringing home to us the fact that the French army was still being maintained on a war basis, and that the younger men who were so badly needed to restore normal conditions were being held in concentration camps.

The train was scheduled to arrive at 11:56 but it was 12:07 when the familiar strains of the National Anthem played by the French military band broke in our ears, and we slowly stopped in the Garde Invalides.

Awaiting the President on the station platform was President and Madame Poincaré, Premier Clemenceau, and all of the other members of the French Cabinet who had not gone to Brest to participate in the official welcome. The usual salutations of welcome were exchanged but there was no formal speech-making, neither was there any formal parade through the streets of the character which had marked our original arrival in France.

Immediately after President Poincaré and Madame Poincaré had shaken hands with the President he turned to Premier Clemenceau, and, warmly shaking his hand, expressed concern over the attempted assassination, and said: "I hope you are not feeling any ill effect from your injury." The reply of the "Tiger of France" emphasized probably more than anything else his absolute disregard for anything or anybody. Instead of expressing a sentiment of having suffered, he said: "On the contrary, I think it did me good."

The President and Mrs. Wilson and the rest of the party were driven to the new White House, which had been prepared for their reception. The White House is located at No. 11 des États-Unis. The new quarters were by no means as commodious and were far less comfortable than the original home at the Murat Palace, but they, like the Murat Palace, had been selected by the French Government, although the President had earnestly requested that he be permitted to choose his own home and to pay for it himself. Premier Clemenceau, however, had insisted that the Republic must have the honor of continuing to entertain the President, so it was necessary to bow to his wishes.

A conference had been arranged between the President and Lloyd-George to take place immediately on the President's arrival, and the British Premier came over from his home at once. It had been intended that this conference would only last a few minutes and that then the President would see Premier Orlando. However, the general situation facing Lloyd-George was such that the conference with the President was extended for more than an hour. Lloyd-George told the President that the general situation in England was very bad. He said that the railway workers were threatening a general strike intended to tie up every piece of transportation in Great Britain, while at the same time there was pending there a proposition on the part of the strong Mine Workers Union to force the Government to take over and operate the mines. Lloyd-George also discussed with the President the big problems that confronted the Peace Commission. He said also that he was very anxious to get back to England without delay because of the labor situation and of the general discontent and could not afford to remain in France much over another week. As a result of the extension of the conference between Lloyd-George and the President the meeting with Premier Orlando had to be put over until later, and the Italian Prime Minister simply welcomed the President back and agreed to defer his urgent business for a time.

Immediately after lunch the President proceeded to the Hotel Crillon, where all of the American Commissioners were waiting to see him. The conference was highly important inasmuch as each Commissioner did his best to acquaint the President with the matters that had been left to them, and it lasted until very late in the afternoon. One of the things which developed as a result of the conference was that the President found it necessary to criticise the Commission for apparently failing to keep the League of Nations covenant to the fore, and also for having failed to keep America's position on the German territorial situation always definitely defined. The fact that the French had officially announced that one of the terms of peace would be the creation of a Rhenish Republic, which the French claimed was necessary as a buffer state to take in the territory between Alsace-Lorraine and the Rhine, presented an embarrassment and the President said so. As a result of the President's frank criticism the American position was straightened out immediately.

The President returned to the house for dinner, and after dinner conferred with Premier Orlando of Italy. The Italian situation was admittedly fraught with grave danger, inasmuch as Orlando had been compelled to break with some of his ministerial associates, and the Italian campaign to force the Peace Commission to turn over Dalmatia to Italy was being pushed to an extent that already had threatened a clash with the Jugo-Slavs. It was understood that Orlando and the President talked over the situation freely, and that Orlando told the President that while he wanted to do everything possible to conciliate yet the Italians themselves had been aroused very much by the widespread belief that the United States was not prepared to be fair to them. The conference did not result in any definite plan, but had a good effect inasmuch as after Orlando left the President he sent for the Italian newspaper correspondents and told them that it would be very embarrassing to him personally and to Italy if they continued their propaganda against the United States.

After Orlando had left the President saw Admiral William S. Benson, Chief of Operations of the Navy, who told him what had been done in connection with the naval terms that had been drafted for Germany.

From the Diary of Colonel House

March 14, 1919.

I went up on Wednesday evening, after our dinner and reception, on the President's special train to meet him at Brest. It was a hard trip and the weather was as bad as weather can be even at Brest.
. . .

I arranged that none of the people who went to meet the President before should go this time, with the exception of the French Ambassador and Mme. Jusserand, whom I could not prevent going if I would. I desired to have the President alone so as to place him *au courant* with the situation here during his absence. I did not go out to the George Washington to meet the President and Mrs. Wilson but met them at the landing stage. I had but little talk with him that night because Jusserand thought it necessary to entertain the President.

However, I had ample opportunity this morning to go over the entire situation with him and to get from him his story of his visit to the United States. He said, "Your dinner to the Senate Foreign Relations Committee was a failure as far as getting together was concerned." He spoke with considerable bitterness of the manner in which he was treated by some of the Senators. Knox and Lodge reamined [remained] perfectly silent, refusing to ask any questions or to act in the spirit in which the dinner was given. However, I told the President that the dinner was a success from my viewpoint which was that it checked criticism as to his supposed dictatorship and refusal to consult the Senate about foreign affairs. He admitted this. I told him that it also had a good effect upon the people, even if it had failed to mollify the Senators themselves.

The President comes back very militant and determined to put the League of Nations into the Peace Treaty.

There was a large crowd at the Gare des Invalides when we arrived, including the President of the Republic, M. Clemenceau, M. Pichon etc. etc. I had arranged for the President to meet Lloyd George at twelve and he was waiting for him at No. 11 Places des Etats Unis, the President's new domicile here. I had arranged for him to meet in the afternoon in my rooms at the Crillon, Clemenceau and Lloyd George. They remained together from three to five o'clock discussing the Western Boundary question and the amount of reparation Germany should be forced to pay. During the latter part of the afternoon they had Montagu,[1] Davis and Loucheur on hand. I also had Tardieu and Mezes in the event they needed them.

The Prime Ministers have skirted around the different questions long enough and I am determined that they shall get at them, troublesome as they are, and settle them this week if it is possible. The President is willing, but first Lloyd George and tehn [then] Clemenceau shies. The reason I wanted them to meet in my rooms was to keep my hand on the situation. If they go to the Quai d'Orsay or the Ministry of War or to the President's house, matters get out of hand.

The people I have seen today are almost without number, but I have not the time or the inclination to go into the subjects discussed. My main drive now is for peace with Germany at the earliest possible moment, and I am determined that it shall come soon if it is within my power to force action. I have the Northcliffe Press at my disposal in this effort, and every day editorials and articles appear which have a tendency to frighten, persuade or coerce.

¹ Edwin Samuel Montagu, Secretary of State for India; one of India's two representatives at the peace conference.

From Joseph Patrick Tumulty

The White House, March 14 [1919]
No. 10. Publicity from European end doing great damage here.
Tumulty.

T telegram (WP, DLC).

From Eleuthérios Vénisélos

Mr. President: Paris, March 14, 1919.

I apologize if immediately on your return, I take the liberty to trouble you with the affairs relating to my country. But I do this with the conviction that I am endeavouring to prevent an injustice being done and a violation of the high principles which you have enunciated and which the Allied Nations have accepted as a basis for the future peace.

The question relates to the Hellenism of Western Asia Minor. I am well aware how fully occupied every hour and every minute of your stay in Europe will be, but I dare nevertheless to ask you to devote sufficient of your valuable time to peruse my enclosed memorandum.¹

Should you even, after reading this, have any doubts in your mind as to the justice of the Greek claims, I would ask you to do me the honour to grant me an appointment for the purpose of discussing with you any points that might still be in doubt.

It being a question relating to the future of the oldest of the democratic nations, I am sure that you will kindly sacrifice the necessary time for the sake of looking into the justice of its national aspirations and considering how far they conform with your principles, so that this nation, which "has long suffered the indescribable agonies of being governed by the Turk and has called out to the world generation after generation for justice, liberation and succour"—to quote one of the most memorable sentences of your New York address—should not run the risk of "not being heard" by the Conference.

I am quite confident, Mr. President, that the rendering of justice to the Hellenism of Asia Minor, with the consequent realization of the national unity of the Greek people, will enable them to further the progress of civilization and Democracy in the Near East in a manner and in a measure which will not prove to be wholly unworthy of the services already rendered by Greece in the past.

With renewed apologies, I remain, Mr. President,

Yours faithfully,   E. K.[2] Vénisélos

TLS (WP, DLC).
[1] "MEMORANDUM," TS MS (WP, DLC).
[2] Vénisélos' father's given name was Kyriakos. It was Greek custom at this time, and still is, for a man to use his father's given name as a middle name, but only to signify that he was (is) "Eleuthérios, son of Kyriakos," and not as a true middle name according to usage in most western nations.

From Sir Robert Borden

Confidential.

Dear Mr. President,   Paris, 14th March, 1919.

During the early part of this week I have been enabled to give pretty careful consideration to the provisions of the Covenant of the League of Nations, and as a result I have circulated to the members of the British Delegations a memorandum embodying certain suggestions on behalf of my colleagues and myself.[1] It seems to me desirable that I should send to you the enclosed copy of the memorandum. You will understand, I am sure, that it is my desire to be helpful and not critical. I fully realize the immense difficulties which have been overcome in presenting to the world this supremely important document upon which the future of humanity so greatly depends. I appreciate also the danger of undertaking amendments which may renew differences that the committee found it difficult to compose.

May I venture to add a word of earnest and intense appreciation

passage of League of Nations in Senate, 491-92,n1

McIlhenney, John Avery, 290; resignation of, 330,n1

McKellar, Kenneth Douglas, 297

McManus, George Henry, 412,n8

meat-packing industry: and foreign-born labor, 286-87

Meda, Filippo, 332,n1

Meeker, Royal: on labor and Whitley Councils, 91,n1

Meloney, Marie Mattingly (Mrs. William Brown), 392n1

Mensheviks, 161n1

Mesopotamia, 7, 27, 82, 142

Meteor, S.M.S., 432

Metropolitan Opera House: WW prepares speech for, 410, 411; WW's address on League of Nations at, 413-21

Mexican Constitution, 353,n1, 355

Mexico: and Germany, 354

Mexico and the United States, 351-52,n1; H. P. Fletcher on, 352-56

Mezes, Sidney Edward, 499; and Rhineland, 475n1,2

Military Affairs, Committee on (House of Reps.), 150

Military Affairs, Committee on (Senate), 150

Miller, David Hunter: diary reveals progress and activities on Covenant revision, 67, 118-19, 154; on pending amendments of League of Nations, 68-70; on U.S. representatives to Supreme Economic council, 148; distributes copies of Covenant, 192; photograph of, *illustration section*

Milner, Alfred, 1st Viscount, 145; and Supreme War Council meetings, 13, 14-15, 15, 61-62, 62, 107, 182-83

Milwaukee Leader, 92n1

Missouri: and judgeship appointment, 207

Mitchell, Allan, 423n1

Mitchell, Silas Weir, 465,n3

Moewe, S.M.S., 432

Mohrenschildt, Ferdinand de: *see* De Mohrenschildt, Ferdinand

Moldavia, 373

Moltke, Helmuth Karl Bernhard, Count von, 508,n1,2

Monroe Doctrine: WW on, 271, 275, 295, 328-29; other comments on, 293, 312n1, 437, 491, 492

Montagu, Edwin Samuel, 499,n1

Montenegro, 29n2, 30, 32, 33

Moore, Edward Caldwell, 486,n2

Morawetz, Victor, 248

Moresnet, Belgium, 109

Morgan, H. Arthur, 157,n1

Morgan & Company: *see* J. P. Morgan & Company

Morgenthau, Henry, 438n3; on WW and Taft together endorsing League of Nations, 288-89, 329

Morley, John, Viscount Morley of Blackburn, 338

Morris, Roland Sletor, 39, 493

Morrison, Frank, 280; on preventing unhealthy labor conditions in U.S., 262; on Burleson's labor policies, 364-65

Morrow, Dwight Whitney, 451,n7,8,9

Moseley, George Van Horn, 180,n3

Moton, Robert Russa: and House's invitation to go to Paris, 335, 341, 404

Muhammad Ali, 383n2

Muhu (Mukhu) Island, 545,n1

Muldoon, Peter James, 422,n2

München, S.M.S., 427

Munich, Germany, 423n1

Murat Palais, Paris, 193

Murmansk, Russia: *see* Russia—Murmansk and Archangel, intervention in

Murmansk Railroad, 190

Murphy, Joseph E., 237

Muskoka Lake, Ontario, 282

My Diary at the Conference of Paris, with Documents (Miller), 67n,n2, 119n, 154n, 192n

My Memoir (E. B. Wilson), 488n2

Napoleon I, 109

Nassau, S.M.S., 23, 427

National Civil Liberties Bureau, 224,n1

National Civil Service Reform League, 330n2

National Security and Defense Fund, 351, 447

National Union of Women's Suffrage Societies, 145n4

National War Labor Board: Stability, Social Justice, and the Voluntary State in World War I (Conner), 365n1

Nauen, Germany, 40, 430

naval peace terms: discussed at Supreme War Council meetings, 16-17, 20-26; Daniels on, 424-25; draft of, 425-32; Benson on, 432-36, 515-21, 522-24, 539; House, Lloyd George and Clemenceau discuss, 458-59

Navy, Department of the, 537

Nearing, Scott, 337,n1

Negroes: WW on Bolshevism and, 471

Nelson, Harold I., 475n2

Netherlands, The, 110; and Belgian restoration, 83; issue of passage of troops and supplies through, 178-80; WW thanks Queen Wilhelmina for offered hospitality, 219-20

Nevin, John Edwin, 221,n1, 222, 409, 479, 480

New Haven, Conn., 237

New London, Conn., 237

New Mexico, U.S.S., 207, 217

newspapers: leak to on possible relocation of peace conference, 66, 88; anti-Wilson propaganda campaign and French press, 66, 88, 94, 120, 153, 266, 489-90; British labor Socialist paper backs WW, 87,n2; WW meets with correspondents before Plenary Session, 161, 195; British press gives false reasons why WW absent from Supreme War Council meeting, 530-31; *see also* under the names of the individual newspapers such as *New York Times*

with respect to the great part which you have taken in the accomplishment of this momentous task.

Faithfully yours,   R. L. Borden.

TLS (WP, DLC).

¹ R. L. Borden, "The Covenant of the League of Nations," T MS (WP, DLC). The memorandum consisted of printed copies of the articles of the draft Covenant pasted on pages, followed by typed proposed amendments and explanations for these amendments. Borden permitted some articles to stand unchanged and suggested minor stylistic changes in others. But in many cases, notably in Articles XII-XIII and XV to XVII, he strongly criticized the ambiguity of the existing language and proposed changes to clarify the meaning and make clear the responsibilities of the signatories to the Covenant. He did not propose any specific amendments to Article VIII but suggested that it needed basic revision to clarify the powers of the Council to bring about arms reductions.

However, the most important of Borden's criticisms was that of Article X. "It is submitted," he wrote, "that this Article should be struck out or materially amended. It involves an undertaking by the High Contracting Parties to preserve the territorial integrity and existing political independence of all States members of the League. The Signatories to the Covenant are called upon to declare (a) that all existing territorial delimitations [delimitations] are just and expedient, (b) that they will continue indefinitely to be just and expedient, (c) that the Signatories will be responsible therefor. The undertaking seems to involve initially a careful survey, consideration and determination of all territorial questions between the various States who become parties to the Covenant. Even if such a survey were practicable, it is impossible to forecast the future. There may be national aspirations to which the provisions of the peace treaty will not do justice and which cannot be permanently repressed. Subsequent articles contemplate the possibility of war between two or more of the Signatories under such conditions that the other Signatories are not called upon to participate actively therein. If, as a result of such war, the nation attacked occupies and proposes to annex (possibly with the consent of a majority of the population) a portion of the territory of the aggressor, what is to be the operation of this Article?"

A Translation of a Letter from Ferdinand Foch, with Enclosure

Mr. President: [Paris] March 14, 1919

With the expression of my regret at troubling you upon your arrival, I have the honor to send you the enclosed note of mine on establishing the military frontier of Germany.

With warmest regards, I remain,

Sincerely yours,   F. Foch

Translation of TLS (WP, DLC).

E N C L O S U R E

C.-in-C. Allied Armies.   G.Q.G.A., 10th January, 1919.

The following memorandum, laid by the Marshal Commanding-in-Chief the Allied Armies before the Plenipotentiaries, states, from the point of view of the military security of the Allied and Associated Powers, the problem of the German Western Frontiers.

The question of the frontiers, special to France and Belgium, is not examined, but only the European collective and international guarantees necessary for the whole mass of States, which, after having fought for right, freedom, and justice, intend to prepare, on new bases, inspired by these three ideas, the relations between Nations.

MEMORANDUM.

Without any doubt, we may rely, in an uncertain future on a development of civilisation and of the moral sense of nations, such that it will be possible to find in a Society or League of Nations, strongly organised, an efficient barrier to wars of conquest. But, in order that this rising society should acquire an authority so strong, that it may be by itself a guarantee of the preservation of peace, it is necessary that this society should receive, at once a sufficiently secure basis and an especial strength that will ensure its development. Therefore we must know the past situation of nations, so as to settle the future, in starting from the situation of to-day, and also take into account the peace securities, which a costly victory has put in the hands of the Allied Nations, thanks to their perfect co-operation, and which could not be given up, without endangering in the future the preservation of peace.

I.

Germany of 1914 is a result of a steady work 150 years long, began by Frederick II, methodically continued by his successors, and which had lead to the prussification of Germany.

From the very outset the Hohenzollern have based the Prussian power upon an exaggerated militarism, for instance, the keeping-up of an army, whose strength was much larger than would be consistent with the total of the population. Thanks to this inflated military organisation Prussia played an important part in the wars of the eighteenth century, realised important territorial expansion, and took an important part in the wars of 1813, 1814 and 1815. In the same way, she soon secured, among European Powers, a rank very superior to the one which should have been allotted to her on account of her natural means, population, trade, industry.

In fact, the investment of its resources in a strong army, produced by personal and compulsory service and the practice of war as an industry of national conquests have given to Prussia serious profits. She was going to apply them to a triumph of her policy.

Thus, in 1866, by the victory of SADOWA, she expelled Austria from the German territory, upset the German Confederation, and took the control of reorganised Germany, so as to militarise it, according to the Prussian model and under Prussian hands.

Thus, in 1871, in the days which followed a victorious campaign, she created the Empire, in view of making Germany a stronger unity, more in Prussian hands, always on the same basis of compulsory service, and of Hohenzollern command.

But, at the same time, Prussian activity exercised itself far beyond purely military ground. All classes, all resources of action or production, all associations as well as all individuals were drilled, centralised and militarised. An ingenious State monopoly system, applied by a covetous and despotic monarchy, was always backed by a strong aristocracy and making use of an undenied military superiority and of profitable wars, that is, the supremacy of might. Public education was soon imbued with the same principles, and compulsory schools, a fairly old institution in this country, found, thanks to an acute management the means of spreading these principles, and of creating a German state of mind, "Kultur," with its own morals. The rule is that might is above right. Might creates right, for its benefit. Lastly Germany more and more believed in a superior nature, in a special fate and mission, which justified the most unjust doings, the most cruel methods, provided that they lead to German victory. Morals are summed up in a word: "DEUTSCHLAND UBER ALLES." The German ideal and the driving power, which justifies its existence, are to dominate the world for the Germans' benefit.

Besides, the centralised authority of the King of Prussia, who has concentrated in his hands all the forces thus created, so as to apply them, at the time he chooses, to the development of Germany by war, has given by the "Rights of the Native," a privileged situation to each of his subjects. The Bavarian, the Saxon, the Wurtemberger, the inhabitant of Baden is above all a German subject. He is protected and claimed by the Empire, interested therefore in the preservation and greatness of the Empire. Once more, on the physical and moral power of Germany the King of Prussia laid his hand and used it as a buttress for his system.

All this explains the irresistible, unanimous and blind rising, of 1914, called by William II.

After having, at the highest degree, exaggerated the military organisation so as to make of it a war machine ready for conquests, after having strained the morale of his people, and roused, in appealing to his interest the devotion of the individual to the Prussian Emperor's cause, it is on the whole an army of scientific and convinced hooligans, which Prussified Germany has turned out, against all treaties, on the peaceful population, and even on the countries of Europe vowed to neutrality, and lastly, on the seas of the world.

It is against this whole fabric of forces, result of a hundred years' continuous drilling, that the Entente has taken up the struggle, without being prepared, in the name of the principles of Right, and Liberty of Peoples, and soon followed in the fight by a mass of nations, urged by the same principles, the United States in the first rank.

Thanks to the effort of all, and at the price of a victory, which has been costly, especially for the first nations engaged in the fight, the crisis is now at an end, but it may start again.

II.

So as to prevent it from being renewed, it shall not be enough, without any doubt, to change the form of the German Government. Now that the Hohenzollerns have left, under conditions, which are of especially disqualifying character for this dynasty, and for all military monarchies, the reinstalment of the Imperial system appears to be improbable at least for some time. But a Republic, built on the same principles of centralised authority and militarism, taking in hand the whole of Germany, will be as dangerous, and remain as threatening for European peace. It might be perhaps easily realised* in a country, imbued with the Prussian spirit, Prussian methods, militarist theories, and where, as much on account of the natural characters as of historical traditions, reveals in a supreme way the principle of authority and of centralisation. Moreover, a German Republic, freed from the hindrance due without any doubt to the existing small principalities, has a chance of finding a surplus of forces in her unity thus completely achieved, and also in the vitality and activity, specially on economic grounds, of a country now more in touch with its government.

It is only in so straightening minds, brought back by defeat and free discussion, to a more correct conception of right and justice, and by the sharing, in a large proportion of the control of executive power, that may be brought a democratic working of institutions, in appearance republican, which should have otherwise all the strength of a despotic authority. We shall not see the coming out of such an evolution without some time, a long time, without any doubt, as we are decided not to quicken the work of persuasion by using force, not to interfere in the internal working of German affairs. But then, full of respect for German tenure, can we be so

---

* To create the Empire in 1871, it has only been necessary to include in the Northern Confederation the Southern States and to replace, in the Constitution, the word "BUND" by "REICH" and the word "PRAESIDIUM" by "KAISER." A move in the contrary direction, which should replace in the Imperial Constitution, the word "REICH" by "BUND" and the word "KAISER" by "PRAESIDIUM" would have for result to maintain, under a form only republican in appearance, all the power embodied in the Empire.

over-confident as to endanger our principles Liberty and Justice, even our existence, by a shifting opinion and by a reactionary force which may take place on the other side of the Rhine, and can immediately throw in a new war regimental staffs and numerous classes of well-drilled soldiers, that is a very strong Army?

Thus, Germany remains, for yet a long time, until the achievement of its political and philosophical change, a dangerous menace. Therefore, the Entente, embryo of a Society of Nations, is absolutely compelled by mere prudence to take towards Germany systematic measures of a purely defensive character, first emergency precautions. At the same time, these will be plain enough, so as to show that the Allies have well made up their mind to reach the goal, peace, and make it impossible for Germany to start again a war of conquest, to take up once more her plan of armed domination.

In view of this lasting German threat, what forces can we call out?

III.

During a great part of the war, which is coming to an end, Russia, with her large armies, has detained a fair number of the German forces. Thus, in 1915, 1916 and even during the greater part of 1917, the Allied powers have been superior in numbers on the Western front.

To-day, the future of Russia is uncertain, probably for many years. Therefore, Western Europe, cradle of and necessary guarantees of the future organisation of nations, can rely only on her own strength for studying, preparing, and ensuring her prospects towards Germany, and in case of a possible attack.

To play this part, Western Europe cannot have a superiority of numbers. In fact, whichever type of political organisation should be agreed to in the near future by the people on the other side of the Rhine, there will always remain, on the eastern bank of the river, a German population of 64 to 75 millions of inhabitants** naturally bound together by common language, and therefore by common ideas, as by common interest.

** German Empire 1914		68,000,000
German Provinces of Austria		7,000,000
German Poland	2,100,000	
Alsace-Lorraine	1,900,000	
Rhine-Lands of the Western bank	5,400,000	
Schleswig-Holstein	1,600,000	
	11,000,000	75,000,000

BALANCE: 64,000,000.

To these German forces, Belgium, Luxembourg, Alsace-Lorraine and France can oppose only a total of 49 millions of inhabitants. Only with the co-operation of the countries on the other side of the sea, can they reach the level of the enemy's figures, as they did in 1914-1918, and yet this help must be waited for, and for how long, especially for the United States.

Now then, what has been the cause of the present calamity? Above all the fact that Germany was tempted by the possibility of striking, with one blow, only in stretching the fist, our vital parts. Without this conviction, she certainly would have hesitated. Impressed with that conviction, she did not even look for pretexts, "We can't wait," said BETHMANN-HOLLWEG.

Therefore, to put an end to the encroachments on the West of Germany, which has always been warlike and covetous of others' property, which lately had been prepared and trained for conquering by force, against all right, and with methods the most inconsistent with law, which can start without delay a terrific war—if we want at least to postpone the decisive battle—we must first of all appeal to the help of nature. Nature has provided a barrier on the road to invasion, but only one: the RHINE. The Rhine must be used and defended, and therefore occupied and organised since peace-time. Without this fundamental precaution, Western Europe remains deprived of her natural frontier and open, as in the past, to the dange[r] of invasion, which may be stronger. Without this precaution, the industrial and peaceful countries of N. W. Europe are immediately drowned under the flow of barbarous wars, which no dike checks.

The Rhine, in itself a serious obstacle, renders especially difficult the crossing at a time, when the machine guns of the defence compel the assailant to resort to the use of tanks. From Switzerland to Holland, on a front of more than six hundred kilometres, this continuous obstacle covers the allied countries, without possibility of being outflanked.

Further, on account of fortified towns, by which it is reinforced, the means of communication (roads and railways) which converge on it, or run laterally along it, it is a magnificent basis of manoeuvre for a counter-offensive.

Mayence [Mainz], Coblens, Cologne are only at three days march from each other. Any attempt by the enemy to affect a crossing between these towns would be threatened in flank and in the rear, on both banks of the river, as each bridge-head, which we are in possession of, on the Rhine, flanks its neighbour and enables such an offensive to be dealt with in the flank or from behind.

Marshal von Moltke,[1] considered the Rhine to be the German military frontier, and concluded certain studies of his by writing: *"The extraordinary strength of our centre of operations on the Rhine cannot be ignored. It could only be compromised, should we undertake a premature offensive on the left bank, with insufficient forces." And farther: "The defensive front of Prussia against France is made up by the Rhine and its fortresses. This line is so strong that it should be far from requiring all the forces of the Monarchy."*[2] The situation is to-day reversed for the benefit of the coalition. She can't give up the advantage thus secured and abandon the defensive shield in this area,—the Rhine—, without seriously endangering its future. "Wacht am Rhein" must be its rallying word.

Henceforward the Rhine ought to be the western military frontier of the German countries. Henceforward Germany ought to be deprived of all entrance and assembling ground, that is, of all territorial sovereignty on the left bank of the river, that is, of all facilities for invading quickly, as in 1914, Belgium, Luxemburg, for reaching the coast of the North Sea and threatening the United Kingdom, for outflanking the natural defences of France, the Rhine, Meuse, conquering the Northern provinces and entering upon the Parisian area.

This is for the time being in the near future, *an indispensable guarantee of peace*, on account of:

1. The material and moral situation of Germany.
2. Her numerical superiority over the democratic countries of Western Europe.

IV

The Rhine, military frontier, without which cannot be maintained the peace aimed at by the coalition, is not a territorial benefit for any country. It is not a question, in fact, of annexing the left bank of the Rhine, of increasing France or Belgium's territory, or of the protection against German revendication, but to hold securely on the Rhine, the *common* barrier of security necessary to the League of Democratic Nations. It is not a question of confiding to a single power the guarding of this common barrier, but to ensure by the co-operation, either moral, either material of all the democratic powers the defence of their existence and of their future, by forbidding Germany once for all from carrying war and its influence of domination across the river.

---

[1] That is, Field Marshal Helmuth Karl Bernhard, Count von Moltke (1800-1891).

[2] Moltke did indeed write a fervent defense of Germany's claims to the left bank of the Rhine, in H. K. B. von Moltke, *Gesammelte Schriften und Denkwürdigkeiten* (2 vols., Berlin, 1892), II, 173-228; also H. K. B. von Moltke, *Essays, Speeches, and Memoirs*, trans. Charles F. McClumpha, C. Barter, and Mary Herms (London, 1893), pp. 169-220. However, if any one of these books was the source from which Foch or his aide was quoting, then it has to be said that the quotation was invented.

It must be understood that it will be for the treaty of peace to lay down the status of the populations of the left bank of the Rhine, not included within French or Belgian frontiers.

But this organisation, whatever form it may take, must take into account the essential military factor stated above, as follows:

1. The total prevention of German Military access to and political propaganda in the territories on the left bank of the Rhine; perhaps even the covering of these territories by military neutral zones on the right bank.

2. The ensuring of the military occupation of the territories of the left bank of the Rhine by Allied forces.

3. The guaranteeing to the territories on the left bank of the Rhine the outlets necessary for their economic activities, in uniting them with the other Western States by a common system of customs.

Under these conditions, and in conformity with the principles, admitted by all, of the liberty of peoples, it is possible to conceive the constitution on the left bank of the Rhine of new autonomous States, administering themselves under the reservations stated above, a constitution which, with the assistance of a strong natural frontier, the Rhine, will be the only means capable of securing peace to Western Europe.

V.

To sum up, the Powers of the Coalition, France, in spite of her legitimate claims and her ever-present rights, Belgium controlled by neutrality, Great Britain in her insular position, never prepared an offensive against Germany, but in 1914 were brutally assailed by this State. For a certain time, the situation may again arise. If in 1914, 1915, 1916 and 1917, these Powers were able to resist Germany, to give time to Great Britain to develop fully her Armies, notably by her compulsory service and other improvised measures, and to enable the United States to arrive with her decisive support, it was because Russia was fighting on their side, and on this account they were able to maintain during a certain period numerical superiority on the Western Front. Russia is no longer of assistance, for a time, which it is impossible to foresee. It becomes necessary, therefore, that the Western barrier against German invasion should be more strongly constituted than in the past, and that the Powers of the Entente, which are geographically in the front row of the defenders of civilisation, be organised henceforth on a military basis to render possible the timely intervention of the other States which are the defenders of civilisation.

The organisation defensively of the Coalition is therefore essential.

This defensive organisation involves, before all, a natural frontier; the first barrier placed to withstand the German invasion. Only one exists: the Rhine. It must until further orders be held by the forces of the Coalition.

VI.

The object of this decision, which is purely defensive and to be adopted at once, is to withstand an attack by Germany and to answer the first needs created thereby. It is an essential organisation, for war, as soon as it breaks, lives only on realities, on material forces brought into play under definite conditions of time: natural lines of defence or defensive organisation, numbers, armament. These are the conditions laid down above as necessary. They could be carried out, as has been seen, under the supervision and patronage of the Nations founding the League of Nations of Right: Belgium, England, United States and France.

Under the protection of these defensive measures, and to provide them with a moral support, the League of Nations, securely established, would be strengthened by those Nations which have come to defend the same principles of Right and Justice, and it would establish definite statutes, henceforward practicable of execution.

The League once thus founded, with its statutes and powers of coercion, could progressively develop into the League of Nations, by the successive adhesion of other Nations; neutral Nations first, enemy Nations afterwards. The results aimed at, once achieved, would be of such a nature as to diminish by degrees the military burdens of the nations, which the League will be composed.

That is an ideal to be realised in a future, which is necessarily indefinite.

It will only be possible of achievement under the protection of the defensive measures explained above, without which civilisation will be placed in danger by a new German attack, which this time it would not be possible to stop in time.

The fortune of war has placed the line of the Rhine in our hands, thanks to a combination of circumstances and a co-operation of Allied Forces, which cannot for a long time be reproduced. The abandonment to-day of this solid natural barrier, without other guarantee than institutions of a moral character and of distant and unknown difficulty, would mean, from the military point of view, the incurring of the greatest of risks.

The Armies moreover know how many lives it has cost them!

F. Foch

CCS MS (WP, DLC).

From Tasker Howard Bliss, with Enclosure

My dear Mr. President: Paris, March 14th, 1919.

Mr. House told me this afternoon that you desired a brief memorandum on the subject of the Military Terms of Peace with Germany. The final draft of these terms has not yet been prepared by the Drafting Committee but I am informed that I shall get it about nine o'clock in the morning. I feel quite sure, from the work already done, that the attached memorandum is a sufficiently accurate analysis to enable you to know the general purport of the document.[1] The document is filled with many petty details which cannot be enforced except by a perpetually continuing military control of Germany. My personal opinion is that it would be wiser if our colleagues would put a little more trust in the growing democratic feeling of that country and in a League of Nations, both of which will be a better protection for France and the rest of Europe than the harassing control which they propose to maintain. You will note that I am opposed to this continuing military control, so far as the United States is concerned. In this attitude I have been supported by my colleagues on the American Peace Commission. I do not think that the United States should allow strings to be tied to her by each one of a number of European nations which, if done, will be with the deliberate intent on their part of being able to drag us into war whenever they please.

My hope has been that the document would be such that we could have reasonable assurance that Germany would accept it. This I am inclined to think Germany would do if the document be presented to her together with all of the other final peace terms. If it be presented to her separately, and without any knowledge on her part of what the other terms of peace will be, I am afraid that she will reject it.   Respectfully yours,   Tasker H. Bliss.

TLS (WP, DLC).
[1] That is, the document embodied in the minutes of the Supreme War Council printed at March 17, 1919.

ENCLOSURE

MEMORANDUM.

Brief Analysis of the Military (not including
Naval and Air) Terms of Peace with Germany.

1. The Military Terms are set forth in successive chapters entitled as follows:

CHAPTER I.   Strength and Organization of the German Army.
CHAPTER II.   Armament, Munitions and Materiel.

CHAPTER III. Method of Raising the Army and Military Instruction.
CHAPTER IV. Fortifications.
CHAPTER V. General Requirements.

2.   CHAPTER I.

The German Army is never to exceed 100,000 men, of which number not more than 4,000 can be officers.

The remaining Articles of this Chapter provide for an organization as set forth in a table annexed to the draft, limits the number of staffs, abolishes the German Great General Staff, fixes the number of officers who may be attached to the ministries of war in the states of Germany, and fixes the number of civil employees in the administrative services of the War Department.

NOTE: One of the Articles as thus submitted to the Drafting Committee contained the following provision:

"Public servants such as Gendarmes, Customshouse Officials, Forest and Coast Guards and local and municipal Police Officials shall never be assembled to take part in any military training."

It is understood that the French military officers will propose (probably as an additional Article to the above Chapter I.) a new Article which will provide that customshouse officials and forest and coast guards shall not exceed the number of such employees in 1913. Further, it is understood that the new Article will provide that the gendarmes and all employees in the local and municipal police forces shall at all times bear the proportion to the local populations which they bore in the year 1913. In my opinion, this provision cannot be enforced and any attempt to do so will lead to perpetual international difficulties.

CHAPTER II.

This Chapter reduces the armament of the new German Army to the numbers and kinds fixed in an attached table and also provides for a small amount of additional corresponding material for replacements.

It provides for a restricted manufacture of arms and munitions.

All excess material is to be delivered to the Allied and Associated Governments to be destroyed or put out of use. The same is to be done with excess special machinery for manufactures.

The importation into Germany of arms and munitions, as well as the manufacture of such things in Germany for foreign use, is prohibited.

The use of asphyxiating and poisonous gases, their manufacture and importation, as well as the manufacture and importation of armoured cars, tanks or any similar engines for war purposes is forbidden.

CHAPTER III.

This Chapter abolishes universal obligatory service and provides that the German Army must be formed from volunteers.

It fixes a term of service for non-commissioned officers and privates of twelve continuous years; and provides that they can leave the service only on account of physical disability, the number being so discharged not to exceed 5% per annum of the total forces allowed.

Officers already in the army must agree to serve to not less than the age of forty-five years; and those hereafter appointed must agree to serve not less than twenty-five continuous years. Officers can leave the service only under the conditions fixes [fixed] for non-commissioned officers and enlisted men.

Certain military schools are abolished and the others are limited to the number and capacity necessary for supplying annual vacancies.

No society, nor association, nor establishment for instruction, nor university, shall train or allow the training in the use of military arms.

All provisions for mobilization are forbidden.

CHAPTER IV.

This Chapter provides for the disarmament and dismantling of all fortifications on German territory west of a line drawn at fifty kilometers east of the Rhine. It also provides that there shall be no construction of any fortification of whatever character within this zone. Fortifications on the southern and eastern frontiers of Germany are to be perpetually maintained in their present condition.

CHAPTER V.

This provides for the embodiment in the German laws of the foregoing provisions.

3. CONTROL.

NOTE: In the first draft submitted by the French for the consideration of Marshal Foch's Committee, there appeared, under the above head of "CONTROL," provisions which contemplated the perpetual occupation of Germany by a great Inter-Allied Commission the function of which would be to see that for all time to come Germany did not vary in any respect from the requirements and prohibitions imposed upon her by these Military Terms. This Commission would have its headquarters in Berlin and its sub-agencies all over Germany. It seemed obvious to me that it was a provision for war and not for peace. The exercise of the functions of this Commission would evidently result in perpetual friction, to say the least. Any officer of the Allied or Associated Powers on this Commission could throw the world into turmoil and into the dread of renewed war, whenever he pleased, by declaring that Germany was violating any one of the many irritating conditions imposed upon her. Moreover, it seemed to me most likely that before long this Inter-Allied Commission and its sub-agencies would be demanding armed forces for their protection.

I felt sure that such a provision would·jeopardize this part of the Peace Treaty when it came to the ratification of the United States Senate. I consulted my colleagues Mr. Lansing and Mr. House on this subject and found that they were strongly of my opinion. They concurred with me that nothing should be done,—after accomplishing the initial reduction of the German military forces and the reduction in German armament,—nothing should be permitted by an American delegate which left a string tied to the United States by which any one of our present Associated Powers could drag us into war at any time in the future.

I, therefore, declined to give assent to this provision. As it was, of course, necessary that there should be some supervision by the Allies [Allied] and Associated Powers over the execution of the provisions relating to the reduction of the Germany [German] Army, its reduction in armament, and the disarmament and dismantling of its fortifications; and as the execution of all of these provisions could be supervised within a period of three months (most of them within a period of two months), I consented to an Inter-Allied and Associated Powers Commission, to exercise its functions for this maximum time alone, counting from the date of signature of the Convention. This was accepted by the Committee, although frequent efforts were subsequently made to introduce the provision for perpetual control. At the time of writing this memorandum, the Drafting Committee has not completed its work on the Article relating to the subject of CONTROL; but it is understood that when the draft of this Article is finally submitted it will be expressed in such terms as will, to say the least, leave it doubtful whether limited or perpetual control is intended. This, in my opinion, is a point on which there should be no possibility of doubt, with all its chances of subsequent grave friction and in regard to which the rights and interests of the United States should be fully guarded. Whenever, therefore, the draft is submitted for final action, I suggest that this subject be most carefully scrutinized by the American Delegates.

NOTE 2: The proposed draft contains many details which I consider unnecessary and the execution of which will be provocative of endless and dangerous friction.

T MS (WP, DLC).

From William Shepherd Benson, with Enclosure

My dear Mr. President: [Paris] 14 March, 1919.

Realizing the tremendous importance of the final disposition of the enemy war vessels, we have given the subject most earnest and careful thought and study, and our views are as concisely and clearly expressed in the attached paper as we can put them.

Due to the importance of this subject, I hope you will pardon me for strongly urging upon you the advisability of reading this entire paper, as we have tried to make it cover every single point involved in this question.

Should there be any doubt in your mind, or should you wish to ascertain what I believe to be the professional opinions of the officers of the foreign Navies with whom I have been associated in the various conferences in Paris, I would appreciate very much an opportunity of discussing this matter personally with you.

I fully appreciate the value of your time and have therefore tried to make the paper as short as possible consistent with clearness and completeness.   Sincerely yours,   W. S. Benson.

TLS (WP, DLC).

E N C L O S U R E

CONFIDENTIAL.

U. S. NAVAL ADVISORY STAFF, PARIS.

MEMORANDUM NO. XXIV.

SUBJECT: *Disposition of German and Austrian Vessels of War.*

13 March, 1919.

MEMORANDUM.

The following naval vessels are, by the proposed naval terms of peace, to be surrendered to the Allies and the United States—

Battleships	21 (3 Austrian)
Battle Cruisers	6
Light Cruisers	19 (3 Austrian)
Destroyers	101 (9 Austrian)
Submarines (about)	135 (15 Austrian)

There is now under consideration by the Peace Conference two methods of disposing of these vessels:

(1) Destruction.

(2) Distribution among the Great Powers.

REASONS FOR DESTRUCTION.

(a) The covenant for a League of Nations, Article VIII states "The High Contracting Parties recognise the principle that the maintenance of peace will require the reduction of national armaments to the lowest point consistent with national safety."

The destruction of the German Austrian vessels would be a practical demonstration to the world of the sincerity of the High Contracting Parties in their determination to reduce armaments. The distribution of the German Austrian vessels would increase the strength of the naval armaments of the great powers about 30%. Great Britain, the United States, Japan, France and Italy have now 85 Dreadnoughts and Battle Cruisers. The German Austrian Dreadnoughts and Battle Cruisers awaiting disposition number 27.

(b) The fact that the menace of German Austrian naval power is removed renders unnecessary any increase in the strength of the navies of the European powers. On the contrary, the logical result of the elimination of this menace should be a reduction in European naval armaments.

(c) The addition of German Austrian ships to the navy of any European power would be an increased economic burden to that power. As the United States is called upon to assist financially the great powers of Europe which are already heavily in our debt and now nearly bankrupt, it is to our financial interest to oppose any unnecesary increase of their financial obligations.

(d) The distribution of German Austrian vessels would arouse dissatisfaction and jealousy between states that were not satisfied with their respective shares and would tend to stimulate armament construction to restore former relative naval strength. It is physically impossible to make an equitable distribution of the German navy among the Great Powers. The ships are of a variety of types of greatly varying value, so that it is not a question of numbers, but rather a vastly intricate naval question. We consider it dangerous to permit this question to be opened at all, since the problems presented by it cannot be solved without compelling some of the powers to accept semi-obselete vessels, thus giving them grounds for future bitterness.

(e) The United States should not participate in the distribution. America is proud to claim that she came into this war with clean hands and will come out with empty hands. We cannot stultify our position by accepting any spoils of war.

(f) It is essential that the United States have a navy as large as that of Great Britain. The League of Nations must be strong enough to restrain, if necessary, its strongest member.

No international navy made up of ships of heterogenous types, training, language, custom and command could hope to cope with the British fleet. There must exist in such an international force a single unit of the same nationality of equal strength to the navy of

Great Britain. Such a unit with the assistance of the forces of the League would be able to enforce the mandates of the League against any power. The United States has its ambitions satisfied and can be relied upon to support loyally the League of Nations. The nations of the world know this and have faith in us. Should we ever fail in our international obligations there would exist the forces of the League with the fleet of Great Britain to apply the remedy.

Any distribution of the German Austrian ships on the basis of losses or of naval effort in the war would give the lion's share to Great Britain, which would mean that the American taxpayer must pay hundreds of millions of dollars to restore equality of strength.

(g) The German capital ships were built for a special purpose— to oppose the British fleet.[1] They are of short steaming radius, built to fight near home and are unsuitable for overseas operations. They have German guns, German equipment and depend on German shops and yards for replacements and upkeep. They would be un-economical and inefficient as a part of a foreign navy. They are inferior in type to the later British and American ships and will soon be obselete. Any country that gets them will find the cost of maintenance out of proportion to their value. Great Britain alone might afford to keep them as a re-enforcement to her Channel fleet, thereby releasing her own modern types for operations abroad.

(h) There are in the world but two great Powers whose existence depends on naval strength. These are Great Britain and Japan. In the past Great Britain built with the exclusive idea of keeping a safe superiority over the German fleet. In future her sole naval rival will be the United States, and every ship built or acquired by Great Britain can have in mind only the American fleet.

Japan has no rival in the Pacific except America. Every ship built or acquired by Japan can have in mind only opposition to American naval strength in the Pacific.

The United States, in its desire to maintain the peace of the world and to help all nations, must not forget the necessity of national safety. Any reduction in our relative naval strength will weaken our influence in the world and will limit our ability to serve the League of Nations.

While distribution of the German Austrian vessels to other powers than Great Britain or Japan would not be so serious for us, it must be borne in mind that Great Britain is in a position in Europe to compel, if necessary, a naval alliance that would add these ships to her fleet.

(i) There is no means of guaranteeing that once the distribution

---

[1] Wilson drew a double line along the right-hand side of this paragraph.

was made on an agreed basis, participating powers would not sell or exchange their vessels or others which they replace to some other power and thereby affect the relative naval strength of states in a manner not contemplated in the distribution.

(j) The German Austrian submarines should not be distributed—they should be destroyed. Not only should these submarines be destroyed, but all submarines in the world should be destroyed, and their future possession by any power forbidden. They serve no useful purpose in time of peace. They are inferior to surface craft in time of war except in ability to treacherously attack merchant ships. In the present war, 99% of submarine attacks were illegal attacks on merchant ships. Civilisation demands that naval war be placed on a higher plane and confined to combatent vessels. So long as the submarine exists it will be used in the stress of war to attack neutral trade. High officers of the British Admiralty have justified the unrestricted use of submarines by Germany on the grounds of military necessity.

REASONS FOR DISTRIBUTION.

(a) The chief reason advanced for not destroying the German Austrian vessels is that it is unsound to destroy good vessels already built that cost millions of dollars, while naval powers are spending money to build new ships. The soundness of this argument is more apparent than real. The distribution of the German Austrian ships would so disturb the relative naval strength of the powers that it would necessitate a building programme greater than any now necessary or contemplated, and in the end would only add the burden of the upkeep of the new ships to those acquired by the distribution. This result would particularly affect the United States who would be compelled to bear the brunt of matching the increased naval strength of Great Britain.

(b) The particular desire on the part of France for distribution of the German Austrian ships is based on the claim that while naval powers like Great Britain and the United States were enabled by their war effort to increase the power of their fleets, France was compelled to devote all her effort to the manufacture of materials for land warfare, which leaves her at the end of the war in an unfair position relative to other naval powers whose chief effort was on the seas.

The justice of this claim must be admitted at once, but it is not admitted that the distribution of German Austrian ships would in any way serve as a compensation. The financial condition of France does not warrant any addition to her armament burdens. The elimination of the fleet of her ancient enemy renders any addition to her fleet unnecessary. Aside from these reasons, even though a very real benefit would come to France from this distribution, such benefit to a single nation should not outweigh the interests of the rest of the world.

The following table illustrates the result of a distribution of the German Austrian Capital ships as affecting the relative naval strength of the five great naval powers. It is assumed that minor types would be distributed in the same proportion.

Two assumptions are made—(1) that distribution would take place on a basis of relative naval effort in the war, in which case the least favourable treatment of Great Britain would demand that her share should be twice as great as that of any other Power (the United States not participating); or (2) that the distribution should be on the basis of absolute naval losses of the war, in which case the share of Great Britain would be still greater.

	I	II	III
	Before Distribution	After Distribution on 2 to 1 basis, U. S. not participating.	After Distribution on basis of absolute losses.
Great Britain	43	53	63
United States	17	17	17
France	7	13	12
Japan	13	18	13
Italy	5	11	7

To be noted in connection with Column I.

(a) With the German navy wiped out and before any distribution takes place, Great Britain has 43 capital ships; all other great powers together have 42 capital ships. (Great Britain has also a corresponding superiority in destroyers and submarines.)

(b) The United States must build 26 more capital ships than Great Britain does in an equal period of time in order to have a navy equal to Great Britain's.

To be noted in connection with Column II.

(c) If the German navy is distributed on the 2 to 1 bases [basis], the United States not participating: Great Britain will have 53 capital ships. All other great powers together will have 59 capital ships.

(d) The United States will have to build 36 more capital ships than Great Britain does in an equal period of time in order to have a navy equal to Great Britain's.

To be noted in connection with Column III.

(e) In case the German navy is distributed on the bases [basis] of absolute losses, Great Britain will have 63 capital ships; all other great powers together will have 49 capital ships.

(f) The United States will have to build 46 more capital ships than Great Britain does in an equal period of time in order to have a navy equal to Great Britain's.

(g) If a distribution of the German navy is made, the naval armaments requiring to be supported by the five great powers will be increased immediately from 85 capital ships to 112 capital ships, and this at a time when we are talking disarmament and when the world is burdened with a debt that it cannot pay.

Should the United States and Great Britain participate in the distribution but sink their respective shares, the result would be as follows—

	I	II	III
	Before Distribution.	After Distribution on 2 to 1 basis.	After Distribution on basis of absolute losses.
Great Britain	43	43	43
United States	17	17	17
France	7	11	12
Japan	13	17	13
Italy	5	9	7

NOTE. A distribution on this 2 to 1 basis would leave Japan with the same number of capital ships as the United States.

We believe it to be essential that the disposition of the German Austrian vessels be settled at once and by the terms of the Peace Treaty. Unless the matter is decided now as a part of the peace terms there will be an inevitable loss of interest in this vital matter and an increasing difficulty in reaching a unanimity of agreement that may in the end result in a disposition of these vessels that will be favourable to the strongest naval power and vitally affect our relative naval strength.

Since, so far as known, there will be but one treaty and that with Germany, and since the disposition of the German Austrian ships is one of the principal points to be decided by that treaty, if the disposition of these vessels is not definitely stated in that treaty there will be no binding provision between the Allies and the United States that will determine the final disposition of the German Austrian fleets.

The controlling reasons why the German Austrian vessels of war should not be distributed may be summarised briefly as follows:

The covenant of the League of Nations requires reduction of armaments. *Distribution* increases the naval armaments of the Great Powers by over 30%.

A stable League of Nations requires two equally great navies. *Distribution* makes it impossible during many years to come for the American navy to overtake the British Navy.

World conditions demand taxation be reduced. *Distribution* will increase taxation.

World conditions demand the removal of sources of friction. *Distribution* will be an endless source of friction and ill-feeling, not only on the part of Germany, but among the Allies.

World interests demand that no single power may rule the sea against all comers. *Distribution* will establish a single power more firmly than ever in a position that dominates the sea completely.

The morale of the world requires a dramatic herald of better days. *Distribution* will herald preparations for a continuance of warlike measures.

American interests in the League of Nations compels her to accept the burden of a navy equal to Great Britain's. *Distribution* makes that burden too great.

France wants Distribution. All other countries want destruction.

CONCLUSION.

We conclude that—

(1) The disposition of the German Austrian vessels of war should be incorporated in the peace treaty.

(2) In order that the disposition may be carried out as agreed upon, the disposition should be stated in the terms submitted to Germany and Austria.

(3) That the terms of the peace treaty signed by Germany and Austria should provide for the destruction of the German Austrian vessels of war.

T MS (WP, DLC).

From William Shepherd Benson, with Enclosure

My dear Mr. President: [Paris] 14 March 1919.

The Military and Naval Terms of Peace with Germany will come to your notice to-morrow. I esteem it my duty to invite your special attention to the general character of these terms. They may be divided into two separate categories—

1. Steps to be taken to disarm Germany.
2. Measures to be continued into the future to ensure that she shall remain permanently disarmed.

From the beginning of the work of the Committee of Admirals to formulate the Naval Terms of Peace, I have opposed all those measures which were intended to limit the sovereignty of Germany once her naval and military power had been reduced and a Treaty of Peace signed. I considered that, no matter how desirable it might be that Germany should cease to be strong in a military sense, nothing short of the continuous application of force or the threat of its application would be effective in maintaining Germany in a disarmed condition. It was not conceivable to me that a nation of 75 million people would submit through the years to come to a permanent curtailment of its sovereignty, to a suzerainty that would in effect make it a vassal State. I believed, and still believe, that the restrictions, proposed to be placed upon German sovereignty by the military and naval terms of Peace will do more to create, than to prevent war.

If the clauses on which I have made reservation in the Naval Terms of Peace, together with the corresponding clauses in the Military Terms, are embodied in the Treaty of Peace without any reservation on the part of the United States, we shall become party to a perpetual Treaty of Alliance against Germany. It appears to me that this, from an American point of view as well as from a world point of view, is highly undesirable. Further, when the several clauses of the proposed terms are examined, it will be seen that they are so detailed in their provisions, so annoying in their restrictions, as inevitably to cause a perpetual series of incidents of such a character as to be dangerous to the continuance of Peace.

I have in a separate Memorandum No. 24, brought to your notice the necessity for having a provision included in the Treaty of Peace to the effect that the German and Austrian vessels of war should be destroyed. This provision occurs in the terms which will be discussed by the Supreme War Council in three places (Clauses 4, 5 and 8) and in each of these places the specific provision has been reserved for decision.

The Article dealing with the Kiel Canal has not yet taken its final

ARTICLE XXXII. Same reservation as in ARTICLE XXI. Complete reservation regarding the last paragraph of ARTICLE XXXII.

ARTICLE XXXIII. No comment.

ARTICLE XXXIV. Same reservation as in ARTICLE XXI.

ARTICLE XXXV. Complete reservation regarding the destruction of harbors.

ARTICLE XXXVI. No comment.

ARTICLE XXXVII. I do not agree to a continuing limitation of Germany's right to defend her coasts after the Treaty of Peace has been signed.

ARTICLE XXXVIII. Comments already submitted. I recommend that nothing be agreed to that could possibly be used as a precedent in the case of the Panama Canal or any other American waterway.

ARTICLE XXXIX. No comment.

ARTICLE XL. I have opposed the transfer of the ownership of these cables except that transfer be made by the decision of the Prize Court, as it was to American interests that direct communication between the United States and Germany should be possible. The cables listed include the only two cables furnishing that service.

ARTICLE XLVII. Same reservation as in ARTICLE XXI.

ARTICLE XLVIII. No comment.

ARTICLE XLIX. No comment.

ARTICLE L. No comment.

ARTICLE LI. No comment.

ARTICLE LII. No comment.

ARTICLE LIII. No comment.

ARTICLE LIV. I made reservation regarding that part of the last paragraph of this article which requires Germany to deliver designs of her warships, etc., and I also made reservation regarding the participation by Naval representatives of the United States of America in any commissions that might hereafter have to deal with the execution of those parts of ARTICLES XXI, XXIII, XXX, XXXII, XXXIV, XXXV, XXXVI, and XXXVII that limited the future strength of the German Fleet once its present strength has been reduced or that, in any other way, limited the sovereignty of Germany after her disarmament as prescribed by the peace terms is completed.

[W. S. Benson]
Admiral, U. S. Navy,
Chief of Naval Operations.

T MS (WP, DLC).
[1] Benson comments below on the naval terms embodied in the minutes of the Supreme War Council printed at March 17, 1919.

From George Lansbury

Dear President Wilson: London E.C. 4 March 14th 1919.

It was very good of you to send me your letter of February 14th. I quite understand how difficult it was for you to see anyone during those last days in Paris.

I write now to say that if it is at all possible for you to see me I should be very glad indeed of an opportunity of doing so, but it would be necessary for me to have a week's notice in order to get my papers in order. The new DAILY HERALD of which I am to be Editor comes out on March 31st. If it were possible to see you one evening during the week ending March 29th I should be grateful.

There is still in this country a good deal of uneasiness about the constitution of the League, but all people of my social and political colour are very much disturbed about the economic conditions prevailing in Europe generally. It is not that we are afraid of the advance of Socialism—because lots of us here, myself included, are Socialists—but what we dread is the march towards downright chaos which appears inevitable unless the situation is grappled with without further delay, and grappled with on lines of international cooperation rather than international rivalry and competition. The new social order that we have all talked about so much during the war—both for our own people and people in other countries—is apparently being built on foundations of hatred and violence. I saw a little of the conditions in Cologne a week or two back and I get information from Austria and Poland, all of which prove that starvation, imperialism, desire for domination is still rampant and all these in turn produce the inevitable reaction towards violence and disorder and those forces which lead to hunger, starvation and unemployment.

Somehow there needs to go from Paris a call to the democracies and I am wondering whether it would be possible for Lloyd George, Clemenceau, Orlando and yourself to sign a really big appeal to the nations of the world. You yourself have again and again made this appeal, but people feel that you are being out-weighted; that you are being, as it were, struck down by the dead weight of imperialism which seems to be abroad. No one disagrees with the proposal to disarm Germany but what very few can understand is why our country should wish to build up a much larger army than in pre war days; to have a huge air fleet and a tremendous navy. Or why France and Italy should want all these things. If Germany is disarmed this should lead towards disarmament everywhere, and the little nations who are now fighting amongst themselves for spoils of the war should be compelled to fall into line with the bigger nations in a sincere effort to release the world from the thraldom of armaments and imperialism, by a refusal to recognise their claims or to give them economic assistance, unless they fall into line with your proposals for a true peace.

I know you will forgive me writing all this; you will have thought it all out before, but most of us feel that the the world's future rests with you just now and on your ability to carry your programme through in its entirety. We want to see you able to say at the end that the League and disarmament have been secured on democratic foundations. And we also want to be sure that the people of Germany, having got rid of their autocracy, having done their best to make amends as far as a nation can make amends, for all the wrongdoing that she has committed, shall be admitted to the Comity of Nations and given a chance not merely to redeem herself but by redeeming herself assist the whole world to recover from the fearful horrors of the war.

I hope you are very well and that it may be possible to see you soon.

I remain,   Yours very truly,   George Lansbury

TLS (WP, DLC).

From Henry Pomeroy Davison

Dear Mr. President: Paris, March 14, 1919.

The world is to be congratulated upon your safe return to Paris. I myself am perfectly delighted and wish for you all that you wish for our own people, and one could wish no more.

As to our Red Cross plan, on the whole it is progressing very satisfactorily. Each move has been made on schedule time and results have been all that could have been expected. I have found opposition from no one and especially enthusiastic approval from scientists and those who are in a position to estimate the value of our plan. And may I say that however much I thought of it, the more it develops and the more I know of conditions in the world, the more I regard it as an essential movement at this time and under conditions now existing. I have been impressed with the fact that your various statements relative to the League of Nations might have been taken as a presentation of the purposes of our Red Cross program. It harmonizes in every particular and can be made an immediate demonstration of the spirit of your conception and purposes.

There is one problem looming up which affects the program materially; in fact, may completely change one of its most important

features. I had supposed that a declaration of peace meant that
there would be peace indeed and that the peoples of the countries
affected would meet at least as occasion required. As you will recall,
I proposed that the International should issue a call for a conference
of the Red Cross societies of the world at Geneva, thirty days after
peace shall have been declared, this date to enable them to adhere
to their principles of neutrality and to insure the acceptance of the
societies of the Central Powers. I am hearing from some quarters
that certain of the British and of the French organizations say that
they do not propose to meet in conference with the Germans even
after peace shall have been declared. I am also getting the impression, which I confess is a new thought to me, that the German
Government is not to be admitted as a member of the League of
Nations for some time after peace.

If these facts prove to be true, then we must elect one of two
alternatives for our program:

First To postpone for an indefinite period our Conference at
Geneva, or

Second To proceed in some relations with the League of Nations.

As to the *First*, I should regard it as most unfortunate because
it will be difficult if not impossible to develop an organization with
the spirit and following which we have been able to do under present conditions. Still another and more important reason is that the
world is bleeding and needs help *now* rather than at some future,
indefinite time.

As to the *Second*, there are advantages and disadvantages. The
disadvantages are that the movement would not be in the interest
of all the peoples and furthermore we are largely committed to the
International, assuming of course that they will play their part and
assume the responsibility. For your information, I have been much
disappointed in them. I find the organization very weak and without
imagination or courage.

In response to the joint request of the Red Cross societies of the
United States, Great Britain, France, Italy and Japan, the International have issued a call to all the Red Cross societies for a conference to be held at Geneva thirty days after peace and I, as chairman of the "Committee of Red Cross Societies," have communicated
with the Red Cross societies of the Allied and most of the neutral
countries, informing them of our program and asking their cooperation. I mention these facts to show you that we are fairly well
along in our plan with the International. But if conditions are to be
different than I anticipated, I feel the responsibility of reconsidering
this fundamental point in our plan.

As our endeavors and purposes are exactly those of the League of Nations, it is most natural that we should be allied to the League, to effect which would not necessarily conflict with the International as it now exists. It could function as heretofore in case of war, but it would amount to little in times of peace, which however has been the case heretofore.

There is one important consideration, however, and that is that the Red Cross was born in Geneva and for sentimental reasons it would be quite too bad to have a development which would rob Geneva or Switzerland of its prestige in this particular. On the other hand, as a new world is being formed and precedents count for little, the question is forced upon us, would it be better to organize a League of Red Cross Societies to be composed of the Red Cross societies of the nations constituting the League of Nations, to be domiciled at the home of the League of Nations, its organization to be modelled after that of the League of Nations?

This would be a move in complete harmony and sympathy with the League and to the advantage of those peoples of the nations constituting the League. It will be obvious to you that I could not contemplate making a decision upon this point or even discussing it with my associates without first receiving your advice and approval.

Thinking you might like a definite recommendation from me, I will, with my present light and understanding, submit the following:

First If Germany is to be admitted to the League of Nations upon the signing of the preliminary peace, and if the International will assume the responsibility, I should proceed with the Geneva plan.

Second If Germany is not to be admitted to the League of Nations upon the signing of the preliminary peace, I would recommend that *upon invitation* from those now organizing the League of Nations there should be formed a League of Red Cross Societies to be composed of the societies of the nations, members of the League of Nations, the headquarters to be located at the same place as the headquarters of the League of Nations. The League of Red Cross Societies should be modelled after the League of Nations, but the League of Red Cross Societies should be a voluntary organization under which the relationship of each member to its government should remain unchanged.

Perhaps you know I have funds appropriated for this organization sufficient, I believe, to continue it for three years. It could, therefore, become immediately operative, the importance of which is obvious. One cannot estimate the value, for example, of the coordinated endeavor of the Red Cross societies of the League of Nations, if they should be organized and ready to go into Russia when that day comes, as it will.

It was your appreciation of the value of the plan and encouragement, together with the cordial and constant support and cooperation of Colonel House, which has made possible the progress up to date. It is needless to say that I regret taking one second of your time but you have made me feel free to do so. I shall be more than delighted to discuss this with you or, if it would better save your time, a letter from you will serve the purpose.

With sincere regards, believe me, my dear Mr. President,

Very cordially yours,   H. P. Davison.

TLS (WP, DLC).

Joseph Patrick Tumulty to Cary Travers Grayson

The White House, March 14, 1919

There appears to be a complete breakdown in publicity at that end. Is there anyone in charge? Now that you are in Paris we look for better results. Suggest to President that warm letter of thanks for what Creel has done would be wise. Mrs. Grayson and baby fine.   Tumulty

T telegram (WP, DLC).

From the Diary of Dr. Grayson

Saturday, March 15, 1919.

After breakfast the President conferred with Premiers Lloyd-George and Clemenceau. The latter had called ostensibly to explain the agreements that had been reached in connection with the drafting of the German peace terms. It developed almost immediately that the President could not agree to the program that had been mapped out by Lloyd-George, Clemenceau and the other members of the "big ten." Their program called for the side-tracking of the constitution of the League of Nations, for the preparing immediately of the military and naval and indemnity terms to be imposed upon Germany, and for the calling together of the Germans not later than the 20th of March to present them with these terms. Colonel House had practically agreed to the proposition to side-track the League of Nations. This the President not only would not agree to but he made it very plain to Lloyd-George and Clemenceau that any such program would be a direct violation of the resolutions adopted at the initial Plenary Session at which all of the Allied delegates had agreed that the League of Nations must be the initial compelling paragraph of any peace treaty. The conference developed a unanimity of purpose after the President had explained his attitude personally to the two Premiers. He told them very frankly that there were so many collateral questions which must be referred to the League of Nations when created that its creation must be the first object, and that no treaty could be agreed upon that would deal only with military, naval and financial matters. The President was opposed to a preliminary treaty. It would be in his opinion only a waste of time and his reasons were so sound that before Lloyd-George and Clemenceau left they had agreed that he was right, and it was also agreed that the President and Clemenceau and Orlando would unite in a personal letter to Lloyd-George asking him to sacrifice his own interests in England and remain in Paris until the general form of the initial peace treaty could be drafted. After the conference broke up the President sent word to the Supreme War Council that he would not be able to sit at a session arranged for that afternoon. Colonel House sat in his place. As a result of this an incident developed which gave rise to considerable feeling. The British press bureau representatives without making any effort whatever to determine why the President did not sit in at the Supreme War Council session put forth a story declaring that he was determined to "rule or ruin," and that he had served notice on Clemenceau and Lloyd-George that they must follow his wishes and adopt the League of Nations program or he would have nothing further to do with the work here. The actual facts in this case were that the President had not had the complete report of the proceedings of the Supreme War Council nor the military terms that were to be imposed upon Germany before him. In fact, they had not even been translated from the French into English, and the President realized that if he attended the meeting of the Supreme War Council he would be asked to cast a vote on a subject with which he was in no way familiar. Every other member of the Supreme War Council knew this and realized it, and it is only fair to say that the erroneous version made public by the British was done so without the knowledge or consent of either Lloyd-George or any of the other British representatives. However, it simply showed that the British themselves did not care whether their news accounts were or were not accurate so long as they did not seem to embarrass British interests. As a result of the President's failure to attend the session of the Supreme War Council that body did not take up the final terms but left them to wait until the President had fully digested the reports which were hurriedly translated and sent to him.

The President spent the afternoon studying the reports which had been presented to him. Between six and seven o'clock he and Mrs. Wilson went for a long walk. After dinner the President went down to the Crillon where he talked in plain terms to the members of the American Commission and told them that their acceptance of the French suggestions that a peace treaty could be made without any reference to a League of Nations not only was embarrassing in the United States but it was embarrassing in Great Britain, and he prophesied before many days were over this would be conclusively proven. The result of the President's talk to the Commission was a distinct and decided change in their attitude, and from that time on there was no more talk of a "preliminary treaty."

From the Diary of Ray Stannard Baker

Saturday the 15th [March 1919]

A whirl of doings. The President called me on the telephone about 11 o'clock & asked me to deny the report, now being circulated, that there would be a separate preliminary treaty with German[y] excluding the League of Nations. Partly this report represents a genuine belief in some circles that such a preliminary peace would be valuable in helping solve immediate difficulties; but it is also being used by enemies of the league here & in America to delay & obstruct the whole L of N. plan. I drew up a statement in accordance with the President's ideas & submitted it to him after the noon conference. He approved it & we put it out.[1] It will cause a fluttering in the dove-cotes. Here is a man who *acts*: and has *audacity*.

[1] The key sentence of this statement, dated March 15, 1919, read as follows: "The President said to-day that the decision made at the Peace Conference at its plenary session, January 25, 1919, to the effect that the establishment of a League of Nations should be made an integral part of the Treaty of Peace, is of final force and that there is no basis whatever for the reports that a change in this decision was contemplated." The balance of the statement quoted the resolution on the League of Nations adopted at the plenary session of January 25, for the text of which see n. 2 to the minutes of that session printed at Jan. 25, 1919, Vol. 54. The full statement is printed in Baker, *Woodrow Wilson and World Settlement*, I, 311.

To Joseph Patrick Tumulty

Paris (Received March 15, 1919.)

The Plenary Council has positively decided that the League of Nations is to be part of the peace treaty. There is absolutely no truth in report to the contrary.   Woodrow Wilson.

T telegram (J. P. Tumulty Papers, DLC).

From Edward Nash Hurley

The White House, March 15 [1919]

[No. 13] Following from Hurley: "After a careful investigation and much study I have worked out all the details of a shipping plan [policy] which should satisfy the country and offset the growing criticism that has been caused by a [our] necessary delay. I have conferred with Judge Alexander[1] and I am authorized to say for him that he endorses this plan. While there are features of the plan which will cause some criticism from the shipping interests, I am convinced that these features are absolutely [essential] not merely for the protection of small ship operators, but for the benefit of the public. You will note that while the plan [policy] avoids the _____ [inertia] and financial entanglements that might embarrass [come from] government ownership, it nevertheless provides all safeguards that could be derived from such ownership.

The total number of steel cargo ships owned by the government, as of February 1, 1919, is 555 of 3,385. 47 fishing smacks [3,385,475] dead weight tons. In addition there are 1,336 [ships of 9,275,006] dead-weight tons building and under contract. If the _____ attempted [our present] programme is carried out, there will be under the American flag next year 16,732,70[0] dead weight tons (figures garbled) [of] steel cargo and passenger ocean-going ships. This standard [fleet] should be sufficient to care for most of the needs of American commerce for the next few years. The government will own more than seventy per cent of it.

The principal plans suggested _____ [for handling] this large fleet, all of which have been considered carefully, have been the following:

1. Government ownership and operation.
2. Government ownership and operation for the benefit of the government through the medium of a private corporation.
3. Government ownership and private operation for private account.
4. Government ownership with ships chartered to private companies.

5. Ownership and operation by a single private corporation.

6. Private ownership and operation.

After weighing the arguments for and against these possible plans, the policy that seems best for the country as a whole, and which offers the best encouragement to shippers, is one whereby all vessels would be sold under a method which will secure the advantages of private ownership and operation, under strict governmental supervision, making possible a wide expansion of our foreign commerce over both old and new trade routes, without involving the government in the possible large expense of actual ownership and yet preserving private initiative. The policy which we all agree will bring about this result and which I feel should be made public as soon as possible is as follows:

That the ships be sold to and operated by American citizens under no restrictions other than the text [terms] of the bill of sale and the fixation of maximum freight rates, either as provided in section eighteen of the Act approved September 7, 1916, or as may be agreed by the government and the operator in some [specific] instances.

The ships should be sold at a price which fairly reflects the current world market for similar tonnage.

Twenty-five per cent of the purchase price of each ship should be paid down, the remainder falling due and payable in graded annual installments over a period not exceeding ten years. The government should take and hold a mortgage for the unpaid balance, charging interest thereon at the current [customary] commercial rate of five per cent. One-fifth of this interest, representing the difference between the customary government interest of four per cent and the customary commercial rate, should be paid into a merchant marine development fund, to be described hereafter.

The purchaser should be required to agree to insure and keep insured with an American maritime [marine] insurance company his part [equity] in the vessel, and because the American marine insurance market has not at present sufficient resources to undertake [underwrite] all the vessels the government has to sell, the government should carry in its own fund, as at present, but for purchasers' account, hull and machinery insurance, covering that part of the vessel for which payment has not been made. Our policy [experience] in operation shows that the government can carry this insurance for at least one per cent less than the open market rate. However, it is proposed that the open market rate be charged, and that the difference be paid into a [the] merchant marine development fund.

It is understood that no transfer of a vessel to foreign registry should be permitted without express permission of the government.

Each purchaser who shall [wishes to] operate in the foreign trade should be obliged to incorporate under federal charter, the necessary legislation for which should be passed by Congress without delay. Such a charter should provide that no stock shall be issued in excess of the money value actually paid in on vessel property, and that no stock can be issued or transferred to an alien.

It should also provide that one member of the board of directors for each company shall be named by the government.

This director should draw no salary, either from the steamship corporation or from the government. He should receive only the customary director's fee for each meeting he attends.

The same legislation should provide for periodical meetings of these government-named directors, in the city of Washington, where they will constitute an official body which will confer with and advise the Shipping Board, or other designated government agency, on the problems arising in, or the questions affecting the welfare of, the American merchant marine, and the administration of the merchant marine development fund.

This fund, drawn from the sources previously indicated, should be used to relieve such financial difficulties as may be encountered in the development of an adequate and well-balanced American merchant marine. For instance:

It is foreseen that a number of trade routes important to the immediate or future welfare of American commerce must be established and developed. Some of these routes may not yield their [steamship] operating profits until their existence shall have attracted an increasing [increased] volume or better balance of trade. Revenue derived from the carriage of mails, and possible fees for the training of seamen and cadet officers, may partly compensate losses incurred in these routes. Still, in cases where the government sells a ship upon condition that it be operated in a route which may not prove profitable at once, it will be necessary to provide for the payment of defaulted interest from the merchant marine development fund, in the discretion of the Shipping Board or other government agency, upon recommendation of the board of government directors, until such time as the route may begin to yield profit. When the ships in the route earn their annual interest rate and a profit, one-half the profit earned each year should be paid into the merchant marine development fund until all the money drawn from the fund on account of the vessels [vessel] in question shall have been replaced. The other half should go to the steamship stockholders.

Such vessels cruising in routes which fail to prove susceptible of profitable development and which do not serve any purpose of the Government of the United States, may be transferred by the government to other routes. However, should the government become convinced that any vessel has failed to make expenses solely or chiefly because of incapable management, it may foreclose its mortgage on that vessel.

On the basis of one billion dollars' worth of all the ships, the merchant marine development fund would be $15,000,000. This amount, investigation convinces me, would be more than sufficient to care for all deficiencies likely to develop due to this [during this period].

Until sold under the terms just stated, all vessels should remain the property of, and should be operated by, the Government of the United States.

[Summarizing] We have here a policy which I believe can be criticised only by selfish shipping interests anxious to keep out smaller companies. It will enable the smaller companies, with smaller resources, to obtain ships which will be operated in competition with the ships of the larger companies. The provision which forces all companies to buy ships on the same terms will prevent the larger companies from taking advantage of capital, which is more available to them than to the smaller companies. The plan also prevents discrimination by insurance companies and yet the merchant marine development fund, which will be created automatically, will avoid any recourse to the United States Treasury, and be available for the encouragement of new trade routes. The writing off_____ [of war costs], incidentally, will be automatic, requiring no appropriation, as the ships will simply be sold at market prices. The drift of the world's market for tonnage leads me to believe that this write off will be about twenty per cent, which is much less than all of us had feared. The government directors will be able to keep the government fully informed as to the profits and management of the companies, and yet the plan avoids both government ownership and subsidies.

After consulting with Judge Alexander and making other inquiries, I am hopeful that you will give me your judgment so that the present period may be utilized to create favorable sentiment. Congressional approval, of course, will be necessary, and it is my thought that by acting promptly we have the opportunity to head off any reactionary tendencies."   Tumulty.

T telegram (WP, DLC).
[1] That is, Representative Joshua Willis Alexander.

From Walker Downer Hines

The White House, March 15 [1919]

No. 14. At the request of Hines, Director General of Railroads, I am sending following message:

"Have been devoting nearly all of my time since adjournment [of Congress] to the question of averting danger of the financial crisis which threatens to grow out of the non-passage of the railroad appropriation. Conferences with the Secretary of the Treasury, Federal Reserve Board and War Finance Corporation, and also with railroad executives, representatives of the equipment companies and various bankers have been held. As a result [information], the following plans have been tentatively agreed upon, and we believe will meet the situation:

First, the War Finance Corporation is making direct loan of $50,000,000 to Railroad Administration;

Second, efforts are being made to get War Department and other labor [Governmental] departments to expedite the payment of large amounts which they owe the Railroad Administration, approximating $100,000,000;

Third, it will be necessary between now and the end of July for the railroad companies to obtain approximately $300,000,000 cash in order to meet interest and dividend requirements and a portion of their maturing obligations. We are contemplating dealing with this by issuing certificates reciting that the Railroad Administration is indebted to the railroad corporations, specifying the amounts. Such certificates will bear interest probably at six per cent and can be used by the railroad companies as collateral to notes upon which they can borrow money at the banks. The success of this plan will be insured by the War Finance Corporation announcing that it will lend at six per cent on such collateral in all cases where the banks are not willing to do so.

Fourth, it will be necessary to raise approximately $300,000,000 to pay equipment companies and supply companies for amounts due and to become due to them up to the end of July. It is probable that this situation will be met by the equipment companies drawing a ninety-days draft on the Director General. The Director General will accept this draft which can then be discounted in bank and can be re-discounted by the Federal Reserve Bank. The Federal Reserve Board today has ruled that such acceptances will be subject to re-discount.

Fifth, it is anticipated that with improvement thus brought about in the financial situation, the railroad companies will be able to collect [borrow] substantial amounts on the other collateral which they own and also will be able to issue and place car trust obligations against equipment now being delivered and in this way can reimburse the Railroad Administration to a substantial extent for advances herein [heretofore] made. These plans are all tentative for the present, but there is reasonable probability of their being adopted."

Tumulty.

T telegram (WP, DLC).

From Carter Glass

Washington March 15, 1919

VERY URGENT. For President from Glass.

Have had financial condition War Risk Bureau reviewed, and beg to advise you following serious situation. Because failure Sundry Civil Bill, which made appropriation for family allowances to dependents of soldiers and sailors immediately available, Bureau will be unable to pay such family allowances due and payable in May and June, deficiency amounting to $22,765,000. More immediate problem is question of meeting Bureau's payroll March 31 and afterwards, as well as other current expenses. Revised statement indicates payroll deficiency this fiscal year $4,560,000, other current expenses $338,000, making total deficiency in this connection $4,898,000.

Deeply regret necessity of drawing matter to your attention at this time, but situation so serious as to have vital bearing upon your decision respecting date for extra session. In view of the fact that no funds are available for payment of family allowances, due and payable in May and June, I see no escape from extra session of Congress not later than May 1st. If that meets with your approval I recommend that sufficient money to carry the Bureau's payroll and incidentals to May 15th be provided from your fund if possible. Since last report your fund has been reimbursed by War Department $2,250,000 and by Navy Department $118,000 making your balance $3,753,874.57. To carry Bureau to May 15th it will be necessary to provide $2,840,000 for payroll and miscellaneous incidentals. I beg to request that you allot the above mentioned amounts reimbursed by the War and Navy Departments, aggregating $2,368,000 to War Risk for purposes payroll, stationery, printing, binding, rentals, traveling and other incidentals, and that remainder of required amount for these purposes be allotted from such further reimbursements as may be made to your fund by the Departments. As directed, I have requested Departments to return such amounts as may be possible, with proper regard for remaining demands of fiscal year.   Polk,   Acting.

T telegram (WP, DLC).

From the Diary of Dr. Grayson

Sunday, March 16, 1919.

On Saturday night late I noticed that the President was very much exhausted, and as a result of his hard work and the natural effect of his slight illness on shipboard,—so I persuaded him to make Sunday a day of absolute rest. The result was that the President remained in his apartment until lunch time, combining breakfast and lunch.

In the afternoon he went for a three-hour motor ride with Mrs. Wilson. In the evening he again conferred with Premier Orlando on the Italian situation. He also talked with Lord Robert Cecil and Colonel House on the League of Nations situation. Lord Robert Cecil, who has been earnestly in favor of the League of Nations at all times, told the President that he also was fully convinced that the League of Nations must be an integral part of the peace treaty and that he (Cecil) intended making a very strong statement to that effect both to the British and American newspapermen.

From the Diary of Colonel House

March 16, 1919.

When I left Balfour, I crossed the street for a conference with the President and Lord Robert Cecil. We were together for an hour and a half going over the Covenant for the League of Nations and discussing how it should be amended if at all. I am in favor of some amendments and some clarifications. By doing this it will make the Covenant a better instrument, and will meet many of the objections of our Senate. The President, with his usual stubborness in such matters, desires to leave it as it is, saying that any change will be hailed in the United States as yielding to the Senate, and he believes it will lessen rather than increase the chances of ratification. Of course, I totally disagreed with him and so did Lord Robert, but rather more diplomatically than I.

When we left, it was agreed that we should dine with the President Tuesday evening at seven and spend the evening together and determine what changes, if any, should be made.

I drove Lord Robert to the Majestic and he seemed depressed. I tried to cheer him by assuring him that the necessary changes would probably be made and that he must not take the President's attitude too seriously.

The President gave me a draft of the Military Terms[1] and asked if I would not go over them and indicate which articles we had already agreed upon so that at tomorrow's meeting he might confine himself to such articles as had not been acted upon. I pressed this action upon him the other day when he was in the mood for reopening the terms from start to finish.

[1] The printed copy, *Dispositions à Imposer à l'Allemagne*, is in WP, DLC. The terms are printed in parallel columns in French and English.

From the Diary of Lord Robert Cecil

March 16 [1919].

At six o'clock I went to see the President with House, and discussed the League of Nations. I found him in a very truculent mood, fiercely refusing to make any concessions to Republican senators. Indeed, we had to be quite careful to avoid making any allusion to the fact that any change in the Covenant that we desired was one recommended by these worthless beings. However, House was quite calm, and driving away with me told me that he was quite sure the President would in fact make considerable concessions. It was arranged that I should draft what was proposed, and have another interview on Tuesday, when the President was good enough to ask me to dinner.

A Memorandum by William Shepherd Benson

MEMORANDUM.   [Paris] 16 March 1919.

Subject: Naval Terms.

Except in the case of Heligoland, Article 35, the Kiel Canal, Article 38, and the cables, Article 40, the American representative has only objected to the principle of the indefinite limitation of German armaments and sovereignty with the corresponding establishment of inter-Allied commissions of indefinite duration. He has strongly insisted on those clauses requiring the destruction of surrendered German ships and German naval war materiel, which destruction has been opposed by the French representative.

W. S. Benson

CCS MS (WP, DLC).

Two Telegrams from Joseph Patrick Tumulty

The White House, March 16 [1919]

No. 15. Believe your most critical time in setting forward America's position at conference has come. Opposition to League growing more intense from day to day. Its bitterness and pettiness producing reaction. Polls throughout the country indicate strong drift toward League. League of Nations and just peace inseparable. Neither half can stand alone. Know you will not be drawn away from announced programme to incorporate league covenant in treaty. You can afford to go to any length in insisting upon this. There is no doubt of your success here and abroad. The real friends of a constructive peace have not begun to fight.

Everything fine here.   Tumulty.

[The White House] 16 March 1919.

[No. 16] Former President Taft asks if he may cable to you direct, for your consideration only, some suggestions about which he has been thinking a great deal and which he would like to have you consider. He said that these suggestions do not look to the change of the structure of the League, the plan of its action or its real character, but simply to removing objections in minds of conscientious Americans, who are anxious for a league of nations, whose fears have been roused by suggested constructions of the League which its language does not justify and whose fears could be removed without any considerable change of language.

                                                  Tumulty.

T telegrams (WP, DLC).

From William Christian Bullitt[1]

Helsingfors March 16, 1919

Bull 5. Most Secret. For The President, Secretary Lansing and Colonel House only.

After daily conversations in Moscow with Tchitcherin and Litvinov, and conference with Lenine, I received from Tchitcherin on

[1] Colonel House, on February 17, had asked Bullitt to go to Russia to investigate conditions there and to conduct informal talks with Bolshevik leaders about the possibility of a truce in the Russian Civil War and the establishment of more normal relations among the Soviet government, its opponents in Russia, and the Allied nations. Thompson, *Russia, Bolshevism, and the Versailles Peace*, p. 151, suggests that House must have discussed with Wilson on February 14 the sending of a fact-finding mission to Russia. Thompson cites as his main supporting evidence Wilson's remark that evening

March 14th the statement which follows. He explained that the statement had been formally considered and adopted by the Executive Council of the Soviet Government and that the Soviet Government considered itself bound to accept the proposals contained therein, if they should be made by the Allied and Associated Governments on April 10th. I replied that although I had no authority to accept a formal note from the Soviet Government since my visit of inquiry was entirely informal and unofficial, nevertheless, I should be glad to carry the statement of the Soviet Government with me. It was understood that the statement should be regarded as absolutely secret, and that no publicity whatever should be given to it or to the fact of its existence.

Throughout our conversations, I found Lenine, Tchitcherin, and Litvinov full of a sense of Russia's need for peace, and therefore,

---

in the Council of Ten that the Allies might have to imitate Mohamet and go to the Russian governments. See the minutes of the Supreme War Council printed at Feb. 14, 1919. However, as Thompson admits, there is no direct evidence that House discussed the mission with Wilson.

Although Bullitt's mission was usually referred to at the time, except among insiders, as a fact-finding one, Bullitt discussed with House on February 20 or 21 the possible terms of a settlement with the Soviet government and, on the latter date, Bullitt received from Philip Kerr a written memorandum which set forth eight terms for a settlement. Kerr stressed that his paper had "no official significance," and it remains a matter of dispute as to whether he had cleared or discussed it with Lloyd George. However, as it turned out, the proposed agreement outlined in the above telegram conformed closely to the one set forth in the Kerr memorandum. The questions Bullitt asked House and the indications of House's answers, as well as the Kerr memorandum, are printed in William C. Bullitt, *The Bullitt Mission to Russia: Testimony before the Committee on Foreign Relations, United States Senate* (New York, 1919), pp. 34-37.

Lansing gave Bullitt his only official orders, and Joseph C. Grew provided a letter of credence. Both are dated February 18, 1919, and both stated that the American Commissioners Plenipotentiary to Negotiate Peace were sending Bullitt to Russia "for the purpose of studying conditions, political and economic," for the benefit of the commissioners. *Ibid.*, pp. 4-5. It appears that Lansing did not know of Bullitt's projected negotiations with the Soviets, and Henry White and Tasker H. Bliss later asserted that they had had no knowledge of the mission at all until after its departure. The British Foreign and War Offices and the French Foreign Office did not learn of the mission until it was well under way, and the other Allied governments did not find out about it until after Bullitt returned to Paris in late March.

Bullitt chose as members of the mission R. E. Lynch, a stenographer serving in the United States Navy, and Capt. Walter William Pettit, of the Military Intelligence Division of the United States Army, who spoke Russian and had done relief work in Russia in 1916 and 1917. Bullitt also invited Lincoln Steffens to accompany the mission in a strictly informal capacity. The group left Paris on February 22 and went to Russia via London and Stockholm. The party crossed the Russian border on March 8; Lynch remained behind in Helsinki. Bullitt conferred with Georgii V. Chicherin and Maksim M. Litvinov in Petrograd on March 9 and went the next day to Moscow, where he had further talks with Chicherin and Litvinov and an interview with Lenin. The results of these talks were the proposals set forth in the telegram printed above. Bullitt gave his impressions of the situation in Soviet Russia in a second, undated telegram sent shortly after the first; it is printed in *FR 1919, Russia*, pp. 81-84. Bullitt left Moscow on March 14 and returned to Paris on March 25. Future documents in the following volume will reveal the dénouement of his mission.

The most thorough and judicious discussion and evaluation of the Bullitt mission is Thompson, pp. 131-77 and 233-47. See also Mayer, *Politics and Diplomacy of Peacemaking*, pp. 450-87. A selection of documents relating to the mission is printed in *FR 1919, Russia*, pp. 74-98. Other important documents on the subject appear in Bullitt, *The Bullitt Mission to Russia*.

disposed to be most conciliatory; and I feel certain that details of their statement may be modified without it being unacceptable to them. For example, the clause under article 5, "And to their own Nationals who have been or may be prosecuted for giving help to Soviet Russia," is certainly not of any vital importance. On the other hand, as a result of a week of day and night discussions with leaders of the Soviet Government, I am convinced that in the main their statement represents the minimum terms which the Soviet Government will accept.

The statement runs as follows: "The Allied and Associated Governments to propose that hostilities shall cease on all fronts in the territory of the former Russian Empire and Finland on (see footnote one) and that no new hostilities shall begin after this date, pending a conference to be held at (see footnote two) on (footnote three).

The duration of the armistice to be for two weeks, unless extended by mutual consent, and all parties to the armistice to undertake not to employ the period of the armistice to transfer troops and war material to the territory of the former Russian Empire.

The conference to discuss peace on the basis of the following principles, which shall not be subject to revision by the conference: First, All existing de facto Governments which have been set up on the territory of the former Russian Empire and Finland to remain in full control of the territories which they occupy at the moment when the armistice becomes effective, except insofar as the conference may agree upon the transfer of territories; until the peoples inhabiting the territories controlled by these de facto governments shall themselves determine to change their governments. The Russian Soviet Government, the other Soviet Governments which have been set up on the territory of the former Russian Empire, the Allied and Associated Governments, and the other governments which are operating against the Soviet Governments, including Finland, Poland, Galicia, Roumania, Armenia, Azerbaidjan and Afghanistan, to agree not to attempt to upset by force the existing de facto governments which have been set up on the territory of the former Russian Empire and the other governments signatory to this agreement (footnote four).

Second. The economic blockade to be raised and trade relations between Soviet Russia and the Allied and Associated countries to be reestablished under conditions which will ensure that supplies from the Allied and Associated countries are made available on equal terms to all classes of the Russian people.

Third. The Soviet Government of Russia to have the right of unhindered transit on all railways and the use of all ports which belong to the former Russian Empire and to Finland and are necessary for the disembarkation and transportation of passengers and goods between their territories and the sea; detailed arrangements for the carrying out of this provision to be agreed upon at the conference.

Fourth. The citizens of the Soviet republics of Russia to have the right of free entry into the Allied and Associated countries as well as into all countries which have been formed on the territory of the former Russian Empire and Finland; also the right of sojourn and of circulation and full security, provided they do not interfere in the domestic politics of those countries (footnote five).

Nationals of the Allied and Associated countries and of the other countries above named to have the right of free entry into the Soviet republics of Russia; also the right of sojourn and of circulation and full security, provided they do not interfere in the domestic politics of the Soviet republics.

The Allied and Associated Governments and other governments whenever set up on the territory of the former Russian Empire and Finland to have the right to send official representatives enjoying full liberty and immunity into the various Russian Soviet republics. The Soviet Governments of Russia to have the right to send official representatives enjoying full liberty and immunity into all the Allied and Associated countries and into the non-Soviet countries which have been formed on the territory of the former Russian Empire and Finland.

Five. The Soviet Governments, the other governments which have been set up on the territory of the former Russian Empire and Finland, to give a general amnesty to all political opponents, offenders and prisoners. The Allied and Associated Governments to give a general amnesty to all Russian political opponents, offenders and prisoners, and to assist their own nationals who have been or may be prosecuted for giving help to Soviet Russia. All Russians who have fought in, or otherwise aided the armed forces opposed to the Soviet Government, and those opposed to the other governments which have been set up on the territory of the former Russian Empire and Finland to be included in this amnesty.

All prisoners of war of non-Russian powers detained in Russia, likewise all nationals of those powers now in Russia, to be given full facilities for repatriation. The Russian prisoners of war in whatever foreign country they may be, likewise all Russian soldiers and officers abroad and those serving in all foreign armies to be given full facilities for repatriation.

Sixth. Immediately after the signing of this agreement, all troops of the Allied and Associated Governments and other non-Russian Governments to be withdrawn from Russia and military assistance

form. There will be a determined effort to strip this Canal of its defences and to internationalize it. I have opposed all such provisions in the past, as I considered it important that no action taken concerning the Kiel Canal should be of such a nature as to form a precedent adverse to our interests in the Panama Canal or any other strictly American waterway.

Throughout the negotiations in which I have participated, I have expressed my complete accord with measures designed to reduce now the naval and military power of Germany, and I still am in accord with all such measures. My belief however that we should not participate in measures restricting the future sovereignty of Germany within her own borders as established by the Treaty of Peace, is so strong that I suggest the advisability of inserting in the Treaty a provision whereby the United States withdraws from participation in the enforcement or execution of all such measures.

Very sincerely yours,   W. S. Benson

TLS (WP, DLC).

E N C L O S U R E

Notes by Admiral Benson regarding Naval Terms.[1]

I have made the following reservations during the negotiations regarding the Naval terms.

ARTICLE XXI. Reservation. I do not agree to a continuing limitation of the German Fleet once its present strength has been reduced, unless that limitation is imposed by the League of Nations.

ARTICLE XXII. No comment.

ARTICLE XXIII. Same reservation as in ARTICLE XXI.

ARTICLE XXIV. I consider that the last sentence, to the effect that these ships shall be destroyed or broken up, should remain as it is and neither be deleted nor modified.

ARTICLE [X]XV. The only part of this article that was reserved was the first paragraph. I consider it essential that the first paragraph remain as a part of the article and that it be not modified.

ARTICLE [X]XVI. No comment.

ARTICLE [X]XVII. No comment.

ARTICLE [X]XVIII. I consider that the last part of paragraph 2, to the effect that these submarines shall be destroyed or broken up, should be neither deleted nor altered.

ARTICLE XXIX. No comment.

ARTICLE XXX. Same reservation as in ARTICLE XXI.

ARTICLE XXXI. No comment.

to cease to be given to anti-Soviet governments which have been set up on the territory of the former Russian Empire.

The Soviet Governments and the anti-Soviet Governments which have been set up on the territory of the former Russian Empire and Finland to begin to reduce their armies simultaneously, and at the same rate, to a peace footing immediately after the signing of this agreement. The conference to determine the most effective and just method of inspecting and controlling this simultaneous demobilization, and also the withdrawal of the troops and the cessation of military assistance to the anti-Soviet Governments.

Seventh. The Allied and Associated Governments, taking cognizance of the statement of the Soviet Government, in its note of February fourth in regard to its foreign debts,[2] propose as an integral part of this agreement that the Soviet Governments and the other governments which have been set up on the territory of the former Russian Empire and Finland shall recognize their responsibility for the financial obligations of the former Russian Empire, to foreign states, parties to this agreement and to the nationals of such states. Detailed arrangements for the payment of these debts to be agreed upon at the conference, regard being had to the present financial position of Russia. The Russian gold seized by the Czecho-Slovaks in Kazan, or taken from Germany by the Allies, to be regarded as partial payment of the debt due from the Soviet Republic of Russia.

Footnote one: The date of the armistice to be set at least a week after the date when the Allied and Associated Governments make this proposal.

Footnote two: The Soviet Government greatly prefers that the conference should be held in a neutral country and also that either the radio, or a direct telegraph wire to Moscow should be put at its disposal.

Footnote three. The Conference to begin not later than a week after the armistice takes effect, and the Soviet Government greatly prefers that the period between the date of the armistice and the first meeting of the conference should be only three days duration if possible.

Footnote four. The Allied and Associated Governments to undertake to see to it that the de facto government of Germany do not attempt to upset by force the de facto governments of Russia. The de facto governments which have been set up on the territory of the former Russian Empire to undertake not to attempt to upset by force the de facto governments of Germany.

Footnote five. It is considered essential by the Soviet Government

---

[2] See n. 1 to the news report of a press conference printed at Feb. 14, 1919.

that the Allied and Associated Governments should see to it that
Poland and all neutral countries extend the same rights as the Allied
and Associated countries.

The Soviet Government of Russia undertakes to accept the foregoing proposal provided it is made not later than April 10th, 1919."

It was understood, in regard to article number 2, that Allied and
Associated countries should have the right to send inspectors into
Soviet Russia to see to it that distribution of supplies is equitable.

It was specifically understood that the phrase in regard to "official
representatives" in article number 4, does not include diplomatic
representatives.

In regard to Footnote two, the Soviet Government hopes that
conference may be held in Norway. Its preferences thereafter are:
first, some point on the frontier between Russia and Finland; Second, on a large ocean liner anchored off Moon Island;[3] Third, on
a large ocean liner anchored off the Aaland Islands; Fourth, Prin-
kipos, to which the Soviet Government objects greatly.

Lenine, Tchitcherin, Litvinov and all other leaders of the Soviet
Government with whom I talked expressed in the most straight-
forward, unequivocal manner the determination of the Soviet Government to pay its foreign debts, and I am convinced that there
will be no dispute on this point.

There is no doubt whatever of the desire of the Soviet Government
for a just and reasonable peace, or of the sincerity of this proposal,
and I pray you will consider it with the deepest seriousness.

Bullitt

T telegram (WP, DLC).
  [3] Muhu, or Mukhu, an island in the Baltic Sea off the coast of Estonia.

Charles Prestwich Scott to Edward Mandell House

Dear Colonel House: Manchester March 16, 1919.

I am grateful to you for your letter. I recognize fully that no ideal
settlement can be got. What I am concerned about is that the
settlement shall be sound so far as it goes. I make no fetish of the
fourteen points, but two things seem to me vital—that no population
forming an integral part of one State shall be transferred to another
against its will, and that generally the new order shall not render
friendly cooperation in the future between conquerer and con-
quered impossible. The ideal is here essentially also the practical.
If justice is not done to Germany she will be as profoundly a troubler
of the peace as France, so wronged, has been for forty years. She
cannot cooperate sincerely in a League of Peace, she may quite

justifiably refuse to enter it. The foundation of the peace will be wrong and it will work out wrong. The whole edifice must crumble. It may seem a small matter, but I think the forcible transfer of the Saar Valley Coal-field would involve these consequences. It would be the denial of the only principle on which a just peace can rest. So would the forcible separation, under whatever form from Germany, of the rest of German territory west of the Rhine. So would the inclusion of Dantzig in the Polish State, which amounts in fact to the dismemberment of Germany. So (though in a less degree) would be the denial to the Austrian-Germans of the right to Trieste, if they so desire with the rest of Germany. Therefore it appears to me all these things should be resisted, and I am convinced (though of course you will know best about this) that they can be successfully resisted. France desires them, foolishly and suicidally desires them. They would of course make permanently impossible for a reconciled Germany. She must, if these things are done, stand to arms, as Germany, since 1871, has stood to arms. Germany cannot be rendered permanently impotent. She will revive and danger and dread will revive with her. George, as I said, was quite ready to make concessions. These things are not concessions, they are surrender. George, be it never forgotten, is not a statesman, he is a pure opportunist, with a good many sound and generous instincts, but an opportunist to the hour. If resolutely resisted he will give way. Why should he not? He has worked with the President. He will not break with him if he can help it. He wants to be nice to France, but at a pinch he will always throw over France for America. Her beautiful eyes are worth no real sacrifice. And France alone is powerless. The President, I am convinced, is master of the situation. And George, will if he wished to stand out, can find no support here. The whole instinct of the people will be against him. Pure anti-Germanism is dying out. France can be consoled in other ways. She needs assistance in material things and this might be forthcoming.

Pray forgive this too long letter, which can only be excused by your kind invitation.   Yours sincerely,   C. P. Scott.

TCL (WP, DLC).

ADDENDA

From Robert Lansing

My dear Mr. President: Paris, February 10, 1919.

I desire to call your attention to the telegram quoted below which has been received from the Department of State,[1] in regard to a resolution of sympathy for Irish freedom pending before Congress:

"There is pending in the Foreign Relations Committee a resolution of sympathy for Irish freedom. One proposal goes as far as requesting the President to instruct the Peace Delegates to present the matter for consideration in Paris.[2] I have been able to delay the matter in committee for over a month but I understand it may be forced out this week unless I can tell committee the President would prefer to have it held in committee. Both sides are playing politics with the resolution in order to get the Irish vote and I hesitate to recommend that the President interfere. I, however, feel that I should ask you to lay the matter before him and request that you give me at earliest possible moment his views.

"The Irish Party here are shortly to hold a convention and intend to select delegates to go to Paris to present the Irish cause.[3] Ex-Senator O'Gorman, Bourke Cochrane and others of that caliber mentioned as delegates. I think I have been able to discourage this movement but any prophecy in regard to an Irish meeting is dangerous. If the question of passports for the delegates does not come up now, it is reasonably certain to come up later and I suggest that this matter should also be given consideration."

According to an item which appeared in the London Morning Post of February 8th, "The House of Representatives has passed a resolution approving the report of the Foreign Relations Committee, in which the hope is expressed that Congress will ask the Peace Conference to consider favourably Ireland's claim to self-determination."

I shall be glad to know whether you desire me to make any communication to Mr. Polk in regard to either or both of the paragraphs of the telegram above quoted.

Faithfully yours,   Robert Lansing

TLS (SDR, RG 256, 841D.00/13, DNA).
[1] FLP to RL, No. 552, Feb. 3, 1919 (SDR, RG 256, 841D.00/13, DNA).
[2] The Gallagher resolution, about which see E. F. Kinkead to WW, March 8, 1919, n. 1.
[3] The Irish Race Convention, about which see G. Creel to WW, March 31, 1919, n. 1.

Robert Lansing to Frank Lyon Polk

[Paris, Feb. 15, 1919]

Your 552 February 3 6 PM SECRET The President does not think that it would be wise for him to intervene in the matter discussed in your telegram but has instructed me to advise you to keep up the utmost pressure to see that the matter is not acted on at this Congress.

Lansing

T telegram (SDR, RG 256, 841D.oo/13, DNA).

INDEX

NOTE ON THE INDEX

THE alphabetically arranged analytical table of contents at the front of the volume eliminates duplication, in both contents and index, of references to certain documents, such as letters. Letters are listed in the contents alphabetically by name, and chronologically within each name by page. The subject matter of all letters is, of course, indexed. The Editorial Notes and Wilson's writings are listed in the contents chronologically by page. In addition, the subject matter of both categories is indexed. The index covers all references to books and articles mentioned in text or notes. Footnotes are indexed. Page references to footnotes which place a comma between the page number and "n" cite both text and footnote, thus: "418,n1." On the other hand, absence of the comma indicates reference to the footnote only, thus: "59n1"—the page number denoting where the footnote appears.

The index supplies the fullest known form of names and, for the Wilson and Axson families, relationships as far down as cousins. Persons referred to by nicknames or shortened forms of names can be identified by reference to entries for these forms of the names.

All entries consisting of page numbers only and which refer to concepts, issues and opinions (such as democracy, the tariff, and money trust, leadership, and labor problems), are references to Wilson's speeches and writings. Page references that follow the symbol Δ in such entries refer to the opinions and comments of others who are identified.

Three cumulative contents-index volumes are now in print: Volume 13, which covers Volumes 1-12, Volume 26, which covers Volumes 14-25, and Volume 39, which covers Volumes 27-38.

INDEX

Academy of Political Science in the City of New York, 157n1

Addresses of President Taft on Arbitration, 448,n1

Addresses of President Wilson, Boston, Mass., February 24, 1919 New York, N.Y. March 4, 1919, 245n, 421n

Addresses of President Wilson on First Trip to Europe December 3, 1918 to February 24, 1919, 178n

aerial navigation, 256

Afghanistan, 542

Africa, 7, 171

agriculture: illiteracy problem and, 288

Alabama: Caldwell case appealed, 327-28, 328

Albert, King of the Belgians, 86, 220; on restoration of Belgium, 63-64

Alby, Henri Marie Camille Edouard, 179,n2

Alexander, Joshua Willis, 532,n1, 535

Allenby, Edmund Henry Hynman, 145

Alliata, Enrico, 332,n2

Allied Maritime Transport Council, 451n7

Allied Naval Armistice Commission, 203n3

Allies: *see* under the names of the individual countries

Alsace, 152

Alsace-Lorraine, 30, 52, 506, 507

American Catholic College (Rome), 493

American Commissioners to Negotiate Peace, 404, 511; on principles of reparation, 29-34; and W. S. Churchill's Russian initiative, 208, 232; and Moton, 335; and issue of League of Nations being separate from peace treaty, 305,n1; WW criticizes for position taken on League of Nations and peace treaty, 498, 531; talk of "preliminary treaty" dropped, 531

American Committee for Relief in the Near East, 485, 486n2

American Committee for the Independence of Armenia, 65, 265n1, 446

American Economic Review, 334n1

American Federation of Labor, 262, 284

American Financing of World War I (Gilbert), 334n1

American Heritage, 448n2

Americanization bill: *see* Smith-Bankhead Americanization bill

American Jewish Congress, 368, 377, 386

American Labor party, 450,n6

American Labor party of Greater New York, 450,n6

American Liberals in the League of Nations Controversy (Helbich), 292n1

American Presbyterian Church, Paris, 36,n1

American Railroad Politics, 1914-1920: Rates, Wages and Efficiency (Kerr), 248n2

American Red Cross, 281,n1

American Socialist Society, 337n1

American Society of International Law, 339n1

Amherst, Mass.: public opinion on League of Nations in, 449

Amherst College, 449n1

Ammon, S.M.S., 432

Anglo-Soviet Relations, 1917-1921: Britain and the Russian Civil War, November 1918-February 1920 (Ullman), 181n4

Anschluss movement (Austria-Germany), 317n3

Answald, S.M.S., 432

Antwerp, Belgium, 326

Appropriations, Committee on (House of Reps.), 227, 291

Appropriations, Committee on (Senate), 227, 228, 257

Arabia, 7

Arabs, 4

Archangel, Russia: *see* Russia—Murmansk and Archangel, intervention in

Arco-Valley, Count Anton, 423n1

Armenia, 7, 80, 243, 265n1, 274, 321-22, 459, 542; issue of U.S. troops to, 27-28, 82; American Committee for Independence of, 65-66, 265n1, 446

Armistice: WW on not altering terms of, 14, 15, 40-41; discussions on renewal of, 27, 53, 94, 95-104, 108, 111, 140-41; Supreme War Council on enforcement of financial clauses, 51-58; and war criminals, 59-60; Foch reports Germany's signing of renewal of, 202-203

Armistice Commission (Spa), 51, 60

arms limitation, 11-16, 20, 112, 116, 268-69, 270-71, 275, 404-406, 426-32, 512-15, 516, 521, 539; *see also* demobilization

Ashurst, Henry Fountain, 351n1

Asquith, Herbert Henry, 116

Associated Press, 221n1, 409, 409n5

Athens, University of, 3

Aubert, Louis, 89, 387

Auchincloss, Gordon, 192, 194

Auflösung des Habsburgerreiches: Zusammenbruch und Neuorientierung im Donauraum, 317n3

Augsburg, S.M.S., 23, 427

Austria, 317,n3; and Jews, 383n2

Austria-Hungary, 140-41, 317n3, 414; and naval terms, 21, 26; and war costs, 211

Azerbaidzhan, 542

Baker, Newton Diehl, 39, 150, 188-92, 218, 235, 299, 341, 404; on sending U.S. troops to Armenia and Turkey, 27-28, 81-82; on Moton going to Paris, 335; and Philippine independence mission to the U.S., 391,n1

Baker, Ray Stannard, 479, 496; and news leak that Paris Peace Conference might relocate, 88; on public opinion on League of Nations, 449-52; a personal view of WW, 463-67, 489-91; on Lloyd George, 480; on beginning of breach between House and WW, 488n2; on League of Nations being part of peace treaty, 531,n1; photograph of, *illustration section*

Baker, Raymond Thomas, 409,n2

Balfour, Arthur James, 66, 192, 213, 305, 423; and Council of Ten and Supreme War Council meetings, 10, 11, 17, 53, 54-55,

Balfour, Arthur James (*cont.*)
56-57, 57-58, 59, 95, 98, 100, 102-104, 108, 109, 110, 111, 144, 147, 178; Seymour on, 35; on Armistice renewal, 108-109; on woman suffrage, 146; and Russian situation, 204; WW on rumors of retirement of, 480
Balfour Declaration, 383, 384, 386
Balkan states, 30, 293, 317
Ball, M. Margaret, 317n3
Baltic Sea, 23-24, 429, 429-30, 434
Baltimore, Md.: and Lafayette monument in, 232; WW on his retirement and, 482
Bancroft, Edgar, 187n2
Bankhead, William Brockman: and Americanization bill, 284,n1, 302
Baring, Evelyn, 1st Earl of Cromer, 384n4
Barnes, George Nicoll, 178n2, 195,n4
Barnes, Julius Howland, 252
Barter, C., 508n2
Barton, James Levi, 485-86
Baruch, Bernard Mannes, 90-91, 117-18, 148, 156, 186, 188, 336; on war costs, 210-11
Bauer, Otto, 317n3
Bavaria, 423,n1
Bavarian Soviet Republic, 423n1
Beck, James Montgomery, 337-38,n2
Bein, Alex, 384n4
Beirut (Bayrouth), 142
Beirut College: *see* Syrian Protestant College
Belgium, 41-42, 62, 66, 86-87, 122, 151, 164, 184, 387, 458, 507; reparation, restoration, and requests for loans, 29n2, 30, 31-32, 33, 42, 63-64, 83, 109-10, 200, 220, 305-306, 349; WW's visit is postponed, 86, 326, 349; and war costs, 210; and Rhineland question, 476, 477, 508, 509
Bender, Robert Jacob, 160, 221-22,n1, 409
Beneš, Eduard, 34, 35
Benham, Edith, 40-41, 66-67, 224, 409, 411, 456, 489
Bennett, (Enoch) Arnold, 338
Benson, William Shepherd, 21, 39, 40, 112, 343, 424, 498; on naval and military terms, 27, 425-26, 426, 428, 429, 430, 431, 431-32, 432-36, 522-24, 539; on disposition of German and Austrian war vessels, 515-21
Berlin, Germany, 430
Berlin, S.M.S., 432
Bermuda, 482
Bessarabia: and Jews, 373, 376, 378, 380
Bethmann Hollweg, Theobald von, 507
Bey, Jamil Mardam, 145n3
Bikaner, Maharaja of (Sir Ganga Singh Bahadur), 146
Blacks: *see* Negroes
Blaine, Anita Eugénie McCormick (Mrs. Emmons), 440, 484-85
Blaine, Eleanor Gooding (Mrs. Emmons, Jr.), 440,n2
Blaine, Emmons, Jr., 440,n1, 484-85
Blakey, Gladys C., 334n1
Blakey, Roy G., 334n1
Bliss, Howard Sweetser, 81; on Syria, 86, 141-45, 472-73
Bliss, Tasker Howard, 58, 112, 160, 179-80,

203, 234, 245; on France and Syria, 4; on sending U.S. troops to Russia, 28-29, 150, 188-92; on relationship between peace with Germany and the Russian situation, 214-15; and Churchill's Russian initiative, 232; on proposed military and naval terms, 404-406, 511-14; and Bullitt mission to Russia, 540n1
Bohemia, 317, 423
Bok, Edward William, 253, 303
Bolivia: and Tacna-Arica dispute, 330-31
Bolshevik Propaganda: Hearings Before a Subcommittee of the Committee on the Judiciary, 297n2
Bolsheviks and Bolshevism, 105, 161, 180, 181, 182, 183, 189, 202, 213, 233, 297,n2, 338, 350, 403, 488, 494; and situation in Archangel, 93n2; Bliss on, 214-15; D. R. Francis on, 235; WW on, 314, 319-20, 471; and German food crisis, 458n1, 493
Bon, Ferdinand Jean Jacques de: *see* De Bon, Ferdinand Jean Jacques
Borah, William Edgar: opposition to League of Nations, 214, 225, 270; absent from dinner with WW, 267; and Irish question, 325-26
Borden, Sir Robert (Laird), 501-502,n1
Bosnia, S.M.S., 432
Boston, Mass., 36; WW's sailing for and arrival in, 185, 193-94, 197, 205-206, 218, 218-19, 225, 226, 229, 231, 235-37; WW's address in, 238-45; WW on retirement and, 482
Boston Herald, 450
Boston Publishing Company, 450n2
Bourgeois, Léon, 41, 178n2, 195, 196; and League of Nations Commission, 5, 6, 43, 45, 46, 68, 69, 70, 72-75, 76-77, 79, 80, 120, 123, 124, 126, 155, 156
Boyd, Kate, 266
Brainard, Clinton Tyler, 341,n1, 484
Brandegee, Frank Bosworth, 270, 275, 388n1
Brandes, Georg, 370
Brătianu, Ion I. C., 35, 376
Brazil, 154, 164, 184
Brest, France: U.S. military camps at, 64-65, 149, 151; as port of departure and return for WW, 160, 197, 487-88
Brewing and Liquor Interests and German and Bolshevik Propaganda: Report and Hearings of the Subcommittee on the Judiciary, 297n2
brewing industry: and German propaganda in the U.S., 297n2
Bristol, Mark Lambert, 485,n1
Britain: *see* Great Britain
Britt, James Jefferson, 367,n1
Brockdorff-Rantzau, Ulrich Karl Christian, Count von, 55,n5
Brookings, Robert Somers, 329
Browning, Sir Montague Edward, 203,n3
Brussels, Belgium, 326, 349
Bryan, William Jennings, 65
Bryant, Louise, 297n2
Bryce, James, Viscount Bryce, 338, 379
Bryn, Helmer Halvorsen, 357,n1

Bulgaria, 111, 211
Bullitt, William Christian: and League of Nations Covenant, 67,n2; mission to Russia, 540-45,n1; photograph of, *illustration section*
Bullitt Mission to Russia: Testimony before the Committee on Foreign Relations, United States Senate, 540n1
Bureau of Education, 285
Burleson, Albert Sidney, 327, 330n2; claims of oppressive labor policies of, 364-65
Burnett, Philip Mason, 29n2
Burns, John, 338
Burton, Theodore Elijah, 255, 278
business and industry, 117-18, 156, 188; and importance of Smith-Bankhead Americanization bill, 286-88
Butler, Nicholas Murray, 440

Calderón, Don Ignacio, 330,n4
Caldwell, Edgar, 327-28, 328
Candler, Ezekiel Samuel, Jr., 297,n4
Capper, Arthur, 450,n5
Carranza, Venustiano, 351, 352, 354, 355
Carson, Sir Edward Henry, 455,n2, 481
Cassel, S.M.S., 432
Caucasus, 61
Cavallero, Ugo, 58,n9, 112
Cecil, Robert Arthur Talbot Gascoyne-, *see* Salisbury, 3rd Marquess of
Cecil, Lord Robert (Edgar Algernon Robert Gascoyne-), 58, 118, 178n2, 195; and League of Nations Commission, 4, 42, 45, 46, 70, 71, 78, 80, 120, 121, 122, 124, 125, 139-40, 154, 155, 155-56; on international army, 78, 80; and food for Germany, 458n1; meets with House and WW on League of Nations, 538, 539
censorship, 327
census bill: WW urged to veto, 281,n1, 290
Chadbourne, Thomas Lincoln, Jr.: on Irish issue and Democratic party, 403-404
Chafee, Zechariah, Jr., 347n1
Chamberlain, George Agnew, 356,n6
Chamberlain, George Earle: strained meeting with WW, 298
Chamberlain, Joseph, 384n4,5
Chamber of Commerce of the United States: *see* United States Chamber of Commerce
Chemnitz, S.M.S., 432
Chicago, Ill.: appointments in, 340,n1
Chicherin, Georgii Vasil'evich: answer to Prinkipo Declaration, 161,n1; and Bullitt mission to Russia, 540n1, 541-42, 545
child labor: and League of Nations, 6, 9, 146, 172, 175-76
Chile: and Tacna-Arica dispute, 330-31, 393
China, 164, 184; and Article 21 of the Covenant, 154; and Japan, 294; wants Germany to return Kiaochow, 424
Chinda, Sutemi, 155
Chinese Eastern Railway, 39
Chita, Russia, 400
Churchill, George Bosworth, 449,n1, 450
Churchill, Marlborough, 93n2, 495
Churchill, Winston Spencer: Russian initia-

tive of, 180-81, 182, 183, 202, 203, 208, 230,n2, 323
citizenship: and Smith-Bankhead Americanization bill, 284-88
civil service: and census bill, 281,n1, 290
Civil Service Commission: reorganization plans enables WW to ask for members' resignations, 330,n1,2,3; and Galloway's refusal to resign, 460, 478
Civil War (U.S.), 85
Clagett, Maurice Brice, 409,n5
Clark, Champ (James Beauchamp), 297
Clemenceau, Georges, 35, 148, 149,n1, 160, 178n2, 196, 211, 306, 423, 458n1, 497, 499; controversy with Foch over German prisioners, 3, 40; WW's views of, 3, 160; and Supreme War Council meetings, 9-10, 14, 15, 54, 55, 56, 57, 58, 60, 61, 62, 95, 95-96, 98-102, 104, 105, 106, 107, 109, 110, 111, 180, 181; House on, 195; and Russian situation, 204, 235,n2; assassination attempt on, 209, 213, 279, 335, 497; House meets with, 233-34, 458; and Rhineland, 233, 458, 475n2; WW meets with and insists peace treaty include League of Nations, 529-30
Clémentel, Étienne, 58, 458n1
Close, Gilbert Fairchild, 151, 188, 233n1, 406, 407, 448; photograph of, *illustration section*
clothing industry: *see* garment industry
coal industry, 251, 286-88, 362-63, 397-98, 398
Cobb, Frank Irving, 450
Coblenz, Germany, 475, 507
Cochrane, Bourke, 547
Cohalan, Daniel Florence, 406, 407; WW calls a "traitor" and refuses to meet with, 411-12, 421, 454, 463
Colby, Bainbridge, 302,n1
Cologne, Germany, 475, 507
Colonel House in Paris: A Study of American Policy at the Paris Peace Conference 1919 (Floto), 488n2
Colonel's Folly and the President's Distress (C. T. Grayson), 488n2
Commerce, Department of, 256
Commission on Reparation and Damages: *see* Reparation Commission
Commission on the International Control of Ports, Waterways and Railways, 110
Commission on the League of Nations: *see* League of Nations Commission
Committee on Committees (U.S. Congress), 449n1
Committee on Public Information, 363
Conference of Governors and Mayors: *see* Governors and Mayors, Conference of
Congressional Record: WW on, 310
Congressional Record, 65th Cong., 3d sess., 204n1, 312n1, 351n1, 367n1, 388n1, 469n1
Congressional Record, 66th Cong., 1st sess., 297n2
Conner, Valerie Jean, 365n1
conscription: and *Schenck v. U.S.*, 347n1
Constantinople, 27-28, 322, 459

Constitution (U.S.): see United States Constitution
Contested Election Case of Britt v. Weaver: Hearings Before the Committee on Elections No. 3, House of Representatives, Sixty-fifth Congress, Second Session . . . , 367n1
Continental Trust Company, 247n1
Coolidge, (John) Calvin, 206,n1, 235, 238
Cooper, Henry Allen, 267,n2, 270
Copley-Plaza Hotel, Boston, 226, 236
Cordoba, S.M.S., 432
Cordova Davila, Felix: on appointment of Attorney General of Porto Rico, 158-59, 264-65
Cossacks, 181
cost of living, 89, 358, 359
Cottin, Émile, 209,n1
cotton industry, 38, 157, 252-53, 286-87, 297
Coughlin, John William, 409,n3
Council of Ten, 83n1, 104, 140-48, 202n1, 230, 458n1; and proposal on women, 145-47
Covenant of the League of Nations (memorandum, Borden), 501,n1
Cracow, University of, 3
Crane, Richard, 453
Craven, Hermon Wilson, 290, 330n2
Creel, George, 363-64, 529
Crespi, Silvio Benigno, 58,n8, 113
Creswell, John Andrew Jackson, 366,n2
Croatia, 84
Croats, 87-88
Croly, Herbert (David), 451
Cromer, 1st Earl of: see Baring, Evelyn
Cromwell, Oliver, 383
Cuba and the United States: and sugar industry, 252
Culpeper, Va., 443
Cummings, Homer Stillé, 308, 313
Cummins, Albert Baird: and railroad crisis, 248, 257
Curtis, Lucius Fisher, 409,n7, 479
Curzon, George Nathaniel, 1st Marquess of Kedleston, 116, 480
Curzon, Lady (Mary Victoria Leiter), 480,n3
Czechoslovakia and Czechs, 29n2, 164, 184, 243; and Jews, 371, 380
Czech troops in Russia, 401-402

Dalmatia, 160, 498
Damascus, 4
Dana, Richard Henry, 330n2
Dania, S.M.S., 432
Daniels, Josephus, 266-67, 343, 367, 424; on Palmer for Attorney General, 36, 263-64; on naval terms, 424-25; on Democratic victory in Pennsylvania, 457
Danzig (Dantzig), Poland, 233-34, 387, 546
Danzig, S.M.S., 427
Dartmouth College, 462
Davis, Edward Parker, 265, 266, 410
Davis, Ellen Duane Gillespie (Mrs. Edward Parker): on WW's new grandson, 265-66, 304
Davis, Jefferson, 366

Davis, Norman Hezekiah, 58, 148, 186, 200, 332, 499; on Italy's loan request, 113-14; on war costs, 210-11
Davison, Henry Pomeroy: and Red Cross, 201, 526-29
De Bon, Ferdinand Jean Jacques, 16-17,n3, 21, 112, 426,n3, 427
Deering, Milliken and Company, 486n2
Degoute, Jean Joseph Marie, 58,n7, 112
De Kalb, U.S.S., 434
Delacroix, Léon, 86,n1, 151, 195, 200,n1
demobilization (disarmament), 103, 104-105, 140, 525-26; see also arms limitation
Democratic National Committee, 469; Cummings named chairman, 308; WW's remarks to, 309-24, 456n2
Democratic party: WW on woman suffrage and, 37; and League of Nations, 214, 222; McAdoo on railroad situation and, 259; WW on congressional election results, 309-11; and Irish situation, 348, 403-404, 407
Democratic party in Connecticut, 237,n4
Democratic party in Pennsylvania: congressional victory, 448-49,n1, 457, 458, 495
De Mohrenschildt, Ferdinand, 442,n1
De Mohrenschildt, Nona Hazlehurst McAdoo (Mrs. Ferdinand), 442,n1
Denmark: appointment of U.S. minister to, 185, 194, 439,n1
Department of: see under the latter part of the name, such as Labor, Department of
Derby, 17th Earl of (Edward George Villiers Stanley), 160
De Silver, Albert, 224,n1
Deutschland, S.M.S., 426
Diamandi, Constantin J., 6
Dickinson, Jacob McGavock, 339,n1
disarmament: see arms limitation; demobilization
Disraeli, Benjamin, Earl of Beaconsfield, 384n3
District of Columbia: see Washington, D.C.
Dmowski, Roman, 3, 464; and Jews, 370, 373
Dodge, Cleveland Hoadley, 265, 303, 411
Dodge, Grace Parish (Mrs. Cleveland Hoadley), 265, 303
Doubleday, Page and Company, 290n1
draft: see conscription
Duggan, Grace Elvina Hinds (Mrs. Alfred), 480,n3
Dulles, John Foster, 35
Dune, Germany, 429
Düsseldorf, Germany, 475
Duval, Marie Victor Charles Maurice, 112,n4
Dwight W. Morrow Discusses the Proposed Covenant of the League (New York Evening Post), 451,n9

Eagle, Joe Henry, 297,n4
Ebert, Friedrich, 55,n4, 99, 458n1
Economic Council: see Supreme Economic Council
Edinburgh, University of: and WW's honorary degree, 89,n1

education: and Smith-Bankhead Americanization bill, 284-88

Edwards, Agustin, 331,n5

Edwards, Clarence Ransom, 218,n1, 235

Egan, Maurice Francis: replacement for, 185

Eisner, Kurt, 423n1

El-Arish, 384n4,5

Election of 1920: mentioned, 443, 448, 457

Elkus, Abram Isaac, 289, 290, 411

Emergence of Modern First Amendment Doctrine (Rabban), 347n1

Emergency Fleet Corporation, 398n1; and housing projects, 342

Emerson, George H., 400,n1

Emil George Von Strauss, S.M.S., 432

employment and unemployment: and civil service appointments and census bill, 281,n1

Employment of Soldiers and Sailors: Statement of Hon. W. B. Wilson, Secretary of Labor, before the Committee on Rules, House of Representatives, Sixty-fifth Congress, Third Session, 291n1

Employment Service: *see* United States Employment Service

Erzberger, Matthias, 10, 11, 18-19, 202-203

Espionage Act: movement for repeal of, 224, 337,n1; and amnesty issue, 344, 345, 346, 347, 365, 482n1

Essays, Speeches and Memoirs (Von Moltke; trans. McClumpha *et al.*), 508n2

Estonia (Esthonia), 202

Everett Hotel, New York, 472

Everybody's Magazine, 392n1, 456n1

excess-profits tax, 333-34,n1

Faisal, Prince, 4, 81, 86, 183

Fall, Albert Bacon, 267

Fall River, Mass., 286

famine relief bill, 116

Farhi, Tewfik, 145n3

Farquhar, Arthur Briggs, 439-40,n1

Farquhar Defends League of Nations (*York Dispatch*), 440,n2

Farrand, Livingston, 281n1

Fawcett, Millicent Garrett (Mrs. Henry), 145,n4, 183-84

Federal Reserve Act: success of as example for League of Nations propaganda, 367

Federal Reserve Board: and railroad crisis, 536

Feisal, Prince: *see* Faisal, Prince

Ferris, Scott, 263

Filene, Edward Albert, 199, 447

Finance Committee (Senate): and revenue bill, 334n1

Finland, 202, 233, 542

Fiske, John, 216

Fitzgerald, David Edward, 237,n3,4

Fitzmaurice, Henry Charles Keith Petty-, *see* Lansdowne, Marquess of

Fiume, 160

Fletcher, Duncan Upshaw, 297

Fletcher, Henry Prather: on situation in Mexico, 352-56

Flood, Henry De La Warr, 270

Floto, Inga, 488n2

Foch, Ferdinand, 387; controversy with Clemenceau over German prisoners, 3, 19, 40; and Supreme War Council meetings on Armistice renewal and peace terms, 10, 11, 15, 18, 56, 93, 96, 100, 102, 103, 107, 108, 109, 111-12, 202-203; on immediately dictating peace terms to Germany, 212-13, 230; on the Rhineland, 502-10

food: Glass on prices, 89-90, 358; Hoover on price controls, 251-53; pork prices, 306-307, 307-308

Food Administration, 90; Hoover on price controls and, 251-53; pork prices, 306, 307-308, 343, 362, 393-94, 396, 483; Glass on prices and, 359-60

food relief, 116-17, 117; and German crisis, 458,n1, 493

food relief bill: *see* famine relief bill

Fordyce, Samuel Wesley, 409,n4

Foreign Affairs, Committee on (House of Reps.): mention of WW's proposed meeting with, 82, 184, 194, 197, 198, 221; WW's dinner and meeting with on League of Nations, 267, 268-76; and Irish issue, 469n4

Foreign Relations, Committee on (Senate): mention of WW's proposed meeting with, 82, 184, 194, 197, 198, 221; WW's dinner and meeting with on League of Nations, 267, 268-76, 499; and Mexico, 351n1; and Irish situation, 547

Forster, Rudolph, 481

Fourteen Points: mentioned, 30, 31, 32, 33, 210, 211, 468

France, 164, 184; and Syria, 4; and reparation, 29,n2, 30, 32, 33, 458; and Armistice renewal plans, 94; Clemenceau on devastation in, 100-102; and cotton imports, 157; peace terms and pressure for settlement made by, 162, 189, 213-14, 230,n1; WW's statement on departing from, 197; and war costs, 210; House on financial situation of, 283-84; and Japan, 294; and Belgium's finances, 305-306, 349; and Rhineland, 475-77,n2, 507, 509; and disposal of enemy war ships, 518-19

France and the United States: anti-Wilson propaganda campaign by French newspapers causes tension between, 66, 66-67, 88, 152-53, 153, 266, 489-90; appointment of new U.S. ambassador to France, 194; WW's Paris "White House," 193, 223, 230-31, 497

Francis, David Rowland, 224, 228n1, 297n1; on Russian situation, 234-35, 349-50

Francis, Emelie De Mun Smith (Mrs. John D. Perry), 228,n1

Francis, John D. Perry, 228,n1

Franken, S.M.S., 432

Franklin, Benjamin, 242

Frazier, Arthur Hugh, 185, 195

Frederick II (of Prussia), 503

freedom of speech: Gavit on, 255

freedom of the seas: WW on nonissue of, 160, 162

Free Speech in the United States (Chafee), 347n1

Fuerst Buelow, S.M.S., 432

Fuller, Alvan Tufts, 343,n1

Galicia, 542; and Jews, 370, 371, 372, 378, 378-79

Gallagher, Thomas, 469n4

Gallagher Resolution on Ireland, 469n4, 547

Galloway, Charles Mills: urges WW to veto census bill, 290; and resignation controversy, 330,n3, 460, 478

Galsworthy, John, 338

Ganem, Chekri, 145,n3, 162,n2

Gannett, Lewis Stiles, 92,n2

Gardiner, Alfred George, 115-16, 466

Garfield, Harry Augustus, 294; on coal prices and export issue, 251, 362-63, 397-98

garment industry: and foreign-born labor, 286-87

Garner, John Nance, 297,n4

Garrett, Finis James, 297,n4

Gasparri, Pietro Cardinal, 493

Gavit, John Palmer: on granting amnesty to political prisoners, 255, 344

Gay, Edward James, 297, 368

general deficiency appropriations bill: and railroads, 257, 258, 388; WW on, 277; W. B. Wilson on Employment Service and, 447

Geneva, Switzerland, 127, 152, 490; and Red Cross, 527, 528

George V (of Great Britain): WW on, 228

George Washington, U.S.S., 197, 217, 229, 234n1, 412, 442; WW fondly remembers, 224n1

Gerard, James Watson: and Armenia, 65-66, 446

German Americans, 443, 448

German Austria, 317n3

German propaganda in the United States: investigation of, 297n2; and Cohalan, 411-12

Germany: and issue of repatriation of prisoners, 3, 10-11, 18-19; National Assembly at Weimar and postal facilities, 10, 18; Supreme War Council discusses arms reduction and, 11-16, 20; peace terms and colonies of, 24; and reparations, 29-34, 210-11; and Poland, 203; Foch on peace terms for, 212-13; issue of representation in League of Nations, 276; and German Austria, 317n3; proposed military and naval terms with, 404-406, 425-32, 511-14, 522-24; food crisis in, 423, 458,n1, 493; and Bavaria, 423,n1; and conscription, 459; and Rhineland, 475-77; Foch on background of militarism of, 503-505; empire of 1914, 506; Benson on disposition of war vessels of, 515-21

Germer, Adolph, 92

Gertrud, S.M.S., 432

Gesammelte Schriften und Denkwürdigkeiten (Von Moltke), 508n2

Gibbons, James Cardinal, 454

Gilbert, Charles, 334n1

Gilder, Richard Watson, 472,n1

Gillett, Frederick Huntington, 449n2

Glasgow, William Anderson, Jr., 336,n1, 360

Glass, Carter, 251, 256, 279; on reducing food prices, 89-90, 358-61; on Italian loan, 113, 114, 115, 208, 332-33, 342; and railroad appropriation, 228, 257; and pork prices, 306-307, 395, 396; on Treasury bonds and certificates, 333-34; on foreign loan policy, 396-97; on financial crisis of War Risk Bureau, 537-38

Gleaves, Albert, 412,n8

Goff, John William, 421,n1, 422

Gompers, Samuel, 185, 262, 280, 364

Goodrich, Chauncey William, 36n1

Gould, Norman Judd, 351n1

Governors and Mayors, Conference of, 219, 387; WW's address to, 389-91

Grant, Sir Ludovic James, 89,n1

Grassi, Rear Admiral, 112

Grasty, Charles Henry, 479, 480, 490

Graudenz, S.M.S., 23

Graves, William Sidney, 39; N. D. Baker praises, 399; on Siberian situation, 399-403; and Japan and Russian situation, 493-95

Grayson, Alice Gertrude (Altrude) Gordon (Mrs. Cary Travers), 185, 496, 529

Grayson, Cary Travers, 3, 36, 41, 94, 120, 187, 218, 465, 529, 538; and leak to press that peace conference may relocate, 66, 88; on Plenary Session and completion of Covenant, 159-60; on WW's departure from Paris and arrival in Brest, 160, 197; on WW's activities during sea voyage to Boston, 201, 205, 207, 217-18, 221-22, 224-25, 228-29, 235-38; on WW's arrival and activities in Washington, 254, 294-95, 308-309, 339, 367, 387-88, 409; on WW's dinner meeting with congressional committees, 267; on WW's activities during return trip to France and his arrival in Brest, 409-10, 442-46, 448, 456-57, 460-62, 471-72, 473-75, 479-82, 486-89, 495-96; WW's dependence on, 466; on beginning of House-WW break, 488n2; return to Paris, 496-98; on WW's meeting with Lloyd George and Clemenceau on League of Nations being part of peace treaty, 529-31

Grayson, David (pseudonym): *see* Baker, Ray Stannard

Great Britain, 144, 155, 164, 184; labor problems and Whitley Councils in, 91,n1, 204n2, 497; and Italy's request for U.S. loan, 113, 114; and Russian railroad situation, 150, 187, 189-93, 400-401; and Prinkipo Declaration, 180-83; and war costs, 210; and French Financial situation, 283-84; and Japan, 294; and Belgian loan, 305-306; and League of Nations and U.S. public opinion, 339; and Irish situation, 363-64, 453-55; and Palestine, 381, 383, 383n2; and Japan: refuses to ship coal to U.S. if U.S. ships coal to Italy, 397-98; and Rhineland, 475-77,n2; Benson on U.S. navy and, 516-21; British press gives false reasons why WW absent from Supreme War Council meeting, 530-31

Great Lakes Division for League of Nations, 187

Great Madness, The (pamphlet), 337n1

Greece, 3, 29n2, 164, 184, 500-501

Gregory, Thomas Watt, 409, 411, 463; on granting amnesty, 344, 345-47; WW's praises as Attorney General, 276-77; successor named, 294

Grinnell College, 486n2

Groat, Carl Diedrich, 479,n1

Gundomar, S.M.S., 432

Habsburg, S.M.S., 432

Hague Conferences and Convention: mentioned, 31, 68, 121

Hague Tribunal, 156

Haidar, Rustum, 178n2

Hale, Frederick, 450,n3

Hamburg, Germany, 458n1

Hampton Roads, Va., 37, 193

Hankey, Sir Maurice Pascal Alers, 192, 305

Hannover, Germany, 430

Hapgood, Norman: appointed Minister to Denmark, 185, 194, 439,n1; on League of Nations, 292, 451

Harbin, China, 495

Harbord, James Guthrie, 398,n3

Harper & Brothers, 341n1

Harris, Ernest Lloyd, 494

Harrison, Francis Burton, 391n1

Harrison, Gilbert A., 441n4

Harrison, Leland, 192

Harrison, Pat (Byron Patton), 297,n4

Harts, William Wright, 326

Harvard University, 486n2

Haskins, Charles Homer: on Belgium's restoration, 83

Hatch, Harold Ames, 486,n2

Hatchet, The (ship's newspaper), 224,n1

Hay, John Milton: on Rumania's treatment of Jews, 375

Hayne, Robert Young, 460-62

Hearst, William Randolph, 194

Hebrew language, 372, 382

Heflin, James Thomas, 297,n4

Helbich, Wolfang Johann, 292n1

Helgoland (Heligoland), 23, 425, 429, 434, 539

Helgoland, S.M.S., 23, 427

Henderson, Philip, 384n3

Herald Publishing Company, 341n1

Herford, Oliver, 244

Herms, Mary, 508n2

Herzl, Theodor, 384n4,5

Hewart, Sir Gordon, 59,n10

Hines, Walker Downer, 90, 277; on railroad crisis, 227-28, 246-50, 251, 257-58, 260-61, 536-37

History of the American People (Wilson): WW rejects offer for revision or condensation of, 341n1, 484

Hitchcock, Gilbert Monell: and League of Nations, 198, 214, 263, 267, 270, 275, 437; and Irish question, 324-26

Holland: *see* Netherlands, The

Holmes, Oliver Wendell, Jr.: and Schenck case, 347n1

Home Rule and Conscription (Plunkett), 455,n3

Homes and 'A Few Well-Placed Fruit Trees': An Object Lesson in Federal Housing (Lubove), 341n1

Hood, Edwin Milton, 160n1

Hoover, Herbert Clark, 148, 186, 279; on Belgium, 86-87, 151; on food prices and controls, 90, 91, 251-53, 308, 359, 360, 361, 396; and food relief, 90, 116-17, 117; and food for Germany, 458n1

Hoover, Irwin Hood (Ike): photograph of, *illustration section*

Hope, George Price Webley, 53-54

House, Edward Mandell, 3, 41, 67, 87, 107, 118, 152, 154, 160, 178, 192, 193-96, 212-13, 256-57, 299, 326, 387, 455, 487-88, 514, 529, 538-39, 545; on rumor that peace conference might move from Paris, 88-89; and League of Nations Covenant, 137, 140, 155-56; on WW's Paris residence, 193, 223, 230-31; meets with WW on peace terms and instructions, 193; on being first to use word "covenant," 194; on Plenary Session, 195-96; on Red Cross, 201, 202; on Churchill's Russian initiative, 203-204, 229-30; on war costs, 210-11; activities in Paris during WW's absence, 212-14, 233-34, 245-46, 283-84, 423; advice to WW, 221; on Lloyd George's views on Russian situation, 233; on starting functioning of League of Nations Covenant and separating from peace treaty, 304-305,n1; on Italian-Yugoslav situation, 305; on Belgian loan request, 305-306; and invitation to Moton, 335, 341; on WW coming directly to Paris to meet with Lloyd George, 349; on success of Federal Reserve Act as propaganda for League of Nations, 367-68; WW's concern over House's plan to start functioning of League of Nations, 392; on meeting with Lloyd George and Clemenceau, 458-59; and Rhineland, 472, 475n1,2; consents to separating League of Nations from peace treaty against WW's wishes, 488,n2, 529; beginning of break between WW and, 488,n2; on WW's arrival and meetings, 499-500; on WW wanting League of Nations as part of peace treaty, 499; meets with WW and Lord Cecil on League of Nations, 538, 539

House of Representatives: *see* United States Congress

housing, 341-42

Houston, David Franklin, 219, 360; on pork prices, 343, 395-96, 483; WW on personality of, 482

Houston, Herbert Sherman, 290,n1

Hudgins, T. T., 444,n8

Hughes, Charles Evans, 65

Hughes, William Morris, 155, 160, 178n2, 192

Hulbert, Allen Schoolcraft: and War Department's surplus trucks, 303-304,n1

Hulbert, Mary Allen, 304
Hull, Cordell, 263
Hull, Merlin, 158,n1
Hungary, 317; see also Austria-Hungary
Hurban, Vladimir S., 297n2
Hurley, Edward Nash, 148, 302n1, 341-42, 394, 397, 398; on shipping policy, 532-35
Hurst, Cecil James Barrington, 119
Hylan, John F., 194
Hymans, Paul, 109; and League of Nations Commission, 5, 6, 41, 42, 45, 72, 122, 123, 124, 126

illiteracy in the United States, 284-88
income tax, 334n1
In Defense of Yesterday: James M. Beck and the Politics of Conservatism, 1861-1936 (Keller), 338n2
India, 125, 184, 499n1
Indianapolis News, 472,n2
"Industrie im Besetzten Frankreich," 61
Inter-Allied Commission to Poland, 110
Inter-Allied Economic Commission: see Supreme Economic Council
Inter-Allied Naval Armistice Commission (London), 53
Interim Report on Joint Standing Industrial Councils: see Whitley Report
International Bible Society, 482-83,n1
International Bible Students' Association, 482n1
International Mercantile Marine Corporation, 367n2
International News Service, 221n1, 409
International Radio-Telegraphic Conference, 26, 430
International Red Cross, 527-28
International Socialist and Labor Congress (Bern), 92
Interstate and Foreign Commerce Committee (House of Reps.), 246n3, 247
Interstate Commerce Commission: and railroads, 246n1, 247, 257-58
Interstate Commerce Committee (Senate), 246,n3, 247, 248, 257
Ireland: WW denies making statement on, 324-26; Tumulty recommends WW meet with delegates on, 348; Creel on, 363-64; attempts to make situation an issue at peace conference, 403, 412, 421-22, 474, 547; WW meets with delegates on, 411-12, 421-22; Plunkett on U.S. public opinion and, 453-55; WW on, 480-81
Irish Americans, 363, 364, 403, 407, 407-408, 421-22, 448, 453, 463, 468, 474, 547; WW meets with, 411-12, 421-22; WW on, 443
Irish Race Convention, 407, 411, 421-22, 443, 454, 463, 547
Irish Reconstruction Association (Plunkett), 455n3
Irkutsk, Russia, 495
Ironside, (William) Edmund, 93n2
Irreconcilables: The Fight Against the League of Nations (Stone), 388n1
Ishii, Kikujiro, 436,n1

Italy, 61, 87, 157, 164, 184, 203, 294, 397-98; and reparation, 29n2; T. N. Page on, 84-86; requests for loans, 113-15, 208, 332-33, 342; food relief efforts thwarted by, 117; Orlando on military terms and, 140-41; grants general amnesty, 301; praise for WW, 301-302; and Yugoslavia, 305; Orlando meets with WW, 498

Jamison, John Martin, 448n1
Janin, Pierre Thiébaut Charles Maurice (Maurice Janin), 400
Japan, 164, 184; and submarines, 22; and racial equality resolution (Article 21 of Covenant), 155, 436-37; and Russia, 187, 401, 493-94; has separate negotiations with Allies, 293-94,n1; naval fleet of, 517, 519, 520
Jastrow, Morris, Jr., 438,n1,3, 484
Jehovah's Witnesses, 482-83,n1
Jersey Railways Advertising Company, 468n1
Jews, 438,n3; plight of eastern European, 368-81, 386; and Palestine, 381-85, 386; in Poland, 464
Joffre, Joseph Jacques Césaire, 149,n1
Johnson, Hiram Warren: Russian resolution of, 149,n1
Johnston, Albert Sidney, 85
Jones, Andrieus Aristieus, 297
Jones, Marvin, 297,n4
Journal of American History, 347n1
Journal of Modern History, 383n2
J. P. Morgan & Company, 451,n7
Judiciary Committee (Senate): hearings on Bolshevik and German propaganda, 297n2, 350,n2
Jusserand, Elise Richards (Mme. Jean Jules), 487, 499
Jusserand, Jean Jules, 160, 221, 487, 489, 499
Justice Oliver Wendell Holmes, Jr., Zechariah Chafee, Jr., and the Clear and Present Danger Test for Free Speech: The First Year, 1919 (Ragan), 347n1

Kahn, Julius, 438,n3, 484
Kalmykov, Ivan Pavlovich, 401
Kehl, Germany, 475
Keller, Morton, 338n2
Kenyon, William Squire, 257
Kern, Howard Lewis, 264,n3
Kerr, Kathel Austin, 248n2
Kerr, Philip Henry, 475,n2, 476, 540n1
Keyes, George Thurman, 330n2
Kiaochow, China, 424
Kiel Canal, 24, 108, 430, 434-35, 522-23, 539
Kilby, Thomas Erby, 327-28,n1, 328
King, Alexander Campbell, 478,n1
King, William Henry, 351n1
Kingdom of Serbs, Croats and Slovenes: see Yugoslavia
Kinkead, Eugene Francis: and Irish issue, 468-70,n1
Kirby, William Fosgate, 297,n1
Kitchin, Claude, 334n1

Klotz, Louis Lucien, 51, 54, 60-61, 66, 100,n3, 283, 284, 458n1
Knapp, Harry Shepard, 66,n1
Knox, Alfred William Fortescue, 187, 400, 401
Knox, Philander Chase, 263, 270, 388n1, 499
Kogoma, S.M.S., 432
Kohn, William, 450n6
Kolberg, S.M.S., 23, 427
Kolchak, Aleksandr Vasil'evich, 399-401
Koniggrätz, Battle of: *see* Sadowa, Battle of
Koo, Vi Kyuin Wellington, 140, 178n2
Kramář, Karel (Karl Kramartz), 34, 35, 45, 70
Kurdistan, 7

labor, 185; and League of Nations Covenant, 6, 8-9, 9, 172; and Whitley Councils, 91,n1; and railroads, 247, 248; and Smith-Bank-head Americanization bill, 286-88; and Employment Service, 291-92, 478; and Burleson's policies, 364-65; WW on restoration to prewar conditions, 389-91; supports League of Nations, 450,n6
Labor, Department of: and Employment Service, 291-92, 447
Labor's Solution of the Railroad Problem (Plumb), 248n2
Labour Year Book, 1919, 91n1
Lafayette, Marquis de (Marie Joseph Paul Yves Roch Gilbert du Motier): WW on inscription on monument to, 232
Lamon, Ward Hill, 366,n1
Lamont, Florence Haskell Corliss (Mrs. Thomas William), 120,n1
Lamont, Thomas William, 157,n1
Land and Power: British and Allied Policy on Germany's Frontiers, 1916-19 (Nelson), 475n2
Land of Gilead, with Excursions in the Lebanon (Oliphant), 384n3
Lansdowne, Marquess of (Henry Charles Keith Petty-Fitzmaurice), 384n4
Lane, Franklin Knight, 219, 357; on Smith-Bankhead Americanization bill, 284-88
Lansbury, George, 87,n1, 187, 525-26
Lansing, Robert, 59, 83n1, 88n1, 152, 154, 185, 406, 493, 514; and Supreme War Council meetings, 12, 183; sketches during meetings, 34-35; on Russian railroad situation, 38-39; and passports for Socialists, 92; on situation in Archangel, 93; and H. W. Johnson's Russian resolution, 149; on Churchill's Russian initiative, 202-203; on assassination attempt on Clemenceau, 209; on war costs, 210-11, 231; and idea of separating Covenant from Peace Treaty, 305n1; and Bullitt's mission to Russia, 540n1; on Gallagher resolution, 547
Lapradelle, Albert Geouffre de, 154,n1
Larnaude, Fernand, 118; and League of Nations Commission, 5, 42, 43, 44, 46, 71, 75, 78-79, 79, 120-21, 122, 123, 125, 126, 155
Lawrence, Mass., 286
League of Free Nations Association, 292,n1
League of Nations: varied individual and or-

ganizational support for, 37-38, 158,n2, 198-99, 199, 205, 253,n1, 278, 292, 457, 458, 503, 510, 511; U.S. public opinion on, 38, 197-98, 339, 449-52, 463-64, 540; and Taft's support, 65, 82, 257, 281-82, 289, 357-58, 540; Bullitt on "Assembly of Representatives," 67n2; Miller memorandum on pending amendments, 68-70; Cecil on international army, 80; preamble adopted by commission, 121; Miller on drafting committee meeting on Covenant, 118; text of Covenant, 129-37, 164-73; and Switzerland, 152; WW on, 160, 255, 272, 313-24, 328-29, 340, 489; WW on freedom of seas and neutrality issue, 160, 162; WW presents and explains Covenant to Plenary Session, 164-78; and mandates, 170-72, 176-77, 321-22; Republican opposition to, 214, 225, 254, 312-13,n1, 388n1; WW on importance of U.S. support, 224-25; suggestions for winning support for, 262-63, 280, 292-93, 337-38, 339, 437, 491, 501-502,n1; WW meets with congressional committees to discuss, 267, 268-76; and question of surrender of U.S. sovereignty, 268, 272-73; House activities give rise to idea of separating the Covenant from the peace treaty, 304-305,n1; Lodge's attack on, 312-13,n1; WW on one sentence in Covenant that should be altered, 315-16; and Tacna-Arica dispute, 330, 331; H. P. Fletcher on Mexico and, 354; House on using Federal Reserve Act fight as model for, 367-68; and Palestine issue, 381-85; WW's concern over House's proposal to start immediate functioning of, 392; WW's address at Metropolitan Opera House on, 413-21; and Japan and racial equality resolution, 437, 464; and Irish issue, 470, 474; legal opinion on U.S. membership in, 478-79; WW on membership and withdrawal from, 481; WW learns of House's agreement to separate peace treaty and, 488,n2; idea of separation from peace treaty disturbs U.S. public, 493; Benson on naval terms and, 515, 516, 517, 521; H. P. Davison on Red Cross and, 527-29; WW makes clear to Lloyd George and Clemenceau that peace treaty must include, 529-30; resolution by Plenary Session to include League of Nations in peace treaty stands, 531,n1, 532; WW, Cecil and House meet on, 538, 539; *see also* Paris Peace Conference
League of Nations Commission: meetings on amending Hurst-Miller draft of Covenant, 4-9, 41-51, 70-80, 120-36, 136-40, 154; and mandates (Article 17), 7-8, 49-50; and labor, 8-9, 9; on international army and peacekeeping, 73-80; on racial and religious issue (Article 21), 137-40, 154, 155, 156; prepares report for Plenary Session, 147-48, 154, 184, 189; WW presents Covenant to Plenary Session, 164-78; *see also* League of Nations
League to Enforce Peace, 225, 288, 290n1; supports League of Nations, 37-38, 186

League of Nations societies: Tumulty on WW addressing, 289
League of Nations Society, 278
League of Red Cross Societies (proposed), 528
Lebanon, 142, 143
Lederer, Ivo John, 88n1
Lee, Algernon, 92,n1
Lee, Robert Edward, 85
Left Bank: see Rhineland
Leiter, Mary Victoria: see Curzon, Lady
Lemberg, Poland, 371
Lenin, V. I. (Vladimir Ilich Ulyanov): and Bullitt mission to Russia, 540n1, 541-42, 545
Leorat, Anne Henri Joseph, 160
Lever, Asbury Francis: on Galloway and Civil Service Commission, 478
Lewis, James Hamilton, 296-97, 351n1
Leygues, Georges Jean Claude, 16, 149,n1, 426,n3
Liberty Loan, 200, 227, 259, 333
Life of George Lansbury (Postgate), 87n2
Life of Laurence Oliphant: Traveller, Diplomat and Mystic (Henderson), 384n3
Lille, France, 326
Limburg, Netherlands, 110
limitation of armaments: see arms limitation
Lincoln, Abraham, 365-66, 481
Lindsay, Samuel McCune, 157,n1
Litvinov, Maksim Maksimovich: and Bullitt mission to Russia, 540n1, 541-42, 545
Livonia (Livland), 202,n2
Lloyd George, David, 62, 66, 81, 88, 180, 204n2, 211, 230,n2, 305, 320; varied opinions of, 35, 480, 546; and Russian situation, 233, 235,n2; WW on, 266; plans to return to Paris and meet with WW, 283, 284, 326-27, 349, 423; and Irish situation, 364, 454, 474; House meets with, 458; and Rhine question, 475n2; meets with WW, 497, 499, 529-30; pressured to remain in Paris, 530
Lodge, Henry Cabot, 237, 474, 499; and Armenia, 66; and WW's meeting with congressional committees on League of Nations, 267, 269, 270; attack on League of Nations, 312,n1, 312-13,n1, 367, 388,n1, 437; R. S. Baker on public opposition to, 449, 450
London, Pact of, 160
London Morning Post, 547
London Times, 371
London Weekly Herald, 87,n2
Long, Breckinridge, 279, 349, 436
Lord Palmerston and the Rejuvenation of Turkey, 1830-41 (Rodkey), 383n2
Lorraine, 480; see also Alsace-Lorraine
Los Angeles Times, 205
Lothringen, S.M.S., 426
Loucheur, Louis, 13-14, 15, 458n1, 499
Loudon, John, 219, 220
Lowell, Abbott Lawrence, 225n2; on League of Nations, 65, 187, 199
Lübeck, S.M.S., 427
Lubove, Roy, 341n1
Lucey, Patrick Joseph, 340,n1

Luxembourg (Luxemburg), 306, 387, 423, 507, 508
L'vov, Georgii Evgen'evich, 369
Lynch, R. E., 540n1

Mack, Julian William, 386; on plight of eastern European Jews, 368-81; on Palestine, 381-85
Mack, Karlheinz, 317n3
Maclay, Sir Joseph Paton, 367,n3
Maikarzel, Nejil Bey, 145n3
Main, John Hanson Thomas, 486,n2
Mainz, Germany, 475, 507
Making of a Radical: A Political Autobiography (Nearing), 337n1
Makino, Nobuaki, 6, 72, 146, 178n2; on racial and religious equality (Article 21), 138-39, 155
Malmédy, Belgium, 109
Malone, Dudley Field, 337-38, 407
Manly, Matthias Evans, 444,n5
Mann, James Robert, 449,n2, 469n4
Mannheim, Germany, 475
Manning, Vannoy Hartrog, 286,n2
Mantoux, Paul Joseph, 35
March, Peyton Conway, 150, 404
Marshall, Louis, 386; on plight of eastern European Jews, 368-81; on Palestine, 381-85
Marshall, Thomas Riley, 204n1
Martin, Richard William, 149,n1
Martin, Thomas Staples, 254, 296, 367, 388; and railroad appropriation, 228, 257, 258, 277
Masaryk, Thomas Garrigue: and Jews, 371
Massachusetts: public opinion in, 449-50
Mathieu, Don Beltran, 330,n3
May, George Oliver, 306,n1
Mayer, Arno Joseph, 204n2, 458n1, 540n1
Mayflower, U.S.S., 444
McAdoo, Eleanor Randolph Wilson (Mrs. William Gibbs), daughter of WW and EAW, 204-205, 283, 395
McAdoo, Ellen Wilson, granddaughter of WW, 205
McAdoo, Nona Hazelhurst: see De Mohrenschildt, Nona Hazelhurst
McAdoo, Sarah (Sally) Fleming, 409n5
McAdoo, William Gibbs, 283, 395, 409n5; on League of Nations support, 205; on relinquishing federal control of railroads, 258-60, 260-61; and revenue legislation, 333, 334n1; death of son-in-law, 442,n1
McCall, Samuel Walker, 292-93, 328-29
McCauley, Edward, Jr., 207, 217, 224
McClumpha, Charles F., 508n2
McClure Newspaper Syndicate, 341n1
McCormack, John, 237
McCormick, Vance Criswell, 29n1, 113, 148, 186, 351, 387, 457, 475n2, 493; on Russian railroad situation, 38-39; offers appointment suggestions, 206-207; on war costs, 210-11; resigns as chairman of Democratic National Committee, 308
McCully, Newton Alexander, 39,n1
McCumber, Porter James: suggestions for

New York, N.Y.: A. E. Smith's invitation to WW, 216; WW on his retirement and, 482
New York *Evening Post*, 451,n8, 480n2
New York *Evening Telegram*, 151,n1
New York Herald, 450n6
New York *Maccabean*, 381n3
New York *Nation*, 248n2
New York Peace Society, 278
New York *Sun*, 480n2
New York Times, 88n1, 145n4, 163n, 197n, 224n1, 275, 276n, 299n, 326n, 330n2, 340n, 355n5, 363n1, 386n, 391n,n1, 422n, 438n3, 448n1, 450n6,.480n2, 482n1
New York *World*, 88n1, 409n, 450
Nieto, Rafael, 355,n5
Noble, George Bernard, 66n2
North Carolina: and Britt-Weaver congressional seat, 367,n1
North Carolina, U.S.S., 217
Northcliffe press, 500
North Sea, 429
Nortoni, Albert Dexter, 206-207,n1
Norway, 545
Norway and the United States: and ship settlement, 357, 394
Nubar, Boghos, 80
Nudant, Alphonse Pierre, 18
Nugent, John Frost, 297

O'Brien, Robert Lincoln, 450,n2
O'Brien, Timothy, 407-408,n1
Ochs, Adolph Simon, 438n3
Official Bulletin, 189n2, 347n2
O'Gorman, James Aloysius, 547
O'Hern, Charles Aloysius, 493,n1
Oldenburg, S.M.S., 23, 427
Old-Fashioned Democrat to the Editor of the *Indianapolis News*, 472,n2
Oldfield, William Allen, 297,n4
O'Leary, Jeremiah A., 411
Oliphant, Laurence, 384,n3
Oneal, James, 92n1
Onega, Russia, 190
Orange Publishing Company, 468n1
Organic Law (Porto Rico), 158, 159
Orlando, Vittorio Emanuele, 88, 211, 305, 530; and League of Nations Commission, 4-5, 6, 42, 44, 45, 71, 123, 125, 126; and Supreme War Council meetings, 95, 107; and Council of Ten, 140-41; and Plenary Session, 178n2, 195, 196; praises WW, 300, 301-302; WW meets with, 497, 498, 538
Ostfriesland, S.M.S., 23, 427
Otani, Kikuzo, 401
Otto Bauer und die 'Anschlussfrage' 1918/19 (Steiner), 317n3
Oulahan, Richard Victor, 160
Overman, Lee Slater, 297, 298; and woman suffrage, 37; on hearings on German and Bolshevist propaganda, 297,n2
Oxford, University of, 116

Pacific islands, 8, 50, 171
Pacific Mail Steamship Company, 398n1

Page, Thomas Nelson, 493; on situation in Italy and peace prospects, 83-86
Page, Logan Waller, 219
Palestine, 7, 61; as issue for peace conference, 381-85; WW on, 386; Jastrow on, 438,n3
Palmer, Alexander Mitchell, 338, 482-83; suggested for Attorney General, 36, 193, 206, 263-64, 276, 294; accepts Attorney General appointment, 339, 412
Paris, University of, 241n1
Paris *Herald*, 120
Paris Peace Conference: talk of relocation of, 66, 88-89, 94, 120, 490; and Syria, 86; WW's address to Third Plenary Session presenting the League of Nations Covenant, 164-78; comments on Plenary Session, 159-60, 195-96; House on hastening work of, 213-14; Churchill's Russian initiative dropped by, 232; WW on, 239; WW on needed appropriations for, 277; time schedules discussed, 295, 349, 387; House on starting functioning of League of Nations, 304-305,n1; and Tacna-Arica dispute, 330-31; and securing rights of Jews, 369, 376-77, 380; and Irish issue, 403, 407, 412, 421-22, 443, 453, 468, 469n4, 474, 547; WW on his choice to attend, 408-409; and China and Kiaochow, 424; and Palestine, 438; and Armenia, 446; resolution on League of Nations adopted at Plenary Session, 531n1, 532
peace terms and treaty: Supreme War Council's recommendations for naval terms, 20-26; difference between peace terms and Armistice terms, 95-104; France (Foch, Clemenceau) on immediately dictating terms to Germany, 212-13, 233-34; Bliss on relation of Russian situation to, 215; WW on pressure put on by France to settle quickly, 230,n1; and war costs, 231; Clemenceau on, 233-34; House on progress regarding, 245-46; WW on League of Nations as part of peace treaty, 320, 529-31; proposed final military and naval aviation terms, 404-406; draft of naval terms, 425-32; and Rhineland, 472, 475-77; WW learns of House's agreement to separate League of Nations from peace treaty, 488n2; McCumber on, 492; Bliss on military terms, 511-14; Benson on disposition of enemy ships, 515-21; Benson on naval and military terms, 522-24; talk of "preliminary treaty" dropped, 531; and Bullitt's mission to Russia, 540-45,n1; C. P. Scott on, 545-46; *see also* under the specific subject or geographical unit, such as reparations; Danzig; Rhineland
Paris *Tribune*, 89
Pašić, Nikola, 87-88
Passaic, N.J., 286
Patrick, Mason Mathews, 112,n3
peace conference: *see* Paris Peace Conference

peace treaty: see Paris Peace Conference—peace terms and treaty

Peacock, Captain, 192,n1

Peek, George Nelson, 90, 156, 336

Peet, William Wheelock, 486

Pennsylvania: Democratic congressional victory in, 448-49,n1, 457, 458, 495

Pennsylvania, University of, 438n1

People's Council of America for Democracy and Peace, 337n1

Percy, Lord Eustace, 119, 154, 192

Permanent Court of International Justice (proposed), 168

Pershing, John Joseph, 29, 82, 160; recommends WW view conditions at Brest, 64-65, 149, 151; and L. Wood, 487

Peru: and Tacna-Arica dispute, 330-31

Pessoa, Epitacio, 71, 123-24, 124

Pétain, Henri Philippe Benoi Omer Joseph, 100, 149,n1

Petchenga, Russia, 190

Peters, Andrew James, 194,n2, 206,n1, 225, 226, 235, 237, 238

Petigru, James Louis, 460-62

Petrograd, Russia, 234, 350

Pettit, Walter William, 540n1

Philadelphia, Pa., 410-11, 457

Philadelphia Public Ledger, 253,n1

Philippine Islands and the United States: and mission for independence, 391,n1

Pichon, Stéphen Jean Marie, 57, 107, 149,n1, 283, 487, 499

Picot, Georges, 160n1

Pillau, S.M.S., 23

Pinega, Russia, 190

Pittman, Key, 263

Plaschka, Richard G., 317n3

Plumb, Glenn Edward, 248n2

Plumb plan, 248n2

Plunkett, Charles Peshall, 266n1

Plunkett, Sir Horace: on Irish situation and U.S. public opinion, 452, 453-55

Poincaré, Henriette Benucci (Mrs. Raymond), 196, 497

Poincaré, Raymond, 149, 160, 196, 497, 499

Poindexter, Miles, 450

Poland, 3, 29n2, 42, 57, 66, 79, 96, 110, 164, 184, 202, 233, 243, 317, 387, 542; and Germany, 15, 55, 100, 108, 112, 203; and Danzig, 233-34, 387, 546; Jews and, 370-71, 372-73, 378, 379, 380, 464

Policies and Opinions at Paris, 1919: Wilsonian Diplomacy, the Versailles Peace, and French Public Opinion (Noble), 66n2

Politics and Diplomacy of Peacemaking: Containment and Counterrevolution at Versailles, 1918-1919 (Mayer), 204n2, 458n1, 540n1

Polish National Committee: and Jews, 372, 373

Polish Weekly, 370,n2

Polk, Frank Lyon, 82, 289, 300, 452; and Russian railroad situation, 38, 350-51, 393; and H. W. Johnson's Russian resolution,

149; on Japan's negotiations with Allies, 293-94; on Tacna-Arica dispute, 330-31, 393; on Mexican-U.S. relations, 351-52; on Norwegian ships, 357; on issuance of passports to Irish groups, 406, 407, 547; on General Graves and Russian situation, 493

Poole, DeWitt Clinton, Jr., 93n2

pork industry, 336, 343, 362, 393-94, 395-96, 483

Porto Rico: and appointment of Attorney General of, 158-59, 264-65

Portugal, 43, 121, 164, 184

Posen, S.M.S., 23, 427

Postgate, Raymond William, 87n2

Post Office Department, 327, 338; claims of oppressive policies of Burleson, 364-65

Post-War German-Austrian Relations: The Anschluss Movement, 1918-1936 (Ball), 317n3

Pou, Edward William, 469

Preston, James Harry, 232,n1

Price, Oscar A., 409,n6

Price, Waterhouse & Company, 306n1

Price Fixing Committee (War Industries Board), 91,n1, 329

prices and price fixing: Glass on reducing food prices, 89-90, 358-61; Baruch on, 90-91; Hoover on, 251; and coal industry and railroads, 251; and pork industry, 306-307, 307-308, 336-37, 343, 396; Redfield on steel, 336-37; and wheat, 360

Princeton University, 216n2

Prinkipo Declaration, 180-83; Francis on, 234, 350; Chicherin's answer to, 161,n1, 181; WW on, 319

Prinkipo Island, 545

Probert, Lionel Charles, 221,n1

prohibition: Washington, D.C. and revenue bill and, 237-38; WW signs amendment, 489

Prophets, Priests and Kings (Gardiner), 466

Providence, Rhode Island: WW's remarks in, 237,n2

Prussia, 503-505; and Jews, 372

public opinion in Great Britain, 73, 476

public opinion in the United States: and League of Nations, 38, 65, 73, 76, 80, 175, 197-98, 198-99, 279, 392, 439, 447, 449-52, 463-64, 493, 500, 540; and return of U.S. troops, 81, 82; on troops in Russia, 82; Plunkett on Irish question and, 453-54

Public Opinion Quarterly, 292n1

Puerto Rico: see Porto Rico

Quezon, Manuel Luis, 391n1

Rabban, David M., 347n1

Ragan, Fred D., 347n1

Ragsdale, James Willard, 297,n4

Railroad Administration: and financial crisis, 227-28, 231-32, 277, 536, 537; and coal prices, 251

Railroad Control Act, 257-58

railroads (Russia), 350-51, 393, 400

railroads (U.S.): issue of government ownership, 246-50, 258-60, 260-61; and needed appropriations, 257-58, 277, 536-37
Rand School of Social Science, 92n1, 337n1
Ransdell, Joseph Eugene, 297
Rappard, William Emmanuel, 151-54, 154; on Rhineland and League of Nations, 151-52; on French anti-Wilson propaganda, 153-54
Ratner, Sidney, 334n1
Rawnsley, Hardwicke Drummond, 387,n1
Recollections of Abraham Lincoln, 1847-1865 (Lamon), 366n1
Red Cross, 201, 202, 526-29
Redfield, William Cox, 90, 156, 188, 291; and pork prices, 306-307, 308, 336-37, 343; and steel prices, 336
reduction of arms: *see* arms limitation
Reed, James Alexander, 270, 279, 450
Reed, John, 297n2
Regensburg, S.M.S., 23
Reis, Jayme Batalha, 5, 6, 43, 44, 70, 121, 123, 124
reparation: declaration of principles of, 29-34; and war costs, 231; and naval terms, 431; House meets with Lloyd George and Clemenceau on, 458
Reparation at the Paris Peace Conference: From the Standpoint of the American Delegation (Burnett), 29n2
Reparation Commission, 29n1, 42, 210-11
Republican party: and League of Nations, 94, 198, 214, 254, 263, 274, 289, 387-88,n1, 437; and railroad appropriation, 228, 258-59; and Coolidge, 237; WW on responsibility of and Victory Loan bill, 297-98; and Irish situation, 348; House vote on Britt-Weaver race, 367n1; and obstruction of legislation in Senate, 408, 409
Republican party in Massachusetts, 449-50
Republican party in Pennsylvania: and congressional seat loss, 448-49,n1, 457
Revel, Paolo Thaon di, 21,n6
Revenue Act of 1917, 334n1
Revenue Act of 1918, 334,n1; WW signs, 237-38
Revenue Act of 1918 (Blakey and Blakey), 334n1
Revolution in Bavaria, 1918-1919: The Eisner Regime and the Soviet Republic (Mitchell), 423n1
Rheinland, S.M.S., 23, 427
Rhenish Provinces: *see* Rhineland
Rhineland (Rhenish Provinces), 387; Rappard on, 151-52, 154; France's views on, 233, 245, 458, 498; WW on, 472, 479-80; memorandum on, 475-77; and House-Wilson growing schism over, 488n2
Rhine River: and passage of troops through Holland, 178-80; as western military frontier, 507-10
rice industry, 252-53
Richards, Bernard Gerson, 381,n3, 385, 386
Richmond, Va., 482
Rickard, Edgar: on pork prices, 307-308, 336,

362, 393-94; and wheat prices, 360
Rio Negro, S.M.S., 432
Rio Pardo, S.M.S., 432
Ritter, William McClellan, 395,n1
Robbins, Edward Everett, 448n1
Robert College, 28, 321, 322
Robins, Raymond, 297n2
Robinson, Henry Mauris, 148,n1
Robinson, Joseph Taylor, 263
Rodkey, Frederick Stanley, 383n2
Rogers, Harry Lovejoy, 397-98,n1
Rogers, Walter Stowell, 194,n3
Rolin-Jacquemyns, Edouard Gustave Marie, 72,n1
Roosevelt, (Anna) Eleanor (Mrs. Franklin Delano), 224
Roosevelt, Franklin Delano, 207, 224, 228n1
Roosevelt, Theodore, 466; R. S. Baker on extremes and excesses of, 467; and L. Wood, 486
Root, Elihu, 367, 440
Rosseter, John Henry, 398,n1
Rothschild, Lionel Walter, 2nd Baron Rothschild, 383
Rotterdam, Netherlands, 180
Roumania: *see* Rumania
Ruggles, James A., 93n2
Rugia, S.M.S., 432
Rules Committee (House of Reps.), 291,n1, 469
Rumania (Roumania), 164, 184, 202, 542; and reparation, 29,n2, 30, 32, 33, 317; and Article 21, 154; and Jews, 370, 373-76, 379, 380
Russia: and railroad situation, 38-39, 150, 187-88, 393, 400; comments on withdrawing U.S. troops from, 149,n1, 181-83, 235; Chicherin's answer to Prinkipo Declaration, 161,n1; Churchill's initiative on, 202, 203-204, 208, 229-30, 232; Foch on, 213; Bliss on U.S. attitude toward situation in, 214-15; Lloyd George on, 233; Francis on situation in, 234-35, 350; and Japan, 294; WW on, 319-20; and Jews, 369; Morris on General Graves and, 493-95; Bullitt mission to, 540-45,n1; *see also* Bolsheviks and Bolshevism
Murmansk and Archangel, intervention in: Bliss on Britain's request for U.S. troops, 28-29; situation in Archangel, 39, 93,n2; U.S. public opinion on, 82; WW approves sending railway troops to, 150, 188-92,n1; talk of U.S. troop removal, 182-83, 189-92
Siberia, intervention in: talk of troop withdrawal, 182-83; Graves on, 399-403
Russia, Bolshevism, and the Versailles Peace (Thompson), 161,n1, 202n1, 540n1
Russia from the American Embassy, April, 1916-November, 1918 (Francis), 234n1
Russian Bureau, Inc., 39, 351
Russian Railway Service Corps, 350
Rutherford, Joseph Franklin, 482n1

Saar Valley, 387,n2

Sacco, Nicola, 343n1
Sadowa, Battle of, 503
Salis, John Francis Charles, Count de, 493
Salisbury, 3rd Marquess of (Robert Arthur Talbot Gascoyne-Cecil), 384n3
Samne, Georges, 145n3
Samuel, Maurice, 384n4
Santa Barbara Press, 205
Santa Cruz, S.M.S., 432
Santa Elena, S.M.S., 432
Santa Fe, S.M.S., 432
Santander, Manuel de Freyre y, 330,n1
Sayre, Francis Bowes, 216, 234, 366
Sayre, Francis Bowes, Jr. (Francis Woodrow Wilson Sayre until Feb. 1919), 216
Sayre, Jessie Woodrow Wilson (Mrs. Francis Bowes), daughter of WW and EAW, 265, 266, 304, 366; awaits birth of third child, 216-17; gives birth to son, 234; WW visits in hospital, 410
Sayre, John Nevin: on granting general amnesty, 365-66, 395
Sayre, Woodrow Wilson; birth of, 234,n1, 265-66, 366; WW gets first view of new grandson, 410
Scharnhorst, S.M.S., 432
Scheidemann, Philipp, 55n5, 99, 203, 458n1
Scheldt (Shelde) River, 110
Schenade, Anis, 145n3
Schenck, Charles T., 347n1
Schenck v. United States, 347n1
Schleswig, S.M.S., 432
Schleswig-Holstein, 506
Schuyler, Roy L., 401,n2
Schwab, Charles Michael, 117-18, 188
Schwabe, Klaus, 458n1
Schwaben, S.M.S., 432
Scialoja, Vittorio, 123
Scott, Charles Prestwich, 338, 545-46
Scott, Hugh Lenox, 486
Scott, Sarah, 216,n2
Scott, William Berryman, 216n2
Seaboard Air Line, 247n1
Seligman, Edwin Robert Anderson, 438n3
Semenov, Grigorii Mikhailovich, 401,n3
Senate (U.S.): *see* United States Congress
Serbia, 66, 84, 87-88, 164, 184, 203; and reparation, 29,n2, 30, 32, 33
Seymour, Charles, 34-35
Seymour, John Barton, 91n1
Shackleford, Dorsey William, 267
Sharp, William Graves, 223
Shaw, Anna Howard: on census bill, 281,n1, 299-300
Shengto, Li, 424
Shenkursk, Russia, 93n2
Sheppard, Morris, 297
Sherley, Joseph Swagar, 256, 257, 277-78, 297, 298
Sherman Antitrust Act, 90, 156
Shield, Catherine, 445,n10
shipbuilding: and labor, 262
shipping: Hurley on policy for, 532-35
Shipping Board (U.S.): *see* United States Shipping Board

Short, William Harrison, 37-38, 186, 198-99, 208
Shotwell, James Thomson, 119
Siberia: and railroad funds, 350, 351, 393; *see also* Russia—*Siberia, intervention in*
Sierra Ventana, S.M.S., 432
Silesia: and Jews, 372
Simmons, Furnifold McLendel, 254, 296
Sims, Thetus Willrette, 246,n3
Sims, William Sowden, 39
Sinn Fein, 348, 363, 364, 474
Slaughter, Homer Havron, 402,n4
Slovenes, 87-88
Smith, Alfred Emanuel, 411; invitation to WW to speak on League of Nations in N.Y., 216, 289
Smith, Ellison DuRant, 246,n3, 297, 478; on cotton situation, 38
Smith, Hoke, 297; and Americanization bill, 284,n1
Smith, Robert Freeman, 355n5
Smith-Bankhead Americanization bill, 284-88,n1, 302
Smuts, Jan Christiaan: and League of Nations Commission, 4, 122, 125, 321; WW on, 266
Snow, Thomas L., 282
Socialist party (U.S.): and passports, 92; and *Schenck v. U.S.*, 347n1
Social Research, 341n1
Society of Free Nations (Morrow), 451,n8
Solling, S.M.S., 432
Sonnino, Sidney, 107, 180, 182, 305
Soroka, Russia, 190
South-West Africa (German South-West Africa), 7-8, 50, 171
Spa, Belgium, 458n1
Spellacy, Nellie Walsh (Mrs. Thomas Joseph), 228,n1
Spellacy, Thomas Joseph, 228,n1
steel industry, 286-87; and prices, 336
Steffens, Lincoln: and Bullitt mission to Russia, 540n1
Steigerwald, S.M.S., 432
Steiner, Herbert, 317n3
Stettin, S.M.S., 427
Stevens, John Frank, 39, 350, 351, 494, 495
Stevens, Raymond Bartlett, 302n1
Stone, Ralph, 388n1
Stralsund, S.M.S., 23
Strassburg, S.M.S., 23, 427
Straus, Oscar Solomon, 195, 200
Strauss, Albert, 186, 306n1
Stringher, Bonaldo, 113,n1
Stuart, Henry Carter, 91,n3, 396,n2
Stuttgart, S.M.S., 23, 427
Styer, Henry Delp, 402,n5
submarines: peace terms and, 22, 26, 425, 426-27, 433, 518
sugar industry: and prices, 252
Sullivan, Roger Charles, 340,n1
Sulzer, Hans, 151
Supreme Court: *see* United States Supreme Court
Supreme Economic Council: formation of, 17,

Supreme Economic Council (*cont.*)
52, 53, 54, 55, 60, 61, 111, 458n1; U.S.
representatives to, 148
Supreme War Council: and Foch-Clemen-
ceau controversy over German prisoners, 3,
40; meetings of, 9-26, 51-62, 95-104, 104-
13, 175-83; on arms limitations, 11-16, 20;
on naval terms, 20-26; Benham reports on,
40; on enforcement of Armistice terms, 51-
58; on war criminals and trials, 59-60;
Grayson reports on, 94; on difference between Armistice renewal terms and peace
terms, 95-104; and renewal of Armistice
terms, 104-12; on passage of troops through
Holland, 178-80; on Prinkipo Declaration,
180-83; British press gives false reasons why
WW absent from, 530-31
Swanson, Claude Augustus, 263, 270, 297;
and woman suffrage, 368; and League of
Nations resolution, 388,n1
Swem, Charles Lee: photograph of, *illustra-
tion section*
Switzerland, 92, 152, 154
Swope, Herbert Bayard, 160
Syria, 4, 7, 61, 160; H. S. Bliss on, 86, 141-
45, 472-73,n1
Sykes, Frederick, 112
Sykes-Picot Agreement, 160,n1
Syrian Protestant College, 321-22

Tacna-Arica dispute, 330,n2, 393
Taft, William Howard, 225,n2, 281-82, 467;
supports League of Nations, 37, 65, 82, 187,
199, 257, 282, 315-16, 418, 419, 439, 540;
and speech at Metropolitan Opera House
with WW on League of Nations, 289, 289-
90, 328, 329, 357-58, 411, 413, 448; WW
on as presidential candidate, 448
Takeshita, Isamu, 21,n7
Talley, Truman H., 161
Tardieu, André Pierre Gabriel Amédée, 11,
13, 14, 160, 209, 245, 283, 284, 350, 387,
458, 499; and Rhine question, 475-77,n2
taxation: and Revenue Act of 1918, 334n1
Taxation and Democracy in America (Rat-
ner), 334n1
Temple, Henry John, Viscount Palmerston,
383n2
Territet, Switzerland, 152
Teschen, 163
Theodore Herzl: A Biography (Bein), 384n4
Thomas, Charles Spalding, 316
Thomas, Evan Welling, 366,n3
Thompson, John Means, 161n1, 202n1, 540n1
Thompson, William Howard, 297,n3
Thüringen, S.M.S., 23, 427
Thwaites, William, 58,n6
*Timeless Affair: The Life of Anita McCormick
Blaine* (Harrison), 441n4
Todd, George Carroll: WW accepts resigna-
tion of, 394; on legal question of U.S. early
membership in League of Nations, 478-79
Trans-Caucasia, 61, 62
Trans-Siberian Railway, 38-39, 187, 350
Transylvania: and Jews, 371, 373, 376, 378,
380

Treaty of Berlin (1878): and Jews, 373, 373-
75, 376
Treaty of Bucharest, 376
Trèves, Germany, 52, 212
*Trial of Scott Nearing and the American So-
cialist Society*, 337n1
Trier, Germany, 52, 212
Trieste, 117, 546
Trotsky, Leon (Lieb or Leb Davydovich), 320
Trumbić, Ante, 88n1
Truth about the Treaty (Tardieu), 475n2
Tumulty, Joseph Patrick, 162, 184, 194, 198,
222, 229, 254, 278, 279, 324, 340, 347, 392,
407, 409, 410, 411, 448-49, 458, 493, 495,
500, 529, 532; on parade in Washington
for returning soldiers, 36, 37; on U.S. public opinion on League of Nations, 197-98,
214, 540; plans for WW's arrival in Boston,
205-206, 218, 218-19, 222, 223, 225, 226,
231; suggests WW address various League
of Nations societies, 289-90; on granting
amnesty, 344, 344-45; recommends WW
meet with Irish contingent, 348; and woman
suffrage, 368; WW on Irish and, 474
Turkey, 7, 111, 317; and war costs, 211; recommendations from American Relief Committee for, 485-86
Turkish Empire, 61, 62, 459; issue of U.S.
troops to, 27-28, 81, 82; and mandates, 171;
WW on, 414
Tygodnik Polski, 370,n2
Tyler, David Gardiner, 444,n6
Tyler, Lyon Gardiner, 444,n7

Ughet, Serge, 351,n2
Ullman, Richard Henry, 184n4
Underwood, Oscar Wilder: and railroad ap-
propriation, 228, 231-32
United Press, 221n1, 409, 479n1
United States Army: issue of U.S. troops to
Turkish Empire, 27-28, 81-82; conditions
at Brest, 149, 151,n1; welcome home parade in Washington, D.C., 294; WW on,
416-17
United States Chamber of Commerce, 249
United States Civil Service Commission: *see*
Civil Service Commission
United States Congress: and Russian railroad
situation, 39; and loans outside the U.S.,
113, 115; WW's plans to meet with foreign
affairs committees on League of Nations,
163, 184, 194, 198, 221, 262-63; WW determined not to call extra session, 206, 222,
250, 254, 261, 267, 295, 296, 297-98, 388n1,
409, 537; and railroad appropriations, 248-
49, 257; and food and price control, 251,
252, 253; WW's meeting with representatives of foreign affairs committees, 267, 268-
76; and League of Nations and disarmament (Article 8), 268-69, 270; and appropriations for Employment Service, 291-92;
WW on election results, 309-11; WW on
importance of keeping in touch with constituents, 311-12; and Mexican situation,
351,n1; kills general deficiency appropriations bill, 388; before adjournment WW

praises (draft), 408; and German vessels seized in U.S. ports, 434; and League of Nations and treaty-making power versus legislative power, 478-79

House of Representatives: and railroad appropriation crisis, 227, 232; and census bill, 290; Britt-Weaver contest, 367,n1; and general deficiency appropriations bill, 447; and Pennsylvania election, 448-49,n1, 457, 458, 495; and Irish question, 469,n4; *see also* under the names of the individual committees, such as Appropriations, Committee on; Foreign Affairs, Committee on

Senate: Johnson's resolution withdrawing troops from Russia, 149,n1, 204,n1; debate, filibuster and opposition to League of Nations, 199, 205, 270-71, 274, 294, 367, 388n1, 439, 465, 538, 539; and railroad appropriation, 228, 277; WW on direct election of senators, 228-29; and census bill, 290; debate over Irish question, 324-25; and Mexico, 351n1; WW on obstruction of legislation by a group of senators, 408-409, 409; and general deficiency appropriations bill, 447; McCumber's suggestions for changes in Covenant to help passage in, 491-92; Foch on ratification of peace treaty and, 514; *see also* under the names of the individual committees, such as Appropriations, Committee on; Foreign Relations, Committee on

United States Constitution, 76, 273, 295

United States Employment Service: W. B. Wilson on financial crisis of, 291-92, 447, 478

United States: European relief, credits, and postwar reconstruction: and cotton industry, 38; and Belgium, 63-64; Glass on reducing food prices, 89-90; and labor and Whitley Councils, 91,n1, 262; and Italy's requests for loans, 113-15, 208, 332-33, 342; Hoover on, 116-17, 117; and U.S. business and industry, 117-18, 156, 188; WW on, 161; and Belgium's requests, 200; and war costs, 210-11, 231; W. B. Wilson on importance of Employment Service, 291-92; and foreign loans, 333, 396-97; WW on disposition of U.S. housing projects, 341-42; *see also* food relief

United States Shipping Board, 398n1, 442n1, 534; Colby resigns from, 302; and Norwegian ships, 357, 394

United States Supreme Court: and *Schenck v. U.S.*, 347,n1; WW on Daniel Webster and, 462

United States and Revolutionary Nationalism in Mexico, 1916-1932 (Smith), 355n5

University of Chicago Law Review, 347n1

Valentino, Pietro Arone di, 300,n1, 301

Van Dyke, Henry, 199,n1

Vanzetti, Bartolomeo, 343n1

Varela, Don Francisco Tudelay, 330n1

Venable, William Webb, 297,n4

Vénisélos, Eleuthérios, 3, 6, 44, 45, 71, 118, 124, 140, 500-501,n2; and Plenary Session,

178n2, 195, 196; WW on, 266, 315

Vergennes, Comte de (Charles Gravier), 242

Vesnić (Vesnitch), Milenko, 5-6, 43, 44-45, 46, 68, 69, 71, 88,n1, 118, 123

Victor Emmanuel (King of Italy): *see* Vittorio Emanuele III

victory loan bill, 297-98

Villa, Francisco (Pancho), 352

Virginia Bill of Rights, 319

Vittorio Emanuele III: grants amnesty for political and military offenses, 301

Vladivostok, Russia: and zemstvo, 403

Von Steuben, U.S.S., 434

Wagner, Charles C.: photograph of, *illustration section*

Wallace, Hugh Campbell: appointed ambassador to France, 194, 308

Wallachia, 373

Walsh, Francis Patrick, 422, 469

Walsh, Thomas James, 262-63, 263, 280, 297n2

Waltraute, S.M.S., 432

Warburg, Paul Moritz, 248

War Department, 537; sale of surplus trucks, 303-304,n1

Warfield, Solomon Davies, 247-48,n1

War Finance Corporation, 409n4, 536

War Industries Board, 90, 188

War Lords (Gardiner), 466

war profits tax, 333-34,n1

War Risk Bureau, 537-38

Warsaw, Poland: and Jews, 372

War Trade Board, 351; and pork prices, 306, 307-308, 343, 362, 393, 396, 483; Glass on prices and, 361

Washington, George, 419, 482; Farewell Address mentioned, 312n1

Washington, D.C.: parade for returning soldiers in, 36, 37, 294; revenue bill makes city "dry," 237-38; WW on, 311, 482

Washington, D.C. Herald, 341n1

Watch Tower and Tract Society: *see* Jehovah's Witnesses

Ways and Means Committee (House of Reps.), 334n1

Weaver, Zebulon, 367,n1

Webster, Daniel, 460-61, 462

Weeks, John Wingate, 449

Wemyss, Rosslyn Erskine, 3, 16, 17, 21, 40, 112

Wentz, Daniel Bertsch, 398,n2

Westfalen, S.M.S., 23, 427

Weygand, Maxime, 11, 95, 102

What I Remember (Fawcett), 145n4

wheat: and prices, 252, 360

Wheeler, Eleanor Josephine McPartland (Mrs. Howard Duryee), 456,n3

Wheeler, Howard Duryee, 456,n1

Wheeler Newspaper Syndicate, 341n1

Whipple, Sherman Leland: and Norwegian ships, 357,n2; suggested for Attorney General, 193, 222

White, Henry, 152, 154, 187-88, 234; on Belgium and reparations, 200; and Bullitt mission to Russia, 540n1

White, John Campbell, 187,n1
Whitley, John Henry, 91n1
Whitley Councils, 91,n1
Whitley Councils Scheme (Seymour), 91n1
Whitley Report, 91,n1
Whitmarsh, Theodore F., 253, 358, 360
Wilhelmina, Queen of the Netherlands, 219-20
William II (of Germany), 504; George V on, 228
William and Mary College, 444
Williams, John Sharp, 198, 270, 325, 326, 412; and woman suffrage, 37; and Armenia, 65-66
Wilmington, Delaware, 410
Wilson, Edith Bolling Galt (Mrs. Woodrow), 36, 41, 65, 66, 265, 266, 269, 281, 283, 308, 309, 409, 410, 440, 531; voyage to and arrival in Boston, 204, 205, 218, 226; departs for France, 442; activities aboard ship, 456, 465, 471, 489, 490, 491; WW's dependence on, 466; arrives at Brest, 487; on WW's appearance after revealing conference with House, 488n2
Wilson, Sir Henry Hughes, 112, 180; requests U.S. troops be sent to Murmansk and Archangel, 28; on meeting with Foch on peace terms, 212-13,n1
Wilson, Janet Woodrow (Mrs. Joseph Ruggles), mother of WW, 473
Wilson, John Haden: congressional victory of, 448n1, 457, 458
Wilson, Margaret Woodrow, daughter of WW and EAW, 440
Wilson, William Bauchop, 91; on importance of Employment Service, 291-92, 447, 478

WOODROW WILSON

offered many honorary degrees, 3, 89, 116; Fourteen Points mentioned, 30, 31, 32, 33; plans for parade for returning soldiers in Washington, D.C., 36, 37, 94; on anti-Wilson propaganda and French press, 66, 88, 94, 120, 153, 266, 489-90; and Number 13, 120, 156; sends autographed photographs to French dignitaries, 149,n1; holds press conference before leaving Paris, 161; catches a few winks of sleep during Syrian poet's recitation, 162; address to Third Plenary Session of peace conference presenting League of Nations Covenant, 164-78, photograph of, *illustration section*; wishes to discuss League of Nations with foreign affairs committees of Congress, 184; voyage and arrival in Boston, 185, 205-206, 218, 218-19, 221, 222, 223, 224, 225, 226, 229, 231, 235-37; new residence and servants in Paris, 193, 223, 230-31, 246, 256-57, 327; statement on departing from France, 196, 197; on assassination attempt on Clemenceau, 209; on not calling extra session of Congress, 222, 254, 295, 296, 297-98, 409; congratulates *The Hatchet* on its first anniversary, 224,n1; on inscription on Lafayette monument, 232; address in

Boston, 236, 238-45, photograph of, *illustration section*; trip from Boston to Washington, 237-38, 254; dinner and meeting on League of Nations with congressional foreign affairs committees, 268-76; news reports of meetings at the Capitol, 295-98; greeting for Senator Chamberlain, 298; on League of Nations being part of peace treaty, 320, 531, 532; denies making statement on Ireland, 324-26; and amnesty issue, 338, 344-47, 365-66; talk of third term, 340; address to Governors and Mayors Conference, 389-91; condemns group of senators who have obstructed necessary legislation, 408-409; leaves Washington for New York, 409-12; meets with Irish Americans, 411-12, 443; address at Metropolitan Opera House on League of Nations, 413-21, 447; departure for France, 442; R. S. Baker on, 464-65; arrives at Brest, 487; beginnings of break with House, 488,n2; arrives in Paris, 497; *see also* League of Nations

APPEARANCE AND IMPRESSIONS OF

tired from stress and constant callers, 162, 298, 412; as he leaves Paris, 196; at Washington press conference, 295; looks rested, 448, 490; R. S. Baker on, 463, 489; upon emerging from revealing conference with House "He seemed to have aged years," 488n2

APPOINTMENT SUGGESTIONS,
APPOINTMENTS AND RESIGNATIONS

Palmer appointed Attorney General, 36, 193, 206, 222, 263-64, 276-77, 294, 412; and Attorney General of Porto Rico, 158-59, 264-65; Hapgood appointed Minister to Denmark, 185, 194, 439,n1; Ambassador to France appointed, 194; judgeship in Missouri, 206-207; Colby resigns from Shipping Board, 302,n1; resignation of McIlhenny from Civil Service Commission, 330,n1; WW requests Civil Service Commission resignations, 330,n3; on judgeship in Chicago, 340,n1; Palmer accepts Attorney-General position, 339; Creel resigns from Committee on Public Information, 363,n1; accepts resignation of Assistant Attorney General, 394; J. Skelton Williams as Comptroller of Currency, 412; Galloway refuses to resign from Civil Service Commission, 460, 478

CABINET

251, 254, 266; and prices, 90, 306; House on geographical representation in, 193

FAMILY AND PERSONAL LIFE

praise and love from the McAdoos, 204-205; news from Jessie awaiting her third child, 216-17; becomes grandfather again, 234,n1; Ellen Davis reports on WW's new grand-

Woodrow Wilson, cont.

son, 265-66; wants to hold on to property in Ontario, 282; keeps the McAdoos informed of his activities, 283, 395; punctuality of, 296; sends regards to Mrs. Hulbert through her son, 304; thanks Ellen Davis for note on his new grandson, 304; and financial appeal for Fred Yates' family, 387; visits Jessie and newborn grandson, 410; Mrs. Blaine on her deceased son's personal feelings for WW, 440-41; reminisces on teaching, 442-43; likes to tease, 443-44; enjoys puns, limericks and puzzles, 465-66; R. S. Baker on temperance of, 466-67; wishes he had a good picture of his mother, 473; on cities to retire to, 482

HEALTH

Benham on strain on, 66; tired, 201, 298; rests in room aboard ship, 202; catches colds aboard ship, 217-18, 457; Grayson examines, 410; sore throat and fever, 462; sore gum, 462; severe stroke of 1906 leaves one eye almost blind, 465,n2; good health of attributed to Grayson, 465; nonsmoker, 466-67; stays in bed all day, 471; WW on his ailments, 473; jokes that his health related to gases generated by Republican senators, 473; sleeps late aboard ship, 486; recovered from sickness, 495; exhaustion, 538

OPINIONS AND COMMENTS

on German arms reduction, 12, 14, 15-16; on renewing Armistice for short period, 56; on freedom of seas as nonissue, 160, 162; I should say of this document that it is not a straitjacket, but a vehicle of life. A living thing is born, and we must see to it that the clothes we put upon it do not hamper it—a vehicle of power, but a vehicle in which power may be varied at the discretion of those who exercise it and in accordance with the changing circumstances of the time. And yet, while it is elastic, while it is general in its terms, it is definite in the one thing that we were called upon to make definite. It is a definite guarantee of peace, 175; We are depending primarily and chiefly upon one great force, and that is the moral force of the public opinion of the world—the cleansing and clarifying and compelling influences of publicity—so that intrigues can no longer have their coverts, so that designs that are sinister can at any time be drawn into the open, so that those things that are destroyed by the light may be properly destroyed by the overwhelming light of the universal expression of the condemnation of the world, 175; Many terrible things have come out of this war, gentlemen, but some very beautiful things have come out of it. Wrong has been defeated, but the rest of the world has been more conscious than it ever was before of the majesty of right. People that were suspi-

Woodrow Wilson, cont.

cious of one another can now live as friends and comrades in a single family, and desire to do so, 177; So I think I can say of this document that it is at one and the same time a practical document and a humane document. There is a pulse of sympathy in it. There is a compulsion of conscience throughout it. It is practical, and yet it is intended to purify, to rectify, to elevate, 177; on W. S. Churchill's Russian initiative, 208; on direct election of senators, 228-29; on the hope and confidence vested in the U.S., 240-45; Speaking with perfect frankness in the name of the people of the United States, I have uttered as the objects of this great war ideals, and nothing but ideals, and the war has been won by that inspiration, 241; on party loyalty, 310-11; The wrong opinion is generally better organized than the right opinion, 311; on contempt he feels for opponents of the League of Nations, 322-24; We are at last learning that the business of government is to take counsel for the average man. We are at last learning that the whole matter of the prosperity of peoples runs down into the great body of men and women who do the work of the world, and that the process of guidance is not completed by the mere success of great enterprises—it is completed only by the standard of the benefit that it confers upon those who in the obscure ranks of life contribute to the success of these enterprises, 390; Intrigue cannot stand publicity, and if the League of Nations were nothing but a great debating society it would kill intrigue, 414; I do mean not to come back until it's over over there, and it must not be over until the nations of the world are assured of the permanency of peace, 417; The only place a man can feel at home is where nothing has to be explained to him. Nothing has to be explained to me in America, least of all the sentiment of the American people, 419; on Covenant, 419; on more employer-employee partnerships, 471-72; on education, 473-74; on Irish problem, 474, 480-81; compares British to Americans, 474-75; on Rhineland, 479-80; on sentencing of Jehovah's Witnesses, 482-83,n1; on L. Wood, 486-87

RECREATION

takes automobile rides, 36, 66, 367, 538; takes walks aboard ship's deck, 202, 207, 456, 471, 474, 481; attends movies aboard ship, 207, 443, 448, 456, 457, 465, 474, 490; takes walks, 308-309, 531; plays solitaire (Canfield), 442; reminiscences of visit to Yorktown, Va., 444-45; enjoys games and puzzles, 465-66; plays shuffleboard aboard ship, 471, 481, 490; golf and golf stories, 479, 489; Grayson reads R. S. Baker's stories aloud to WW, 491; sings with ship's crew, 491

Woodrow Wilson, cont.

RELIGIOUS LIFE

attends church, 36,n1, 66, 201, 367; R. S. Baker on, 467

WRITINGS

remarks that he'll be an historian again, 323, 340; on not abbreviating his *History of the American People* for general use, 341,n1, 484; unable to write article for *Everybody's Magazine*, 392,n1; remarks that he'll be historian again prompts publishing offers, 456,n2

End of Woodrow Wilson entry

Wilson Will Fight League Foes Anywhere (Philadelphia *Public Ledger*), 253,n1
Wingo, Otis Theodore, 297,n4
Wise, Stephen Samuel, 368, 386; on plight of Eastern European Jews, 368-81; on Palestine, 381-85
Wiseman, William, 195
Wisconsin: supports League of Nations, 158,n1,2
Wolcott, Josiah Oliver, 263
Wolf, Simon, 438n3
Woman's Committee: discontinuation of, 299-300
woman suffrage: WW continues effort for passage of, 37, 368; amendment defeated, 94; and peace conference, 145-47; WW explains decision of peace negotiators on Covenant and, 183-84
women: and League of Nations, 6, 9, 122, 145-47, 172, 175-76; and census bill,

281,n1; and war work, 299-300
Wood, Leonard: WW on, 486-87
Wood, Spencer Shepard, 235,n1
Woodrow Wilson and World Settlement (R. S. Baker), 488n2, 531n1
Woodrow Wilson, Revolutionary Germany and Peacemaking, 1918-1919: Missionary Diplomacy and the Realities of Power (Schwabe), 458n1
Woolley, Clarence Mott, 308,n1, 336, 357
Work, John McClelland, 92n1
World's Court League, 278
World's Work, 290n1
W. R. Grace & Company, 398n1

Yager, Arthur, 264,n2
Yap Island, 24
Yates, Emily Chapman Martin (Mrs. Frederic), 282,n2, 387
Yates, Frederic, 282; death of, 282n3, 387
Yates, Mary, 282n2, 387
Yiddish language, 372
Yitang, Wang, 424
Yorck, S.M.S., 432
York Dispatch, 440,n2
Yorktown, Va.,: WW's visit to, 444-45
Young, James, 297,n4
Young, Riley S., 158n2
Yugoslavia, 84, 85, 87-88, 243, 305; and Jews, 380
Yugoslavia at the Paris Peace Conference: A Study in Frontiermaking (Lederer), 88n1

zemstvo, 403
Zionism, 381-85, 386, 438
Žolger, Ivan, 88n1
Zorn, Anders Leonard, 225,n3